Examining International Land Use Policies, Changes, and Conflicts

G. N. Tanjina Hasnat
University of Chittagong, Bangladesh

Mohammed Kamal Hossain
University of Chittagong, Bangladesh

IGI Global
PUBLISHER of TIMELY KNOWLEDGE

A volume in the Advances in Public Policy and Administration (APPA) Book Series

Published in the United States of America by
IGI Global
Information Science Reference (an imprint of IGI Global)
701 E. Chocolate Avenue
Hershey PA, USA 17033
Tel: 717-533-8845
Fax: 717-533-8661
E-mail: cust@igi-global.com
Web site: http://www.igi-global.com

Library of Congress Cataloging-in-Publication Data

Names: Hasnat, G. N. Tanjina, 1988- editor. | Hossain, Mohammed Kamal, editor.
Title: Examining international land use policies, changes, and conflicts / G.N. Tanjina Hasnat and Mohammed Kamal Hossain, editors.
Description: Hershey, PA : Engineering Science Reference, [20201] | Includes bibliographical references and index. | Summary: "This book contain research on international land use policies, changes, and conflicts"-- Provided by publisher.
Identifiers: LCCN 2020013991 (print) | LCCN 2020013992 (ebook) | ISBN 9781799843726 (h/c) | ISBN 9781799857259 (s/c) | ISBN 9781799843733 (eISBN)
Subjects: LCSH: Land use. | Land use--Government policy. | Land use--Planning.
Classification: LCC HD111 .E93 2021 (print) | LCC HD111 (ebook) | DDC 333.73/13--dc23
LC record available at https://lccn.loc.gov/2020013991
LC ebook record available at https://lccn.loc.gov/2020013992

This book is published in the IGI Global book series Advances in Public Policy and Administration (APPA) (ISSN: 2475-6644; eISSN: 2475-6652)

British Cataloguing in Publication Data
A Cataloguing in Publication record for this book is available from the British Library.

Advances in Public Policy and Administration (APPA) Book Series

ISSN:2475-6644
EISSN:2475-6652

Mission

Proper management of the public sphere is necessary in order to maintain order in modern society. Research developments in the field of public policy and administration can assist in uncovering the latest tools, practices, and methodologies for governing societies around the world.

The **Advances in Public Policy and Administration (APPA) Book Series** aims to publish scholarly publications focused on topics pertaining to the governance of the public domain. APPA's focus on timely topics relating to government, public funding, politics, public safety, policy, and law enforcement is particularly relevant to academicians, government officials, and upper-level students seeking the most up-to-date research in their field.

Coverage

- Government
- Law Enforcement
- Political Economy
- Politics
- Public Administration
- Public Funding
- Public Policy
- Resource Allocation
- Urban Planning

IGI Global is currently accepting manuscripts for publication within this series. To submit a proposal for a volume in this series, please contact our Acquisition Editors at Acquisitions@igi-global.com or visit: http://www.igi-global.com/publish/.

The Advances in Public Policy and Administration (APPA) Book Series (ISSN 2475-6644) is published by IGI Global, 701 E. Chocolate Avenue, Hershey, PA 17033-1240, USA, www.igi-global.com. This series is composed of titles available for purchase individually; each title is edited to be contextually exclusive from any other title within the series. For pricing and ordering information please visit http://www.igi-global.com/book-series/advances-public-policy-administration/97862. Postmaster: Send all address changes to above address.

Titles in this Series

For a list of additional titles in this series, please visit: http://www.igi-global.com/book-series/advances-public-policy-administration/97862

Effects of E-Authoritarianism and E-Protest on Contemporary Society
Nygmet Ibadildin (KIMEP University, Kazakhstan)
Information Science Reference • © 2020 • 300pp • H/C (ISBN: 9781799828631) • US $185.00

Historical Examinations and Current Issues in Turkish-American Relations
Hüseyin Işıksal (Near East University, Nicosia, Turkey) and Ozan Örmeci (Istanbul Gedik University, Istanbul, Turkey)
Information Science Reference • © 2020 • 300pp • H/C (ISBN: 9781799837527) • US $195.00

Handbook of Research on Recent Developments in Internet Activism and Political Participation
Yasmin Ibrahim (Queen Mary University of London, UK)
Information Science Reference • © 2020 • 368pp • H/C (ISBN: 9781799847960) • US $245.00

Political Identity and Democratic Citizenship in Turbulent Times
Niels Noergaard Kristensen (University of Aalborg, Denmark)
Information Science Reference • © 2020 • 333pp • H/C (ISBN: 9781799836773) • US $195.00

Historical and Future Global Impacts of Armed Groups and Social Movements Emerging Research and Opportunities
Pablo Alberto Baisotti (University of Costa Rica, Costa Rica) and Pablo Pozzi (University of Buenos Aires, Argentina)
Information Science Reference • © 2020 • 292pp • H/C (ISBN: 9781799852056) • US $195.00

Utilizing Decision Support Systems for Strategic Public Policy Planning
Mohamed Timoulali (GTOPIC sarl, Morocco)
Information Science Reference • © 2020 • 269pp • H/C (ISBN: 9781799819165) • US $185.00

Reshaping Social Policy to Combat Poverty and Inequality
Augustine Nduka Eneanya (University of Lagos, Nigeria)
Information Science Reference • © 2020 • 218pp • H/C (ISBN: 9781799809692) • US $185.00

Citizen-Responsive Urban E-Planning Recent Developments and Critical Perspectives
Carlos Nunes Silva (University of Lisbon, Portugal)
Information Science Reference • © 2020 • 409pp • H/C (ISBN: 9781799840183) • US $195.00

IGI Global
PUBLISHER of TIMELY KNOWLEDGE

701 East Chocolate Avenue, Hershey, PA 17033, USA
Tel: 717-533-8845 x100 • Fax: 717-533-8661
E-Mail: cust@igi-global.com • www.igi-global.com

Table of Contents

Detailed Table of Contents

With the acceleration of China's new urbanization and industrialization process, the expanding demand for construction land will continue to expropriate a large number of cultivated land. Under the strict land management system, the policy of land requisition and compensation balance will continue to protect China's food security and the bottom line of 1.8 billion mu of China's cultivated land. Based on China's land management law, agricultural law, and other land management policies, the authors analyzed the dilemma and development trend of China's policy of land requisition and compensation balance, combining with the case study of building R railway dry port in Q County, Western China. By analyzing the balance policy of land requisition and compensation, this chapter tries to find the defects and future development trend of China's cultivated land protection policy.

The ideological clash between Muslim-Malay is predominant in Thailand, which undoubtedly led to conflicts between the separatist groups and the central government. It is a source of risk to development efforts that might harm the sensitivity of the conflict situation. Hence, this chapter aims to explore the impacts of development efforts in the conflict-affected areas of the Deep South region of Thailand. The data is collected from secondary sources and analyzed through descriptive statistics. Results showed that the development efforts from the central government in the southernmost provinces resulted in significant improvement of basic infrastructure, education, and the healthcare system. Due to a high degree of government intervention, the impact of the NGOs on development is considerably limited.

It is suggested that the communities should be strengthened in their capacity to increase their role and share the local political power, reduce the monopolizing of local politicians, and increase the accuracy of the development project to the communities' actual needs.

This critical review explored the current scholarship of the experiences and challenges faced by Gullah Geechee midlife women heirs' property owners along the Gullah Geechee Cultural Heritage Corridor. Past researchers have noted these women often experience invisibility due to the concurrent burdens of management of jointly owned property along the corridor in addition to legacy experiences of cultural isolation, land dispossession, voice dispossession, and ancestry enslavement. Past researchers have called for ongoing collaborative research by both non-indigenous and indigenous researchers as a gap continues for gendered perspectives for current corridor heirs' property challenges and land dispossession with respect to power, trauma, economic impact, Gullah Geechee ways of knowing, land-based cultural values, heritage tourism, governmental dispossession, and the legacy of enslavement for critical inquiry from the transformative paradigm.

The land use of the Belihuloya catchment area in Sri Lanka has been changing over a long period mainly due to the human activities. The study was aimed to find out the spatial and temporal changes of land use in the Belihuloya Mini Catchment area of 1956 to 2015, and obtain the local people's perception of the effects of land-use changes in Belihuloya. To study the people's perceptions of land use change, a questionnaire survey was conducted among randomly selected 180 households. Aerial data of 1956 and satellite data of 2015 were used to analyze the land use changes. The vegetation cover maps of 1956 and 2015, demonstrated the drastic changes of land use in Belihuloya. More than 50% of the respondents in the study area perceived that the land use has been changing due to the construction activities, forest fires, illegal loggings, pine and tea cultivation and the expansion of built-up areas. The deforestation has badly effected on water resources in the Belihuloya. The reforestation programs, including community-based reforestation programs can be introduced to minimize the impacts. It is necessary to implement existing legal frameworks with supports of different stakeholders to conserve the Belihuloya.

is one of the first investigations conducted to identify the various dimensions of youths' willingness to accept agriculture entrepreneurship in the Nepalese context.

Zia Ur Rahman Farooqi, Institute of Soil and Environmental Sciences, University of Agriculture Faisalabad, Pakistan
Zahoor Ahmad, Department of Field Crops, Faculty of Agriculture, University of Cukurova, Adana, Turkey
Muhammad Ashar Ayub, Institute of Soil and Environmental Sciences, University of Agriculture Faisalabad, Pakistan
Wajid Umar, Szent Istvan University, Gödöllő, Hungary
Muhammad Nadeem, Institute of Soil and Environmental Sciences, University of Agriculture Faisalabad, Pakistan
Hina Fatima, School of Applied Biosciences, Kyungpook National University, South Korea
Abbas Shoukat, Institute of Soil and Environmental Sciences, University of Agriculture Faisalabad, Pakistan
Tasawar Ali, Institute of Soil and Environmental Sciences, University of Agriculture Faisalabad, Pakistan
Muhammad Imran Ashraf, Institute of Soil and Environmental Sciences, University of Agriculture Faisalabad, Pakistan

Arable lands are the major source of food production worldwide. Increasing crop cultivation in the response to population pressure and the use of synthetic fertilizers and chemicals are the main reasons for the conversion of arable lands into problematic soils. Increasing food demand requires to increase the per acre yield of agricultural crops resulting in over exploitation of soil resources. This is a major contributor to soil degradation which is the major threat to the food security of the world. Climate change and poor-quality irrigation are the other problems are also affecting crop productivity and the conversion of arable lands into problematic lands. Deforestation and urbanization are the main reasons behind the conversion of agricultural land into infrastructure. Adopting precision agriculture, vertical farming and good agricultural practices are the only ways to conserve arable lands. This chapter provides a keen overview of world arable land issues with the focus on threats to arable land and possible solutions to overcome this issue.

for deteriorating living standards and quality of life for humans in major metropolitan cities around the world. The urban ecosystem leaves a major impact on world renewable resources and carbon footprint. Urban vegetation and forests can help in net balancing and buffering of immense pollutant surge intro urban ecosystems being done due to urbanization. Extensive urbanization is responsible for more and more wastewater and gaseous pollutant release in the environment which urban forests can help tackle effectively. Moreover, city vegetation also plays a critical role in decreasing city surface temperatures thus helping shrinkage of the urban heat island. The present draft presents the role of urban vegetation in effective management and buffering of urban microclimate.

This chapter provides a holistic understanding of the existing conditions of urban green spaces in Sabah by reviewing relevant past studies and publications. Nature serves as the foundation in the establishment of pocket parks, urban parks, and forest protected areas that are made available for public access within and outside of the major urban areas in Sabah. Presently, both native and exotic flora and fauna species are coexisting at the local urban green spaces, although some invasive exotic species have developed into urban pests of Sabah. Moreover, the importance and functions of urban green spaces in maintaining the well-being of mankind and ensuring the survival of indigenous wildlife species are acknowledged by society. Nevertheless, much research is required to fill up the research gaps of urban forestry, and also to provide solutions to the existing problems that happened at the urban green spaces in Sabah.

In Pacific Small Island Developing States (PSIDS), the degradation of mangroves advances at a fast pace, especially in urban places. Rural to urban migration let urban settlements grow tremendously in the past 60 years. People built many informal settlements straight into mangrove forests. Health implications are severe, but settlements in mangrove forests provide protection against eviction. The case study provides insight into people's lives, perception and actions in a degraded mangrove forest in the eastern part of Suva, the capital of Fiji. The major question is why people are exposing themselves to serious environmental health hazards. Based on recent changes, the chapter also looks at development efforts that threaten residents of informal settlement to get evicted from the locations they right now reside. Investigations concentrate on people's actions in space, particularly, the role degraded urban mangroves play in their decision to reside in a particular place. A major explanation is that people want to reduce risk and enhance security: security from eviction.

Preface

Land is a finite resource and most important gift of nature to human beings. Land is not only important resource to the human but also for wildlife, natural vegetation, and other ecosystems. About 95% of our basic needs are obtained from land directly or indirectly. Due to increasing population, the land use and land cover is changing gradually. Rising of land conflicts and land use conflicts are now the global problem. The land is under various competing pressures from urbanization, industrialization, infrastructures, and increased demand of food. To give the space for over population and meet the extra demand for these populations, natural forests and agricultural lands are converted into urban and industrial land and diminishing day by day.

Increasing competitive demand for a land for different uses due to growing population, conflicting views arise and thus land use conflicts occur. Natural land cover of earth has been changed with natural phenomenon and human intervention over time. The detrimental land cover changes and alteration due to human activities was detected since 1700 AD. The Geographic Information System (GIS) and satellite based Remote Sensing (RS) are the modern technologies uses for assessing and analyzing land use changes.

Considering the gradual increase of land use changes and conflicts this book deals with the land use policy, land use conflicts, land use changes, GIS, RS, land regulation, land tenure, urban vegetation, land use planning and sustainable development from different aspects of different countries. This book has five parts. The first part "Land Use Policy and Conflicts" discusses with the policy of cultivated land requisition in China, impacts of development efforts in the conflict-affected areas of Muslim-Malay and Thai predominant in Thailand, and the Heirs' property challenges at Gullah Geechee in America. The second part "Land Use Changes, GIS & RS" discusses the land use changes and local perception towards these changes in Sri Lanka, vegetation transformation at Rajasthan in India, and the urban sprawl visual investigation of Beijing, China. The third part "Land Regulations, Tenure and Local Land Use" discusses about the land regulation, tenure and local land use of Sri Lanka, youths' perception to agricultural entrepreneurship in Nepal, worldwide threats to the arable land, and precision agriculture for sustainable land use. The fourth part "Urban Vegetation" encloses a general description on the role of urban vegetation, urban forestry in Malaysia, and the mangrove degradation in urban setting and its socio-economic impacts in Fiji. The fifth part "Land Use Planning & Sustainable Development" encompasses the land use planning, management, and sustainable development in India, Sri Lanka, and Nepal.

Land use conflicts and changes are the emerging and time demanding issues. This book is a combined effort of different authors from different countries. Land use researches from different areas are gathered in one compilation will be a supportive document to the academians, researchers, global policymakers, students, developers, and to the governmental works of different countries.

Chapter 1
A Study on the Policy of Cultivated Land Requisition–Compensation Balance of China With Q County R Railway Dry Port as an Example

Hongbin Ding
Research Center for Security and Development in Western China, Sichuan University, China

Danli Gao
Chongzhou Court Research Office, China

ABSTRACT

With the acceleration of China's new urbanization and industrialization process, the expanding demand for construction land will continue to expropriate a large number of cultivated land. Under the strict land management system, the policy of land requisition and compensation balance will continue to protect China's food security and the bottom line of 1.8 billion mu of China's cultivated land. Based on China's land management law, agricultural law, and other land management policies, the authors analyzed the dilemma and development trend of China's policy of land requisition and compensation balance, combining with the case study of building R railway dry port in Q County, Western China. By analyzing the balance policy of land requisition and compensation, this chapter tries to find the defects and future development trend of China's cultivated land protection policy.

INTRODUCTION

The balance of land requisition and compensation is an important policy to protect cultivated land confirmed by China's land management law. It means that if the non-agricultural construction needs to expropriate the cultivated land for a long time, the new cultivated land with the same quantity and quality

DOI: 10.4018/978-1-7998-4372-6.ch001

shall be supplemented by the requisitionists according to the principle of " how much cultivated land is expropriated and how much is compensated "(Tian Yufu 2005). Article 31 of China's land management law stipulates that the government shall protect cultivated land and strictly control the conversion of cultivated land to non cultivated land use. The government implements the system of compensation for land requisition. If the non-agricultural construction is approved to expropriate the cultivated land, the person who expropriates the cultivated land shall be responsible for reclaiming the new cultivated land equivalent to the quantity and quality of the expropriated cultivated land in accordance with the principle of " how much cultivated land is expropriated and how much is compensated ". If there are no conditions for reclamation or the cultivated land reclaimed does not meet the requirements, the cultivated land reclamation fee shall be paid in accordance with the provisions of the provincial government and shall be used exclusively for the reclamation of new cultivated land. The provincial government shall formulate plans for the reclamation of cultivated land, supervise the expropriators of cultivated land to reclaim the land in accordance with the plans, and conduct acceptance inspection. The establishment of this system marks the beginning of the balance policy of land requisition and compensation in China. Some Chinese scholars believe that the balance policy of land requisition and compensation does not play a significant role in maintaining the bottom line of 1.8 billion mu of cultivated land, but only slows down the encroachment of urbanization on cultivated land. The cultivated land resources are just being swallowed by urbanization rapidly, but gradually eroded by urbanization. The bottom line of 1.8 billion mu of cultivated land is hard to get rid of the fate of being broken through(Li Wuyan et al. 2006). Other Chinese scholars believe that the policy can effectively prevent the breakthrough of the bottom line of cultivated land and maintain the steady increase of cultivated land(Xu Lili et al. 2015).

In this chapter, the author has the following main points: first, in the practice of land requisition and compensation balance in China, the quality of the requisitioned cultivated land is high, and the newly reclaimed cultivated land is difficult to reach the quality level of the requisitioned cultivated land. Second, reclamation of cultivated land resources, rural land consolidation and new cultivated land quota transaction are the three most important methods to compensate the cultivated land. However, the reclamation of land reserve resources did not pay attention to ecological protection, resulting in many ecological problems. Third, there are two implementation modes of the policy, among which the mode of "first compensation for cultivated land, then expropriation of cultivated land" is widely supported by Chinese scholars of cultivated land protection, and will become the future development direction of cultivated land protection policy. Fourth, because the index of grain output level is easy to quantify, it will become an important index for China to determine the quality and quantity conversion coefficient between the requisitioned cultivated land and the compensated cultivated land. A detailed discussion of the above points will be the objective of the following context.

CHINA'S POLICY OF CULTIVATED LAND REQUISITION, COMPENSATION AND BALANCE

Cultivated Land Requisition

Definition and type of cultivated land. According to the classification of China's second national land survey, cultivated land refers to the land where crops are planted, including paddy field, irrigated land and dry land. Among them, paddy field refers to the land used to grow aquatic crops such as rice and lotus root. Irrigated land refers to the cultivated land with water source guarantee and irrigation facilities, which can irrigate normally and grow dry crops in general years. Dry land refers to the land without irrigation facilities, mainly relying on natural precipitation to grow dry crops. From the perspective of cultivated land protection law, there are two types of cultivated land: the first type is permanent basic cultivated land. According to Article 33 of China's land management law, permanent basic cultivated land mainly includes the following four categories. First, cultivated land in the production bases of grain, cotton, oil, sugar and other important agricultural products approved by the competent agricultural and rural departments of the central government of China or the local governments at or above the county level. Second, the cultivated land with good water conservancy and soil and water conservation facilities, or the cultivated land with middle production rate and low production rate that is undergoing transformation, or the cultivated land with high standard that has been built. Third, vegetable production base. Fourth, agricultural research and teaching experimental fields. The second type of cultivated land is other cultivated land except permanent basic cultivated land. Other cultivated land is generally distributed around the permanent basic cultivated land and can grow limited varieties of trade crops and food crops, but its soil, slope, water conservancy, sunshine and other conditions are slightly inferior to the permanent basic cultivated land. China's land management law stipulates that the permanent basic cultivated land designated by the provincial governments shall generally account for more than 80% of the cultivated land. Permanent basic cultivated land is quite different from other cultivated land in terms of land requisition principle, compensation standard and approval procedure.

Reasons for requisition of cultivated land. First, expand residential areas. Increasing the number of houses has become a way for the Chinese government to meet the needs of citizens. The houses of Chinese citizens can be roughly divided into two categories, one is low standard houses with resettlement nature, the other is high standard houses with commercial nature. Houses for poverty alleviation and houses for victims of natural disasters belong to low standard houses of resettlement nature. Houses built for the purpose of exchange and profit are commercial houses. Commercial housing and China's economy are tied together, and they are highly correlated. For the construction of commercial houses, a large amount of cultivated land has to be expropriated. Second, build infrastructure. Public infrastructure such as energy, transportation, electric power, water conservancy, communication, postal service, national defense construction, science and technology, education, culture, health, sports, ecological environment and resource protection, disaster prevention and mitigation, cultural relics protection, community comprehensive services, social welfare, municipal public utilities, preferential treatment and resettlement, heroic protection, etc. need to requisition cultivated land. Third, industrial land for economic development. China has a wide land area and rich mineral resources. Many cultivated land stores a large number of oil, natural gas, ore and other resources. In order to exploit and utilize these resources and develop oil, gas and ore industries, it is necessary to requisition cultivated land. In addition, the general economic activities of citizens also need to requisition cultivated land, such as building shopping malls or vegetable markets. Fourth, in addition to land requisition for construction, disaster damage, ecological conversion and agricultural structural adjustment also encroached on a large number of cultivated land. In China, cultivated land requisitioned for disaster damage, ecological conversion and agricultural structural adjustment is not under the jurisdiction of the policy of land requisition compensation balance.

Compensation for Cultivated Land Requisitioned

The compensators of the cultivated land requisitioned. According to the assessment policy of cultivated land requisition and compensation balance, there are four types of responsible persons for compensation of cultivated land: first, if the cultivated land is used in a separate site selection project, the builder is the responsible person for compensation of cultivated land. Second, if cultivated land is used for urban construction, the municipal and county governments shall be the persons responsible for the compensation of cultivated land. Third, if villages and towns use cultivated land for construction, the rural collective economic organizations involved are the responsible units for compensating cultivated land. Fourth, if there is no condition for reclamation or the cultivated land reclaimed does not meet the requirements, the original land reclamation obligor or the company must pay the land reclamation fee in accordance with the provisions of the provincial government, and the local government or the relevant department that collects the land reclamation fee shall be the responsible unit for compensating the cultivated land. In practice, the situation that the constructors are directly responsible for the reclamation of cultivated land is less, mostly in the form of paying land reclamation fees, and the government comes out to reclaim cultivated land.

Source of cultivated land for compensation. In a county, there are three ways to compensate cultivated land: reclamation of new cultivated land, land consolidation and cultivated land reclamation again. The first is to cultivate new cultivated land. Reclamation of new cultivated land means that forest land, River land, grassland and bare land can be reclaimed as cultivated land. We know that forest land, river beach land, grassland and bare land are the key points of China's cultivated land reserve, but generally speaking, these lands are far away from the farmers' settlements, the soil quality is fragile, the reclamation is difficult and the cost is high. The second way is land consolidation. Reducing the number of rural houses is the most common way of land consolidation in China. Arranging farmers to live in high-rise buildings can reduce the number of rural houses, save cultivated land resources and improve the efficiency of land use. Another way of land consolidation is to increase the area of cultivated land by integrating the ridges, terraces and roads in the field. There are six typical patterns of land consolidation in China: first, the pattern of large-scale agricultural consolidation in Northeast China, the pattern of changing drought into water consolidation, and the pattern of water-saving consolidation. Second, the water-saving and saline alkali land consolidation modes in North China. Third, the middle region of waterlogged land consolidation model, hill land consolidation model. Fourth, the high standard cultivated land ecological consolidation model and the farmer housing reclamation model in the southeast region. Fifth, the ecological consolidation model of Loess Hilly and gully area in Northwest China. Sixthly, the slope land consolidation model, river beach land consolidation model and karst rocky desertification land consolidation model in Southwest China. Third, cultivated land reclamation again. Cultivated land reclamation again refers to the reclamation of abandoned land which was originally used as cultivated land, because of some reasons, is not suitable for cultivation or the yield of cultivated land is not high. In terms of the way that the land reclamation obligors choose to compensate the cultivated land, the proportion of land consolidation is the highest (6 million hectares), accounting for 45%, followed by new cultivated land (5.8667 million hectares), accounting for 44%, followed by cultivated land reclamation again (1.5333 million hectares), accounting for 11%(Pan Hongyi et al. 2006).

The Balance Between Cultivated Land Requisition and Compensation

First, quantity balanced. According to Article 11 of the assessment policy for the balance of requisition and compensation of cultivated land, the amount of cultivated land compensated through reclamation of new cultivated land shall not be less than the amount of cultivated land requisitioned for construction. Article 31 of China's land management law stipulates: "the government shall protect cultivated land and strictly control the conversion of cultivated land to non cultivated land use. The government implements the system of compensation for land requisition. If the non-agricultural construction is approved to expropriate the cultivated land, the person who expropriates the cultivated land shall be responsible for reclaiming a new cultivated land equivalent to the quantity and quality of the expropriated cultivated land in accordance with the principle of " how much cultivated land is expropriated and how much is compensated ". These two regulations establish the quantity balance rules between cultivated land requisition and compensation.

Second, quality balanced. Article 11 of the assessment policy for the balance of requisition and compensation of cultivated land also stipulates that the new cultivated land to be reclaimed shall have the same or higher grade as the cultivated land to be requisitioned. In other words, the quality of cultivated land newly reclaimed should be basically the same as that of cultivated land requisitioned. The quality is equal or unequal, the key is the grade of cultivated land. With regard to the grade of agricultural land, the Chinese government divides the cultivated land from high to low into one to fifteen according to the factors such as slope, altitude, soil thickness, parent material of soil formation, thickness of cultivated land and composition of cultivated land. In China, the cultivated area evaluated as the first to the fourth class is 498 million mu, accounting for 27.3% of the total cultivated area in China. This part of cultivated land has a high basic soil capacity, and there is basically no obstacle of cultivation layer. Therefore, the first to fourth class cultivated land should be used in the way of using and maintaining at the same time to ensure its stable and rising quality. The cultivated land area evaluated as grade 5-11 is 818 million mu, accounting for 44.8% of the total cultivated land area in China. This part of cultivated land is basically suitable for the environment and climate conditions, with good cultivated land infrastructure conditions and no obvious obstacles in the cultivation layer. It is the key area for grain production in China in the future. The cultivated area evaluated as grade 11-15 is 510 million mu, accounting for 27.9% of the total cultivated area in China. This part of cultivated land has relatively poor basic soil capacity, obvious obstacles of cultivation layer, and it is difficult to get fundamental improvement in a short time. In addition, with regard to the level of cultivated land, Chinese scholars of cultivated land protection have the views of four levels of cultivated land, six levels of cultivated land and ten levels of cultivated land. Scholars who hold the view of six grades of cultivated land advocate that the quality grade of cultivated land should be determined by taking the assurance rate of water source, buried depth of groundwater, irrigation and drainage facilities and road accessibility as supplementary indexes, and the cultivated land should be divided into flat paddy field, terraced field, flat watered field, terraced dry land, flat dry land and sloping dry land(Liu Shuixing 2002). Scholars who hold the view of ten grades of cultivated land advocate to use the existing results of cultivated land grading, and increase organic matter, topsoil, salinization, irrigation assurance rate, soil configuration as important indicators of cultivated land quality evaluation(Yu Lei 2009).

Two Models of the Balance Policy of Land Requisition and Compensation in China

The first is the traditional mode of "first requisition and then compensation". Companies or individuals that need to requisition cultivated land shall first pay cultivated land reclamation fees to the land management department, and can directly use cultivated land after some certain procedures. Since then, the government will make a unified investment, and will choose and entrust a third-party organization specialized in cultivated land reclamation to undertake the specific task of compensation for cultivated land by means of bidding (Zhang Zhanlu et al. 2010).

The second is the cultivated land ticket mode of "compensation cultivated land first, requisition cultivated land then ". Companies or individuals that need to requisition cultivated land have the right to choose not to pay cultivated land reclamation fees, and companies and individuals can implement or invest to entrust a third-party organization to implement cultivated land consolidation or reclamation projects. Reclaim qualified new cultivated land, or purchase compensation cultivated land quota from the new cultivated land quota transaction market, and obtain corresponding cultivated land use certificate after necessary examination and approval procedures, and then expropriate cultivated land with the type and quantity of cultivated land recorded in the land ticket (cultivated land use certificate).

A CASE STUDY ON THE BALANCE OF CULTIVATED LAND REQUISITION AND COMPENSATION——CONSTRUCTION OF R RAILWAY DRY PORT IN Q COUNTY

Brief Introduction of Q County and The Bottom Line of Cultivated Land in Q County

Brief introduction of Q county. Q county is located in the eastern foot of the Qinghai Tibet Plateau and the northeast of Chengdu Plain, covering an area of 378.56 square kilometers. It is 31.6km long from the east to the West and 28.4km wide from the south to the north, with a northwest southeast trend. The terrain is relatively flat, including plain, hill and low mountain (36%, 39% and 25% respectively). The northwest is a plain with an altitude of 451-480 meters, the middle is a hill with an altitude of 480-700 meters, and the southeast is a low mountain area with an altitude of 546-915 meters. The terrain of the whole area is high in the southeast and low in the northwest. Q county's land use is mainly agricultural land, accounting for 79.72% of the total land, of which cultivated land is the main part, accounting for 64.24% of the agricultural land area. Q county has obvious regional differences in land use, the southeast is dominated by forest land, cultivated land and garden land, and the Northwest has a large proportion of urban and rural construction land(figure 3).

The origin of the bottom line of cultivated land in Q county. Taking 15 years as a cycle, the central government of China has arranged the national land use plan for 2006-2020. According to the plan, by 2020, the bottom line of cultivated land in Q county is 19247 hectares, which can not be changed without extremely special circumstances (earthquakes, landslides and other serious natural disasters). The bottom line of 19247 hectares of cultivated land is arranged step by step: first, the central government of China plans to have a bottom line of 124333300 hectares (1865 million mu) of cultivated land nationwide by 2020. Then, according to the requirements of the central government, Sichuan provincial government determined that the bottom line of cultivated land conservation in Sichuan Province in 2020 is 5.888 million hectares. Thirdly, according to the requirements of Sichuan provincial government, Chengdu municipal government has determined that the bottom line of cultivated land reserve in Chengdu in 2020 is 420800 hectares or more. Finally, according to the requirements of Chengdu municipal government, Q county government determined that the bottom line of cultivated land conservation in 2020 is 19247.00 hectares. Q County governs 11 towns, but the town government is not the responsibility unit of the balance of land requisition and compensation. Q county government is the most basic legal responsibility unit of the balance of land requisition and compensation in China(Figure. 1). However, because the town government is under the management of the county government, the county government is actually arranging the bottom line of cultivated land for each town government, but this task arrangement is not open to the public. At the beginning of 2021, the central government of China will investigate or sample the completion of the bottom line task of cultivated land protection in each administrative region step by step. If the ability to compensate cultivated land is insufficient or the balance policy of requisition and compensation of cultivated land is not well implemented, the main officials in charge of the government will be severely punished, and the local government will also be reduced the corresponding plan of requisition of cultivated land for construction. The following is an empirical case of Q County R railway dry port construction to open up the policy picture of China's land requisition and compensation balance.

Figure 1. The origin of the bottom line of cultivated land in Q county

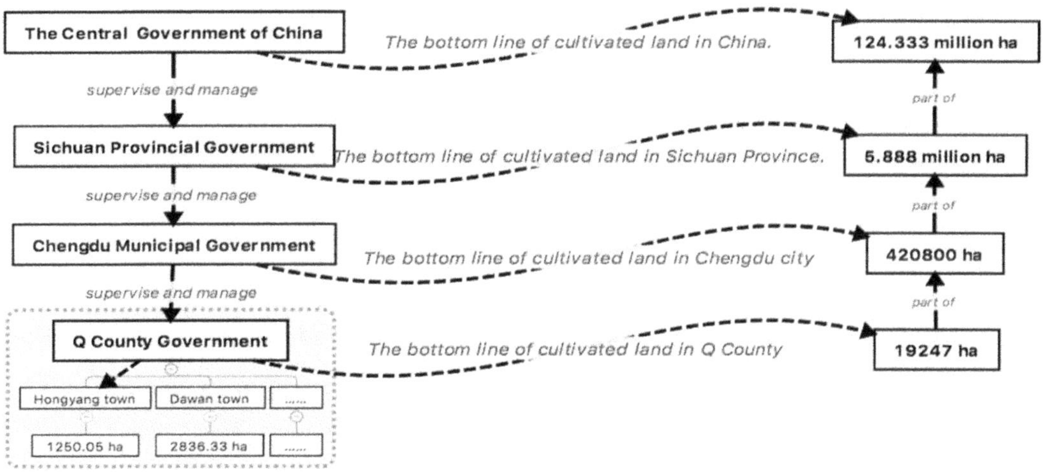

Cultivated Land Requisitioned for Construction of R Railway Dry Port

In 2016, Q County embarked on a major Logistics industrial park project construction - R railway dry port. The largest dry port in Asia, with a total planning area of about 22 square kilometers, needs to expropriate a lot of cultivated land, which seriously affects the bottom line task of 19247.00 hectares of cultivated land in Q county(figure 2).

Figure 2. Satellite map of cultivated land requisition for R railway dry port

R railway dry port (Figure 3) covers an area of 2235.51 hectares, accounting for 8% of the total land area of Q county. Three types of land need to be expropriated for the construction of the port: 1031.19 hectares of agricultural land, 1175.42 hectares of construction land and 28.90 hectares of other land. Among them, agricultural land includes 1004.31 hectares of cultivated land, 10.05 hectares of garden land, 7.81 hectares of forest land and 9.02 hectares of other agricultural land. Construction land includes 685.53 hectares of urban land, 289 hectares of rural residential areas, 6.58 hectares of mining land, 171.20 hectares of transportation land, 15.12 hectares of water conservancy facilities land and 1.93 hectares of other construction land. Other land, including 28.90 hectares of water area.

Figure 3. Satellite map of R railway dry port location

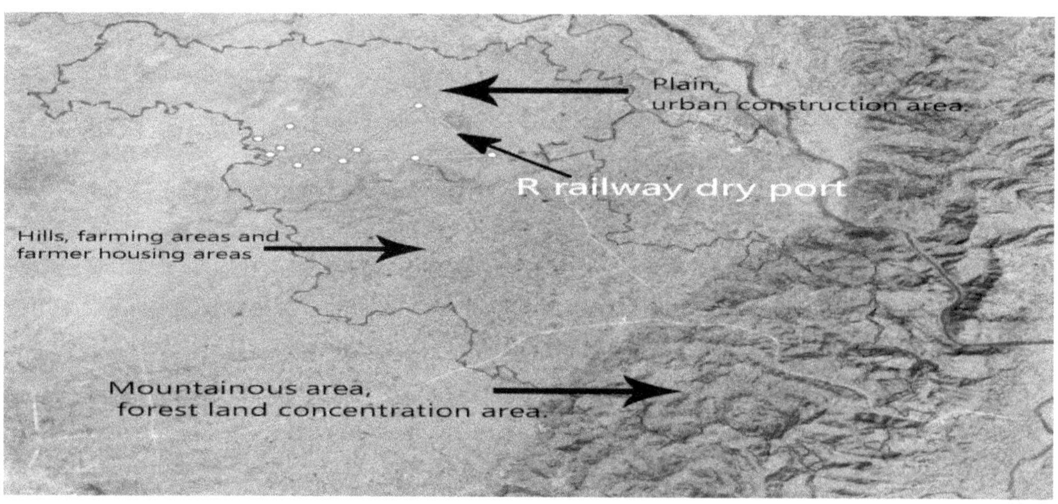

Compensation for Cultivated Land Requisitioned by R Railway Dry Port

According to the balance policy of cultivated land requisition and compensation, Q county must compensate 1004.31 hectares of cultivated land requisitioned. Q county has three ways to develop new cultivated land(figure 4):

Figure 4. Land use of Q County in 2019

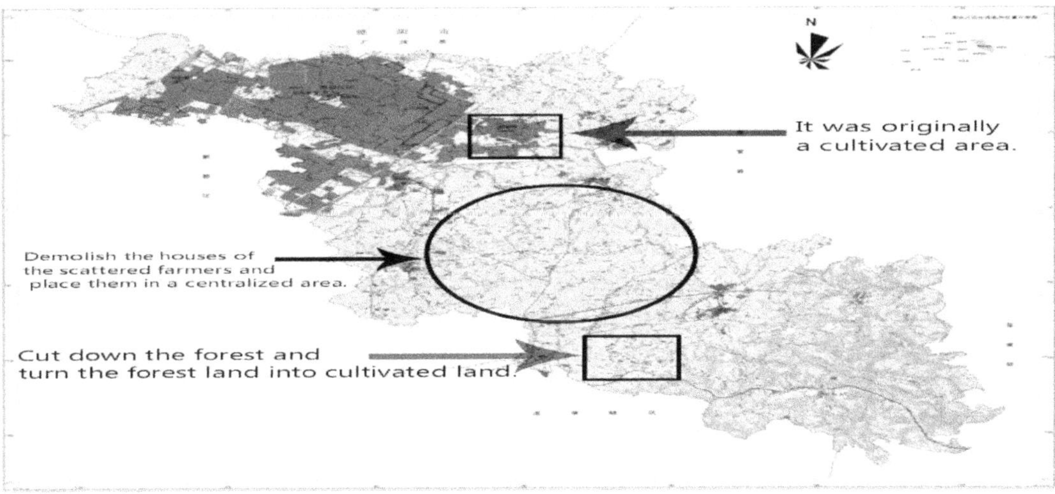

Figure 5. Reclaim new cultivated land from the forest land

First, reclaim the reserved land resources in Q County. The way is transforming the forest and economic forest into cultivated land. It is impossible to reclaim cultivated land in high mountain areas. Therefore, the mountainous area that can become cultivated land can only be the transition zone from hills with gentle slope and complete water conservancy facilities to mountainous area. Through deforestation, Q county has developed 21 hectares of cultivated land in Fuhong town and Qingquan town(figure 5).

Second, land consolidation. Land consolidation is to change the land occupied by farmers' houses or inefficient land into cultivated land. As shown in Figure 6, since 2014, Q county plans to reclaim the scattered farmers' houses and land and reclaim 881.63 hectares of cultivated land from the forest land in six years to compensate for the land requisitioned for the construction of R railway dry port. Because the land consolidation needs a lot of financial support in the early stage, Q county tried their best to get a part of municipal cultivated land reclamation fees. The city level cultivated land reclamation fee, plus Q county's own land consolidation fund, forms the capital fund. With this capital fund, Q county supports the establishment of a land consolidation project company, which is specially responsible for the demolition of farmers' houses, the construction of the farmer's new resettlement houses and the reclamation of cultivated land in Q County. In order to reduce the difficulty of comprehensive land consolidation and improve the efficiency of conversion of residential land to cultivated land, Q county further allocated 881.63 hectares of land consolidation tasks to 11 township governments under its jurisdiction, as shown in table 1. As the land of Chengxiang town and Xiangfu town is mainly expropriated by R railway dry port, Q county mainly allocated 334.74 hectares and 181.51 hectares of land consolidation and reclamation to Xiangfu town and Chengxiang town, because Chengxiang town and Xiangfu town benefit from the economy development chance a lot.

Figure 6. One of the ways of land consolidation: demolishing the houses of farmers

Third, purchase the quota of new cultivated land from other counties outside Q county. Due to resource constraints, land consolidation can not fully meet the land needs of R railway port, Q county has to purchase new cultivated land from other counties. In Chengdu rural property rights trading company, the third level cultivated land is 900000 yuan per hectare, and the sixth level cultivated land is 300000 yuan per hectare. Q County spent a total of 81.786 million yuan to purchase 101.68 hectares of new cultivated land in S county. Both s and Q counties are under the management of Chengdu municipal government. As S county is located in the easternmost edge of the Qinghai Tibet Plateau, which belongs

Table 1. Q county allocated 881.63 hectares of land consolidation tasks to 11 township

	Area name	Allocation of land reclamation tasks
Q County	Hongyang town	65.99 ha
	Dawan town	71.93 ha
	Mimu town	141.61 ha
	Datong town	31.75 ha
	Chengxiang town	181.51 ha
	Xiangfu town	334.74 ha
	Yaodu town	6.22 ha
	Qingquan town	23.37 ha
	Longwang Town	8.64 ha
	Fuhong town	11.11 ha
	Renhe Town	5.76 ha
Total		881.63 ha

to the impact plain of the lower reaches of the glacier melt water river, its forest land resources and cultivated land reserve resources are relatively rich. County S vigorously develops agriculture and often reclaims new cultivated land, so there are surplus cultivated land quota available for sale. According to the regulations of Chengdu municipal government, the sale of new cultivated land in the city must be listed and sold by Chengdu rural property rights trading company, not privately. After Q county and S county reached an agreement on the transaction of new cultivated land, Chengdu municipal government increased the bottom line of cultivated land in S county by 101.68 hectares and reduced the bottom line of cultivated land in Q County by 101.68 hectares. During the planning period from 2006 to 2020, Q County purchased 1220 hectares of new cultivated land from different places. After that, Chengdu will reduce the cultivated land protection task of Q County, and adjust the bottom line of 19247 hectares of cultivated land to 18027 hectares. In other words, by 2020, the bottom line of cultivated land in Q county will change from 19247 hectares to 18027 hectares(figure 7).

Figure 7. Logic chart of new cultivated land quota transaction

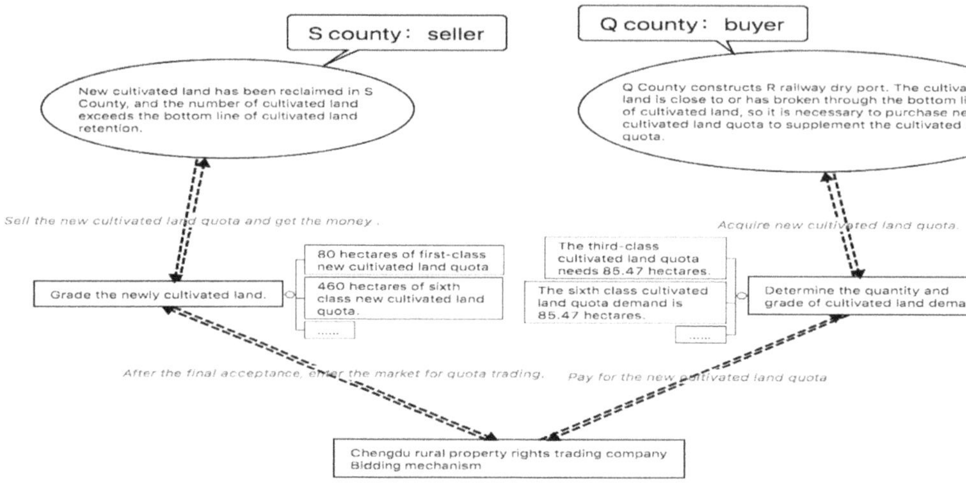

"Quantity" and "Quality" Balance between Land Acquisition and Land Compensation of R Railway Port in Q County

First, the balance of quantity. Among the 1004.31 hectares of cultivated land expropriated, there are 85.47 hectares of third class cultivated land, 370.17 hectares of sixth class cultivated land, 246 hectares of seventh class cultivated land and 302.4 hectares of ninth class cultivated land. In Q County, a total of 902.63 hectares of new cultivated land were obtained through 21 hectares of cultivated land and 881.63 hectares of cultivated land were newly increased through land reclamation reserve resources and land consolidation. By purchasing new cultivated land from S county, Q county obtained 101.68 hectares of cultivated land quota, and completed the task of land requisition and compensation balance in quantity.

Second, the balance of quality. According to the regulations of Sichuan provincial government, the cultivation layer of the third-class cultivated land shall be sandy loam or loamy clay, mainly loamy clay, with a thickness of 16-18cm, organic matter of 2.4-3.9, nitrogen content of 0.108-0.233, phosphorus content of 4-14 and pH value of 5.0-7.5. The cultivation layer of the sixth class cultivated land should be sandy soil or clay, mainly clay, with the thickness of 11-17cm, organic matter of 1.7-4.4, nitrogen content of 0.087-0.242, phosphorus content of 3-14 and pH value of 4.5-8.3. Q County in the region through land consolidation of cultivated land can reach the sixth, seventh and ninth class of cultivated land indicators, but it is difficult to achieve the third class of cultivated land standards. Therefore, Q county must purchase 85.47 hectares of third-class cultivated land and 16.21 hectares of sixth class cultivated land from Chengdu rural property rights trading company, so as to meet the requirements of quality balance with the cultivated land requisitioned.

Four Things Need to Be Clarified in The Case of Q County Cultivated Land Requisition Compensation Balance

First, the requisition of forest land and garden land does not need the balance of land requisition and compensation. In this case, in addition to cultivated land, Q county also cut down 10.95 hectares of forest and 10.05 hectares of garden land to obtain 21 hectares of new cultivated land. According to China's land management law, forest land can be used to compensate cultivated land. However, without special and sufficient reasons, cultivated land cannot be converted into forest land. After the reduction of forest land, it is not necessary to find other kinds of land for conversion of cultivated land to forest or afforestation. It is enough to reduce the forest statistics of the central or local governments. Up to now, China has only defined the bottom line of cultivated land, but not the bottom line of forest land. Therefore, except for 1004.31 hectares of cultivated land that has been expropriated, the balance of land requisition and compensation is not needed for other land types.

Second, the compensation for the cultivated land requisitioned in Q county is a kind of data compensation, not a substantial compensation for the right to use or ownership of the new cultivated land. First of all, the right to use the new cultivated land in Q county does not belong to the farmers who have lost the cultivated land. Generally, the new cultivated land obtained through forest cutting development and land consolidation in the area is given priority to the farmers of the original expropriated cultivated land, but the right to use the new cultivated land does not have to belong to the farmers of the expropriated cultivated land or the farmers of the land consolidation area. Generally speaking, the newly reclaimed cultivated land is far away from the farmers who have been expropriated. If the right to use the newly increased cultivated land is allocated to the farmers who have been expropriated, there is a high probability that the newly increased cultivated land will face the awkward situation of no farming. Second, what County S has sold to county Q is the quota of new cultivated land, not the use right or ownership of new cultivated land. Q County paid 81.786 million yuan to buy 101.68 hectares of new cultivated land in S county, and obtained the Permission of Chengdu municipal government to reduce the bottom line of local cultivated land. The use of new cultivated land in S county is arranged by S county government. In practice, the S county government delivers part of the newly reclaimed cultivated land to the nearby farmers for cultivation, and the farmers pay a little bit cultivated land contract fee to the S county government. For the other part of cultivated land, the S county government has a corresponding agreement with the cultivated land reclamation company, stipulating that the newly reclaimed cultivated land shall be used by the cultivated land reclamation company free of charge for 30 years, because the company that reclaims the new cultivated land has paid the cost of reclaiming the new cultivated land.

Third, before the new cultivated land compensated by S county is sold to Q County, it has passed the strict qualification examination. In order to enter into the transaction market held by Chengdu rural property rights trading company, the newly reclaimed cultivated land of S county must be preliminarily inspected and accepted by the Land Bureau of S county and the Agriculture Bureau of S county. After the preliminary acceptance, the land department of Sichuan Province shall organize the final inspection and acceptance. After the final inspection and acceptance, the land department of Sichuan Province will issue the acceptance certificate of new cultivated land to S county government. After the land department of Sichuan Province submits the cultivated land acceptance report to the Ministry of land and resources of China for filing, the new cultivated land of S county can be listed and traded in the market held by Chengdu rural property rights trading company. The final inspection and acceptance includes 12 first-class indicators: terrain position, soil parent material, slope structure, water type, winter groundwater level, thickness of arable layer, texture of arable layer, physical barrier level, drainage and irrigation conditions, physical and chemical properties of soil, maturity and food output level.

Fourth, the cost of reclaiming new cultivated land should be borne by the companies and individuals who expropriate or want to expropriate the cultivated land(Yang Lina 2013). A company or individual who wants to enter the R railway dry port industrial area and use the land in the industrial area needs to pay the reclamation fee of the new cultivated land first. After paying the fee for new cultivated land reclamation, the company or individual may not need to cultivate new cultivated land by themselves anymore, and the government will organize the reclamation or purchase new cultivated land outside the region. In general, the government needs to pay the cost of new cultivated land reclamation in advance, no matter in or out of the region. A large part of these costs come from the new cultivated land reclamation fees paid by companies or individuals. If the company or individual pays the cultivated land reclamation fee, it is deemed to have fulfilled the obligation of new cultivated land reclamation.

PROBLEMS ENCOUNTERED IN THE IMPLEMENTATION OF THE POLICY OF CULTIVATED LAND REQUISITION AND COMPENSATION BALANCE IN CHINA

Problems in The Process of Requisition of Cultivated Land

First, the practice of expropriation of forest land and grassland to compensate cultivated land has been abused, which leads to an increase in the risk of ecological environment damage and more cultivated land in the risk of natural disasters caused by ecological environment damage. For a long time, in order to pursue the balance of the amount of cultivated land, some governments blindly reclaim some vulnerable areas of ecological environment as new cultivated land, "reclaim the lake to build cultivated land", "destroy the forest to build cultivated land", "reclaim the riverbed to build cultivated land". The reclamation of new cultivated land in the fragile ecological environment area has seriously damaged the ecological environment. The original ecological balance has been broken, resulting in frequent water and soil loss, flood disaster, serious loss of ecological benefits, and new cultivated land unable to cultivate because of the threat of natural disasters. What's worse, natural disasters and land pollution in turn cause a lot of cultivated land loss. The amount of cultivated land lost is even more than the newly reclaimed cultivated land. For the purpose of ecological environment protection, China has implemented the policies of returning cultivated land to forest, grassland and lake. Since the implementation of the policies, about 143 million mu of cultivated land has been converted into forest land, among which there are some newly developed cultivated land due to the balance of land requisition and compensation.

Second, the approval authority of requisition of cultivated land is gradually decentralized, and the risk of large-scale requisition of cultivated land is increased. According to Article 45 of China's land management law, the requisition of the following land shall be approved by the central government of China: (1) basic cultivated land; (2) over 35 hectares of cultivated land other than basic cultivated land. The approval standard of this kind of cultivated land requisition is very high, which to a large extent prevents the cultivated land from being expropriated for construction. However, the recent implementation regulations (Draft) of China's land management law have changed this approval standard. The above two types of cultivated land can be expropriated only with the approval of the provincial government, and then the provincial government reports the expropriation plan to the central government of China for filing. The decentralization of examination and approval authority may lead to the local government to over expropriate cultivated land for political achievements(Xiao Ye 2019).

Third, there is no unified legal system to support the balance method of "first compensating cultivated land, then expropriating cultivated land". The practice of "first using cultivated land and then compensating cultivated land" has been criticized by both theorists and practitioners. This practice has led to three phenomena, the first one is that the cultivated land is expropriated without compensation, the second one is that more cultivated land is expropriated but less cultivated land is compensated, and the third one is that the high-quality cultivated land is expropriated while the low-quality cultivated land is compensated. Chinese scholars generally hold the view that the root cause of the three phenomena is "get on the train first, make up the ticket then ". Although we all agree that the practice of "first compensation for cultivated land, then expropriation of cultivated land" has obvious advantages, but the current situation is that the provincial governments are still making their own rules, lacking national unified laws and operational guidelines. In the early practice of the policy of land requisition compensation balance, the quality and grade of cultivated land requisitioned were ignored, and a large number of excellent cultivated land was requisitioned, which was only compensated according to the standard of ordinary cultivated land. The biggest advantage of "first to compensate cultivated land, then to expropriate cultivated land" is that it is convenient to check whether the quality of the compensation cultivated land meets the standard according to the quality of the expropriated cultivated land. Now, many places in China have begun to require that companies or individuals who expropriate cultivated land must prepare a feasibility study report. In addition, the company or individual shall add the basic information such as the level, quality and quantity of the cultivated land to the feasibility study report. Only after the feasibility study report is examined and approved by the land management department of the government, can the company or individual expropriate the cultivated land.

Fourth, there is no uniform standard for the collection of new cultivated land reclamation fees. Some governments charge for new cultivated land reclamation fees by calculating the new cultivated land reclamation fees per mu of first-class cultivated land at twice the land acquisition fees. The cultivated land reclamation fee of the second-class cultivated land is calculated as one time of the land acquisition fee per mu. Land acquisition fee includes land compensation fee, seedling fee, land attachment compensation fee and residence compensation fee. Another way for some governments to charge for new cultivated land reclamation is to charge for cultivated land reclamation according to the grain output of the requisitioned cultivated land. For example, the output of first-class cultivated land is about 13500kg / ha, and that of ninth class cultivated land is about 3000kg / ha. Therefore, the cultivated land reclamation cost of cultivated land is 4.5 times of that of ninth class cultivated land. Companies or individuals that need to expropriate cultivated land need to pay one-off or installment of 20-year cultivated land reclamation fees. It can be seen from this that there is no uniform standard for the collection of cultivated land reclamation fees in China.

Problems in The Process of Compensation For Cultivated Land

First, it is difficult for the newly reclaimed cultivated land to reach the quality level of the expropriated cultivated land. Most of the cultivated land requisitioned for urban construction is located in the high-quality cultivated land with flat terrain, convenient transportation and fertile soil around the city, while many new cultivated land reserve resources are mostly located in mountainous or hilly areas. The terrain conditions of these plots are relatively poor, the slope is large, the traffic is inconvenient, the water source is lack, the area of continuous cultivated land is small, and the qualified cultivated land reserve resources available for reclamation and consolidation are extremely limited. It is very difficult to achieve the quality level of the previously requisitioned cultivated land, and the cost is very high. Therefore, the detailed rules of China's land management law stipulate that the newly increased cultivated land obtained through land consolidation can only compensate the original cultivated land expropriated in the proportion of 1:0.6. The reason for this regulation is that it is difficult for the newly reclaimed land to reach the quality level of the expropriated land.

Secondly, the balance method of land requisition and compensation which uses a large number of low-level cultivated land for a small amount of high-level cultivated land is abused, resulting in the decrease of high-level cultivated land and the continuous expansion of low-level cultivated land. As shown in figure 8, 1 mu of first-class cultivated land can be compensated for 2.5 mu of tenth class cultivated land. The government thinks that it is too complicated and expensive to change the tenth class of poor cultivated land into the first class of high quality cultivated land according to the standard of high standard cultivated land transformation rules(Qian Fengkui et al. 2008). However, it is simple, easy to operate and low cost to reclaim new cultivated land by increasing the number of low-level cultivated land(Yu Lei et al. 2009). Under the guidance of this new cultivated land reclamation thinking, the high-grade cultivated land in China is rapidly reduced, the low-grade cultivated land is continuously expanding, the proportion of high-quality cultivated land and low-quality cultivated land is seriously out of balance, and the land resources are seriously wasted(Chen Bosong et al. 2009).

Figure 8. Conversion coefficient between cultivated land grades
Source:(official website of The Ministry of Natural Resources of China,2019)

占用等别 Grade of requisition	补充等别 Grade of compensation														
	1等	2等	3等	4等	5等	6等	7等	8等	9等	10等	11等	12等	13等	14等	15等
1等	1	1.07	1.15	1.25	1.36	1.5	1.67	1.88	2.14	2.5	3	3.75	5	7.5	15
2等	1	1	1.08	1.17	1.27	1.4	1.56	1.75	2	2.33	2.8	3.5	4.67	7	14
3等	1	1	1	1.08	1.18	1.3	1.44	1.63	1.86	2.17	2.6	3.25	4.33	6.5	13
4等	1	1	1	1	1.09	1.2	1.33	1.5	1.71	2	2.4	3	4	6	12
5等	1	1	1	1	1	1.1	1.22	1.38	1.57	1.83	2.2	2.75	3.67	5.5	11
6等	1	1	1	1	1	1	1.11	1.25	1.43	1.67	2	2.5	3.33	5	10
7等	1	1	1	1	1	1	1	1.13	1.29	1.5	1.8	2.25	3	4.5	9
8等	1	1	1	1	1	1	1	1	1.14	1.33	1.6	2	2.67	4	8
9等	1	1	1	1	1	1	1	1	1	1.17	1.4	1.75	2.33	3.5	7
10等	1	1	1	1	1	1	1	1	1	1	1.2	1.5	2	3	6
11等	1	1	1	1	1	1	1	1	1	1	1	1.25	1.67	2.5	5
12等	1	1	1	1	1	1	1	1	1	1	1	1	1.33	2	4
13等	1	1	1	1	1	1	1	1	1	1	1	1	1	1.5	3
14等	1	1	1	1	1	1	1	1	1	1	1	1	1	1	2
15等	1	1	1	1	1	1	1	1	1	1	1	1	1	1	1

Third, the new cultivated land reclamation fees are not fully used in the reclamation of new cultivated land. According to the detailed rules for the implementation of the land management law of China, the land management departments of the governments at or above the county level that have approved the use of land shall be responsible for collecting the land reclamation fees. The allocation of cultivated land reclamation fees shall be 20% for provincial government, 20% for municipal government and 60% for county government(Xiong Dongyang 2015). The cultivated land reclamation fee shall be turned over to the account of the financial department of the government, and shall be used exclusively for the reclamation of cultivated land, the transformation of low grain output fields, and the protection and management of permanent basic cultivated land. After receiving the reclamation fee for new cultivated land, the government shall arrange 50% for the land department and 50% for the agricultural department (Zhang Fengrong et al. 2002). The drawback of the above regulations is that the county-level government usually undertakes the task of new cultivated land reclamation, but the county-level government can only receive 60% of the cultivated land reclamation fee, and 60% of the cultivated land reclamation fee can not meet the task demand of supplementing new cultivated land. What's worse, because the cost of reclaiming new cultivated land can be wholly or partially borne by the users of the new cultivated land, many governments regard the 60% of the land reclamation fees received as the government's net income, ignoring the nature of its dedicated to reclaiming new cultivated land.

Fourth, the trading mechanism of new cultivated land quota is not perfect, and there are still obstacles in the trading of new cultivated land across provincial governments. First, there is a lack of bidding mechanism. China's new cultivated land transaction is not a multi buyer to multi seller bidding. After the buyer and the seller reach an agreement and obtain the approval of the superior, the buyer pays the price under the insufficient competition, sells the house and delivers the detailed data of the new cultivated land, and the transaction is declared to be completed. In fact, this kind of transaction is also an indicator allocation under the instruction of the superior. Secondly, the new cultivated land purchased by the buyer cannot be traded twicc. According to China's land management law, the government should carefully calculate the amount of cultivated land and purchase new cultivated land. If there is surplus to the purchased cultivated land, it cannot be resold without special and sufficient reasons. The motivation of this regulation is easy to understand. It is mainly to prevent the government from hyping the data of new cultivated land quantity, which leads to excessive premium of the data of new cultivated land quantity. The data transaction mechanism of new cultivated land quantity in China, with low degree of marketization and strong color of regional protection, leads to difficulties in cross provincial government transactions.

Fifth, the lack of supervision on the use of new cultivated land causes waste of cultivated land resources and the phenomenon of abandoning cultivated land (Zhao Yuntai et al. 2012). There are three reasons for no cultivation in the new cultivated land area: first, the responsibility of management and protection of the new cultivated land is not in the right place. Some land consolidation projects did not select the project area according to the local actual situation, and ignored the analysis and investigation of the soil conditions, ownership, ecological environment and location conditions of the project area. Especially after the final acceptance of the land consolidation project, if the person in charge of management and protection is not found or the agreement on management and protection responsibility is not signed with the person in charge of management and protection, there is a high probability that no one will cultivate the new cultivated land. Second, the farmers are arranged in high-rise houses, the rural population is rapidly urbanized, and the rural farming labor force is gradually insufficient. One of the costs of reducing the land use of farmers' houses is that many farmers are transformed into residents. They no longer use farming as a means of livelihood. The farming labor force in rural areas is greatly reduced, and many cultivated land will be abandoned(Tan Zhi Zhi et al. 2014). Third, the cost of using new cultivated land is too high due to the lack of infrastructure, narrow roads, inconvenient transportation, incomplete water conservancy facilities, and difficulties in later stage fertilization. Because of the inconvenience of transportation and the unsatisfactory irrigation conditions, some of the new cultivated land compensated indirectly raised the cost of cultivation, so that the enthusiasm of farmers to use the new cultivated land was not high, and many of the new cultivated land was in a state of extensive and wasteful use.

FIVE DEVELOPMENT TRENDS OF THE BALANCE POLICY OF LAND REQUISITION AND COMPENSATION IN CHINA

First, the government will purchase more and more professional third-party services to reclaim new cultivated land. In the past, farmers and ordinary companies could participate in the cultivation of new cultivated land. However, it is obvious that farmers and general companies have a single way to reclaim cultivated land, and the efficiency of reclamation is low, so they can not fully reclaim the potential of cultivated land, and the quality of cultivated land is uneven. The professional new cultivated land reclamation company, with larger scale, more professional technicians and more complete equipment, can give full play to the land potential and reclaim cultivated land with higher quality level(Zhang Lin et al. 2007).

Second, the level of grain output will become an important index to determine the conversion coefficient of cultivated land grade between the requisitioned cultivated land and the compensated cultivated land. There are many indicators to measure the quality of cultivated land (as shown in Figure 9). In addition to the level of grain output, other indicators are difficult to quantify. Therefore, many scholars of cultivated land protection in China advocate the level of grain output as an important basis for the conversion of cultivated land quantity and quality. For example, the grain output of the first level cultivated land is 4.5 times that of the Ninth level cultivated land, so 4.5 hectares of the Ninth level cultivated land is equivalent to 1 hectare of the first level cultivated land. Replacing "quantity balance" with "productivity balance" of cultivated land can stimulate citizens' interest in the transformation of low yield land. Through a large number of low-yield cultivated land transformation, the problem of decreasing high-quality cultivated land and increasing low-quality cultivated land in China can be quickly reversed(Guan Wenrong 2006). It is easy to quantify the level of grain output, and it can also form a unified national acceptance system standard for new cultivated land as soon as possible.

Figure 9. Index chart of cultivated land quality evaluation

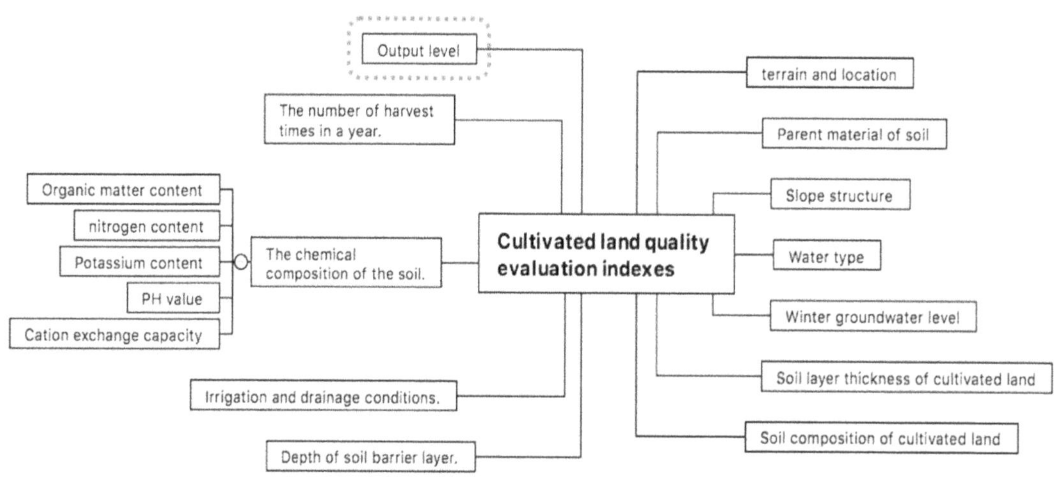

Third, to strengthen ecological protection when reclaiming new cultivated land will become a new direction for the development of the policy of land requisition and compensation balance. On the premise of confirming that it will not cause serious damage to the ecological environment and natural disasters, forest land can be reclaimed step by step. When starting the project of compensation for new cultivated land, governments should introduce the assessment mechanism of ecological environment damage. Through strict examination and approval of new cultivated land projects, the ecological damage caused by the cultivation of cultivated land may be contained. In addition, the central government of China will also establish the awareness of ecological red line and cultivated land red line for the lower level governments, and make clear the boundaries of reclaimable areas and prohibited areas. In the future, China will establish the bottom line mechanism of forest land, grassland and garden land, and implement the ecological red line mechanism.

Fourth, the methods of "first requisitioning cultivated land, then compensating cultivated land", "while requisitioning cultivated land, while compensating cultivated land" will be abandoned, "first compensating cultivated land, then requisitioning cultivated land", "with cultivation capacity, determining the amount of compensation cultivated land" will become an important content of China's cultivated land protection laws and regulations.This kind of arrangement is not only a simple adjustment in order, but also an innovation in land use planning, management concept and mode under the new situation. The practice of "first compensating cultivated land, then expropriating cultivated land" has fundamentally blocked the loopholes of "first getting on the train, then buying tickets" or even "not buying tickets" in the expropriation of cultivated land for non-agricultural construction projects(Huang Meijun 2013). This kind of innovation will also effectively curb the bad habits of the government, companies or individuals who arbitrarily expropriate cultivated land and start construction projects. This kind of innovation improves the consciousness of the government, the company or the individual to use the land intensively, and makes the government, the company and the individual carefully choose the project of expropriating and compensating the cultivated land. The method of "determining the amount of compensation cultivated land with the farming capacity of rural society" considers the responsibility of management and protection of the newly reclaimed cultivated land in advance, avoiding the situation of abandoning the new cultivated land after the new cultivated land is reclaimed because the supervision is not in the right position.

Fifth, the transaction of new cultivated land will develop towards marketization, forming a centralized bidding mechanism of multiple sellers and multiple buyers. In addition, the national unified mechanism of new cultivated land trade across provincial governments will gradually mature(Shao Ting et al. 2011). The multi seller to multi buyer bidding mechanism makes the government who purchases the new cultivated land quota not have to agree with the government who sells the new cultivated land quota face to face. The new cultivated land quota becomes the commodity without special mark, which can improve its circulation efficiency. The rural land and mineral rights trading company set up by the government is responsible for supervising the abnormal information, such as abnormal premium, or the rapid increase of the number of new cultivated land transactions. For the new cultivated land quota acquired through bidding transaction, it will be allowed to be transferred again. With the introduction of the new cultivated land bidding trade mechanism to the whole country, this kind of auction like system can promote the cross provincial government trade of new cultivated land quota.

CONCLUSION AND DISCUSSION

As a whole, the balance policy of land requisition and compensation is of great significance for China to keep the bottom line of 1.8 billion mu of cultivated land. However, due to the defects of the policy itself, there are many problems in the practice of cultivated land protection in China.

From the perspective of the policy itself, there are still many loopholes and deficiencies in the policy. First, the approval power of cultivated land requisition has been gradually decentralized, and the provincial government has obtained greater approval power of cultivated land requisition. The management of the central government of China on cultivated land requisition tends to be loose. Secondly, forest and grassland are not suitable for the balance policy of land requisition and compensation, and the rules that allow the requisition of forest and grassland for the purpose of reclaiming new cultivated land exist, which has hidden dangers for ecological damage. Third, the method of "first use of cultivated land, then compensation of cultivated land" is still the mainstream in the government's practice of land requisition and compensation. The method of "first compensation of cultivated land, then requisition of cultivated land" has not been supported by uniform legal rules. Fourth, there are no unified standard rules for the collection and expenditure of cultivated land reclamation fees. Fifthly, the degree of marketization of data trading of new cultivated land quantity is not high, and the data trading of cultivated land quantity across provincial areas has not been supported by the unified relevant rules of the central government of China.

From the perspective of the problems encountered in the practice of the balance policy of land requisition and compensation, these problems can be summarized as the problems in the process of land requisition and compensation. The problems encountered in the process of requisitioning cultivated land include: first, it is difficult for the newly reclaimed cultivated land to reach the quality level of the requisitioned cultivated land. Second, the practice of expropriating forest land and grassland to compensate cultivated land has been abused, which leads to increased risk of ecological environment damage. The problems encountered in the process of compensation for cultivated land include: first, the method of compensation balance for requisition of cultivated land with a large number of low-level cultivated land for a small number of high-level cultivated land has been abused, resulting in the decrease of high-level cultivated land and the continuous expansion of low-level cultivated land. Second, the lack of supervision on the use of new cultivated land has resulted in the waste of cultivated land resources and the phenomenon of abandoning cultivated land.

From the perspective of the future development of the policy, it will continue to play an important role in China's cultivated land protection. In conclusion, the policy has the following development trends. First, when the government, companies or individuals reclaim new cultivated land, they will enhance their awareness of ecological protection, which will become a priority for the development of the policy of land requisition and compensation balance. The government will be more cautious in approving projects to reclaim new cultivated land on forest and grassland. Secondly, the methods of "first compensation for cultivated land, then expropriation of cultivated land" and "determining the amount of compensation cultivated land with the cultivation capacity of the newly reclaimed cultivated land society" will become the mainstream of the government practice of land requisition compensation balance in China. Third, the government will purchase more professional third-party services to reclaim new cultivated land. Fourthly, the trade of new cultivated land will develop towards marketization, and the national unified mechanism of new cultivated land trade across provincial governments will gradually mature. Fifthly, the level of grain output will become an important index to determine the quality and quantity conversion coefficient between the requisitioned cultivated land and the compensation cultivated land.

From the perspective of the whole world, the policy of balance of land requisition and compensation is only one of many ways to protect cultivated land in the world. Although the balance policy of land requisition and compensation has opened up a new situation for China's cultivated land protection, whether the policy is replicable and can provide China's experience to the world is still worthy of in-depth consideration. China's economy relies heavily on real estate. It can be said that the real estate market drives and dominates the land requisition activities in China. Therefore, strictly controlling the conversion of cultivated land into commercial real estate and controlling the expansion of real estate market as much as possible may be another way or a better way to protect cultivated land. The policy of land requisition and compensation balance is only a remedy to slow down the rapid decrease of cultivated land. Relying only on the policy of land requisition and compensation balance can not reverse the rapid decrease of cultivated land in China. The policy has its special political background and institutional environment. It may work well in China, but it may not work well in other countries.

REFERENCES

Chen, Juan, Yuchun, & Jihua. (2009). Index system and method of agricultural land grade monitoring. *Journal of Agricultural Engineering*, *25*(13), 272–276.

Guan, & Li. (2006). Broadening the thinking of protecting cultivated land -- the task and thinking of the investigation and evaluation of the comprehensive production capacity of agricultural land. *China Land, 0*(3), 17-18.

Huang, Zhu, Jun, & Xin. (2013). Reflections on improving the land ticket system in Chongqing -- from the perspective of land ticket nature and function. *China Land Science*, (6), 48-52.

Lei, Y., Yong, Z., Yun, W., & Xia, X. (2009). Equal conversion of farmland share and compensation balance based on farmland classification results. *Journal of Agricultural Engineering*, *25*(1), 244–248.

Li & Xu. (2006). The application of agricultural land classification results in the balance of cultivated land requisition and compensation: a case study of Zhejiang Province. *China Land Science, 20*(2), 15-18.

Lin, Z., Zhang, F., Xue, Y., & Yan, L. (2007). Prediction of the balance trend of cultivated land in China. *Ziyuan Kexue*, *29*(6), 114–119.

Liu, & Bo. (2002). The application of farmland grading and evaluation results in the balance of cultivated land requisition and compensation. *Regional Research and Development*, (3), 82-84.

Pan, Jing, Ting, Ma, Yi, & Li. (2015). Study on the sequence of agricultural land consolidation under planning guidance and cultivated land quality constraints. *China Land Science*, (8), 81-88.

Qian, Wang, Dong, Dong, Bian, & Jia. (2008). The application of Farmland Grade conversion results in the balance of farmland requisition and compensation. *Journal of Agricultural Engineering*, (8), 110–113.

Tan. (2014). Coexistence of strict control and incentive: policy context and local implementation of land increase and decrease. *China Social Sciences*, (7), 125-142.

Tian. (2005). It is necessary to establish the quality evaluation system of supplementary cultivated land -- further discussion on the balance of cultivated land requisition and compensation. *China Land*, (3), 36-38.

Ting, Cui, Fan, & Xu. (2011). Land use efficiency, inter provincial differences and the balance between different regions. *Economics: Quarterly*, (3), 358-375.

Xiong. (2015). Research on fiscal and tax policies to protect the quality of cultivated land in China. *Tax and Economy*, (2).

Xu, L., Li, B., Yuan, Y., Gao, X., Liu, H., & Dong, G. (2015). Analysis on the effect of China's policy of cultivated land change and cultivated land requisition compensation balance in 2000-2010. *Ziyuan Kexue*, *37*(8), 1543–1551.

Yang. (2013). *Study on the influencing factors and guarantee mechanism of the later stage management and protection of rural land remediation project: a case study of Yunyang County in the Three Gorges Reservoir area*. Academic Press.

Ye. (2019). New law is coming into effect, and reform has a long way to go -- written at the time of the adoption of the amendment to the land management law. *China Land*, (9).

Zhang & Pingli. (2002). Quality control of newly cultivated land. *China Land, 0*(3), 22-24.

Zhang & Zhang. (2010). The pattern of rural residential area consolidation in urban suburbs based on the current situation survey. *Geographical Research*, (5), 127–134.

Zhao, Huang, Zhong, & Zhang, Du, & Zhang. (2012). Evaluation of the balance effect of the implementation of land supervision system on the quantity of cultivated land expropriated and supplemented. *Journal of Agricultural Engineering*, *28*(25), 1–7.

KEY TERMS AND DEFINITIONS

Compensation for Cultivated Land: Compensation for cultivated land requisitioned. In particular, if one hectare of cultivated land is expropriated, one hectare of the same cultivated land must be compensated.

Cultivated Land Requisition: The government purchases land owned by farmers. Then the government will hand over the purchased land to a third-party company or a third-party individual for use.

Cultivated Land Reclamation Again: The land originally used as cultivated land is abandoned because there is no one to cultivate it. Now, the land is reclaimed again.

Expropriated Cultivated Land: Cultivated land will be occupied for more than 20 years.

Land Consolidation: Land consolidation is to reallocate the elements of land, in order to make the best use of land.

New Cultivated Land Quota Transaction: Each county has a bottom line of cultivated land. The quota data of new cultivated land exceeding the bottom line of cultivated land can be used for transaction.

New Cultivated Land Reclamation Fee: The fee that a company or individual needs to pay to the government for requisition of cultivated land. The name of this cost is to reclaim new cultivated land with the same quantity and quality as the expropriated cultivated land.

Reclamation of New Cultivated Land: Reclaim the uncultivated forest, grassland and other land into cultivated land.

Chapter 2
Development Efforts and Response to the Regional Conflicts in Socially Sensitive Areas of South Provinces, Thailand

Chanon Nunbhakdi
Asian Institute of Technology, Thailand

Mokbul Morshed Ahmad
https://orcid.org/0000-0002-4003-0920
Asian Institute of Technology, Thailand

Shahab E. Saqib
https://orcid.org/0000-0003-0326-5197
Higher Education Department, Mardan, Pakistan

ABSTRACT

The ideological clash between Muslim-Malay is predominant in Thailand, which undoubtedly led to conflicts between the separatist groups and the central government. It is a source of risk to development efforts that might harm the sensitivity of the conflict situation. Hence, this chapter aims to explore the impacts of development efforts in the conflict-affected areas of the Deep South region of Thailand. The data is collected from secondary sources and analyzed through descriptive statistics. Results showed that the development efforts from the central government in the southernmost provinces resulted in significant improvement of basic infrastructure, education, and the healthcare system. Due to a high degree of government intervention, the impact of the NGOs on development is considerably limited. It is suggested that the communities should be strengthened in their capacity to increase their role and share the local political power, reduce the monopolizing of local politicians, and increase the accuracy of the development project to the communities' actual needs.

DOI: 10.4018/978-1-7998-4372-6.ch002

1. INTRODUCTION

Like other developing countries, Thailand has no exception in the prevalence of violent conflicts. Due to the current unrest in the Malay-Muslim provinces of southern Thailand has got international, national, regional and local attention due to the highly frequent and mass scale attacks (Chalk 2008). The conflict between the Thai state and Muslim Malay insurgencies in the Deep South regions of Thailand has been carrying on along with the history of predominant Thai and Muslim-Malay relationship. Thai culture which was not suitable for intense Muslim culture and undoubtedly led to the conflicts between the local aristocrats and the bureaucrats from the central government at various levels (Aphornsuvan 2003).

In the early 21st century, an international community has acknowledged the collective framework imposing development direction known as Millennium Development Goals, and the recently Sustainable Development Goals. Specific issues such as poverty, environment, and livelihoods at the community level are now gaining essential attention from the development perspective. Of all-important development dimensions, security is considered as the most important contribution to sustainability. Additionally, security is expected to build sustainability with the incisive process. Therefore, the overall process ranged from imposing policy to the implementation should be done with an inclusive approach and at the very local level instead of national (UN 2015; UNDP 2016). The overall goal of sustainable development (SD) is the long-term stability of the economy that can only be attainable by integration and acknowledgment of economic, environmental, and social concerns throughout the decision-making process (Emas 2015). The economy-oriented development theory clearly showed its ineffective ability to deal with a conflict situation. Consequently, generated a great extent of inequality in many levels of the globe while increasing the national income of the developing countries. The issue of inequality is impeding the whole global security as it represents the increase of the national and international incidents such as migrations, terroristic. To address the conflict, it is also impossible to neglect other factors of development of those particular areas in which implementation takes place (Mac Ginty and Williams 2009).

To respond to each incident, the root cause of the conflict needs to be understood. The historical background of particular adversarial groups is mostly accounted for the explanation of the cause of typical conflict (Ray and Esteban 2017). On the other hand, despite the historical root of the conflict, unequal development distribution is believed to be a major factor contributing to and sustaining the conflicts. Many researchers have specified the actual contribution of the conflict as inequality in access to certain resources through several factors such as; unequal economic distribution, social exclusion, and the limitation of natural resources, has resulted in the growing trend of modern intrastate violent conflicts (Collier and Hoeffler 1998; Cramer 2005; Humphreys 2005; Justino 2011). By acknowledging the risk of development efforts that may harm the sensitivity of the situation and iterating the complexity of the conflict, global debates on development in the conflict-affected areas have now become an important controversial topic in the development field. Therefore, it is needed to review the literature and published documents to identify the factors contributing to the development approach performed by the Thai authorities in the Deep South provinces of Thailand.

2. BACKGROUND

The number of intrastate violent conflicts in recent decades is almost two times greater than what we have faced in the past (Dupuy et al. 2017). Although violent conflicts are generated by various factors including poor political and administrative institutions, historical grievances, ethnic issues, etc., and underdevelopment issues remain highly accounted for the most important factor increasing the trends of violent conflict (Harding 2007). Note that most of the intrastate conflicts in this century occurred in under-develop countries (e.g. Sub-Sahara countries) where the state's functions are poor and the distribution of development limits. Surely, when particular groups of the population lack access to certain important resources by poor state's functions which resulted from improper development, there are plenty of reasons to mobilize the likelihood of violent conflicts (Justino 2011). Ikejiaku (2009), pointed out that political corruption is one of the most crucial factors that led to state dysfunction, poor development, spreading of poverty, and social discontentment. World Bank (2010), suggests that lagging regions have experienced more than three times the number of terrorist incidents per capita, compared with leading regions, and almost twice as many deaths per capita in such incidents. Therefore, conflict and development areas are recognized as one of the associated processes that seek to prevent and resolve the conflicts that generally occur in underdeveloped countries (Duffield 2007). Collier and Hoeffler (1998), point out that the risk of civil war is correlated to the national economic condition where the country who has a better economy, tends to have a lower risk of conflict. Specifically, the countries in which the government incapable to fulfil the basic needs of their people. Therefore, due to corruption, mismanagement, or other issues, may end up with a higher risk of conflict and due to disparity, the people can reclaim their right to use force in the resolution of their discontentment (Hegre 2014). Consequently, development has become key element of achieving a major reduction of global violent conflicts (Ikejiaku 2009).

The conflict between the Thai state and Muslim Malay insurgencies in the Deep South regions of Thailand has been carrying on along with the history of predominant Thai and Muslim-Malay relationship (Chalk 2008; International Crisis Group 2017). Until recently, the conflict has not yet signed any possibility of its end, it has been transforming itself throughout the times to survive the government's suppression and increase the complexity of the situation. Long-lasting ideology clash between Malay extremist patriotic and the Thai government has resulted in ranges of chronic issues such as; unending regional poverty, smuggling, and various kinds of illegal activities that greatly obstructing the regional development (Chalk 2008). Tremendous efforts from the Thai government in these particular areas during the past several decades reveal that the government, who can survive the regional communism threats throughout the country, has failed to deal with the situation of the Muslim-Malay separatists (Asia Foundation 2013), particularly in southern provinces. Since 2006, successive national administrations have been primarily preoccupied with their political survival in an environment of national political instability, and have not prioritized bringing peace to the Deep South. Since the resumption of violence in the Deep South in 2004, there have been five prime ministers, a military coup, and violent protests in Bangkok in 2010 that resulted in 90 deaths and 2,000 injuries (Asia Foundation 2013). These armed conflicts may affect land use in Thailand.

Changes to land systems over time can be due to urbanization or economic growth or drastic shocks, such as sudden socio-economic, environmental (Sekizawa et al. 2015) political changes (Baumann et al. 2011) or armed conflicts (Baumann et al. 2015). Armed conflicts effect agricultural production, also can disturb the investment in agriculture sector, land use policies and its distribution, which ultimately and impact food trade. Consequently, socio-economic shocks backed by armed conflicts have adverse impacts on food security (Eklund et al. 2017). Armed conflict may lead to deaths and outmigration from conflict areas, causing agricultural production decline and land abandonment (Baumann et al. 2015; Eklund et al. 2017). Tensions over land use and community rights also help fuel the ethnic nationalist conflicts in Thailand's Deep South. In 2015, plans to build coal-fired power plants in Pattani were met with protests from the Malay Muslim community, because the work would result in the forcible relocation of people, mosques, and cemeteries and expose them to environmental damage (The Asia Foundation 2017). Therefore, the Thai Malay Muslim confects effect the regional land use and agricultural activities.

3. FOCUS OF THE CHAPTER

The concept of development in conflict situations has been introduced to Thailand for more than half of a century since the country encountered a communist threat back in the 1950s. The implementation of development in that particular period was claimed to be one effective process that can overcome such an important threat of the era. However, there is another conflict in the Deep South region that has not been solved for long times and still going in the present days. Following the global trend, that the number of intrastate conflicts has been increasing throughout the world, especially the South's states, the recognition of the development efforts in the conflict-affected situation is now receiving emphasis from the international platform. The approaches of development that will be carried on in the conflict situation have been changed to be specific when comparing with the previous time. Therefore, the chapter provides insights regarding the development efforts in response to the conflicts in southern Thailand. The chapter will provide a review of the literature that how geopolitics in the regions triggered the unrest in the south region of Thailand.

4. MATERIAL AND METHODS

Inferences in the chapter have mainly been derived by reviewing government documents and other significant secondary source data. For this purpose, three Southern Provinces of Thailand refer to the distinctive region next to the Thai Malaysia border were selected. Where the majority of the residents are native Malay Muslim people. The three provinces including Pattani, Yala, Narathiwat have always had a high level of violence between radical Muslim insurgencies and Thai authorities. The study has used several secondary information sources, i.e. National Economic and Social Development Board, Bureau of Budget, South Border Provinces Administrative Center, Deep South Watch, Office of Royal Development Projects Board. Besides, the data and information were analyzed through graphs and pie charts.

5. FINDINGS AND DISCUSSION

5.1 Brief History of the Conflicts in Thailand

The events since the kingdom of Siam invaded and took over Malay's Pattani kingdom in the 17th century (Reid 1988). The emergence of violence in contemporary time began during the 19th century when His Majesty King Rama V modernized the Thai administration system (Table 1). The central government, located in Bangkok, replaced the local Sultan with delegates from Bangkok and provided them authority to rule over the Muslim kingdom. These administration reforms also divided the Muslim kingdom into three provinces which are Pattani, Yala, and Narathiwat. The contents of this table include the Thai government's action and how the separatist insurgencies react to the government's implementation.

The deep-south had been calm for more than 50 years with less unrest occurring each year until the rise of the authoritarian regime of Thai militarists stepped on to the power. Started from Field Marshal Plaek Phibunsongkhram[1] and subsequent junta governments. The policies for Deep South's affairs have been overwhelmed by nationalism idea. Forced cultural assimilation along with severe punishment for those who were against the state authorities. Indeed, iterated an existed historical grievance, increased the number as well as the intensity of resistance from the local people. The insurgencies which then operated in the jungle moved to the urban areas and blended to the civilians caused more difficult for security forces to settle. Thousands of incidents were recorded within the initial phase of the conflict outbreak. This situation has brought the following government after militarist regimes to realize that the cultural assimilation policy had failed in those areas. Moreover, it also worsened the situation by fueling up discontentment and violence. The later government, therefore turned to a more political-cultural integration policy to compromise with the local Muslim population. Due to setting up of the Southern Border Provinces Administrative Center (SBPAC) in 1981, the amount of violence has been reduced those areas. Even though incidents still occurred, but the number and frequency were reduced. In Yala and Pathani, over 5,500 innocent Muslims, Buddhists; men, women, and children were died due to Islamic separatist movements (Antonio 2017). The common civilians who were unarmed were fired by soldiers. In the years between 2004 and 2014, in Krung Thep, the Krue Se mosque debacle in April 2004 and the Tak Bai massacre in October 2004. These two tragedies happened during the Thaksin administration.

Table 1. Historical events in the three southern provinces of Thailand

Period	Events	Consequences
17th C	Invasion of Siamese kingdom	Originate the historical grievances
19th C	Administrative reformation	Local aristocracies' riot
The 1940s	Cultural assimilation policy	Dusun Nyor Rebellion[2]
1950-1970s	Infrastructure development and intense suppression	Strongly resistance from the local population
The 1980s	Establishing of SBPAC	Reducing the violence
2002- Present	Dissolving of SBPAC	The eruption of the intense violence

Source: Authors' review of the literature.

The statistical data in Figure 1 shows that the number of violent events sharply increased from 100 incidents per year before 2004 to around 1,800-2,000 times per year afterward. However, the information also indicated that the trends of violent incidences in early 2008 has slightly decreased (Deep South Watch 2016).

Figure 1. Number of incidents in three southern provinces and some parts of Songkhla Province
Source: Deep South Incident Database, 2016

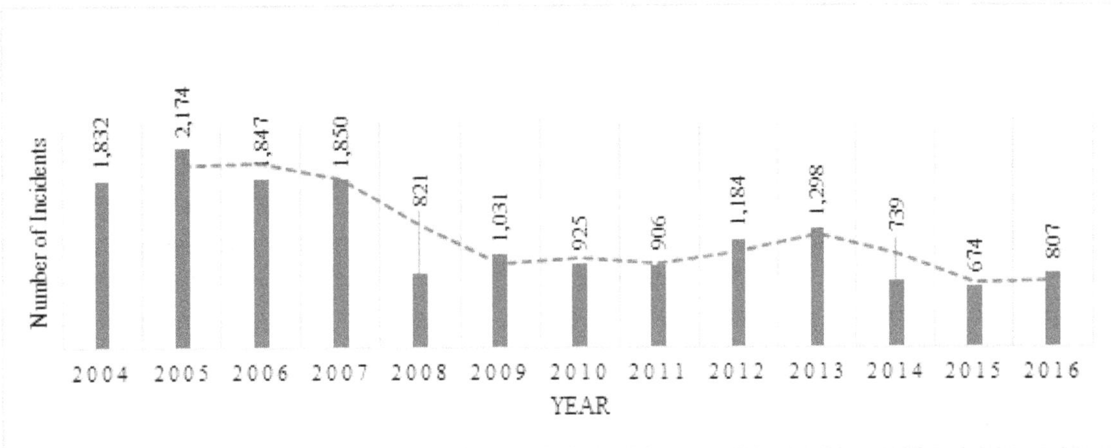

5.2 Development Process in Thailand

The development process has been carried out since 1930. Nevertheless, the implementation of substantial development in Thailand has been initiated during the intensified cold war period (Kelly et al. 2012), this was led by the United State of America and its allies, a great amount of aids in terms of finance and other support flowed to Thailand intended to develop the country in all dimension to tackle the communism threats. The development process emphasized the improvement of basic infrastructure and simultaneously promoted the commercial and industrial economy. The strategy was employed to increase national income in addition to the macroeconomic development concept. Also, this period was an initial phase of the National Economic and Social Development Plan (NESDP). It had been carried on in close cooperation between the Thai technocrats and other Western advisers to make the macroeconomic changes and drive the country's development with rapid growth. Commercial growth and industrial economic expansion were supported by top-down administration structure. There was no policy devised for equal growth distribution in this period of rapid development. An investment was put particularly on those areas which had the most economic potentials and already more well-off (Kelly et al. 2012).

Most of the economic activities have been done in potential areas. Especially, Bangkok impacted other aspects such as the improvement of education and the healthcare system (OECD 2013). Development in this phase resulted in a significant improvement in overall Thailand's economy. The top-down policy had generated a huge gap between the rich and poor which also became a cause of other subsequent inequality issues. This rapid growth was affected only at the national level and failed to improve the majority of the population. Chaleampong (2014), states that between 1986 and 2011, Thailand's economic growth had significantly decreased the issue of poverty. However, income distribution hardly changed over that period; did leave many people behind with income inequality.

A great turning point occurred in the late 1990s after the Asian Economic Crisis. Highly dependency on the global market of the Thai economy made Thailand that it has severely suffered from the aftermath. The consideration of a development strategy, thus, was shifted towards other alternative concepts aimed at finding the way to overcome the global economic dependency. Before the implementation of the 8th

NESDP in 1997, most of the policies regarding rural development, that had been focused on infrastructure and industrial improving without- or less- focusing on sustainable development, are accounted for a factor that intense the crisis's impacts (NESDB 2002) In the 8th National NESDP, rural and regional development strategy started to embrace more sustainable development approach. The concept of communities' capacity improvement, decentralization, and natural resources conservation (NESDB 2002; NESDB 2007), This plan has been gradually emphasizing as the concept for rural development in Thailand. Simultaneously, the promotion of a sustainable development approach as guided by MDGs started to influence Thai rural development. In 2002, the United Nations (UN) held the World Summit on SD which rose the recognition of SD for the implementation plan for the countries pursuing this conference (WSSD 2002). The concept of SD, as mentioned in the World Summit on Sustainable Development was emphasized on building integration of economic, social, and environmental dimensions of SD in the implementation process of the member countries (UN 2015).

Later on, the National Economic and Social Development Board published the "Sustainable development in the Thai context", as a component of the 2003 annual conference. The report pointed out that overall development progress, emphasizing economic boosting in the prior NESDP, resulted in certain negative consequences prevented further development. Also, the importance of the SD concept in the global context was acknowledged in the report and delivered into certain approaches for the implementation of the national development plan (NESDB 2003). Until now, the SD concept is mentioned in the later NESDP as presented in the 9th to 12th NESDP emphasized on the development implication for Thailand (NESDB 2002; NESDB 2007; NESDB 2011; NESDB 2017).

5.3 Development Efforts in the Conflict-Affected Areas of Thailand

The development in the conflict situation of Thailand can be divided into several phases based on the historical event. The concept of development was initiated and implemented in the 1950s (period of countering the communist insurgencies). Western liberal countries, especially the United States, learned from their prior operations in other countries such as Vietnam, Lao, and the Philippines that under-developing creates a potential for the communism to recruit their participants. Therefore, the initial phase of development in Thailand aimed at improving basic infrastructure and connecting isolated parts of the country under the state security purposed (Bergin 2016; Heymann Jr 1969).

Until now, the implementation of the development process by each government is designed and influenced by factors from both internal and external key actors. The trends of development in the conflict situation of three southernmost provinces region can be categorized into three phases. According to (Photongkhanong 2009), the phases of each implementation can be differentiated by using the National Economic and Social Development Plans as a reference for the study's orientation (Table 2). Before the establishment of the National Economic and Social Development Plan, development policy under the fascist regime of Plaek Pibulsongkram was merely emphasized on cultural assimilation in addition to his nationalist ideology. Forced assimilation policy was aimed at intervening local predominant Muslim belief by using the central government's authority regardless of the actual development. This policy, thus, resulted in a huge failure to integrate the Malay minority. Instead, it led to strong resistance from the local population and reproduced the historical grievance discourses (Pitsuwan 1985).

Note that the establishment of the National Economic and Social Development Board during the outbreak of the Cold War era was correlated with international influence. As discussed prior, the promotion of the development concepts is mostly conceptualized by the countries from the North which have been raised many debates on how it was improperly designed in the circumstances countries from South (Mac Ginty and Williams 2016). Due to the close tie between the Thai government and developed Western countries, especially the United States, the NESDPs are a clear reflection of the implication of the western development theories in Thailand's conditions.

During the 1st to 3rd NESDP that had been implemented under a long period of junta regime. It emphasized on intervening local institution through the centralization policy and simultaneously suppressing the Muslim insurgencies. However, in this period for the first time, the concept of development, and wellbeing of the population, was emphasized in the central government policy. The ideology of development at that time was implemented around national security purposes and was delivered throughout the country where the conflict between state-authorities and communist insurgencies took place. The objectives of development in the conflict situation at that time were to gain popularity and prevent people from joining the communist insurgencies resulted in satisfying results. The efforts for development in a conflict situation, at that time, was highly effective in most of the areas except the southernmost region because most of the population throughout the country are already integrated by a similarity of culture. Nevertheless, in particular areas of the southernmost region, where the distinct culture remains strongly resistant to the national culture, development efforts seem to have resulted in a contradicted way comparing with other parts of the country (Pitsuwan 1985). Negative impacts of over suppression and extreme cultural assimilation policies are far greater than the impact of the positive consequence of infrastructure development. Despite basic infrastructure and industrial based economic improvement, the development in other aspects was not carried out substantially. As a result, heavy suppression throughout the long reign of the dictator government on the other hand urged the violent conflict by giving the local institutes intervention as the insurgence reason for their operations (Photongkhanong 2009).

In the 4th and 5th NESDP, there was a significant change in the development approach to the conflict situation of the southernmost region. The 4th and 5th NESDP were on the reformation of the administrative system in those particular areas. Following the localization trends, several specific agencies (e.g. SBPAC) were formed to localize the administration and provide opportunities for local peoples' participation (Photongkhanong 2009). Even though the degree of decentralization was still low, and the Muslim minority were not completely integrated through the integration, but this attempt could, to some extent, create a positive psychological impact on the population. Furthermore, another key turning point is that the government had recognized the importance of culture, social, and other sensitive aspects despite macro-economy into their planning and implementation. They also shift their emphasis from suppression to integration as part of the development in a conflict situation for that time. One of the most well-known policies called "United front for Thailand's development" after the issue of 66/2523 Prime Minister Act that allowed every insurgency, who are mostly communism, surrender to the government without any guilt or charge so the government would ensure the resettlement process.

This policy ended the confrontation between the insurgencies and governmental authorities throughout the country that lasted for more than two decades under the military regime (CFR 2008). The chronic violent conflict of the three southernmost regions also affected this change. The changes of policy reduced conditions for the Muslim insurgencies to claim for their operations which later on reduce the role of suppressing policy in the conflict-affected areas. Consequently, the integration process helped the Malay population gradually accepted the authority of the central government and dilute the tension between these actors (CFR 2008).

However, it is not yet claiming that all the development in the conflict situation of the southernmost region can eliminate violent conflict. Ever since, the major cause of this conflict based upon ethical oppression, which is deeply stuck into the ideological level of both insurgencies and government, has not been touched. As a result, the violent conflict in the southernmost region of Thailand is still smoldering and ready to be escalated at any time. Table 2, summarizes the changes of development emphasize in the Deep South region referring to the implementation of different National Economic and Development Plan.

Table 2. Implementation of National Economic and Social Development Plan in the Deep Southern Region

NESDPs	Key focuses for the Deep South Region
1st-3rd (1961-1966)	Promoted Pattani province for the hub of the Deep South region
2nd – 3rd (1967-1971)	Integrate the Deep South region into the development plan for remote-underdeveloped areas
4th (1972-1976)	Imposed Pattani, Yala, Narathiwat, and Satun to be the Southern intensive developing provinces
5th -6th (1977-1991)	Emphasized on specific regional and areal facing critical poverty or insecurity
7th (1992-1996)	Songkhla, Pattani, Yala, and Narathiwat provinces become both commercial and administrative hub that distributed development to the Deep South region
8th (1997-2001)	Promote the role of the civil sector in the development
9th (2002-2006)	Integrate His Majesty King Rama IX sufficiency economic theory into the plan by emphasizing more on sustainability
10th (2007-2011)	Rebuilt government's trust through peace, reduce poverty and improve living conditions
11th (2012-2016)	Improve rubber production, promote cultural and environmental tourism, improve logistic system

Source: National Economic and Social Development Board, 1997-2012

5.4 A Case Study of the Development in Conflict Situation of the Three Southern Provinces of Thailand

In the present day, development has been recognized by the government as a key measure of conflict resolution. The suppression policy that emphasized security establishment is now shifted towards a more peaceful approach. By integrating with other concerned government agencies and local institutions, SB-PAC is assigned to be a leading governmental agency responsible for the development implementation in the southernmost region of Thailand. Framework and direction of the development conducted by this agency heavily rely on His Majesty King Rama IX's sufficiency economic theory and the principle of "Understand, reach out and develop". Nevertheless, specific legal enforcement of martial law is still there in those particular areas. It helps to predominate the governmental organizations' role in the development process as well as shape the limited non-state organizations' movements.

After the outbreak of conflict in 2004, the response from concerned actors has been carried on by the national government, and non-governmental organizations. Note that the involvement of government sectors are accounted for the majority of development implementation in this case. The principal objectives of the Thai government's development in southernmost region conflict were a bear close resemblance to national integration approaches adopted in the 1960s and 1970s, in response to the threat posed by Communist insurgency (Asia Foundation 2013).

The national budget for Deep South conflict resolution has been allocated to the southernmost region to ensure the effectiveness of the concerned agencies on the operation in that particular area (Figure 2). The budget was spent on several projects such as basic infrastructure construction aims at uplifting living conditions, aids, palliation, and some cultural promotions aim at increasing participation and cultural assimilation. Some initiatives demonstrate considerable willingness to modify national approaches. The Thai Government Departments have made efforts reach to the Malay Muslims through programs and some policy adaptations. For instance, the government made easy the local students entry to universities, community centers were built, health services centers were increased, media initiatives were taken. In addition to this, local NGOs were provided several grants for activities ranging from income generation to youth exchanges with other parts of Thailand.

Figure 2. National budget for deep south conflict resolution projects
Source: Bureau of Budget, 2016

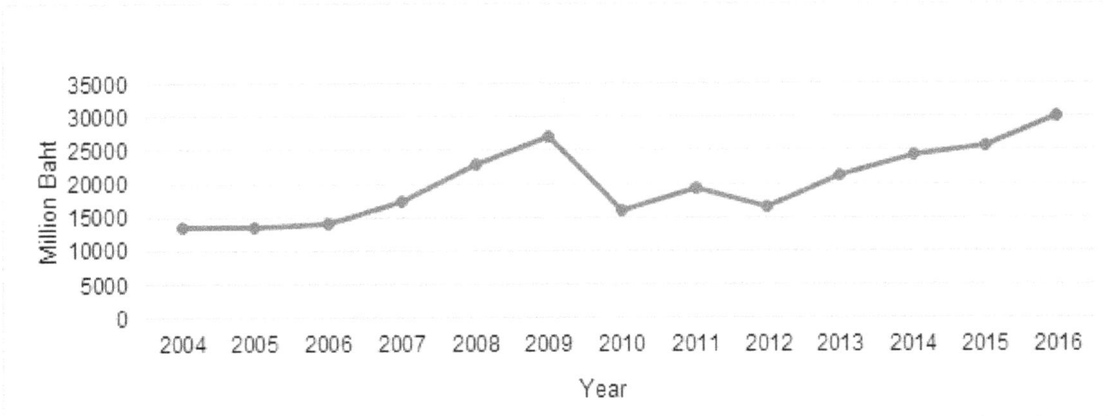

Lomlim (2015), pointed out that the production values of regional administration and security sectors between 2004 and 2010 considered around 11.81% of the non-agricultural production of the three southernmost provinces of Thailand. When comparing with the inflation rates before the outbreak of conflict, the values of the budget allocated for administration and national defense such as; spatial development and security forces deployed in that particular area has increased tremendously (Figure 2).

The implication of development in conflict-affected areas of the southernmost provinces is framed under the three years Five Special Provinces Development Plan, which is also supervised by SBPAC (NESDB 2009). According to the plan, the collective tasks of the southernmost region's development is divided into four aspects. First of all, the three years development plan is expected to uplift the living condition of the local population in addition to the sufficiency economic theory. This task also seeks to contribute sustainability and peace by supporting the local's dignity, as well as the security of lives and property through the promotion of socio-economic equality. Secondly, the plan seeks to acquire local trust in the authorities by ensuring justice, rule of law, palliation, and participation of the local people in the justice process. Third, the plan aimed at integrating society through cultural and religious integration and social services provision. Lastly, the plan aimed at strengthening the local economy upon the cultural identity of the local population. Several economic development plans such as promoting international collaboration with that particular region and distributing economic development to the local population (NESDB 2009).

5.5 The Role of South Border Provinces Administrative Center (SPBAC)

The direction and obligation of the SBPAC, into three aspects according to the Southern Border Provinces Administration Act B.E.2553, include; First, preparing the regional development plans by cooperating with the committees who are comprised by stakeholders from different sectors and ensure that the implementation has been carried on in addition to the plan; Second, entitling and enhancing right for the victims of the violence, both who are governmental staff and civilians, to have access to the palliation when they are affected by the violence. Lastly, promoting local participation in the conflict resolution process, as well as promoting local tradition and multi-culturalism in that particular area (SBPA 2010).

The 2015's information reveals that budged allocated for SPBAC's operations was around 90.47 million Baht (Figure 3). The budget allocated for supplementary projects contributes to the greatest values of overall spending in other aspects. It includes ranges of various projects namely; palliating and aids for the violence's victims, rehabilitation project, security establishment, maintaining security, basic infrastructure construction, etc. Of all projects, uplifting living conditions and security strengthening projects for the communities live in conflict-prone are accounted for the highest spending of 2015's expenditure. Budget spending in addition to these projects was allocated for the construction of basic infrastructures such as roads, water supply systems, utility buildings, etc. Additionally, palliating and aids for the violence's victims makes up second-most of the expenditure (SBPAC 2015).

Figure 3. 2015 SBPAC expenditure
Source: *Bureau of Budget, 2016*

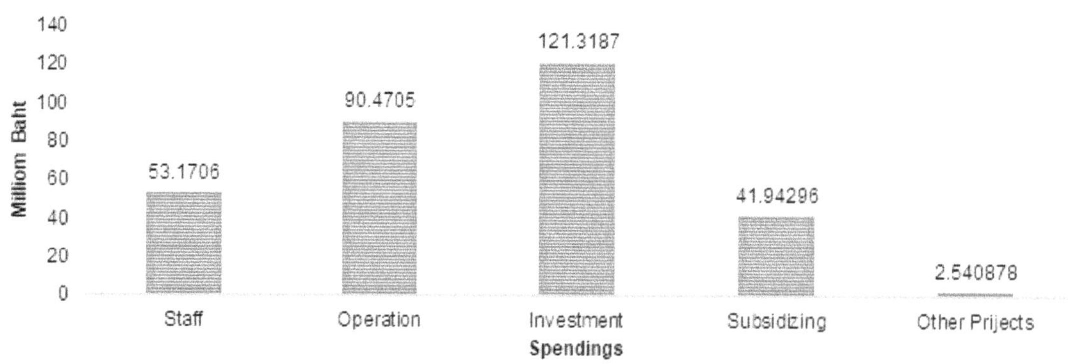

5.6 Non-Governmental Organizations (NGOs) and International Aid

Interestingly, the civil sector in the Deep South region has impressively increased since 2004 and reach around 400 organizations by 2015. These NGOs operate in various fields of development such as education, culture, human rights, academy, community, women, and youth. In all aspects, NGOs working in the youth's field make up the highest contribution followed by women, media, and economy respectively (Deep South Watch 2016). Likewise, the emphasis of social sectors is put into the politics, violence, and peacebuilding dimensions. It also involves several advocative activities in response to significant violence events. Also, innocent people, women, and youths are the key emphasis by the social sectors in their avocations.

Suthisak (2014), suggests that non-governmental organizations, particularly legal assistance, in the southernmost region can obtain more thrust from the local people because they do not have government image, and more importantly, the staff are all native. On the other hand, operation from the government side seems to have less success. The reason behind their failure is their passive approach and issue of trust. Particularly, within the peacebuilding process, some academic points out that the dynamic conflict is driven by the impact of movement between state authorities and separatist insurgencies. Unfortunately, innocent civilians within this dynamic suffer the most, both direct and indirectly. Within this context, the civil sector seems may bring balance to the power competition of both sides (Jitrbhiromsri 2014).

Figure 4 illustrates that NGOs working in the field of women's rights and education, religion, and culture share the greater contribution of the NGOs operating in the southernmost region. In contrast, natural resources and environment, economy, as well as human rights aspects contribute the least share of total active NGOs. This chart also represents the government action on NGOs who operate in the human rights field that interrupt or damage the authorities' image in those particular areas. Recently, there was a new reporting the story of one Deep Southern activist who was sued by the military on the computer crime accuse after he exposed his experience of being abused by the security forces during his detention. This is an example from many cases that shows how the state authorities respond to the NGOs who tried to reveal their excessive power.

However, it is noted that the operation of local NGOs is closely tied to international development agencies. Aid agencies are not allowed to open offices in the Deep South and usually need to gain the permission of several government departments before undertaking any initiative (Burke et al. 2013). In accordance, the USAID report on Violent Extremism and Insurgency in Southern Thailand (2013) also pointed out that the United States is not directly engaged with the development in the conflict situation of the Deep South region. For instance, the projects funded by the international organizations in the Deep South region from 2009 to 2013 include community-driven development (CDD) projects in 27 communities or villages, supported by the close collaboration between the World Bank and the Local Development Institute. Another example is the Save the Children and Sweden's Kampong Suenae program, aimed at building strong communities, in particular for children. Oxfam operates a small community-based project in 23 communities (Burke et al. 2013).

Figure 4. NGOs active in the deep south region
Source: *Bureau of Budget, 2016*

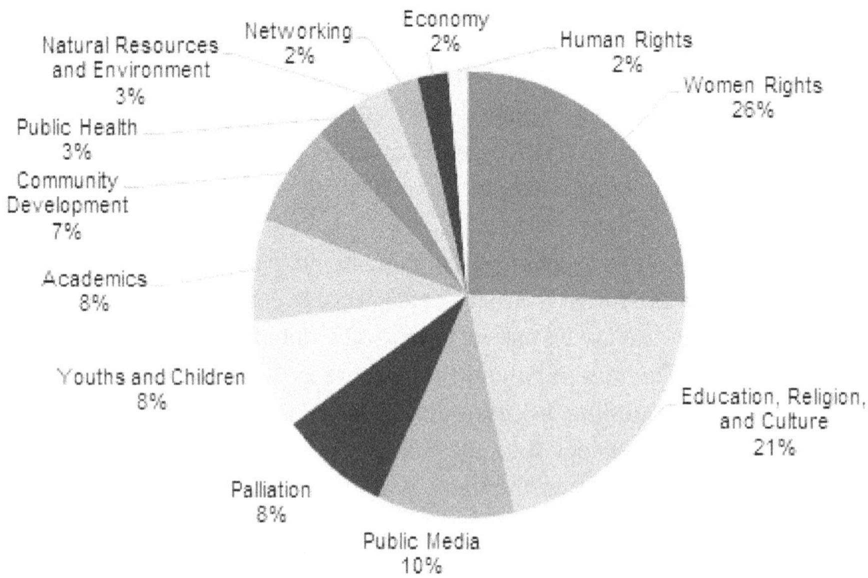

5.6 The Royal Development Projects

Even though the Royal Projects in the Southern region of Thailand have been carried out since 1974, it was not yet having serious support from the central government until the implementation of the 5th National Development Plan. Since then, there was a higher degree of support from the central government for the royal development projects in the three Southern provinces of Thailand (ORDPB 1996). Statistic information (Figure 5) obtained from the Office of Royal Development Projects Board shows that around 80% of projects implemented in the southern region were embarked in the three southernmost provinces areas (ORDPB 2016). The implementation of projects including the small-medium irrigation system construction, road construction, fishery promotion, consumable and cash crops cultivation promotion, Muslim religious schools development, etc.

The implementation of Royal Development projects aimed to facilitate the locals' life by providing more options that are suitable to their lifestyle. To be more specific, most of the projects are implemented to serve agricultural activities such as water resources development projects, natural resources conservation, model farming, and occupation promoting in those particular areas Figure 6. Even though the autonomous implementation of the Royal Development Projects cannot directly reduce the number of conflicts, but its success on poverty reduction. Consequently, the government gradually embrace the royal approach into the regional development plan in 1980 as a part of the Fifth National Economic and Social Development Plan and increasingly emphasized the royal's approach in their following plans (Photongkhanong 2009).

Figure 5. The contribution of royal projects in the three southern provinces
Source: Office of Royal Development Projects Board, 2016

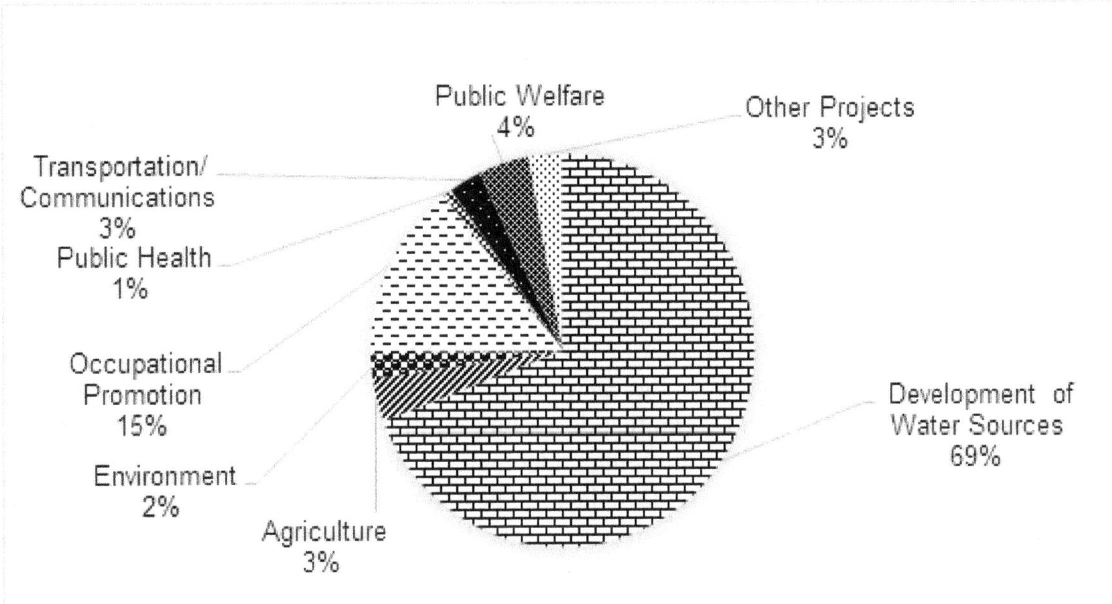

5.7 Factors contributing to the development approach of the Thai Government in the Deep South Provinces of Thailand

Development efforts in the conflict-affected area of Deep Southern provinces are overwhelmingly performed by the Thai state authority. Of all aspects, basic infrastructure construction such as road construction seems to be the only tangible accomplishment from these efforts. In the past decades, Thailand had received enormous support, technically and financially, from the US to improve its basic infrastructure as part of an anti-communist strategy during the Cold War period. Throughout the years, Thai authorities, as well as the private sector, have maximized their experience in this field. Comprehensive road systems and basic infrastructure have contributed tremendously to the country's overall economic improvement (Koonnathamdee 2013). The Thai government thus acknowledges this potential and has relied on the construction of basic infrastructure as a means for development. This explains why most of the SBPAC's budget has been allocated for this matter.

However, along with a high ability for infrastructure construction, corruption is another factor influencing this form of a developmental approach. According to Transparency International (2017), Thailand is ranked 96th in the Corruption Perception Index in 2017. Specifically, construction is the sector that is largely susceptible to corruption in Thailand. UNDP (2016), indicates that public work contracts and construction are the sectors most prone to corruption since there are many of procurements occurring throughout each project where some officials ask for bribes and irregular payments from private companies in exchange for the government contracts. This huge amount of investment opens opportunities for corrupt officials to be involved with the public procurement process in which they can benefit from surplus money and the bidding companies.

Besides, the study also reveals the structural issue of the Thai administration. A high degree of hierarchical and top-down oriented administration prevents the possibility of horizontal decentralization where most of the political power is clustered among state authorities and local politicians. This also helps to explain why there are fewer NGOs and international agencies involved in the development process of the Deep Southern region since the central government retains a high degree of influence on the access and scope of involvement of the NGOs under the use of martial law and security concerns (Deep South Watch 2016).

5.8 Impact of development efforts on the conflict resolution process

Many studies which have been mentioned at the beginning of this paper, have suggested that this violent conflict has its root cause from the suppression of ethnic identity that has been reinforced over time through mistreatment and negligence by the Thai authorities (CFR 2008; Deep South Watch 2016; Koonnathamdee 2013). It is rationally seen that development efforts in the Deep South have had little impact on the transformation process of this ethnic ideological conflict toward peace.

While many local people, especially ethnic Malays, are heavily engaged in poverty, basic infrastructure development and the agriculture-related projects from the RDPs seems to have had very little impact on the improvement of their living (Burke et al. 2013). Despite a more convenient road system, the economy of the Deep Southern region still underperforms when compared with other regions, or even with neighboring Malaysia. The employment rate is low, as well as economic activities. The majority of the population still heavily depends on the cultivation of economic crops such as rubber tree and palm oil that are currently suffering from a decline in demand due to the global economic downturn (CFR 2008). Therefore, improving basic infrastructure is virtually not enough to bring this region out of poverty and violent conflicts. Development processes should be carefully designed and implemented continuously to cover all details and sensitivities. Unfortunately, the development policy for the Deep Southern region has changed over time corresponding to the political instability of the central government. Without proper and continuous implementation, the government fails to resolve the problems burdening regional economic development and leaves many of the ethnic Malay population marginalized (CFR 2008). The critical factor of discontentment remains unresolved.

Last but most importantly, the human rights issue in the Deep Southern region has been the main controversy between the Thai government and NGOs for some time (Deep South Watch 2016). Accordingly, this issue is one of the reasons that Malay separatists claim their right to fight with the Thai authorities. Negligence of the Thai authorities towards the human rights issue, as represented by the low number of NGOs operating in that topic, thus becomes an insincere move from the perspective of the local people. Moreover, NGOs are the actors without critical dissension from both separatists and insurgencies (Suthisak 2014). These organizations can build collective links, facilitate reconciliation, and increase the capacity of the development process. Blocking the NGOs from involvement in the development process may, indeed, create a major burden for the transformation process of this ideological and ethical conflict toward peace. The impact of the NGOs on development is considerably limited. Due to a high degree of government's intervention, most of the development implication, as well as resources are, to some extent, directly or indirectly under government control. However, the study reveals that numbers of aids from international agencies urge the formation of small-local NGOs in the areas. The expansion of non-state organizations also contributes to an awakening of social sectors and the local community to advocate for their political rights and participation in the transformation and development process. Tan-Mullins (2009), revealed that one of the respondents in his study stated that, "our fights for our children and the legacy (land and resources) given to them by Allah (may peace be upon him). It implies that the people in the south region of Thailand are for their land and territories.

6 LIMITATIONS AND CHALLENGES TO THE RECENT DEVELOPMENT

The government is considered as a key performer for determining the development direction in the conflict-affected areas of the southernmost region. Due to its high degree of intervention, most of the development efforts, as well as resources are controlled by the central government. The Predominating role of the government in delivering the development is considered a great criticism of the development in the conflict situation of Thailand. Indeed, it creates subsequent limitation that later on becomes challenging for the development in several aspects. Even though previous development efforts are not a complete attempt in vain since the regional economy and local's living conditions have improved tremendously, but the issues of national unity and regional insecurity problems have increased. However, misaddressing of key important factors- politics is accounted for the struggling towards sustainable peace establishment.

Practically, development policies in the southernmost region were not effectively implemented in every dimension. Many types of research pointed out that the results of these development attempts are only restricted in particular aspects such as economic and social issues. Critically, some even claim that these measurements, which emphasized economic development, have few impacts on the conflict resolution process. Chalida (2017) points out that it is inappropriate to blame poverty for an incentive of insurgency recruitment. Due to their difficult living condition, joining separatists will impede their household's economic status because they will no longer work normally. Therefore, the development that heavily emphasized developing regional economy instead of political and administration reformation is not seemed to be a true resolution for this violence. Critically, the Asia Foundation (2013) research on the southernmost region conflict found that government programs were more likely to exacerbate conflict conditions. The roots of violence in the Deep South stem from the area's political marginalization, a problem that spending large development budgets through existing government channels risks exacerbating rather than transforming (Burke et al. 2013).

Nevertheless, political aspects are the most important concern that has not been seriously emphasized by the government. Many surveys have suggested that local needs for development in political aspects are the highest in every aspect. These surveys are also interrelated with previous researchers that pointed out the political problems, caused by misunderstanding and centralizing of the central government's authorities, as a core of the conflict's incentive (CSCD 2014). Besides, a political aspect of the development process has not been pragmatically touched by the government. Even though SBPAC is intentionally established for promoting social integration and shifting the decision making to the regional level, but the component of this agency, especially in the policy and implicational level, is mostly comprised of concerned governmental and security agencies regardless of contributing stakeholders from the local level.

As a result, most of the local administrative structure is still under strong intervention from the security forces and agencies, while local participation in the political process is relatively low. Even though the NGOs and social sectors are performing a significant role in the development process by international financial assistance, their role in political aspects is still limited by the governments. On the other hand, the delivery of development through the government's operational structure can also sustain the monopolizing of local political power. Instead of improving participation, the development efforts seem to be suspended as the providing of commodities and aids, not enhancing any kind of transformation.

Another challenge is the issue of implementing justices by the government. The implementation of political and justice aspects have not been seriously carried on throughout the history of the government's involvement in this conflict. It is seen that excessive suppression and abuse, which have been performed by security forces during the operation are the main concerned mentioning in the Five Special Provinces Development Plan. Numbers of reports on the excessive use of power by the authorities in justice processes such as ill-treatment and torturing are still regularly seen in human rights organization reports (Amnesty International 2014; World Bank 2016). The security forces were given explicit powers in Narathiwat, Pattani, and Yala provinces when the Martial Law was imposed in 2004. These powers to security forces included: a common man could be kept in detention for seven days without any approval from the court or any other government department approval. In addition to these seven days detention, the people were detained for 30 days per Emergency Decree (USAID 2013). Likewise, aids and subvention of the conflict victims' families that belong to the justice process, sometimes, have been used for the wrong purposes. A great amount of those aids and grants allocated for the victims of the violent conflict sometimes are not willing to help the victims' families. While compensation is paid in those cases, families sometimes allege that such is only to "cover over" extrajudicial executions by security forces—essentially "blood money" (Amnesty International 2014). These measures sometimes create more discontentment between the local population and security officers.

7 CONCLUSION

In general, immense development efforts from the central government in the southernmost provinces resulted in a significant improvement of basic infrastructure, education, and the healthcare system. Budgets from the central government spending in this particular region did contribute a significant improvement of the regional economy, creating employment- especially in the government's sectors. However, current debates on the previous development attempts revealed that the development process is still slow. The impact of the NGOs on development is considerably limited. Due to a high degree of government intervention, most of the development implications, as well as resources are, to some extent, directly or indirectly under government control. The government is considered as a key performer for determining the development direction in the conflict-affected areas of the southernmost region. Due to its high degree of intervention, most of the development efforts, as well as resources are controlled by the central government. Although national security is the main priority emphasized by the Thai government resulted in a high degree of intervention in every aspect of the development, the government especially those who work in the Deep South region should acknowledge the importance of community-driven development as part of the development mechanism. To maximize the quality of development towards the sustainability approach, the government should enhance a suitable environment for communities to participate in every level of the development process, starting from the political aspect. Communities should be strengthened their capacity to increase their role and share the local political power, reduce the monopolizing of local politicians, and increase the accuracy of the development project to the communities' actual needs.

REFERENCES

Amnesty International. (2014). *Thailand submission to the United Nations committee against torte (52nd session).* Amnesty International Publication. Available at: https://www.amnesty.org/download/Documents/8000/asa390032014en.pdf

Antonio, R. (2017). *The King and the making of modern Thailand: Routledge.* Taylor and Francis Group.

Aphornsuvan, T. (2003). *History and Politics of the Muslims in Thailand.* Bangkok: Thammasat University. Retrieved September 20, 2017, from https://seap.einaudi.cornell.edu/sites/seap/files/MuslimThailand.pdf

Asia Foundation. (2013). *The Contested Corners of Asia: Subnational Conflict and International Development Assistance.* Available at: https://asiafoundation.org/publication/the-contested-corners-of-asia-subnational-conflict-and-international-development-assistance/

Baumann, M., Kuemmerle, T., Elbakidze, M., Ozdogan, M., Radeloff, V. C., Keuler, N. S., Prishchepov, A. V., Kruhlov, I., & Hostert, P. (2011). Patterns and drivers of post-socialist farmland abandonment in Western Ukraine. *Land Use Policy, 28*(3), 552–562. doi:10.1016/j.landusepol.2010.11.003

Baumann, M., Radeloff, V. C., Avedian, V., & Kuemmerle, T. (2015). Land-use change in the Caucasus during and after the Nagorno-Karabakh conflict. *Regional Environmental Change, 15*(8), 1703–1716. doi:10.100710113-014-0728-3

Bergin, B. (2016). Defeating an Insurgency—The Thai Effort against the Communist Party of Thailand, 1965–ca. 1982. *Studies in Intelligence, 60*(2), 25–36.

Burke, A., Tweedie, P., & Phūčhārœ̄n, R. N. (2013). *The Contested Corners of Asia: Subnational Conflict and International Development Assistance: the Case of Southern Thailand.* Asia Foudation.

CFR. (2008). *The Muslim Insurgency in Southern Thailand.* Council on Foreign Relations. Available at: https://www.cfr.org/backgrounder/muslim-insurgency-southern-thailand

Chaleampong, K. (Producer). (2017). *Relationship between growth, inequality and poverty and pro-poor growth in Thailand: 1986-2011.* Retrieved from https://www.slideserve.com/pearl/relationship-between-growth-inequality-and-poverty-and-pro-poor-growth-in-thailand-1986-2011

Chalida, B. (2017). Economy and development in southernmost border provinces of Thailand: a criticized exploratory. In A decade of anthropology and sociology of southernmost border provinces study (pp. 29-68). Bangkok: O.S. Printing House.

Chalk, P. (2008). *The Malay-Muslim Insurgency in Southern ThailandUnderstanding the Conflict's Evolving Dynamic.* RAND National Defense Research Institute. Available at https://www.rand.org/content/dam/rand/pubs/occasional_papers/2008/RAND_OP198.pdf

Collier, P., & Hoeffler, A. (1998). On economic causes of civil war. *Oxford Economic Papers, 50*(4), 563–573. doi:10.1093/oep/50.4.563

Cramer, C. (2005). Violent conflict and the very poorest. *Chron Poverty Res Cent*, 4-26.

CSCD. (2014). *Men and Youth in Thailand's Conflict-Affected Deep South*. Center for Conflict Studies and Cultural Diversity. Available at: https://www.deepsouthwatch.org/sites/default/files/men_and_male_youth_english_web_version.pdf

Duffield, M. (2007). *Development, security and unending war: governing the world of peoples*. Polity Press.

Dupuy, K., Scott, G., Håvard, M. N., Ida, R., Siri, A. S., Håvard, S., & Henrik, U. (2017). *Trends in Armed Conflict, 1946–2016*. Oslo: Peace Research Institute. Available at: https://www.prio.org/utility/DownloadFile.ashx?id=1373&type=publicationfile

Eklund, L., Degerald, M., Brandt, M., Prishchepov, A. V., & Pilesjö, P. (2017). How conflict affects land use: Agricultural activity in areas seized by the Islamic State. *Environmental Research Letters, 12*(5), 054004. doi:10.1088/1748-9326/aa673a

Emas, R. (2015). *The concept of sustainable development: definition and defining principles*. Florida International University.

Harding, S. (2007). Man-made disaster and development: The case of Iraq. *International Social Work, 50*(3), 295–306. doi:10.1177/0020872807076041

Hegre, H. (2014). Democracy and armed conflict. *Journal of Peace Research, 51*(2), 159–172. doi:10.1177/0022343313512852

Heymann, H., Jr. (1969). *Seminar on Development and Security in Thailand: Part 1. The Insurgency*. Rand Corp. Available at: www.dtic.mil/dtic/tr/fulltext/u2/500943.pdf

Humphreys, M. (2005). Natural resources, conflict, and conflict resolution: Uncovering the mechanisms. *The Journal of Conflict Resolution, 49*(4), 508–537. doi:10.1177/0022002705277545

Ikejiaku, B.-V. (2009). The relationship between poverty, conflict and development. *Journal of Sustainable Development, 2*(1), 15. doi:10.5539/jsd.v2n1p15

International Crisis Group. (2017). *Thailand: Malay-Muslim Insurgency and the Dangers of Intractability*. Available at: https://www.crisisgroup.org/global/8-watch-list-2017-second-update

Jitrbhiromsri, S. (2014). An inconvenient peace in the Deep South's violence: The paradox between knowing enemy hypothesis and intrinsic balancing forces. *Peace Studies Journal, 1*(1), 155–198.

Justino, P. (2011). Poverty and Violent Conflict: A Micro-Level Perspective on the Causes and Duration of Warfare. *IDS Working Papers, 2011*(385), 1-25.

Kelly, M., Yutthaphonphinit, P., Seubsman, S., & Sleigh, A. (2012). Development policy in Thailand: From top-down to grass roots. *Asian Social Science, 8*(13), 29–39. doi:10.5539/ass.v8n13p29 PMID:23814630

Koonnathamdee, P. (2013). *A Turning Point for the Service Sector in Thailand*. Asian Development Bank Economics Working Paper Series No. 353.

Lomlim, C. (2015). The driving of three southern provinces' economy under the conflict situation. *Rusamila Journal, 35*(2), 25-40.

Mac Ginty, R., & Williams, A. (2009). *Conflict and development*. Routledge. doi:10.4324/9780203880005

Mac Ginty, R., & Williams, A. (2016). *Conflict and development*. Routledge. doi:10.4324/9781315714059

NESDB. (2002). *The Ninth National Economic and Social Development Plan*. Bangkok: National Economic and Social Development Board. Available at: http://www.nesdb.go.th/ewt_dl_link.php?nid=3784

NESDB. (2003). *Sustainable development in the Thai context*. Bangkok: National Economic and Social Development Board. Available at: www.nesdb.go.th/ewt_w3c/ewt_news.php?nid=3157

NESDB. (2007). *The Ten National Economic and Social Development Plan*. Bangkok: National Economic and Social Development Board. Available at: http://www.nesdb.go.th/ewt_news.php?nid=5747&filename=develop_issue

NESDB. (2009). *Five Special Provinces Development Plan B.E.2552-2555*. Bangkok: National Economic and Social Development Board. Available at: http://eris.nesdb.go.th/pdf/351000-001.pdf

NESDB. (2011). *The Eleventh National Economic and Social Development Plan*. Bangkok: National Economic and Social Development Board. Available at: http://www.nesdb.go.th/ewt_news.php?nid=5748&filename=develop_issue

NESDB. (2017). *The Twelfth National Economic and Social Development Plan*. Bangkok: National Economic and Social Development Board. Available at: http://www.nesdb.go.th/ewt_news.php?nid=6420&filename=develop_issue

OECD. (2013). Southeast Asian [*With Perspectives on China and India*. Available at: http://www.oecd.org/dev/asia-pacific/Thailand.pdf]. *Economic Outlook, 2013*, •••.

ORDPB. (1996). *Philosophy of Sufficiency Economy*. Office of the Royal Development Projects Board. Available at: http://www.rdpb.go.th/en/Sufficiency

ORDPB. (2016). *Philosophy of Sufficiency Economy*. Office of the Royal Development Projects Board. Available at: http://www.rdpb.go.th/en/Sufficiency

Photongkhanong, D. (2009). *The Development Policy of Thai Government toward the Three Southernmost Provinces, A.D.1938-1986 Master*. Kasetsart University.

Pitsuwan, S. (1985). *Islam and Malay Nationalism: A Case Study of the Malay-Muslims of Southern Thailand*. Academic Press.

Ray, D., & Esteban, J. (2017). Conflict and Development. *Annual Review of Economics*, *9*(1), 263–293. doi:10.1146/annurev-economics-061109-080205 PMID:28202148

Reid, A. (1988). *Southeast Asia in the Age of Commerce, 1450-1680: Expansion and crisis* (Vol. 2). Yale University Press.

SBPA. (2010). *Five Special Provinces Development Plan B.E.2552-2555*. Bangkok: Southern Border Provinces Administration Act B.E.2553. Available at: www.codi.or.th/downloads/laws/law/Other-5.pdf

SBPAC. (2015). *National Security Policy B.E. 2558-2564 (2015-2020)*. Bangkok: National Security Council.

Suthisak, D. (2014). Role of legal aid organizations in the southernmost provinces of Thailand during 2012-2013. *Peace Studies Journal, 1*(1), 221–242.

Tan-Mullins, M. (2009). Armed conflict and resolutions in Southern Thailand. *Annals of the Association of American Geographers, 99*(5), 922–931. doi:10.1080/00045600903260689

The Asia Foundation. (2017). *The State of Conflict and Violence in Asia* Bang Rak, Bangkok, Thailand. Available at: https://asiafoundation.org/wp-content/uploads/2017/10/Thailand-StateofConflictandViolence.pdf

Transparency International. (2017). *Corruption Perceptions Index*. Berlin, Germany: TI. Available at: https://www.transparency.org/news/feature/corruption_perceptions_index_2017

UN. (2015). *Resolution adopted by the General Assembly on 25 September 2015*. Washington, DC: United Nations. Available at: http://www.un.org/ga/search/view_doc.asp?symbol=A/RES/70/1&Lang=E

UNDP. (2016). *Conducting a Conflict and Development Analysis*. Available at: https://undg.org/wp-content/uploads/2016/10/UNDP_CDA-Report_v1.3-final-opt-low.pdf

USAID. (2013). *Violent Extremism and Insurgency in Southern Thailand: A Risk Assessment*. United States Agency for International Development.

Watch, D. S. (2016). *Summing up the situation of unrest in the southern border provinces in 2014*. Deep South Incident Database. Available at https://www.deepsouthwatch.org/en/node/6596

World Bank. (2010). *Conflict and Development: Where is Conflict Concentrated in South Asia*. WB. Available at: http://blogs.worldbank.org/endpovertyinsouthasia/conflict-and-development-where-conflict-concentrated-south-asia

World Bank. (2016). *Unheard Voices: Men and Youth in Thailand's Conflict-Affected Deep South*. World Bank. Available at: http://www.worldbank.org/en/news/feature/2016/09/21/men-and-youth-in-thailands-conflict-affected-deep-south

WSSD. (2002). *World Summit on Sustainable Development. (September, 2002)*. Report of the World Summit on Sustainable Development. Available at: www.un-documents.net/aconf199-20.pdf

ENDNOTES

1 Field Marshal Plaek Phibunsongkhram stepped into power by overthrowing the civilian democratic government in 1938before the beginning of the Greater East Asia War. He implemented the National Integration Policy aimed to unite the diversity of the ethnics' population under the mainstream Thai nationalist culture. Consequently, this action finally urged the escalation of the modern time conflict in the Deep South region.

2 Dusun Nyor Rebellion is the first local resistance against the Thai state in the modern era. Back in 1948, an implementation of intense cultural assimilation policy caused discontentment to the Malay population by forcing them to abandon their religious-related practices to embrace Thai culture instead. In comprising with other preceding discontentment, the situation reached its final straw in the April of 1948 when some local people in Dusun Nyor Sub-District, Narathiwat province started to riot. The riot then followed by an intense counterattack from the security forces and ended with high Malays casualties. It is noted that the consequence of this rebellion is significant. It has been placed at the center of the controversy over Thai authorities' suppression. Above and beyond, this incident hitherto becomes the symbol of the resistance against the Thai state.

Chapter 3
A Critical Review of Gullah Geechee Midlife Women and Heirs' Property Challenges Along the Gullah Geechee Cultural Heritage Corridor

H. Shellae Versey
Fordham University, USA

Robin Throne
https://orcid.org/0000-0002-3015-9587
University of the Cumberlands, USA

ABSTRACT

This critical review explored the current scholarship of the experiences and challenges faced by Gullah Geechee midlife women heirs' property owners along the Gullah Geechee Cultural Heritage Corridor. Past researchers have noted these women often experience invisibility due to the concurrent burdens of management of jointly owned property along the corridor in addition to legacy experiences of cultural isolation, land dispossession, voice dispossession, and ancestry enslavement. Past researchers have called for ongoing collaborative research by both non-indigenous and indigenous researchers as a gap continues for gendered perspectives for current corridor heirs' property challenges and land dispossession with respect to power, trauma, economic impact, Gullah Geechee ways of knowing, land-based cultural values, heritage tourism, governmental dispossession, and the legacy of enslavement for critical inquiry from the transformative paradigm.

DOI: 10.4018/978-1-7998-4372-6.ch003

INTRODUCTION

This critical review explores experiences and challenges faced by Gullah Geechee (GG) midlife women heirs' property owners along the Gullah Geechee Cultural Heritage Corridor (GGCHC). Previously, the authors and other researchers have noted that these women often carry the burden of management of jointly-owned property, referred to as heirs' property, along the Corridor, as well as legacy experiences of cultural isolation, land dispossession, voice dispossession, and ancestry enslavement (Boley & Gaither, 2016; Center for Heirs' Property Preservation [CHPP], 2019; Derickson, 2016; Throne, 2020).

The GG people are descendants of enslaved Africans on the rice, indigo, and cotton plantations of the lower Atlantic coast. Many came from the rice-growing regions of West Africa. The nature of their enslavement on isolated islands and coastal plantations created a unique Black American culture fused with African customs that survives today throughout the coastal areas of North Carolina, South Carolina, Georgia, and Florida. The GGHC communities in the Southeast region of the United States have farmed, cultivated, and depended on the land for the past four hundred years. However, their ability to protect their communities and cultural heritage through land ownership and retention has been an ongoing challenge. This review centers the experiences of GG women using an intersectional lens. Historical experiences of land usage (e.g., sharecropping), land transfer, and heirs' property specifically (also commonly referred to heir or heir's property) are examined as a contextual lens to current research, which has contributed to cumulative disadvantage for the GG community broadly, and for women in particular.

Other researchers have called the marginalization of midlife women in the GG community a "silent demographic" who bears great family and community responsibility (Botwick, 2018; Troutman & Johnson, 2018; Wright, 2008). Women heirs' property owners often experience invisibility amidst immense responsibility for family property, elder care, childcare, discrimination, and preservation of their land-based cultural heritage. The GGCHC research consortium has noted the need to better understand indigenous ways of knowing (Auslander, 2017; Dickens, 2019; Gould, 2017; Rosengarten, 2018; Rosengarten & Wigfall, 2019; Throne, 2016) and an annual conference has been established at the Charles Joyner Institute for Gullah and African Diaspora Studies Coastal Carolina University focused on the advancement and dissemination of GG research (Coastal Carolina University, 2020).

In addition, the authors noted declarations of positionality by non-indigenous researchers have been shown to improve transparency and reduce researcher bias and reflexivity as an ongoing practice to examine gender and cultural power dynamics (Throne, 2018). This chapter was intended to view the complexities of the GG land culture for relational aspects of earth, land as agency, and coastal access as well as to examine the scholarship surrounding voice and land dispossession specifically for GG midlife women.

The chapter proceeds in four parts. First, a background of the historical and current scholarship for GG land dispossession and constructs specific to GG women are presented. Second, the intersectionality framework is reviewed as a basis for exploring gender and land loss within the GGCHC. Third, a historical context for GG as a subset of larger Black agricultural community in the southeastern United States and the literature is discussed alongside the contemporary wave of large-scale land loss related to heirs' property, including its challenges and difficulties. Within this context, an overview of GG women represents the challenges of land retention within this community.

BACKGROUND

Heirs' property is defined as parcels of residential, commercial, agricultural, or vacant land inherited by multiple living descendants. In contrast to structures that facilitate property transfer through wills or estates, heirs' property is real property passed down without a clear title or properly administered will to the owner's children and successive generations as 'tenants in common' (Thomas et al., 2004). In other words, when an individual dies without a probated will, their property becomes heirs' property shared communally amongst all living heirs. Family members receive a fractional portion of the land based on the number of generations removed from the deceased. As a collective, no one person "owns" the land. Descendants have equal access to the property, regardless of who maintains it, lives on it, or pays taxes on it (Dyer & Bailey, 2008). The primary objective of this review was to seek further illumination of the construct of *invisibility* among GG women heirs' property owners along the GGCHC, as a gap exists in the exploration of the land retention challenges faced by this specific silent demographic.

In examining land loss and the consequential decline in the protection and preservation of GG communities, this critical review reveals the challenges associated with heirs' property have collectively framed significant economic and social disadvantages that shape important life outcomes for Southern Black families, such as loss of potential wealth from land ownership, lack of access to credit, segregation, relegation to marginal and hazard-prone land, natural disasters, and systemic discrimination.[1] Given women's centrality in the GG culture, the authors further explore these issues from overlapping perspectives of gender, class, race, and geographical region–as well as other perspectives of social stratification used to view inequities of dispossession.

Previous researchers have noted the gap in the scholarship related to the specific aspects of GG land retention and called for continued research into the role of heirs' property in larger preservation efforts (Gaither, 2016; Gaither & Zarnoch, 2017; Hitchner et al., 2017). Others have echoed this call in the context of rural and coastal land loss, as well as a newly developed predilection for cultural tourism (Moore, 2017). Therefore, this review highlights some of the contemporary legal and socioeconomic challenges to heirs' property within a larger civil rights and intersectional lens, one that is focused on unjust processes in order to encourage transparency and advocacy. The focus on midlife GG women further illuminates bodies at the center of dispossession debates as the research is limited and in so doing, the issue of land dispossession becomes a metaphor through which claims of land ownership among indigenous groups can be highlighted and explored further. This examination may chart useful recommendations for preserving and retaining Black-owned land and sacred spaces managed by GG women landowners and women heirs as members of community landowners.

CONCEPTUAL FRAMEWORK

Black women, particularly those with the fewest resources, have long been at the center of spatial battles over land and housing rights. Culturally, land represents connections to ancestral roots, traditions, and familial ties, particularly among the GG. When land is lost, these connections are weakened. Perry (2013) used an intersectional approach in her work examining women's neighborhood organizations and land rights in Brazil. Perry's foundational research and calls from others (e.g., Rice et al., 2019) highlight previously obscured grassroots efforts by women of color and indigenous women to resist dispossession. Unfortunately, these struggles have not largely been recognized in the larger academic literature.

In this chapter, southern rural property becomes the geographical site used to explore how GG women's connection to land has, in some ways, sustained it. Contemporary critical race theory and Crenshaw's (1991, 1998) intersectionality framework highlight overlapping perspectives of gender, class, race, and geographical region as well as other perspectives of social stratification and dispossession. Intersectionality advances the idea that systems of oppression—namely, racism, classism, sexism, ableism, and heterosexism—work together to create a set of social conditions under which Black women and other women of color live, labor, and provide care (Hill Collins, 2019). Crenshaw articulated these co-constitutive arrangements after encountering Black women who were discriminated against not solely on the basis of gender or race, but from the specific position of being *Black women.* This position, or intersectionality, encapsulates and collectively names a body of Black feminist work about the intersection of social problems that simultaneously highlight interlocking systems of dominance and subordination, while at the same time, centering the lived experiences of Black women (Hill Collins, 2000, 2019; Hill Collins & Bilge, 2016).

In much the same way that Crenshaw sets the stage for illuminating invisibility within oppressive systems, this chapter highlights disparities in land ownership and land retention among Southern Black and GG women of African descent. Specifically, experiences of Black women as stewards of heirs' property are highlighted to draw attention to the less known narratives between gender and land relationships. In addition, the unique roles and responsibilities of women navigating complex judicial process at midlife are explored from a life-course perspective. This work aims to center issues of legal and social import among the GGCHC, with a specific emphasis on heirs' property and institutional power that marginalizes GG women (Hill Collins & Bilge, 2016; Throne, 2020).

GULLAH GEECHEE HEIRS' PROPERTY STEWARDSHIP

Following the Civil War, Blacks acquired approximately 15 million acres of land between 1865 and 1910 (Bloome & Muller, 2015; Moses, 2018; Woofter, 1930). By 1870, almost 1,200 formerly enslaved Africans owned land in Beaufort County, South Carolina – the highest estimated number of landowning Blacks for any county in the South. Many enslavers fled the area and sold their land to the formerly enslaved Africans along the Sea Island plantations in small land parcels (Guthrie, 1996; Moses, 2018; Woofter, 1930). These land parcels were used for farming to sustain whole communities. With limited mainland contact, these island communities were able to retain their land, dialect, and cultural traditions following emancipation, maintaining their way of life and land stewardship, based on an agricultural economy and barter system. Land ownership served as an indicator of community membership, kinship ties, and defined community boundaries (Hitchner et al., 2017; Woofter, 1930). Even as communities grew and expanded, land remained in the possession of one or more family members, sustaining the intact social structure and operations of the GGCHC until the 1950s (Dyer & Bailey, 2008; Guthrie, 1996).

About a decade following Emancipation (a time when many whites were losing land), approximately one-fifth of Blacks who operated farms in the South had become landowners (Schweninger, 1990). However, this period was followed by a period of sharp decline in ownership in the 1940s and 1950s due in large part to discriminatory practices and illegal land seizures (The Emergency Land Fund, 1980). During the same time, land owned by White upper-class families increased (Hitchner et al., 2017; Zabawa et al., 1990). Currently, in areas where the GG once comprised 90 percent of the population, they now comprise for as little as 10 percent (Byrd, 2018). For GG communities, the loss of approximately 700 acres in the Hilton Head area of South Carolina alone has been due to forced sales (or partition sales) of heirs' property sold at auctions for a fraction of the value (Dyer & Bailey, 2008). This process has impeded lend retention, asset accumulation, and endangered the survival of the GG people inhabiting these coastal areas (see Figure 1; Gaither, 2016).

Figure 1. Black Belt counties (red) in the U.S. South. (Source: J intela, CC BY-SA 3.0 license.)

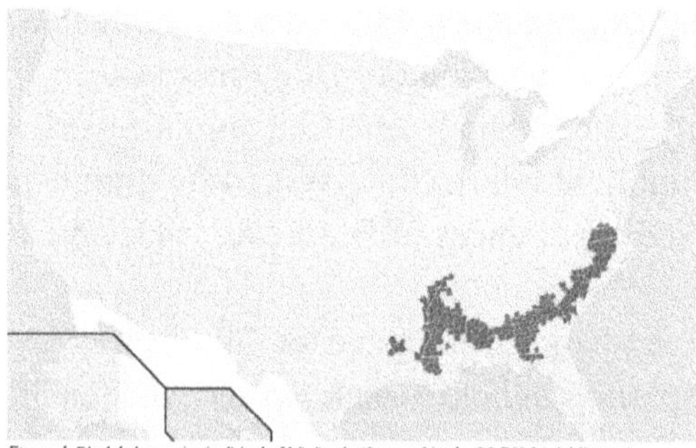

Figure 1. Black belt counties (red) in the U.S. South. (Source: J intela, CC BY-SA 3.0 license.)

The Southern Black Belt is where most heirs' property is located, including the GGCHC, and mostly rural counties from southern Virginia across the Carolinas. In 1980, the Emergency Land Fund estimated that 41 percent of all Black-owned land in the Black Belt South was heirs' property (Gaither, 2016). Land evictions in the South Carolina Lowcountry, where GG families are most concentrated, drew large-scale attention to the issue of heirs' property in this region, showing the need for research and policy efforts focused on coastal and rural communities (Baab, 2011; Bartelme, 2000, 2001, 2002; Chandler, 2005). Therefore, heirs' property is an important case study that demonstrates the gradual erosion of opportunities for both individual and community economies to thrive, resulting in poverty, housing instability, and generational cumulative disadvantage.

Heirs' property is widespread in many communities in the southeast and is disproportionately found among low-income, rural Black families. Heirs' property also includes use and sale restrictions that impacts its profitability. For example, when land becomes heirs' property, it is not divided, nor is the deed to the property (Copeland, 2015; Craig-Taylor, 2000; Hinson, 2018; Hitchner et al., 2017). Therefore, any decisions regarding use of the land, such as tax payment, building permanent structures, using the land as collateral for loans, harvesting timber or leasing plots, must be agreed upon by all those entitled to the land. Securing agreement for decisions is often difficult as one land parcel can have up to hundreds of co-owners. As a result, the economic value of heirs' property as a source of income or repository of wealth is limited because of difficulties associated with collective ownership.

Heirs' property is usually managed by one heir or by a small group of heirs. Managing the property and staying current with property taxes can be challenging due to confusion about who owns what, how much is owed, and who should be paying taxes. Heirs managing tax payments and stewardship may have trouble establishing contact with other heirs (especially those who live far away) and organizing to save property due to collective ownership (Dyer et al., 2009). These challenges can lead to lapses in property tax payments in which the land is recouped by tax offices or real estate speculators, who acquire the land by paying the taxes themselves (i.e., adverse possession) (Brooks, 1979; Gilbert et al., 2002).

Partition or Forced Sales of Heirs' Property

Since the very nature of heirs' property prevents a clear title, there are several legal complications, including ineligibility for housing programs, inability to secure a mortgage, sell timber, and vulnerability to land loss through partition and forced sales. Forced sales by real estate investors and speculators is the most significant way in which land has been lost by Blacks in the U. S. South generally, and for the GG specifically. (Casagrande, 1986, Craig-Taylor 2000, Rivers, 2006). Over time, prime waterfront property owned by GG farmers has been sold, traded or stolen by real estate developers through forced sales and some cases, seizure (Faulkenberry et al., 2000; Zabawa et al., 1990).

Partition sales occur when one heir/descendent decides to sell their share of land, often to a developer, then asks to have this share sold—thereby forcing the sale of the entire property significantly below market value (Zabawa, 1991). Co-owners do not require the consent of other heirs before seeking such a sale. Other heirs or family members who live on the land are usually unable to out-bid resource-rich developers and real estate speculators, therefore losing property that could have otherwise been saved and kept within family ownership (Brooks, 1979; Thomas et al., 2004; Tinubu & Hite, 1978). Any proceeds from the sale (often marginal) are distributed among the co-owners according to their fractional interests, but only after the costs of conducting the sale and attorney fees are deducted (Thomas et al., 2004). In addition to receiving less profit than the property is worth, legal fees associated with the cost of sale can consume as much as twenty percent of the proceeds (Zabawa & Baharanyi, 1992).

As a commodity that has become increasingly valuable over time, coastal GG land has been subject to multiple threats to support a new industrial landscape (Jones-Jackson, 1987). Besides seizure, one of the most pressing contemporary issues facing the GG community has been an increased interest in large-scale development and tourism. As a result, the GGCHC has experienced a transition from an agricultural-based economy to one based on industry, recreation, and tourism (Faulkenberry et al., 2000; Hardy et al., 2017). This transition has resulted in the displacement of many GG people. While incoming corporate development to the GGCHC has increased land value and property taxes, it has also contributed to the loss of large tracts of land (e.g., due to inability to pay taxes). In addition, GG communities have been forced to abandon their primary means of agricultural subsistence, farming, because the "rent value" of the land has become too great (Faulkenberry et al., 2000). Over time, landowners have been pressured, tricked, and forced to sell their land to developers forcibly displacing their communities and significantly diminishing the prospect of wealth generation and land transfer to subsequent generations (Hitchner et al., 2017). More recently, environmental threats (e.g., storms and hurricanes) have exacerbated these issues with property laws and retention, forcing large numbers of GG families to leave their homes (Byrd, 2018).

At the center of many of these transactions are women of the community: either as primary stewards of the land, or as managers tasked with overseeing logistical and legal processes to save property or facilitate family contacts. Taken together, the intersectionality of these complications of managing heirs' property often result in dispossession and destabilization, which largely cripple communities that live off the land, such as the GG. In this way, GG women, families, and communities who might have benefitted from land ownership are not only restrained from making sizable profits through fair market sales but may also be unable to use the land in a way that is economically feasible. Entities that do profit from heirs' property sales are real estate investors, developers, and attorneys. Despite these problems, heirs' property is still common, particularly across the GGCHC, and many families make no attempts to clear their titles, given the long, cumbersome process and expense associated with doing so.

LAND AS A SOCIAL GOOD AND CULTURAL DISPOSSESSION

While the current literature surrounding GG land dispossession has grown some recently, the gap remains to explain heirs' tenure specifically in relation to Southern Black women or GG women landowners. As Rice et al. (2019) noted, critical research can illustrate theoretical concepts faced by Black women currently and historically. The nexus of intersectional oppressions demands transformational views of relationships to resources and land (Carastathis, 2016 as cited by Rice et al., 2019). For GG women along the GGCHC, these trends have included the erosion of family enclaves and post-Civil War rural Black settlements (Rosengarten, 2018).

Literary writers have been especially adept in expressing the sentiments tied to protecting and losing land. Since a monetary value cannot be placed on family relations and stability, land often serves as the connective tissue that holds these elements together. Living together in close proximity to relatives provides a source of social support and collective familial resource that can be used and cultivated into additional resources. For example, Pearce (1973) described difficulties with land retention as "problems" and "pitfalls," and Mitchell (2019) referred to heirs' property land seizure as a "devastating land loss." These descriptions have been useful to highlight a crucial point beyond legal and policy implications of heirs' property: land as a social good. For example, Batteau (1982) described land as central to the "control of kin, marriage, reputation, and localities" (p. 453). Likewise, Falk (2004) explained how important land is to rural Black communities. For in these communities, the issue is not dollars and cents, but rather a cultural identity tied to the land (p. 131). For the GG specifically, working the land and owning it was a reflection of self-determination and freedom, serving as an historical source of sustainability and resilience.[2] More research is needed to better understand the gendered contexts of these historical and contemporary experiences and value for this land-based culture.

Indigenous communities living on reservations, secluded areas, or close to waterways are rich in culture, language, and have a deep sense of love and connection to the land. Yet, harsh realities accompany land ownership. In one chronicle of children and grandchildren of sharecroppers, Stack (1996) tells the story of a woman who left her husband in the North, to return to her birth home in the South. Besides the land, this woman owned little. Yet, she lived on a plot so overgrown that she could not walk the perimeter, and never determined exactly how much land she owned. Still, she considered it home, raised her children there, and later died there. Stack recounts another story of how land was so significant to one family, when their ownership was threatened, the father killed himself to provide his wife with enough income to hold on to the land. "Nora," another woman in the rural South found herself the target of envy because she had inherited her father's land–10 acres. However, one stipulation was that Nora could never sell the land. According to Stack, "Nora believed that this limitation was a great comfort for her and all the family. The land tied them all together. It gave focus and purpose to family relationships – the land itself was a family relationship" (Stack 1996, p. 31). For Nora and others, it is the land that holds value and holds families together. In many ways, these accounts mirror the realities of other indigenous communities at the center of battles about land tenure, residency rights, and land ownership. Yet they are the same groups on the front lines of intense legal and illegal challenges to keeping and protecting their land from human and environmental threats. GG women have also faced intense threats over the years both due to their close proximity to valuable waterfront property, and as a function of weak legal protections for heir's property owners.

VOICE and IDENTITY AMONG GULLAH GEECHEE MIDLIFE WOMEN

Sabir (2018) noted GG women's voices in relation to the issues of oppressed land-based cultures have been constructed primarily through artistic representations rather than peer-reviewed research, such as in Julie Dash's *Daughters of the Dust* or Beyonce's *Lemonade*. Both visual art projects retell the narrative of GG women, yet the setting–the land itself–is the backdrop that imbues the stories with meaning. Morris Johnson (2017) notes how, in both cases, rituals and a sense of communion with other women reflects introspection of self and shapes identity. These artistic representations may not specifically name or highlight dispossession as much as they reconstruct a broader narrative about sacred lands and the value it holds for women in particular, as stewards of the GG community. Campbell (2017) notes Beyoncé's short film rendition of Dash's original piece centers on GG women's narratives of resistance and uses voice to demonstrate courage and bravery, themes too often reserved for men. The artistic depictions also include water as an integral component of the communal space necessary to GG culture and history riddled with trauma, survival, and hope (Campbell, 2017).

With new threats of environmental concern, these narratives continue as noted by Byrd (2018) who described the increasing challenges to land ownership as coastal regions are often the hardest hit and the slowest to recover from hurricanes and tropical storms. Historically, the GG people have resisted evacuating their land in times of distress, due to deep ties to the land, a respect for tradition, and economic limitations. "We are people of faith and that is the reason that people do not just leave...Our souls are tied from the land." Queen Quet Marquetta L. Goodwine, the elected Chieftess of the Gullah/Geechee Nation explains (Goodwine, 1997). Yet environmental change brings more climate-related hurricanes, placing the GG community at greater displacement risk. If homes damaged or destroyed, rebuilding or receiving federal funds for relief present significant barriers. Aside from those concerns, developers and speculators may seek to profit from tragedy, buying land during times when community resilience and family connections may be weakest (Hinson, 2018). As younger generations live further away from home, connections that could hold generations of land in-tact remain fragile.

GULLAH GEECHEE AND BLACK SOUTHERN WOMEN AS LAND STEWARDS AND PRESERVATIONISTS

Structural racism, past and present, continues to contribute to land loss among southern Black farmers and the GG (Daniel, 2013; Gilbert et al., 2002; Lewan & Barclay, 2001; McIver, 2003; Mitchell, 2005, 2019; Thomas et al., 2004; Williams, 2005). What is less known, however, are mechanisms linking how these processes continue in a contemporary context, and how adjacent framings of environmental justice, cultural preservation, settler colonialism, displacement, and spatial/environmental racism speak to issues facing GG communities (Bullard, 1993, 1996; Pellow, 2016; Pulido, 2016; Saturnino et al., 2013; Whyte, 2018). For example, environmental justice research has only recently considered the larger social, ecological, cultural, economic, and political factors that shape rural precarity for some populations (Pellow, 2016). These accounts suggest heirs' property presents a sizable hindrance to land retention; yet little has been done to ease the process for rural families with few resources most likely to be recipients of heirs' property (Mitchell, 2019).

The gaps in this literature particular to the experiences of GG women clearly demonstrate the need for additional research to fully understand how current policies and legal restrictions on heirs' property continue to accelerate land loss in the GGHCH and the specific experience of the intersectional oppression and challenges that often face GG women at midlife. The impact of land dispossession is important to women's rights and the well-being of women, who are more likely to be marginalized within rural contexts compared to other groups (Millar, 2015; Tsikata, 2009). However, history also suggests that Black women serve as critical social agents, facilitating land ownership for other Black women, as well as their own families to maintain financial security (Bell, 2018). For example, through church involvement and participation in female benevolent societies that encouraged women to save and invest in land following Emancipation, Southern Black women were able to provide a sense of stability for their families during Reconstruction. In the African Methodist Episcopal (A.M.E.) church, as well as in other churches, committees seeking to establish homesteads pursued landowning opportunities and specifically established committees devoted to land acquisition.

Benevolent societies were popular throughout the southeast (Bell, 2018). As key members of GG and Black committees, Black women often ensured the foundation of the church not only through raising funds for buying land, but in some instances by providing land (Bell, 2018). For example, Selina Stewart, a Savannah, Georgia resident, sold a small parcel of the inherited estate of her father to Mt. Zion C.M.E. church to "promote the welfare of the church." In Savannah, Georgia, another site where large numbers of land-owning Sea Islanders resided in the GGHCH, Black women benevolent societies enabled aspiring women the opportunity to form independent wealth and power within their communities. Members in associations such as the Sons and Daughters of Jerusalem, the Sons and Daughters of Mount Sinai, and the Sons and Daughters of Zion, coordinated activities with the goal of acquiring land for self-sufficiency. However, whether this practice extended fully to large numbers of GG women, who were more likely to be poorer and live outside of main city centers, is uncertain. Many rural women—some single and widowed—found it difficult to purchase land because of low wages and familial responsibilities.

Over time, complications with maintaining heirs' property mount considerably and limited research has focused on cultural understandings of heirs' property among the GG and the concerns for future generations and the well-being of the culture itself. Despite the challenging realities faced, 117 Black women in Savannah-Chatham County became landowners by 1876, most of whom were formerly enslaved. In 1870 and 1880, women headed one-fourth of Black families in Savannah (Bell, 2018). In other instances, women purchased land for their children through an "internal land trade" where they gained access to small parcels of land. Less is known about these informal types of internal transactions and who all benefitted; therefore, additional research that expands and deepens our understanding of land ownership by Black women can separate important differences between formerly enslaved GG communities and Black communities without Sea Island ties in the South.

More recently, ethnographic interviews of GG women in Beaufort, South Carolina revealed several important patterns associated with new development and heirs' property loss in the area (Faulkenberry et al., 2000). According to several respondents in a study on the effects of tourism on the area, new development has had an inverse effect, compared to the collective efforts at the turn of the century. Incoming tourism, for example, has contributed to weakened land control and political power. In describing the many challenges of passing land down through family generations without a will, women now find themselves at the center of complicated deeds and long legal processes required to clear those deeds. In addition, maintaining taxes when taxes are steadily increasing makes land more difficult to develop. According to one woman who owned heirs' property,

"At one time they were going to develop Fripp Plantation.... we would've been sandwiched in between golf courses which would've made the land taxes go up to the point where you couldn't farm it anymore."

Another respondent noted that,

"The only thing they [family] know for sure," she says, "is that they own a piece of property." That they own an undivided interest "doesn't sink in." As time goes by titles become more entangled: "That's the problem – when folks start dying off, (family members) forget that interest out there."

The discrepancy between the ability of outside, capital-rich developers to transform the GGHCH into extravagant resorts while the original owners and stewards of the land face poverty and displacement reflects decades of attempting to circumvent GG landowners through intimidation, threats, and even violence (McIver, 2003). In many of these cases, no action has been taken by local or federal authorities in order to prevent or remedy deceptive tactics to take coastal land (McIver, 2003). Furthermore, resistance efforts can be difficult, especially since landowners in the GGCHC generally have limited access to legal counsel (Gilbert et al., 2002; Mitchell, 2019; Thomas et al., 2004). Lacking knowledge about legal rights, many GG families have fallen prey to speculators and unscrupulous attorneys who receive land at a deep discount and sell it to developers for large profits (Hinson, 2018).

At the center of processes fighting to keep and preserve remaining land and create productive land use strategies, are Southern Black and GG women. Our review finds that women heirs' property owners consider land as a place to call home and a way to keep familial ties strong (Gilbert et al., 2004; Thomas et al., 2004; Zabawa, 1991). While not well documented, there is growing evidence that Southern Black and GG women are primary land stewards and often assume responsibility for navigating legal and judicial strategies associated with preserving heirs' property in GGCHC. In one well-known example, Shirley Sherrod, a longtime agricultural and farming advocate, co-founded New Communities, a Black farming community in rural Georgia during the civil rights era. At the time, New Communities was the largest tract of Black-owned land in the United States and the country's first community land trust – described by the organizers as "a nonprofit organization to hold land in perpetual trust for the permanent use of rural communities."

With anticipated assistance from consultants and a planning grant from the Office of Economic Opportunity, the group planned to build 500 family homes, a railroad track, health and educational systems, and a farm operation. While the group managed to build some infrastructure, discrimination from local White farmers and federal agencies eventually led New Communities to close in foreclosure proceedings. In 1985, an auction was held to sell off the land the New Communities farmers had built, a wealthy white buyer paid $1 million for the land–$950,000 of which he borrowed from the FHA, the same U.S. Department of Agriculture (USDA) office that had refused to loan money to New Communities previously. Eventually, Sherrod and New Communities filed a case under the *Pigford v. Glickman* class action lawsuit against the USDA that alleged racial discrimination against Black farmers between 1981 and 1986 in its allocation of farm loans and other assistance. New Communities was eventually awarded a $12M settlement, in large part due to Sherrod's efforts and persistence and they were able to rebuild a thriving farm community that still exists today.

Currently, approximately 80 percent of the land gained by 1969 by Black and GG families has been lost, primarily as a function of heirs' property sales. While no definite solutions to resist land takeovers have been established, there are several strategies that may be useful in stemming the tide of dispossession.

Used in the Sherrod case, land trusts are one strategy of collective ownership that has been used with some metric of success in other areas across the country to preserve valuable land and prevent displacement in high-poverty areas (Meehan, 2013). In addition, recent policy and legal advocates attempt to protect landholding stewards of heirs' property by educating landowners on their rights, assist in clearing titles, and endeavor to have the land generate some benefit for families (CHPP, 2019; Stephans, 2015). Still, loss remains a concern and heir property still an important component in that concern as heir property is commonly cited as the "traditional form of farmland ownership among blacks" (Zabawa et al., 1990, p. 113). As long as heir property exists, there are Black landowners.

The Uniform Partition of Heirs Property Act, the first, significant step in addressing the cultural aspects of heirs' property ownership may be one of the most significant steps towards alleviating some burdens of heirs' property (Hinson, 2018). The Act, sponsored by the National Conference of Commissioners on Uniform State Laws, has been enacted in Alabama, Arkansas, Connecticut, Georgia, Montana, Nevada, and South Carolina, and has been introduced in Hawaii, Mississippi, and West Virginia (Baba et al., 2018; Uniform Law Commission, 2016). Some of the key provisions of the Heirs Property Act are: (a) a clearer definition of heirs' property; (b) in the event of a property sale, those heirs not wishing to sell could purchase the interests of the seller, and the former would have to match only the amount that the seller had invested in the property rather than the land's larger fair market value; and (c) crucially, the court must consider both economic and noneconomic factors in determining whether property should be partitioned in kind or sold.

CONCLUSION

This chapter presents a review of several challenges related to heirs' property in the South, specifically focusing on the role of Southern Black and GG women in providing the foundation for Black women landownership, and the difficulties associated with maintaining ownership. Despite gaps in the current research, the authors highlighted central issues of legal and social import among the GGCHC, with a specific emphasis on heirs' property and institutional power that contributes to land dispossession. Due to significant gaps in the literature for midlife GG women and the construct of invisibility, the authors call for continued research into the noneconomic aspects of GG land tenure to include intangible sentiments, attachments, and gendered histories associated with land ownership as these must be further considered (Gaither, 2016; Mitchell, 2005, 2019). Finally, the experiences of midlife GG women specific to voice dispossession and invisibility have not yet been highlighted within the current scholarship and deserve further empirical investigation to examine gendered land relationships along the GGCHC.

ACKNOWLEDGMENT

With gratitude to the Gullah Geechee Cultural Heritage Corridor Commission Research Consortium and the Gullah Nation of North America for their support of this work and for their ongoing dissemination of GGCHC research. Additional appreciation to The Wesleyan University College of Environment Climate Scholar Award and Northcentral University for the Faculty Research Capacity Award in support of this social justice research.

REFERENCES

Auslander, M. (2017). Rose's gift: Slavery, kinship, and the fabric of memory. *Present Pasts*, *8*(1), 1. Advance online publication. doi:10.5334/pp.78

Baab, C. H. (2011). Heir property: A constraint for planners, an opportunity for communities—The legacy of Steve Larkin. *Planning & Environmental Law*, *63*(11), 3–11. doi:10.1080/15480755.2011.630283

Baba, A., Zabawa, R., & Zekeri, A. (2018). Utilization of property among African American heir and titled landowners in Alabama's Black Belt. *The Review of Black Political Economy*, *45*(4), 325–338. doi:10.1177/0034644619838378

Bartelme, T. (2000). Heirs property tangle leads to loss of land. *The Post and Courier.* http://archives.postandcourier.com/archive/arch00/1200/arc1224276403.shtml

Bartelme, T. (2001). Families evicted from heirs' property: Deputies enforce court's directive after relative's lawsuit leads to sale order. *The Post and Courier.* http://archives.postandcourier.com/archive/arch01/0901/arc0928311298.shtml

Bartelme, T. (2002). Heirs land at risk. *The Post and Courier.* http://archives.postandcourier.com/archive/arch02/0602/arc0623648840.shtml

Batteau, A. (1982). Mosbys and Broomsedge: The semantics of class in an Appalachian kinship system. *American Ethnologist*, *9*(3), 445–466. doi:10.1525/ae.1982.9.3.02a00010

Bell, K. C. (2018). *Claiming freedom: Race, kinship, and land in nineteenth-century Georgia*. University of South Carolina Press. doi:10.2307/j.ctv6wghxq

Bloome, D., & Muller, C. (2015). Tenancy and African American marriage in the postbellum South. *Demography*, *52*(5), 1409–1430. doi:10.100713524-015-0414-1 PMID:26223562

Boley, B. B., & Gaither, C. J. (2016). Exploring empowerment within the Gullah Geechee cultural heritage corridor: Implications for heritage tourism development in the Lowcountry. *Journal of Heritage Tourism*, *11*(2), 155–176. doi:10.1080/1743873X.2015.1080712

Botwick, B. (2018). Gullah-Geechee settlement patterns from slavery to freedom: Investigation of a Georgia plantation slave quarter. *North American Archaeologist*, *39*(3), 198–228. doi:10.1177/0197693118793795

Brooks, J. (1979). The Emergency Land Fund: A rural land retention and development model. In L. McGee & R. Boone (Eds.), *The Black Rural Landowner – Endangered Species: Social, Political, and Economic Implications* (pp. 117–134). Greenwood Press.

Bullard, R. D. (1993). Environmental racism and land use. *Land Use Forum: A Journal of Law. Policy & Practice*, *2*(1), 6–11.

Bullard, R. D. (1996). *Unequal protection: Environmental justice and communities of color*. Sierra Club.

Byrd, A. (2018). Congress investigates EPA for refusing NASA's help after hurricane Harvey. *Color lines*. https://www.colorlines.com/tags/environmental-racism

Campbell, A. (2017, April 7). *Beyond say: Water, spirituality, and the womanist autoethnography in Beyonce's Lemonade*. The National Conference on Undergraduate Research, University of Memphis, TN. http://ncurproceedings.org/ojs/index.php/NCUR2017/article/view/2244/1264

Carastathis, A. (2016). *Intersectionality: Origins, contestations, horizons*. University of Nebraska Press. doi:10.2307/j.ctt1fzhfz8

Casagrande, J. G. Jr. (1986). Acquiring property through forced partitioning sales: Abuses and remedies. *Boston College Law Review, 27*(4), 755–783.

Center for Heirs' Property Preservation. (2019). *Protect your land*. https://www.heirsproperty.org/

Chandler, A. B. (2005). "The loss in my bones": Protecting African American heirs' property with the public use doctrine. *The William and Mary Bill of Rights Journal, 14*(1), 387–414.

Coastal Carolina University. (2020). *International Gullah Geechee and African Diaspora Conference*. https://www.coastal.edu/joynerinstitute/conference/

Copeland, R. W. (2015). Heir property in the African American community: From promised lands to problem lands. *Professional Agricultural Workers Journal, 2*(2), 2-9. https://tuspubs.tuskegee.edu/pawj/vol2/iss2/2

Craig-Taylor, P. (2000). Through a colored looking glass: A view of judicial partition, family land loss, and rule setting. *Washington University Law Review Quarterly, 78*(3), 737–788.

Crenshaw, K. (1998). Demarginalizing the intersection of race and sex: A Black feminist critique of antidiscrimination doctrine, feminist theory, and antiracist politics. *Feminism and Politics*, 314-343. doi:10.4324/9780429499142-5

Crenshaw, K. W. (1991). Mapping the margins: Intersectionality, identity politics, and violence against women of color. *Stanford Law Review, 43*(6), 1241–1299. doi:10.2307/1229039

Daniel, P. (2013). *Dispossession: Discrimination against African American farmers in the age of Civil Rights*. The University of North Carolina Press.

Derickson, K. D. (2016). The assassination of Clementa Pinckney. *Southeastern Geographer, 56*(1), 38–44. doi:10.1353go.2016.0012

Dickens, N. (2019, March 7). *Reinventing Erzulie's past for literature's future*. Inaugural International Gullah Geechee and African Diaspora Conference, Coastal Carolina University, Conway, SC.

Dyer, J., Bailey, C., & Tran, N. (2009). Ownership characteristics of heir property in a Black Belt county: A quantitative approach. *Southern Rural Sociology, 24*(2), 192–217.

Dyer, J. F., & Bailey, C. (2008). A place to call home: Cultural understandings of heir property among rural African Americans. *Rural Sociology, 73*(3), 317–338. doi:10.1526/003601108785766598

Emergency Land Fund. (1981). *The impact of heir property on Black rural land tenure in the Southeastern region of the United States*. Report submitted to the U.S. Department of Agriculture.

Falk, W. W. (2004). *Rooted in place: Family and belonging in a Southern Black community*. Rutgers University Press.

Faulkenberry, L. V., Coggeshall, J. M., Backman, K., & Backman, S. (2000). A culture of servitude: The impact of tourism and development on South Carolina's Coast. *Human Organization*, *59*(1), 86–95. doi:10.17730/humo.59.1.353730461t724j02

Gaither, C. J. (2016). *"Have not our weary feet come to the place for which our fathers sighed?": Heirs' property in the southern United States*. https://www.treesearch.fs.fed.us/pubs/53186

Gaither, C. J., & Zarnoch, S. J. (2017). Unearthing 'dead capital': Heirs' property prediction in two US southern counties. *Land Use Policy*, *67*, 367–377. doi:10.1016/j.landusepol.2017.05.009

Gilbert, J., Sharp, G., & Felin, M. S. (2002). The loss and persistence of Black-owned farms and farmland: A review of the research literature and its implications. *Southern Rural Sociology*, *18*(2), 1–30.

Gilbert, J., Wood, S. D., & Sharp, G. (2002). Who owns the land? Agricultural land ownership by race-ethnicity. *Rural America*, *17*(4), 55–62.

Goodwine, M. (1997). *Gwad dun smile pun we: Beaufort Isles*. Kinship Publications.

Gould, G. (2017). The Black feminine on screen. *Sight and Sound*, *27*(6), 42–45.

Guthrie, P. (1996). *Catching sense: African American communities on a South Carolina Sea Island*. Bergin and Garvey.

Hardy, R. D., Milligan, R. A., & Heynen, N. (2017). Racial coastal formation: The environmental injustice of colorblind adaptation planning for sea-level rise. *Geoforum*, *87*, 62–72. doi:10.1016/j.geoforum.2017.10.005

Hill Collins, P. (2000). *Black feminist thought: Knowledge, consciousness, and the politics of empowerment* (2nd ed.). Routledge.

Hill Collins, P. (2019). The difference that power makes: Intersectionality and participatory democracy. In *The Palgrave Handbook of Intersectionality in Public Policy* (pp. 167–192). Palgrave Macmillan. doi:10.1007/978-3-319-98473-5_7

Hill Collins, P., & Bilge, S. (2016). *Intersectionality*. Wiley.

Hinson, W. R. (2018). Land gains, land losses: The odyssey of African Americans since Reconstruction. *American Journal of Economics and Sociology*, *77*(3-4), 893–939. doi:10.1111/ajes.12233

Hitchner, S., Schelhas, J., & Gaither, C. J. (2017). "A privilege and a challenge": Valuation of heirs' property by African American landowners and implications for forest management in the Southeastern US. *Small-scale Forestry*, *16*(3), 1–23. doi:10.100711842-017-9362-5

Jones-Jackson, P. (1987). *When roots die: Endangered traditions on the Sea Islands*. University of Georgia Press.

Jones-Jackson, P. (1987). *When roots die: Endangered traditions on the Sea Islands*. University of Georgia Press. muse.jhu.edu/book/11406

Jordan, P. K. (2016). "Ain't gonna let nobody turn me around": Spirituals as embodied acts of resistance. *The Black Scholar*, *46*(1), 37–45. doi:10.1080/00064246.2015.1119623

Manigault-Bryant, L. S. (2016). Where Black bodies lie: Historiography, race, and the place of Eros. *Theology and Sexuality*, *22*(3), 165–174. doi:10.1080/13558358.2017.1329884

McIver, L. (2003). Blacks driven and cheated out of their land. *The Black Collegian*, *33*, 100–101.

Meehan, J. (2013). Reinventing real estate: The community land trust as a social invention in affordable housing. *Journal of Applied Social Science*, *8*(2), 113–133. doi:10.1177/1936724413497480

Millar, G. (2015). "We have no voice for that": Land rights, power, and gender in rural Sierra Leone. *Journal of Human Rights*, *14*(4), 445–462. doi:10.1080/14754835.2015.1032219

Mitchell, T. W. (2005). Destabilizing the normalization of rural Black land loss: A critical role for legal empiricism. *Wisconsin Law Review*, 557–615.

Mitchell, T. W. (2019). Historic Partition Law Reform: A game changer for heirs' property owners. In C. J. Gaither, A. Carpenter, T L. McCurty, & S. Toering (Eds.), *Heirs' property and land fractionation: Fostering stable ownership to prevent land loss and abandonment.* US Department of Agriculture, e-General Technical Report. https://www.srs.fs.usda.gov/pubs/gtr/gtr_srs244.pdf

Moore, L. (2017). Gullah Geechee families: Land and culture. *Contemporary Rural Social Work, 9*(1), 1–14.

Morris Johnson, N. M. (2019). Janie's Gullah/Geechee seekin journey in "Their eyes were watching God,". *South Atlantic Review*, *84*(1), 72–90.

Moses, S. K. (2018). Enslaved African conjure and ritual deposits on the Hume Plantation, South Carolina. *North American Archaeologist*, *39*(2), 131–164. doi:10.1177/0197693118773252

Ochiai, A. (2001). The Port Royal Experiment revisited: Northern visions of reconstruction and the land question. *The New England Quarterly*, *74*(1), 94–117. doi:10.2307/3185461

Pellow, D. N. (2016). Environmental justice and rural studies: A critical conversation and invitation to collaboration. *Journal of Rural Studies, 47*(A), 381-386. doi:10.1016/j.jrurstud.2016.06.018

Perry, K.-K. Y. (2013). *Black women against the land grab: The fight for racial justice in Brazil*. University of Minnesota Press.

Pulido, L. (2015). Geographies of race and ethnicity I: White supremacy vs white privilege in environmental racism research. *Progress in Human Geography*, 1–9. doi:10.1177/0309132514563008

Rice, C., Harrison, E., & Friedman, M. (2019). Doing justice to intersectionality in research. *Cultural Studies Critical Methodologies*, 1-12. doi:10.1177/1532708619829779

Rivers, F. R. (2006). Restoring the bundle of rights: Preserving heirs' property in coastal South Carolina. *Proceedings of the 17th annual estate planning symposium*. https://www.americanbar.org/content/dam/aba/events/real_property_trust_estate/symposia/2006/12_property_preservation.authcheckdam.pdf

Rose, W. L. (1964). *Rehearsal for reconstruction: The Port Royal Experiment*. Bobbs-Merrill.

Rosengarten, D. (2018). Babylon Is falling: The state of the art of Sweetgrass basketry. *Southern Cultures, 24*(2), 98–124. doi:10.1353cu.2018.0022

Rosengarten, D., & Wigfall, N. (2019, March 9). *Babylon is falling: The state of the art of Sweetgrass basketry.* Inaugural International Gullah Geechee and African Diaspora Conference, Coastal Carolina University, Conway, SC.

Sabir, W. A. B. (2018). Sweeping conversations: Julie Dash's *Daughters. The Journal of Pan African Studies, 11*(6), 231–247. https://www.jpanafrican.org/docs/vol11no6/final-Kim-26-Sabir.pdf

Schweninger, L. (1990). *Black property owners in the South, 1790-1915.* University of Illinois Press.

Snow, K. C., Hays, D. G., Caliwagan, G., Ford, D. J. Jr, Mariotti, D., Mwendwa, J. M., & Scott, W. E. (2016). Guiding principles for indigenous research practices. *Action Research, 14*(4), 357–375. doi:10.1177/1476750315622542

Stack, C. B. (1974). *All our kin.* Harper and Row.

Stack, C. B. (1996). *Call to home: African-Americans reclaim the rural South.* Basic Books.

Stephens, J. L. (2015). *Don't sign anything!* Center for Heirs' Property and Preservation., https://heirsproperty.org/wp-content/uploads/2018/04/2014_Fall_Newsletter.pdf

Stewart, T., Throne, R., & Evans, L. (2020). A critical review of gender parity and voice dispossession among executive women in higher education leadership. In G. Berg & L. Venis (Eds.), *Accessibility and diversity in the 21st century university.* IGI Global. doi:10.4018/978-1-7998-2783-2.ch005

Thomas, M., Pennick, J. & Gray, H. (2004). *What is African-American land ownership?* Federation of Southern Cooperatives Land Assistance Fund.

Throne, R. (2016). Past as prologue: Sea Island Cotton as heuristic metaphor for the Port Royal Experiment. *SAGE Open, 6*(3), 1–8. doi:10.1177/2158244016662105

Throne, R. (2018). The letter: Fidelity in researcher positionality to exhume dispossessed voices for Leavy's concept of coherence in feminist narrative research. *Gender and Women's Studies, 2*(1). http://riverapublications.com/journal/gender-womens-studies

Throne, R. (2020). Dispossession of land cultures: Women and property tenure among Lowcountry heirs in the Gullah Geechee Corridor. In U. Onyebadi (Ed.), *Multidisciplinary issues surrounding African Diasporas* (pp. 152–174). IGI Global. doi:10.4018/978-1-5225-5079-2.ch007

Tinubu, G. B., & Hite, J. C. (1978). *Intestate holding of rural land in South Carolina: Empirical evaluation of the dimensions of the heirs' property problem. South Carolina Agricultural Experiment Station.* Clemson University.

Troutman, S., & Johnson, B. (2018). Dark water: Rememory, biopower, and Black feminist art. *Taboo: The Journal of Culture & Education, 17*(3), 73. doi:10.31390/taboo.17.3.08

Tsikata, D. (2009). Gender, land and labour relations and livelihoods in Sub-Saharan Africa in the era of economic liberalization: Towards a research agenda. *Feminist Africa, 12*, 11–30.

Versey, H. S. (2017). Caregiving and women's health: Toward an intersectional approach. *Women's Health Issues*, *27*(2), 117–120. doi:10.1016/j.whi.2017.01.009 PMID:28258803

Versey, H. S., Cogburn, C. C., Wilkins, C. L., & Joseph, N. (2019). Appropriated racial oppression and its role for health in Whites and Blacks. *Social Science & Medicine*, *230*, 295–302. doi:10.1016/j.socscimed.2019.03.014 PMID:31054520

Woofter, T. J. (1930). *Black yeomanry: Life on St. Helena Island*. Holt.

Wright, N. E. (2008). Property rights and possession in "Daughters of the Dust." *Melus*, *33*(3), 11–25. doi:10.1093/melus/33.3.11

Zabawa, R. (1991). The Black farmer and land in South-Central Alabama: Strategies to preserve a scarce resource. *Human Ecology*, *19*(1), 61–81. https://link.springer.com/content/pdf/10.1007/BF00888977.pdf. doi:10.1007/BF00888977

Zabawa, R., Siaway, A., & Baharanyi, N. (1990). The decline of Black farmers and strategies for survival. *Southern Rural Sociology*. https://egrove.olemiss.edu/jrss/vol07/iss1/9/

ADDITIONAL READING

Amaker, M. (2017). *empath*. CreateSpace.

Bailey, A. C. (2017). *The weeping time: Memory and the largest slave auction in American history*. Cambridge University Press. doi:10.1017/9781108140393

Campbell, E. (2008). *Gullah cultural legacies: A synopsis of Gullah traditions, customary beliefs, art forms and speech on Hilton Head Island and vicinal Sea Islands in South Carolina and Georgia* (3rd ed.). BookSurge.

Cooper, M. L. (2017). *Making Gullah: A history of Sapelo Islanders, race, and the American imagination*. University of North Carolina Press. doi:10.5149/northcarolina/9781469632681.001.0001

Georgia Appleseed Center for Law & Justice. (2013). Unlocking heir property ownership: Assessing the impact on low and mid-income Georgians and their communities. http://www.gaappleseed.org/media/docs/unlocking-heir-property.pdf

Goetcheus, C., & Brabec, E. (2014). The interrelationships of land, culture and heritage: The Gullah Geechee communities of the Southeastern United States. In K. Taylor, A. St. Clair, & N. J. Mitchell (Eds.), *Conserving Cultural Landscapes* (pp. 127–146). Routledge.

Gullah Geechee Cultural Heritage Corridor Commission. (2012). Management plan. National Park Service, Denver, CO. https://www.gullahgeecheecorridor.org/resources/

Jones-Jackson, P. (2011). *When roots die: Endangered traditions on the Sea Islands*. University of Georgia Press.

Manigault-Bryant, L. S. (2014). *Talking to the dead: Religion, music, and lived memory among Gullah/ Geechee women*. Duke University Press. doi:10.1215/9780822376705

McGill, D. (Producer/Director), & Duvall, S. (Producer/Editor). (2019). *The Gullah Project* [Documentary series]. United States. https://thegullahproject.org/

Moore, G. C. (2017). *Maternal metaphors of power in African American women's literature: From Phillis Wheatley to Toni Morrison*. University of South Carolina Press. doi:10.2307/j.ctv6wggmx

Smith, T. K. (2018). *Wade in the water*. Graywolf.

Throne, R. (2019). *The cotton breath, an allegorical novella*. Anaphora Literary Press.

Walker, S. (2018). *African American girls and the construction of identity: Class, race, and gender*. Rowman & Littlefield.

KEY TERMS AND DEFINITIONS

Gullah Geechee Cultural Heritage Corridor (GGCHC): The Gullah Geechee Cultural Heritage Corridor (GGCHC) is a federal national heritage center. It extends along the southeastern Atlantic coast to include North Carolina, South Carolina, Georgia, and Florida and the Gullah Geechee people. Gullah has been identified with those living along the Carolina segment of the corridor and Geechee with those along the Georgia and Florida segment of the corridor. Boley and Gaither (2016) noted the formation of the GGCHC brought together the GG reference, which may obscure distinctions among people with cultural or community alliances than the federally-defined GGCHC.

Heirs' Property: Heirs' property is a form of tenancy in common and the term is commonly used along the GGCHC to refer to common land owned by multiple heirs whereby the original owner often died intestate and the land is typically passed down generation to generation outside of probate. Some report heirs' property as a leading cause of land loss along the Corridor.

Intersectionality: Originally founded within Black feminist and critical race theories, intersectionality has been defined as the intersection of oppressive forces that lead to marginalization and contribute to explicit bias and discrimination. The term is often used within social justice research and may carry various contextual denotations and connotations in contemporary research.

Invisibility: Invisibility has been used to address marginalized identities, underrepresented individuals who experience voice dispossession and/or are silent, and those who experience oppression and/or discrimination.

Land-Based Culture: The terms land culture or land-based culture are often used in reference to indigenous cultures that view their responsibility as land curators versus landowners. As such, land is also often connected to the identity and spirituality of individuals within the culture (Throne, 2020).

Lowcountry: The Lowcountry has been traditionally referred to as the 200-mile (322-kilometer) stretch of coastal South Carolina and Georgia.

Voice Dispossession: Voice dispossession involves the filtered, silencing, or reduction of vocality of opinions, ideas, and innovation among specific groups due to oppressive hierarchies, gendered obstacles or barriers, or other societal power domains. Fear or threat of consequences may also impede vocality of individuals amid these societal structures, which can result in decreased wellbeing, unfair or imbalanced dialogue, repressed innovation, barriers to social justice, and land dispossession (Stewart et al., 2020; Throne, 2018).

ENDNOTES

1 For more extensive scholarship of the socio-legal aspects of GG land tenure, see the Center for Heirs' Property Preservation https://www.heirsproperty.org/ and the Georgia Appleseed Center for Law & Justice https://gaappleseed.org/initiatives/heir

2 See Rose (1964) and Ochiai (2001) for detailed accounts of the economic and sociopolitical context of GG land tenure since the since the Port Royal invasion in 1861.

Chapter 4
Perception of Local People on Land Use Change:
Belihuloya-Mini Catchment Area, Sri Lanka

H. M. Paba Herath
Sabaragamuwa University of Sri Lanka, Sri Lanka

K. W. G. Rekha Nianthi
University of Peradeniya, Sri Lanka

ABSTRACT

The land use of the Belihuloya catchment area in Sri Lanka has been changing over a long period mainly due to the human activities. The study was aimed to find out the spatial and temporal changes of land use in the Belihuloya Mini Catchment area of 1956 to 2015, and obtain the local people's perception of the effects of land-use changes in Belihuloya. To study the people's perceptions of land use change, a questionnaire survey was conducted among randomly selected 180 households. Aerial data of 1956 and satellite data of 2015 were used to analyze the land use changes. The vegetation cover maps of 1956 and 2015, demonstrated the drastic changes of land use in Belihuloya. More than 50% of the respondents in the study area perceived that the land use has been changing due to the construction activities, forest fires, illegal loggings, pine and tea cultivation and the expansion of built-up areas. The deforestation has badly effected on water resources in the Belihuloya. The reforestation programs, including community-based reforestation programs can be introduced to minimize the impacts. It is necessary to implement existing legal frameworks with supports of different stakeholders to conserve the Belihuloya.

INTRODUCTION

Land is the basic natural resource of mankind. The land supports all the human activities, providing goods (resources) and services (regulations) (Turner II et al, 2007) and receiving disposal. Land use is being dynamically shaped under the influence and interaction of two broad sets of forces – human needs and environmental features and processes (Briassoulis, 2006). Land use is the way how people have used

DOI: 10.4018/978-1-7998-4372-6.ch004

the land by man. In other words, land use, simply means the use to which the land is being put or the utilization of land devoted to human activities. Sekliziots (1980) defined, land use as the human function of a given area while land cover is the physical surface of the land. The land use/land cover change analysis has become a central component in current strategies of managing and monitoring environmental changes. Changes are occurring in the land use on different spatial and temporal levels (Argawal et al, 2002). These changes are beneficial and sometimes have detrimental impacts (Briassoulis, 2006), which can affect the structure and functioning of ecosystems (and ultimately, the earth system) as well as the human well-being (Turner II et al, 2007). Definition and description of land cover, land use and land use change, vary with the purpose of the application and the context of their use. The land cover is the biophysical state of the earth's surface and immediate subsurface, while the land use denotes the human employment of the land (Turner II & Meyer 1994, Briassoulis 2006) and land-cover type (Skole 1994, Briassoulis, 2006).

Over the past two decades, there has been a rapid increase in large-scale land acquisitions to produce fibre, biofuels, feed and food for international markets, which has impacted ecosystems, agro-ecosystems and societies, predominantly across the Global South (D'Odorico et al. 2017). Socio-environmental changes in the context of large-scale land acquisitions are highly complex and associated with several sustainability challenges, like deforestation (Davis et al. 2015), water scarcity and pollution (Dell'Angelo et al. 2018). Mark and Kudakwashe (2010) in a study in Shurugwi district in Midlands Province of Zimbabwe observed the increase in cropland. He attributed this increase to the Land Reform and Resettlement Program. Large areas of forests were cleared for different farm related activities like opening new farming plots, wood for fuel, poles for building both homes and cattle pens, among other activities. Begum (et al. 2010) revealed the built-up area around the water bodies in Davangere city, Karnataka, India has almost doubled between 1970 and 2005, at the cost of the agricultural land and scrub land. Prakasam (2010) studied land use/land cover change over a period of 40 years in Kodaikanal Taluk, Tamil Nadu. In this study major changes have been observed like area under built-up land and harvested land has increased, whereas the area under forest and water body has decreased. Javed and Khan (2012) studied land use land cover change during due to mining activities from 2001 to 2010. The study revealed that significant decrease has been observed in dense forest area, cultivated land and water body, however settlement, wasteland land and uncultivated land has increased mainly due to anthropogenic activities.

The most recent scientific land use mapping exercise was undertaken by the Survey Department of Sri Lanka during 1983-1988 period and identified 7 major categories of land use such as Arable lands, Built- up and residential lands, Forests, Rangelands, Wetlands, Barren lands and Water bodies. The sparsely used croplands include "Chena" lands (slash & burn agriculture) and abandoned plantations, which are cultivated now and then. The category of urban and residential lands includes built up lands, associate non-agricultural lands (archaeological reservations) and homesteads. The forestlands include natural forest and forest plantations. The rangeland consists of scrub lands and grasslands. Grasslands comprise of both natural (Patana & Villus) and cultivated grasslands. The marshy lands and mangroves are grouped as wetlands. Rocky lands and erosional remnants are grouped as barren lands. All natural water bodies and reservoirs in the inland are included in the category of water bodies (National Atlas, 1988).

Public perception of land use change appeared to have increased the interest with the present land use change patterns by means of their drivers. There is a need to recognize the wide range of perceptions and preferences of relevant societal actors, not least those who are most impacted by, and vulnerable to, social and environmental change (Schneider and Rist, 2013). Indigenous observations can strengthen land-change research as a rich source of environmental history and as a framework for formulating research questions because they provide a valuable opportunity to uncover local concerns (Nightingale, 2003, Carothers et al. 2014). Participatory methodologies have thereby been argued to be empowering, for example by legitimizing local knowledge, To sum up, land-use change associated with large-scale land acquisition is an area of research that would benefit from methodological expansion toward novel qualitative and participatory approaches, as it (1) allows people who are affected yet underrepresented to influence the research focus and uncover local concerns that can be further researched, (2) creates a platform to explore desirable alternatives and preferences expressed by the people in place, and (3) helps to understand and communicate the complexity of situated human–nature interactions and lived experiences by people who are dependent on and vulnerable to (but could also benefit from) social and environmental change. A joint production of visual art is one possible way of complementing conventional research methods as it enriches discussions and communication both during and after fieldwork. Participatory art workshops were used in this study as a means to explore how people perceive the past, present, and future in relation to socio-environmental change (Johansson, and Eigen, 2017).

STUDY AREA

Belihuloya Mini Catchment area spatially lies between 6°39" and 6°45'13''N and 80°44 and 80°49"E and comprise a total area of 42 km^2. The Belihuloya stream is one of the major tributaries of the Walawe river basin, and the Mini Catchment area of Belihuloya is found in the upper tributary of the Walawe River typical of mountainous landscape. The Belihuoya tributary originates from Horton plains, grassland and the study area Belihuloya is surrounded by Horton Plains from North, the Samanalawewa reservoir from the South, Paraviyangala peak and Hirikatuoya from east and Hagala peak from the west.

The study area spreads over 7 Grams Niladari Divisions (Yakdehiwala, Belihuloya-upper, Belihuloya-lower, Muththetuwegama, Kinchigune, Kumburuteniwala, and Karagastalawa), belong to the Imbulpe Secretariat Division, Rathnapura District in Sabaragamuwa Province in Sri Lanka. Belihuloya lies under IU3b and IM2b Agro-Ecological Zones, of Sri Lanka (CEB, 1992). The mean annual rainfall of IU3b is >1700mm and IM2b is >1600mm. The study area receives precipitation mainly from the Northeast monsoon and Inter-monsoons. Study area receives high intensity of rainfall from late December to late April, and average day temperature is between 22-25°C. Between December and March, night temperature goes down to 15°C, between August and October (dry period) day temperature goes up to 30°C and night temperature varies around 20°C (Francois Molle et al 2004).

The vegetation of Belihuloya mini-catchment includes areas afforested with pines, secondary thick forests, tea estates, grasslands, chena lands, and paddy fields irrigated by ani-cuts. In the 1950's grasslands, forests and the new tea lands were predominant vegetation types in Belihuloya. In 1956 most of the grasslands were invaded by the natural forests. Pine was the main land use type in 1996 in the area because of the afforestation programme Extent of the paddy land remains constant as all potential paddy lands were developed before the colonial era. During the 1956-1975 periods, pine cultivation was introduced to the area with the aim of reducing soil erosion and the authorities converted most grasslands to pine lands. Destruction of forest cover for logging, chena cultivation, fuel wood for tea factories, timber for construction are major causes of deforestation. Fires are kindled by people raising animals who need to expand pastures for them, or by hunters chasing away animals to ambush them (François Molle et al, 2003).

The present-day study aimed to assess the spatial and temporal changes of land use in the study area from 1956 to 2015, and to examine the people's perception on effects of land use change in the study area, therefore, following research questions were formulated.

i. What are the land use categories that show spatial and temporal changes in Belihuloya over the last 60 years?
ii. Has paddy land expansion lead to drying up springs and decreasing the volume of the streams in the area?
iii. Has tea land expansion lead to drying up wells and springs in the area?
iv. Does the pine plantation lead to decrease water resources in the area?
v. Does the decreasing forest cover in the area lead to drying up springs?
vi. Has forest fires leads to decrease ani-cut water and the water volume of stream water in the area?
vii. Does the build-up area expansion has led to decrease the volume of water in the streams in the area?

METHODOLOGY

The method and materials involved in the study are different for different parameters, but guided to solve the main problem of study. Thus, the methodology has been divided into various steps based on techniques employed and data used. These are categorized into field work, GIS methods, and statistical methods (Figure 2).

Field observations and Questionnaire Surveys

The objective of the study is to assess the spatial and temporal changes of land use in the study area from 1956 to 2015, and to examine the people's perception on effects of land use change in the Belihuloya Mini Catchment area which is located in the Imbulpe Secretariat Division of Rathnapura District in Sabaragamuwa Province. To obtain people's perceptions related to land use change in the selected area, a questionnaire survey was conducted, thus 30 households were randomly selected from each GN Division, 180 house –holds were interviewed among seven (7) GN Divisions namely Yakdehiwala, Belihuloya-upper and Belihuloya-down (together), Muththetuwegama, Kinchigune, Kumburuteniwala, and Karagastalawa.

GIS and Remote sensing techniques

The present study also based on the combined implementation of GIS and Remote sensing techniques as follows.

Figure 1. Study area in the Imbulpe Divisional Secretariat Division, Rathnapura District
Source: Generated from 1956 Ariel data and 2015 Satellite data

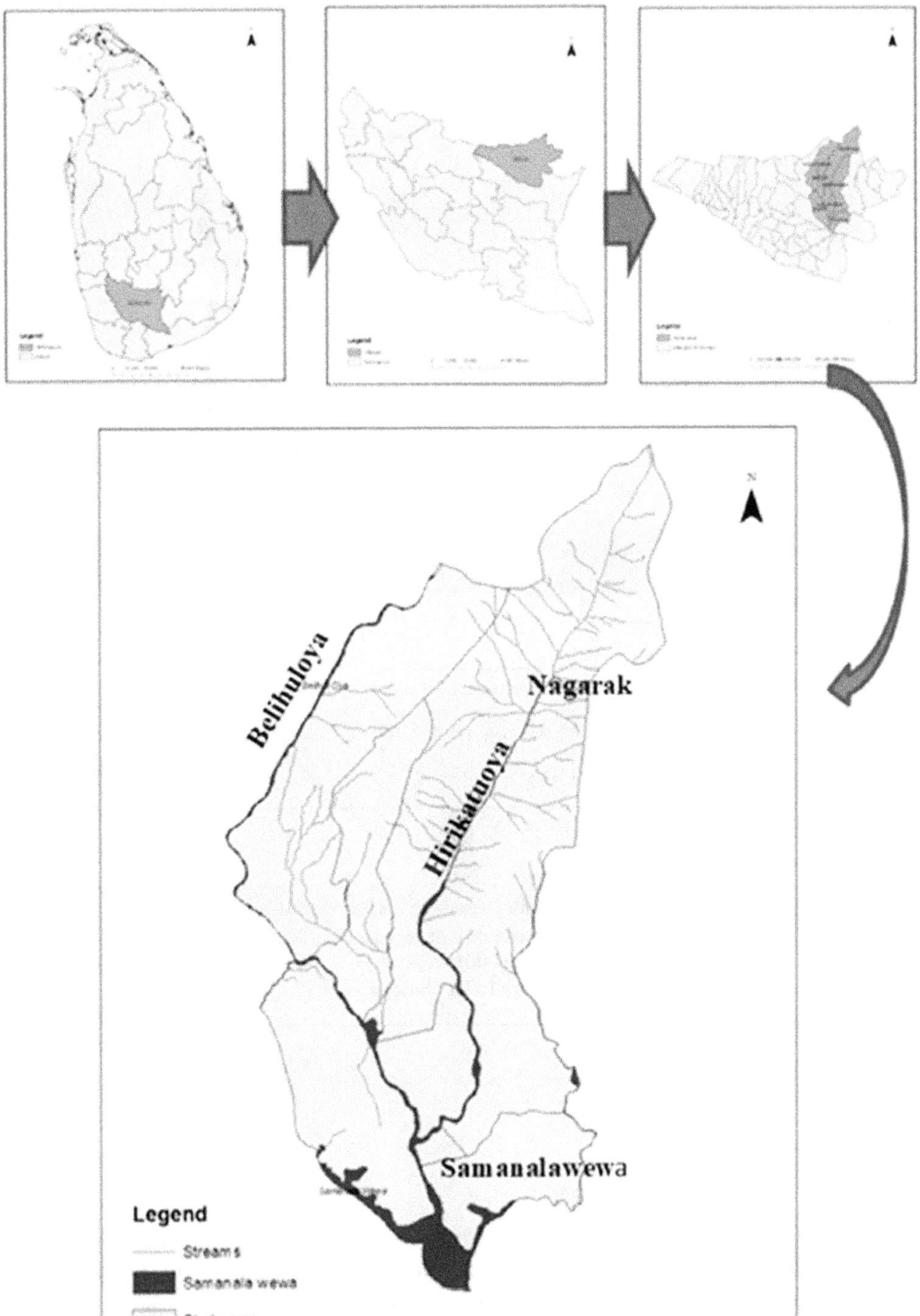

Figure 2. Methodology

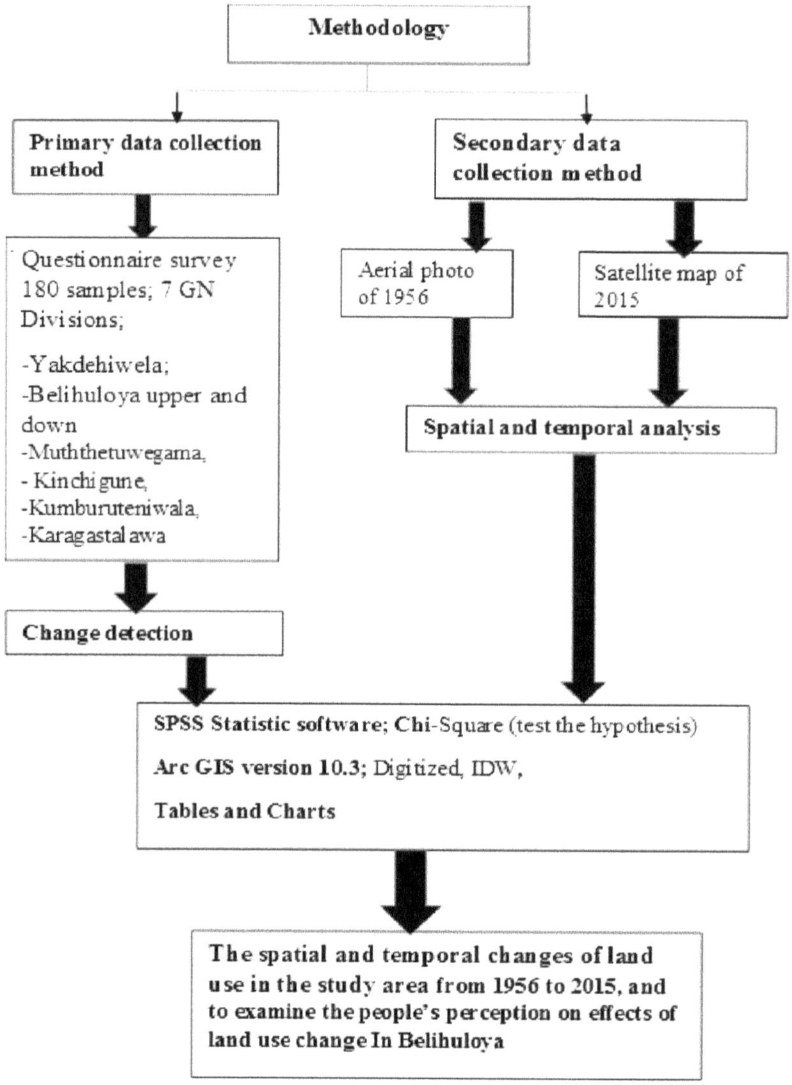

Construction of a Digital Database

I. Geo-referencing: The thematic maps including Base map, Drainage map, Land use/ Land cover map were generated from Aerial Photograph of 1956 and Google-earth satellite image of 2015. Aerial Photograph was in a photographic TIFF (Tagged Image File Format) format and were finally registered to a Universal Geographical Coordinate system. To locate the Ground Control Points

(GCP's) has been selected at the intersection points of latitude & longitude lines. The thematic maps were initially projected in Geographical latitude /longitude coordinate system.

II. Digitization: The second step involved is the on-screen digitization of themes like, drainage, land use/ land cover, etc. In the form of feature data line, polygon and point. The process of digitization was done in ArcView 10.3 GIS software

III. Cleaning and Building Topology: The process of cleaning and building topology has been done by first changing the format of the data from shape file for Arc coverage and then the tools like clean vector layer and Build Vector layer topology are operated to do the required task.

Digital Image Analysis

Digital image processing is an extremely broad subject, but the methodological procedure of the present study has been confined to the following steps.

A. Acquisition of satellite data
B. Processing
C. Image Enhancement and Sub-setting.
D. Image Classification

Analysis and quantification of differences in Land use/ Land cover and preparation of the final maps

The land use/land cover statistics obtained from the attributes tool of raster module of the software were analysed to draw certain inferences. The absolute change in land use/ land cover of the two dates was obtained by the difference of the values of different dates of the same category, while percentage change was calculated by dividing it with the total area and multiplying by hundred.

$$\text{Percentage Change} = \frac{Absolute\,Change}{Total\ area} \times 100$$

The ArcView 10.3 was used in preparation of final outputs in the form of maps. They were then exported to photographic formats for hard copy output.

Statistical methods used for analysing data from questionnaire surveys

The socioeconomic data collected from the questionnaire were entered, processed, coded, and analysed using the Statistical Package for Social Sciences (SPSS) version 20 and subsequently descriptive-statistical analysis was used to describe socioeconomic variables of the households in Belihuloya. A nonparametric test (Pearson's chi-square) was used to ascertain the differences/associations between public perceptions on land use change variables and perceptions of effects of land use change in the area respectively.

RESULTS

Land use Change in Belihuloya Mini Catchment area 1956

The land-use map of 1956 in the Figure 7 has revealed, the forest as the dominant land-use with a total area of 16.9 km^2, which constitutes 40.3% of the study area followed by grass lands (both Savannah and Patana) occupying 4.47 km^2 which is 17.7% of the total study area. Scrub lands is the second major land category spread over lower-catchment area of 6.2 km^2 occupying 14.7% of the study area. After scrub lands, Tea represents an area of 5.5 km^2 showing 13.1%, followed by paddy occupies 3.364 km^2, which is 8% in the area (Figure 3).

Figure 3. Land-use categories in 1956
Source; Generated from digitized data 1956

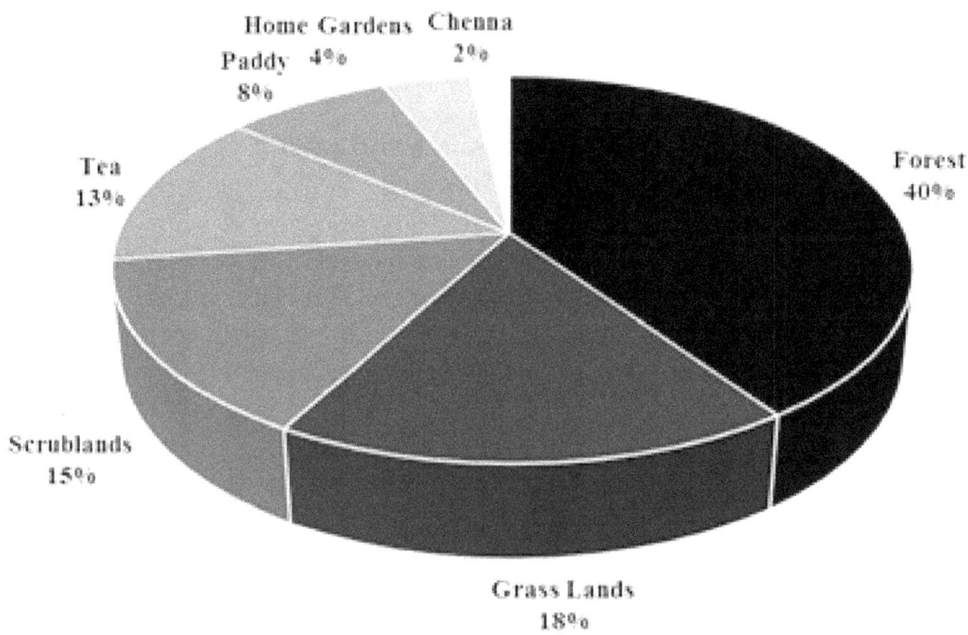

Home gardens mostly extend in both upper and lower-catchment area covering 1.2 km^2 with 3%, while Chena spread over an area of 0.8 km^2 occupying 2% of the area. Area under degraded forest represents 0.2 km^2 with 0.6% of the study area Belihuloya.

Land-use of Belihuloya Mini Catchment area 2015

The land-use map of 2015 in the Figure 7 revealed, forest as the dominant land-use with a total area of 15.5 km2 which constitutes 36% of the study area followed by grass lands (both Savannah and Patana) occupies 4.28 km^2 which is 10% of the total study area. Paddy is the next major land use category spread over an area of 3.6 km^2 occupying 8% of the study area. After paddy, home garden represents an area of 3.3 km^2 showing 8%, followed by pines occupies 3.3 km^2, which is 7% in the area. Scrub lands, mostly extends into down-catchment area signifies an area of 2.9 km^2 with 7%, while built-up area spreads over an area of 2.7 km^2 occupying 6%of the study area of Belihuloya (Figure 4).

Figure 4. Statistics of Land-use categories in 2015
Source; Generated from digitized data, 2015

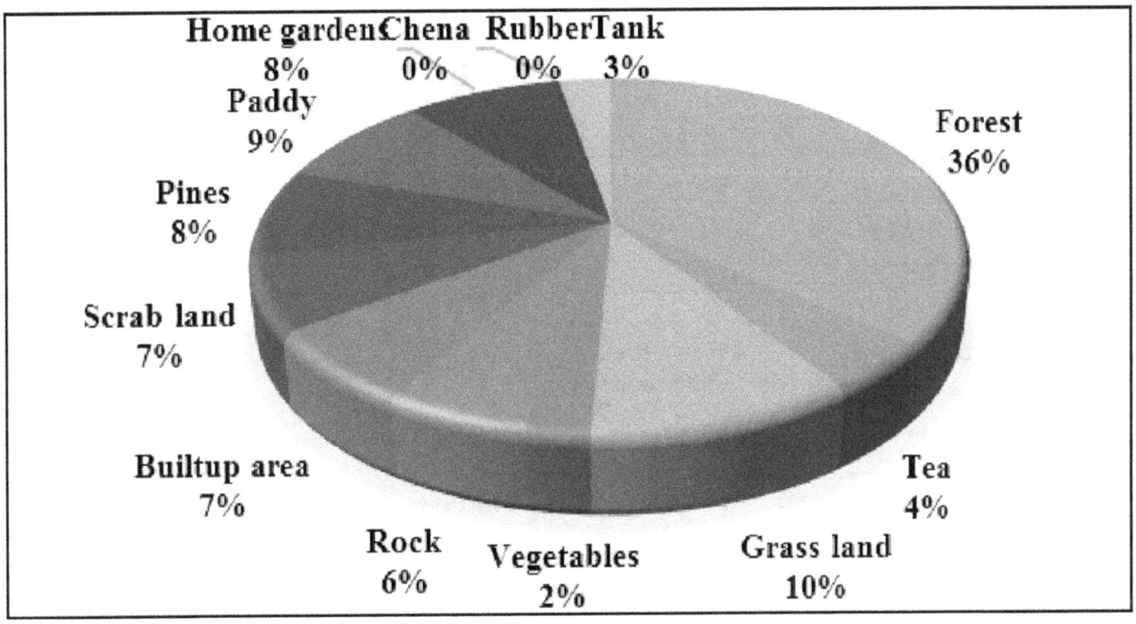

Drivers of Land-use changes in Belihuloya Catchment

The land use pattern of Belihuloya Mini Catchment is quite varied and includes areas afforested with pines, secondary thick forests, tea estates, grasslands, scrublands, Chena (shifting cultivation) lands, and paddy fields. The pattern of the settlement in the study area is characterized as rugged, inaccessible and sparsely populated with 60% of its land is under patana, savannah grasslands, scrub and forest. In most trees are it halted to preserve an idyllic natural environment and a rich human heritage due to this inaccessibility, in spite of being situated in close proximity to the main A4 road linking Sabaragamuwa and Western province and just a few miles from Balangoda, one of the main towns in the Province (CEB, 1992).

Village settlements are more of the ribbon type than of the cluster type. Population densities are lower than the basin average in upper catchments but this is because of the large portion of the land under state reservation or on too steep a slope to be cultivated. But, land use change from 1956 to present gives a broad picture of the discrepancy in land use expansions under certain circumstances in the area. This discrepancy in land use can be broadly discussed with main driving forces attached to them.

According to the results of the questionnaire survey (Figure 5), Tea plantations in both upper and lower catchments, pine cultivation in upper catchments, construction of Samanalawewa, and construction of the Sri Lanka Sabaragamuwa University is considered to be mega driving forces in changing the landscape of the area. Introduction of photosensitive High-Yielding Varieties for paddy and double cropping, expanding infrastructure after establishment of SHEP[1], rainfall variations, and changing the

Figure 5. Drivers of Land-use changes in Belihul-Oya Catchment
Source: Identified based on the questionnaire survey, (2014)

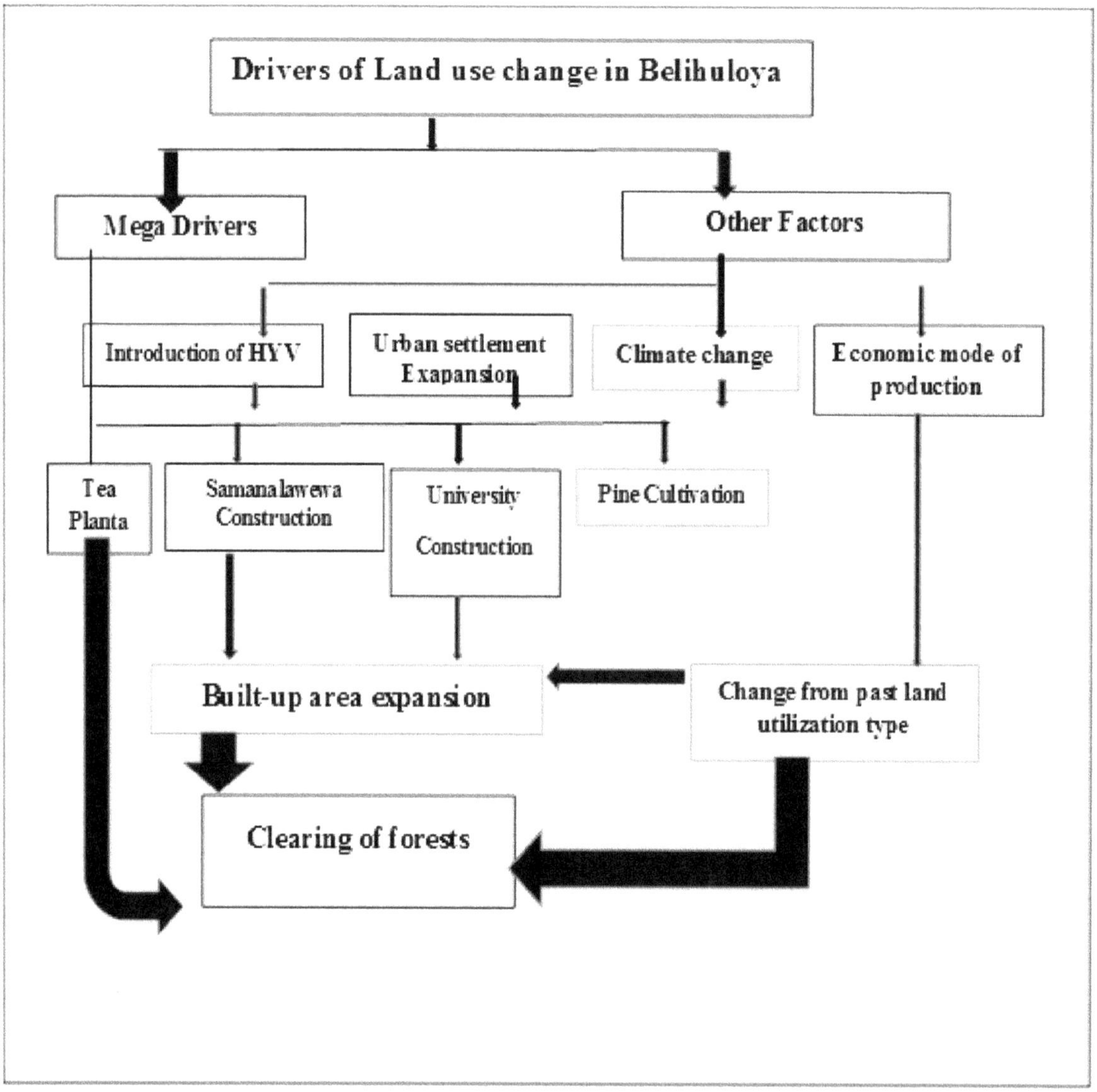

economic mode of production are considered to be other factors determining the changing landscape in the study area at the present. The vegetation of the upper part of the study area, mostly constitute with Montane and sub-Montane evergreen forests, patana grasslands and tea estates.

DISCUSSION

Changes in Land Use Categories of Belihuloya Mini Catchment Area, 1956-2015

Total percentage and the decline in the growth of different land use/land cover categories in the study area appears significant. Some land use/land cover categories have recorded a positive growth while others have witnessed a negative growth.

I. **Forest and Dense Forest;** Forest and dense forest cover have reduced from 40.3% in 1956 to 36.0% in 2015, thus registering negative growth of (-08.6%). Decrease in forest and dense forest cover means more and more degradation of the environment. Deforestation, agricultural expansion and increasing built-up areas expanding tremendous pressure on the forest resources of the study area.

II. **Grasslands;** The northern part of the study area is mostly covered by the grasslands have shown a reduction as tea from 17.7% in 1956 to 10.1% by 2015, thus registering a negative growth of -42% in the Belihuloya mini-catchment area. Expansion of pines and HG[2] related phenomena resulted in decreasing this land-use category in the study area.

III. **Scrub lands;** scrub is one of the major land cover categories in Belihuloya Mini Catchment and has registered a further negative growth of -53% from 1956 to 2015. The degradation of forests due to various reasons over a long period of time transforms them into scrublands in the area.

IV. **Paddy;** Next to Scrub lands paddy as a main land-use category in the study area registered a slightly increasing trend from 08% in 1956 to 08.5% in 2015. It has shown a total growth of +7 in the study area.

V. **Home Garden**; HG being the dominant land use in the whole of the Belihuloya basin and got maximum area under it. It has witnessed a total growth of 163% and expanding towards the higher reaches of the study area at the expose of forests.

VI. **Chena;** It constituted 01.9% in 1956 and 0.3% in 2015, thus shown a negative growth of -83% in the study area. Expansion of Built-up area and HG remain a main factor in reducing this land –use category in the area respectively.

Drivers of Land-Use Changes in Belihuloya Catchment

Tea plantations in both upper and lower catchments, pine cultivation in upper catchments, construction of Samanalawewa, and construction of the Sri Lanka Sabaragamuwa University is considered to be mega driving forces of changing the landscape in the area. Introduction of photosensitive High-Yielding

Figure 6. Total growth in different land-use/land-cover categories in Belihuloya Mini Catchment area 1956-2015
Source; Generated from digitized data 1956-2015

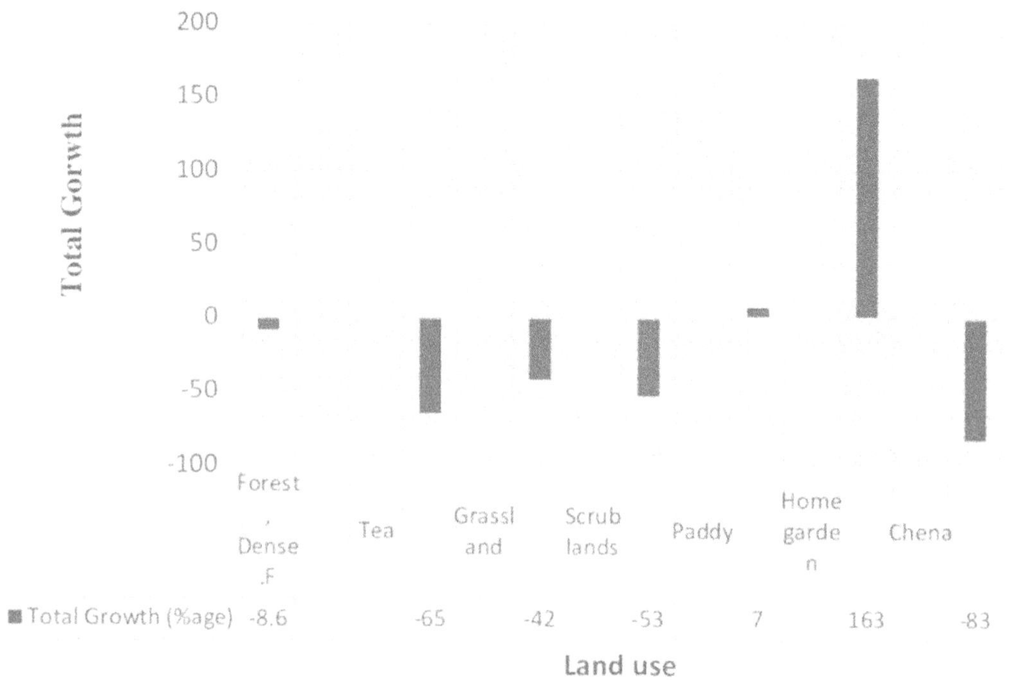

Varieties for paddy and double cropping, expanding infrastructure after establishment of SHEP, rainfall variations, and changing the economic mode of production are considered to be other factors determining the changing landscape in the study area at the present. The vegetation of the upper part of the study area, mostly constitute with Montane and sub-Montane evergreen forests, patana grasslands and tea estates.

According to the 1958-1959 Aerial photographic survey of the (Canada, Ceylon Colombo Plan Project), 38% of the land area of the basin comprised of forests which was extensive on the upper-slopes of the west and central parts of the escarpment. According to the Canada-Ceylon Colombo Plan Project report of 1960 more than 40% of the upland Platform consists of Savannah forests. Intermediate and dry zone forests (26%) occupy the lower slopes and valleys having moist soils (CEB, 1992). In the past farmers cultivated both paddy and chena crops in the area. Paddy fields provided them rice and chena provided them cereals and vegetables. Forest supplied fruits, bee honey, meat, wood for building houses and medicals. The buffaloes were used to plough the paddy fields. There were enough grasslands to feed their cows. Cow dung was put into fields as fertilizers and used to smooth the house floor. During the British period tea was introduced into uplands such as Bogawantalawa and Nonpareil (Upper part of the Belihuloya basin) leading to the destruction of dense forests. Consequently, less land was available for chena cultivation in the basin area.

Some locals started working as labourers in the tea states. After the introduction of the Paddy Land Act in 1956, tenant farmers received user rights to the lands they were cultivating at that time by paying a smaller rent. Some Government lands were also distributed among the landless people under this Act.

In the 1990's tomato was introduced to this area and succeeded. This success encouraged farmers in the neighbourhood to start growing tomato. The tomato became popular because of its resistance to pest

Table 1. Total Growth in Different Land-use/land-cover Categories in Belihuloya mini-catchment area 1956-2015

Land-use/ land cover category	Area in Sq. Km (%) 1956	Area in Sq. Km (%) 2015	Total Growth (%)
Forest and Dense forest	40.3	36.0	-08.6
Tea	13.1	04.5	-65.0
Grassland	17.7	10.1	-42.0
Scrub lands	14.7	06.9	-53.0
Paddy	08.0	08.5	+07.0
Home garden	03.0	08.0	+163.0
Chena	01.9	00.3	-83.0

Source: Generated from digitized data 1956-2015

and disease attacks and high selling prices. According to the Department Agriculture, a few years after its introduction, some 40% of total production of tomato in Sri Lanka was produced in the Belihuloya region. In 1994-2000 period, nearly 60 ha of lands was occupied by tomato cultivation (Francois Molle et al, 2004).

LOCAL PEOPLE'S PERCEPTIONS OF LAND USE CHANGE IN BELIHULOYA CATCHMENT

Expanding Built-Up Area and Changing Pattern of Forest Cover in the Area

In 1956, predominant vegetation types were grasslands, forest and the new tea lands. Pines were the main land use type in 1996 map because of the afforestation program. During the 1965-1975 period, pine cultivation was introduced to the area with the aim of reducing soil erosion and the authorities converted grasslands to pine lands (Francois Molle et al, 2004). 1981 and 1985 period Belihuloya area is covered with forest plantations, natural forests, grasslands and scrub lands. The Belihuloya forest plantation was found to be the largest of 1328 hectares, mainly under the pines. In the same year under the natural forests, much of the area was covered with dense forests, including parts of the and the wilderness Natural Reserve.

Expanding built-up area and other development projects have decimated the forest cover gradually to what it is at present. Deforestation can be seen at a large-scale lower catchment. Population concentration in the area is now expanding speedily with the construction of the Samanalawewa Hydro Electricity Project and the "Gamudawa" succeeded by the Sabaragamuwa University of Sri Lanka. Depletion of the natural forest cover in the area has been going on long before the project was even conceived of due to adverse land use practices over the years. This is evidenced by the existence of large extents of anthropogenic ally derived savannah scrublands and degraded forests, sometimes even within in the forest reserves. However, for the construction of SHEP large scale forest clearance was needed in the reservoir bed command areas. Especially for dam, quarry, spoil dumps, workshops, storage areas, power station, Japanese and British construction camps and miscellaneous. Vegetation removals and the impoundment of the reservoir have been resulted in the loss riverine forest (CEB, 1994).

After the establishment of the Sabaragmauwa University of Sri Lanka in 1991, forest in the area was further removed. Initially the University was started on abandoned residences of SHEP. But at present, gradually emerging new Faculties, Hostels and expanding attach residential areas have degraded the surrounding forest cover rapidly. According to the survey, villagers pointed out a number of reasons behind the degrading forest cover in the area, 28% viewed construction as the foremost factor among them (Figure 7). In addition, 38% pointed out forest fires as a main reason behind degrading of forest cover in the Belihuloya.

Figure 7. People's view on reasons behind degrading forest cover
Source: Field survey 2013-2014

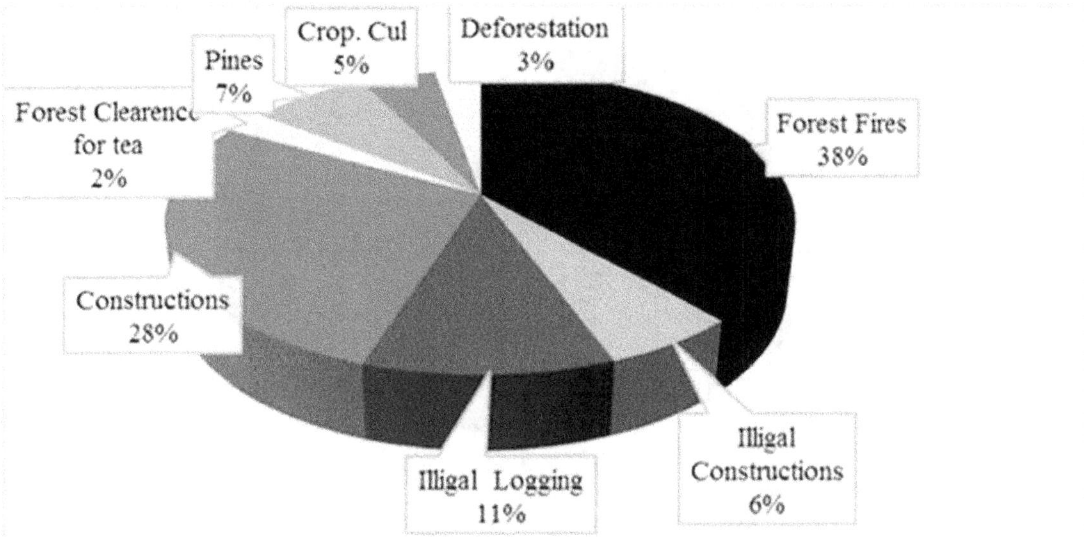

People perceived forest fires as the main reason behind decreasing forest cover in the catchment. Forest fires found to be a usual phenomenon in the area, especially in the dry season. Some Villagers engage forest fires for hunting and agricultural purposes and some believed it as a continuing practice in the area. In dry seasons lots of savannah and scrub lands were found under fire. Sometimes those fires found to be expanded over even dense forest areas. Illegal logging marked the third largest among above reasons where 11% villagers perceived it with political interferences. Other than above reasons, illegal constructions, forest clearance for tea, pines, forest clearance for crop cultivations, and deforestation, are found related to degrading forest cover in the area.

Villagers are also heavily involved in illicit felling of wood for timber and fuel wood/ forest fuel other than obtaining medicinal plants. According to the survey, 51% were obtaining fuel wood/ from the forest, 24% were involved in obtaining herbs and 23% of them were obtained timber from the nearer by forest, only 2% utilize the forest for other purposes. Villagers also utilize fuel wood as the main cooking resource instead of gasoline, kerosene, and electricity (Figure 8).

Figure 8. Utilization of forests
Source: Field survey, 2013-2014

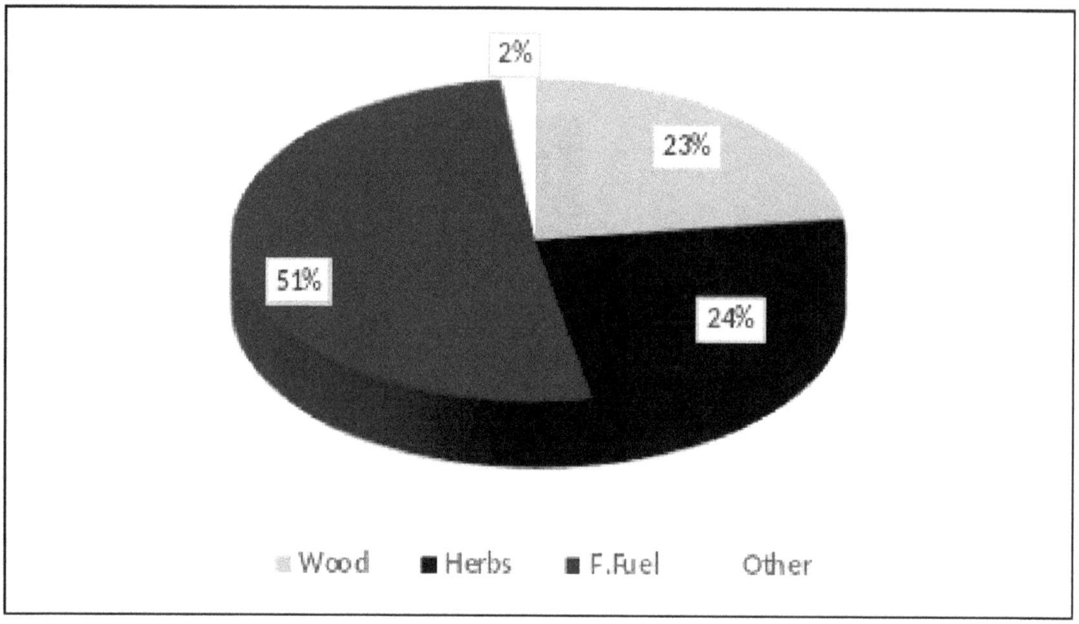

Out of the total sample, 66% utilize fuel wood as main burning resource for cooking, 20% utilize gasoline, 11% use kerosene and only 3% utilize electricity in the area.

Effects of Land-use Change on Water Resources

Effects of paddy and tea land change on water resources

As mentioned above paddy land remained constant at 1956 as all potential paddy lands were developed before the colonial era and tea was introduced to uplands such as Bogawantalawa and Nonpareil (Upper part of the Belihuloya basin) leading to the destruction of dense Montane forests. In the past farmers cultivated paddy and chena crops. They cultivated paddy only in "Yala "[3]season and production surplus was stored for "Maha"[4] season. This could be achieved due to low population and land availability. In the 1970s Sri Lanka government sought economic self-sufficiency for the country, thus food commodity was not freely imported into the country and had led to a food shortage in the country, causing hardship in remote areas like Belihuloya. To meet food requirements everyone had to cultivate their lands. As a result of this, Belihuloya area became intensively cultivated with vegetables, roots and tuber crops.

Figure 9. Cooking energy sources
Source: Field survey, 2013-2014

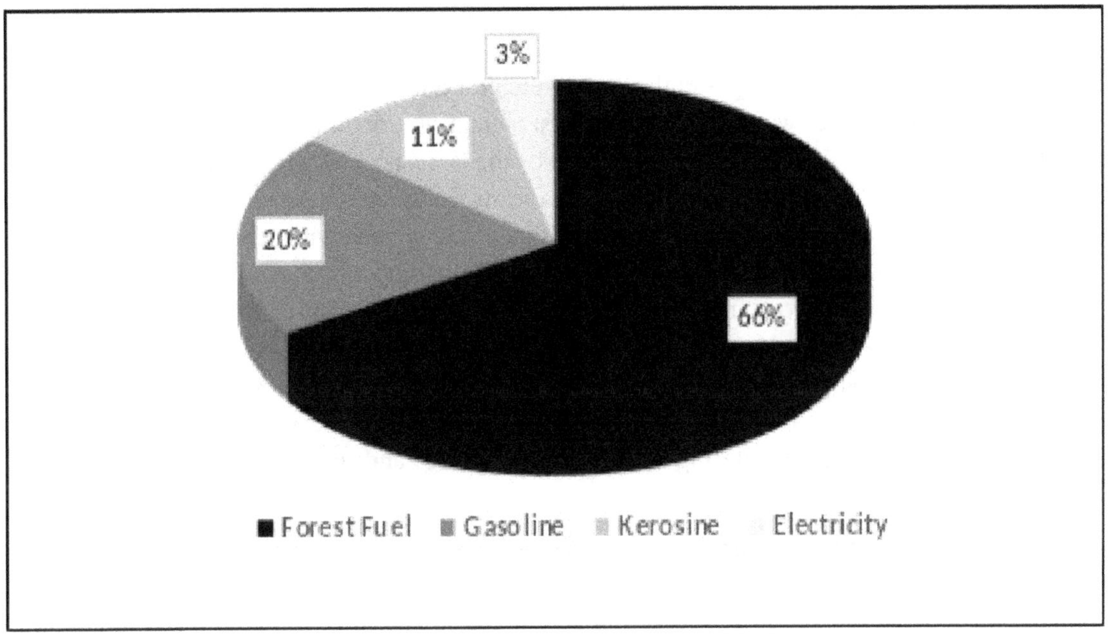

Farmers grew paddy in every inch of potential land. While the government opened the economy in 1977, and farmers shift from traditional low yielding varieties to high yielding varieties. With the introduction and spread of non-photosensitive High-Yielding Varieties, double-cropping was quickly adopted in the study area. In most cases, water supply was sufficient to raise two crops per year. According to the survey, most paddy farmers depend upon rain water (100%), and ani-cut water (90%) while homestead farmers depended upon irrigation water (45%) and well water (85%).On the other hand it reflects that most paddy farmers relied on spring water and ani-cut water rather than rain water for paddy cultivation in the area.

But at the same time, they observed a decreasing trend of water resources due to over utilization of water resources for paddy and tea cultivation for long periods of time. Pumping more water for agricultural activities may further decrease the amount of available water in streams and wells in the area. On the other hand, utilization of more ani-cut and well water for crops may have also decreased the level of water table in the area. Significant differences were found among the interviewed households in perceptions regarding paddy land expansion is significant in drying up springs ($p < 0.001$), paddy land expansion is significant in decreasing the volume of the stream water in the area ($p < 0.001$), tea land expansion is significant in drying up of springs ($p < 0.001$), and tea land expansion is significant in drying up wells ($p < 0.001$). Therefore, people in the study area believed, paddy land and tea land expansion as main reasons behind drying up of springs, decreasing the volume of the stream water in the area, and tea land expansion as a reason for drying up wells. As mentioned earlier, paddy lands in the area are disappearing rapidly, therefore drying up springs and decreasing the volume of the stream water might have not been caused due to expansion of paddy lands in the area but may be due to extraction of more water.

Effects of Built-Up Area and Forest Cover Change on Water Resources

In 1956, predominant vegetation types in the basin were grasslands, forest and the new tea lands. By the 1981 to 1985 period land area was covered with forest plantations, natural forests, grasslands and scrublands. The Belihuloya Forest plantation was found to be the largest consisting of 1327.5 hectares, mainly under pines, varieties. In the same period the natural forests, most areas have covered with dense forests, including peak wilderness (Natural Park). An expanding built-up area with other development projects such as Samanalawewa Hydro Electricity Project, and establishment of the Sabaragamuwa University of Sri Lanka have declined above mentioned forest cover gradually. This can be seen on a large scale in lower catchments leading to decrease in the water levels of most of wells, springs and streams in the area. In explaining the people's perception related to altering water resources in the area, pine plantations and deforestation were prioritized. Some 38% villagers strongly recognized pinus plantations and deforestation, mainly influenced altering water levels in springs and streams (Figure 10).

Figure 10. People's view on Reasons Behind Alteration of Water Resources
Source: Field survey 2013-2014

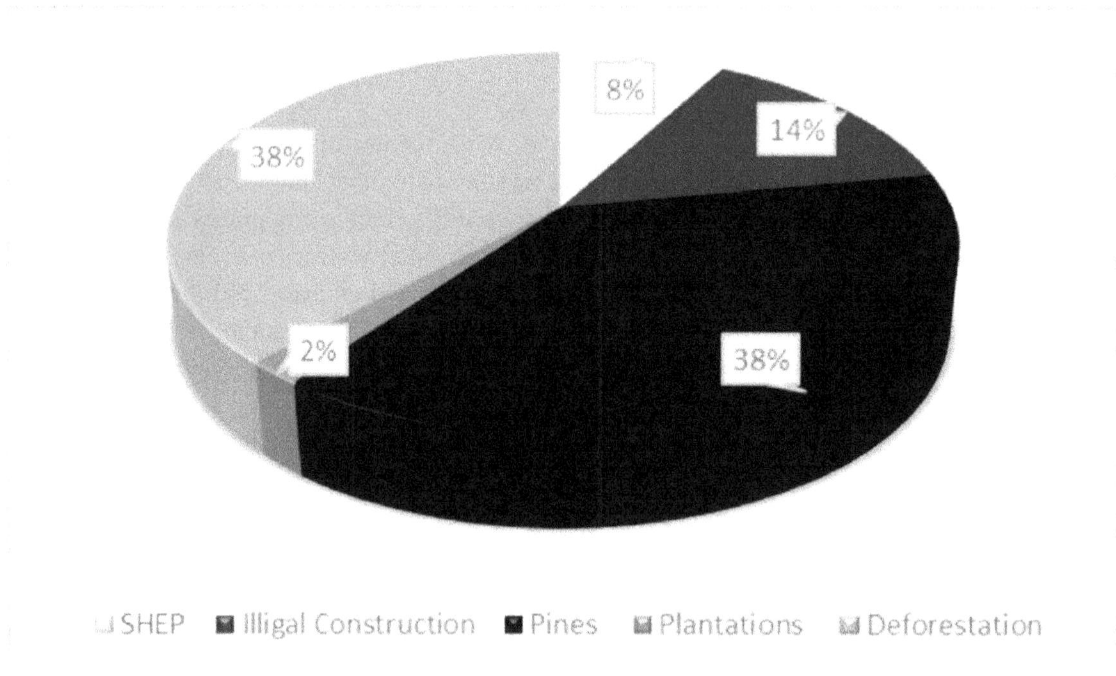

From the upper catchments, as an example, people believed that, "Himbiliya gaha spring", "Namagastenna spring", and "Kumbukgediya spring" have dried up due to pine plantations in the area. Pines in the area were introduced in 1965-1975 period by the government for the purpose of reducing soil erosion converting grasslands to pine lands. According to Francois Molle, people in the area Belihuloya, reported negative effects of pines on existing natural resources, for example, 75% of the villagers perceived rain fall and water flows were reduced due to pines, as called "Thirsty Devils" as they allegedly absorbing ground water excessively. According to the villagers there is no ground cover or either any grass inside the pines. Pines compete with other trees and plants for water and reduce the base flow in the rivers. They believe that the pine needles excrete some toxic compound or gas that also reduces the growth of other plants. They report that in the rainy period water does not infiltrate into the soil because fallen needles cover the ground just like a wax layer and water directly runs off to the river.

Significant differences were found among the interviewed households in perceptions regarding pine plantation is significant to decreasing water resources in in Belihuloya ($p < 0.001$). Next to pine, 38% villagers believed deforestation as the second highest reason behind altering water levels in the area. In addition, illegal constructions, Samanalawewa project, establishment of the Sabaragamuwa University, chena/ plantations are also emphasized. Under the Samanalawewa Hydro Electricity Project (SHEP) deforestation in borrowing areas and for purposes of constructing access roads/workshops/offices/ contractor's housing complexes such as the Kapugala complex have significantly altered the vegetation.

Figure 11. People's View on Stream Water Availability area
Source: Field survey 2013-2014

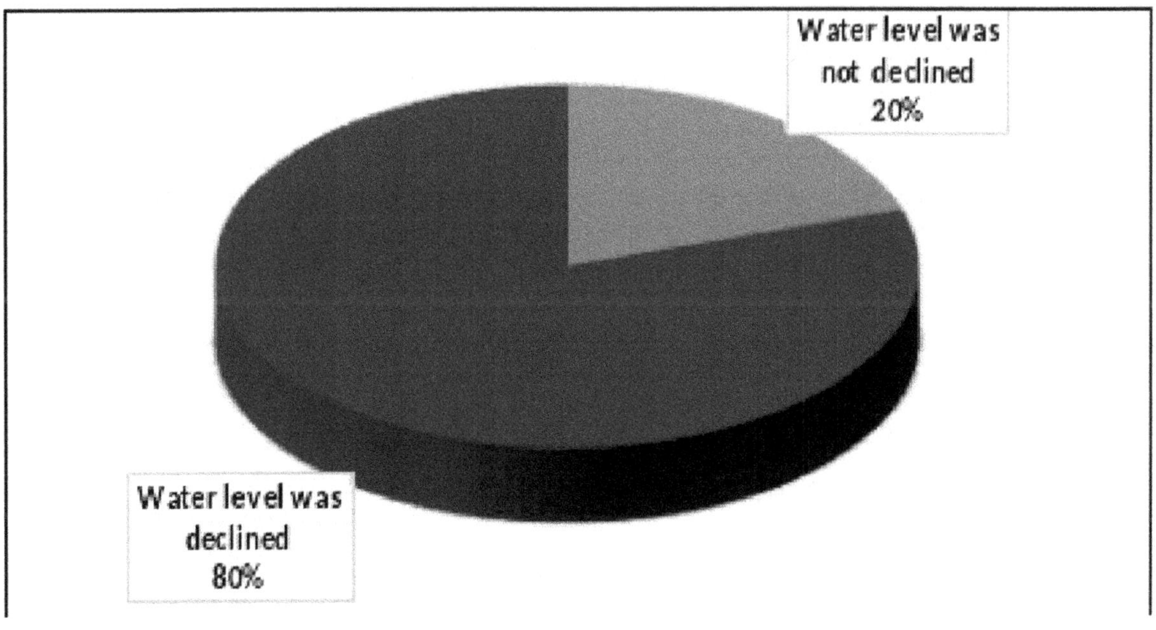

Roads that are to be permanent features of the landscape as well as temporally access roads would have resulted in vegetation alternations in the area. On the other hand, with the construction of the Samanalawewa power tunnel, ground water table was depleted in certain areas. As a result of this, many dug wells and springs have dried up in both upper and lower catchments in the area, but mostly in lower catchment areas, causing immense hardship to the people. According to present survey, 80% believed water levels of streams have declined, while 20% mentioned as not declined in the area (Figure 11). Significant differences were found among the interviewed households in perceptions regarding decreasing forest cover is significant to drying up springs in the area ($p < 0.001$). Thus, people in the study area believed deforestation as one reason for drying up springs in Belihuloya. Instead of pine plantations, forest fires caused a decrease in water resources in the area under deforestation activities. Most of the villagers from lower catchments perceived forest fires have largely affect on decreasing water resources in the area at the present.

Accordingly, significant differences were found among the interviewed households in perceptions regarding forest fires are significant in decreasing ani-cut water in the area ($p < 0.001$), forest fires are significant in decreasing the volume of the stream water in the area ($p < 0.001$). After the forest fires, built- up area expansion has caused the highest deforestation within three decades of a time in the area, especially the establishment of SHEP and Sabaragamuwa University of Sri Lanka at present. Surrounding two institutions, built-up area, including, infrastructure, houses, retail shops, complexes, hotels, restaurants, student's hostels, staff quarters, hospitals, religious institutions, have speedily been constructing and expanding in the area.

Sabaragamuwa University of Sri Lanka established in 1991 on the abandoned territory of SHEP. At present, SUSL operates with five Faculties and 19 Departments, offering 27 ofDdegree programs for about 4,000 students per year. The university employs 760 academic and non-academic staff. The university has a Water Supply Scheme, which extracts water from Hirikatu Oya with a capacity of 500 m^3/day, while the present demand is about 900 m^3/day. Demand of further expanding its student intake to 12,000 along with additional staff may lead further declining of water levels of steams in Belihuloya. On the other hand, the University scheme is unable to extract more water from the source because of the objections from the farmers in the downstream who also use the same source for their cultivations, thus water in the area became more conflicting topic breaking human connections. Significant differences were found among the interviewed households in perceptions regarding build-up area expansion is significant to decrease the water volumes of the streams in the area ($p < 0.001$). Thus, people in the study area believed expansion of the built - up area as a one reason behind decreasing water volume of the streams in Belihuloya.

CONCLUSION AND RECOMMENDATIONS

The Land use change in Belihuloya-Mini Catchment area in the Walawe Basin, Sri Lanka have taken place in the last decades. This study attempted to estimate the land use changes in the area. The results revealed occurrences of newly emerged and decreasing land-use categories within the period of 1956 to 2015 in Belihuloya. Three forest types together dense forests, forests and degrading forests were observed in 1956 land-use map and further both dense forests and forests continued to decrease in 2015.

In contrast to 1956, land-use categories as built-up area, pines, vegetables, rubber, and tank area have been observed in 2015 in the study area., The highest change (decreased) has observed in tea cultivation from 1956 to 2015. The scrublands and grasslands have also shown decreasing trends. Paddy and home garden have shown slightly increasing trends. However, most of the Montane and sub-Montane forests, savannah grasslands from upper catchments, forests from lower catchments, most of the tea lands from upper and down catchments have shown notable decreasing trends by 2015 compared to 1956. Above phenomena can further be explained, with villager's perceptions of land use changes. At the same time, they perceived, decreasing levels of water in streams and drying up springs due to the expansion of built-up area and deforestation. According to them, paddy and tea lands are declining rapidly due to the expansion of built-up area. They believed that the paddy harvests have been decreased due to decreasing rainfall in the area. Thus, most of the villagers believed declining rainfall in "Maha season" while other believed declining rainfall in "Yala season" in Belihuloya. However, according to present conditions, they believed forest fires have declined the anicut-water, while pine plantations and Samanalawewa Hydro-Power Project further altered water sources in Belihuloya.

Since, farmers adopted HYV for paddy, utilization of water for farming in the area increased while farmers attempting to cultivate two times per year using ani-cuts in the area. Hence farming within drought seasons where with lower water levels in the stream was further utilized by the farmers. Continuous agricultural practices extracted volumes of water in the Belihuloya and Hirikatuoya streams in the area, to further drying up of springs. Tea lands appeared to be decreasing, but since after introducing tea lands in the uppermost areas in Belihuloya, abstracted more water resources of streams for 70 years (1940-2016) that, created larger problems of decreasing stream water for lower catchment paddy farmers. Earlier, this issue constructed conflicts between Estate owners and the village community. Therefore, villagers strongly believed tea and paddy cultivations create water scarcity problems in Belihuloya.

Tackling rapid deforestation, including forest fires in the area, needs of effective coordination to reduce forest fires and deforestation prioritize rather other issues, since it influences other main issues such as decreasing water quality and quantity in Belihuloya, hence considering different types of stakeholder partnership (training institutions, universities, agencies, and community-based organizations) programme could be introduced to the area in conserving forest resources. Reforestation programmes including community-based reforestation programmes can be introduced by the SUSL with supports of NGOs and the Forest Department of the Belihuloya catchment while strengthening and implementing the legal framework of catchment area conservation practices. Since the tea is no longer profitable crop in Belihuloya, unprofitable tea areas can be converted to "Tourism Protected Area" due to attraction revealed by tourists even at present.

The study reflected the effects of utilizing HYV equivalent to chemical fertilization with the changing economic mode of production within 60 years of a period in the area. In contrast, lower levels of the above parameters in groundwater (wells and springs) and surface water (stream water) were observed along forests, scrublands, and grasslands in the area. Hence continuous monitoring of groundwater and surface water quality in the area and guide the levels of vulnerability of groundwater sources in the area known as necessary to avoid the potential health hazards of the people in the area. Fertilizer associated parameters in ground and surface water in the study area too have shown a serious health threat to people living in the area signifying the need for using bio-fertilizers. Awareness's should be created on the hazards due to use of chemical fertilizers in agriculture in the area. Some paddy and HG farmers have introduced bio-fertilizers; hence bio-fertilizers can be introduced to all paddy and HG farmers. Apart from that, to reducing and preventing the leaching and build-up in NO_3 in groundwater and surface water-efficient irrigation water management practices need to be introduced to in the catchment correspondingly.

According to the survey, effective water management practices are needed beside decreasing rainfall and stream discharge in Belihuloya. Increase the local forest awareness programmes for villagers, encourage building home gardens and different Agroforestry systems by the local agricultural and forest authorities in the Belihuloya could be considered as very effective programmes for addressing the existing issues. Hence ancient water management practices like "Mura method" should be re-established as an adaptation practice for water scarcity.

Villagers and farmers should encourage establishing RWH[5] system (National and micro-scale) in the catchment. It is necessary to develop agro-climate tools to support managing climate risks of water resources at the watershed level and farm level for that it is must install stream gauges and rain gauges in both streams in the area arises much essential at present. It is also, essentially to implement structural and non-structural measures to protect existing surface water resources in Belihuloya. Further studies are necessary to have the proper conclusion of the main reasons for this issue at farm level activities that increase the knowledge and skills of farmers to prevent further issues on water resources in Belihuloya. Village level in forest and watershed protecting committee and legislate reforms conferring greater responsibility to individuals, local communities and relevant authorities in the area while encouraging farmers to cultivate paddy in abandoned paddy lands to enhance the food security in the area.

This research received no specific grant from any funding agency in the public, commercial, or not-for-profit sectors.

REFERENCES

Agarwal, C., Green, G. M., Grove, J. M., Evans, T. P., & Schweik, C. M. (2002). *A review and assessment of land-use change models - Dynamics of space, time, and human choice. USDF Forest service.* North-eastern Research Station.

Begum, N., & Narayana, J., & SL, A. K. (2010). Land Use/Land Cover Changes in the Catchment of Water Bodies in and Around Davangere City, Karnataka. *International Journal of Ecology and Environmental Sciences*, *36*(4), 277–280.

Briassoulis. (2006) Changes in land use and land cover: A global perspective. In *Global land use and land cover change: An overview* (pp. 3-10). Cambridge University Press.

Carothers, C., Brown, C., Moerlein, K. J., López, J. A., Andersen, D. B., & Retherford, B. (2014). Measuring perceptions of climate change in northern Alaska: pairing ethnography with Glassman, M., and G. Erdem. 2014. Participatory action research and its meanings: vivencia, praxis, conscientization. *Adult Education Quarterly*, *64*, 206–221. doi:10.1177/0741713614523667

D'Odorico, P., Rulli, M. C., Dell'Angelo, J., & Davis, K. F. (2017). New frontiers of land and water commodification: Socio environmental controversies of large-scale land acquisitions. *Land Degradation & Development*, *28*(7), 2234–2244. doi:10.1002/ldr.2750

Davis, K. F., Yu, K., Rulli, M. C., Pichdara, L., & D'Odorico, P. (2015). Accelerated deforestation driven by large-scale land acquisitions in Cambodia. *Nature Geoscience*, *8*(10), 772–775. doi:10.1038/ngeo2540

Dell'Angelo, J., Rulli, M. C., & D'Odorico, P. (2018). The global water grabbing syndrome. *Ecological Economics*, *143*, 276–285. doi:10.1016/j.ecolecon.2017.06.033

Javed, A., & Khan, I. (2012). Land use/land cover change due to mining activities in Singrauli industrial belt, Madhya Pradesh using remote sensing and GIS. *Journal of Environmental Research and Development*, *6*(3A).

Johansson, E. L., & Isgren, E. (2017). Local perceptions of land-use change: Using participatory art to reveal direct and indirect socio environmental effects of land acquisitions in the Kilombero Valley, Tanzania. *Ecology and Society*, *22*(1), 3. doi:10.5751/ES-08986-220103

Mark, M., & Kudakwashe, M. (2010). The rate of land-use/land-cover changes in Shurugwi district, Zimbabwe: Drivers for change. *Journal of Sustainable Development in Africa*, *12*(3), 107–121.

Molle, F., Jayakody, P., & de Silva, S. (2003). *Anicut systems in Sri Lanka, The case of upper Walawe basin*. IWMI.

National Atlas. (1988). *Survey Department of Sri Lanka*.

Nightingale, A. J. (2003). A feminist in the forest: Situated knowledges and mixing methods in natural resource management. *ACME: An International E-Journal for Critical Geographies*, *2*(1), 77–90.

Prakasam, C. (2010). Land use and land cover change detection through remote sensing approach: A case study of Kodaikanal Taluk, Tamil Nadu. *International Journal of Geomatics and Geosciences*, *1*(2), 150.

Samanalawewa Hydro Electricity Project Environmental Post Evaluation Study. (1992). Ceylon Electricity Board.

Schneider, F., & Rist, S. (2013). Envisioning sustainable water futures in a transdisciplinary learning process: Combining normative, explorative, and participatory scenario approaches. *Sustainability Science*, *9*(4), 463–481. doi:10.100711625-013-0232-6

Sekliziotis, S. (1980). *A Survey of Urban Open Space Using Colour-infrared Aerial Photographs. Aston*. University of Aston.

Skole, D. (1994). Data on global land-cover change: Acquisition, assessment, and analysis. In Changes in land use and land cover: A global perspective. (pp. 437-471) Cambridge University Press.

Turner, B. L., II, Lambin., E.F., & Reenberg, A. (2007). The emergence of land change science for global environmental change and sustainability. *Proceeding of the National Academy Sciences of the United State of America (PNAS)*.

Turner, B. L., II, & Meyer, B. L. (1994). Changes in land use and land cover: A global perspective. In Global land use and land cover change: An overview (pp. 3-10). Cambridge University Press.

ENDNOTES

1 SHEP: Samanalawewa Hydro Electricity Project.

2 HG: Home Gardens

3 Farming seasons

4 Farming seasons

5 RWH: Rainwater Harvesting System

Chapter 5
How and Why the Land Resources Changed:
A Chronological Change of Land Use and Land Cover in Sri Lanka

Lasantha Manawadu
Department of Geography, University of Colombo, Sri Lanka

M. D. K. L. Gunathilaka
Department of Geography, University of Colombo, Sri Lanka

V. P. I. S. Wijerathne
Department of Geography, University of Colombo, Sri Lanka

K. L. W. I. Gunathilake
Department of Geography, University of Colombo, Sri Lanka

ABSTRACT

Human activities have recognized in recent years as the most significant force shaping the biosphere. This is completely true concerning rapid changes in the land surface. Concerning land resources, it is important to understand how this change happens. Thus, this chapter aims to review how this change has occurred throughout the history of Sri Lanka. A piecemeal approach in the unsustainable manner of land resource utilization towards severe land changes illustrates and compares the land use and land cover changes in significant phases in the history of Sri Lanka. This was further revitalized as well as influenced by the land-use policies introduced throughout history. The absence of a clearly defined land-use policy in the country after independence is problematic when addressing land-related issues. Consequently, chronological changes in land use and land cover existed within the country has now doubled and more intensified than ever.

DOI: 10.4018/978-1-7998-4372-6.ch005

INTRODUCTION

The land comprises a range of biophysical components and subjected to various effects and also land in its natural condition undergoes regular rejuvenation. The range of biophysical components embedded in the landscape is used for different purposes. Thus land use (LU) has become one of the main concerns of many disciplines. Though the topic is debatable among researchers, academics, and scientists much have been contributed to 'LU' rather than 'preservation or restoration of the land' (Mather, 1986). Its principles are mostly those of economics and ecology, but it is the product of human decisions operating within social, political, and legal frameworks. Land is classified among basic natural resource, and in classical economics (Abegunawardhana & Senarathne, 2002), the land is considered as one of the three factors of production along with capital and labour. Throughout human history, man has drawn most of his sustenance and fuel, clothing, and shelter from the land. The land has been man's living space and key resource to avoid hunger. Therefore the use of land should have been of key consideration to man is not surprising. What is more surprising is the man's attachment to the land and his persisting concern for it into the industrial and post-industrial ages. In the developed countries man has been detached from the land. His food comes from the supermarkets rather than directly from the soil. Much of his clothing is of synthetic fiber. In place of firewood, he uses fossil fuels from deep below the land surface. Days, weeks, or months may pass when his only landscape is townscape. Yet the man is still concerned about the use of the land from which he has become largely separated. A man who may be living in the city would have a general concern for the use of both rural and urban land. The use of more natural resources invariable evokes concern, but the use of land seems to stand out in attracting special attention. No clear identification between man and land is expressed than in the Hebrew language; man is *Adam* and land is *Adama* (Mather, 1986).

The term LU refers to human activities associated with a specific piece of land, whereas Land Cover (LC) relates to the type of features present on the surface of the earth. Furthermore, both LU/LC are synonymous in the scientific community. LU/LC are two ways of observing the earth's surface. LC Land cover is a feature that can be used in different disciplines (geography, ecology, geology, forestry, land policy, and planning, etc.) as a geographical reference (e.g., for land-use, climatic or ecological studies). In modern geographic databases, due to its relatively easy spatialization, LC has become a sort of "boundary object" between different disciplines. In more detail, the LC consists of physical characteristics of the earth's surface with relation to the distribution of vegetation, water, soil, and other physical features. LU is how the land has been utilized by humans and their habitats such as agriculture, settlements, industry (Kaul and Sopan, 2012). Burns & Hart (1970) have observed: *Land as an object, tends to produce benefit, gives a social advantage, pleasure, happiness.....to the party whose interest is considered.* These non-materials are mostly based on personal objectives. Thus, non-personal objectives differ from personal objectives. In that aspect, the objectives of land may be an economic, social, or cultural phenomenon. These phenomena may spatially and temporally vary in a country like Sri Lanka. LU has changed over time and is changing in the country under different perspectives.

This chapter begins with an introduction to the background of Sri Lanka and then moves to the LU/LC pattern of Sri Lanka, focusing on LU/LC changes during the colonial period. Then the attention has been drawn to the post-independence period highlighting the changes of LU/LC with the introduction of liberalized economic policies. The final concern gave on planning and sustainable developments are decisive measures of LU management in Sri Lanka.

Historical Background of Sri Lanka

The first entries in the Mahavansa or Great History date back to 543 BCE, coincides with the arrival of Prince Vijaya. The early Anuradhapura Period commenced with King Pandukabhya as the first ruler in Sri Lanka. In the 3rd century BCE, Buddhism gifted from India established with the corporation of Sinhalese King Tissa. Anuradhapura dynasty flourished for nearly 1500 years before moving to Polonnaruwa in 1070. It remained for 150 years. The coastal zone of the country was fallen to Portuguese and Dutch administration for 300 years and in 1815 whole country was fallen to British colonial. Unrest under colonial rule saw the Ceylon National Congress formed in 1919, uniting Sinhalese and Tamils. A constitution wrote and some concessions provided, but it wasn't until the 1947 constitution came into effect. Ceylon gained independence in 1948. The socio-economic background of the country shaped concerning the administrative development since the arrival of the Prince Vijaya to Thambapanni which is known as Mannar. Simple socio-economic behaviours transferred to complex socio-economic structures and behaviours throughout a long history. The society, commerce, economic, cultural, and technology are consequences of such a sequential development. The economy and social aspects were shaped by the different policies adopted under the reign of different European powers. Liberalized and the industrialized economy is what we are experiencing now is the recent influential economic policy that shaped both the economic and social status of the country. The dynamic socio-economic conditions manipulate the environment as well. The absolute location of the country positioned her like a tropical island that experiences a wide array of environmental conditions and consists of many natural resources. The country mainly includes economically important agricultural land use, forests and biodiversity, water and mineral resources. Step by step, the environmental attributes have been degrading and highly threatened the environment of the country.

HISTORICAL PERSPECTIVE OF LAND USE IN SRI LANKA

Pre-Colonial Era (543BCE-1505 Anno Domini (AD)

When considering the tenure system of ancient Sri Lanka, the king was the centre. The absolute lord of the soil and land property and all the descriptions originated from him. Ariyapala (1956) and Ralph Pieris (1956) states king as the sole mighty of the land property of the country. The irrigated civilization of the country woven around water tanks (*Wewa*). The tank-based Hydro-Paddy Culture Civilization (H-PCC) has had a large surplus of rice in the past. The Golden era of the rice cultivation was the period of king Prakramabahu (1153 - 1186). During his period, the country called the 'granary of eastern' (Mahavansaya, 1986). The Hydro-Paddy Culture Civilization is mainly evolved from the dry zone of the country. The civilization has first emerged around natural lakes and streams *i.e.,* Malwathu Oya - Anuradha Grama and Upatissa Grama, Kala Oya - Uruwela Grama. These settlements clustered around a source of water. Later these primitive pond-reservoirs converted into tanks (Brohier, 2000). Subsequently, early settlers developed rainwater-harvesting methods to make the existence possible in the other areas of the dry zone (FAO, 2017). More logical water harvesting methods introduced after the establishment of the agrarian society until the end of the sovereignty of great king Prakramabahu's (Mahavansaya, 1986). The dry zone of the country became more prosperous with numerous small, medium, and large scale tanks (Deraniyagala, 1992). Agricultural LU undoubtedly dominated by paddy cultivation during this time.

Anuradhapura particularly located by adopting water management measures to control the water supply from seasonal rainfall, streams, and perennial rivers flowing across the dry zone (Deraniyagala, 2002).

Figure 1. A model of an ancient village -dry zone land use
Source: (Dharmasena,2010)

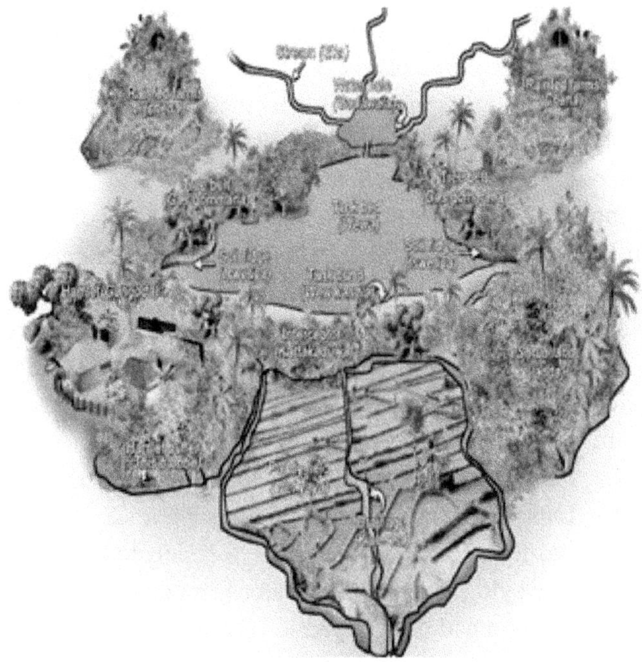

Although paddy dominated the agricultural LU, the farming system included secondary agricultural types; Chena and Home Garden as well (Dharmasena, 1993). Dharmasena has further emphasized this as a threefold farming system evolved from the tank-villages: rainfed upland cultivation, lowland paddy cultivation (wela), and dwelling gardens (gangoda).

According to the model developed by Thennakoon (1986) on the spatial organization of the village agricultural, LU system, forests, tanks, settlement, old filed, field block, parkland, and canal are distinguished. This is quite similar to the traditional tank-based village system as shown in figure 1. Literary evidence proves that the spatial organization of ancient agriculture directly depends on the tank system. With reserved forests on top of the tank and paddy fields beneath could be cultivated during both seasons. The demand for the old field high due to the adequate water supply. The field blocks used for double cropping is highly uncertain even in a year of normal rainfall which was the first sign of changing LU pattern as people wanted to cultivate the field blocks for their subsistence with the population growth. Parkland used for grazing for cattle. The settlements in the open area consisted of short grass and shrubs where no one claimed for the land. The settlements demonstrated a clustered pattern. The outer area covered with natural forests and people had access to the forest for shifting cultivation. According to Tennakoon (1986), the proportionate zonal distribution of land differs significantly according to the size of the village. Further Tennakoon (1986) emphasized about 8% of the total land area in a village is occupied by water in the village tank. Another 14% of the land was in the old field and the field blocks almost in equal proportions. All the lands are irrigational with the village tank water are in these two zones. The homestead gardens situated near the tank occupied further 10% from the village land. The remaining parkland zones and the forest zone occupied nearly 68% from the land areas in a ratio of 1:1 to 1:2 respectively. All these literary pieces of evidence illustrated simple and monotonous ancient LU pattern in the Dry zone of Sri Lanka.

The king had the power to demarcate different LUs in the surrounding areas of the water tanks. This can be considered a kind of LU/LC controlling system is practiced in the present world. Under this zoning system, distribution of home gardens, paddy lands, forest areas, and strictly reserved forest areas demarcated. Strictly reserved forest areas inaccessible by the general public for their daily requirements. Several modern concepts, such as environmental conservation, water management, soil conservation, LU regulations, and controlling zones were behind this system.

As in many Asian countries, shifting cultivation is the oldest method of farming in the country. With a less population, villagers had access to plentiful forests separated settlements from one another, and slash and burn agriculture (also known as Chena cultivation or shifting cultivation) was in standard practice. However, the early prescriptions mentioned the king himself had declared the forests as strictly reserved areas (Bandara, 2007). A collection of tanks built by ancient engineers by diverting rivers and streams and many other early technologies (Bandara, 2007). One of the most fascinating technologies used valve pits, complex canal systems, and giant tanks. Slope and elevation considered when creating such massive hydraulic systems. e.g. the slope of the first 17 miles of the Jaya Ganga canal is 6 inches per one mile (Mahavansaya, 1986). Tanks connected one by one in such a way it creates a cascade of tanks in the dry zone landscape. A cascade tank-village system is 'a connected series of tanks organized within a micro-catchment; storing, conveying and utilizing water from an ephemeral rivulet'. Based upon this cascade LU, wetland rice cultivation had been expanded throughout the dry zone of the country during the middle historic period driven from 300 A.D. to 1000 A.D. (Panabokke, 2009).

The 13th century was a remarkable phase in the history of the LU evolution of the country. Until 13th century village farming communities mainly distributed in Anuradhapura and Polonnaruwa areas. Later only they shifted to Southwest with South Indian invasions; Kalinga Mag(h)a, a South Indian invader caused vast destruction in traditional LU pattern whereas drastic changes took place under the European powers as well. The demand for Chena declined with the expansion of permanent cultivation, commercial pressure, and population expansion.

Colonial Period (1505-1948AD)

During the Colonial period, the LU determined by mostly market-led based policies. With the introduction of plantations, the traditional system of LU commercialized. The laissez-faire system highly recognized. It is the theory or practice of governmental abstention from interference in the workings of the market. During the European colonial rule, land uses were featured by mono-cropped large units of operation, estates or haciendas, intensive use of waged labour and export-oriented production (Peris, 1996). The overall LU of the country particularly in the hill country has drastically changed by replacing traditional subsistence systems with introduced plantations.

At the beginning of the plantation economy, Cinnamon also drew to an end. Less interest gave on other species and commodities such as chanks, pepper, cardamom, and areca nut. The rapid downfall of the prices of Cinnamons further proved this. The situation emphasized no detectable changes in LU/LC until the emergence of glamour crop 'coffee'. Coffee introduced by the Arabs in the medieval period prevailed only as a garden crop. Subsequently, the dominance of coffee detected only in the wild. However, the technical assistant displaced the coffee as the primary economic crops.

Booming of coffee reported in the 1830s. In the beginning, more or less as a cottage industry, Sir Edward Barnes the first person to be acknowledged for the success of large scales coffee plantations in the country (Mahavansaya, 1986; Holsinger, 2002). George Bird considered the father of the plantation industry in Sri Lanka. George Bird identified slopes as the most suitable locations for coffee plantations and settled on the slopes of Sinhapitiya hill at Gampola. The beginning of a mass catastrophe applied his technique in a jungle clearing and planting operations bringing labourers from South India. At first, the British failed to plant up virgin jungles with coffee. Thus, successful plantations operated in the Midlands of the country by 1835. It evidenced coffee exports of Sri Lanka reached its zenith by becoming the world's largest coffee producer. There were approximately 1,760,000 acres of coffee cultivation lands in 1869 (Mahavansaya, 1986) that the year evaded coffee cultivation. When coffee destroyed due to *Haemelia vastratix*, a fungus distributed all over coffee plantations in 1869 and the production decreased. It could wipe out almost 250,000 acres of coffee within two decades (Sri Lankan History IV, 2007). However, the British government statistics of 1878 mentioned about 334,686 acres of land area in the midlands of the country under coffee cultivation (Holsinger, 2002). With the large extent of coffee cultivation, the labour force requirements fulfilled by importing labourers from India. Further, the government statistics of 1900 stated there were only 11,392 acres of land under coffee cultivation (Holsinger, 2002). During the period of 1839s, coffee was supremely delighted among economic crops, tea cultivation was insignificant and it was grown as a home garden crop at an experimental level. In 1867 the first commercial plot of tea was planted on Loolcondera estate (Holsinger, 2002).

Meanwhile, several decisions had been taken by the political authority to acquire the lands. Thus, Europeans prohibited to owe land outside the vicinity of cities. Europeans resided in the country tried to rescind this law. During this period, especially the British military personnel acquired more virgin lands in the country. The embargos on land ownership withdrew during the governing period of Thomas Maitland between 1805-1811 leading virgin lands into a catastrophe. The land ownerships permitted for Europeans and British could purchase or receive grants of the land up to 4000 acres (Holsinger, 2002). Therefore, land sales and auctions regularly conducted. Surprisingly, the price of an acre of a virgin jungle was only five shillings. The reprehensible wasteland act of 1824 has allowed purchasing large tracts of virgin forest lands by legislation led to perish almost half of the virgin forests in the hill country. During the period from 1883 to 1889, the export of Ceylon tea grew from 1,000,000 pounds to 28,500,000 pounds. The first tea auction of the country held in 1893 by Somerville and Co. demonstrated the total land-use change. The annual production of tea was about 2,000,000 pounds (Holsinger, 2002). The income generated from rubber, coconut, cocoa, and other crops was not as high as the income generated by tea. This clearly emphasizes the significance of LU change due to tea cultivation at that time. It is important to mention that during the governance of Sir William Henri Gregory (1872-1877), 6000 acres of land were under cinchona cultivation (Mahavansaya, 1986).

Although the virgin jungles cleared, urban and rural populations still concentrated in the traditionally occupied areas along with the massive hill country virtually devoid of human habitation. The large-scale opening up of estates in the uplands and required massive inputs from logistical support and infrastructure. The gradual movement of a largely immigrant labour force particularly towards the highlands made great demands on several supply centres. Basic needs, infrastructure and even luxury items developed, and these further changed the LU. The agrarian style economy of the country, the traditional feudal system of land tenure and tenancy, subsistence farming, and slash and burn cultivation gradually usurped by the new wave of industry and commerce. Though Sinhala Monarchy had recognized the importance of the virgin forest cover and had declared all highland rain forests as strict nature reserves, the British had not bothered about the denudation of highlands (Holsinger, 2002; Sri Lankan History IV, 2007).

Post-Colonial Period (After 1948)

The transitional period had both colonial features and initial phases of Post-Colonial LU could be distinguished between the colonial and post-colonial periods. This transitional period politically identified as the period introduced the Representative Government to Sri Lankan political system (Silva, 2007). Still, tea was the major crop in the hill country. At the beginning of 19th century, the total extent of tea was about 380,000 acres. Tea required a higher labour input than coffee. Lower elevations, specifically below 2000 feet also opened up for cocoa and rubber. These land-use practices ruined subsistence farming and paddy lands. Coffee cultivation was there only about 11,932 acres for production, whereas 417,448 acres were tea by 1900 (Holsinger, 2002). Tea always the major economic crop with around 50% of exported commodities originated from tea products. In 1915, 45% land (426,816 acres) out of 1,664,643 acres of cultivated land accounted for tea cultivation (Table 1). The total extent of tea has been increased to 457,000 acres in 1931, and coconut and rubber have also reached a higher land extent dominating among the pioneering economic crops (Table 1).

Table 1. Dominating economic crop-based land use areas in Sri Lanka during 1915 and 1931

Crop Type	Acreage under cultivation 1915*	Acreage under cultivation 1931**
Tea	426,816	457,000
Rubber	198,588	354,000
Coconut	997,701	1,100,000
Cocoa	41,538	34,000
Total	1,664,643	1,945,000

Source: (Holsinger, 2002*; Sri Lankan History IV, 2007**)

Accordingly, the LU of the post-colonial period can be identified under different categories as listed below.

- Export-oriented commercial agriculture
- Subsistence agriculture/farming
- Minor export crops
- Home gardens

Tea, rubber and coconut became the major economic crops cultivated for commercial purposes. Paddy cultivation considered as subsistence farming since the beginning of the hydraulic civilization.

Export-Oriented Commercial Agriculture

Dramatic changes seem to be continued in the same manner even after independence. The land extent of tea had been increased up to 498,000 acres in the early 20th century while decreasing coffee to 830 acres. The cultivated acreage of tea reached 560,000 acres before the 20th century. By 1961, the registered extent of tea lands significantly exceeded 200,000 or 500,000 hectares (Holsinger, 2002) and tea exports exceeded 2,000,000 metric tons (440,000,0001b). At the end of the first quarter of the 20th century, over one million acres of land planted with tea, rubber, and coconut. Slight fluctuations noticed in the extents of registered tea lands (Fig 2) during the post-colonial period.

The plantation was operated by the private sector until the 1970s. The government of the 1970s nationalized the plantations by introducing land reform laws in 1972 and 1975. Consequently, the government acquired 503 tea, rubber, and coconut estates and assigned them to two State Corporations; Janatha Estates Development Board and Sri Lanka State Plantation Corporation. By 1990, these two corporations accounted for approximately 51% of tea production, 32% of rubber production, and 2% of coconut production in the country (Holsinger, 2002). Along with the nationalization of plantations, adverse fiscal and monetary policies and haphazard regulatory policies declined the export agriculture. Yet, again the plantation sector privatized for liberation. Tea is the ailing giant since 1994, and it has become the largest economic crop that has allowed Sri Lanka to stand among the world's largest tea exporters.

Figure 2. The chronological changes of tea cultivated area by elevation in Sri Lanka*
Source: (Holsinger, 2002)
** Data from the Land Use survey is indicated for 1994/95. The statutory requirement that owners should register their Tea Lands with the Tea Commissioner was repealed at the end of 1992.*

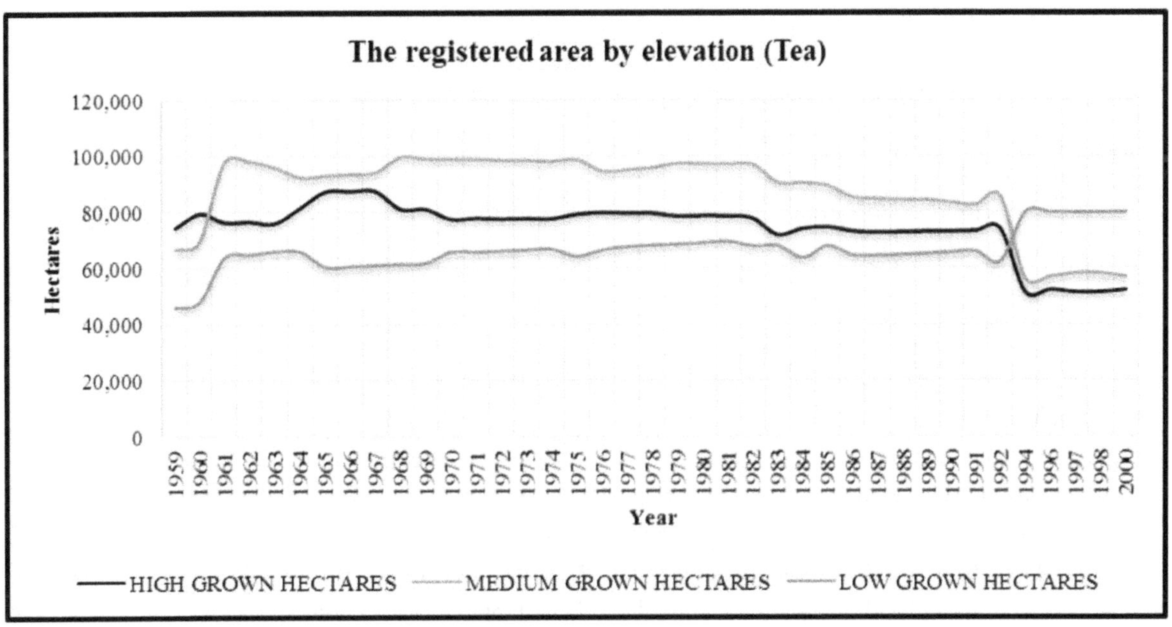

The total land extent of tea, rubber, and coconut has fluctuated in the areas with middle elevations till 1992. Most of the districts have shown a rapid decrease in the cultivated land extent, while several districts have shown a particular increase in tea and coconut. Among them, Kalutara, Hambanthota, Moneragala, and Ratnapura depicted a salient increase in tea and Matale, Nuwara Eliya, Hambanthota, and Badulla had shown an increase in coconut (Table 2). The second major commercial crop is the rubber grows in the ridges and valleys in the interior of the wet zone of the country. About 80% of cultivated land out of 159,000 hectares harvested and 96.6 million kilograms of rubber produced in 1999. The third major economic crop coconut and its production in 1999 accounted for 2,828 million nuts are the highest recorded output since 1986. As coconut is one of the major ingredients used in food preparation in Sri Lanka, nearly 65% of the output locally consumed. The remainder exported in the form of desiccated coconut, coconut oil, copra, coconut cream, and coconut milk powder (nation's encyclopaedia, 2000).

Table 2. District wise changes in tea, rubber and coconut cultivation area (ha)

District	Tea		Rubber		Coconut	
	1982	2002	1982	2002	1982	2002
Kaluthara	3,586	7,170	Decreased			
Hambanthota	142	440	67	71	20,430	20,733
Matale					9,296	10,299
Nuwara Eliya	Decreased				833	1,043
Badulla					885	2,715
Moneragala	797	922	Decreased			
Ratnapura	24,064	38,352				

Source: (Census department, 2019)

Table 3. Land-use changes in major cash crops in hectares from 2007 to 2014

Crop	2007	2008	2009	2010	2011	2012	2013	2014
Tea	212,715	221,969	221,969	221,969	221,969	221,969	221,969	221,969
Rubber	116,478	116,478	124,000	127,000	130,280	132,904	132,904	132,904
Coconut	394,836	394,836	394,836	394,836	394,836	394,836	394,836	394,836

Source: (Census department, 2019)

A significant change is noted in the tea cultivated area of the country during the post-colonial period. It slightly directed towards the middle and low elevated areas such as Rathnapura and Kalutara districts. During the colonial period, tea mainly concentrated in Kandy and Nuwara Eliya areas. These spatial changes noticed with the introduction of tea smallholders of the country who not-existed during the colonial period. Kalutara and Rathnapura districts reported an increase of land area under tea cultivation from 1982-2002, by about 3,584 ha and 14,288 ha respectively (Table 2). Accordingly, the total land extent of tea and rubber has been increased from 2007-2014 while remaining coconut in the same position as it was in 2007 (Table 3).

Subsistence Agriculture

The rapid changes in LU/LC mainly woven around the plantation economy during the colonial period. Less attention paid for paddy cultivation due to the lack of irrigational development. Although the plantation economy has invaded hill country and middle elevation areas of the country, the wet zone and the lower peneplains had a less from plantation economy. Less attention paid on irrigation development under the colonial rule due to the differences in personal interests of governors and the abundance of lakes and tanks in the dry zone; the trend prevailed till 1948. Thus, people tend to move towards Chena cultivation. Most of the parts in the dry zone consisted of Chena while the Ampara district dominated with paddy for a long time. Significantly identify home gardens with coconut in the wet zone, mentioned as 'uyan' in Sandesha Kavya (Sri Lankan History iii, 2007). According to Mahavnsaya (1986), thousands of acres of land in the dry zone including Anuradhapura, Minneriya, Batticaloa, Thissamaharamaya occupied by the government under Sir William Henri Manin who encouraged to cultivate paddy and other cereals. Further, the Mahavansaya (1986) has stated for 913,239 acres of paddy lands in 1945 and dramatically increased to 10,850,011 acres in 1952. Although the land extent occupied by paddy cultivation increased, 64% and 32% of paddy lands were less than one acre and half an acre respectively in size (Mahavansaya, 1986).

The Gal Oya Scheme, the first basin development project, started during 1948. Gal Oya reservoir developed to cover an area of 120,000 acres while left bank alone could irrigate an area of 80,000 acres. However, the areas under irrigation were only 65,000 acres. Uda Walawa provided irrigation for about 71,000 acres. About 10,000 acres from the total area constituted for existing irrigated rice fields. The area used to grow rice increased from 6 times reaching 546,249 hectares (1960-2000). Modernized farming methods such as high-yielding seeds, tractors, and chemical fertilizers also affected on the increased productivity in the rice sector. The rice yield per hectare has been doubled from 1,877 square kilograms - 3,672 square kilograms (1960-1999). Also, there were significant fluctuations in paddy extent from 2007-2014 (Table 4). The recent data highlighted Ampara, Batticaloa, and Polonnaruwa were among the major districts for paddy cultivation.

Table 4. Changes in paddy cultivation area (ha) with time

Year	2007	2008	2009	2010	2011	2012	2013	2014
Area (ha)	816,713	1,052,995	1,065,281	1,091,049	1,066,617	1,227,248	1,227,248	964,268

Source: (Census department, 2019)

Minor Export Crops

The history of minor export crops goes back to Dambadeni kingdom. Greek, Roman and Arabs maintained relationships through the spice trade; cinchona, cinnamon, coffee, cocoa popular since the colonial period. Though Portuguese accidentally stranded near the country, they expedited for spices and to spread Christian. This proves that Sri Lankan spices had obtained a particular favourite among the consumers. The list of spices cultivated in the colonial period extended up-to-date including perennials pepper, cardamom, clove, nutmeg, vanilla, betel, citronella, lemongrass, areca nut, goraka, ginger and turmeric; today known as Minor Export Crops.

Additionally, to rice, many other food crops are produced in the irrigation schemes and home gardens for local consumption (nation's encyclopaedia, 2000). They include yams, pulses, grains, vegetables, and fruits. Most of these crops are cultivated in home gardens except potatoes and sugar. Sugar cane is cultivated in the dry zone, and only 15% of its domestic consumption is produced by Sri Lanka. The LU for other crops; kurakkan, maize, meneri, sorghum and green grams salient due to the increase of total cultivated land extent from 2007 - 2014. When comparing with major economic crops, a slight decrease could be identified in the land extent of minor export crops; cinnamon, coffee, cocoa and cardamom (Table 5).

Table 5. Land use change pattern in hectare under cultivation of minor export crops

Crop	2007	2008	2009	2010	2011	2012	2013	2014
Cinnamon	25,760	26,770	28,090	29,163	30,432	30,090	30,090	29,512
Coffee	10,170	8,790	8,720	8,686	8,458	8,740	8,740	8,340
Cocoa	2,350	2,690	2,740	2,548	2,534	2,257	2,257	2,170
Pepper	30,520	34,070	37,340	36,431	37,825	39,493	39,493	39,650
Cardamom	1,850	1,320	1,530	1,547	1,510	1,692	1,692	1,680
Kurakkan	5,410	6,080	5,900	6,570	5,345	5,195	5,953	7,420

Source: (Census department, 2019)

Home Gardens

Home gardens have been identified as an integral part of the landscape throughout history is mixed with cultural aspects as well. Throughout the known literature, Kandyan home gardens have obtained much attention, as a subset of home gardens in Sri Lanka. Home gardens in historical Kandy and adjacent districts such as Badulla, Kegalle, Kurunegala, Matale, Nuwara Eliya, and Ratnapura are considered as Kandyan home gardens. Although attention was given for fruits and vegetable cultivations in home gardens by colonials, much attention has been given by the recent governments on home gardens. However, there is a lack of accurate data relevant to home gardens as no recent studies done.

The land extent under home gardens in Sri Lanka reported as 781,000 ha and 858,100 ha in 1983 and 1995 respectively (FSMP, 1995). According to the reports of Ariyadasa (2002) and FAO (2009), 14.3% of the land extent of the country was under home gardens. It is important to note that statistics of those reports have covered only 20 districts, excluding Jaffna, Kilinochchi, Mannar, Mullaitivu, and Vavuniya. According to the census and statistics, 76,484 ha (1.2%) of the land extent covered by home gardens in 2002 (considering only the home gardens of less than 0.25 acres). This indicates there is an ambiguity over the extent of home gardens in Sri Lanka.

Home garden areas in Sri Lanka has been increased annually by about 1% (8,000 ha) from 1980 to 1992 (FSMP, 1995). There were about 1.42 million home gardens in Sri Lanka by 2002 with a holding size below 0.25acres (Census, 2002). The total number of home gardens has also continued to grow at an annual rate of 1.6%. A comparison of LU data from 1956 to 1980 also revealed the area under home gardens has steadily increased. A similar trend related to the change of areas of home gardens has been reported from the upper Mahaweli catchment area as well (FSMP, 1995). FAO (2009) reported both the number of home gardens and the total land extent under home gardens are increasing in Sri Lanka due to the establishment of new settlements and land fragmentation. Perera & Tsuchiya (2009), has mentioned there is a reduction in forest cover by 50%, doubling the areas of home gardens in their assessment of LU/LC and its change from 1987-2006 in south-eastern Sri Lanka. The extent of home gardens in Nilwala river basin in the southern province was 20% in 1940-1956, and it has increased to 26% in 1965-1972 and later decreased to 15% in 1985-1995 mainly due to the conversion of home gardens to monoculture tea plantations (Mungai et al., 2004).

Home gardens are distributed in all districts of Sri Lanka varying from 2.4% of the total land area of the Mannar district to 36.2% of the Matara district. According to FSMP (1995) report, the extent of forest cover exceeds the national average forest cover (22.4%) only in the areas of the dry zone of the country whereas the percentage area of home gardens exceeds the national average (13.1%) largely in areas of the wet zone of Sri Lanka (Fig 3). Home gardens in the highly populated Wet zone have suffered in the past two decades due to fragmentation and urbanization (FSMP, 1995; MENR, 2009; ME, 2010; Dela, 2011). However, Premakantha et al. (2008) in a recent assessment using the same methodology, suggested the area of home gardens in Nuwara Eliya district was 27,440 ha or 16% from the total land area.

Figure 3. Home Gardens cover in Sri Lanka by district
Sources: (FSMP, 1995)

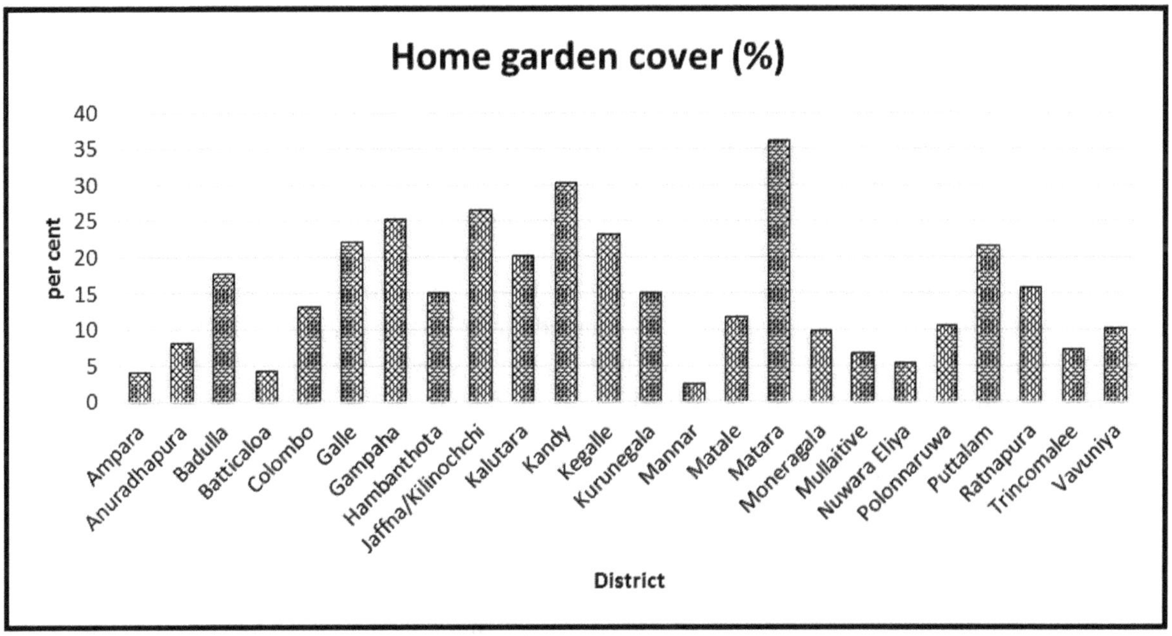

Accelerated Land-Use Change and Loss of Forest Cover

Cultural features of the country too began to change drastically with the fluctuation of agricultural LU. Except for paddy lands and marshy areas, much of the lands re-filled for settlements. Increasing demand for settlements become a threat that accelerated the urbanization related LU. The accelerated urban expansion usually associated with economic factors (He et al., 2006). Oduwaye (2001) mentioned urban land as a place full of diversity used for different purposes. Those included residential areas, low medium to high densities commercial and central areas, offices, industrial areas, warehouses, public and semi-public areas, and circulation and recreational spaces.

LU change in urban areas is directly connected with infrastructural development (Bhagawat, 2011). Urban centres are concentrated mainly in coastal belt in Western and Southern parts of Sri Lanka. Colombo city being the metropolitan region, it has a high urbanization growth rate. The report 'State of Sri Lankan Cities in 2018' has given a wider view of the spatial distribution of the settlement expansion. Colombo and the Western Region Megapolis are identified as rage urban conurbations that have experienced rapid spatial growth over the past decade.

Rural-urban migration has increased with the development of infrastructure and urban facilities in the country. Consequently, the urban expansion has accelerated and the land extent occupied by settlements has been doubled within a few years. This trend has created a significant spatial pattern in the LU of the western province while showing less significance in the other parts of the country. The commercial and administrative capital and the urban centres (1st,2nd, 3rd, and 4th places of the urban hierarchy at the national level) are situated in Colombo and suburbs (Ranaweera & Rathnayake, 2017). The new ring represents the newly established urban centres such as Maharagama, Kaduwela, Kesbewa and illustrating a rapid change. For example, Kaduwela divisional secretariat; nearly 60% out of the total land is used for residential purposes during the year 2005. The built-up area has increased from 8.6 km^2 to 22.9 km^2 during 1975-2016. Within the country, rates of urban expansion varied across the country. The rate of built-up area expansion, about 6.16% per year reported for the Colombo municipality based on the area of interest of Colombo which includes the urban area of Colombo, Kotte, and Dehiwala municipal councils and outside fringe areas. This figure shows an accounting of additional land of 333 km^2 of urban areas in the period of 1995-2017. Another notable feature in LU of settlements was some cities expanded from a small urban base in 1995, and in some cases remained small urban areas in 2017. Therefore, cities like Ratnapura expanded at a fast rate. The amount of additional urban areas this accounted for was small when compared with larger cities like Colombo. In Ratnapura, urban LU was 0.4 km^2 (0.15%) of the area of interest (AoI) in 1995, increased up to 3.5 km^2 (1.3%) of the AoI by 2017 (SoSLC, 2018).

In contrast, AoI of the Colombo urban LU accounted for 122.1 km^2 (22%) out of all the AoI in 1995 and 455.2 km^2 (73%) in 2017 (SoSLC, 2018). These examples show the diverse rapid expansions of the cities of the country over the past two decades. Urban sprawling is another aspect revealed in the spatial analysis of urban expansion. A precursor to sprawl is ribbon development. Urbanization took place in 1956-1994 resulted in ribbon development along Colombo-Katunayake road from Welisara to Ja - Ela and again from Seeduwa to Negombo and along Galle road from Kudawaskaduwa to Katukurunda. The ribbon development process in urban LU can be significantly observed in the city of Colombo, Kurunegala, Galle, and Kalutara as well as along Negombo-Minuwangoda road and Colombo-Kandy road. Ribbon expansion of the urban LU in settlements is depicted through the concentration of urban settlements from 1995-2017. A significant sprawling expansion found in the urban and semi-urban area across the area of interest which is dispersed with the non-built up area. Low-density semi-urban space will transition to urban sprawl if remedial policy actions are not taken. The scale of this issue is most obvious in the case of the western region megapolis which covers an area of 3,684 km^2, where around 70% of the built-up area is low-density semi-urban. The antidote to this sprawl is compact cities. Compact urban expansion refers to the densification of mixed urban land use over a small area and is widely viewed as preferable to low-density sprawl. The exception of this trend is the Colombo municipal council. Remote sensing shows that 90% of the Colombo municipal council fits into the urban land use category (SoSLC, 2018).

Furthermore, these rapid changes in LU have severely affected the forest cover of the country. By the dawn of the 19th century, the estimated forest cover was 70% of the total land area. After the drastic change in LU policy with the British invasion in the 19th century, the natural forests denudated. According to the Global Forest Resources Assessment, 80% of unspoiled forest coverage had decreased to 44% by 1956, 30% by 1996 (Table 6). Further supporting FAO (2010) reported the forest coverage has reduced 25% in 2010. Although deforestation is a widely distributed phenomenon throughout the country, the consequences of this drastic loss of natural forest cover significant in the wet zone of the country. Peiris (1996) identified mass development programmes from 1956-1981 took place in the country as the main root cause to drop the wet and intermediate zone forests from 16-11%. However, some particular events took place in history to clear the forests for development activities. Brohier (2000) has mentioned some of such events in his book 'Seeing Ceylon' (page 44) as follows -

Minneriya, together with its colonies Hingurakgoda and Hathamuna, designed and constructed to bring fifty thousand acres of virgin wild to the service of his country... Year by year, the work of reclaiming from the jungle the rice fields once worked by the ancient kings, proceeded on a set plan.

Table 6. A chronological change in forest coverage since 1956 to1996

Total forest cover			Difference			Annual depletion (%)
Year	Area (ha)*	% of the land area	Period	Area (ha)	Percentage	
1956	2,898,842	44.2				
1983	2,458,250	37.5	1956-1983	-440,592	15.2	0.6
1992	2,046,599	31.2	1983-1992	-411,651	16.7	1.9
1996	1,942,219	29.6	1992-1996	-104,380	5.1	1.3

Source: *(FAO, 2009)*

Table 7. Closed canopy forest cover change in Sri Lanka 1983-2001

Year	Forest of total area (%) *	Forest of total area (%) †	Forest area (ha) *	Forest area (ha) †	Annual change*	Annual change†
1983	27.1		1,757,995			
1992	24.4	26.0	1,585,858	1,685,278	-1.1	
1996	24.1	25.8	1,560,639	1,673,671	-0.4	-0.1
2001		24.8		1,604,834		0.5

Source: *(*Ratnayake et al., 2002; †Government of Sri Lanka, 2000).*

The data are shown in Table 7 rather differs from the data in table 6. Table 7 shows the data comparing two studies to detect the closed canopy cover changes from 1983-2001. Though the data are different, both studies have shown a decline in forest cover. Natural forest cover has decreased from 1,170,000 ha during this period while 60% of the land has become wastelands (Peiris, 2006).

The forest cover changes have taken place at a rate of 7,147 ha/year from 1992 to 2010, particularly in the dry zone. Figure 4 represents the forest cover changes in 1992 and 2010. This illustrates the significant differences that have been taken place in LU in the recent past.

Figure 4. Forest cover changes over time in Sri Lanka due to land use and land cover changes
Source: (Fernando et al., 2015)

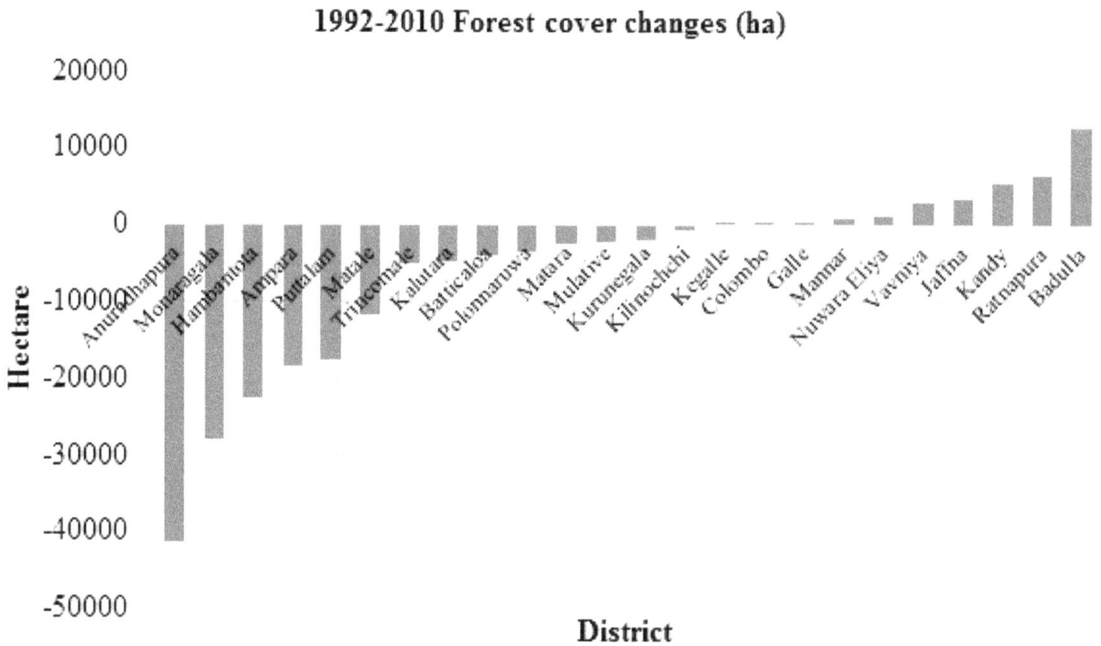

The graphical presentation indicated in figure 4 carries a general picture on the forest cover changes implying the highest rate of deforestation took place in Anuradhapura in which the loss of forest cover has shown spread more or less uniformity over the district. Other highlighting hotspots of declined land cover are Moneragala, Hambanthota, and Ampara. Puttalam districts also identified as a hotspot while Kalutara and Ratnapura districts account for the only hotspot of the wet zone. The proximate drivers of deforestation in this period are encroachments, development projects and private agriculture ventures and the illicit felling. The root cause behind the increasing rate of deforestation is population growth. This is further proved by the inverse relationship identified between the population growth and the forest cover change. Nonetheless, a much broader study could provide further socio-economic factors to such LU/LC change in the country.

Such a wider point of view is possible to achieve through satellite remote sensing is ideal for mapping of LU/LC changes. A recent study carried out by Rathnayake et al. (2020) clearly emphasizes the annual total area changes/disturbed (ha) across all land cover types and significant historical events along with socio-economic conditions (Fig 5) that took place from 1993-2018 are strongly matched to the land-use change occurred within the given period. Most of the changes detected far from Colombo, dry zone specifically. Many of the protected areas in the dry zone have been notably impacted due to the increasing human population and urbanization. Also, this impact remarkably at the proximity of district capitals (Fig 6). Most of the LU/LC changes occurred through the period of 2004-2008 and 2014-2018.

Figure 5. Annual total area changes/disturbed (ha) across all land cover types and significant historical events took place in Sri Lanka from 1993-2018
Source: (Rathnayake et al., 2020)

Between 2010 and 2013, several giant road developments took place making Hambantota, Galle, Matara, Kandy, and Jaffna as the hubs of road and railway development. Apart from that, several reservoirs including Moragahakanda (2014-2018), Deduru Oya (2014), Lunugamwehera (2013-2014), Upper Kothmale (2011), and Rambaken Oya reservoir (2007-2013) establishment also contributed for LU/LC changes in the recent history. Warnasuriya (2015) well explained the shift of this pattern of LU/LC changes took place after 2009. Significant infrastructure development created new suburbs such as Hambanthota, along with Monaragala, Ampara, and Batticaloa. While the dry zone LU changed in such a way, Colombo expanded by reclaiming new land from the ocean will add a particular extent of land to the country.

Figure 6. Distribution of land cover changes and disturbances by defined periods from 1993-2018
Source: (Rathnayake et al., 2020)

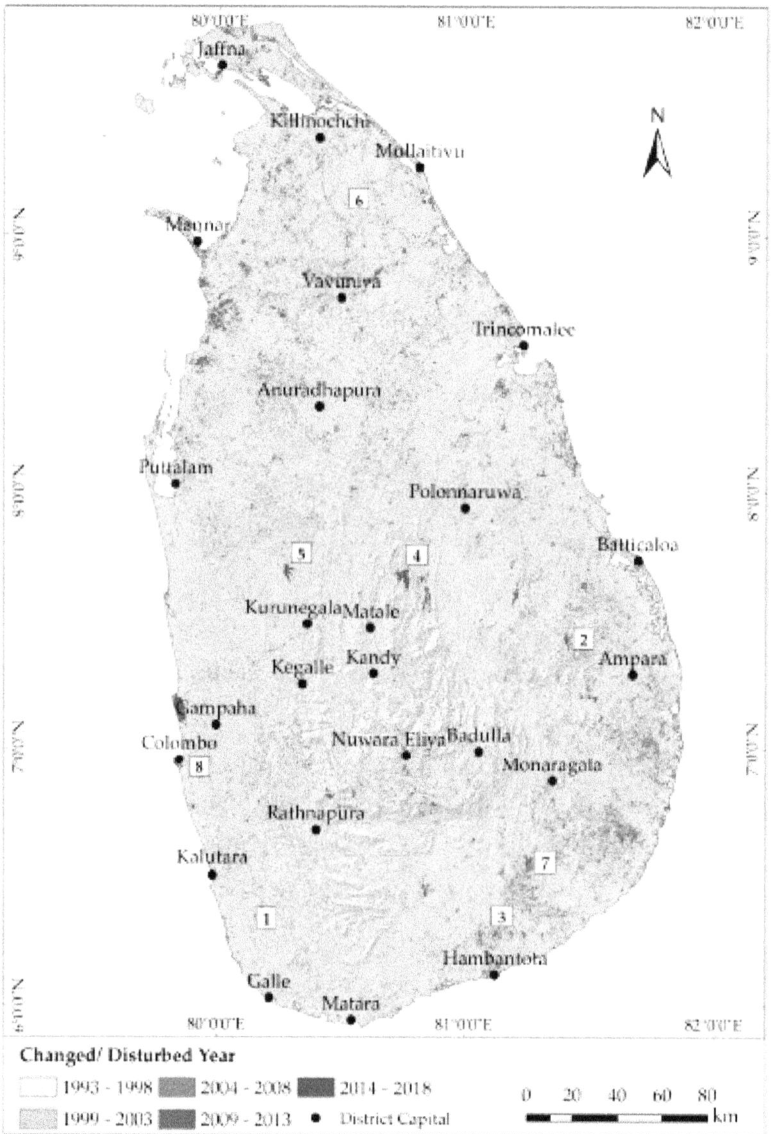

It is noticed that the protected areas in the country are being impacted by ongoing LU/LC changes. In this respect, forest fragmentation has raised highly and biodiversity refugees are created harming the biodiversity of the area, threatened genetic diversity, specifically. Focusing Colombo district alone (Saparamadu & Zongping, 2018), recent remote sensing studies on LU/LC changes show 11% loss of agricultural land and 7% of wetland in a relatively short period (fewer than 10 years). These changes ranged from the form of hard surface cover, mainly consisting of residential and industrial use and related transportation infrastructure.

Sri Lanka is a developing country possessing urban policy structures that lack the human and financial infrastructure for a comprehensive implementation, for example, lack of expertise, multi-disciplinary environmental assessments without political intervention and scientific support in the decision making process. Therefore, it is worth to study the land-use policies in the country.

LAND-USE POLICIES THROUGHOUT THE HISTORY

In ancient Sri Lanka, the "King" or ruler of the country had all the rights and ownership of the lands. Hence, the king himself gave himself the honourable titles such as "Maheepathi", "Bhupathi", etc., whatever liked by the king, the sole owner of the land. The land gave out to the people by his grace either as a payment or in return to some kind of services (Ariyapala, 1956, as cited in Dharmasiri, 2009). But some historians have disagreed with this statement regarding the role of king as lord of lands and they have argued on king's role on land to clarify whether it is absolute over-lordship or only a trusteeship (Siriweera, 1994; Herath, 2006).

Apart from the king's role as the sole owner of lands, some adopted land ownership and tenure patterns existed during the ancient king's era in Sri Lanka. According to Dharmasiri (2009), land ownership could be classified as follows,

a) Land directly controlled by King
b) The land gave to religious institutions or individuals by the king
c) Land controlled by temples or officials
d) Land controlled by individuals.

As per the above classification, the land ownership based on the feudal and semi-feudal systems in which land rights mainly held up by the king and religious institutions. Also, most of these lands utilized for cultivation by tenants and temple serfs (Herath, 2006).

The colonial period in Sri Lanka started with Portuguese rule. During that period, no significant change in the existed land right system recorded. At the beginning of the Dutch era, they claimed for sovereign rights for all the lands. Under that, different paddy land ownership patterns such as lands with and without service tenure identified (Silva, 2000; Dharmasiri, 2009).

With the invasion of the British in 1815, existed land ownership and tenure system of Sri Lanka based on traditional feudal and semi-feudal systems completely changed (Herath, 2006). Many land policies and legislations formulated in Sri Lanka and those could be categorized into two main groups as the pre-independence and post-independence period. Pre-independence land policies included Crown land encroachment ordinance, Wasteland ordinance, Land development ordinance and Irrigation land ordinance. Post-independence land legislation included Land reform law and National land-use policy.

The first major legal enactment on LU in Sri Lanka was introduced by the British in 1840. It is also known as "Crown Land Encroachment Ordinance". The primary purpose of this ordinance was to acquire the lands to meet the demand for land for the expansion of plantation activities. This resulted in large scale conversion of natural forests in low, mid, and up-country regions of the wet zone into cultivation lands for the expansion of plantation crops such as coffee, tea, rubber, and coconut. The plantation sector began to grow rapidly compelling the British rulers to seek new lands with the Waste Land Ordinance of 1897 (succeeded partially due to the difficulties in establishing claims for lands that have already been developed) (Peiris, 1996).

The first land commission formed in 1927, and it had recommended the conversion of vast expanses of "underdeveloped crown lands" in the dry zone into the lands for food production. The mainland legislation enacted after the land commission of 1927 enforced "Land development ordinance" in 1935. This ordinance marked the first change in the traditional colonial attitude to the land policy of Sri Lanka. The principle of government initiative in alienating lands introduced by this policy and a Land Commissioner's Department established to supervise and control the alienation and use of Crown land (Herath, 2006). Excluding that, the "Irrigation Land Ordinance" was introduced in 1946 to assist the irrigation requirements of the alienated lands of the dry zone under Land Development Ordinance of 1935.

The introduction of "Land reform law/act" in 1972 was a revolutionary step in land policies of Sri Lanka after independence. The main focus of the law was to establish the limits on private ownership of land by imposing land ceiling and granting power to acquire land above the ceiling to dispose of the property. In 1979, "Mahaweli Authority Act" enacted to implement the Accelerated Mahaweli Development Program. Under the program, new lands opened for new farmers and landless communities (Herath, 2006).

Apart from the above-discussed land policies, few other land-related legal enactments such as Land settlement ordinance (1931), State land ordinance (1947), Land acquisition act (1950), Land grants act (1979), Title registration act (1998), etc. are also available to address different land matters. Some legal enactments on specific LUs are Forest ordinance (1885), Fauna and flora protection ordinance (1937), Soil conservation act (1951), Tea and Rubber land fragmentation act (1958), urban development authority act (1978), Coast conservation act (1979), Agrarian development act (2000), etc.

Likewise, several different land policies and LU planning legal enactments have been introduced to address many land-related issues in the country. But the absence of a clearly defined land-use policy in Sri Lanka, after years of independence was problematic. In 2007, "National LU Policy of Sri Lanka" was introduced by the Department of Land use policy planning under Ministry of land. The main principles of the policy included LU based on zoning, balanced regional development, adoption of an integrated approach to land management, utilization of land-based on physical suitability, and the functioning of the state. These principles of the policy will keep the state as "trustee" to ensure the sustainability of the LU (National LU Policy of SL, 2007). This policy has been presented in three main themes as "Land and People", "Agriculture and Food Security" and "Land Nature".

However, the formulation of a land-use policy alone would not ensure the sustainability of the utilization of the land resources of this country. So, legislation should be enacted, and institutional arrangements should be made to monitor and see whether these resources are utilized under the sound principles of LU planning and management. Unsustainable land-use practices will lead not only to capital loss and human resources but also could permanently damage the precious forest cover.

CONCLUSION

The chapter discussed how the land use and land cover changed over time in Sri Lanka under three significant periods. The pre-colonial period is identified as the most influential and protective period for better land use and land cover maintenance. Introducing of export crops under the colonial period led to devastating early patterns of land use and destroyed most of the virgin forests. Post-colonial period, especially after the independence the massive loss of forest cover, reported due to mass development programmes took place in the country. An increasing trend is identified in the decline of forest cover parallel to the population growth accelerates the settlement growth and related LU. Recent trends on national level demand for food and bioenergy have raised the concerns on the impact of LU/LC changes can ultimately impact on biodiversity and other socio-economic-environmental contexts. Thus, it is necessary to implement sustainable LU planning while achieving sustainable development. Therefore, a debate has been formed on the role of market-based instruments to reduce land-use conversions and other environmental issues. Forest certification and eco-labelling are more successful market-based instruments for sustainable forest harvesting and management become. Based on the existing status, it is highly recommended to enhance-the payments for ecosystem services are identified as fairly a successful method for low and medium-income countries to have sustainable LU and LC system.

Funding Information

This research is based on critical literature review thus received no particular grant from any funding agency.

REFERENCES

Abegunawardhana & Senarathne. (2002). *Natural resources and environmental economics*. Author publication.

Ariyadasa, K. P. (2002). *Assessment of tree resources in the home gardens of Sri Lanka*. FAO Regional Office for Asia and the Pacific.

Ariyapala, M. B. (1956). Society in Medieval Ceylon. Academic Press.

Bhagawat, R. (2011). *Urban Growth and land use/land cover Change of Pokhara Sub-Metropolitan City, Nepal*. Retrieved from; https://docs.google.com/ viewer? A=v&q=cache

Brohier, R. L. (2000). *Seeing Ceylon*. Suriya publications.

Burns, J. H., & Hart, H. L. A. (1970). The Collective Workers of Jeremy Bentham: An Introduction to the Principle of Morals and Legislation. University of London.

Department of Census and Statistics. (2002). *Agricultural census*. Author.

Department of Census and Statistics. (2019). *Agricultural census*. Retrieved from: http://www.statistics.gov.lk/agriculture/index.htm

Deraniyagala, S. U. (1992). *The prehistory of SL, parts I, II*. Archaeological Survey Department.

Deraniyagala, S. U. (2002). A note on man and water in SL: from prehistory to history. In *Mendis DLO Water Heritage of Sri Lanka*. Sri Lanka Pugwash Group.Dharmasiri, R. K. (2009). *Land use land tenure and agricultural productivity in Sri Lanka A spatiotemporal analysis*. Retrieved from http://hdl.handle.net/10603/175107

Dharmasena, P. B. (1993). Man environment interaction in-tank village home gardens: the trends in vegetations. *Proceedings of the 4th Regional Workshop on Multipurpose Trees*, 12-14.

Dharmasena, P. B. (2010). Essential components of traditional village tank systems. *Proceedings of the National Conference on Cascade Irrigation Systems for Rural Sustainability*.

FAO. (2009). *Asia Pacific Forestry Sector Outlook Study II*. Working paper No APFSOS II/WP/2009/29. Sri Lanka Forestry outlook study, regional office for Asia and the Pacific. Bangkok 2009.

FAO. (2010). *Global Forest Resources Assessment 2010*. Available at: http:// foris.fao.org /static/data/ fra2010/FRA2010_Report_1oct2010.pdf

FAO. (2017). *The cascade tank village system in the dry zone of Sri Lanka*. Retrieved from https:// www. fa o.org/fileadmin/templates/giahs_assets/GIAHS_test/02_GIAHS_around_the_world/01_Designated_sites/02_Asia_and_the_Pacific/07_Sri_Lanka/Mar_6th_rev_GIAHS_Proposal_Sri_Lanka_March_2017.pdf

Fernando, S., Senaratna, A., Pallewatta, N., Lokupitiya, E., Manawadu, L., Imbulana, U., … Ranwala, S. (2015). *Assessment of key policies and measures to address the drivers of deforestation and forest degradation in Sri Lanka. Final report of a consultancy awarded to the Colombo Science and Technology Cell*. Faculty of Science, University of Colombo, by United Nations Development Programme for the Sri Lanka UN-REDD Programme.

FSMP. (1995). Sri Lanka forestry sector master plan. Forestry Planning Unit, Forest Department, Ministry of Agriculture, Lands and Forestry, Colombo, Sri Lanka.

GOSL. (2000). *Forest Cover Mapping 2000*. Forest Inventory Division. Forest Department.

He, C., Okada, N., Zhang, Q., Shi, P., & Zhang, J. (2006). Modelling urban expansion scenarios by coupling the cellular automata model and system dynamic model in Beijing. Academic Press.

Herath, J. (2006). Distributional impacts of land policies in Sri Lanka. Sri Lanka n Agriculture Economics Association (SLEA) and Movement for National Land and Agricultural Reform (MONLAR), Sri Lanka.

Holsinger, M. (2002). *History of Ceylon Tea*. Undergraduate thesis.

Kaul, H.A. & Sopan, I. (2012). Land use land cover classification and change detection using high-resolution temporal satellite data. *Journal of Environment*, *1*(4), 146-152.

Mahavansaya. (1986). *Wimalojothi Thero*. Buddhist Cultural Centre.

Mather, A. S. (1986). Land Use. Longman Group.

Mungai, D. N., Ong, C. K., Kiteme, B., Elkaduwa, W., & Sakthivadivel, R. (2004). Lessons from two long-term hydrological studies in Kenya and Sri Lanka. *Agriculture, Ecosystems & Environment*, *104*(1), 135–143. doi:10.1016/j.agee.2004.01.011

Nasstrom, R., & Mattsson, E. (2011). *Land-use change and forestry at the national and sub-national level; country report Sri Lanka*. Focali.

National Land Use Policy of Sri Lanka. (2007). *Land use Policy Planning Department*. Retrieved from http://www.luppd.gov.lk/web/images/content_image/downloads/pdf/national_land_use_policy.pdf

Oduwaye, A. O. (2001). *Residential Land Use and Land Values in Metropolitan Lagos* (Unpublished PhD Thesis). Urban and Regional Planning Department, Obafemi Awolowo University, Ile-Ife, Nigeria.

Panabokke, C.R. (2009). *Small village tank system of Sri Lanka: their evolution, setting, distribution and essential functions*. Hector Kobbekaduwa Agrarian Research and Training Institute.

Peiris, G.H. (1996). *Development and change in Sri Lanka – Geographical Perspectives*. International Centre for Ethnic Studies.

Peiris, G. H. (2006). Sri Lanka, Challenges of the New Millennium. Kandy Books.

Perera, K., & Tsuchiya, K. (2009). Experiment for mapping Land Cover and its change in southeastern SL utilizing 250 m resolution MODIS imageries. *Advances in Space Research*, *43*(9), 1349–1355. doi:10.1016/j.asr.2008.12.016

Pieris, R. (1956). *Sinhalese Social Organization; the Kandyan Period*. The Ceylon University, Press Board.

Premakantha, K. T., Pushpakumara, D. K. N. G., & Dayawansa, N. D. K. (2008). Identification of tree resources outside forests in the upcountry of Sri Lanka using medium resolution satellite imagery. *Tropical Agricultural Research*, *20*, 354–365.

Ranaweera, D. K. D. A., & Ratnayake, R. M. K. (2017). Urban land-use changes in Sri Lanka with special reference to Kaduwela town from 1975 to 2016. *International Journal of Innovative Research and Development*, *6*(6), 52–64p. doi:10.24940/ijird/2017/v6/i6/JUN17014

Rathnayake, C. W.M., & Jones, S., & Benelov, M. S. (2020). Mapping LC changes over 25 years (1993-2018) in Sri Lanka using Landsat time series. *Land (Basel)*, *9*(27), 2–19p.

Ratnayake, J., Abeykoon, M., & Chemin, Y. (2002). *District-wise forest area variation in Sri Lanka from 1992 to 2001 for supporting the National Physical Planning Policy*. Available at: https://www.gisdevelopment.net/aars/acrs/2002/for/015.pdf

Saparamadu, S., Yi, Z., & Zongping, Z. (2018). Temporal Changes of Land use Land Cover and Environmental Impacts: A Case Study in Colombo, Sri Lanka. *Int J Earth Environ Sci*, *3*(1), 150. doi:10.15344/2456-351X/2018/150

Silva, M. U. (2007). History of Sri Lanka. Representative Government, 4.

Sri Lanka Agriculture. (2020). Retrieved from https://www.nationsencyclopedia.com/ economies/Asia-and-the-Pacific/Sri-Lanka-AGRICULTURE.html#ixzz6GxxE3Olh

Sri Lanka History Volume III. (2007). Education Publication Department.

Sri Lanka History Volume IV. (2007). Education Publication Department.

Tennakoon, U. V. M. (1986). *Drought Hazard and Rural Development*. Central Bank of Sri Lanka.

Warnasuriya, T. W. S. (2015). Mapping land-use pattern using image processing techniques for Medium resolution satellite data: A case study in Matara District, Sri Lanka. *Proceedings of the 15th International Conference on Advances in ICT for Emerging Regions*, 106–111.

ADDITIONAL READING

Andrews, J. R. T. (1961). *A Forest Inventory of Ceylon, a Canada-Colombo Plan Project*. Hunting Survey Corp Ltd.

FAO-UNEP. (1997). *Negotiating a Sustainable Future for Land*. FAO/AGLS.

Kendaragama, K. M. A., & Bandara, T. M. J. (2000). *Changes in Land Use pattern in paddy lands, natural resource management centre*. Department of Agriculture.

KEY TERMS AND DEFINITIONS

Cascade Tank System: A cascade tank system is a connected series of tanks organized within a micro-catchment.

Colonial Period: A country or a region subjected to administration by colonials.

Export-Oriented Commercial Agriculture: Foreign market-oriented large scale production of crops for sale, widely distributed and harvested perennially and sold to world markets.

Land Use and Land Cover: How people utilize land and physical land types such as forests.

Plantation Economy: Economy based on mass agricultural production limited to a few crops which are grown in large areas.

Shifting Cultivation: A form of agriculture, the ground is cleared and cultivate with vegetables, pulses, for few years and abandoned to fertilize naturally.

Subsistence Agriculture: Farmers grow food crops to meet their needs of themselves.

Water Management: Planning, developing, distributing, sustainable utilization of water resources under clearly defined water policies and regulations.

Chapter 6
Transformation in Vegetation and Urban Sprawl in Gotan and Surrounding:
A Sustainable Development Approach for Land Use Change and Socioeconomic Issues

Rizwan Ahmad
https://orcid.org/0000-0002-1445-1924
Interdisciplinary Department of Remote Sensing & GIS Applications, Aligarh Muslim University (UN GGIM Academic Network), India

Ramaraju Sudarshana
United Nations Compensation Commissions, India

ABSTRACT

The main driving forces associated with transformation of vegetation cover and urban sprawl, are undoubtedly climate change and human intervention. Finding the truth behind transformation of Gotan, Rajasthan Landsat TM/ETM+ data of the years 1987,1990, 1995, 2000, 2003, 2010, 2015, and 2018 were used. These time series data comprising total of nine scenes were selected to measure the urban and green cover transformation in the past four decades. Landsat TM/ETM+ data were used because it is inexpensive, with high monitoring frequency and covers large areas. The Normalized Difference Vegetation Index (NDVI) of 1987–2018, derived from the remote sensing dataset along with the application of statistical methods and GIS techniques, were used to quantify vegetation cover change. The results show that human-induced factors can explain most variations at sites with significant cover change. It has been a well-known fact that sustainable development presents a system in order to accomplish economic growth, bring about social justice, implement environmental awareness and most certainly the fortification of government sector.

DOI: 10.4018/978-1-7998-4372-6.ch006

INTRODUCTION

GIS and remote sensing is defined as the science and technology of detection and measurement of spectral properties of objects and phenomena related to earth, atmosphere, and sea from a far distant and analyzing the collected data (Gerland, 2014). This technology is useful in investigation and recognition of features and natural resources. Scanning large area with repetition cycle, providing up-to-date thematic maps, knowing environment and the factors affecting it are among the factors which are useful in reaching sustainable development (Meiyappan et al., 2018). Therefore, utilizing remote sensing technology is one of the effective tools in social & environmental studies.

The bird's-eye view, means that the satellites have allowed the people to see large areas of earth at one time, and therefore the satellites can collect more data, even more quickly than the instruments on the ground, that's why it was decided to see and measure the Gotan sustained transformation from the sky. It has the capability to reach in inaccessible areas and to make the desktop information ready for study.Satellites can also see into space better than telescopes at earth's surface. That is because satellites fly above the clouds, dust and molecules present in the atmosphere that can block the view from ground level. Effective use of the information in satellite imagery can have a transformational impact on humanity's most significant challenges, such as helping global scientists, resource planning managers and politicians. Further it can enable in better monitoring, protection of fragile ecosystems, assurance of resilient infrastructure, managing climate risks, enhancing food security, building more resilient cities, reducing poverty and improving governance among others (Wunder, 2001).

GIS is an excellent tool for data management and planning as it stores spatial information on a digital map. A digital base map can be overlaid with data or other layers of information onto a map in order to view spatial information and associations (Gerland, 2014). Sophistication in satellite sensor technology in capturing geometrically accurate images of earth's surface coupled with GIS technology holds the capability of large scale mapping of land and resources.

DATA USED

Transformation of Gotan i.e. Trans-Gotan study has been considered under different datasets covering spatial and non-spatial parameters, but for creation of base map Landsat time series data has been explored exclusively. Landsat, TM/ETM+ data for the years 1987,1990, 1995,2000, 2003, 2010, 2015 and 2018 were used for finding the truth behind transformation, and were freely downloaded from USGS service website http://glovis.usgs.gov. A total of nine scenes comprising the path and row cover the whole study area. Landsat TM/ETM+ data was used because it is inexpensive, with high monitoring frequency and covers large areas. Landsat TM/ETM+ sensors (Tables 1) of time series datasets have been collected. Both the Landsat TM and ETM+ data were geo-referenced to Universal Transverse Mercator Projection (UTM) with WGS 84 datum. Corresponding toposheets of the study area were downloaded from website of the Survey of India, Dehradun.

Table 1. Landsat ETM & TM data Specification

Landsat ETM data Specification				Landsat TM Specification		
Band	**Spectral band (µm)**	**Resolution**	**Use**	**Spectral band (µm)**	**Resolution**	**Use**
1	0.45 – 0.515	30m x 30m	Ground/plant differentiation/coastal zones	0.45 – 0.515	30m x 30m	Ground/plant differen-tiation/ coastal zones
2	0.52-0.60	30m x 30m	Vegetation	0.52-0.60	30m x 30m	Vegetation
3	0.63-0.69	30m x 30m	Differentiate plant species	0.63-0.69	30m x 30m	Differentiate plant species
4	0.70-0.90	30m x 30m	Biomass	0.70-0.90	30m x 30m	Biomass
5	1.55-1.75	30m x 30m	Snow/cloud differentiation	1.55-1.75	120m x 120m	Snow/cloud differentiation
6	10.4-12.5	60m x 60m	Thermal	10.4-12.5	30m x 30m	Thermal
7	2.09- 2.35	30m x 30m	Lithology	2.09- 2.35	30m x 30m	Lithology
PAN	0.50-0.90	15m x 15m		0.50-0.90	15m x 15m	
Senor Altitude		705 Km				
Swath		185 Km				
Spatial Resolution		15 m PAN 30 m (bands 1-5, 7) 60 m band 7				
Radiometric Resolution		8 bit				
Temporal Resolution		16 days				
Source:Lillesand, T.M., & Kiefer, R. W. (2002)						

Table 2. Time series Landsat legacy data used for Trans-Gotan(Transformation of Gotan) Study

Year	Path	Row	Date of Acquisition	Sensor Type	Spatial Resolution
1987	148	42	27 December 1987	TM	30m
1990	148	42	03 September 1990	TM	30m
1995	148	42	04 December 1995	TM	30m
2000	148	42	10 December 2002	TM	30m
2002	148	42	04 April 2004	TM	30m
2010	148	42	13 December 2010	ETM	30m
2015	148	42	27 December 2015	OLI	30m
2018	148	42	22 March 2018	OLI	30m

Landsat data band combination is applied to represent an image in natural color and therefore best approach in studying the appearance of the landscape in reality for theTrans-Gotan region. Band 3 detects chlorophyll absorption in vegetation (thus low reflectance). Band 2 detects the green reflectance from vegetation. Band 1 is more suited for penetration in water, in clear water and this can be some 25 meters penetration. On the other hand, one can also derive information about sediment transportation in water from this band. Band 1 also differentiates between soil and vegetation and hence distinguishes among forest types.

Socioeconomic Data CIESIN

Tabular data from the Primary Census Abstract (PCA) and Village Directory (VD) for each village/town were downloaded from the online digital database of the Census of India for 1991, 2001 and 2011. The official published survey of India toposheets was utilized to finalize the vector data set for the village/town boundaries that correspond to the census data. It has been further validated with Center for International Earth Science Information Network (CIESIN) data of Columbia University.These data sets are combined with satellite-derived or meteorological data sets to better understand the spatial changes in various socio-economic characteristics of the Indian population. Thus, this data set will provide a useful social science application of GIS.

The data set can also be used to track socio-economic changes in the Indian population over the decades. For example, when combined with census data from other years e.g. 2011, this data set can also be used to identify spatial-temporal changes in different demographic categories, such as male, female, urban, rural, level of education, etc as has been proposed by Meiyappan et al. (2018).

STUDY AREA

The study area belongs to the central- western part of India, the district Nagaur of the desert state of Rajasthan (Fig. 1). Nagaur is located in the transitional zone (The Department of Agriculture, Govt. of Rajasthan). The encroachment of Thar Desert towards its eastern border has become a serious problem to these districts. A large number of population and animals of this region are at risk due to shifting of sand dunes, dust storms, and consequently decreasing agricultural productivity. This region gets rainfall during the onset of southwest monsoon which starts on the last week of June and lasts until mid-September. *The* study site as shown in Fig. 1 has marginal average annual rainfall which, ranges from 20 to 30 cm in Bikaner and about 30–40 cm in Nagaur, and neighboring district, Churu. The maximum daily temperature varies from 40 to 45 °C, whereas the minimum daily temperature ranges from 20 to 29 °C in this region. This region is covered by sandy soil with exposed bare rocks and sand dunes. Vegetation cover is very less, mainly composed of thorny scrubs, grasses, along with some xerophytes species like Babul, Khejri, *Accacia senegal*, *Prosopis spicigera*, and *Prosopis juliflora*.

METHODS OF ANALYSIS OF SATELLITE DATA

Procedure for Trans-Gotan is a systematic, theoretical analysis of the methods applied to the field of study, or in other words theoretical analysis of the body of methods and principles associated with a branch of knowledge. It, typically, encompasses concepts such as paradigm, theoretical model, quantitative and qualitative techniques.

Figure 1. Landsat Time series data of Gotan and surrounding Villages a. 27 Oct 1978, b. 3 Sept 1990, c. 12 April 1995, d. 21 April 2000, e. 10 Dec 2002, f. 13 Dec 2010, g. 27 Dec 2015, h. 22 March 2018

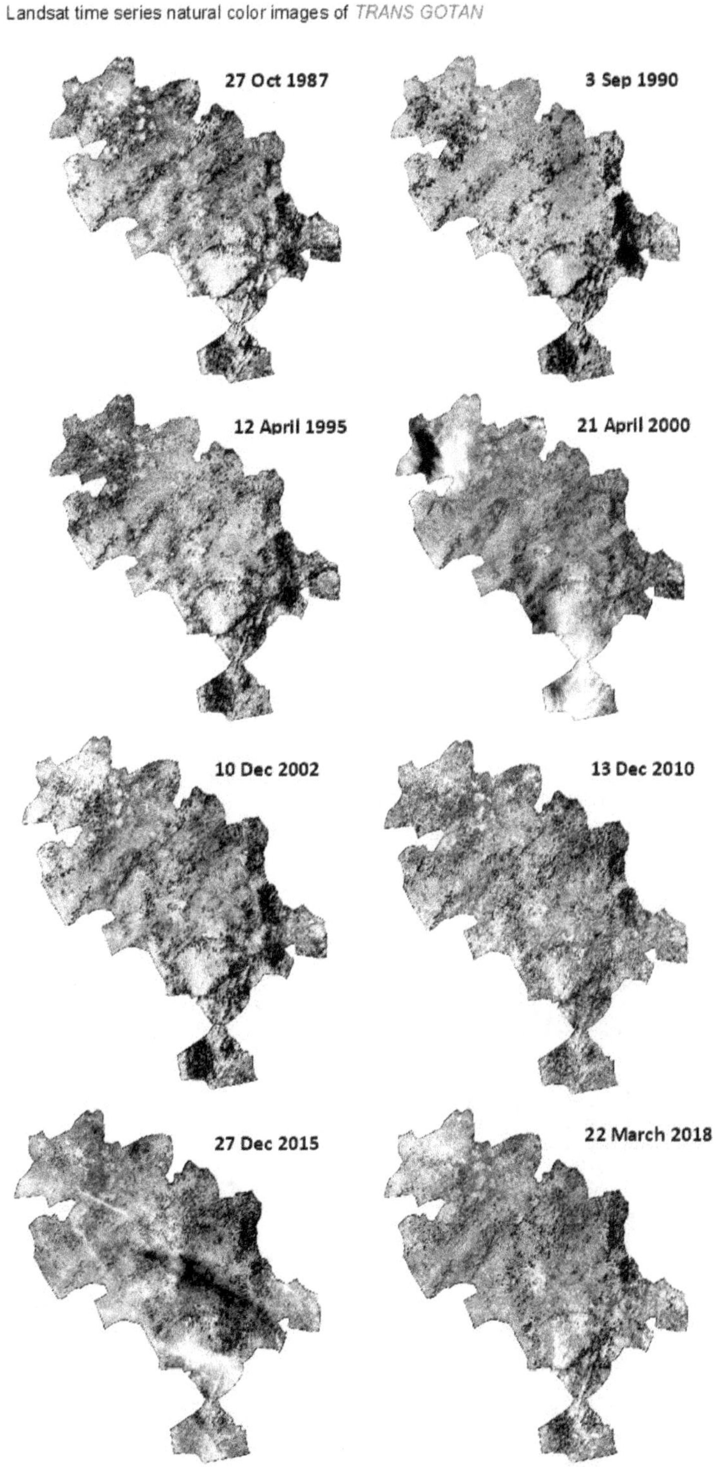

Figure 2. Selected villages for measuring transformation from CIESEN data in GIS

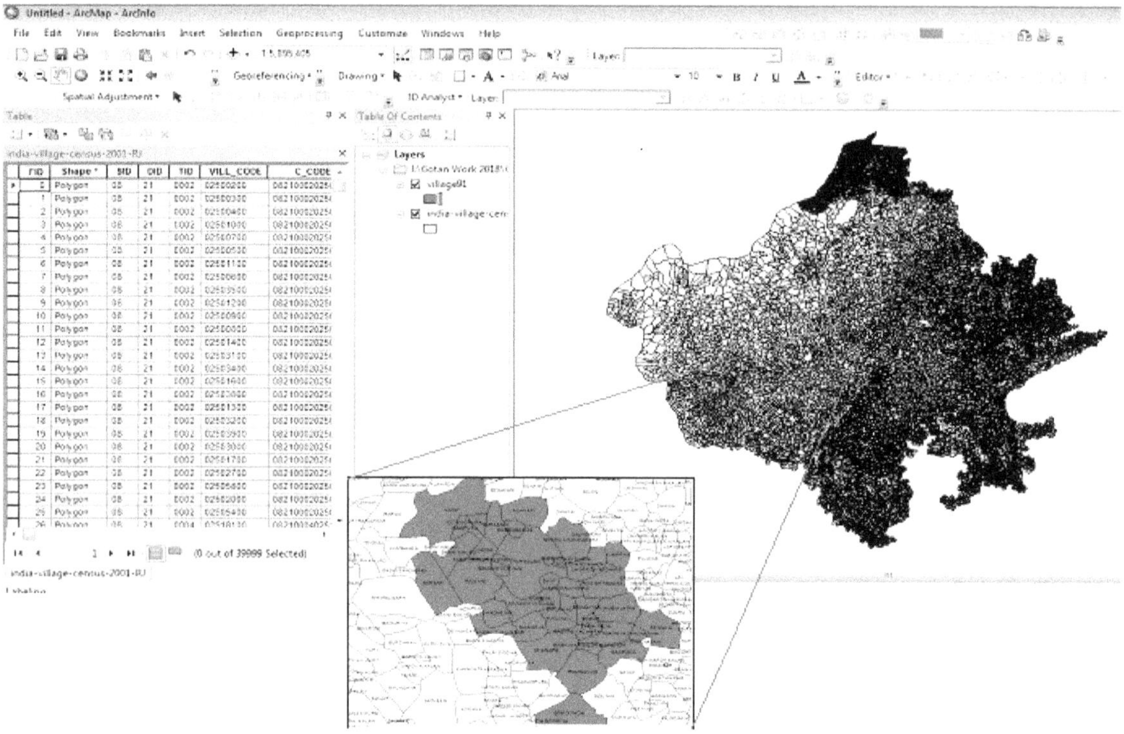

Figure 3. GIS Database generation and organization

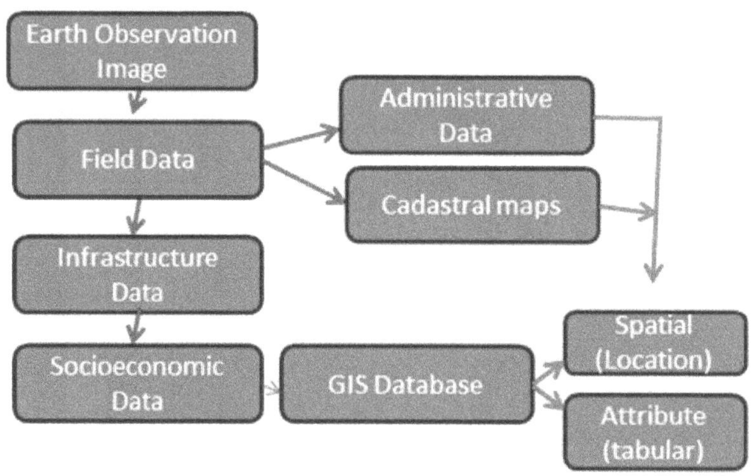

Figure 4. Flow chart showing methodology adopted for Trans-Gotan study under GIS domain

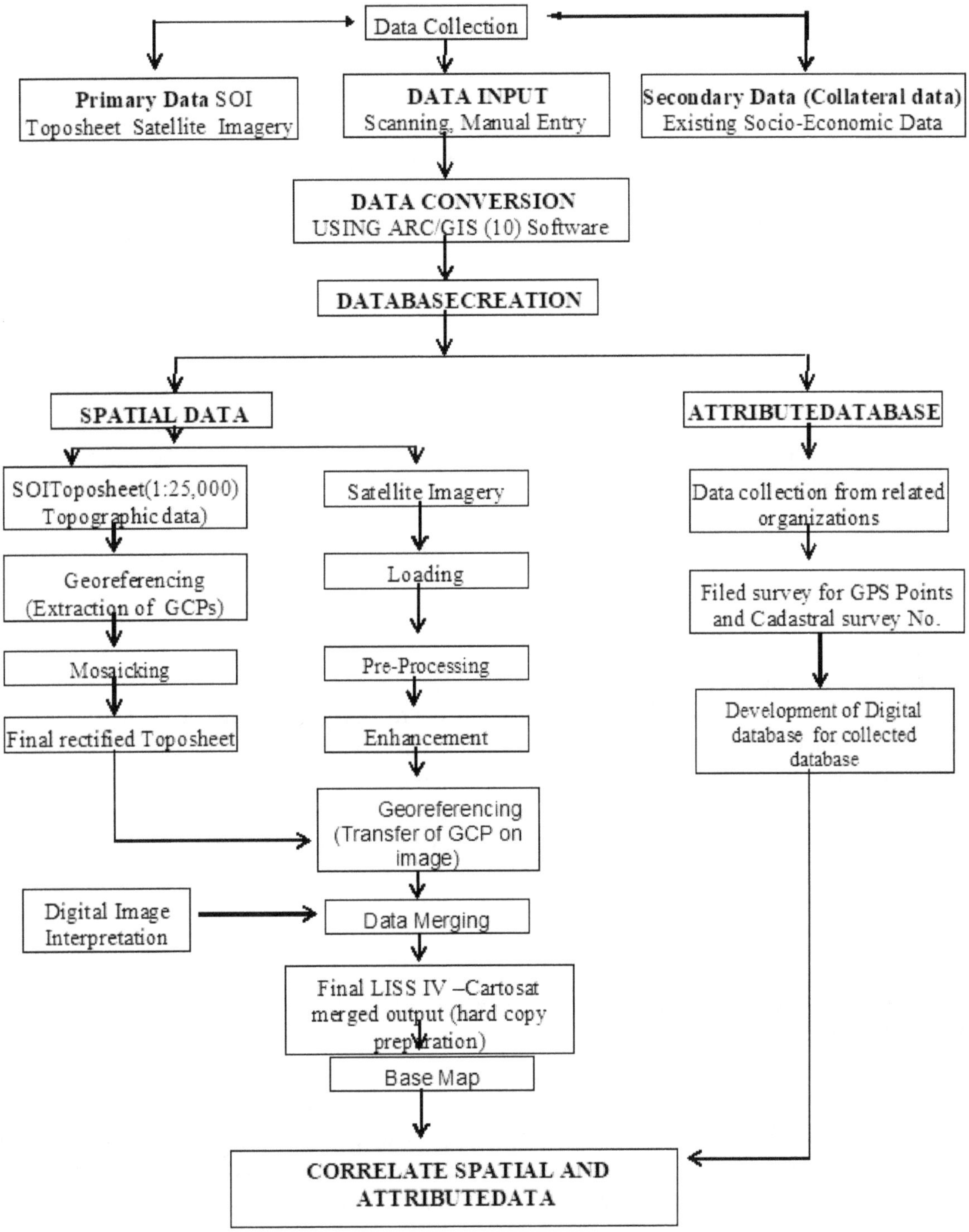

The Trans Gotan study is a micro level study covering an entire city. Therefore, the analysis is purely based on qualitative and quantitative data collected from different sources. Primary data are collected by field visit of villages and filling the qestionnaire of SDGs method. For that purpose detailed and comprehensive information is prepared and gathered and through interview from the villagers, government, non government offices. Secondary data are obtained from census handbook, district statistical department and socio- economic review of Nagaur district, through the literature available. Survey and field knowledge of present scenario have also been used to supplement the qualitative and quantitative analysis of the present study. The steps involved in transformation study of Gotan Trans in GIS domain have been displayed in the flow diagram.

In setting up a statistical GIS, attention must be given on hardware and software compatibility, standardization of data formats, spatial referencing conventions, and in the selection and definitions of spatial data themes and indicators which have been discussed by Lillesand and Kiefer (2002) and Meiyappan, et al. (2018) in their previous works. Practical steps include, for example, such basic requirements as standard classifications, common geographic codes and administrative structure as well as common file formats for data and maps. Since the source and type of data can be very heterogeneous, it is very important to store all relevant meta-information describing the series. This is necessary as one needs to know numerous aspects pertaining to data. This may include key code, definition of the variable, periodicity, unit of measure, universe covered, number of terms recorded, base year (for an index), adjustment applied, and so on. A minimum dataset of versatile indicators should consist of those variables that are useful for a wide range of applications, and are consistently available across space and time, and also whose characteristics are clearly defined.

The Normalized Difference Vegetation Index (NDVI) is a simple graphical indicator that can be used to analyze remote sensing measurements, typically, but not necessarily, from a space platform, and assess whether the target being observed contains live green vegetation or not.Interpreting NDVI values vary depending on the radiation absorption by chlorophyll in the red spectral reflectance in the near infrared region. These values are between -1 and +1, expressing consistency of green vegetation. The closer to 1 (light colors) is a high consistency of specific vegetation indicating towards hardwood. Values close to -1 (dark tones) are barren land, with soil or rock to date. A value of 0 (mid tones) is associated with lands meadows. NDVI is useful in areas with vegetation mapping, vegetation typology, health of vegetation and land use patterns. The method to quantify NDVI is shown by the mathematical representation as $NDVI = (NIR - R)/ (NIR + R) = (B5 - B4) / (B5 + B4)$.

PROCESS OF MAP SELECTION, MAPPING, VECTORIZATION AND SEGREGATION OF VILLAGES

GIS deals with three types of spatial objects: point, line and polygon. However, in most population-related activities, the information is collected at the point level (individual, household, house, community) and almost always aggregated to existing spatial entities (i.e. administrative units) to allow tabulations according to various data attributes. The spatial dimension of the information is being forgotten most of the time. Geography is only used to collect data(Bohnet, 1995; Clarke &Rhind, 1992).

Mapping is a process, which can be used to generate a series of outputs to be transferred into a Geographic Information System (GIS). Transferred information permits for various ways of processing, analyses, and presentation and can be easily updated according to the specific objective (Gerland, 1996).

The process of conducting participatory mapping contains several steps-preparatory work, fieldwork, data processing, feedback to and from stakeholder.

In the present study,segregation of villages at parcel level has been visualized for resource use in order to facilitate discussions without communication barriers and to motivate participants to reflect and discuss about land issues. Further, it has been done to allow a rapid identification of social, economic, and environmental problems of the village by determining and debating issues related to natural resource use with the active participation of the community. Common understanding among local land users and administrative authorities on spatial distribution and status of resources and resource use has also been established. Another aspect is to provide a basis for joint and demand-driven decision-making between different villages and between villages and state entities. Moreover, the aim is also to acquire accurate spatial data on a large scale on the basis of local knowledge and provide options for participatory impact monitoring for rural development investments from government and other donors. Last but not least, the study aims at mediating and solving prevailing boundary conflicts and to generate accurately scaled information on land use that can be officially approved for management purposes.

RESULT AND DISCUSSION

Trans-Gotan study is based on Geospatial Data Integration in relation to measuring the socio-economic study of the region. The data of four decades time series of Landsat NDVI has proved sufficient for deriving statistically significant trend values for 60% of transformation of Gotan i.e. Trans-Gotan surface. Areas showing positive and negative trends of NDVI, coincides with areas of land cover class change indicating an increase or a decrease in vegetation, respectively. Precipitation changes in the same time period seems to have had an influence on large NDVI trend areas. The NDVI time series trend analysis methodology was applied and it successfully detected changes due to deforestation, mining activities, urban expansion, and fallow land regeneration. These findings demonstrate that NDVI time series trend analysis is suitable for detecting vegetation change areas and for identifying land degradation and regeneration especially in case of Asop, Asawari villages in north and Dhanapa village in the west and Borunda in the south of Trans-Gotan.

Finally, NDVI product is used for agriculture expansion from dismal to numbers and spreading of urban sprawl with time and space. Time series trend analysis shows various procedures of vegetation changes. Increasing or decreasing trend of vegetation cover and bare soil fraction was mapped on a per pixel basis through the time trend analysis. The vegetation cover at the beginning of the study period was taken into consideration, as identical magnitudes of change have a dissimilar meaning depending on the particular base level. For the present study, Landsat TM/ETM+ satellite data (10-year interval) was used to extract the pure pixel of two major class, urban area and vegetation fraction area and other categories were mapped.Socio-economic phenomena are linked to people and their activities. Therefore, their distribution over space is often extremely uneven and heterogeneous.Trans-Gotan study has investigated the major transformation in terms of agriculture, urban sprawl, and land use/land cover in past 4 decades. In this regard, we have critically analyzed the satellite data of time series.

Figure 5. NDVI time series trend of Transformation of Gotan region a. 1987, b. 1990, c. 1995, d. 2000, e. 2002, f. 2010, g. 2015, h. 2018

Land Use/Land Cover of Trans-Gotan Region

The desert is undergoing land transformation mainly due to better management, irrigation facilities and mining/industrial activities. Land use/land coverto derive Level-I classification using multi-temporal Landsat TM datasets was taken into consideration for the present study.Land cover relates to the bio-physical cover of the earth's terrestrial surface, identifying vegetation, inland water, bare soil or human infrastructure. Distinct land cover types provide specific habitats and determine the exchange of energy and carbon between terrestrial and atmospheric regions (Colditz et al. 2011). Biophysical processes occurring on the land surface have an impact on the climate system and also on habitat diversity and the capacity of ecosystems to support human needs. As discussed by Gomez et al. (2016), land cover, recognized as an essential climate variable, is the most important element for description and study of the environment and is a key input to models of ecosystem services.

Table 3.Landuse classes in time series in terms of area in sq km

Class Name	1987	1990	1995	2000	2002	2010	2015	2018
Open Land	99.63	94.54	91.92	87.19	87.19	80.71	79.03	78.69
Water Body	0.97	0.97	0.97	0.97	0.97	0.97	0.97	0.97
Forest Land	9.27	11.10	14.17	12.90	13.70	13.99	14.21	14.70
Build up Land	21.13	26.22	29.53	34.40	34.40	41.68	44.55	45.02
Agriculture Land	847.28	847.28	846.60	846.55	846.55	845.74	844.56	844.42

Table 4. Statistics of vegetation and urban area in time series

Area in sqkm derived from Landsat time series data								
	1987	**1990**	**1995**	**2000**	**2002**	**2010**	**2015**	**2018**
Vegetation	9.27	11.10	14.17	12.90	13.70	13.99	14.21	14.70
Urban Area	21.13	26.22	29.53	34.40	34.40	41.68	44.55	45.02

The Geospatial technique enables us to study dynamics, particularly in desert area using remote sensing (RS), geographic information system (GIS) and global positioning system (GPS) (Meiyappan et al. 2018). Remote sensing is being used to obtain quicker and higher quality information about natural resources.

Data from Landsat satellites are often used to create information products like the one shown in Table 4. This land-cover classification layer displays land cover information for all areas in the region. Trans Gotan land cover changes are related to life transformation including natural processes like anthropogenic activities (e.g., urbanization, agriculture). Time series land cover information has proved valuable to aid in formulation of socio-economic level and data provision for environmental applications (e.g., vulnerability and risk assessment), which is directly related to the sustainable development of the region. The rate of change and the nature of land cover transition differ in time and space. Some regions are relatively stable (e.g., permanent vegetation); whereas, other areas are subject to rapid and persistent transformation (e.g., urban expansion of previously vegetated areas). Increased human population and technological development have been found to accelerate land cover changes. Assessing the location, extent, type, and frequency of land cover transitions, as well as identifying spatial and temporal patterns of change through interpretation and analysis of frequent land cover maps, most certainly provide insights into underlying processes and drivers of change.

Figure 6. Landuse/land cover map of study area of different time period a. 1987, b. 1990, c. 1995, d. 2000, e. 2002, f. 2010, g. 2015, h. 2018

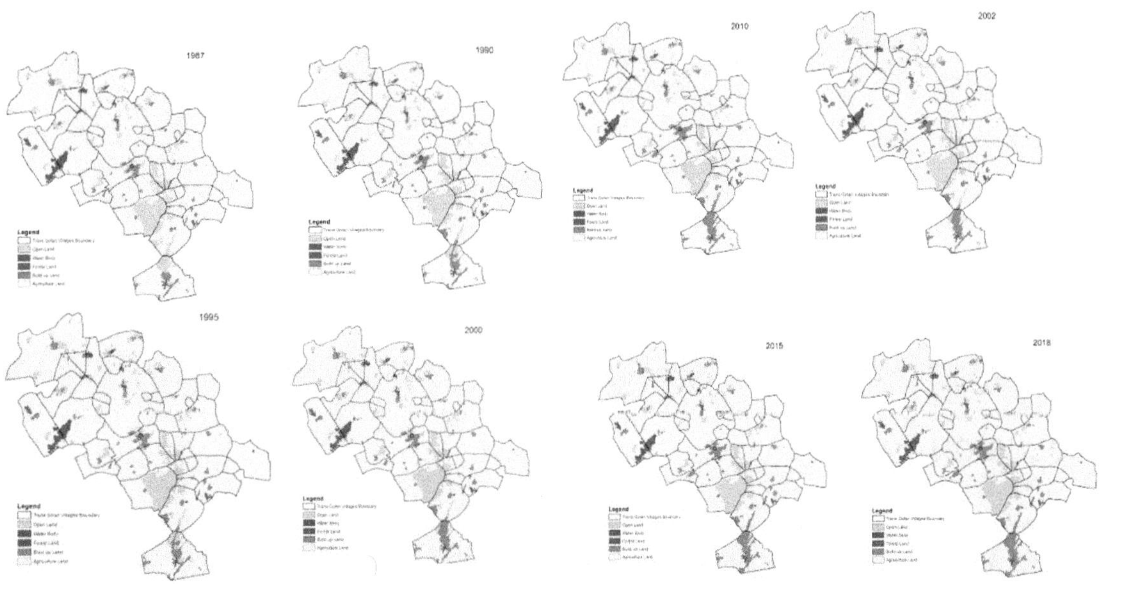

URBAN BUILT UP AREA

Urban built-up area is defined as land characterized by buildings, asphalt, concrete, suburban gardens, and a systematic street pattern. It also includes the area under residential, commercial, industrial, transportation, communications, all places with a municipality, corporation, cantonment board or notified town area committee, etc. according to NRSA (1991).All other places that satisfy the following criteria: i) a minimum population of 5,000; ii) at least 75 per cent of the male main working population engaged in non-agricultural pursuits; and iii) a density of population of at least 400 persons per sq. km. are therefore included in urban built up area category (Census of India, 2011).

A series of meticulously analyzed satellite images showcase the gradual increase of urban sprawl in the cluster of 29 villages. Beginning from about 21 to 26 sq.km in 1980s, the transformation of the built-up area has gradually risen to over 45 sq.km in 2018. This remarkable change is a visual summary of growing prosperity and bettering habitat conditions in the Gotan region.

Figure 7. Urban sprawl map of study area for different time period a. 1987, b. 1990, c. 1995, d. 2000, e. 2002, f. 2010, g. 2015, h. 2018

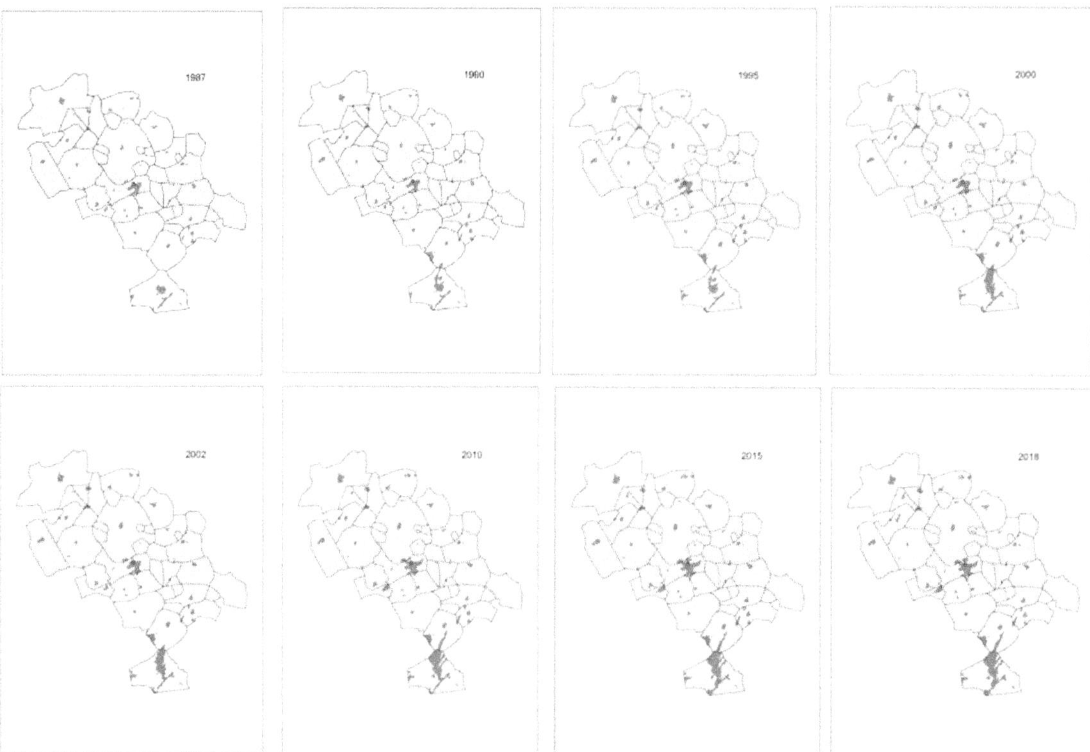

CONCLUSION

Over the past 30 years, a considerable effort towards sustainable development in Trans-Gotan region has been made. Actions and multiple approaches have been applied to sustainable development to eliminate poverty, hunger, and improve health, promoting awareness on sanitation and bringing equality etc., especially after the SDGs were commenced. However, people appear to live in a less sustainable world, far away from the society of advanced technology. Today, because of increasing population and consumption, loss in biodiversity, reduction in forest area, pollution of air and water,it cannot be denied that the world is in great danger. Nonetheless the other factors posing problems are spread of diseases, threat of terrorism, extreme climate conditions, hydrological events and depletion of the stratospheric ozone layer. The Trans-Gotan study has focused on understanding socio-economic condition of the region to articulate the method of implementation of sustainable development goals undertaken by the United Nations.

The research strategy employs statistical analysis of a cluster of 29 villages using GIS data. These include remote sensing data on land cover and Geo-referenced socio-economic data from censuses and household surveys. Future work will look at other aspects of land use, change and urban growth. The socio-economic parameters are being taken as one of the major inputs to measure the real change of Trans-Gotan region.For this, village wise summary of sustainable development and gaps have been analysed under self-defined scaling system, which is based on socioeconomic indicators. In this regard, 16 variables have been taken in which 6 are broad indicators, like literacy of total population, education facilities, health services, water resources, work participation and basic amenities. All the 16 variables have been clumped in broad indicators that have been further measured village wise.

GIS and mapping technologies offer a unique opportunity to address the problems scientifically which were earlier traditionally associated with data collection, validity and management. GIS enables information from one sector (such as health and sanitation) in providing a comprehensive picture of the situation in any given community or a district to another level i.e. region or a country. By this way, it facilitates the setting of priorities for control and surveillance activities, the rationalization of the use of scarce resources and effective district level planning. The framework also provides a link between micro and macro aspects of sustainable development goals through appropriate indicators.

Trans-Gotan study has investigated the major transformation in terms of agriculture, urban sprawl, and land use/land cover in the past four decades. In this regard, we have critically analyzed the satellite data of time series. Finally, NDVI product for agriculture expansion from dismal to numbers and spread of urban area sprawl with time and space was understood both quantitatively and qualitatively.

Physical transformation has been measured in terms of agricultural and urban sprawl in the region, and it was found that agricultural production was at its lowest rate since decades. In an expansion of the clusters of 29 villages, agriculture was reasonably flourishing in only 9.27 sq km, making the establishment of the industry and its ancillary businesses a timely vision. The transformation has doubled in terms of built up area forthe last three decades. This remarkable change is a visual summary of growing prosperity and a way towards bettering habitat conditions in the Gotan region.

REFERENCES

Bohnet, D. (1995). Integration of Socio-economic data into GIS - a case study of the CRDA Bizerte, GTZ, Bonn, F.R. Germany. Paper presented in AfricaGIS'95. UNITAR / CNTGI / OSS / UNSO.

Census of India. (2011). *Provisional Population totals.* Urban Agglomerations and Cities.

Clarke, J., & Rhind, D. W. (1992). *A Review of Spatial Population Database Design and Modeling. Population Data and Global Environmental Change. Paper prepared for the UNEP/GRID and CGIAR, NCGIA*. Asia Population Database Documentation.

Deichmann, U. (1996). *Technical paper and digital database*. NCGIA.

Colditz, R. R., Schmidt, M., Conrad, C., Hansen, M. C., & Dech, S. (2011). Land cover classification with coarse spatial resolution data to derive continuous and discrete maps for complex regions. *Remote Sensing of Environment*, *115*(12), 3264–3275. doi:10.1016/j.rse.2011.07.010

Gerland, P. (1996). *Socio-economic data and GIS: Datasets, databases, indicators and data integration issues*. UNEP/ CGIAR Arendal III Workshop on the Use of GIS in Agricultural Research Management.

Gómez, C., White, J. C., & Wulder, M. A. (2016). Optical remotely sensed time series data for land cover classification: A review. *ISPRS Journal of Photogrammetry and Remote Sensing*, *116*, 55–72. doi:10.1016/j.isprsjprs.2016.03.008

Lillesand, T.M., & Kiefer, R.W. (2002). *Remote Sensing and Image Interpretation*. John Wiley & Sons, Inc.

Meiyappan, P., Roy, P. S., Soliman, A., Li, T., Mondal, P., Wang, S., & Jain, A. K. (2018). India Village-Level Geospatial Socio-Economic Data Set: 1991, 2001. Palisades, NY: NASA Socioeconomic Data and Applications Center (SEDAC). doi:10.7927/H4CN71ZJ

NRSA. (1991). *Manual of Nationwide Land use Land Cover Mapping using digital techniques*. NRSA.

Roy, D. P., Wulder, M. A., & Loveland, T. R. (2014). Landsat-8: Science and product vision for terrestrial global change research. *Remote Sensing of Environment*, *145*, 154–172. doi:10.1016/j.rse.2014.02.001

Wunder, S. (2001). Poverty alleviation and tropical forests-what scope for synergies? *World Devopment*, *29*(11), 1817-1833.

Chapter 7
Google Earth Engine-Based Visual/Qualitative Investigation on Urbanization:
Quick Urban Sprawl Visualization in Beijing, China

Muhammad Ashar Ayub
University of Agriculture Faisalabad, Pakistan

Zia Ur Rahman Farooqi
https://orcid.org/0000-0003-2398-1895
Institute of Soil and Environmental Sciences, University of Agriculture Faisalabad, Pakistan

Wajid Umar
Szent Istvan University, Gödöllő, Hungary

Muhammad Nadeem
Institute of Soil and Environmental Sciences, University of Agriculture Faisalabad, Pakistan

Tasawar Ali
Institute of Soil and Environmental Sciences, University of Agriculture Faisalabad, Pakistan

Hina Fatima
School of Applied Biosciences, Kyungpook National University, South Korea

Zahoor Ahmad
Department of Field Crops, Faculty of Agriculture, University of Cukurova, Adana, Turkey

Muhammad Naveed Arshad
Aberystwyth University, UK

ABSTRACT

An increase in the global population has led to a net shift of the global community to move towards cities from per-urban and village areas due to various reasons. This population pressure has made a net expansion of cities over time making urban-periurban fringe quite non-distinguishable in past decades. Especially in developing countries, these cities' expansion is often done on agricultural lands resulting in fast depletion of the most important natural resource responsible for feeding the globe. Google Earth Engine is an open access multi-functional remote sensing platform that can be effectively used to monitor urban sprawls. In this chapter, after a brief introduction of urbanization, google earth engine-based investigation is presented to visualize urban sprawl patterns in Beijing China. Visual presentation and

DOI: 10.4018/978-1-7998-4372-6.ch007

high spatial resolution of google earth engine have proven to be very beneficial in this regard and the author strongly recommends using it for quick multi temporal urbanization study.

INTRODUCTION

a. Introduction to Urbanization

What urbanization stands for? Generally, it is defined as the locomotion of the population from rural areas to urban areas (Hussain & Imitiyaz, 2018). However, the definition of urbanization is still controversial since it is varied concerning the country under discussion. For instance, in the case of Argentina if an area has inhabitants ^{3} 2000 it is referred to as "urban". However, in Sweden if inhabitants are ^{3} 200 and houses in that specific area are 200m apart it is called an urban area. In Japan to be denoted as an "urban" that area should fulfill three conditions (1) it should contain ^{3} 50,000 residents (2) ^{3} 60% of the houses should be in core built-up area (3) ^{3} 60% of the area's population should be involved in the urban-type of businesses. On the other hand, in the case of India urban areas should contain (1) residents ^{3} 5000 (2) 75% of the male workers should be involved in pursuits other than agriculture (3) minimum 400 residents per square km (Ritchie & Roser, 2020).

In 2018 a report published by The United Nations about the world's urbanization prospects collected the data of 233 countries including their urban and rural population. Some of the key facts mentioned by this report were as follows (1) worldwide more people dwell in urban areas compared to rural areas (2) >55% people were residing in urban areas in 2018, this figure was 30% in 1950 and is expected to increase up to 68% in 2050 (3) in 1950 the urban population was 751 million which increased dramatically and turned into 4.2 billion in 2018 (4) in 2018 the most urbanized regions of the world were North America, Latin America & Caribbean, Europe, Oceania, Asia and Africa with a population of 82%, 81%, 74%, 68%, 50%, and 43% respectively. Conversely, since 1950 a slower growth trend was observed in the world's rural population which was 3.4 billion in 2018 and it is expected to decrease to approximately 3.1 billion in the year 2050 (United Nations, 2018).

b. Urban Extent Worldwide

In 2018 data for the degree of urbanization was comprehensively compiled in the form of a report by the United Nations department of economic and social affairs, population division. In this report data of 233 countries/areas were assembled from 1950 until the present even anticipated future trends up to the year 2050. The World's urbanized areas are increasing with time. For instance, in 1950 only 3 countries (Singapore, Macao & Belgium) out of 201 countries had an urban population ^{3} 90%. By 2018 this figure increased to 20 countries/areas having > 90% urban inhabitants including China, Kuwait, Singapore, Hong Kong, Réunion, Qatar, Guadeloupe, Belgium, United States Virgin Island, Uruguay, Guam, Malta, Iceland, Puerto Rico, Israel, Argentina, Japan, Netherland, Luxembourg, and Jordan. However, in 2050 more than 42 countries/areas are anticipated to have > 90% of their population in urban areas with Kuwait leading the list (United Nations, 2019). Migration to the metropolitan areas happened very recently, according to UN estimates more people migrated from rural to urban areas in the year 2007(Ritchie & Roser, 2020). Nevertheless, by careful observation of urbanization statics, it was found that 90% of the global population used to live in the rural areas until 1800 however from

1900 urbanization increased gradually with the United States at top of the list with 40% of its population living in urban areas followed by India and China with 10% and 7% respectively. In 1950 US urban share reached 64% followed by Japan, India, and China with 53%, 17%, and 11% respectively. However, in 2001 Japan Overtook United states with 80% of urban share followed by China and India with 37% and 27% respectively. Until 2016 Japan remained at the top with 91.30% urban inhabitants placing the United States, China, and India on 2nd, $3^{rd,}$ and 4th rank (Kuroda, 1990; Bairoch, 1991; Forstall, 1996; Ritchie & Roser, 2020). Nevertheless in 2018 China with 837 million urban inhabitants headed the list followed by India and the United States (United Nations, 2019).

c. Increase in Urban Population Worldwide

Since there is no present international standard to set a boundary line for an area to be referred to as "city". Currently, there are three terms "city proper" "urban agglomerations" and "metropolitan area" each having its respective definition. Globally size and population of cities are growing dramatically. In 2018 United Nations presented a report about the increasing population of the world's cities from 1950-2030. According to this report by 2000 cities with ^{3} 1 million dwellers were 371 which increased to 548 in the year 2018. Further, in 2030 this number is projected to reach 706 cities with ^{3} 1 million dwellers. A city with ^{3} 10 million populations is generally termed as "megacity". In 2018 there were 33 megacities worldwide. This number is anticipated to reach 43 by the year 2030. Moreover, in 2018 there were 48 cities with a population between 5 to 10 million inhabitants. 10 out of these 48 cities are foretold to become megacities and 66 cities are going to have a population between 5 and 10 million by 2030 (United Nations, 2018).

A city with a population of> 20 million can be termed as "meta" or "hyper" city. For instance, in 2018 twenty countries were reported to have 33 urban agglomerations with ^{3} 10 million inhabitants. In 2018 Tokyo is the world's most populated city had a population of 37 million, followed by Delhi, Shanghai, São Paulo & Mexico City, and Cairo with 29 million, 26 million, 22 million, and 22 million population respectively (United Nations, 2019). However, some cities also exhibited a decline in population growth. Since 2000 most of the countries with stagnant or decelerating populations were from Asia and Europe. From 2000-2018 a population decline was observed in Nagasaki (Japan) and Busan (Republic of Korea). Nevertheless, several cities of Europe *i.e.,* Bucharest, La Habana, and Riga also suffered from population decline. This population loss was owing to less fertility, emigration, a shift in the political regimes and economic policies (United Nations, 2018, 2019).

d. Effects of Urbanization

Impacts of urbanization are diverse, it not only influences the environment (water quality, habitat fragmentation & food wastes) but also has health and social effects (nutrition, asthma, crime, and mental health). In 2017 Wang and Zhao conducted a study to identify the effect of urbanization on CO_2 emission. They found that improvement in the standards of living and technology significantly increased the CO_2 emission (Wang & Zhao 2018; Liu & Bae, 2018). In the same year, an Australian study unveiled the combined effect of urbanization and climate change on the urban temperature. It was found that the increase in the urban population had a significant effect on heat islands and urban temperature which was recorded 5°C in some cities (Chapman et al., 2017). Another study revealed the combined effect of urbanization and climate change on surface water quality. The study unveiled that the effect of climate change and urbanization in combination were responsible for deteriorating the quality of surface water owing to the doubled release of phosphorus from the combined sewer overflows (Franco et al., 2018; Luo et al., 2018). A review paper by Gruebner and coworkers comprehensively discussed the pros and cons of urban life. For example, it was reported that people living in urban areas are more prone to severe mental illness compared to people living in rural areas. It might be owing to traffic, noise, and an unhealthy environment. In contrast, cities offer better health, employment, and education facilities. A proper balance of both harmful and beneficial factors would help reduce the hazards of mental illness (Gruebner et al., 2017; Hotez, 2017; Qing, 2018). Also, the effects of urbanization on biodiversity are well known. Urbanization can lead to the division of habitat, isolating the species from their original environment. This change can affect the survival and sustenance of the respective species. Appropriate management can avoid the habitat fragmentation conserving biodiversity (Liu et al., 2016; Guetté et al., 2017).

BRIEF HISTORY OF GOOGLE EARTH ENGINE

Google Erath Engine (GEE) was introduced by Google in December 2010 (U.S. Geological Survey, 2010). Changes to the earth's surface over time can be analyzed by using the image data from the previous 40 years or more available online due to this geospatial analysis platform (Houseman et al., 2010). Presence of millions of servers of GEE all over the world makes it possible for the scientist to analyze the huge number of images at a time (Dong et al., 2016). The GEE is a web portal that allows the cloud-based computing, algorithm, and software access to process the data (Gorelick et al., 2017). The data is available from several satellites like Land sate series, National Oceanographic and Atmospheric Administration Advanced very high-resolution radiometer (NOAA AVHRR), Moderate Resolution Imaging Spectrometer (MODIS. Advanced Land Observing Satellite (ALOS), Sentinel 1, 2 and 3, etc. Initially, the GEE setup only consists of remote sensing data, but after that layers of climate and weather data, social demographic, Huge amount of vector, and digital elevation models have been added (Moore & Parsons, 2011). Images from GEE can be exported in the TFRecord format of GeoTIFF. Data from GEE can be transferred to Google cloud storage or Google drive account easily.

USES OF GOOGLE EARTH ENGINE

GEE can be used in research projects in different ways like vegetation mapping and monitoring, Land cover mapping, Agricultural applications, and for disaster management and in earth sciences.

a. Vegetation Mapping and Monitoring

Several articles explain the use of GEE for mapping and monitoring of vegetation. This includes the estimation of the absorption of photosynthetically active radiations, the Leaf area index, vegetation cover fraction, and the water contents of the canopy by using the historical data from MODIS (Campos-Taberner et al., 2018). In Vietnam vegetation was mapped by web-based GEE application using EVI products derived from MODIS at planetary scale (Poortinga et al., 2018). Rangeland monitoring was also carried out by using historical land sat data in an environment of cloud computing. In Brazil 17 pastureland maps were produced with an accuracy of 80% by using 2000-2016 data from MODIS (Parente & Ferreira, 2018). An increase in the pasture area was observed in most of the mapped areas.

b. Land Cover Mapping

Several researchers assessed the change in land cover by using GEE. GEE provides access to advanced analytical techniques and advanced data. Lee et al. (2018) fused the data from Landsat with globe cover, 2009 by using Bayesian Updating of Land Cover (BULC) algorithm, which improved the spatial resolution from 300 m to 30 m in Brazil. The GEE is also used to analyze the effect of the land cover change on urban heat island by using the long-term temperature data from the climate tool engine (Ravanelli et al., 2018). Apart from land sat data, data from Sentinel 1 and 2 was also used for the mapping of wetland extent in Newfoundland Canada at the provincial scale (Mahdianpari et al., 2019). In that study, GEE based advanced machine learning algorithms and computational power were used.

c. Agricultural Applications

Remote sensing applications in agriculture like mapping of crop area, assessment of suitability, pest and disease vulnerability, and estimation of crop yield among others are important in enhancing productivity and food security. GEE can be used at varying scales for agricultural applications. (He et al., 2018) fused the Landsat and Terra MODIS data to evaluate the productivity of 7 crops in Montana, the USA at a spatial resolution of 30m from 2008-2015. High spatial resolution data from World View 2 was also used to estimate the cropland area in the South African environment of Mali (Aguilar et al., 2018).

d. Disaster Management and Earth Sciences

The studies which address the disaster exposure, extent, and response and the studies related to earth sciences were carried out by using the GEE platform. A Snow cloud hydro model was developed by using MOD10A1 applicable in the USA, Spain, and Chile in different environments (Sproles et al., 2018). That model mapped the areas covered with snow and used to forecast the streamflow during snowfall. For disasters, (Liu et al., 2018) developed a system by using the GEE platform to respond and prevention of flood. By using soil moisture as an indicator, GEE can be used to analyze the moisture stress globally (Sazib et al., 2018).

Other applications in this regard included mapping of mining area using Sentinel data (Lobo et al., 2018), cloud masking (Mateo-García et al., 2018), monitoring of surface sediments (Markert et al., 2018).

Table 1. Uses of Google Earth Engine in different sectors

No.	GE/GE based tools	Uses	References
1	GEE, Landsat series	Land surface temperature estimation	Ermida et al. (2020)
2	GEE	Response evaluation of seasonal indicators to drought stress	Lai et al. (2020)
3	GEE, Sentinel 1 and 2	Wetland mapping	Mahdianpari et al. (2019)
4	GEE	Impact of land cover change on urban heat island	Ravanelli et al. (2018)
5	GEE, BULC-U	Land use/land cover classification	Lee et al. (2018)
6	GEE	Disaster management	Liu et al. (2018)
7	GEE	Streamflow forecasting in snowfall areas	Sproles et al. (2018)
8	GEE	Draught assessment	Sazib et al. (2018)
9	GEE, Sentinel-2	Monitoring and mapping of seagrass	Traganos et al. (2018)
10	GEE, Sentinel-2/MSI	Mapping of mining areas	Lobo et al. (2018)
11	GEE	Biophysical variable estimation	Campos-Teberner et al. (2018)
12	GEE	Cloud masking	Mateo-García et al. (2018)
13	GEE	Land use and vegetation mapping	Tsai et al. (2018)
14	GEE, Landsat	Surface Sediment monitoring	Markert et al. (2018)
15	GEE	Fire severity Metrix	Parks et al. (2018)
16	GEE, Sentinel-2	Satellite-derived bathymetry estimation	Traganos et al. (2018)
17	GEE	Planetary scale vegetation monitoring	Poortinga et al. (2018)
18	GEE	Mapping of the smallholder farming system	Aguilar et al. (2018)
19	GEE, MODIS	Spatial assessment of the dynamics of the Brazilian pasture lands	Parente and Ferreira, (2018)
20	GEE, Landsat-MODIS	Yield estimation and crop productivity	He et al. (2018)
21	GEE	Ecosystem assessment	Goldblatt et al. (2017)
22	GEE, Landsat-8, Sentinel-2	Mapping the extent of cropland	Xiong et al. (2017)
23	GEE	Derivation of NDVI product	Robinson et al. (2017)

ANALYSIS OF IMAGERY FOR URBAN AREA EXTRACTION OF BEIJING, CHINA

A wide number of research publications has reported a surge in urbanization in various metropolitans of the world (Hassan, & Southworth, 2018; Shakrullah et al., 2015; Mahboob et al., 2015; Zhang et al., 2016). Though remote sensing-based observations are very much quantitative Realtime and instant visualization of urban sprawl important for authorities and residents to track built up in surroundings. Google earth engine-based observations in this regard are very helpful and needed.

METHODOLOGY

Study Area

Beijing (39^{0}55’N 116^{0}23’E), the capital of China, is the 3rd most populated city of the world and the world’s most populous capital city. It was established in 1045 BC. It covers the total municipality area of 16410 km^2 in which urban areas cover 4144 km^2. Its urban population exceeds 21 million in 2018. It is the 2nd largest city in China after Shanghai in terms of the urban population. Beijing was established in 1045 BC. It is the hub of culture, business, science, language, politics, and economy. The climate of Beijing is characterized by humid, hot summers and windy, dry, cold winters with mean annual precipitation of 570 mm and monthly min. mean temperature in January -3.7^{0}C and max. in July i.e. 26.2^{0}C. Rapid urbanization in previous decades has caused manifold anthropogenic emissions due to which air quality and atmospheric conditions of the city are compromised. Being the capital city of China, Beijing has always been a magnet towards the working community making it a dream destination for all. The past 30 years account for the extraordinary economic growth of China which has triggered extensive urbanization in Beijing.

Remote Sensing Data Source

To access urban built up, multispectral and multitemporal Landsat 7 imagery was used from 2000 to 2018. Second last of Landsat series, Landsat 7 has enhanced thematic mapper (ETM) sensor, and various descriptions regarding it are given in Figure 1. Landsat cloud-free and clear imagery for each year were selected for classification purposes with one composite image for each year.

Figure 1. Characteristics of Landsat 7 (Source: https://www.usgs.gov/media/images/landsat-7-band-designations)

	Landsat 7	Wavelength (micrometers)	Resolution (meters)
Enhanced Thematic Mapper Plus (ETM+)	Band 1	0.45-0.52	30
	Band 2	0.52-0.60	30
	Band 3	0.63-0.69	30
	Band 4	0.77-0.90	30
	Band 5	1.55-1.75	30
	Band 6	10.40-12.50	60 * (30)
	Band 7	2.09-2.35	30
	Band 8	.52-.90	15

Figure 2. Basic Layout of Google Earth Engine window

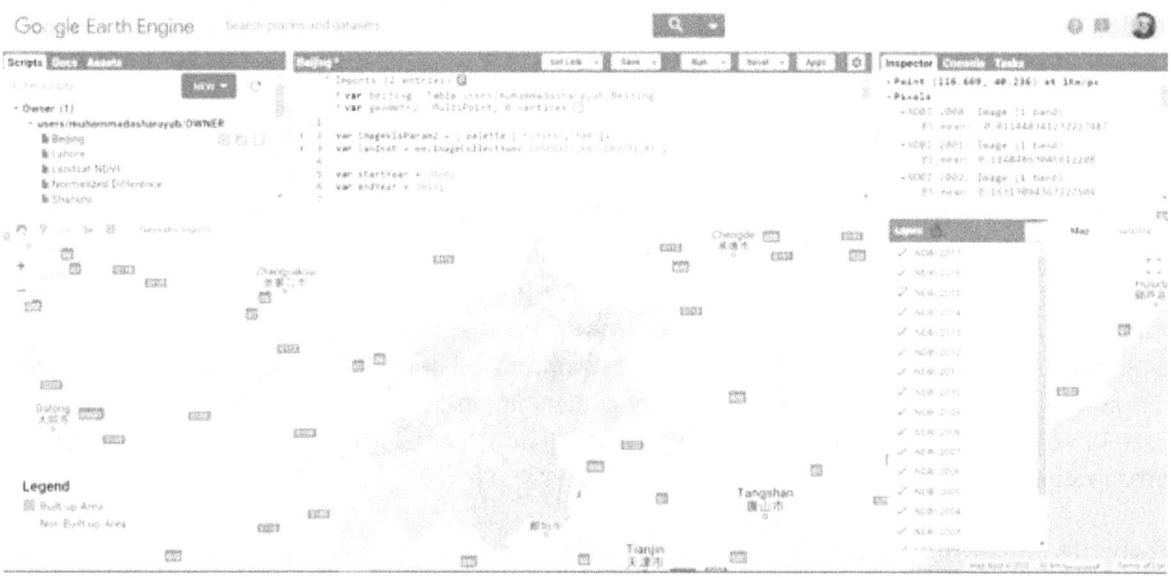

Urbanization Detection Using Google Earth Engine

Google earth engine is a coding-based plate form where remote sensing (satellite remote sensing) data sets are available to be used for free Figure 2. Earth engine coder was used to write a code for the quantitative determination of Normalize Difference Built-Up index (equation 1) using Landsat 7 whose value range between -1 to 1 with 0-1 being built-up area while 0 to -1 was designated as non-built-up.

$$\text{Normalized difference Built-Up Index}=\frac{SWIR-NIR}{SWIR+NIR}$$

Where, SWIR=Short Wave Infra-Red Band and NIR=Near Infra-Red Band

Below mentioned is the code used for the determination of NDBI.

The basic mechanism of Urbanization detection was as shown in Figure 3 and the code for google earth engine is presented in Figure 4.

Figure 3. Basic Layout for urbanization de-linting using Google Earth Engine

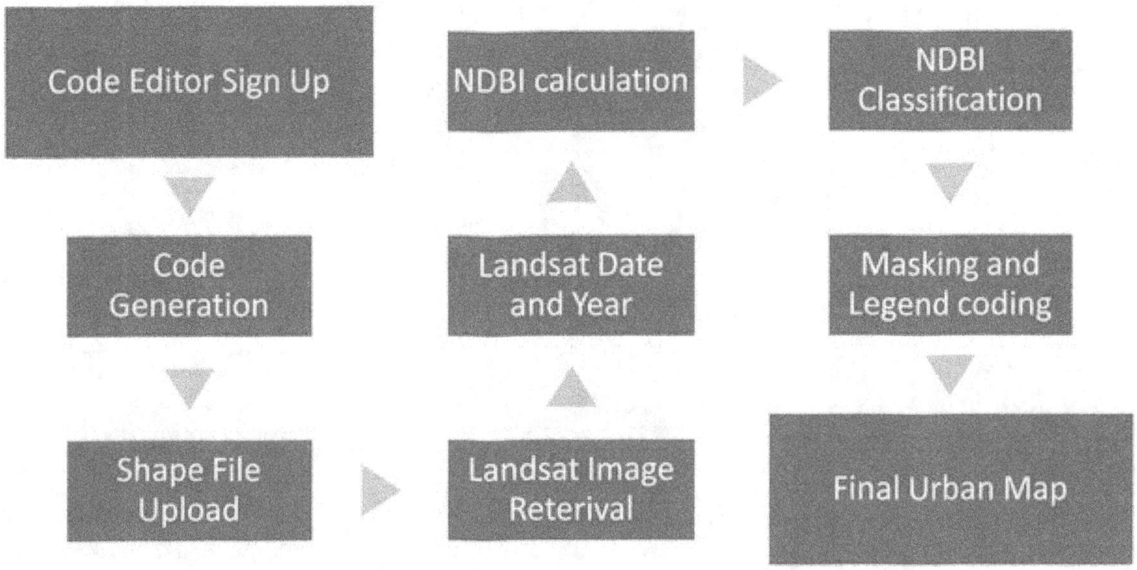

SUMMARIZATION OF RESULTS

Visual Interpretation of urban sprawl using the google earth engine is quite easy and evident. The classified urban sprawl in Beijing city can be seen in Figure 5. Furthermore, license-free platforms like GOOGLE EARTH ENGINE should be used by policymakers worldwide to plan better for urban growth in the coming years.

Figure 4. Google Earth Engine code for urbanization detection in Beijing from 2000-2017

```
var imageVisParam2 = { palette:["f6f4f4","f00"]}
var landsat =
ee.ImageCollection('LANDSAT/LE07/C01/T1_RT')
var startYear = 2000;
var endYear = 2018;
var startDate=ee.Date.fromYMD(startYear,01,01);
var endDate=ee.Date.fromYMD(endYear+1,12,31);
//SDA
var StudyArea = beijing;
//ANALYSIS: Annual Averages
var year_list = ee.List.sequence(startYear, endYear);
//LANDSAT filter based on date and study area
var collection = landsat.filterBounds(StudyArea)
            .filter(ee.Filter.lt('CLOUD_COVER',10));
print(collection);
var NDBI_collection =
ee.ImageCollection.fromImages(year_list.map(function
(ynz)
{
 var img = collection.filter(ee.Filter.calendarRange(ynz,
ynz, 'year'))
        .mean()
       var ndbi = img.expression(
 "(SWIR-NIR)/(SWIR+NIR)",
 {'SWIR': img.select('B5'),
 'NIR': img.select('B4')});
        return ndbi.set('year', ynz)
        .set('month', 1)
        .set('date', ee.Date.fromYMD(ynz,1,1))

.set('system:time_start',ee.Date.fromYMD(ynz,1,1));
}).flatten());
print(NDBI_collection);
var NDBI_chart =
ui.Chart.image.series({imageCollection:
NDBI_collection,
                    region:StudyArea,
                    reducer: ee.Reducer.mean(),
                    scale: 1000
})                         .setOptions({title: "NDBI MEAN",
pointSize: 3});
print(NDBI_chart);
 var year = 2000;

for (var i=1;i<=18;i++)
{var NDBI_mean = NDBI_collection.select('B5')
                .filterDate(ee.Date.fromYMD(year,1,1))
                .reduce(ee.Reducer.mean());
var clipped = NDBI_mean.clip(beijing);
Map.addLayer(clipped,imageVisParam2,'NDBI '+year);
year=year+1;
}
var xvalues = ee.Array(NDBI_collection.get('B5'));
//////////////
// set position of panel
var legend = ui.Panel({
 style: {
  position: 'bottom-left',
  padding: '8px 15px'
 }
});
// Create legend title
var legendTitle = ui.Label({
 value: 'Legend',
 style: {
  fontWeight: 'bold',
  fontSize: '18px',
  margin: '0 0 4px 0',
  padding: '0'
  }
});
// Add the title to the panel
legend.add(legendTitle);
// Creates and styles 1 row of the legend.
var makeRow = function(color, name) {
   // Create the label that is actually the colored box.
   var colorBox = ui.Label({
 style: {
    backgroundColor: '#' + color,
    // Use padding to give the box height and width.
    padding: '8px',
    margin: '0 0 4px 0'
   }
  });
  // Create the label filled with the description text.
  var description = ui.Label({
   value: name,
   style: {margin: '0 0 4px 6px'}
  });
  // return the panel
  return ui.Panel({
   widgets: [colorBox, description],
   layout: ui.Panel.Layout.Flow('horizontal')
  });
};
// Palette with the colors
var palette =['f4977f', 'f6f4f4'];
// name of the legend
var names = ['Built-up Area','Non Built-up Area'];
// Add color and and names
for (var i = 0; i < 2; i++) {
 legend.add(makeRow(palette[i], names[i]));
 }
Map.add(legend);
/////////// Save //////////
// Make a collection of points.
Export.image.toDrive({
 image: clipped,
 description: 'NDBI-beijing',
 scale: 30,
 maxPixels: 1e13,});
```

Figure 5. Urban Sprawl in Beijing

REFERENCES

Aguilar, R., Zurita-Milla, R., Izquierdo-Verdiguier, E., & De By, A, R. (. (2018). A cloud-based multi-temporal ensemble classifier to map smallholder farming systems. *Remote Sensing*, *10*(5), 729. doi:10.3390/rs10050729

Bairoch, P. (1991). *Cities and economic development: from the dawn of history to the present*. University of Chicago Press.

Campos-Taberner, M., Moreno-Martínez, Á., García-Haro, F. J., Camps-Valls, G., Robinson, N. P., Kattge, J., & Running, S. W. (2018). Global estimation of biophysical variables from Google Earth Engine platform. *Remote Sensing*, *10*(8), 1167. doi:10.3390/rs10081167

Chapman, S., Watson, J. E., Salazar, A., Thatcher, M., & McAlpine, C. A. (2017). The impact of urbanization and climate change on urban temperatures: A systematic review. *Landscape Ecology*, *32*(10), 1921–1935. doi:10.100710980-017-0561-4

Dong, J., Xiao, X., Menarguez, M. A., Zhang, G., Qin, Y., Thau, D., Biradar, C., & Moore, B. III. (2016). Mapping paddy rice planting area in northeastern Asia with Landsat 8 images, phenology-based algorithm and Google Earth Engine. *Remote Sensing of Environment*, *185*, 142–154. doi:10.1016/j.rse.2016.02.016 PMID:28025586

Ermida, S. L., Soares, P., Mantas, V., Göttsche, F. M., & Trigo, I. F. (2020). Google Earth Engine Open-Source Code for Land Surface Temperature Estimation from the Landsat Series. *Remote Sensing*, *12*(9), 1471. doi:10.3390/rs12091471

Forstall, R. L. (1996). *Population of States and Counties of the United States: 1790 to 1990 from the Twenty-one Decennial Censuses. National Technical Information Services.* NTIS.

Franco, S., Gaetano, V., & Gianni, T. (2018). Urbanization and climate change impacts on surface water quality: Enhancing the resilience by reducing impervious surfaces. *Water Research*, *144*, 491–502. doi:10.1016/j.watres.2018.07.058 PMID:30077910

Goldblatt, R., Rivera Ballesteros, A., & Burney, J. (2017). High spatial resolution visual band imagery outperforms medium resolution spectral imagery for ecosystem assessment in the semi-arid brazilian sertão. *Remote Sensing*, *9*(12), 1336. doi:10.3390/rs9121336

Gorelick, N., Hancher, M., Dixon, M., Ilyushchenko, S., Thau, D., & Moore, R. (2017). Google Earth Engine: Planetary-scale geospatial analysis for everyone. *Remote Sensing of Environment*, *202*, 18–27. doi:10.1016/j.rse.2017.06.031

Gruebner, O., Rapp, M. A., Adli, M., Kluge, U., Galea, S., & Heinz, A. (2017). Cities and mental health. *Deutsches Ärzteblatt International*, *114*(8), 121. PMID:28302261

Guetté, A., Gaüzère, P., Devictor, V., Jiguet, F., & Godet, L. (2017). Measuring the synanthropy of species and communities to monitor the effects of urbanization on biodiversity. *Ecological Indicators*, *79*, 139–154. doi:10.1016/j.ecolind.2017.04.018

Hassan, M. M., & Southworth, J. (2018). Analyzing land cover change and urban growth trajectories of the mega-urban region of Dhaka using remotely sensed data and an ensemble classifier. *Sustainability*, *10*(1), 10.

He, M., Kimball, J. S., Maneta, M. P., Maxwell, B. D., Moreno, A., Beguería, S., & Wu, X. (2018). Regional crop gross primary productivity and yield estimation using fused landsat-MODIS data. *Remote Sensing*, *10*(3), 372. doi:10.3390/rs10030372

Hotez, P. J. (2017). Global urbanization and the neglected tropical diseases. *PLoS Neglected Tropical Diseases*, *11*(2), e0005308. doi:10.1371/journal.pntd.0005308 PMID:28231246

Housman, I., Tanpipat, V., Biswas, T., Clark, A., Stephen, P., Maus, P., & Megown, K. (2015). *Monitoring forest change in southeast Asia: case studies for USAID Lowering Emissions in Asia's Forests*. US Department of Agriculture, Forest Service, Remote Sensing Applications Center.

Hussain, M., & Imitiyaz, I. (2018). Urbanization Concepts, Dimensions and Factors. *International Journal of Recent Scientific Research*, *9*(1), 23513–23523.

Kuroda, T. (1990). Urbanization and population distribution policies in Japan. *Regional Development Dialogue*, *11*(1), 112. PMID:12316641

Lai, P., Zhang, M., Ge, Z., Hao, B., Song, Z., Huang, J., Ma, M., Yang, H., & Han, X. (2020). Responses of Seasonal Indicators to Extreme Droughts in Southwest China. *Remote Sensing*, *12*(5), 818. doi:10.3390/rs12050818

Lee, J., Cardille, J. A., & Coe, M. T. (2018). BULC-U: Sharpening resolution and improving accuracy of land-use/land-cover classifications in Google Earth Engine. *Remote Sensing*, *10*(9), 1455. doi:10.3390/rs10091455

Li, X., Zhou, W., & Ouyang, Z. (2013). Forty years of urban expansion in Beijing: What is the relative importance of physical, socioeconomic, and neighborhood factors? *Applied Geography (Sevenoaks, England)*, *38*, 1–10. doi:10.1016/j.apgeog.2012.11.004

Liu, C. C., Shieh, M. C., Ke, M. S., & Wang, K. H. (2018). Flood prevention and emergency response system powered by google earth engine. *Remote Sensing*, *10*(8), 1283. doi:10.3390/rs10081283

Liu, X., & Bae, J. (2018). Urbanization and industrialization impact of CO2 emissions in China. *Journal of Cleaner Production*, *172*, 178–186. doi:10.1016/j.jclepro.2017.10.156

Liu, Z., He, C., & Wu, J. (2016). The relationship between habitat loss and fragmentation during urbanization: An empirical evaluation from 16 world cities. *PLoS One*, *11*(4), e0154613. doi:10.1371/journal.pone.0154613 PMID:27124180

Lobo, F. D. L., Souza-Filho, P. W. M., Novo, E. M. L. D. M., Carlos, F. M., & Barbosa, C. C. F. (2018). Mapping mining areas in the brazilian amazon using msi/sentinel-2 imagery (2017). *Remote Sensing*, *10*(8), 1178. doi:10.3390/rs10081178

Lozano-Fuentes, S., Elizondo-Quiroga, D., Farfan-Ale, J. A., Loroño-Pino, M. A., Garcia-Rejon, J., Gomez-Carro, S., ... Dominguez-Galera, M. (2008). Use of Google EarthTM to strengthen public health capacity and facilitate management of vector-borne diseases in resource-poor environments. *Bulletin of the World Health Organization*, *86*(9), 718–725. doi:10.2471/BLT.07.045880 PMID:18797648

Luo, K., Hu, X., He, Q., Wu, Z., Cheng, H., Hu, Z., & Mazumder, A. (2018). Impacts of rapid urbanization on the water quality and macroinvertebrate communities of streams: A case study in Liangjiang New Area, China. *The Science of the Total Environment*, *621*, 1601–1614. doi:10.1016/j.scitotenv.2017.10.068 PMID:29054671

Mahboob, M. A., Atif, I., & Iqbal, J. (2015). Remote sensing and GIS applications for assessment of urban sprawl in Karachi, Pakistan. Science. *Technology and Development*, *34*(3), 179–188. doi:10.3923td.2015.179.188

Mahdianpari, M., Salehi, B., Mohammadimanesh, F., Homayouni, S., & Gill, E. (2019). The first wetland inventory map of newfoundland at a spatial resolution of 10 m using sentinel-1 and sentinel-2 data on the google earth engine cloud computing platform. *Remote Sensing*, *11*(1), 43. doi:10.3390/rs11010043

Markert, K. N., Schmidt, C. M., Griffin, R. E., Flores, A. I., Poortinga, A., Saah, D. S., ... Someth, P. (2018). Historical and operational monitoring of surface sediments in the lower mekong basin using landsat and google earth engine cloud computing. *Remote Sensing*, *10*(6), 909. doi:10.3390/rs10060909

Mateo-García, G., Gómez-Chova, L., Amorós-López, J., Muñoz-Marí, J., & Camps-Valls, G. (2018). Multitemporal cloud masking in the Google Earth Engine. *Remote Sensing*, *10*(7), 1079. doi:10.3390/rs10071079

Moore, R., & Parsons, E. (2011). *Beyond SDI, bridging the power of cloud based computing resources to manage global environment issues*. In *INSPIRE Conference*, Edinburgh, UK.

Parente, L., & Ferreira, L. (2018). Assessing the spatial and occupation dynamics of the Brazilian pasturelands based on the automated classification of MODIS images from 2000 to 2016. *Remote Sensing*, *10*(4), 606. doi:10.3390/rs10040606

Parks, S. A., Holsinger, L. M., Voss, M. A., Loehman, R. A., & Robinson, N. P. (2018). Mean composite fire severity metrics computed with Google Earth Engine offer improved accuracy and expanded mapping potential. *Remote Sensing*, *10*(6), 879. doi:10.3390/rs10060879

Poortinga, A., Clinton, N., Saah, D., Cutter, P., Chishtie, F., Markert, K. N., ... Bean, B. (2018). An operational before-after-control-impact (BACI) designed platform for vegetation monitoring at planetary scale. *Remote Sensing*, *10*(5), 760. doi:10.3390/rs10050760

Qing, W. A. N. G. (2018). Urbanization and Global Health: The Role of Air Pollution. *Iranian Journal of Public Health*, *47*(11), 1644. PMID:30581779

Ravanelli, R., Nascetti, A., Cirigliano, R. V., Di Rico, C., Leuzzi, G., Monti, P., & Crespi, M. (2018). Monitoring the impact of land cover change on surface urban heat island through Google Earth Engine: Proposal of a global methodology, first applications and problems. *Remote Sensing*, *10*(9), 1488. doi:10.3390/rs10091488

RitchieH.RoserM. (2020). *Urbanization*. Retrieved from https://ourworldindata.org/urbanization

Robinson, N. P., Allred, B. W., Jones, M. O., Moreno, A., Kimball, J. S., Naugle, D. E., Erickson, T., & Richardson, A. D. (2017). A dynamic Landsat derived normalized difference vegetation index (NDVI) product for the conterminous United States. *Remote Sensing*, *9*(8), 863. doi:10.3390/rs9080863

Sazib, N., Mladenova, I., & Bolten, J. (2018). Leveraging the google earth engine for drought assessment using global soil moisture data. *Remote Sensing*, *10*(8), 1265. doi:10.3390/rs10081265 PMID:32021700

Shakrullah, K., Shirazi, S. A., & Sajjad, S. H. (2015). Spatio-temporal analysis of land cover changes of Dhaka City in Bangladesh. *Pakistan Journal of Science*, *67*(4), 413.

Sproles, E. A., Crumley, R. L., Nolin, A. W., Mar, E., & Lopez Moreno, J. I. (2018). Snow Cloud Hydro—A New Framework for Forecasting Streamflow in Snowy, Data-Scarce Regions. *Remote Sensing*, *10*(8), 1276. doi:10.3390/rs10081276

Traganos, D., Aggarwal, B., Poursanidis, D., Topouzelis, K., Chrysoulakis, N., & Reinartz, P. (2018). Towards global-scale seagrass mapping and monitoring using Sentinel-2 on Google Earth Engine: The case study of the aegean and ionian seas. *Remote Sensing*, *10*(8), 1227. doi:10.3390/rs10081227

Traganos, D., Poursanidis, D., Aggarwal, B., Chrysoulakis, N., & Reinartz, P. (2018). Estimating satellite-derived bathymetry (SDB) with the google earth engine and sentinel-2. *Remote Sensing*, *10*(6), 859. doi:10.3390/rs10060859

Tsai, Y. H., Stow, D., Chen, H. L., Lewison, R., An, L., & Shi, L. (2018). Mapping vegetation and land use types in fanjingshan national nature reserve using google earth engine. *Remote Sensing*, *10*(6), 927. doi:10.3390/rs10060927

United Nations (2018). *World urbanization prospects: The 2018 revision–key facts*. Author.

United Nations, Department of Economic and Social Affairs, Population Division (2018). *The World's Cities in 2018—Data Booklet (ST/ESA/ SER.A/417)*. Author.

United Nations, Department of Economic and Social Affairs, Population Division. (2019). *World Urbanization Prospects: The 2018 Revision (ST/ESA/SER.A/420)*. United Nations.

U.S. Geological Survey. (2010). *U.S. Geological SurveyThousands of Landsat Scenes in Google's Earth Engine*. https://landsat.usgs.gov/google-earth-engine

Wang, Y., & Zhao, T. (2018). Impacts of urbanization-related factors on CO2 emissions: Evidence from China's three regions with varied urbanization levels. *Atmospheric Pollution Research*, *9*(1), 15–26. doi:10.1016/j.apr.2017.06.002

Zhang, Z., Li, N., Wang, X., Liu, F., & Yang, L. (2016). A comparative study of urban expansion in Beijing, Tianjin and Tangshan from the 1970s to 2013. *Remote Sensing*, *8*(6), 496. doi:10.3390/rs8060496

Chapter 8
Land Regulations, Tenure, and Land Use of Sri Lanka: A Historical Analysis on Agricultural Lands

Jeevika Weerahewa
Faculty of Agriculture, University of Peradeniya, Sri Lanka

Dilini Hemachandra
Faculty of Agriculture, University of Peradeniya, Sri Lanka

Gamini Pushpakumara
Faculty of Agriculture, University of Peradeniya, Sri Lanka

ABSTRACT

Present land use and tenure of a country is a result of the social norms and regulations. Land use manifests a country's priorities with implications on the economic development. Land tenure has implications on the investment decisions on land and hence efficient allocations of land. Sri Lanka, a country with a history of king's reign, colonial rule and then an elected government has its unique journey in the evolution of laws and regulations and institutions governing land and the resultant land use. This chapter chronicles the evolution of laws and regulations and institutions governing agricultural land and the resultant land use and tenure arrangements. At present, the governance of agricultural land is complex as it involves many regulations and many competing institutions.

INTRODUCTION

Government regulations governing lands, among other things, largely determine land use pattern of any country either directly or indirectly. Some regulations impose direct restrictions on the use of a particular land while some others indirectly influence the use by altering the incentives. It may be the choice of sector to invest in, the crops to cultivate or to leave the land fallow which ultimately have implications on the sustainable management of lands. For agricultural lands, the types of crops grown will determine

DOI: 10.4018/978-1-7998-4372-6.ch008

food security of the country, foreign exchange earnings, and living standards of people and hence overall economic development of the country.

Land regulations govern land tenure as well. Land tenure is concerned with who owns the resource, and who uses, manages and makes decisions about the resources, including control over benefits as well as transfer of rights. It is characterized by the bundles of rights, rules, and institutions that define individual or community access to land. Rights of access, withdrawal, management, exclusion and alienation and authority to sanction are considered as critical rights (Ostrom and Schlager 1996, USAID 2011). In most cases, those who have rights to a resource have a stronger interest to sustainably manage the resource and land is no exception. Higher land tenure security is often associated with higher investments on lands, lesser land degradation and higher land productivity. Land tenure is shaped by both de-jour and de-factor rights. De-jour tenure rights are defined through government regulations and de-factor rights are perceptions of the community on land tenure.

When regulations are not conducive for land consolidation, fragmentation is unavoidable with the growth of rural populations. Small holdings are generally not economical for commercial cultivation of crops and hence the degree of fragmentation influence the choice of crops cultivated by farmers. Fragmented lands are detrimental to conservation and subjected to degradation constraining agricultural development. Certain government regulations such as nationalization programs generally dismantle communal lands and paves the way for encroachment. Breakdown of common property regimes in return leads to land fragmentation and hence land degradation (Niroula and Thapa, 2005). When tenure rights are weakly defined and enforced, it leads to disputes and inefficient allocation of resources.

The nexus among land use, regulations, and tenure in Sri Lanka, evolved over time, can be considered unique among global experiences. Of the total surface area of 6.57 million ha, almost 83% (5.45 million ha) is owned by the state and the remaining 17% (1.12 million ha) is privately owned according to the data available at the Land Commissioner General's Department of Sri Lanka. Over 2 million ha are under agricultural usage of which 1.38 million ha are state-owned agricultural land. They are farmed by private farmers under varying tenure arrangements. Privately owned agricultural lands comprise 0.88 million ha and they are largely located in the Wet Zone of the country (World Bank, 2008). The administration and management of agricultural lands in Sri Lanka is governed by around 40 operational laws, which are vested with the Ministry of Agriculture, Ministry of Lands and Land Development, Ministry of Mahaweli and Ministry of Irrigation. Different user and transfer rights have been given to recipients of land settlement schemes administered by the government agencies in terms of land grants and permits. Apart from these, a variety of informal arrangements to own, manage and access to agricultural lands are also evident in rural settings often disregarding regulations. They include varying rotational tenure forms (such as *thattumaru* and *kattimaru*[1]), share tenancy arrangements (*ande* and *viporonduwa*), absentee landlordism (*gambaraya*) and ownership rights acquired through long term use (*paraveni*). Encroachment of state land is also a widespread phenomenon, especially in the Dry Zone where shifting (Chena) cultivation was commonly practiced (Gunasena and Pushpakumara, 2015; Marawila, 2007). The government of Sri Lanka has imposed restrictions on maximum and minimum sizes for agricultural holdings yet informal land transactions take place violating these limits. Different regulations have been formulated for management of various uses of agricultural lands particularly relating to cultivations of paddy and plantation crops and forestry. The objective of this chapter is to chronicle land regulations of Sri Lanka with a special emphasis on their direct and indirect effects on land use pattern, tenure and fragmentation of agricultural lands.

This chapter is organized as follows. The next section reports the changes in land distribution and land use pattern in Sri Lanka over time, associated changes in land size, number of holdings and the tenure arrangements. The third section illustrates the extent to which land regulations implemented by the government of Sri Lanka influenced land use, fragmentation and tenure and thereby land degradation and productivity. The forth section provides the challenges for development and the final section provides a way forward.

LAND DISTRIBUTION, LAND USE AND TENURE: PAST and PRESENT

Extent and Size of Agricultural Lands in Sri Lanka

By 1946, the total extent of agricultural lands in Sri Lanka was reported as 1.73 million ha and the per capita agricultural land was 3.85 persons per ha. The total extent of agricultural lands was increased to 1.89 million ha in 1962 and the per capita agricultural land became 5.54 persons per ha illustrating an increase in population per unit of agricultural land (Census of Agriculture, 1962). Figure 1 shows how the extent of agricultural lands changed during 1961-2016 period. Agricultural lands as a fraction of total extent of lands in the country which amounts to 6,27 million ha changed from 37.2% in 1970 to 43.7% in 2016 (World Development Indicators, 2020). Even though land area under agriculture has increased, the size of a holding has decreased over time as shown in Tables 1 and 2. The number of agricultural holdings of less than 20.23 ha (50 acres) has increased several folds since 1962 (Table 2).

According to the Agricultural Household Survey conducted in 2016/2017 by the Department of Census and Statistics, there are 2.1 million farm households. The average household size is 3.8 persons making the total farming population of 8.1 million. Of this population, 36.1% are agriculture operators, 26% are contributing to agricultural activities and 37.9% are not contributing to agricultural activities as far as people above 15 years old are concerned.

Land Use Pattern

The agricultural sector in Sri Lanka is divided into two sub-sectors: plantations and smallholdings. The former consists of three main crops: tea, rubber and coconut, commercially oriented and medium to large-scale in operations. The smallholding (or domestic or non-plantation) sub-sector consists of paddy, other field crops and fruit and vegetables. It is semi-subsistent and consists mainly of small-scale operations.

According to Mapa et al. (2002), land use changes of Sri Lanka since independence in 1948 has been surveyed and well documented at regular intervals than in many Asian countries. Tables 3 and 4 show the land use pattern in 1961 and 2018 respectively.

The changes in the major crop areas show a decrease in extent under tea, rubber and coconut and an increase in paddy extent. The latter was due to opening of large areas of land with irrigation facilities under land settlement schemes in the Dry Zone. The rubber lands decreased drastically owing to diversification and settlement schemes in the Wet Zone of Sri Lanka.

Figure 1. Agricultural Land as a percentage of land area
Source: World Development Indicators (Downloaded on March 18, 2020)

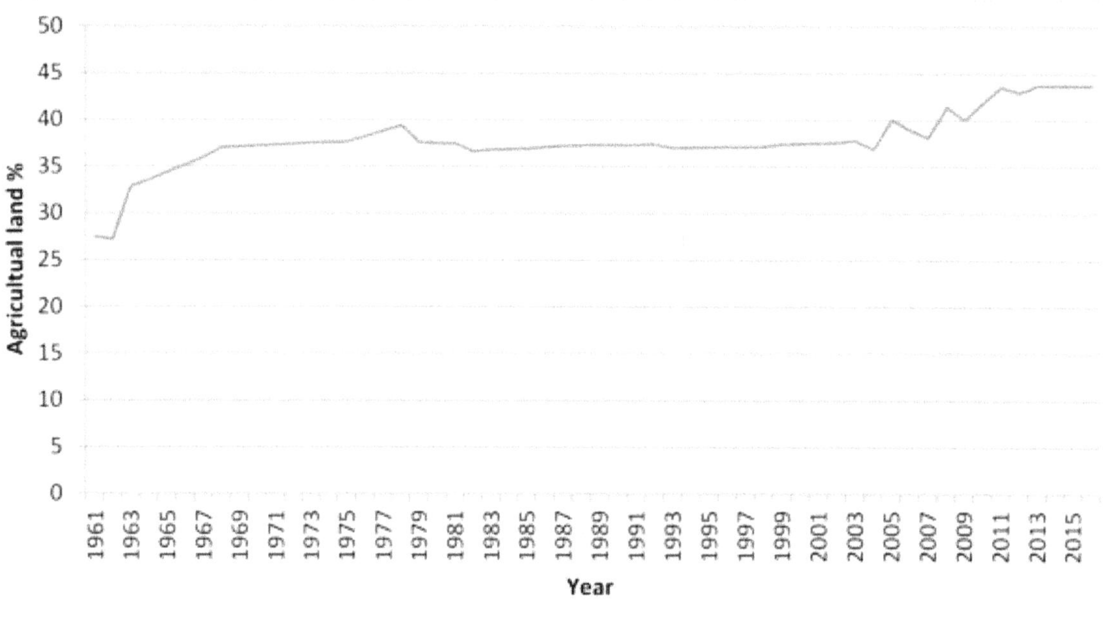

Figure 1: Agricultural Land as a percentage of land area
Source: World Development Indicators (Downloaded on March 18, 2020)

Table 1. Number and area of total agriculture land holdings

Year	Number of holdings	Extent (ha)	Average extent per holding (calculated) (ha)	Source
1982	1,800,000	1,973,652	1.10	Economic Census (2013/2014)
2002	3,253,000	1,941,277	0.59	Economic Census (2013/2014)
2014	4,353,000	2,283,641	0.52	Economic Census (2013/2014)

Table 2. Number and area of agriculture land holdings below 50 acres (20.23 ha)

Year	Number of holdings	Extent (ha)	Average extent per holding (ha)	Source
1946	849,527	1,140,387	1.34	Agriculture Census (1962)
1962	1,168,214	1,265,040	1.08	Agriculture Census (1962)
2002	3,211,245	1,556,444	0.49	Economic Census (2013/2014)
2014	4,294,767	1879472	0.44	Economic Census (2013/2014)

Table 3. Land Use Pattern in 1961

	Land use		Extent (ha)	Percentage %
1	Settlements and associated non-agricultural lands		19,535	0.3
2	Horticulture		574,180	9.0
3	Tree and other perennial crops:			
	a	Tea	257,479	3.9
	b	Rubber	227,378	3.5
	c	Coconut	250,469	3.8
	d	Others	54,031	0.7
4	Cropland:			
	a	Paddy	510,688	7.8
	b	Land under development	43,420	0.7
	c	Other	1,009,725	15.3
5	Improved permanent pasture		2,493	-
6	Grassland and scrubland		425,743	6.4
7	Woodland		2,899,518	44.2
8	Swamp and marsh		32,788	0.5
9	Unused land		43,149	0.7
10	Inland waters		204,739	3.2
	Total		6,567,475	100.0

Source: Aerial Survey based on Canada – Colombo Plan Project – (1961)

Land Tenure

Land tenure arrangements in contemporary Sri Lanka can best be termed as "complex". They are a reflection of composite effects of government interventions, the population pressure on land and cultural norms of the society. Accordingly, the resulting tenure arrangements are region specific. The earlier stated rotational tenure forms (such as *thattumaru* and *kattimaru*) are found mainly in the densely populated and paddy land scarce districts in the Wet Zone of the country. Various forms of share tenancies (such as *ande, karuande, koottuande, vi poronduwa,* and other forms) involving different arrangements of labour and input sharing and allocation of use rights on a temporary (seasonal) basis or on the basis of affixation exist in these areas. Tenancy rights are permanent and inheritable in the Wet Zone. The lands owned and managed by Buddhist and Hindu temples, known as *Vihargam* and *Devalagam*, are found in Central Highlands and districts of the Dry and Intermediate Zones of the country. In these lands, temples extract a combination of crop shares and prescribed servitudes from 'tenants' who occupy the land (Ratnayake, undate).

Absentee landlordism associated with the *gambaraya* system is concentrated in the South-East Dry Zone Districts and the *podiyar* system is found in the Eastern Province with exploitative rent collecting and grazing rights exerted by representatives (overseers) of absentee landowners. Similar, albeit more commercialised contractual transactions are found in certain districts (Vavuniya and Mullaitivu) (Kumara, 2016).

Table 4. Land Use Pattern in 2018

		Land use	Extent (ha)	Percentage (%)
1.	Nonagricultural lands			
	Built up Areas		85,094	1.3
2.	Home Garden		1,192,925	18.18
3.	Plantation crops			
	a	Tea	228,118	3.48
	b	Abandoned Tea	5,855	0.09
	c	Rubber	186,334	2.84
	d	Abandoned Rubber	2,359	0.04
	e	Coconut	208,368	3.18
4.	Paddy		983,550	14.99
5.	Abandoned paddy		40,356	0.62
6.	Palmyrah		15,833	0.24
7.	Oilpalm		8,781	0.13
8.	Cinnamon		21,015	0.32
9.	Other Feld Crops		57,041	0.87
10.	Mixed tree and Other perennials		82,228	1.25
11.	Sparsely used Croplands/Chena		307,311	4.68
12.	Forest lands			
	a	Forests	1,848,548	28.17
	b	Forest Plantations	68,103	1.04
	c	Scrubs	599,787	9.14
13.	Water Bodies		374,553	5.71
14.	Other (Marsh, mangroves & Streams etc)		85,442	1.30
15.	Balance Area*		159,399	2.43
	Total		6,561,000	100.00

Source: Department of Land Use and Policy Planning and Ministry of Lands and Land Development
Extracted from: AgStat, 2019
*Note: Rocky area, sandy area, unutilized lands and bare lands etc.

Small tank based land ownership and land use systems found mainly in the North Central and North-Western Provinces in particular, still retain much of the communal ownership character in homestead land as well as paddy land. In the traditional village paddy tract (*purana vela*), individual rights claimed over land parcels tend to become subordinated to a communal decision to cultivate a limited extent of the tract, with a reduced number of individual land parcels. This is termed as the *bethma* arrangement and practiced in times of water shortage in the tank. Similar communal ownership exists in the case of *paraveni* (ownership rights through long term use) *chena* (shifting cultivation) and *kurulupaluwa* (areas allocated for birds) strips of land in *purana* (traditional) small tank villages. Tenancy rights for private lands are permanent and heritable in these small tank based systems as well (Shah, 2013).

The land tenure of the Dry Zone agricultural system is still characterized by the indigenous system comprising the old-fields (*purana vela*), acre/leased fields (*akkara vela*) and *chena* lands under communal ownership (Abeywardena et al., 2019). Tenancy rights for private lands in the Dry Zone are also permanent and inheritable. In irrigation settlement schemes however, land is owned by the government and farmers are given varying degrees of rights through various land lease arrangements. Illegal land transactions are also present in these areas.

Tenure arrangements for plantation crops are specific to types of cultivation. Small holdings mostly have private ownership to the lands. The large estates are owned by the State and are managed by the Regional Plantation Companies (RPCs) under a long-term lease agreement (Herath, 2016).

LAND REGULATION AND MANAGEMENT

Institutional Set-Up Governing Land

The Ministry of Land, the key institution governing lands, was established in 1932. The objectives of the Ministry are to formulate and implement state land policies, conserve state lands, and implement activities related to land settlement and land acquisition for public purposes (About the Ministry). This Ministry's vision is the optimum utilization of land resources for sustainable development and its Ministry's mission is to effectively and efficiently manage land resources to an optimal level contribute to the country's socio-economic development while maintaining environmental equilibrium (About the Ministry). The Survey Department, the Land Commissioner General Department, the Land Title Settlement Department, the Land Use Policy Planning Department, Land Survey Council, Institute of Surveying and Mapping and Land Reform Commission fall under the purview of the Land Ministry.

The custodian of the land acquired to the Crown (The British rule) and not vested to other institutions is under the Land Commissioner General. The Land Commissioner General's Department alienate land to the public as per the need. Land parcels are first alienated as permits. The permit requests from the public comes to the Divisional Secretariat of area who is the local custodian of the land under the Land Commissioner. The requests are evaluated based on the intended use of the land and the landlessness of the requester. Priorities are given to blood relatives of the person who used the land before. Land is thus alienated for agricultural use and residential use. The land permits will be later considered for land grants (*Swarnabhoomi, Jayabhoomi* deeds). Number of permits and grants issued are presented in Table 5. A land granted with a *Swarnabhoomi* or a *Jayabhoomi* deed cannot be sold. The land may be divided and be transferred to the next generation subjected to a minimum size.

Table 5. Land Statistics in Sri Lanka – 2019

Criteria	Extent (ha)
Total land	6,561,000
State land	5,403,809
Percentage of state owned land[2]	83%
No. of issued land permits (up to 2019)	2,952,542
No of Issued land grants (up to 2019)	1,361,391
No. of surveyed lands	701,398
No. of plots yet to be surveyed	436,993
No. of issued long term leased land permits (up to 2019)	261,572
No. of lands plots yet to be regularized	600,000

Source: Land Use and Policy Planning Department, Land Commissioner General's Department

The Land Commissioner General Department is governed by two Ordinances. The Land Development Ordinance (1935) and the State Land Ordinance (No. 7 of 1947 ad No. 8 of 1949). The State Land Ordinance stipulates provisions for the grant and disposition of state lands in Sri Lanka; for the management and control of such lands and the foreshore. The Land Development Ordinance (No. 19 of 1935) provides for the systematic development and alienation of State land in Sri Lanka. It marked the beginning of an era of rapid land settlement and starting from mid-1930s. It continued up to the implementation of the accelerated Mahaweli Development Project in mid-1980s.

The Mahaweli Authority of Sri Lanka was established in 1979 by a Parliamentary Act with the mandate for implementing the Mahaweli Development Programme to develop agricultural land and human settlements in the Dry Zone of Sri Lanka. Nearly, 365,000 ha of public and private land were earmarked for this programme. The new settlers were granted an acre of lowland and a half an acre of homestead per family with restrictions for on transfer and sale of land.

At present, a number of institutions perform key functions in land related matters as well as a number of institutions that perform related auxiliary functions. Box 1 provides a list of land related institutes together with their functions.

Box 1. Land and Land Managemengt Related Institutions in Sri Lanka

1. Ministry of Lands and Land Development: Responsible for the formulation and implementation of land policies and land development programmes. The Ministry id also responsible for the management of land settlement; land acquisition; surveying; land use planning and alienation of land and development of settlement projects.
Following institutes fall within the ministry.
a. The Survey Department
b. Land Settlement Department
Title registration is being implemented by the Survey and Land Settlement Departments. Operates within the Registration of Title Act No. 21 of 1998.
The title register is maintained by the Registrar General's Department. By 2014 405,813 titles had been registered under the National Land Titling Program (*Bim-Saviya*). The Survey Department has developed a national Cadastral Map in SLG99 for title registration and by the end of 2014 had surveyed close to 1 million land parcels. In 2015 the Registrar General's Department recorded 25,500 transactions for titles. Title registration was intended to replace deeds registration, but the implementation of title registration has taken longer than anticipated and there are clearly issues in both survey and adjudication processes in acquiring title.
c. Land Use Policy and Planning and Department
d. Land Reform Commission
2. **Registrar General's Department**: There are 45 Land Registries in Sri Lanka managed by the Registrar General's Department of the Ministry of Public Administration and Management (MOPAM). The Land Registry records deeds, mortgages, leases and other documents on land and property. It covers approximately 7 million land parcels (of the estimated total of 13 million land parcels in Sri Lanka). Registration is not mandatory and there is no legal guarantee on the rights that are registered. Over 1.1 million deeds were registered in 2015.
3. **National Physical Planning Department**: Operates under the Ministry of Urban Development, Construction and Public Utilities with the mandate for formulation and implementation of a national physical planning policy.
4. **Valuation Department**: provides compensation values for the land acquisition and suggests lease levels for the government including to Provincial Councils and local authorities.
5. **Mahaweli Authority**: Administers land is areas declared for the Mahaweli Ganga Development Scheme (about 39% of Sri Lanka has been declared).
6. National Land Commission: The National Land Commission that was specified in the 13th Amendment (1987) of the Constitution with the responsibility of formulating land policy with respect of state lands has never been established.
7. **Provincial Council:** Land administration and management powers were intended to be devolved to the Provincial Councils under the 13th Amendment (1987) to the Constitution (1978). There are uncertainties in the devolution of responsibilities to the Provincial Councils and hence has not functioned as yet.
8. **Divisional Secretariat:** Function as the local custodian of state land. Applications and requests from the public are evaluated, processed and recommended to the Land Commissioner General.
9. Forest Department
10. Department of Wild Life conservation
Source:http://www.fao.org/gender-landrights-database/country-profiles/countries-list/land-tenure-and-related-institutions/en/?country_iso3=LKA
World Bank, 2017

Regulatory Framework Governing Agricultural Lands

The following section summarizes the key regulations governing agricultural lands in Sri Lanka with special emphasis on the resulting tenure rights, land sizes and land uses. For comprehensives reviews on the implications of land regulations in Sri Lanka see Amerasinghe (1976), Ellman et al. (1976), Herath (2006), Marawila (2010) and Wanigaratne et al. (1979),. For pioneering work on land tenure in Sri Lanka see Obeysekera (1967), Peiris (1978) and De Silva (1992). Box 2 provides a list of land regulations implemented during 1840 – 2020.

Box 2: List of Land Regulations pertaining to Agricultural Land

Ordinances, Acts and Laws Related to Land Ordinance/Act/Law

Crown Lands (Encroachments) Ordinance No. 12 of 1840

Waste Lands Ordinance No. 1 of 1897

Land Development Ordinance No. 19 of 1935

Irrigation Ordinance of 1946

Paddy Lands Act, No. 1 of 1953 and 1958

Land Reform Law, No.1 of 1972

Land Reform (Amendment) Law, No. 39 of 1975

Agrarian Services Act, No. 58 of 1979

Agrarian Development Act, No. 46 of 2000, 46 of 2011

Land Grants (Special Provisions) Act, No. 43 of 1979

Registration of Title Act, No. 21 of 1998

Source: Samaratunga and Marawila, 2006.

Rajakariya System During Pre-Colonial Period

The pre-colonial period of Sri Lanka refers to the reign of local kings which prevailed until 1815. During this period, all lands were considered as belonged to the King. Lands were granted to people either for a payment or as a return for a services rendered. The latter system was termed as a *Rajakariya* (Zubair,2005). The services expected were of two kinds: (i) public works such as construction of roads, bridges, and irrigation infrastructure, and (ii) special services elicited on the basis of a person's caste-related occupation[3]. The lands given out to people for their service to the King were known as "*Nindagam*". Some lands were given out to religious activities and the lands given out to Buddhist temples were known as "*Viharagam*" and those given to Hindu temples were known as "*Dewalagam*". Three categories of land tenancies have been identified for *Paraveni* tenure. They are (i) share cropping (*Ande paraveni*), (ii) tenancy ownership of less fertile lands (*Otuparaveni*), and (iii) non-service tenancy ownership (*Ovita paraveni*).(Wijeyewardene,1956)

During this period, Sri Lanka has self-sufficient in its requirement of rice, the staple food crop. Excess rice has even been exported to neighbouring countries. Hence, the dominant land use was paddy cultivation. Extensive irrigation networks that consist of a large number of village tanks, gigantic reservoirs and network of water canals connecting these tanks were constructed by the kings to facilitate rice production particularly in the Dry Zone. A tax on agricultural lands was charged by the kings (Marambe, 2017).

The inheritance rule practiced during this period did not require division of lands between sons and daughters. The daughters take their share in the form of a monetary dowry and other assets and the sons inherit land only when they stay at home and reside patri-locally. This resulted in a system of patrilineal descent associated with the holding of large undivided estates (Leach, 1959). This system avoided land fragmentation.

Crown Lands during Colonial Period

Sri Lanka was colonized by the Portuguese (1505 - 1658), Dutch (1658 – 1796) and British (1796 – 1948). The emphasis of the colonial rulers was on a trading economy hence subsistence agriculture was neglected during the colonial period and instead export crops were given prominence. The Portuguese and Dutch ruled only the coastal belt of the country and significant changes in the traditional land management system during their reign was not visible. Some drastic changes to the land use and tenure were made during the British rule. Under the British ruling, the Crown Land (encroachment) Ordinance No. 12 of 1840 was enacted and it acquired almost 90% all the lands to the Crown. Gradually this system created a landless peasant sector in the country. Traditional institutions, such as land tenure by accommodessan (the granting of land for cultivation, as opposed to its outright sale), was abolished. *Rajakariya* system was found to be an organization that retard growth of private enterprises, inhibit creation of land markets, interfere with free movement of labor and morally not acceptable. The land tenure system introduced by Crown Land (encroachment) Ordinance No. 12 was unfamiliar to native people. Since documentary evidences were not in use at the time, peasants who could not prove ownership lost their land to the Crown. Some land appropriated to the Crown, were sold to private investors. In 1897, the Waste Land Ordinance was enacted to prevent the encroachment of Crown waste lands by the peasantry. This further marginalized peasants. The lands acquired were later given to various government departments, projects and alienated for land settlements, land grants and leaseholds. The Department of Forest Conservation, Department Wild Life and Conservation, the Railway Department and the Mahaweli Authority are the largest recipients (Mapa, 2002).

In 1927, the first Land Commission was established by the colonial government mainly to improve the welfare of peasants (MaddumaBandara, 1990; Goonawardene and Hatten, 1990). The recommendations of the Commission led to the enactment of the Land Development Ordinance (LDO) in 1935 which set the future course of land development of Sri Lanka (Goonawardene and Hatten, 1990; Jayawardana, 1990; MaddumaBandara, 1990; Abeysinghe, 1979). It marked the beginning of an era of rapid land settlement starting from mid-1930s and continued up to the implementation of the Accelerated Mahaweli Development Project in mid-1980s. The initial objectives of the LDO were to protect the interests of the peasantry. The tenure rights of LDO lands were subjected to a number of conditions. The recipients had the rights to cultivate the land but the rights of selling, leasing and mortgaging, and abandoning of lands were regulated. The holding size of the lands alienated during this period was as large as 8 acres.

Land Acquisition and Alienation during 1948 – 1977

The Land Acquisition Act of 1950 acquired lands and alienated among the landless. The settlers were provided with water, free of charge, through the canal system managed by a separate irrigated office for each settlement and were granted with two acres of highlands. The extent of low lands granted varied over time. The early settlers were granted five acres and the allocation reduced to three acres to two acres in subsequent allocations. These provisions were introduced through the LDO in 1935. The provisions provided by the ordinance restricted further subdivisions and all forms of transactions. Later, amendments to LDO introduced a legal minimum of 1.5 acres to a low land plot. In addition, a farmer with a valid deed was given transfer rights subjected to the sanction of the government administrative officer of the respective settlement area.

According to Ellman et al. (1976), there has been a marked difference in selecting settlers in the programmes implemented in 1935 and 1960s. During the early phase, the government was of the view that peasants should be protected and assisted. Social justice, more than agricultural efficiency, was the priority. Hence landless were selected in alienating crownland. Latter, educated youth was chosen for settlements and collective tenure was promoted to improve resource use efficiency.

The Irrigation Ordinance of 1946 which was amended in 1951 and 1968 specified the division of responsibility between the cultivators and the Irrigation Department for maintaining and operating the irrigation system.

Issues were reported with respect to tenure arrangements, i.e., share cropping, *Thattumaru* and *Kattumaru*, in the Wet Zone in early 1950s. By 1954, 25-30% of paddy lands were cultivated under share tenancy. Owner-tenant disputes were common and tenant exploitation was also common. In order to ensure tenure security and to regulate the rent paid by tenants to the landlords,the government enacted two tenure reform programmes, Paddy Lands Acts of 1953 and 1958.

The Paddy Lands Act of 1958 generated important tenancy reforms in the paddy sector by protecting the rights of *ande* tenants (share croppers). It achieved greater social justice, but failed to increase productivity. This was offset by the introduction of high-yielding paddy varieties in the following period. Today, tenant protection measures continue to operate under the Agrarian Development Act (Amendment) 46 of 2011.

With respect to landlord-tenant relationship however, the two acts turned out to be more detrimental than beneficial. Between 1958 and 1972 about 43,000 tenants were reported to have been evicted (Gamage, 2000) and only 18 per cent ended in a final restoration.

With growing shortage for land for new settlement in the Wet Zone and rising cost of developing land for colonization in the Dry Zone, pressure for the takeover of private estate became acute (Ellman et al., 1976). Two land reform Acts were passed in 1972 and in 1976 to address this issue. The Land Reform

Act of No. 01 of 1972 established the Land Reform Commission (LRC)..A ceiling (of 50 acres of highland and 25 acres of lowland) on private ownership was imposed through the two acts. Large extents of plantations (mainly tea plantations) were nationalized and were vested with two state companies, Janatha Estate Development Board (JEDB) and State Plantations Corporation (SPC). Approximately 981,160 acres of land have been acquired under the Land Reform Commissions and of them about 10 per cent has been granted to the low income groups (blocks of 0.25 acre to 1 acre were distributed among the landless and most of which were marginal). The majority of the lands (e.g. >60% of the tea land) was vested with state agencies, further shrinking the privately-owned productive agricultural land and limiting the access to productive lands by the poor (Land Watch Asia). Wanigaratne et al. (1979) states that declared objectives of solving problems of landlessness and unemployment have not been satisfactorily achieved by the land reforms implemented during 1972-1975.

The LRC leases land for 35 years. The public could identify land plots under LRC and apply for long term leases with an investment plan. In 1995 the government leased out plantations under the JEDB and SPC to the private plantation companies for a 55 year lease period.

According to Ganewatte and Edwards (2000), the lands brought under the management of two state organizations; JEDB and SPC were subjected to many changes to make the estate management more efficient until 1992 when the plantation restructuring begun. All the actual and potential profit making tea estates were grouped in to 21 regional plantation companies and assigned their management to selected private companies at initial stage. Then, ownership of the estate was gradually transferred to the private sector. However, JEDB and SPC continue with the marginal unproductive lands in mid grown area of the country. Subsequent land distribution after land reform and attractive prices for low grown tea helped to develop small holder sector extensively in the country. Land ownership regulation and unavailability of large land blocks did not permit further growth of estate sector. Poor performances of the estate sector with its incapability to expand the production to meet the increased demand further induced small holder expansion.

Agriculture Productivity Law No. 22 of 1972 was enacted to ensure that lands acquired, private lands and lands in settlement are properly utilized and developed.

Later, the Land Sales (Special Provisions) Act No. 43 of 1973 provided freehold tenure to allotees subject to certain conditions on sale and subdivisions.

Agrarian Services Act of 1979 also aimed at securing tenure rights of tenant cultivators of paddy and improving productivity of such lands. It is considered as a more realistic approach in solving the problem of the paddy sector. This policy was also considered to be in complete conformity with open economic policies and the macroeconomic needs to affect higher flexibilities in basic resources governing food production, employment and income creation (Alwis and Wanigarathna, 2001). Agrarian Development Act No. 46 of 2000 has identified the necessity of setting a national policy to safeguard the rights of tenant cultivators. It also tries to ensure maximum utilization of agricultural land by imposing restrictions on conversion of agricultural land into non-agricultural uses.

With respect to the tenure that was given to the recipients of land settlement schemes, a clear distinction can be observed in most of the new types of settlement initiated after 1970 compared to those initiated in 1935. The concept of individual ownership has been introduced over collective ownership in alienating lands under the old settlement schemes. The individual ownership and management devolved the ultimate responsibility on the officials, since settlers had become so dependent on government assistance for solving their problems. In the case of the new settlement schemes, there has been a positive attempt to encourage self-reliance and management. The encouragement of non-traditional forms of cultivation has been another important difference between the two types of settlements. In the old colonization schemes a perpetuation of the peasant rural economy centered on paddy cultivation had been encouraged, while on the new settlement schemes, market oriented production of cash crops and livestock has been encouraged (Amerasinghe, 1976).

Enhancing Land Rights during 1978 - 2020

The Government of Sri Lanka opened the economy in 1977 yet retained the achievement of food self-sufficiency, particularly with respect to rice, as one of its key policy objectives. Mahawelli Development project took a new turn with respect to settling people in the dry zone of Sri Lanka and the Accelerated Mahaweli Development Program was initiated in 1977. The State Land (Recovery of Possession) Act No 07 of 1979 and Land Grant (Special Provisions) Act No 43 of 1979 were enacted to distribute lands under Mahaweli Development Program.

Land Development (amendment) Act No. 27 of 1981 provided legal provisions to mortgage the lands only to prescribed banks and institutions, the amendment Act No. 22 of 1993 empowered mortgaging lands in State Banks, and the amended Act No. 20 of 1996 enabled mortgaging in private banks. The Department of the Land Commissioner General (DOLCG) is responsible for promoting the society with undisputed lands as the predecessor of government land administration.

The Title Registration Act No 21 of 1998 was enacted with the objective of transforming deeds and other documents (such as permits) into clear titles, and eliminating certain restrictions imposed on lands under leases, grants and permits. The elimination of these restrictions enabled a process of conversion from grants into full ownership and provided about 1.4 million hectares freehold titles to their land.

The Agrarian Development Act No. 46 of 2000 and the Amendment Act No. 46 of 2011 constituted legal environment on matters relating to landlords and tenant cultivators of paddy lands. They established provision for the utilization of agricultural lands in accordance of the agricultural policy framework of the country.The Agrarian Development Act restricts cultivation of paddy (low) land only to paddy. As successor to the Paddy Lands Act of 1957 and the Agrarian Services Act of 1979, Agrarian Development Act No. 46 of 2000 sought the establishment of agricultural tribunals, farmer organizations, and agrarian development councils that promote the interests of the farming community.

In order to strengthen ownership of land by providing secure titles to those possessing or utilizing a parcel of land, the Ministry of Land and Land Development launched the Land Title Registration Programme in 2007 known as *Bim Saviya*. Under the provision of the Registration of Title Act No. 21 (1998), this programme surveys, defines boundaries, and ensures ownership under a title certificate issued free of charge. It is anticipated that clear and secure land titles will lessen land disputes and litigation, while improving land security and its marketability. This programme seeks to introduce title registration (in place of deed registration), to resolve or make arrangements to resolve the ownership of unsettled lands, and to establish a Digital Land Information System for better land administration.

CONTEMPORARY ISSUES

The issues pertaining to the management of the agricultural land in contemporary Sri Lanka as stated earlier is a result of the legacy of the pre-colonial and colonial rule and regulations enacted by the successive local governments. They could be identified as limited availability of land for agriculture, tenure insecurity, informal land markets, land fragmentation and degradation, land encroachment, land conflicts and lack of institution coordination. They are discussed below in relation to the historical developments.

Limited Availability of Land for Cultivation

The appropriation of land during the colonial period and the land reforms in the 1970s, resulted in about 83% of the land under the State ownership. Even though most of these lands are alienated for the public (except for the 1.95 million ha of land gazetted under the Departments of Forest Conservation and Wildlife Conservation and land given to other State Departments) in small allotments, it is done so withholding the ownership status with the State. While these lands are having user rights (e.g. residential and agricultural), they are not saleable. This is often criticized and cited as a hindrance to the efficient allocation of land resource in Sri Lanka. Private investors find it difficult to access lands for large agricultural or forest plantation investments as the State ownership has blocked the functioning of a land market for most of the agricultural land and hence, the productivity of agriculture sector in Sri Lanka is lowest among its Asian counterparts. There has been attempts by the government to provide freehold titles to these lands, but it often loses momentum due to the fear of land grabbing leading to again a class of landless rural poor.

Insecurity in Land Tenure Rights

The land alienation by the State discussed above has also lead to the problem of inadequate tenure rights. This has been identified as another factor that demoralize cultivators to do productivity enhancing investments. Of the agricultural lands, 52% were inherited and 16.8% were granted by the government (see Table 6 presents the distribution of tenure types).

Table 6. Tenure of Agricultural Lands

Type	Category	Percentage
Inherited		52
Granted	Government	16.8
	Others	1.6
Purchased	With title	9.9
	Without title	1.8
Rent/leased	Government owned	0.4
	Private owned	6.0
Borrowed for free		2.2
Encroached		5.9
Fallowed paddy fields		0.1
Other		2.8

Source: Agriculture Household Survey 2016/2017

This situation is predominant in irrigation settlements in Sri Lanka. With various amendments to the Land Development Ordinance over time, the restrictions now consist of the following: (i) the land cannot be sold or disposed of except with the prior consent of an authorized Government Agent, (ii) the land can be mortgaged but only to selected financial institutions stipulated by the Government, (iii) the allottee cannot lease or sub-lease the land, except in cases of extenuating circumstances, such as illness, and then only for up to one year, (iv) the allottee cannot dispose of a portion of the land, which is less in extent than the prescribed minimum unit of subdivision, and (v) the allottee cannot dispose of the land or a part of it that would lead to co-ownership. Transferability of land is restricted to persons belonging to the same class with the prior approval of the Government Agent.

Wickramarachchi and Weerahewa (2016) revealed, using data gathered from 935 farmers who cultivated 1230 plots in total in *Maha* 2013/2014 in three irrigated settlements namely *Mahakanadarawa, Rajanganaya, Kagama- Katiyawa* settlements in Anuradhapura district, that land tenure differences affect land investment and thereby they affect land productivity. A security in tenure encourages land investment and hence has the ability to increase land productivity. It was found that farmers who do not possess documents to prove tenure are of the view that their rights to land is weak and hence spend less time on investing on the lands, particularly on application of organic manure, and the plots with high tenure security are more productive. The average productivity of a plot is kg 4,148 per ha and the highly secure plots demonstrated a productivity of kg 4,951 per ha.

Informal Land Markets

It is evident that the distribution of lands by the government to the first generation settlers was guided by the LDO. As time passes, the settlers found that the conditions stipulated in the LDOs, i.e., prohibitions on sales, mortgages and subdivisions, have been stringent and hence started informal transactions of land allotments.

Even though formal land transactions are restricted for most of the alienated land to the public under land alienation programmes or irrigation settlements informal land transactions are quite common place. There are informal sales of lands, land subdivisions and land transformations. Table 7 lists the types of informal land transactions and the percentages. By means of informal transactions there is a tendency to acquire more land plots by entrepreneurial farmers leading to increase in the size of land. The presence of informal land market is evident that the enforcement of land laws are weak and inadequate. Further, the government has been unable to stop land grabbing even though the informal land markets allocates resources more efficiently. Moreover, the land values are misrepresented by the informal land markets. Paranage (2018) provides a good overview on the consequences of restricting rights to lands. How the rules of minimum sub-divisions have been disregarded was illustrated. Despite the permissible minimum sub-divisions of land, land sub-divisions and land transfer to next generations take place. Again, due to the poor enforcement of the laws, the protection provided for the land against fragmentation has been ineffective.

Table 7. Links between Erosion and Tenure

Land Tenure	Soil Depth Highland Average	Soil Depth Homegarden Average
Sole owner	4.40	3.34
Co owner	4.43	3.18
Allotments granted under the Land Development Ordinance	5.27	3.53
Encroached (Private)	5.00	5.33
Encroached (Government)	2.00	1.50
Leased in	4.10	--
Leased out	2.94	2.00
Rented in	4.00	--

Source: HARTI-Socio Economic Survey (1998)

Land Fragmentation

The initial equal size land allocation was sub-divided and distributed among the second and third generation farmers. A decrease in land sizes by 45% to 60% after thirty years period of the establishment of settlements can be observed and cultivating lowland with an extent of 0.25 acres is not uncommon (Wanigarathne, 1995 and Chandrasiri, 2009). Land Watch Asia states that nearly 300,000 share tenants and 1.2 million landowning farmers who live in similar, dismal conditions. Any action to improve the plight of share tenants must also take into account the conditions of small land-owning cultivators. Wickramarchachi and Weerahewa (2018) find a significant variability in productivity has been observed by size class, number of plots, distance to plots, shape of the plots, and tenure arrangement. It was revealed that land productivity decreases when a farmer cultivates more plots, plots that are far from home, and irregular shaped plots keeping all other factors affecting productivity at constant levels, total farm productivity increases until the farm size reaches 1.708 hectares and it declines thereafter and productivity of plots increases with size. An increase in size by one hectare will increase land productivity by 185 kg.

Land Degradation

Land degradation has emerged as a serious problem in Sri Lanka over the last century. Around 11.8% of the land area of Sri Lanka is categorized under high hazard level of erosion while 4.8% is under very high level of hazard (Jayasekara et al, 2018). Both these categories are not suitable for any land use in terms of sustainable productivity. In the long run these are leading to loss of water resources, vegetation, biodiversity and ecosystem services, and less climate resilient in agricultural production systems.

Furthermore, more than 44% of the soils in the country are under some form of degradation. For example, soil fertility has affected agricultural land productivity making 1.2 million ha (Sustainable Sri Lanka, 2030), mostly in the Dry Zone, unproductive and of limited use while marginal lands have led to the loss of land productivity in annual and perennial cropping and animal production.

According to Agriculture Household Survey 2016/2017, of the agriculture households, 54% do not engage in any form of soil erosion control. Terraces and bunds are being used by 27% of the population each. A survey was conducted by Hector Kobbakaduwa Agrarian Research and Training Institute (HARTI) in 1998 to ascertain the relationship between soil erosion and insecurity of tenure. The topsoil was thinnest in encroachments on Government lands where the occupants had no security of tenure. See Table 7. Further, annual leases by government and temporary leases granted by the private sector do not create the motivation required for the farmers to adopt soil conservation practices because the benefits of investments on land conservation are realized only in the long term. This applies also to leasing of agricultural lands by entrepreneurs, very often on short-term basis, to cultivate commercial crops such as potato, vegetables and pineapples. The tenurial arrangements leave little incentives for the lessees to adopt conservation measures (UNEP, 2001).

About 14% of the island's total land area is under state ownership as protected areas of which 12.3% is administrated by the Department of Wildlife Conservation and the balance 1.7% by the Forest Department, designated as different categories of reserves under the protected area network. The boundaries of reserves are being surveyed and marked to prevent encroachments. However, still deforestation and forest degradation due to encroachment, tree felling are still continuing. During the last three decades, the importance of community participation in biodiversity conservation has gained much recognition. Forest zoning and buffer zone management, participatory forest management is being increasingly considered in the protection of conservation areas, particularly in the buffer zone development activities with limited success in Sri Lanka. In forest plantation establishments, thaungya system, community forestry and participatory forestry approaches have been used but again with limited success due to lack of land rights for cultivators. Forest users have been registered and permits have been granted to collect non-timber forest products, but again with limited success.

Chena (shifting cultivation) continues in most Dry Zone areas despite restrictions, contributing to land degradation and thwarting efforts to introduce alternative farming systems. About a million farmers depend on chena for their livelihoods or as a secondary source of income (Land Watch) (Gunasena and Pushpakumara, 2015).

Land Conflicts

In the war-affected areas of Sri Lanka, land use for agricultural production has been severely affected by the conflict because people had to abandon their land or cannot access it due to the war. The current volatile and fuzzy land entitlements seriously threaten the societal bonds across communal boundaries, constrain development efforts and contribute to confirm old and create new socio-political cleavages among the communal (ethnic) groups in the Trincomalee district (Fonseka and Raheem, 2010).

Encroachment

The last encroachment survey was conducted in 1979, and no similar survey has been done since. The island-wide survey done by the Department of Land Commissioner General (DOLCG) in 1979 revealed that an extent of 386,038 ha was encroached, out of which, about 155,803 ha were distributed among encroachers in all districts in the country by 1980. Since then, the DOLCG has undertaken further clearances of encroachment. It may be assumed that there are nearly half a million encroachments despite periodic regularization. Evicting encroachers may not be a good political option, but allowing "business-as-usual" not only increases proneness to natural hazards such as floods and landslides, but encourages further encroachments.

Institutional Coordination

There are numerous policies, laws, action plans and institutions involved in addressing the land use and land tenure issues in Sri Lanka. Having multiplicity of agencies enhances inefficiencies in coordination. Poor land recording (all compounded by a heavily centralized administration with the Land Commissioner's Department). As an example, there has been much concern about bringing the Forest Department and the Department of Wildlife Conservation under one ministry. Further, in 1979 the Land Use Policy Planning Division (LUPPD) was set up under the Ministry of Lands and District Land Use Planning Committees (DLUPC) were set up at each district consisting of 10-12 district level officers. More recently a District Land Use Planner was appointed to each district who is supposed to coordinate planning at national, district and local levels.

CONCLUSIONS

This chapter provides an overview of regulations governing agriculture lands in Sri Lanka with special emphasis on their implications on land tenure, size of the holdings and land use. It was evident that the government of Sri Lanka adopted diverse regulatory measures to achieve the political objectives of the rulers at the time.

During the pre-colonial era, the objective of the rulers, i.e., kings, was to make the country self-sufficient in food and a hydraulic civilization was promoted. Accordingly, a semi-feudal arrangement was in place to distribute lands for cultivation among various communities under different tenure systems. The King, who owned lands in the entire country obtained taxes, mostly in kind or as services, to earn the needed revenue. Paddy and other field crops were the main crops cultivated. Cultivation of spices, mainly cinnamon, was evident during Kings era mainly for export purposes in exchange for clothing.

During the colonial rule, the objective was to export agricultural commodities to earn foreign exchange (in form of gold and silver) and commercial cultivation of spices, coffee, tea, rubber and coconut was promoted. The land tenure system prevailed in the country did not facilitate acquisition of lands for commercial cultivation and hence regulations were formulated to declare all uncultivated lands and waste lands as crown lands. Simultaneously, the *Rajakariya* system was abandoned with the objective of releasing workers from their designated enterprises to the plantation sector.

With the promotion of export agriculture, domestic agriculture was neglected. Domestic production of rice was not sufficient to meet the local demand. As a result, rice had to be imported. When world prices escalated with the World War I, the colonial government found it difficult to finance the import bill and it resolved to promote domestic food production. To facilitate this move, land colonization schemes were initiated. The LDO of 1935 was enacted for this purpose.

The first Sri Lanka prime-minister of the Independent Sri Lanka continued the above movement. River diversion programs were initiated to support colonization and the expanded agriculture and regulations were enacted to secure rights of the tenant farmers.

During 1970s, the government took Marxist view of Economic Development. A maximum ceiling of 50 acres was imposed for single ownership of land. Remaining lands was appropriated to reduce the income disparity among people and to even out asset distribution. Large plantations were nationalized and management of the plantations was given out to two plantation companies holding the ownership with the state. Land were alienated in small plot sizes keeping ownership with the state.

The effects of the above regulations on degradation and productivity of agricultural lands has been a source of concern among many. A number of regulations were enacted to address this issue. A minimum size for the holding was imposed to deter further fragmentation of lands. The present day programmes seek clear demarcation of lands and provision of more rights to the occupants of lands.

A complete assessment of implications of the above regulations is way beyond the scope of this chapter but the above discussions indicate that they shaped up tenure rights, size of the holdings and land use pattern of the country. A revisiting of regulations governing agricultural lands is required to address the issues of availability and access to agricultural lands, land fragmentation, tenure insecurity, under-developed land markets, encroachment of state lands and weak institutional coordination.

Acknowledgements

The support provided by the AHEAD/DOR/52 project administered by the Faculty of Agriculture, University of Peradeniya, Sri Lanka is gratefully acknowledged.

REFERENCES

Abeysinghe, A. (1979). *Ancient land tenure to modern land reform in Sri Lanka*. Academic Press.

Abeywardana, N., Schütt, B., Wagalawatta, T., & Bebermeier, W. (2019). Indigenous agricultural systems in the dry zone of Sri Lanka: Management transformation assessment and sustainability. Sustainability, 11(3), 910. doi:10.3390u11030910

Alwis, J., & Wanigaratne, R. D. (2001). *Agrarian reforms and agricultural productivity: A status review of Sri Lanka's experience.* Report of the Asian Productivity Organization Meeting.

Amerasinghe, N. (1976). An overview of settlement schemes in Sri Lanka. *Asian Survey*, *16*(7), 620–636. doi:10.2307/2643162

Bastian, S. (2009). The politics of land reform and land settlement in Sri Lanka. Kathmandu, Nepal: Panos South Asia.

Caron, C. M. (2018). Pursuing gender-transformative change in customary tenure systems: Civil society work in Zambia. *Development in Practice*, *28*(7), 872–883. doi:10.1080/09614524.2018.1480896

Chandrasiri, J.K.M.D. (2010). *Impact of informal land transactions in settlement schemes in Sri Lanka.* HARTI-Research Report, 132.

Chandrasiri, S. (2009). Labour market trends and informal sector of the economy. *Sri Lanka Economic Journal*, *2*(1), 89–106.

Chokkalingam, U., & Vanniarachchy, A. (2011). *Sri Lanka's REDD+ potential, myth or reality?* Forest Carbon Asia.

De Silva, M. U. (1992). Land tenure, caste system and the rājakāriya, under foreign rule: A review of change in Sri Lanka under Western powers, 1597-1832. *Journal of the Royal Asiatic Society of Sri Lanka, 37*, 1–57.

Ellman, A. O. (1976). *Land settlement in Sri Lanka, 1840-1975: A review of the major writings on the subject*. Academic Press.

Felloni, F. &McGrenra, D. (2013). *Democratic Socialist Republic of Sri Lanka*. Academic Press.

Fonseka, B., & Raheem, M. (2010). *Land in the eastern province: politics, policy and conflict*. Centre for Policy Alternatives.

Gamage, D. (2000). *Little space for maneuvering: agrarian structure, land tenure regimes and agrarian development in Sri Lanka. Sri Lanka agriculture for the next decade: challenges and opportunities*. HARTI.

Ganewatta, G. & Edwards, G. W. (2000). *The Sri Lanka tea industry: economic issues and government policies*. Academic Press.

Goonewardene, L. K. P., & Hatten, C. J. (1990). Rationalizing land use. *Economic Review, 15*(10).

Gunasena, H. P. M., & Pushpakumara, D. K. N. G. (2015). Chena cultivation in Sri Lanka: prospects for agroforestry interventions. In Shifting Cultivation and Environmental Change: Indigenous People, Agriculture and Forest Conservation. Routledge, Taylor & Francis.

HARTI. (1998) A Study on Socio Economic Aspects of Soil Erosion for Ministry of Forestry and Environment. Hector Kobbakaduwa Agrarian Research and Training Institute, WijeramaMawatha, Colombo 7, Sri Lanka.

Herath, J. (2006). *Distributional impacts of land policies in Sri Lanka. Sri Lankan Agriculture Economics Association (SLEA) and Movement for National Land and Agricultural Reform*. MONLAR.

Herath, J. (2006). *Distributional impacts of land policies in Sri Lanka. Sri Lankan Agriculture Economics Association (SLEA) and Movement for National Land and Agricultural Reform*. MONLAR.

Jayasekara, M. J. P. T. M., Kadupitiya, H. K., & Vitharana, U. W. A. (2018). Mapping of soil erosion hazard zones of Sri Lanka. *Tropical Agricultural Research, 29*(2), 135–146. doi:10.4038/tar.v29i2.8284

Korf, B. (2002). Ethnicised entitlements in land tenure of protracted conflicts: The case of Sri Lanka. *9th Biennial IASCP Conference*, 17-21.

Kumara, K. K. (2016). Agrarian change in the peasant economy of a paddy producing village in the Southern dry zone of Sri Lanka: The Gambaraya system in transition. *Sri Lanka Journal of Social Sciences, 0*(0), 77. doi:10.4038ljss.v0i0.7431

Land Watch Asia. (2012). *Land ownership and the journey to self-determination*. Sri Lanka Country Paper.

Leach, E. R. (1959). Hydraulic society in Ceylon. *Past & Present, 15*(1), 2–26. doi:10.1093/past/15.1.2

Leach, E. R. (1961). *PulEliya: a village in Ceylon*. Cambridge University Press.

MaddumaBandara, C. M. (1990). Land use policy. *Economic Review, People's Bank, 15*(10).

Mapa, R. B., Kumaragamage, D., Gunarathne, W. D. L., & Dassanayake, A. R. (2002). Land use in Sri Lanka: past, present and the future. *Proceedings of the 17th World Congress of Social Science (WCSS)*, 14-21.

Marambe, B., Silva, P., & Athauda, S. (2017). Agriculture and rural development under central government and provincial council setup in Sri Lanka. In *Decentralization and Development of Sri Lanka Within a Unitary State* (pp. 111–145). Springer. doi:10.1007/978-981-10-4259-1_6

Marawila, D. (2007). Revitalizing small-scale agriculture: Rental policies of alienated state lands of Sri Lanka. *Sri Lankan Journal of Agricultural Economics*, *9*(0), 23–42. doi:10.4038jae.v9i0.1831

Mundial, B. (2008). *Land reforms in Sri Lanka: a poverty and social impact analysis*. PSIA.

Nanayakkara, V. K. (2006). Agrarian reform and rural development: issues, concerns and future challenges: *Twenty-second meeting of CIRDAP technical committee (TC-22)*.

Niroula, G. S., & Thapa, G. B. (2005). Impacts and causes of land fragmentation, and lessons learned from land consolidation in South Asia. *Land Use Policy*, *22*(4), 358–372. doi:10.1016/j.landusepol.2004.10.001

Obeyesekere, G. (2008). *Land tenure in village Ceylon: a sociological and historical study*. Cambridge University Press.

Obeysekara, G. (1967). *Land Tenure in Village Ceylon*. Cambridge University Press.

Ostrom, E., & Schlager, E. (1996). The Formation of Property Rights. In Rights to Nature: Ecological, Economic, Cultural, and Political Principles of Institutions for the Environment. Washington, DC: Island Press.

Parakrama, A. (2006). Rural Land Sector In Sri Lanka: Major Characteristics, Determinants and Implications for Land Policy. Institute of Policy Studies.

Paranage, K. (2018). The consequences of restricting rights to land: understanding the impact of state-land tenure policies in Sri Lanka. *Sustainability: Science, Practice and Policy*, *14*(1), 46–54.

Peiris, G. H. (1978). Land reform and agrarian change in Sri Lanka. *Modern Asian Studies*, *12*(4), 611–628. doi:10.1017/S0026749X0000634X

PrabathWitharana, D. D. (2014). *The impact of land consolidation programme on land productivity in traditional agricultural land tenure system in the wet zone of srilanka* (Doctoral dissertation). Sri Lanka Institute of Development Administration.

Samaratunga, P. A., & Marawila, D. (2006). *Rural Land Sector in Sri Lanka: Major Characteristics, Determinants, and Implications for Land Policy (No. 7)*. Institute of Policy Studies.

Samaraweera, V. (1982). Land Reform in Sri Lanka. *Third World Legal Stud.*, 104.

Shah, T., Samad, M., Ariyaratne, R., & Jinapala, K. (2013). Ancient small-tank irrigation in Sri Lanka: Continuity and change. *Economic and Political Weekly*, 58–65.

UNEP. (2001). *State of the Environment Sri Lanka – 2001. United Nations Environment Programme*. Regional Resources Centre for Asia and the Pacific.

Wanigaratne, R.D. (1995). *Informal tenure conditions in irrigated settlements in Sri Lanka: A review of empirical research evidence.* Land Tenure Center, University of Wisconsin.

Wanigaratne, R. D., Gooneratne, W., &Shanmugaratnam, N. (1979). *Policies and implementation of land reform in selected villages of Sri Lanka.* ARTI Research Study (Sri Lanka). no. 32.

Wickramaarachchi, N.C., & Weerahewa, J. (2018). Relationship between Land Size and Productivity: Empirical Evidence from Paddy Farms in Irrigation Settlements of Sri Lanka. *Sri Lanka Journal of Economic Research.*, *5*(2), 125–142.

Wickramarachchi, N.C., & Weerahewa, J. (2016). Land Fragmentation and Land Productivity: Empirical Evidence from Land Distribution Schemes of Sri Lanka. *International Academic Research Journal of Business and Management.*, *5*(1), 11–21.

Wijeyewardene, E. A. L. (1956). *Report of the Commission on Tenure of Lands of Viharagam, Dewalagam and Nindagam.* Ceylon Sessional Paper, 1-1956.

Zubair, L. (2005). Modernisation of Sri Lanka's Traditional Irrigation Systems and Sustainability. *Science, Technology & Society*, *10*(2), 161–195. doi:10.1177/097172180501000201

ENDNOTES

1 *Thattumaru* and *kattimaru* are rotational cultivation practices of a land plot by a group of farmers. Under these traditional methods of land tenure, the lands are not divided but held jointly by a number of cultivators (owners and tenants), each of whom take over a small area in rotation depending on his share in the join holding. The cultivators keep changing every year and there is no single cultivator always working the land. *Thattu* means tray or plot and *Maru* means exchange or shift hence rotation. *Thattumaru* is the rotation of farmer groups and *Kattimaru* is the rotation of land parcels while the land is constant, by years. The basic idea of *Thattumaru* and *Kattimaru* system was to avoid over fragmentation while maintaining high degree of equity.

2 This includes all land vested in government institutes mainly the Department of Forest Conservation, Department of Wild Life Conservation, Department of Railway, Mahaweli Authority and Land Commissioner General's Department.

3 Leach (1959) refers this as "caste feudalisms" in which specialised occupations are professed not by individuals but by whole groups (sub-castes), and, provided these sub-caste groups are physically immobile, complex organic structures of specialized labour division can be maintained from generation to generation without any intervention of a money medium. The economic contract is a permanent one between settled groups continuously resident in particular localities. He further,notes that, as to their main occupation, all these castes are peasant cultivators, cultivating irrigated rice lands according to identical techniques. Where the castes differ from one another is in the service duties which they formerly owed to their feudal lords in payment for their land. Thus the farmers rendered military service or tax in kind but the lower castes rendered their profession: i.e. the washerman washed clothes, the blacksmith made tools, the potter made pots.

Chapter 9
Youth Willingness to Accept Agricultural Entrepreneurship in Bedkot Municipality, Kanchanpur, Nepal

Niranjan Devkota
https://orcid.org/0000-0001-9989-0397
Quest International College, Nepal

Ashok Joshi
Quest International College, Nepal

Udaya Raj Paudel
Quest International College, Nepal

ABSTRACT

One of the major factors that aids in economic growth, sustainability, and poverty reduction of a developing nation is agriculture. With the passage of time, contribution of agriculture in GDP seems decreasing and youths' involvement towards agricultural entrepreneurship has been increasing in Nepal. Agro-entrepreneurship is rising due to technological innovation and transformation in production process that will provide higher output aiding in income generation. This study aims to identify youths' willingness to accept agriculture entrepreneurship and provincial role for its development. This study is based on explanatory research design with 324 samples from farmers of Bedkot municipality. Both primary and secondary data are used for the study based on a structured questionnaire. Tobit model has been used to generate results, along with several variables based on descriptive and inferential analysis. The study depicts that agriculture information has positive significance with overall awareness of youths' willingness to accept agriculture entrepreneurship. Likewise, youths' acceptance of agro-entrepreneurship is significant to annual income, land size, market information centre (MIC) as well. Training and awareness of agricultural entrepreneurship need to be focused more by policy-makers. This is one of the first investigations conducted to identify the various dimensions of youths' willingness to accept agriculture entrepreneurship in the Nepalese context.

DOI: 10.4018/978-1-7998-4372-6.ch009

1. INTRODUCTION

Youth agricultural entrepreneurs came together to share their experiences and skills among the participants in the first agro Entrepreneurship Symposyum 2016 organized by 4-H Nepal in Kathmandu, which formed a network entitled 'Youth Agro-Entrepreneurs' Association' . The members of this network have been involved in advocating and facilitating the issues of agriculture and access to youth entrepreneurs in various districts of Nepal (Pande et al., 2016). Nepal is experiencing unique socioeconomic changes, including massive out-migration of the youth, which has made larger agricultural areas to become unused, particularly in those areas that are near to forests, far away from settlements and with low productivity, as examined by (Paudel et al., 2014). The youth negotiation brought together over 100 Nepali youth from various sectors are benefitted to identify and acknowledge the spirit of the Nepali youth and to support the role of the youth in the development of Nepal (ILO, 2016). Agriculture is more effective than other sectors for reducing poverty and throughout the world agriculture sector produces more healthy food for improving the livelihood of growing population, especially to the poor (World Bank Agriculture, 2014). As mentioned by Budhathoki et al. (2019), sectorial ministries of Nepal have issued and implemented gender equality and social inclusion policies in the agricultural sector as well in order to encourage participation in agricultural activities from every level.

Nepal is a small land-linked country with diverse agro-ecologies, culture, and agriculture sector, where agriculture is a key source of economic growth, poverty reduction, and environmental sustainability in Nepal (Gauchan & Shrestha, 2017). Nepal is an agriculture based country and its one-third of GDP comes from agriculture. There are various opportunities in agriculture sector because of mixed agro-climate occupied in the country (Paudel, 2016; Devkota and Phuyal, 2018). In Nepal, the availability of arable land is declining rapidly. More than 55% of the holdings are smaller than 0.5 hectares (ha) in 2010 (CBS, 2011). Similarly, out of 56.6 million households, 4.25 million farming households are landless, and half of them are deprived of a piece of land, even for housing (CSRC, 2012).

The contribution of agriculture sector has shrunk to 27.6% in fiscal year 2017/18 compared to 28.8% in FY 2016/17, and the average annual growth rate of agriculture sector remained 2.9% in FY 2017/18 which is less than 1.5% compre to FY 2016/17 (MOF, 2018). For the purpose of self-employment to poor and unemployed youth, there is a provision of maximum Rs. 200 thousand per entrepreneur without any collateral or securities through Youth and Small Entrepreneurship Self-employment Programs (Sunder, 2018). In 2018, 12,622 people have been provided the orientation training, and 658 people have been provided skill-based training through Youth and Small Entrepreneurship Self-employment Programs. Further, to encourage youths with higher education to start their own businesses, the arrangements have made to provide loan of up to Rs. 700 thousand with 5 percent subsidy in interest rate against collateral of their academic certificates (Sunder, 2018).

Several questions have been aroused from the perspective of youth agriculture entrepreneurship in the context of Nepal, which needs to be answered in this study. Some questions are: what is the understanding of people about agricultural entrepreneurship? what is the best agricultural entrepreneur practice adopted in Nepal? how has agriculture been converted to be entrepreneurship? what are the factors associated with the province roles? what are the barriers to those factors? what is the strategy adopted for agricultural entrepreneur? Thus, a proper assessment is required to explore these questions in the context of Nepalese youth agriculture entrepreneurs. Therefore, the aim of this research is to analyze the youth's willingness to accept agricultural entrepreneurship in Bedkot municipality, Kanchanpur, Nepal.

This research explores the interest and perception of youth toward agriculture and agricultural entrepreneurship. It also shows the need of agricultural entrepreneurship and identifies the subsidies and other facilities provided by the provincial government to youth entrepreneurs. Similarly, this research helps to determine the proper management strategy for youth entrepreneurial roles. This research is beneficial to the future researcher, youth farmer of Sudurpaschim provincial government, policymakers, various farmers, and other interested people as well.

The remaining part of this paper is organized as section 2 represents the literature review; section 3 discusses materials and methods with data collection techniques and study area; section 4 covers the results and findings of the study; section 5 presents the discussion; and conclusions and policy recommendations are presented in section 6.

2. LITERATURE REVIEW

2.1. Agriculture Entrepreneurship

Traditionally, agriculture was seen as a low-tech industry with restricted dynamics dominated by several small families (farmers), which mostly focuses on doing things better is changed doing new things and from the last decade, the situation has been changed entirely by the cause of economic liberalization, to protect reducing agricultural markets, which is a fast-changing, (Lans et al., 2011). Agricultural entrepreneurship was hypothesized into the strategic orientations, social orientation, growth orientation, and financial conservatism. Nowadays, social farmers and new farmers who are more socially oriented seem to have the best response to the demands of today's agricultural entrepreneurship (De Lauwara, 2005). The average age of youth farmers all over the world has been increasing because of agriculture was not the first choice of youths. Agriculture entrepreneurships are creative, innovative, self-motivated, and have the ability to optimally take advantage of available opportunities (Khan et al., 2013). It was conceptualized into the strategic orientation, social orientation, growth orientation, and financial conservatism, in positive, "tough" personal characteristics affect agricultural entrepreneurship positively and negative personal characteristics affect it negatively (De Lauwere, 2005). Agricultural innovation policies should not seek to fully plan, control and manage the agricultural innovation system but to operate on the probability of events, to increase the odds of desired outcomes, and reduce the chances of undesired results (Hall et al., 2003; Spielman et al., 2010; Poncet et al., 2010).

According to Anderson and Jack (2002), entrepreneurship is the development of ideas into valuable business propositions and the pulling together of resources. Entrepreneurship in the farming sector is seen as a means to transform the sector as well as to bring new economic development in rural areas (Alsos et al., 2011). Macher (1999) stated that agriculture entrepreneurship presence visionary, innovativeness, opportunity recognition and evaluation, resilience, risk tolerance and self-efficacy. Among other entrepreneurship, sustainability and profitability are the underlying principles of any agriculture entrepreneurship venture. Agricultural entrepreneurship may arise from internal factors such as personal interest as well as external factors like as influence by family members, friends, and mentors (Buli & Yesuf, 2015; Carr & Sequeira, 2007). Agricultural entrepreneurship has received much attention in the last decade, in developed and developing economies and recent studies show that agricultural entrepreneurship is not only wishful thinking or a new hype, it has a weighty impact on business growth and existence (Lans et al., 2011; Verhees et al., 2011).

Thus, from the above definitions, the agricultural entrepreneur develops ideas, economies, and personal interests. Similarly, agriculture entrepreneurship involves creating a product or provides services related to agriculture and make higher productivity and innovation in agriculture for enhancing income level and improve livelihood. Likewise, agriculture entrepreneurship arises from internal factors; they have vision, innovativeness, risk-taking capacity, generate opportunity, and self-sufficiency among others.

2.2. Agriculture Entrepreneurship in Nepal

Today, the scope of agriculture in Nepal is environmentally friendly farming, ecological farming, bio-dynamic agriculture, regenerative agriculture, natural farming, permaculture, and sustainable agriculture (Tamang et al., 2011). Nowadays, farmers are modifying their agriculture into agriculture entrepreneurship for higher productivity and expansion of agriculture sectors. In Nepal, the first agro-entrepreneurship symposium held in 2016 and second in 2018 to promote agriculture sectors. In present context, the youth force is currently migrating in foreign employment that has caused agriculture sector currently suffering from labor force and entrepreneurship deficits. Nepal is going through a youth bulge approximately 61% of the age group 16-40 years; they are utilizing their skill and talents in agriculture fields. Only youth can transform agriculture sector by using modern technology and new thinking. Dhital (2017) states that 'the agriculture sector of Nepal is currently suffering from human resources and entrepreneurship deficit because the youth force is presently directed towards foreign employment. Thus, Selling off land and cattle to arrange money for a job in a foreign land is a growing trend, which does not bode well for the sector regarded as the backbone of the national economy.

Tandukar et al. (2019) urge that banking, finance, and corporate sectors are taking commendable initiatives in order to aid and promote agricultural sector. Agriculture development bank was established to promote agriculture sectors; that provides various facilities to the youth farmer, developing remote area, provide different insurance and other essential facilities to promote agriculture of the nation. Similarly, the government of Nepal is also providing various subsidies in diverse forms to make sustainable agriculture development. Today, youths are motivating in agriculture sector and they invest certain fund themselves and government also support them to enhance agriculture industry. In 2019, the financial minister separated the Nepalese Rupees 8 billion for the prime minister agriculture plan to promote agriculture sectors. Almost all the commercial banks are providing credit facilities a lower interest rate for encouraging youths in agriculture sectors. There are various rules and regulation formulated by different governments to promote agriculture sectors that helps reducing costs. In Nepal, there is zero value-added tax (VAT) in the agriculture sector for enhancing agriculture. However, Devkota et al. (2017) stated that if the government boosts agriculture activities in Nepal, it could help in the development of agricultural sector.

B.K. et al. (2019) mentioned that Sustainable Development Goals (SDG) Nepal (goal number 2) provides emphasis on ending hunger, achieving food security, improving nutrition, and promoting sustainable agriculture. Agriculture is the main source of income, food, and employment of Nepal. The agriculture sector contributes 27.6% in GDP and provides 66% of the people livelihoods in the nation, but farmers have limited technology, unavailable seed sources, and they are using traditional systems in farming sector (ILO, 2018). The government of Nepal directly as well as indirectly promotes the agriculture entrepreneurship of the nation with the help of loans and subsidies, trainings, increasing awareness programs, promoting agriculture programs, and so on. The government of Nepal introduces various plans to expand the agriculture sectors and encourages youths. In a developing country like

Nepal, agriculture is the main source of food, income, and employment of the nation. In every year, agriculture sector's contribution to GDP is decreasing, but the employment rate on agriculture is almost the same. The government of Nepal imports the agricultural products like rice, vegetables, in higher quantities, despite comparatively higher cultivable land. Farmers are following the traditional system for agriculture production, which cause lower productivity and lower earning. So, to enhance productivity in the agriculture sector, we must need agricultural entrepreneurship that helps to export the agriculture product or stay on the balance of payment of the agriculture sectors. If the agriculture sector is modified, that will help to enhance per capita income of the nation.

3. RESEARCH METHOD

This research is based on explanatory research design. The research is conducted to identify the extent and nature of cause and effect relationships, and this study falls in explanatory research design category because it is a survey. A significant weigh is given to both the quantitative and qualitative data collenction and analysis in the study. Morgan (1998) argued that such coverage is integrated part of the study. Researchers must initially conceptualize the variables and provide a clear conceptual definition (Neuman, 2003). Therefore, this study tries to analyze the relation between dependent and independent variables.

3.1. Conceptual Framework

A farmer's choice is understood through the willingness to participate in agri-environmental measures model. This theory explains that people are more willing to join in a group to cooperate (or to solve) a common problem if they perceive that they will receive a benefit from their cooperation. Here, team members have related backgrounds and goals, they can trust other members of the group and they have strong social connections (Ostrom, 1990; Pretty, 2003). Also, there are various factors which can be recognized to individual behavior, perceptions and participation in agro-environmental measures argue such measures as representation for familiarity and environmental concerns (Drake et al., 1999; Devkota et al., 2018).

3.2. Theoretical Framework

Apart from decision subject characteristics, decision making characteristics play vital roles for farmers' willingness to accept. Individual characteristic is one of the determinants for their subjective judgment. People from different geographic location, different ages and aptitudes may perceive the same scheme differently. Hence, knowledge about entrepreneurship and its advantages, entrepreneurs and level of education could be enhancing factors for willingness to accept agro-entrepreneurship among the farmers. Farm characteristics also may influence in a different way. It can be assumed that farm size and structure has a potential influence on decision-maker characteristics. Often small farm size/landholders have less willingness to accept any regulatory and other decision support characteristics. With the decision, this research assumes willingness to accept for agricultural entrepreneurship that may be influenced by both decision support characteristics and decision-makers' characteristics, but their intensity to influence is to check by empirical analysis, which is the primary goal of this research.

Figure 1. Conceptual model of willingness to participate in agro-environmental measurement
Source: Modified from Vanslembrouck et al. (2002)

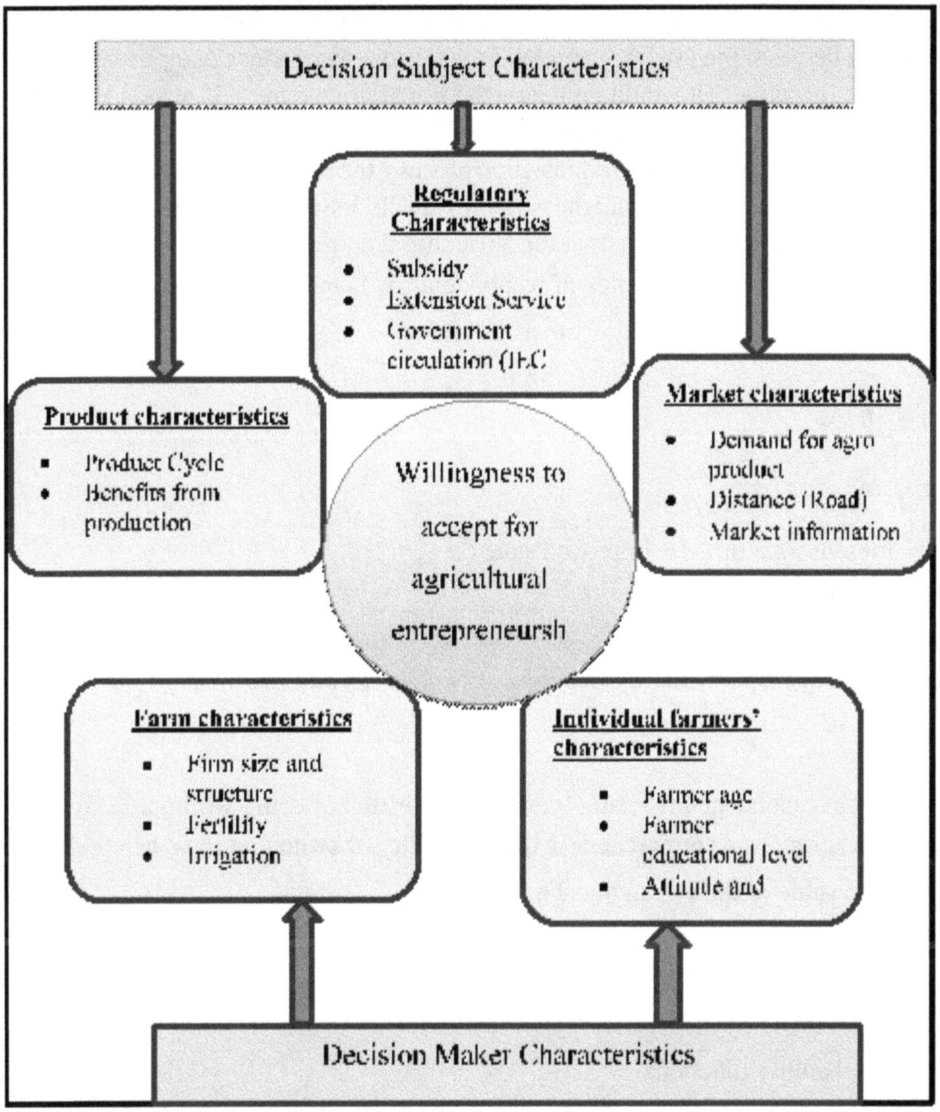

In order to transform conventional agricultural practices to agriculture entrepreneurs, it is essential to create a favorable environment for the farmers where they live and work. The willingness to accept could be one of the approaches for this transformation. This approach of agriculture has various advantages from providing commercial farming and products with demand. In this study, we identify the change to agriculture entrepreneur as the object of the value estimation and contingent valuation method, which is suitable for the hypothetical bias. In order to overcome this biasness, Cummings & Taylor (1999) recommended a cheap talk technique. The cheap talk was acquired from the game theory. This technique explains the hypothetical bias to survey parties. Similarly, it is a way to announce in advance that there should be careful decision making for reducing that biasness.

The premium price would be fixed between the minimum price (WTA–) and the maximum price (WTA+),. This study tired to test whether the youth farmer would be willing to change from conventional farming to agriculture entrepreneur under the condition that the premium price was set at the (WTA), randomly selected between the (WTA–) and (WTA+). If the respondent A replied 'yes,' there was no follow-up question (because that would go below the stated price range). If respondent A said 'no,' we asked the (WTA+) at what revenue level he/she would switch to.

To provide a specific explanation of the selection process, the factor influencing farmers' willingness' to accept the agriculture entrepreneur and the variables are discussed in the form of utility function mode. This model is based on the assumption that the agricultural entrepreneur (i), individual respondent (j), personal income (y_j), the characteristics of respondent (z_j), and an unknown error (ε_{ij}). Hence, the equation of the individual utility function are as follows:

$$u_{ij} = u_i\left(y_j, z_j, q^i, \varepsilon_{ij}\right) \tag{1}$$

i = 0, 1 [(0= present state (q^0), 1= improved state (q^i)]
j = individual respondent
$y_j = personal\ income$
$z_j = characteristics\ of\ respondent\left(age, sex, educational\ background, residence\right)$
$\varepsilon_{ij} = unknown\ error$

A condition of a respondent answering 'yes' to the question of being willingness to accept the price of b_j to switch to agriculture entrepreneur is that the utility of switching must be greater than or equal to rejecting it. The value of utility can thus be expressed as:

$$u_1\left(y_j + b_j, z_j, q^1, \varepsilon_{1j}\right) \geq u_0\left(y_j, z_j, q^0, \varepsilon_{0j}\right) \tag{2}$$

Expressed as a probability function:

$$\Pr\left(yes\right) = \Pr[u_1\left(y_1 + b_j, z_j, q^1, \varepsilon_{1j}\right) > u_0\left(y_1, z_j, q^0, \varepsilon_{0j}\right) \tag{3}$$

The total number of respondents (T_j) is the sum of those that say 'yes' (Y_j) and those that say 'no' (N_j). The 'no' answer of the cumulative probability is shown in the equation (v). If cumulative probability (f_j) is not monotonically increasing, a monotonic increase in force can occur through a comprehensive process. Adjusting the cumulative probability (f_j) is shown in the equation (vi):

$$T_j = Y_j + N_j \tag{4}$$

$$f_j^* = \frac{N_J}{T_j} = \frac{N_j}{N_j + Y_j} \tag{5}$$

$$f_j^* = F_j - F_{j-1} \tag{6}$$

Here, we shall present similar Product-Limit estimator in the agricultural sector. This estimator, which has no closed method, is based on an iterative procedure and has been suggested by Turnbull (1976). The Turnbull method for estimating the cumulative probability (F_j) of negative responses is as follows. Therefore, the minimum boundary (b_d^j) and the maximum boundary (b_u^j) can be summarized into three cases: (yes), (no, yes), and (no). By considering each case is expressed as (M_y^j), $\left(M_{ny}^j\right)$ and $\left(M_n^j\right)$, the total number of respondents is thus:

$$N^j = M_y^j + M_{ny}^j + M_n^j \tag{7}$$

Estimating the probability is shown in the Equations (viii) and (ix):

$$r = Pr_1\left(b_d^j \geq WTA\right) = \frac{M_y^j}{N^j} \tag{8}$$

$$Pr = Pr_2\left(b_u^j \geq WTA\right) = \frac{M_{ny}^j + M_y^j}{N^j} \tag{9}$$

For a higher price of (j), the equation is equal to the lowest price of (j +1), and ($b_u^j = b_d^{i+1}$) and thus the Equation (ix is valid.

$$\Pr\left(b_u^j \geq WTA\right) = \Pr\left(b_d^{j+1} \geq WTA\right) \tag{10}$$

The Equation (x) indicates the average WTA computed by using the Turnbull model and the Equation (xii) demonstrates the variance in the WTA:

$$E_{meanB}\left(WTA\right) = \sum_{j=0}^{M} b_j \times f_j^* + 1 \tag{11}$$

$$V(E_{meanB}\left(WTA\right) = \sum_{j=1}^{M^*} \frac{F_j^*\left(1-F_j^*\right)}{T_j}(b_j - b_{j-1})^2 \tag{12}$$

3.3. Tobit Model

Tobit model was developed by James Tobin (1958) to describe the relation between non-negative variables and independent variables. Tobit model was used to classical farmers WTA using maximum likelihood estimation procedures. Tobit model or censored regression model is used to estimate the willingness to accept (WTA) for youth agricultural entrepreneurs because the government provides subsidies, trainings, irrigation facilities, insurances, and seeds for agricultural entrepreneurs. Tobit Model considers the nature of the data, either a left changed, or a right changed. Tobit model was used to analyse the attempting behavior for youth agricultural entrepreneurs. This model is also called a censored regression model, which is designed to estimate linear relationships between variables. The main interest is focused on the most important needed effects, and possible interactions were ignored. In general, the Tobit model can be expressed as:

$$y_i^* = \beta' x_i + u_i, u_i \sim N\left(0, \sigma^2\right)$$

$$y_i = y_i^* \ if\ y_i^* > 0\, or\, 0 \quad if\ y_i^* \leq 0$$

Therefore, the expected willingness to accept for consumer i can be computed as:

$$Ey_i^* = E\left(\frac{y_i}{y_i} > 0\right) \times f\left(\frac{y_i}{y_i} > 0\right) + E\left(\frac{y_i}{y_i} = 0\right) \times F\left(y_i = 0\right)$$

$$= [x'\beta + \sigma » \left(2'\, x/\sigma\right)] \times \varnothing\left(\frac{\beta' x_i}{\tilde{\sigma}}\right) + 0$$

$$= \beta' x_i \varnothing\left(\frac{\beta' x_i}{\tilde{\sigma}}\right) + \sigma\varnothing\left(\frac{\beta' x_i}{\tilde{\sigma}}\right)$$

Where the inverse Mills ratio ($»^2{}'\, x/\sigma$) is equal to $\varphi(\beta' x / \sigma) / \varnothing(\beta' x / \sigma)$ and the marginal effect for the continuous variable x_j is:

$$\frac{\partial E(y_i)}{\partial_{xj}} = \varnothing\left(\frac{\beta'_{xj}}{\sigma}\right)\beta_j$$

Assessing that the censor point is zero, the empirical model can be written as:

$Y = \alpha_0 + \beta_1 age + \beta_2 sex + \beta_3 education + \beta_4 marital\ status + \beta_5\ farm\ income + \beta_6 experience + \ldots + \beta_{17}$ farm structure $+ \varepsilon$

Where, Y = Dependent variable, β_1 - β_{17} = Independent variables (Independent variables are explained in detail in table 2) and ε = Error term.

The study assumed following hypothesis:

H_0: Youth farmers' from Bedkot Municipality are not willing to accept for agricultural entrepreneurship
H_1: Youth farmers' from Bedkot Municipality are willing to accept for agricultural entrepreneurship

The definition measurement and priori sings of the variables used in the study are illustrated in table 1.

3.4. Method of Data Collection

This section includes the study area, source and nature of population and sample, data analysis, and relevant other things. This study is based on both primary and secondary data.

3.5. Study Area

The study area selected for this research is Bedkot municipality of Kanchanpur district. It lies on 28^0 32' to 29^0 08' North latitude and 80^0 32' to 80^0 33' East longitude, which is located in Sudurpaschim Province of Nepal. The populations in the district composed of Brahman (15%), Chhetri (28%), Kami (10%), and Sarki (13%) and others include Thakuri, Sanyasy, Tamang, Magar, and Damai and the overall literacy rate of Kanchanpur district is 59.3%.

Sudurpaschim province is located in the western-most part of Nepal. In this province there are nine districts, out of those two districts (Kanchanpur and Kailali) are located in Terai regions and the other seven districts are located in Hilly and Himalaya regions. The total population of province seven was 2,552,517 and the population of Kanchanpur district was 451,248 in 2011 (CBS, 2011).

India lies in the west as well as south and Tibet (China) lies in the north of Sudurpaschim province Thus, the region has the good agriculture potentiality of external trade. Kailali (Dhangadhi), Dadeldhura, Kanchanpur (Mahendranagar), and Dipayal are the major trde center of this province where the main productive crops are wheat, rice, mustard, maize, and cotton. The District Agricultural Development Offices (DADOs) is located in Kanchanpur (Mahendranagar).

This province has both remote and development challenges; 44% of this province is Hills and 49% is Himalayan districts, which lies below the poverty. All these targets for food and nutrition security of the people seeking entrepreneurship in agricultural field and agricultural commodities. Hence, the study area provides careful observation and suggestions for foods and nutrition security for this region.

Table 1. Variables and expected signs of variables

Variables	Description	Value	Expected Sign
Age	Respondents' age	Years	±
Sex	Respondents' sex	1 = male, 0 = female	±
Education	Formal schooling	1 = Educated, 0 = Uneducated	+
Marital status	Marital status of the respondent	1 = Married, 2 = Unmarried	±
Farm income	Annual income	In Nepali Rupees	+
Experience	Work experience	In Years	±
Family types	Types of family	1= Nuclear, 0= Joint	±
Agricultural training	Agriculture training taken or not	1= Yes, 0= No	+
Farm size	Size of the land	In hectors	+
Irrigation	Flow of irrigation in cultivated land	1= Yes, 0= No	+
Product cycle	Production in years	1= 2 and more, 0= One	±
Market information Center in your area	Availability of marketing information center	1= Yes, 0= Others	+
Subsidy	Farmers received any form of subsidy	1= Yes, 0= No	+
Available of IEC materials	Available of IEC related service	1= Yes, 0= No	+
Demand for agro product	Demand of product in the market	1= Yes, 0= No	+
Fertility of land	Fertile land	1= Yes, 0= No	+
Farm Structure (sloppy, plain, wetland)	Types of land	1= Plain, 0= Others	+

3.6. Source and Nature of Data

The specific data required for this study are collected from both primary and secondary sources. Primary data are collected from questionnaire survey at Bedkot municipality of Kanchanpur district and also collected from key informants' interviews (KIIs) with experts. Similarly, secondary data were collected from different sources of information such as NPC, MOF, MOA, agricultural policy, land policy, labor act, etc., and by browsing electronic media, . Secondary data has been used for enhancing research and its finding helps to provide evidence for this study.

3.7. Study Population and Sample

Youth farmers of the Bedkot municipality are the population for this study. In this area, the total population was 49490, where total males are 23501 and females 25989 (CBS, 2011). In this area, the main economic sources are livestock and poultry, and others are cottage industries and trading. In this district, 75.65% households are based on agriculture. We used non-probabilistic sampling for our study. It is a sampling technique in which the researcher selects samples based on the particular judgment of the researcher rather than random selection, but it does not include all the members of the population, which have chance for participation in this study like probability sampling. Purposive sampling was used under non-probabilistic sampling and this method is based on characteristics of the population and objective of the study. In this sampling, the researcher has their own judgment when selecting the member of the population to participate in this study.

Figure 2. Location map of the study area

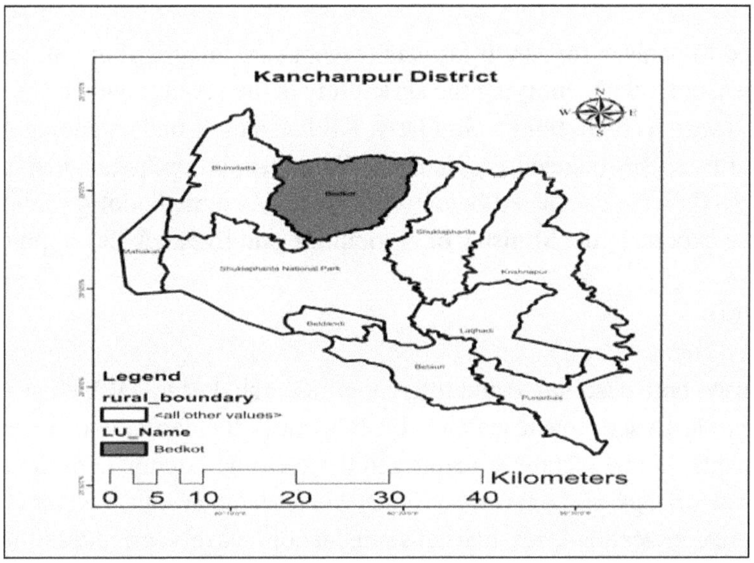

The following formula was used to calculate the sample size.

$n = z^2pq/l^2$ (Singh and Masuku, 2014)

where,

n_0 = sample size required for the study

Standard tabulate value for 5% level of significance (z) = 1.96

P = prevalence or proportion of an event 50% = 0.50

So, p =0.5 and q = 1-p, = 0.5
Allowable error that can be tolerated (e) = 6%
Total population for the study $n_0 = z^2pq/l^2$

$= (1.96)^2*0.5*0.5/(0.06)^2$

= 266.78

Non-responses error 5%, i.e. 266.78*5/100

= 13.34

Thus, sample size taken for study was (266.78+13.34) = 280.12 (≈280)

3.8. Research Instruments

KIIs were conducted to analyze the youth farmers' acceptance in agriculture and also to identify the agricultural entrepreneurs' role, identifying the agriculture in the seven provinces, government policies, market analyses, and various other things. Similarly, KII helps us in understanding Nepal's agriculture scenario, issues, and problems related to agriculture like irrigation problems, market problems, transportation problems. KIIs were conducted before starting research methodology, and this KII has been conducted with three experts in the Ministry of Agriculture and livestock development.

3.9. Data Analysis

In this section, we used both descriptive and inferential research designs. Which are:

Descriptive research: Descriptive research helps to identify the participants in an accurate way and describe all participants. In this section, we analyzed the socio-demographic of the farmers, provincial role, and management strategy of the farmers. Under this research design, we calculate data on the basis of farmer's age, sex, education level, marital status, income level, agriculture training, government roles, and so on.

Inferential statistics: In this section, inferential statistical analysis of studied samples are made which will be helpful to define significance of this study. Under this section, we use Tobit model and order logistics models to analyze summary statistics, correlation, regression, post estimation test, multicollinearity, and so on. For this study, STATA software was used for data analysis, and Microsoft Excel was used for data entry and tabulation. STATA software helps to analyze mode, median, mean and standard deviation.

4. RESULTS

4.1 Youth Farmer's Socio-Economic Characteristics

Youth involved in agricultural entrepreneurship are found to be in age group between 14-54. Highest numbers of respondents (30.86%) are between 31-40 ages. However, the lowest farmers are aged 50 above i.e., 8.02%. The study also shows that both males and females are involved in agriculture. It depicts that a total of 62.04% male and 37.96% female are involved in agriculture entrepreneurship. Similarly, the majority of respondents are from joint families (63.27%) and rather than nuclear families (36.73%). 80.56% of the respondents are married, among them, almost half respondents (50.62%) are married to joint families. The result shows that 62.5% of respondents are male educated respondents and 37.5% are female educated respondents. 93.82% people are literate and only 6.17% are illiterate. Among these respondents, 43.75% are from secondary level education background, which includes 24.34% male and 19.40% female. However, only 2.63% of the respondents are male who hold master's degrees in education.

Only 6.79% of the respondents are involved in agriculture training program and 93.21% of the respondents did not receive any training program. The result shows that 55.24% of the respondents are from agriculture backgrounds, which include 31.79% male and 23.45% female. Similarly, 25.31% of the respondents are from business backgrounds, which include 18.21% male and 7.09% female. However, 0.62% of the respondents (male) have industry background and no female entrepreneurs are found from industry background.

Results present that two-fifth of the respondents have less than 10 Kattha and one-third of people have 11-20 Kattha land. However, only a few respondents have more than 50 kattha land i.e., 6. In the same way, 90% of the respondents have their own land and are using leasehold land and communal land. Similarly, 285 respondents have plain land, 34 respondents have sloppy land and only 8 respondents have wetland.Almost all of the farmers have access to irrigation in their cultivated land by tune-well (46%) as well as canal (50%), but very few people (i.e. only 4%) use the rainwater for irrigation. Similarly, the result shows that one-third of the farmer responses that there is the market information center in this area, and 60% of the farmer responses that there is no market information center. The remaining farmers have very little or no knowledge about market information center . Likewise, those farmers who respond positively, they are nearest to the agriculture office and nearest to the highway.

Result shows that almost 90% of the farmers response that their families practice in crop cycle is two times in a year. 170 farmers get agriculture related information and 80% of them respond that this information is relevant to their agriculture activities. Most of the farmers receive information through television and radio, where few people receive from newspaper. Similarly, educated farmers response that mobile phone is the more practiced for information.

4.2. Youths' Perception on Agricultural Entrepreneurship in Bedkot Municipality

The results show that 5% of the farmers are involved in agriculture entrepreneurship i.e., poultry, vegetable, livestock, and fish farming. Most of the entrepreneurs are involved in less than five years in entrepreneur's activities, and their initial capital is less than 500000. Only a few entrepreneurs received supports from the government, which is less than 20%. Results show that vegetable farmers' entrepreneurship activities are in profit. It also reveals that there are more male agriculture entrepreneurs compared to females.

More than half respondents provide positive responses for getting ealy loan for agricultural activities in this area. The responses are dual, the less income farmers (i.e. ammual income 200000 or less) provides negative response while other income level respondents provide positive responses for getting easy loan. Similarly, the third-fourth of the respondents provide positive responses for a government subsidy is helpful for agriculture. Likewise, almost half of the total respondents provide positive responses for the credit facilities at commercial banks are available. In Bedkot municipality, there is both an adequate communication system and available electricity. Almost 90% of people are facilitated by the communication system and electricity.

3 out of every 5 responses expressed that the government is not actively supporting the entrepreneurial activities in the country. However, two-third of the sample responds that there is regular exchange of information and easy to access the domestic market. The youth agricultural entrepreneur feels that there is barrier in the market and goods do not get justified prices. 80% of respondents response lack of

general education negatively affecting farming operation; training is essential for profitability farming, and vocational education is important for future agriculture entrepreneurship. However, almost half of the respondents responded that family members influence their choices of farming activities. Most of the women respondents, old age respondents, and entrepreneurs' respondents answered that family members do not influence their choice of firming.

The results present those 3 out of 5 respondents response that taking risk by venturing into the unknown does not help to provide opportunities in the market. However, more than 80% respondents response that pro-activeness is encouraged to farmers that increase the use of information technology that can improve the knowledge and skill of farmers, and new methods of agriculture can improve the quality of products. The results show that 83% of the farmers' pro-activeness encourages emerging farmers, which include the same level of male and female. In the same ways, 84% males and 83% females respond that increasing use of information and technology (IT) can improve the farmers' knowledge and skills.

Responses from 80% of the respondents reveal that farmers require a creative mind to resolve problems, good knowledge of agricultural and farming techniques is necessary for success, and good knowledge of agriculture equipment is important for better soil management to avoid the soil losing quality. However, almost half of farmers respond that they are not adequately equipped with entrepreneurial skills. In the same way, 93% males and 79% females response that good knowledge of agriculture and farming techniques are necessary for success. Among the total respondents, only 15% of the farmers response that the entrepreneurship development scheme is sufficient to attract entrepreneurship in Bedkot municipality. Other farmers respond that there must be necessity of training, subsidies, increase in awareness level, agriculture related education, modern technology at cheaper prices, solve the market and road problem, and so on to attract entrepreneurship. This study shows that one-third of the farmer thinking for vegetable farming and modernized agriculture, one-fifth of the farmer thinking fish and livestock. However, few people want to expand the existing firm. 28% farmers require less than 100000 to invest for starting agro-entrepreneurship, 27% farmers require the 100001-200000, 10% farmers require the above 500000 for starting the entrepreneurship. The higher investment is required for poultry, livestock, and banana farming. Similarly, the result shows that if a subsidy is provided to the farmers, then more than 90% of the farmers become ready to start-up agriculture entrepreneurship.

4.3. Provincial Roles for Enhancing Youths Towards Agricultural Entrepreneurship

Among the sample, two-third of respondents response positively that if any support receives, they are ready for agriculture entrepreneurship. Farmers choose the provincial government for subsidy, training, enhancing agriculture, providing necessary facilities and information. Some of the farmers response that as now the provincial government is new, and it can not do better for the agriculture entrepreneurs as per the expectation of the entrepreneurs. A total of 25.6% farmers, among whom 30.85% are males, 12.8% secondary level educated people, and 30% uneducated people response that the provincial government acted the positive roles for the farmers, . A total of 38% people perceive that training and subsidy from the provincial government could enhance agricultural activities, whereas, 12.96% people express the need of other resources and information from provincial governments. Likewise, 10.5% female need better seeds and necessary materials for higher productivity.

In the same ways, master's degree educated people demand the higher budget, new agriculture programs, sufficient information and some of them respond that the provincial government can play a vital role for the farmers. 45% uneducated people need education and training for higher production. Farmers need other things like road management, market management, irrigation facilities, new methods, necessary materials related to agriculture, and so on. Existing entrepreneurs need the market management, special selling points, and necessary subsidies. Among the 58 respondents, 19 respondents are thinking of starting agro-entrepreneurship. Among these respondents, they start up modern agriculture, poultry farm, livestock, fish farming, vegetable farming, sugar candy, banana farming, expanding the existing farm, and start poly house.

4.4. Management Strategy for Youths' Attraction on Agricultural Entrepreneurship

A total 315 respondents response that there is a possibility of enhancing agriculture entrepreneurship in Nepal. One-fourth of the farmers need the agriculture related training, 26.98% of farmers need subsidy, and 12.06% farmers think that increasing awareness level is helpful to enhance agriculture entrepreneurship. Likewise, 11.43% of the farmers response that market management, road management, irrigation facility, motivation are necessary, and 11.43% farmers need the subsidy to enhance agriculture in this area. Similarly, farmers think that infrastructure, seeds and materials, new development programs, increased communication and providing information in time are essential to develop agricultural entrepreneurship. However, some farmers response that there is no possible space to enhance agriculture, they response that most of the youths are out migrant, land is not suitable, lack of market management, lower technology and traditional method is used in agriculture, so, it may be difficult to enhance agriculture in this area.

One-fifth of the farmers response that the availability of necessary resources (seeds, material, compost) in time is essential for overall development of agriculture entrepreneurship. Similarly, it also shows 25% of the farmers need training, and awareness level is the best strategy for overall development of agriculture entrepreneurs. Likewise, market management, subsidy, development program are essential for entrepreneurship development. The other necessary things are valuable information, irrigation, supervision through government; land in rent is also essential for overall development. However, some of the respondents responded that the government has corrupted bureaucrats and the government cannot take necessary action. So, it is difficult to say the best strategy for overall development of agricultural entrepreneurship in Bedkot municipality.

4.5. Awareness Index on Agricultural Entrepreneurship

This section presents the perception, knowledge, and awareness about the farmers related to agriculture entrepreneurship based on financial and non-financial perspective. This result shows that 55.56% of the farmers have a high level of awareness, 25.6% of the farmers are moderately aware and others are less aware (see Table 2). While analyzing the awareness level of farmers on social and cultural levels, it shows that 55% farmers are less aware, 32.7% farmers are moderate and only 12.3% farmers have higher awareness.

Table 2. Awareness index

Variables	Awareness level			
	Low	Medium	High	Total
Financial and non-financial	61	83	180	324
Social and cultural	178	106	40	324
Education and training	23	98	203	324
Risk taking and innovation	61	134	129	324
Technical and entrepreneur skills	72	146	106	324
Overall	19	191	114	324

Education and training are important for analyzing awareness level, where 62.65% of the farmers have high awareness, 30.25% farmers have medium and 7.1% farmers have less awareness. It shows that farmers need education and training related to the agriculture entrepreneurship that helps to enhance farmers' productivity. However, on the basis of risk-taking and innovation perspective, medium awareness level farmers are higher than other farmers, where 41.36% farmers have moderately awareness level, 39.81% farmers have high awareness and only 18.83% farmers are low aware.

Likewise, on the basis of technical and entrepreneur skills, 45.06% farmers have medium level of awareness, 32.7% farmers have high awareness and only 22.23% farmers have less awareness. It shows that educated farmers have high awareness then uneducated on the perspective of technical and entrepreneur skills. Similarly, compared with overall level of awareness 58.95% farmers have medium level of awareness, 35.18% farmers have low level and only 5.87% farmers are less aware. It means almost all farmers are more or less aware of the agriculture and agriculture related activities.

4.6. Tobit Regression Analysis

In this study, we use tobit regression analysis to analyze the farmers' maximum willingness to accept agriculture entrepreneurship. The study employed Tobit regression model to measure youths' willingness to accept agriculture entrepreneurship. Table 3 shows the overall results.

The first model of this study indicates that four independent variables are significant with respect to awareness of youths to accept agriculture entrepreneurship, among which three are positively significant and one is negatively significant. Three factors namely crop cycle, market information centre in the area, and demand for agro are positively significant whereas, agricultural training is negatively significant. Market information centre at your area and demand for agro are found to be 1% significant with youths' willingness to accept agriculture entrepreneurship and crop cycle is found to be significant at 5%.

Similarly, **the second model** depicts that four independent variables are significant with respect to awareness of youths' to accept agriculture entrepreneurship, among which three are positively significant and one is negatively significant. Similar to the results obtained from model one, three factors namely crop cycle, market information centre in your area, and demand for agro are positively significant whereas, agricultural training is negatively significant. Market information centre at your area and demand for agro are found to be 1% significant with youths' willingness to accept agriculture entrepreneurship and crop cycle is found to be significant at 5%. Hence, hypothesis is accepted as there is a significant relationship with explanatory variables.

Table 3. Tobit Regression Estimation

	UL 10,000,000	*UL 1,000,000*	*UL 100,000*
VARIABLES	**Model 1**	**Model 2**	**Model 3**
annual_income	-3,413	-1,241	2,099
	(7,101)	(6,058)	(1,421)
agricultural_training	**-49,033***	**-42,946***	-6,589
	(27,106)	(24,853)	(7,757)
farm_size	10,918	5,155	-5,116
	(21,437)	(19,083)	(3,818)
access_irrigation	-635.4	847.1	2,596
	(16,404)	(15,899)	(6,613)
crop_cycle	**55,454****	**50,692****	**16,588***
	(23,989)	(22,886)	(9,313)
mic_your_area	**57,861*****	**51,143*****	**9,787*****
	(19,253)	(16,091)	(3,352)
receive_subsidy	1,600	1,688	-511.8
	(9,034)	(8,040)	(2,460)
iec_information	-19,440	-15,191	**5,617***
	(14,281)	(12,544)	(2,900)
demand_agro	**194,564*****	**188,156*****	**89,588*****
	(20,998)	(18,398)	(4,435)
land_type	8,728	5,356	**-8,505****
	(11,759)	(10,204)	(3,332)
Constant	**-67,772****	**-62,390****	**-16,494***
	(32,342)	(30,429)	(9,693)
Sigma	**130,070*****	**111,263*****	**24,877*****
	(23,565)	(15,551)	(2,004)
Left-censored observations	0	0	0
Uncensored observations	324	321	251
Right-censored observations	0	3	73
Observations	324	324	324

Robust standard errors in parentheses
*** $p<0.01$, ** $p<0.05$, * $p<0.1$

Likewise, **the third model** shows that five independent variables are significant with respect to awareness of youths to accept agriculture entrepreneurship, among which four variables are positively significant and one is negatively significant. Four factors namely crop cycle, market information centre in your area, information and demand for agro are positively significant, whereas, land type is negatively significant. Crop cycle and information are found to be 10% significant, whereas, market information centre at your area and demand for agro are found to be 1% significant with youths' willingness to accept agriculture entrepreneurship.

5. DISCUSSIONS

Land that were cultivated for many years are now being abandoned by farmers, for which Paudel et al. (2014) questioned why and how cultivated land are abanded by farmers? This question is significant for developing nations like Nepal, which faces major problems of food security, and this study also tries to include and address similar notions. With the advancement of technology, the use of chemicals, terminator seeds, and adopting high input technology have also increased even in agricultural sector. But in contrast, Tamang et al. (2011) mentioned that Nepal's agricultural scope yet relies upon environmentally friendly farming, natural and ecological farming, bio-dynamic agriculture, permaculture, regenerative and sustainable agriculture. However, several barriers as lack of entrepreneurial skills, low support from government hinder entrepreneurs' development (Kshetri, 2011; Phuyal & Devkota, 2017) and similar hindrances can be substantiated in this study as well.

The findings of the study revealed that 5% of farmers are involved in agriculture entrepreneurship while analyzing youths' perceptions towards agricultural entrepreneurship. Likewise, Mueller and Remaud (2013) unleashed that marginal WTP for agriculture entrepreneurship is three times higher for environmentally responsible claims rather than for specific socially responsible claims. WTP for environmental responsibility is also found to be non-negative across the investigated market, whereas, it is negative for the socially responsible claim in France and Francophone, Canada. However, this study reveals that market information, crop cycle, and demand for agro are some major factors for youths' willingness to accept agro entrepreneurship. Similarly, in the Nepalese context, it seems the profile of entrepreneurs is also impacted by the nature of enterprise and not only by age group. On the similar note, the study shows that male has more entrepreneurial capacity compared to female. 18.83% farmers stated that training is the best medium for development of agriculture entrepreneurship that needs to be initiated by local government. Similarly, Vanslembrouck et al. (2002) also mentioned that agro-environmental policies should be incorporated to reflect environmental concern in farmers' decision making and other behavioral aspects. Thus, the need for various training related to agro entrepreneurship and its development seems to be initiated from policy level.

Government subsidies are considered to be important financial resources for agro- entrepreneurial development stated by farmers, but there are various other factors as well, which would aid in entrepreneurial development. The study shows that farmers are aware of loan (54%) and credit facilities provided by banks (57.5%) under financial resources for agro-entrepreneurial development. In contrary, our study shows that only 12.35% of farmers consider subsidy as the best medium to promote agro-entrepreneurship and 19.14% feel seeds and similar resources are the best medium to promote agro-entrepreneurship. Thus, the quality of seeds and related materials must be improved in the Nepalese context.

6. CONCLUSION AND RECOMMENDATIONS

This study showcases youths' willingness to accept agriculture entrepreneurship in Bedkot municipality, Kanchanpur, Nepal. Some specific objectives of this study are understanding youths' perception on agriculture entrepreneurship, the provincial role for enhancing youths towards agriculture entrepreneurship and various management strategies to attract youths towards entrepreneurship. Results of the study revealed that there are various requirements for development of entrepreneurship among which one-fourth of the farmers stated that they need agriculture related training, 26.98% needs subsidy and 12.06% thinks an increase of awareness level help to enhance agro-entrepreneurship. Likewise, farmers also mentioned that agriculture must be improved to enhance agro-entrepreneurship. Among the respondents, 11.43% felt improvement in market management, road management, irrigation facility and motivation are essential to enhance entrepreneurship. On the other hads, same portion of the respondent (i.e. 11.43%) felt subsidy, development program are essential for entrepreneurial development. Apart from this, other crucial factors for entrepreneurial development are valuable information, irrigation, supervision through government, and land in rent.

After the assessment of overall objectives and results of the study following recommendations are considered for policymakers and further study.

Providing training: After analyzing the results, it was found that only 6.97% farmers have taken agriculture training. Almost 18% of the farmers need training from the provincial government, 26.98% of the farmer respond that training makes it possible to enhance agriculture entrepreneurship in Bedkot municipality. Similarly, 18.83% farmers focus training as the best medium to overall development of agriculture entrepreneurship in this area, which needs to be done by the local government.

Providing subsidy: The results show that 17.28% farmers expect subsidy from the provincial government. Similarly, 11.43% farmers respond that providing subsidy to the farmer helps to enhance agricultural entrepreneurship. Likewise, 12.35% farmers respond that providing subsidy is the best medium for overall development, which needs to be done by the local and provincial governments.

Improve seeds and necessary materials: 5.86% of the farmers need better seeds and other materials from the provincial government to enhance agriculture entrepreneurship. Similarly, 8.89% farmers analyze that seeds help to enhance agriculture entrepreneurship in Bedkot municipality. Likewise, 19.14% farmers think that seeds and other necessary materials are the best medium to enhance agriculture entrepreneurship, for which local government has a crucial role in providing more improved seeds and necessary materials.

Road management and solving market problems: 12.96% of the farmers need to manage resources and solve the problems from the provincial government. Similarly, 6.79% of the farmers think road management and 14.81% of the farmers think market problems required to be addressed. Most of the existing entrepreneurs and awareness people respond that market management is the best medium for overall development. Thus, in order to develop roads and enhance market access, local government needs to develop roads and dissolve market related issues similarly.

Modern technology and equipment: The results show that only 11 people have tractors. Almost 2.76% farmers respond that infrastructure and technology in agriculture sector help for agriculture entrepreneurship. Similarly, 4.4% farmers respond that infrastructure development is essential for enhancing agriculture entrepreneurship, and 5.86% farmers response equipment as essential for agriculture entrepreneurship. For this, the central government needs to allocate adequate level of budget to facilitate the role of the provincial government.

Enhance awareness: Local government needs to educate the local people of Bedkot municipality regarding the awareness of youth entrepreneurship on agriculture so that newer generations can be motivated to involve in agriculture and farming entrepreneurship.

Enhance WTA: Last but not the least, the central government needs to visualize clear policies and sustainable distribution mechanisms in order to increase willingness to accept. For this, appropriate loan needs to be reimbursed and stated in national level policies like fiscal policies so that farmers accept to envisage agricultural entrepreneurship. Recommendation for the provincial government is to identify similar willingness to accept agriculture entrepreneurship area within the province and to encourage it in social and economic development.

REFERENCES

Alsos, G. A., Carter, S., Ljunggren, E., & Welter, F. (2011). Introduction: researching entrepreneurship in agriculture and rural development. The handbook of research on entrepreneurship in agriculture and rural development, 1-18.

Anderson, A. R., & Jack, S. L. (2002). The articulation of social capital in entrepreneurial networks: A glue or a lubricant? *Entrepreneurship and Regional Development*, *14*(3), 193–210. doi:10.1080/08985620110112079

B. K., A., Mahato, A., Thapa, S., Rai, A., & Devkota, N. (2019). Achieving Nepal's sustainable development goals (SDGs) by effective compliance of corporate governance. *Quest Journal of Management and Social Sciences, 1*(1), 50-72.

Budhathoki, P., Sapkota, B., Maharjan, R., Bista, S., & Gosain, A. (2019). Empowerment of diversity in the Nepalese corporate sector. *Quest Journal of Management and Social Sciences*, *1*(1), 96–118. doi:10.3126/qjmss.v1i1.25976

Buli, B. M., & Yesuf, W. M. (2015). Determinants of entrepreneurial intentions: Technical-vocational education and training students in Ethiopia. *Education + Training*, *57*(8/9), 57891–57907. doi:10.1108/ET-10-2014-0129

Carr, J. C., & Sequeira, J. M. (2007). Prior family business exposure as intergenerational influence and entrepreneurial intent: A theory of planned behavior approach. *Journal of Business Research*, *60*(10), 1090–1098. doi:10.1016/j.jbusres.2006.12.016

Central Bureau of Statistics (CBS). (2011). *National population and housing census 2011*. Retrieved from https://unstats.un.org/unsd/demographicsocial/census/documents/Nepal/Nepal-Census-2011-Vol1.pdf

CSRC. (2012). *Land ownership and land reform in Nepal, Centre for community self-reliance, Kathmandu Nepal*. Retrieved from https://csrcnepal.org/

Cummings, R. G., & Taylor, L. O. (1999). Unbiased value estimates for environmental goods: A cheap talk design for the contingent valuation method. *The American Economic Review*, *89*(3), 649–665. doi:10.1257/aer.89.3.649

De Lauwere, C. C. (2005). The role of agricultural entrepreneurship in Dutch agriculture of today. *Agricultural Economics*, *33*(2), 229–238. doi:10.1111/j.1574-0862.2005.00373.x

Devkota, N., & Phuyal, R. K. (2018). Adoption Practice of Climate Change Adaptation Options among Nepalese Rice Farmers: Role of Information and Communication Technologies (ICTs). *American Journal of Climate Change*, *7*(2), 135–152. doi:10.4236/ajcc.2018.72010

Devkota, N., Phuyal, R. K., & Shrestha, D. L. (2017). Cost and benefit analysis of adoption of climate change adaptation options among rural rice farmers in Nepal. *Asian Journal of Agriculture and Rural Development*, *7*(7), 136.

Devkota, N., Phuyal, R. K., & Shrestha, D. L. (2018). Perception, determinants and barriers for the adoption of climate change adaptation options among nepalese rice farmers. *Agricultural Sciences*, *9*(3), 272–298. doi:10.4236/as.2018.93021

Dhital, P. R. (2017). Agricultural extension in Nepal: Experiences and issues. *Journal of Advances in Agriculture*, *7*(3), 1071–1082. doi:10.24297/jaa.v7i3.6287

Drake, L., Bergström, P., & Svedsäter, H. (1999). Farmers' attitude and uptake. *Countryside Stewardship: Farmers, Policies and Markets*, 89-111.

Gauchan, D., & Shrestha, S. (2017). *Agricultural and rural mechanization in Nepal: status, issues and options for future*. Institute for Inclusive Finance and Development (InM).

Hall, A., Sulaiman, V. R., Clark, N., & Yoganand, B. (2003). From measuring impact to learning institutional lessons: An innovation systems perspective on improving the management of international agricultural research. *Agricultural Systems*, *78*(2), 213–241.

International Labour Organization. (2018). *World Employment Social Outlook*. Retrieved from https://ec.europa.eu/knowledge4policy/organisation/ilo-international-labour-organisation_en

Khan, N. R., Awang, M., & Zulkifli, C. M. (2013). Small and medium enterprises and human resource practices in Pakistan. *International Journal of Asian Social Science*, *3*(2), 460–471.

Kshetri, N. (2011). Cloud computing in the global south: Drivers, effects and policy measures. *Third World Quarterly*, *32*(6), 997–1014. doi:10.1080/01436597.2011.586225

Lans, T., Verstegen, J., & Mulder, M. (2011). Analysing, pursuing and networking: Towards a validated three-factor framework for entrepreneurial competence from a small firm perspective. *International Small Business Journal*, *29*(6), 695–713. doi:10.1177/0266242610369737

Macher, R. (1999). *Making your small farm profitable*. Storey Publishing.

Ministry of Finance (MOF). (2018). *Economic Survey 2017/18*. Ministry of Finance.

Morgan, D. L. (1998). Practical strategies for combining qualitative and quantitative methods: Applications to health research. *Qualitative Health Research*, *8*(3), 362–376. doi:10.1177/104973239800800307 PMID:10558337

Mueller Loose, S., & Remaud, H. (2013). Impact of corporate social responsibility claims on consumer food choice: A cross-cultural comparison. *British Food Journal*, *115*(1), 142–166. doi:10.1108/00070701311289920

Neuman, W. L. (2003). *The meanings of methodology: Social research methods*. Allyn.

Ostrom, E. (1990). *Governing the Commons: The Evolution of Institutions for Collective Action*. Cambridge University Press. doi:10.1017/CBO9780511807763

Pande, P. C., Awasthi, P., Bargali, K., & Bargali, S. S. (2016). Agro-biodiversity of kumaun himalaya, India: A review. *Current Agriculture Research Journal*, *40*(1), 16–34. doi:10.12944/CARJ.4.1.02

Paudel, K. P., Tamang, S., & Shrestha, K. K. (2014). Transforming land and livelihood: Analysis of agricultural land abandonment in the Mid Hills of Nepal. *Journal of Forest and Livelihood*, *12*(1), 11–19.

Paudel, M. N. (2016). Prospects and limitations of agriculture industrialization in Nepal. *Agronomy Journal of Nepal*, *4*, 38–63. doi:10.3126/ajn.v4i0.15515

Phuyal, R. K., Devkota, N., & Shrestha, D. L. (2017). Climate change adaptation related hindrances among rice farmers in Nepal: Farm level analysis. *Journal of Development and Administrative Studies*, *25*(1-2), 1–10. doi:10.3126/jodas.v25i1-2.23434

Poncet, J., Kuper, M., & Chiche, J. (2010). Wandering off the paths of planned innovation: The role of formal and informal intermediaries in a large-scale irrigation scheme in Morocco. *Agricultural Systems*, *103*(4), 171–179. doi:10.1016/j.agsy.2009.12.004

Pretty, J. (2003). Social capital and the collective management of resources. *Science*, *302*(5652), 1912–1914. doi:10.1126cience.1090847 PMID:14671287

Singh, A. S., & Masuku, M. B. (2014). Sampling techniques & determination of sample size in applied statistics research: An overview. *International Journal of Economics, Commerce and Management*, *2*(1), 1–22.

Spielman, D., Davies, K., Negash, M., & Gezahegn, A. (2010). Rural innovation systems and networks: Findings from a study of Ethiopian smallholders. *Agriculture and Human Values*, *28*(2), 195–212. doi:10.100710460-010-9273-y

Sunder, S. (2018). *India economic survey 2018: Farmers gain as agriculture mechanisation speeds up, but more R&D needed*. The Financial Express.

Tamang, S., Dhital, M., & Acharya, U. (2011). *Status and scope of organic agriculture in Nepal. In Food and Sustainable Agriculture Initiative, Forestaction*. Lalitpur.

Tandukar, H., Niroula, A., Shrestha, K., & Paudel, U. R. (2019). Assessment of national policy to promote corporate governance in Nepal. *Quest Journal of Management and Social Sciences*, *1*(1), 73–95. doi:10.3126/qjmss.v1i1.25975

Tobin, J. (1958). Estimation of relationships for limited dependent variables. *Econometrica*, *26*(1), 24–36. doi:10.2307/1907382

Turnbull, B. W. (1976). The empirical distribution function with arbitrarily grouped, censored and truncated data. *Journal of the Royal Statistical Society. Series B. Methodological*, *38*(3), 290–295. doi:10.1111/j.2517-6161.1976.tb01597.x

Vanslembrouck, I., Van Huylenbroeck, G., & Verbeke, W. (2002). Determinants of the willingness of Belgian farmers to participate in agri environmental measures. *Journal of Agricultural Economics*, *53*(3), 489–511. doi:10.1111/j.1477-9552.2002.tb00034.x

Verhees, F. J. H. M., Kuipers, A., & Klopcic, M. (2011). Entrepreneurial proclivity and farm performance: The cases of Dutch and Slovenian farmers. *International Journal of Entrepreneurship and Innovation*, *12*(3), 169–177. doi:10.5367/ijei.2011.0039

World Bank Agricultural. (2014). *GDP growth indicator for countries, Nigerian GDP growth rate*. Retrieved from: https://data.worldbank.org/indicator/NY.GDP.MKTP.KD.ZG

Wynn, G., Crabtree, B., & Potts, J. (2001). Modelling farmer entry into the environmentally sensitive area schemes in Scotland. *Journal of Agricultural Economics*, *52*(1), 65–82. doi:10.1111/j.1477-9552.2001.tb00910.x

Yu, X., Gao, Z., & Zeng, Y. (2014). Willingness to pay for the "Green Food" in China. *Food Policy*, *45*, 80–87. doi:10.1016/j.foodpol.2014.01.003

Chapter 10
Threats to Arable Land of the World:
Current and Future Perspectives of Land Use

Zia Ur Rahman Farooqi
https://orcid.org/0000-0003-2398-1895
Institute of Soil and Environmental Sciences, University of Agriculture Faisalabad, Pakistan

Zahoor Ahmad
Department of Field Crops, Faculty of Agriculture, University of Cukurova, Adana, Turkey

Muhammad Ashar Ayub
Institute of Soil and Environmental Sciences, University of Agriculture Faisalabad, Pakistan

Wajid Umar
Szent Istvan University, Gödöllő, Hungary

Muhammad Nadeem
Institute of Soil and Environmental Sciences, University of Agriculture Faisalabad, Pakistan

Hina Fatima
School of Applied Biosciences, Kyungpook National University, South Korea

Abbas Shoukat
https://orcid.org/0000-0002-6186-3657
Institute of Soil and Environmental Sciences, University of Agriculture Faisalabad, Pakistan

Tasawar Ali
Institute of Soil and Environmental Sciences, University of Agriculture Faisalabad, Pakistan

Muhammad Imran Ashraf
Institute of Soil and Environmental Sciences, University of Agriculture Faisalabad, Pakistan

ABSTRACT

Arable lands are the major source of food production worldwide. Increasing crop cultivation in the response to population pressure and the use of synthetic fertilizers and chemicals are the main reasons for the conversion of arable lands into problematic soils. Increasing food demand requires to increase the per acre yield of agricultural crops resulting in over exploitation of soil resources. This is a major contributor to soil degradation which is the major threat to the food security of the world. Climate change and poor-quality irrigation are the other problems are also affecting crop productivity and the

DOI: 10.4018/978-1-7998-4372-6.ch010

conversion of arable lands into problematic lands. Deforestation and urbanization are the main reasons behind the conversion of agricultural land into infrastructure. Adopting precision agriculture, vertical farming and good agricultural practices are the only ways to conserve arable lands. This chapter provides a keen overview of world arable land issues with the focus on threats to arable land and possible solutions to overcome this issue.

INTRODUCTION

In May 2020 there have been under 7.8 billion people living on Planet Earth. It took less than 220 years to increase the world's population by almost eightfold. The increasing population is exerting tremendous pressure on renewable as well as non-renewable natural resources such as soil and water, two major requirements for food production. Also, climate change is making existing challenges more severe (Koubi & Spilker, 2017; Weber, 2011, 2012, 2014). In the current scenario of food insecurity existing resources need to be managed in a sustainable way to meet existing needs without compromising the needs of future generations. To live up to these challenges the world's existing soils must be managed to allow higher crop yields. Degraded soils must be reclaimed/ restored and added to the areas under crop production (Lal, 2016). Globally, one billion hectares of land is arable and 10% of this area is salt-affected costing US$441/ ha amounting to a total global loss of US$ 27.3 billion per year (Abiala et al., 2018). Arable lands are lands with having the capacity to e used as productive lands and these are cumulative of all the soils which can be used as agricultural soils but are being wasted. An increasing percentage of these soils are degraded due to soil salinity, erosion, deforestation, and different types of soil pollution (Blanco et al., 2017; Costantini et al., 2018; Oldeman et al., 2017). Salt accumulation in arable land is one of the major reasons behind degradation. Salts accumulating in soils reduce the nutrients available to plants and limit plant growth and yield. Common salts that cause soil salinity are sodium (Na^+), potassium (K^+), calcium (Ca^{2+}), magnesium (Mg^{2+}), and chlorides (Cl^-) (Blanco et al., 2017). Land degradation, which is a form of soil structure, and texture deterioration also occurs through extensive tillage and soil erosion. Both operations cause soil structure deterioration which leads to the exposure of soil organic matter to heat which increases its decomposition (León et al., 2017). Deforestation accelerates soil erosion and soil degradation (Marichal et al., 2017). Extensive deforestation and other forms of vegetation loss are additional causes that can lead to desertification and loss of fertility (Bouma et al., 2017). Different forms of pollution such as heavy metals pollution, excessive fertilizer, and pesticide use, application of brackish water for irrigation and natural release of salts from soil sediments are also responsible for soil degradation (Cachada et al., 2018; Romero-Baena et al., 2018).

For restoration and rehabilitation of these soils, to be able to use them as productive soils, there are numerous methods. Some of these methods are e.g. the use of recommended agricultural practices which optimizes crop growth and soil requirements of nutrients and water (Emran et al., 2020), use of organic and inorganic amendments for soil fertility rehabilitation and structure (Emran et al., 2020), and treatment of salt-affected soils through chemicals like gypsum, sulfuric and nitric acids (Al-Saedi et al., 2018).

In addition to the soil reclamation and their improvement for crop production, different alternatives of soil as a growth medium for crops have been studied. Scientists have found various technologies where water and air are suitable media for food crop cultivation. Aeroponics, hydroponics, vertical farming, kitchen gardening, and modifying desserts for crop cultivation have been tested. The methods provided good results during trials (Ayipio et al., 2019; Rubio-Asensio et al., 2020). In addition to these innovative technologies, improvements in existing agronomic practices are employed coupled with existing agronomical practices to improve crop yields. Precision agriculture, site-specific practices, and zero tillage are the techniques that give a considerable amount of crop yield increase (Pedersen & Lind, 2017).

This chapter provides the following: (1) it gives a systematic overview of challenges to the soils of arable land, especially from the perspective of how these challenges compromise global food security in an era of climate change. (2) methods are introduced which support efforts to restore/reclaim/rehabilitate these problematic lands, and (3) the importance of modern technologies is discussed, which can help in alleviating challenges to soils of arable land problems and enhance global food security (Crosson, 2017; Lal, 2016; Kopittke et al., 2019).

GLOBAL ARABLE LAND

Arable lands are at one point in time only a limited section of the land can be used for agriculture. This portion of arable land can increase through land-use change (e.g. conversion of forest land in agricultural land, greening deserts, etc.) (Wu et al., 2018). The amount of land available for agriculture can also go down by converting agricultural land to urban, industrial, tourism, and many other uses. Agricultural land can also degrade, meaning losing in quality, which affects yields and can in extreme cases make agricultural use entirely impossible (Kubiak et al., 2018). Many processes such as an increase in resource extraction, population increase, industrial development, food insecurity, and economic development can lead to the reduction of cultivable areas. At the same time in many parts of the world agricultural land is degraded, e.g. badly affected by salts, pesticides, excessive use of fertilizers, and residues from fossil fuel use (Kopittke et al., 2019). Around the world, an area of around 1,407 million hectares (14 mill km^2) is arable. Much of this land is affected by different types of challenges such as soil salinity, degradation, contamination, and erosion (World Bank, 2016). Alone in Pakistan e.g. some 30.4 mha are affected (Lal, 2018). Being an agricultural country, Pakistan is facing a problem of increased arable lands due to water shortage and climate change-induced soil fertility and structure changes.

At least 75 countries have salt-affected areas expanding to 831 mha (Saifullah et al., 2018). Soils are also degraded by other factors such as forest fires (Barlow et al., 2016), soil erosion (Evans et al., 2016; Novara et al., 2018), and farmland ownership fragmentation (Sklenicka, 2016).

THREATS ASSOCIATED WITH ARABLE LANDS

a) Soil Salinity

Salt affected soils are categorized into three major groups, saline, sodic or saline-sodic soils. They cover more than 830 mha of the agricultural lands, where saline soil accounts for 48%. Soil salinity refers to the condition where an accumulation of salts makes the soil infertile / reduces its fertility, whereas sodicity (also called alkalinity) is caused by adsorption of sodium ions on to the soil clay particles. Soil salinity is a universal issue that continues to threaten the productivity of cropland. It is often the first step in the degradation of agricultural land (Hillel et al., 2008). Salt accumulation in soil results in toxicity to plants, reducing soil fertility and causing a significant change in soil's hydraulic properties. It is predicted that 50% of all fertile land will be impacted by salinity by 2040 (Scherr, 1999). To improve food security and lessen the economic loss we are required to have an improved knowledge of crops response to salinity. The area of salinized soil is increasing especially the irrigated soil. Though it is hard to calculate the effects with accuracy, it is estimated that 20% of irrigated land which yields one-third of the world's food is affected by salinity (Vengosh, 2003). In addition to these, excessive irrigation, blind use of synthetic fertilizers, climate change-induced salinity, sea-level rise (Srivastava et al., 2019).

b) Land Degradation

Since the beginning of farming, land degradation was the biggest dilemma in soil productivity and continues to affect the yield and quality of agricultural land (Sullivan, 2004; Balikie, 2019). It is caused by deforestation, over-grazing, salinity, soil erosion, extensive-tillage, etc. (Mohamed, et al., 2019). In the 20th-century land, degradation has been a global issue, and still on the apex of international problem resolving catalog. The topsoil is a source for plant standing support, nutrient, and important microbial fauna required for the efficient growth of plants. Land degradation affects soil water holding capacity, microbial fauna, and nutrient availability for plants. The impact on agriculture by soil degradation is perfectly described by Doran and Parkin as the skinny layer of soil on the surface of earth shows the extinction and survival difference of the most terrestrial life (Doran & Parkin, 1994). Many ecological losses in massive numbers were reported in grassland, forest land, and cropland, because of soil erosion, salinity and soil alkalinity, micronutrient deficiency, water soaking into the groundwater which can lead to groundwater contamination (Miranowski, 1984; Gupta, 2019).

c) Deforestation

Deforestation is the cutting of standing trees and converting land into non-forest land (urban or ranches, farms use). The deforestation rate is high in the tropical rainforest (Bradford, 2015). Countrymen cut down trees for construction, use as fuel, and source of income. The clear land is used for livestock as a pasture, and plantation of specific plant species. However, massive deforestation is caused by poor forest management, lack of environmental protection laws, and their enforcement in developing countries (Sunderland and Rowland, 2019). Deforestation resulted in both natural and human activities. Forest of 2.3 million square km was cut down from 2000 to 2012 worldwide (Conservancy, 2015).

d) Desertification

Desertification is caused by climate change, droughts, overexploitation of natural resources, and deforestation (Becerril-Piña & Mastachi-Loza, 2019). The United Nations Environment Program has listed desertification as a major international concern. Thirty-six million square km of land has been affected by desertification. According to the estimation of the United Nations Convention, it has affected 250 million people's lives already and 136 million people may be displaced in combating desertification by 2040 which makes it one of the most rigorous environmental challenges to humanity. There is a disagreement of the appraisal on coverage of the land degradation ranging from 15% to 63% of global land and 4% to 70% of drylands (Nkonya et al., 2011; Lewis, 2017).

e) Soil Pollution

Soil pollution is the presence of toxic substances or chemicals present at high concentrations. These pollutants can enter into the soil from natural (volcanoes, weathering) as well as anthropogenic sources (industries, agriculture, and municipal wastes) (Rodrigues & Römkens, 2018). In Europe and Eurasia, it has been listed as the third most significant menace to soil functions. The range of pollutants is continually advancing because of agrochemicals and industrial development. According to The Status of the World's Soil Resources Reports, Soil acidification and nutrient imbalances are the two major problems in most parts of the world may be due to the presence of certain pollutants.

Organic and inorganic pollutants are common problems for the environment. Heavy metals and Potentially Toxic Elements (PTEs) are the most important inorganic pollutants in soil. PTEs are also a group of metals and metalloids with high density. Organic and Inorganic pollutants differ adversely in their functioning in soil (Ahmad, Imran, Hussain, & Hussain, 2017). Potentially toxic elements are non-degradable while organic pollutants are easily remediated or decomposed to their less toxic small units. Potentially toxic elements may cause changes in physicochemical conditions of soil and experience decrease or increase in the availability with time. Both pollutants may have a natural or anthropogenic origin. The large portion of soil pollutants is complex mixtures of these two major pollutants (Rodríguez-Eugenio et al., 2018).

f) Exhaustion of Soil Reserves

Exhaustion of soil reserves occurs when soil is no longer able to provide nutrients to plants, it happens gradually. The productivity of land decreases in-spite of using the same conventional cultivation techniques. The incapability of maintaining the thin organic layer between the rocks and vegetation is not just a problem of the past (Usher, 1923).

The plant's root builds a complicated relationship with the soil and may release some substances known as allelopathic substances, that affect the development or growth of the plants from the same family. It may cause slow soil degradation and may leave a long-lasting effect on the soil. This degradation of soil is due to loss of porosity and organic matter reduction which in turn reduces microbiological activity and soil capacity of keeping and exchanging nutrients with water that circulates in the plant body. Changes in the physical properties of the soil are linked with a microbiological course of action in soil and its exhaustion (Jigău et al., 2016).

On one hand use of synthetic fertilizers also effects management of agricultural soil by disturbing ratio cycles (as for Carbon, Nitrogen, Phosphorus and other elements), on the other hand, it is also affected by natural processes that enhance the degree of soil exhaustion (Jigău et al., 2016).

g) Poor Water Application

Water is a vital ingredient for photosynthesis and healthy plant growth. Irresponsive use of irrigation practices has resulted in the loss of cropland which cannot be used for agricultural purposes any longer. Irrigation water conservation is, therefore, to a certain point, a new idea that needs to be translated into feasible management strategies and this is evident that water conservation strategies need to be operationalized using appropriate assessment systems. However, a shortage of good quality water is said to have negative impacts on access to maintain agriculture systems and has led to the degradation of the land (Forouzani & Karami, 2011).

MEASURES TO REVERSE/SLOWDOWN LAND DEGRADATION

a. Good Agricultural Techniques

Good agricultural practices can prevent and reverse the loss of arable land up to a greater extent. These practices, discussed in detail should be adopted at large (Borrelli et al., 2016).

b. Harvest Management

Soil erosion because of winds and water can be minimized by better farming practices. Keeping land covered is important in restoring degraded farming land. Also helpful is the approach to soil shielding from erosion through leaving plant residues on the surface of the ground after harvest (Vořížek et al., 2002).

c. Intercropping

The effect of raindrops on the soil surface is minimized by rapidly growing legumes like beans and cowpeas before cotton or maize canopies are established to protect the field. This method decreases desertification and enables the restoration of agricultural land as it effectively controls agricultural soil erosion agents (Feike et al., 2012).

d. Selection of Crops

If the time from harvesting one kind of crop and planting/sowing the next is too long, then sowing additional crops can be helpful. The resilience of the sustainable farming system is improved by crops that cover the land surface, and the impacts of erosion are minimized by improving soil characteristics and this biological diversity is promoted in the agronomic ecosystem for its potential. Perennial crops are more successful in soil erosion than the annual crops. Sugar cane, fodder grass, and sweet potatoes are more effective (Bhat et al., 2009).

e. Cover Crops

Cover plants are' tight-growing crops which provide soil protection, seeding protection, and soil enhancement through intervals of standard agricultural production or between gardens and vineyard trees. Such crops are also known as green manure. This use of crops is indeed an ancient traditional practice, dating back to ancient cultures in Athens, Rome, China, and other countries. The method of growing crops to cover the surface of the soil is called cover cropping to minimize wind and water erosion. By controlling soil heat and temperature this activity provides a suitable environment for microorganisms (Panagos et al., 2015).

f. Shelterbelts

These techniques are employed to shield the rain-fed and irrigated fields. Their principal role in the current situation is to secure productive cropland and canals for irrigation from spreading sands. That is happening in Northern Africa and North Sudan. Shelterbelts minimize wind speed, enhance the microclimate, and boost livestock production (El-Lakany, 1983).

g. Wastewater Treatment for Irrigation Purposes

The primary objective of wastewater treatment is to enable the disposal of human and industrial effluents without damage to public health or unacceptable harm to the natural habitat. Therefore, the most effective water treatment to be used for irrigation is one that will yield an effluent that satisfies the required chemical and microbiological rules and guidelines for irrigation water at a lower cost with minimal technical and operational needs (Borgman & Chefetz, 2013).

h. Mineral Fertilizers and Organic Manures

Organic manures and fertilizers play a vital role in agricultural land restoration. These provide the essential nutrients to plants for better crop production. The fast-growing crops cover the soil quickly and produce higher yields. Essential nutrients such as phosphorus, potassium, nitrogen, and sometimes Sulphur are provided to plants by inorganic fertilizer (Alewell et al., 2019). According to Yamoah et al. (2002) in West Africa, the combination of fertilizers and crop residues restored the degraded agricultural land and led to the highest straw and millet grain yields.

i. Mulching and the Use of Crop Residues

The spreading of plant materials on the bare soil such as straw, dry leaves, dry grass, sugar cane trash, banana leaves and other crop residues around stems of the plants could be helpful in moisture conservation and controlling soil erosion (Bashir et al., 2017).

j. Organic Agriculture

Organic farming has many benefits some of which include less contamination by herbicides, pesticides, and fertilizers, enhancement of soil carbon sequestration and nutrients, biodiversity increase, genetic diversity conservation of local varieties of animals and plants, and enhancement of natural pest control (Gabriel et al., 2010).

k. Treating Barren Land

Reclaiming or reversing barren land is the method of restoration of agricultural land which has been eroded, damaged, degraded, or destroyed. Regaining barren land needs a variety of strategies based on the barren landform and severity. The reversal of barren land relies on the cause including heavy metal accumulation in the soil or intense salinity, etc. (Saturday, 2018). Barren land conservation activities promote water absorption and enhance soil water retention ability, resulting in reduced flow and degradation. Barren land conservation requires careful management and policy-making for sustaining life now and in the future. Restructuring and preventive measures must be taken in affected areas by land degradation to minimize the risk of flood shocks and drought (Dobson et al., 1997). Consideration may be taken for various measures of barren land reclamation:

NATURAL AND ENGINEERED RESTORATION

Naturally induced transformation can often be a cost-effective technique and can be accomplished by designing pasture plans easily. In several other situations, heavy terracing and hydrology preservation equipment is helpful.

1. Making Use of Correct Tillage Strategies

Tillage procedures must be implemented. Slash and burn, hand tilling, plowing, minimal level tillage, deep tillage are still the main tillage methods (Gebhardt et al., 1985).

2. Use of Manures and Fertilizers

It is quite essential to apply natural manure as well as chemical fertilizers to restore soil fertility. Manure and fertilizers deliver important plant nutrients for enhanced crop production in the soils. Quickly growing plants rapidly cover more soil which produces greater yields.

3. Mulching

The spreading or placing of plant materials on the soil surface such as dead grass, dry leaves, leaves of banana, sugarcane recyclables as well as other crop byproducts helps control soil erosion and also conserve moisture in the soil (Zhang et al., 2005).

4. Agroforestry

Agroforestry refers to growing trees or grasses or to protect natural plants. Trees reduce the extent of splash degradation via minimizing impacts on the surface soil from raindrops. They control soil temperatures, minimizing evaporation of water, and playing a major role in deeper soil nutrients recycling (Thaman et al., 2017).

5. Contour Agriculture

Cultivation across the slope is termed contour agriculture, instead of upward and downward crop cultivation. This approach has confirmed a reduction in soil loss of as much as 50 percent. Water conservation is the principal aim (Wankhade et al., 2017). In conjunction with several other strategies for effectively reclaiming barren land, including physical soil restoration, water reservoir building as well as strip cultivation, etc., and the above-discussed strategies can be taken into consideration.

Climate change is a factor that influences greatly on agriculture by exerting temperature and soil degradation stresses to the agricultural soils. As discussed below;

CLIMATE CHANGE AND ARABLE LANDS

Climate change deteriorates the soil structure and its suitability for agricultural use, that's why hitting different regions of the world drastically with varying intensity and unprecedented impacts on different sectors of life. Climate change cause soil fertility loss, which results in less yield and food insecurity problems., economy (Hsiang *et al.*, 2017), hydropower generation (Fan *et al.,* 2020), water resources (Ortiz-Partida et al., 2020), forest distribution (Seidl et al., 2017), biodiversity (Guisan et al., 2019), animals (McIntyre et al., 2017), human health (Silva et al., 2017) and agriculture (Chandio *et al.,* 2020). Among all mentioned above, agriculture is one of the most vulnerable sectors to climate fluctuations with global food security at stake. Despite the uncertainty, it is now a well-known fact that the climate is changing worldwide. Increased level of greenhouse gasses, elevated temperature leading to global warming, melting glaciers, rainfall, droughts, smog, unexpected weather fluctuations, longer season all are the clear signs of climate change (Lane et al., 2018). The consequences of climate change could be diverse including reduced agricultural productivity, variations in crop planting and harvesting period, and ingress of some new species of pathogens and pests (Tobin et al., 2015).

In the past, several models have been used to predict future trends and to estimate the effects of climate change on crop and forest ecosystems. These models work by regarding future socio-economic factors that could influence the sources and sinks of greenhouse gases and variation in land use (Lozano-García et al., 2017; Metz, Davidson et al., 2007). Moreover, several researchers unveiled the role of soil as "carbon sink" which prompted others to think about the potential factors that can influence the storage of carbon (C) in the soil (Orgill et al., 2018). Land use and its management, temperature, precipitation, soil clay contents & compaction, crop residues, and food industry byproducts are major potential factors that can influence the storage of carbon in the soils (Willaarts et al., 2016; Muñoz Rojas et al., 2012).

Apart from the above-mentioned tactics, climate change activists and researchers have discovered several new ways to tackle with climatic scenarios. For example, in 2017 Yadav and coworkers revealed that reduced tillage with judicial management of nutrients produced grain yield of 5.15 $Mgha^{-1}$ with total sequestered C and rate of soil organic carbon sequestration of 1.30 $Mgha^{-1}$ and 427.kg ha^{-1} yr^{-1} respectively (Yadav et al., 2019). In the same year, a meta-analysis was carried out by De Stefano & Jacobson to identify the role of agroforestry in sequestering atmospheric CO_2 by analyzing the change in the SOC stock at five different soil depth (0- ≥100cm) level by following different land-use transitions. They reported 26, 40, and 34% increase in the SOC at 0-15, 1-30, and 0-100 cm depth by converting agriculture land to forest land (De Stefano & Jacobson, 2018). Later, in 2018 Muñoz-Rojas and coworkers revealed the role of cyanobacteria for carbon and N accumulation in dryland ecosystems. In this study mixture of cyanobacteria with the mine, soil increased the chlorophyll-*a* contents up to 12.2ug/g and soil organic carbon contents from 0.6g/kg to 1.9g/kg exhibiting their ability to improve and restore the dry and infertile soils as a potential reconstructed soil substrate by sequestering C (Muñoz-Rojas et al., 2018). Similarly, an experiment was conducted by Cha-un and colleagues to identify the role of rice rotation systems on GHG_S emission, rice yield, and carbon sequestration. They inferred that corn-rice and sorghum-rice rotations reduced the methane emission by 78-84% also net CO_2 emission with stable gain yield. Hence, it was concluded that rice rotation with corn and sorghum played a role in soil carbon sequestration by stabilizing soil organic carbon stock and rice yield (Cha-un et al., 2017).

Furthermore, abandonment of croplands can also act as a low-cost technique to mitigate CO_2 emissions by human activities and can play a decisive role in carbon storage. Hence, in this regard, Novara and colleagues performed a study to analyze the impact of different regions and bio-climates on the SOC, especially after abandonment. It was deduced that the abandonment of agricultural land increased the soil organic carbon stock (SOC) from 5.4 Mg C/ ha to 26.7 Mg C/ha (Novara et al., 2017). However, others suggested that proper grazing, nutrition, cultivation of legumes and improved grass varieties, irrigation and conversion from croplands to grasslands all above-mentioned approaches augmented soil C from 0.105 to >1 Mg C ha^{-1}yr-1 (Conant et al., 2017; Ghosh et al., 2018; Chen et al., 2018). Also, recently Mandel and coworkers proposed the role of long-term manuring in soil carbon storage and found that the use of 100%NPK+FYM can sequester 1.77 Mg C/ha especially in rice-rice cropping systems (Mandal et al., 2020).

CULTIVATION IN DESERTS

The world population is constantly increasing at a rapid pace and it is expected to touch 10 billion by 2050 and is further expected to reach 11.2 billion by 2100 (Carter, 2018). Feeding 11.2 billion mouths has become a big challenge for the agriculture sector putting global food security at risk. Although, the food demand will increase due to the increase in population. However, agriculture despite all efforts will not be successful in eradicating hunger from the world by 2100. In the present scenario, out of 7.53 billion some 800 million people do not have enough food to eat (De Clercq et al., 2018). Hence there is the need for further innovations in agriculture to cope up with the ever-increasing requirement of food. No doubt the introduction of some advanced techniques like genetic engineering (Ortiz, 2019; Redden et al., 2019), nanotechnology (Elemike & Uzoh, 2019) have done wonders. However, some advanced techniques *i.e.,* hydroponics using seawater, algae feedstock, Bioplastics, seawater farming, vertical/ urban farming, Cultured meat, 3D printing, drone technology, artificial intelligence, and desert farming (De Clercq et al., 2018) can act as a game-changer. Among those mentioned above desert farming is a technique to get production from the deserts. Although growing crops in the regions with the scarcity of both water and nutrition is a challenge. However, this practice has been followed since ancient times. For instance, Negev desert revealed the evidence of "desert cultivation" from 5000 BC. There are also some current examples of desert farming *i.e.,* the imperial valley of southern California, restoration of the desert in Saudi Arabia, Israel, and Australia (Berkofsky et al., 2019; Cordesman, 2019; Crabtree et al., 2019).

Moreover, some of the predominant desert characteristics are as follows (1) Arid environment (2) Extreme temperature (3) low humidity day time and comparatively more humidity at night time (4) Uncertainty of precipitation (5) temporary or permanent drought (6) High wind velocity with the absence of vapors in the air (7) very intense sunlight with high evaporation rate (8) minimal cloud cover (9) Mirage (10) Short plant growth season (11) Minimal vegetation and food available for animals (12) less dense human population (Babayev, 2019). Major causes of desertification can be divided into two categories (1) Anthropogenic, for instance, overgrazing, deforestation, and urbanization (2) Natural include climate change (Glantz, 2019).

However, to tackle these issues innovative cultivation systems are actively being introduced. For example, recently an innovative cultivation system has been introduced by Xie and coworker with the name of "Gobi agriculture". This type of cultivation system is special since it uses solar energy to produce fresh fruits and vegetables on dry deserted lands. Also, they observed 10-27 times higher productivity with 20-35 times greater water use efficiency compared to traditional technology. Also, nutrition was provided using local organically synthesized material which reduced the use of fertilizers. Also, it provided rural employment for the locals (Xie et al., 2018). This system could play a wonder in desert reclamation especially for regions facing the problems of overpopulation and food security like Africa, the Middle East, China, and India.

Moreover, in the same year 2018, a report was presented by De Clercq and his colleagues with the name of Agriculture 4.0. The future of farming technology through the platform of the world's government summit. According to agriculture 4.0, in future agriculture will be no more dependent on the water, fertilizers, and pesticides rather agriculture 4.0. the industry will use resources like solar energy and seawater which are abundant and ubiquitous. Further, this will make it possible to get produce from arid regions by targeting only specific areas (De Clercq et al., 2018). However, another study suggested the use of endophytic bacteria that promote plant growth and protect them from drought stress in arid regions. For instance, a group of researchers extracted endophytic plant growth-promoting bacteria from the roots of date palm trees from the oasis in the Tunisian Sahara. These endophytic bacteria promptly colonized the roots of other plants including native Tunisian date palm and increased plant biomass (Cherif et al., 2015). Similarly, in another study desert cyanobacteria, *Scytonema javanicum* were inoculated into a synthetic wastewater system to evaluate their ability to transfer nutrients from wastewater to the desert. They found that twenty days after inoculation 90% of N and P were removed and bacteria grew well with a maximum biomass yield of 3.91 mg Chl-a L^{-1} (Wu et al., 2018).

SOIL LESS AND VERTICAL FARMING

Since the world's population is increasing perpetually so do the standards of living for human beings. More than half *i.e.,* > 3.765 billion world's population lives in urban areas with the expected addition of 2.5 billion more people by 2050 (De Clercq et al., 2018). Increasing urbanization means the transformation of more agriculture lands to urban lands which eventually will lead to lesser lands available for cultivation. Cultivation systems like vertical farming (VF) could work miracles since this is a technique to grow crops in vertically stacked layers which is a combination of high walled buildings and farms (Kalantari et al., 2017). The concept of VF was the first time given by Dickson Despommier (Platt, 2007). VF with artificial lighting has multiple shelves connected with LED lights and nutrient supply units. Additional equipment is generally required for VF is environment control units, CO_2 supply unit, air conditioner, and air control fans (Kozai & Niu, 2016). Increasing the number of vertical shelves increases the efficiency of land use. This culture system is currently being used in Japan and other Asian countries, the US, Australia (Benke & Tomkins, 2017), and Canada.

It has several advantages over traditional cultivation system among that principal advantage are (1) Not affected by weather/ climate fluctuations (2) Can be constructed anywhere since there is no need of either sunlight or soil (3) 100 times more production compared to traditional cultivation system (4) Products are pesticides free (5) Transportation cost can be reduced by constructing farms in cities (6) Products with longer shelf life (7) Environment can be protected with minimum loss of fertilizers, CO_2

and water. However, there are some constraints and limitations, the predominated ones are (1) Restriction to only leafy vegetables *i.e.,* mostly tomato, lettuce and strawberries (2) High installation cost (3) Production volume is low compared to large acre farming (4) Energy requirement is high (5) Skilled workers are needed (6) Taste and nutrition of the product is unstable (7) High cost of urban lands (Kozai & Niu, 2020, Benke & Tomkins, 2017).

There are three main types of techniques used in VF (1) Hydroponics (2) Aeroponics (3) Aquaponics. Nevertheless, hydroponic is a predominant VF system. In the hydroponic systems, roots of the plants are immersed in water containing both primary & secondary macronutrients and few micronutrients (Son et al., 2020). Hydroponics has exceptional advantages over traditional cultivation systems in the form of high yield and water use efficiency. For instance, a study in 2016 revealed that hydroponic cultivation gave 11 times more lettuce production utilizing 13 times less water (Barbosa et al., 2015). Similarly, another study in Mexico urged on the implementation of a hydroponic system in the Mexican agriculture system to fulfill the demand for food for the country's ever-growing population which is expected to reach 150 million by 2050 (Anda & Shear, 2017). On the other hand, Pascual and coworkers (2018) conducted a study to identify the applicability of hydroponic technology, its sustainability, and acceptability among the onion farmers of the Philippine. They inferred that there was a significant difference in the growth and suitability of onion compared to the traditional system; also, most of the onion farmers were willing to adopt this VF except the issue of high start-up cost (Pascual et al., 2018).

THE second VF renowned technique is aeroponics, a technique to grow plants in the air in the absence of any liquid or solid medium. This practice was originally proposed by NASA to grow plants in the air space (Spinoff, 2006). Aeroponics approach is not as popular as other VF approaches however, it is slowly gaining popularity. In aeroponics water containing the nutrient solution is sprayed on the plants growing in the air chambers thus using 90% less water and 30-50% less fertilizer compared to hydroponics. Still faster and higher yield can be achieved by carefully maintaining optimum pH and nutrient supply. Although the most imperative factor in aeroponics is the proper supply of oxygen to the roots for the efficient growth of plants (Mytton-Mills, 2018).

Aeroponic systems are being used effectively for the growth of the potato, tomato, lettuce, onions, carrot, spinach, cucumber, strawberries, and cotton in different parts of the world. For instance, a study was conducted by Li and coworkers (2018) to compare lettuce growth in the aeroponic system with hydroponic and substrate culture. Results of the study exhibited that lettuce produced under aeroponic culture had higher root length, root/shoot ratio, root biomass however lower shoot growth compared to hydroponics which might be due to limited availability of nutrients and water in the aeroponic culture (Li et al., 2018). Later in 2019, another study on lettuce was conducted by Lakhiar and coworkers (2019) to identify the effect of the different aeroponic atomizer on the growth and quality of lettuce. They observed that atomizer A2 had a significant effect on the growth, polyphenol contents, and antioxidant activity of the crop. Hence, they suggested that the use of proper droplet size for misting nutrient solution is a vital factor to consider (Lakhiar *et al.,* 2019). Apart from this, there are various studies on the potato as well (Oraby et al., 2015; Buckseth et al., 2016; Rykaczewska, 2016; Tessema et al., 2017).

THE third VF technique in use is aquaponics, a technique of growing plants in the soil-less medium which contains nutrient-rich waste from the fish-ponds. This waste solution is first passed through a solid removal filter followed by biofilter to convert ammonia into nitrate. This nitrate is used as a nutrient for plants in vertical farms. Plants purify the wastewater and recycle it back to fishponds. However, this cultivation technique is not as common as hydroponics (Salin & Ataguba, 2018). This practice originated in China back in 1000-2000 BC when the culture of common carps (*Cyprinus carpio*) came into being.

However, currently apart from Carps, Salmonids, Tilapias, Catfishes, Marine finfish, Soft-shelled turtle, Shrimps, Freshwater decapod crustaceans, Bivalve mollusks, and Abalone are being aquacultured *i.e.* in China (Xie et al., 2018; Chen et al., 2018; Li et al., 2018), South Korea (Park et al., 2018; Cho et al., 2019), Philippines (Guerrero & Fernandez, 2018), South Africa (Potgieter, 2018), North Africa (Kara et al., 2018), United States (Lester et al., 2018), etc. Moreover, globally researchers interested in the aquaculture industry are proposing new practices for the sustainability of the aquaculture industry. For instance, a study carried out in Indonesia in 2017 suggested the use of bio floc technology (BFT) in aquaculture which will improve aquaculture production with minimal effect on the environment (Bossier & Ekasari, 2017). By the same token, genetic breeding is believed to have significant positive results on the aquaculture industry especially concerning high production and disease resistance of animals of aquatic systems (Zhou & Gui, 2018). Conversely, some also reported the harms emerging from the aquaculture industry *i.e.,* a comprehensive review was compiled by Chilean researchers to reveal the harms related to increased amounts of antibiotics being used by the aquaculture industry which has become an environmental and public concern (Lozano et al., 2018).

PRECISION AGRICULTURE

In the current scenario of changing climate, sustainable agriculture, and food production is considered very important to ensure food supply for the future world via controlling resources waste and to ensure efficient use. Precision agriculture in this regard can be very helpful as it provides site-specific crop management strategies, pest management, and use of electronic technologies to get sustainable yield and production (Corwin & Plant, 2005).

Accurate yield estimates and improved nutrient management are crucial in agriculture nowadays. Precision agriculture and its allied technologies are being widely used in building decision support tools for contemporary farming systems to improve yield production and nutrient management while reducing operating costs and environmental impact (Chlingaryan et al., 2018; Vuran et al., 2018).

SUMMARY

The accelerated population and agricultural activities have resulted in a loss of soil fertility, salinity, fertilizers and pesticide pollution, soil degradation, and food insecurity. The resultant of all the above are arable lands that can be restored, reacclimated, and used as cultivable soils. Different activities are carried-out to use these soils as cultivable soils like; soil erosion control by crop cultivation, harvesting management, selection of crops which use fewer nutrients to prevent soil fertility loss, intercropping, cultivation of cover crops, use of shelterbelts to prevent soil erosion, mulching, agroforestry and use of treated wastewater for irrigation.

REFERENCES

Abiala, M. A., Abdelrahman, M., Burritt, D. J., & Tran, L. S. P. (2018). Salt stress tolerance mechanisms and potential applications of legumes for sustainable reclamation of salt-degraded soils. *Land Degradation & Development*, *29*(10), 3812–3822. doi:10.1002/ldr.3095

Ahmad, I., Imran, M., Hussain, M. B., & Hussain, S. (2017). Remediation of Organic And Inorganic Pollutants From Soil: The Role Of Plant-Bacteria Partnership. In N. A. Anjum (Ed.), *Chemical Pollution Control With Microorganisms* (pp. 197–243). Nova Sci. Publisher.

Alewell, C., Borrelli, P., Meusburger, K., & Panagos, P. (2019). International Soil and Water Conservation Research. *International Soil and Water Conservation Research (ISWCR), 203.*

Al-Saedi, S. A., Al-Ameri, B. H., & Rasheed, A. G. (2018). Sulfuric acid as a chemical amendment for increasing efficiency of reclamation process of salt affected soils of Iraq. *Net Journal of Agricultural Science*, *6*(3), 49–52. doi:10.30918/NJAS.63.18.022

Ayipio, E., Wells, D. E., McQuilling, A., & Wilson, A. E. (2019). Comparisons between Aquaponic and Conventional Hydroponic Crop Yields: A Meta-Analysis. *Sustainability*, *11*(22), 6511. doi:10.3390u11226511

Babayev, A. G. (2019). Principal Problems of Desert Land Reclamation in the USSR. In *Desertification* (pp. 203–232). CRC Press. doi:10.1201/9780429050893-9

Barbosa, G. L., Gadelha, F. D. A., Kublik, N., Proctor, A., Reichelm, L., Weissinger, E., Wohlleb, G. M., & Halden, R. U. (2015). Comparison of land, water, and energy requirements of lettuce grown using hydroponic vs. conventional agricultural methods. *International Journal of Environmental Research and Public Health*, *12*(6), 6879–6891. doi:10.3390/ijerph120606879 PMID:26086708

Barlow, J., Lennox, G. D., Ferreira, J., Berenguer, E., Lees, A. C., Nally, R. M., & Gardner, T. A. (2016). Anthropogenic disturbance in tropical forests can double biodiversity loss from deforestation. *Nature*, *535*(7610), 144–147. doi:10.1038/nature18326 PMID:27362236

Bashir, S., Javed, A., Bibi, I., & Ahmad, N. (2017). *Soil and Water Conservation*. https://www.researchgate.net/publication/320729156_Soil_and_Water_Conservation

Benke, K., & Tomkins, B. (2017). Future food-production systems: vertical farming and controlled-environment agriculture. Sustainability: Science. *Practice and Policy*, *13*(1), 13–26.

Berkofsky, L., Faiman, D., & Gale, J. (Eds.). (2019). *Settling the desert* (Vol. 16). Routledge. doi:10.4324/9780429287886

Blanco, P. D., Hardtke, L. A., Rostagno, C. M., del Valle, H. F., & Metternicht, G. I. (2017). Soil Degradation in Peninsula Valdes: Causes, Factors, Processes, and Assessment Methods. In Late Cenozoic of Península Valdés, Patagonia, Argentina (pp. 191-213). Springer.

Bossier, P., & Ekasari, J. (2017). Biofloc technology application in aquaculture to support sustainable development goals. *Microbial Biotechnology*, *10*(5), 1012–1016. doi:10.1111/1751-7915.12836 PMID:28941177

Bouma, J., Keesstra, S., & Cerdà, A. (2017). The importance of Soil Science to understand and remediate Land Degradation and Desertification processes. Paper presented at the Geophysical Research Abstracts.

Bradford, A. (2015). *Deforestation: facts, causes & effects*. Live Science.

Buckseth, T., Sharma, A. K., Pandey, K. K., Singh, B. P., & Muthuraj, R. (2016). Methods of pre- basic seed potato production with special reference to aeroponics-A review. *Scientia Horticulturae*, *204*, 79–87.

Cachada, A., Rocha-Santos, T., & Duarte, A. C. (2018). Soil and pollution: an introduction to the main issues. In *Soil pollution* (pp. 1–28). Elsevier.

Carter, E. D. (2018). Overpopulation. In Companion to Environmental Studies (Vol. 76, No. 80, pp. 76-80). Routledge in association with GSE Research.

Chandio, A. A., Jiang, Y., Rehman, A., & Rauf, A. (2020). Short and long-run impacts of climate change on agriculture: An empirical evidence from China. *International Journal Climate Change Stress.*, *7*, 395–402.

Cha-un, N., Chidthaisong, A., Yagi, K., Sudo, S., & Towprayoon, S. (2017). Greenhouse gas emissions, soil carbon sequestration and crop yields in a rain-fed rice field with crop rotation management. *Agriculture, Ecosystems & Environment*, *237*, 109–120. doi:10.1016/j.agee.2016.12.025

Chen, S., Su, Y., & Hong, W. (2018). *Aquaculture of the large yellow croaker. Aquaculture in China: Success Stories and Modern Trends*. John Wiley & Sons.

Chen, S., Wang, W., Xu, W., Wang, Y., Wan, H., Chen, D., Tang, Z., Tang, X., Zhou, G., Xie, Z., Zhou, D., Shangguan, Z., Huang, J., He, J.-S., Wang, Y., Sheng, J., Tang, L., Li, X., Dong, M., ... Bai, Y. (2018). Plant diversity enhances productivity and soil carbon storage. *Proceedings of the National Academy of Sciences of the United States of America*, *115*(16), 4027–4032. doi:10.1073/pnas.1700298114 PMID:29666315

Cherif, H., Marasco, R., Rolli, E., Ferjani, R., Fusi, M., Soussi, A., Mapelli, F., Blilou, I., Borin, S., Boudabous, A., Cherif, A., Daffonchio, D., & Ouzari, H. (2015). Oasis desert farming selects environment-specific date palm root endophytic communities and cultivable bacteria that promote resistance to drought. *Environmental Microbiology Reports*, *7*(4), 668–678. doi:10.1111/1758-2229.12304 PMID:26033617

Chlingaryan, A., Sukkarieh, S., & Whelan, B. (2018). Machine learning approaches for crop yield prediction and nitrogen status estimation in precision agriculture: A review. *Computers and Electronics in Agriculture*, *151*, 61–69. doi:10.1016/j.compag.2018.05.012

Cho, Y., Shim, W. J., Jang, M., Han, G. M., & Hong, S. H. (2019). Abundance and characteristics of microplastics in market bivalves from South Korea. *Environmental Pollution*, *245*, 1107–1116. doi:10.1016/j.envpol.2018.11.091 PMID:30682745

Conant, R. T., Cerri, C. E., Osborne, B. B., & Paustian, K. (2017). Grassland management impacts on soil carbon stocks: A new synthesis. *Ecological Applications*, *27*(2), 662–668. doi:10.1002/eap.1473 PMID:27875004

Cordesman, A. H. (2019). *Guarding the desert kingdom*. Routledge. doi:10.4324/9780429497452

Corwin, D. L., & Plant, R. E. (2005). Applications of apparent soil electrical conductivity in precision agriculture. *Computers and Electronics in Agriculture*, *46*(1), 1–10. doi:10.1016/j.compag.2004.10.004

Costantini, E. A., Priori, S., Giffard, B., Fulchin, E., Tardaguila, J., Schroers, H.J., & Valboa, G. (2018). Causes of soil malfunctioning in degraded areas of European and Turkish vineyards. *EQA–Environmental Quality, 30*, 15-22.

Crabtree, S. A., Bird, D. W., & Bird, R. B. (2019). Subsistence transitions and the simplification of ecological networks in the Western Desert of Australia. *Human Ecology*, *47*(2), 165–177. doi:10.100710745-019-0053-z

Crosson, P. (2017). Degradation: Food Security and Poverty. In Encyclopedia of Soil Science (pp. 574-577). CRC Press.

De Anda, J., & Shear, H. (2017). Potential of vertical hydroponic agriculture in Mexico. *Sustainability*, *9*(1), 140. doi:10.3390u9010140

De Clercq, M., Vats, A., & Biel, A. (2018). Agriculture 4.0: The future of farming technology. *Proceedings of the World Government Summit,* 11-13.

De Stefano, A., & Jacobson, M. G. (2018). Soil carbon sequestration in agroforestry systems: A meta-analysis. *Agroforestry Systems*, *92*(2), 285–299.

Kashyap. (n.d.). *Deserts Characteristics: 21 General Characteristics of Deserts (With Maps),Yours Articles Library.* http://www.yourarticlelibrary.com/deserts- environment/deserts-characteristics-21-general-characteristics-of-deserts-with-maps/64226

Dobson, A. P., Bradshaw, A., & Baker, A. Á. (1997). Hopes for the future: Restoration ecology and conservation biology. *Science*, *277*(5325), 515–522. doi:10.1126cience.277.5325.515

Doran, J. W., & Parkin, T. B. (1994). Defining and assessing soil quality. *Defining soil quality for a sustainable environment, 35*, 1-21.

Elemike, E. E., Uzoh, I. M., Onwudiwe, D. C., & Babalola, O. O. (2019). The role of nanotechnology in the fortification of plant nutrients and improvement of crop production. *Applied Sciences*, *9*(3), 499. doi:10.3390/app9030499

Emran, M., Doni, S., Macci, C., Masciandaro, G., Rashad, M., & Gispert, M. (2020). Susceptible soil organic matter, SOM, fractions to agricultural management practices in salt-affected soils. *Geoderma*, *366*, 114257. doi:10.1016/j.geoderma.2020.114257

Evans, R., Collins, A. L., Foster, I. D., Rickson, R. J., Anthony, S. G., Brewer, T., & Zhang, Y. (2016). Extent, frequency and rate of water erosion of arable land in Britain-benefits and challenges for modelling. *Soil Use and Management*, *32*, 149–161. doi:10.1111um.12210

Fan, J. L., Hu, J. W., Zhang, X., Kong, L. S., Li, F., & Mi, Z. (2020). Impacts of climate change on hydropower generation in China. *Mathematics and Computers in Simulation*, *167*, 4–18. doi:10.1016/j.matcom.2018.01.002

Forouzani, M., & Karami, E. (2011). Agricultural water poverty index and sustainability. *Agronomy for Sustainable Development*, *31*(2), 415–431. doi:10.1051/agro/2010026

Gabriel, D., Sait, S. M., Hodgson, J. A., Schmutz, U., Kunin, W. E., & Benton, T. G. (2010). Scale matters: The impact of organic farming on biodiversity at different spatial scales. *Ecology Letters*, *13*(7), 858–869. doi:10.1111/j.1461-0248.2010.01481.x PMID:20482572

Gebhardt, M. R., Daniel, T. C., Schweizer, E. E., & Allmaras, R. R. (1985). Conservation tillage. *Science*, *230*(4726), 625–630. doi:10.1126cience.230.4726.625 PMID:17797277

Ghosh, A., Bhattacharyya, R., Meena, M. C., Dwivedi, B. S., Singh, G., Agnihotri, R., & Sharma, C. (2018). Long-term fertilization effects on soil organic carbon sequestration in an Inceptisol. *Soil & Tillage Research*, *177*, 134–144. doi:10.1016/j.still.2017.12.006

Glantz, M. H. (2019). The UN and desertification: Dealing with a global problem. In *Desertification* (pp. 1–15). CRC Press. doi:10.1201/9780429050893-1

Gomiero, T. (2016). Soil degradation, land scarcity and food security: Reviewing a complex challenge. *Sustainability*, *8*(3), 281. doi:10.3390u8030281

Guerrero, R. D., & Fernandez, P. R. (2018). Aquaculture and Water Quality Management in the Philippines. In *Water Policy in the Philippines* (pp. 143–162). Springer. doi:10.1007/978-3-319-70969-7_7

Guisan, A., Broennimann, O., Buri, A., Cianfrani, C., D'Amen, M., Di Cola, V., Fernandes, R., Gray, S., Mateo, R. G., Pinto, E., & Pradervand, J. N. (2019). Climate change impacts on mountain biodiversity. In *Biodiversity and Climate Change* (pp. 221–233). Yale University Press. doi:10.2307/j.ctv8jnzw1.29

Hsiang, S., Kopp, R., Jina, A., Rising, J., Delgado, M., Mohan, S., & Larsen, K. (2017). Estimating economic damage from climate change in the United States. *Science*, *356*(6345), 1362–1369. doi:10.1126cience.aal4369 PMID:28663496

Jigău, G., Cernolev, E., & Acciu, A. (2016). Plant Health Risks Arising by the Soil Exhaustion. *Present Environment and Sustainable Development*, *10*(2), 185–194. doi:10.1515/pesd-2016-0036

Kalantari, F., Mohd Tahir, O., Mahmoudi Lahijani, A., & Kalantari, S. (2017). A review of vertical farming technology: A guide for implementation of building integrated agriculture in cities. In *Advanced Engineering Forum* (Vol. 24, pp. 76-91). Trans Tech Publications Ltd. 10.4028/www.scientific.net/AEF.24.76

Kara, M. H., Lacroix, D., Rey-Valette, H., Mathé, S., & Blancheton, J. P. (2018). Dynamics of research in aquaculture in North Africa and support for sustainable development and innovation. *Reviews in Fisheries Science & Aquaculture*, *26*(3), 309–318. doi:10.1080/23308249.2017.1410521

Kopittke, P. M., Menzies, N. W., Wang, P., McKenna, B. A., & Lombi, E. (2019). Soil and the intensification of agriculture for global food security. *Environment International*, *132*, 105078. doi:10.1016/j.envint.2019.105078 PMID:31400601

Koubi, V., & Spilker, G. (2017). Natural Resources, Climate Change, and Conflict. In Oxford Research Encyclopedia of Politics. Academic Press.

Kozai, T., & Niu, G. (2020). Role of the plant factory with artificial lighting (PFAL) in urban areas. In Plant Factory (pp. 7-34). Academic Press.

Kozai, T., & Niu, G. H. (2016). Overview and concept of closed plant production system (CPPS). In *Plant Factory: An Indoor Vertical Farming System for Efficient Quality Food Production*. Academic Press.

Kubiak, K., Wrzosek, M., Przemieniecki, S., Damszel, M., & Sierota, Z. (2018). Bacteria Inhabiting Wood of Roots and Stumps in Forest and Arable Soils. In Endophytes of Forest Trees (pp. 319-342): Springer. doi:10.1007/978-3-319-89833-9_14

Lakhiar, I. A., Gao, J., Syed, T. N., Chandio, F. A., & Buttar, N. A. (2018). Modern plant cultivation technologies in agriculture under controlled environment: A review on aeroponics. *Journal of Plant Interactions*, *13*(1), 338–352. doi:10.1080/17429145.2018.1472308

Lakhiar, I. A., Gao, J., Xu, X., Syed, T. N., Chandio, F. A., Jing, Z., & Buttar, N. A. (2019). Effects of Various Aeroponic Atomizers (Droplet sizes) on the Growth, Total Polyphenol Content and Antioxidant Activity of Leafy Lettuce (Lactuca sativa L.). *Transactions of the ASABE*.

Lal, R. (2016). Feeding 11 billion on 0.5 billion hectare of area under cereal crops. *Food and Energy Security*, *5*(4), 239–251. doi:10.1002/fes3.99

Lal, R. (2018). Managing agricultural soils of Pakistan for food and climate. *Soil & Environment*, *37*(1), 1–10. doi:10.25252/SE/18/61527

Lal, R. (2016). Global food security and nexus thinking. *Journal of Soil and Water Conservation*, *71*(4), 85A–90A. doi:10.2489/jswc.71.4.85A

Lane, D., Chatrchyan, A., Tobin, D., Thorn, K., Allred, S., & Radhakrishna, R. (2018). Climate change and agriculture in New York and Pennsylvania: Risk perceptions, vulnerability and adaptation among farmers. *Renewable Agriculture and Food Systems*, *33*(3), 197–205. doi:10.1017/S1742170517000710

León, P., Espejo, R., Gómez-Paccard, C., Hontoria, C., Mariscal, I., Renella, G., & Benito, M. (2017). No tillage and sugar beet foam amendment enhanced microbial activity of degraded acidic soils in South West Spain. *Applied Soil Ecology*, *109*, 69–74. doi:10.1016/j.apsoil.2016.09.012

Lester, S. E., Gentry, R. R., Kappel, C. V., White, C., & Gaines, S. D. (2018). Opinion: Offshore aquaculture in the United States: Untapped potential in need of smart policy. *Proceedings of the National Academy of Sciences of the United States of America*, *115*(28), 7162–7165. doi:10.1073/pnas.1808737115 PMID:29991573

Lewis, I. D. (2017). Solutions to desertification. *Geodate*, *30*(2), 3.

Li, Q., Li, X., Tang, B., & Gu, M. (2018). Growth responses and root characteristics of lettuce grown in aeroponics, hydroponics, and substrate culture. *Horticulturae*, *4*(4), 35. doi:10.3390/horticulturae4040035

Li, Z., Liu, J., Wang, Q., & Silva, S. S. D. (2018). Inland aquaculture: Trends and prospects. Aquaculture in China: Success stories and modern trends, 25-37.

Lozano, I., Díaz, N.F., Muñoz, S. & Riquelme, C. (2018). Antibiotics in Chilean aquaculture: a review. *Antibiotic use in animals, 3*, 25-44.

Lucas, J. S., Southgate, P. C., & Tucker, C. S. (Eds.). (2019). *Aquaculture: farming aquatic animals and plants*. John Wiley & Sons.

Mandal, M., Kamp, P., & Singh, M. (2020). Effect of Long Term Manuring on Carbon Sequestration Potential and Dynamics of Soil Organic Carbon Labile Pool Under Tropical Rice-Rice Agro-ecosystem. *Communications in Soil Science and Plant Analysis*, 1–13.

Marichal, R., Praxedes, C., Decaëns, T., Grimaldi, M., Oszwald, J., Brown, G. G., & Oliveira, M. N. (2017). Earthworm functional traits, landscape degradation and ecosystem services in the Brazilian Amazon deforestation arc. *European Journal of Soil Biology*, *83*, 43–51. doi:10.1016/j.ejsobi.2017.09.003

McIntyre, K.M., Setzkorn, C., Hepworth, P.J., Morand, S., Morse, A.P., & Baylis, M. (2017). *Systematic assessment of the climate sensitivity of important human and domestic animals pathogens in European Scientific Reports*. Academic Press.

Metz, B., Davidson, O.R., Bosch, P.R., Dave, R., & Meyer, L.A. (2007). *Contribution of working group III to the fourth assessment report of the intergovernmental panel on climate change, 2007*. IPCC Fourth Assessment Report (AR4).

Miranowski, J. A. (1984). Impacts of productivity loss on crop production and management in a dynamic economic model. *American Journal of Agricultural Economics*, *66*(1), 61–71. doi:10.2307/1240616

Monzon, J. P., Calviño, P. A., Sadras, V. O., Zubiaurre, J. B., & Andrade, F. H. (2018). Precision agriculture based on crop physiological principles improves whole-farm yield and profit: A case study. *European Journal of Agronomy*, *99*, 62–71. doi:10.1016/j.eja.2018.06.011

Muñoz Rojas, M., Jordán López, A., Martínez Zavala, L. M., Rosa, D. D. L., Elmabod, A., Mohamed, S. K., & Anaya Romero, M. (2012). Organic carbon stocks in Mediterranean soil types under different land uses (Southern Spain). *Solid Earth*, *3*(3), 375–386. doi:10.5194e-3-375-2012

Muñoz-Rojas, M., Román, J. R., Roncero-Ramos, B., Erickson, T. E., Merritt, D. J., Aguila-Carricondo, P., & Cantón, Y. (2018). Cyanobacteria inoculation enhances carbon sequestration in soil substrates used in dryland restoration. *The Science of the Total Environment*, *636*, 1149–1154. doi:10.1016/j.scitotenv.2018.04.265 PMID:29913577

Mytton-Mills, H. (2018). Reimagining Resources to Build Smart Futures: An Agritech Case Study of Aeroponics. In *Smart Futures, Challenges of Urbanization, and Social Sustainability* (pp. 169–191). Springer. doi:10.1007/978-3-319-74549-7_10

Nkonya, E., Gerber, N., Baumgartner, P., von Braun, J., De Pinto, A., Graw, V., & Walter, T. (2011). *The economics of desertification, land degradation, and drought. Toward an Integrated Global Assessment*. IFPRI Discussion Paper, 1086.

Novara, A., Gristina, L., Sala, G., Galati, A., Crescimanno, M., Cerdà, A., Badalamenti, E., & La Mantia, T. (2017). Agricultural land abandonment in Mediterranean environment provides ecosystem services via soil carbon sequestration. *The Science of the Total Environment*, *576*, 420–429. doi:10.1016/j.scitotenv.2016.10.123 PMID:27792957

Novara, A., Pisciotta, A., Minacapilli, M., Maltese, A., Capodici, F., Cerdà, A., & Gristina, L. (2018). The impact of soil erosion on soil fertility and vine vigor. A multidisciplinary approach based on field, laboratory and remote sensing approaches. *The Science of the Total Environment*, *622-623*, 474–480. doi:10.1016/j.scitotenv.2017.11.272 PMID:29223076

Oldeman, L. R., Hakkeling, R., & Sombroek, W. G. (2017). *World map of the status of human-induced soil degradation: an explanatory note*. International Soil Reference and Information Centre.

Oraby, H., Lachance, A., & Desjardins, Y. (2015). A low nutrient solution temperature and the application of stress treatments increase potato mini-tubers production in an aeroponic system. *American Journal of Potato Research*, *92*(3), 387–397. doi:10.100712230-015-9444-x

Orgill, S. E., Condon, J. R., Conyers, M. K., Morris, S. G., Alcock, D. J., Murphy, B. W., & Greene, R. S. B. (2018). Removing grazing pressure from a native pasture decreases soil organic carbon in southern New South Wales, Australia. *Land Degradation & Development*, *29*(2), 274–283. doi:10.1002/ldr.2560

Ortiz, R. (2019). *Role of Plant Breeding to Sustain Food Security under Climate Change*. Food Security and Climate Change.

Ortiz-Partida, J. P., Sandoval-Solis, S., Arellano-Gonzalez, J., Medellín-Azuara, J., & Taylor, J. E. (2020). Managing water differently: Integrated Water Resources Management as a framework for adaptation to climate change in Mexico. In *Integrated Water Resource Management* (pp. 59–72). Springer. doi:10.1007/978-3-030-16565-9_6

Park, M., Shin, S. K., Do, Y. H., Yarish, C., & Kim, J. K. (2018). Application of open water integrated multi-trophic aquaculture to intensive monoculture: A review of the current status and challenges in Korea. *Aquaculture (Amsterdam, Netherlands)*, *497*, 174–183. doi:10.1016/j.aquaculture.2018.07.051

Pascual, C., Agulto, I., Espino, A., Jr., & Malamug, V. (2019). *Effect of ground heat exchanger for root-zone cooling on the growth and yield of aeroponically-grown strawberry plant under tropical greenhouse condition*. Paper presented at the IOP Conference Series: Earth and Environmental Science. 10.1088/1755-1315/301/1/012006

Pedersen, S. M., & Lind, K. M. (2017). *Precision agriculture: Technology and economic perspectives*. Springer. doi:10.1007/978-3-319-68715-5

Platt, P. (2007). Vertical farming: An interview with Dickson Despommier. *Gastronomica*, *7*(3), 80–87. doi:10.1525/gfc.2007.7.3.80

Potgieter, T. (2018). Oceans economy, blue economy, and security: Notes on the South African potential and developments. *Journal of the Indian Ocean Region*, *14*(1), 49–70. doi:10.1080/19480881.2018.1410962

Prashar, P., & Shah, S. (2016). Impact of fertilizers and pesticides on soil microflora in agriculture. In *Sustainable agriculture reviews* (pp. 331–361). Springer. doi:10.1007/978-3-319-26777-7_8

Redden, R. J., Upadyaya, H., Dwivedi, S. L., Vadez, V., Abberton, M., & Amri, A. (2019). *Role of Plant Genetic Resources in Food Security*. Food Security and Climate Change.

Romero-Baena, A. J., González, I., & Galán, E. (2018). Soil pollution by mining activities in Andalusia (South Spain)-the role of Mineralogy and Geochemistry in three case studies. *Journal of Soils and Sediments, 18*(6), 2231–2247. doi:10.100711368-017-1898-7

Rubio-Asensio, J. S., Parra, M., & Intrigliolo, D. S. (2020). Open field hydroponics in fruit crops: Developments and challenges. In *Fruit Crops* (pp. 419–430). Elsevier. doi:10.1016/B978-0-12-818732-6.00030-7

Rykaczewska, K. (2016). The potato minituber production from micro-tubers in aeroponic culture. *Plant, Soil and Environment, 62*(5), 210–214. doi:10.17221/686/2015-PSE

Saifullah, D., Dahlawi, S., Naeem, A., Rengel, Z., & Naidu, R. (2018). Biochar application for the remediation of salt-affected soils: Challenges and opportunities. *The Science of the Total Environment, 625*, 320–335. doi:10.1016/j.scitotenv.2017.12.257 PMID:29289780

Salin, K. R., & Ataguba, G. A. (2018). Aquaculture and the environment: Towards sustainability. In *Sustainable Aquaculture* (pp. 1–62). Springer. doi:10.1007/978-3-319-73257-2_1

Saturday, A. (2018). Restoration of degraded agricultural land: A review. *Journal of Environmental Health Science, 4*, 44–51.

Scherr, S. J. (1999). *Soil degradation: a threat to developing-country food security by 2020?* (Vol. 27). Intl Food Policy Res Inst.

Seidl, R., Thom, D., Kautz, M., Martin-Benito, D., Peltoniemi, M., Vacchiano, G., & Lexer, M. J. (2017). Forest disturbances under climate change. *Nature Climate Change, 7*(6), 395–402. doi:10.1038/nclimate3303 PMID:28861124

Silva, R. A., West, J. J., Lamarque, J. F., Shindell, D. T., Collins, W. J., Faluvegi, G., Folberth, G. A., Horowitz, L. W., Nagashima, T., Naik, V., Rumbold, S. T., Sudo, K., Takemura, T., Bergmann, D., Cameron-Smith, P., Doherty, R. M., Josse, B., MacKenzie, I. A., Stevenson, D. S., & Zeng, G. (2017). Future global mortality from changes in air pollution attributable to climate change. *Nature Climate Change, 7*(9), 647–651. doi:10.1038/nclimate3354 PMID:30245745

Sklenicka, P. (2016). Classification of farmland ownership fragmentation as a cause of land degradation: A review on typology, consequences, and remedies. *Land Use Policy, 57*, 694–701. doi:10.1016/j.landusepol.2016.06.032

Son, J. E., Kim, H. J., & Ahn, T. I. (2020). Hydroponic systems. In *Plant factory* (pp. 273–283). Academic Press. doi:10.1016/B978-0-12-816691-8.00020-0

Spinoff, N. A. S. A. (2006). *Progressive plant growing has business blooming*. Environmental and Agricultural Resources.

Sullivan, P. (2004). *Sustainable soil management: soil systems guide. Appropriate Technology Transfer for Rural Areas*. ATTRA.

Tessema, L., Chindi, A., Gebremedhin, W. G., Solomon, A., Shunka, E., & Seid, E. (2017). Determination of nutrient solutions for potato (Solanum tuberosum L.) seed production under aeroponics production system. *Open Agriculture, 2*(1), 155–159. doi:10.1515/opag-2017-0015

Thaman, R. R., Clarke, W., Manner, H. I., Decker, B. G., & Ali, I. (2017). *Agroforestry in the Pacific Islands: Systems for sustainability*. United Nations University Press.

The World Bank. (2016). *Arable Land (% of land area).* Data accessed at: https://data.worldbank.org/indicator/AG.LND.ARBL.ZS

Tobin, D., Janowiak, M., Hollinger, D., Skinner, R. H., Swanston, C., Steele, R., Radhakrishna, R., Chatrchyan, A., Hickman, D., Bochicchio, J., & Hall, W. (2015). *Northeast and northern forests regional climate hub assessment of climate change vulnerability and adaptation and mitigation strategies*. USDA Climate Hubs.

Tunio, M. H., Gao, J., Shaikh, S. A., Lakhiar, I. A., Qureshi, W. A., Solangi, K. A., & Chandio, F. A. (2020). Potato production in aeroponics: An emerging food growing system in sustainable agriculture for food security. *Chilean Journal of Agricultural Research*, *80*(1), 1. doi:10.4067/S0718-58392020000100118

Usher, A. P. (1923). Soil fertility, soil exhaustion, and their historical significance. *The Quarterly Journal of Economics*, *37*(3), 385–411. doi:10.2307/1883847

Vengosh, A. (2003). Salinization and saline environments. *Treatise on Geochemistry, 9*, 612.

Vuran, M. C., Salam, A., Wong, R., & Irmak, S. (2018). *Internet of underground things: Sensing and communications on the field for precision agriculture.* Paper presented at the 2018 IEEE 4th World Forum on Internet of Things (WF-IoT). 10.1109/WF-IoT.2018.8355096

Wankhade, R., Patode, R., Nagdeve, M., Gabhane, V., & Pande, C. (2017). Effect of Continuous Contour Trenches on Nutrient Status of the Micro-Catchment. *Current Agriculture Research Journal*, *5*(3), 305–311. doi:10.12944/CARJ.5.3.07

Weber, E. (2012). Climate and environmental change and food security. *Journal of Pacific Studies*, *32*, 99–110.

Weber, E. (2014). Climate change, agriculture and food security in the Pacific Islands. *Journal of South Pacific Agriculture*, *17*(1&2), 20–35.

Weber, E. H. (2011). Climate change and food security–some conceptual considerations. *Journal of South Pacific Agriculture*, *15*(1&2), 85–97.

Willaarts, B. A., Oyonarte, C., Muñoz-Rojas, M., Ibáñez, J. J., & Aguilera, P. A. (2016). Environmental factors controlling soil organic carbon stocks in two contrasting Mediterranean climatic areas of southern Spain. *Land Degradation & Development*, *27*(3), 603–611. doi:10.1002/ldr.2417

Wu, L., Zhu, Q., Yang, L., Li, B., Hu, C., & Lan, S. (2018). Nutrient transferring from wastewater to desert through artificial cultivation of desert cyanobacteria. *Bioresource Technology*, *247*, 947–953. doi:10.1016/j.biortech.2017.09.127 PMID:30060434

Xie, C., Li, J., Li, D., Shen, Y., Gao, Y., & Zhang, Z. (2018). Grass carp: the fish that feeds half of China. *Aquaculture in China: Success Stories and Modern Trends*, 93-115.

Xie, J., Yu, J., Chen, B., Feng, Z., Lyu, J., Hu, L., Gan, Y., & Siddique, K. H. (2018). Gobi agriculture: An innovative farming system that increases energy and water use efficiencies. A review. *Agronomy for Sustainable Development*, *38*(6), 62. doi:10.100713593-018-0540-4

Yadav, G. S., Lal, R., Meena, R. S., Babu, S., Das, A., Bhowmik, S. N., Datta, M., Layak, J., & Saha, P. (2019). Conservation tillage and nutrient management effects on productivity and soil carbon sequestration under double cropping of rice in north eastern region of India. *Ecological Indicators*, *105*, 303–315. doi:10.1016/j.ecolind.2017.08.071

Zhang, D., Liao, Y., & Jia, Z. (2005). Research advances and prospects of film mulching in arid and semi-arid areas. *Agricultural Research in the Arid Areas, 1*, 41.

Zhou, L., & Gui, J. F. (2018). Applications of genetic breeding biotechnologies in Chinese aquaculture. Aquaculture in China: Success stories and modern trends, 463-496. doi:10.1002/9781119120759.ch6_1

Bhat, N., Suleiman, M., & Abdal, M. (2009). Selection of crops for sustainable utilization of land and water resources in Kuwait. *World Journal of Agricultural Sciences*, *5*, 201–206.

Borgman, O., & Chefetz, B. (2013). Combined effects of biosolids application and irrigation with reclaimed wastewater on transport of pharmaceutical compounds in arable soils. *Water Research*, *47*(10), 3431–3443. doi:10.1016/j.watres.2013.03.045 PMID:23591105

Borrelli, P., Paustian, K., Panagos, P., Jones, A., Schütt, B., & Lugato, E. (2016). Effect of good agricultural and environmental conditions on erosion and soil organic carbon balance: A national case study. *Land Use Policy*, *50*, 408–421. doi:10.1016/j.landusepol.2015.09.033

El-Lakany, M. (1983). A review of breeding drought resistant Casuarina for shelterbelt establishment in arid regions with special reference to Egypt. *Forest Ecology and Management*, *6*(2), 129–137. doi:10.1016/0378-1127(83)90017-8

Feike, T., Doluschitz, R., Chen, Q., Graeff-Hönninger, S., & Claupein, W. (2012). How to overcome the slow death of intercropping in the North China Plain. *Sustainability*, *4*(10), 2550–2565. doi:10.3390u4102550

Panagos, P., Borrelli, P., Meusburger, K., Alewell, C., Lugato, E., & Montanarella, L. (2015). Estimating the soil erosion cover-management factor at the European scale. *Land Use Policy*, *48*, 38–50. doi:10.1016/j.landusepol.2015.05.021

Voříšek, K., Růžek, L., Svobodová, M., Šantrůček, J., Strnadová, S., & Popelářová, E. (2002). The influence of grassing and harvest management on microbial parameters after arable land setting-aside. Rostl. *Výr*, *48*(9), 382–388.

Becerril-Piña, R., & Mastachi-Loza, C. A. (2019). Desertification: Causes and Countermeasures. In W. Leal Filho, A. M. Azul, L. Brandli, P. G. Özuyar, & T. Wall (Eds.), *Life on Land* (pp. 1–13). Springer International Publishing.

Mohamed, E., Belal, A.-A., Ali, R. R., Saleh, A., & Hendawy, E. A. (2019). Land Degradation. In H. El-Ramady, T. Alshaal, N. Bakr, T. Elbana, E. Mohamed, & A.-A. Belal (Eds.), *The Soils of Egypt* (pp. 159–174). Springer International Publishing. doi:10.1007/978-3-319-95516-2_9

Rodrigues, S. M., & Römkens, P. F. (2018). Human health risks and soil pollution. In *Soil Pollution* (pp. 217–250). Elsevier. doi:10.1016/B978-0-12-849873-6.00009-1

Srivastava, P., Wu, Q.-S., & Giri, B. (2019). Salinity: An Overview. In Microorganisms in Saline Environments: Strategies and Functions (pp. 3-18). Springer.

Chapter 11
Precision Agriculture to Ensure Sustainable Land Use for the Future:
Precision Agriculture and Arable Land Use

Zia Ur Rahman Farooqi
https://orcid.org/0000-0003-2398-1895
Institute of Soil and Environmental Sciences, University of Agriculture Faisalabad, Pakistan

Muhammad Ashar Ayub
https://orcid.org/0000-0003-1276-9979
Institute of Soil and Environmental Sciences, University of Agriculture Faisalabad, Pakistan

Muhammad Nadeem
Institute of Soil and Environmental Sciences, University of Agriculture Faisalabad, Pakistan

Muhammad Shabaan
Institute of Soil and Environmental Sciences, University of Agriculture Faisalabad, Pakistan

Zahoor Ahmad
Department of Field Crops, Faculty of Agriculture, University of Cukurova, Adana, Turkey

Wajid Umar
Szent Istvan University, Gödöllő, Hungary

Irfan Iftikhar
Institute of Soil and Environmental Sciences, University of Agriculture Faisalabad, Pakistan

ABSTRACT

Global food security is coupled with the preservation and safe use of arable land resources. Land use competition in terms of commercial land use and urbanization has imparted enormous pressure on soil resources. The arable land of the world is already shrinking due to land degradation and desertification while our efforts to ensure commercial land availability is making the current scenario even worse. Soil degradation has put millions of acres of land as devoid of sustainable use over the past few decades and research shows that situation is going to be worse day by day. Precision agriculture can not only ensure the optimal use of available land but also can increase the restoration potential of global agriculture sectors. Integrated nutrient and pest management along with zero tillage, organic farming, and vertical plantation can be visualized as insurance of land and water conservation for the future. This chapter is an effort to contribute comprehensive information regarding the role of precision farming in the restoration and optimal use of global land resources.

DOI: 10.4018/978-1-7998-4372-6.ch011

INTRODUCTION

Precision agriculture is the series of advanced methods for farm management and crop production which uses information technology-based platforms to check and ensure that crops are receiving the right amount of nutrients, water, and other necessary plant supporting elements. This technique was evolved to ensure the economic and environmental gains as well as sustainable development (Carolan, 2017). This technology used information technology, hi-tech drones, and remote sensing and is widely adopted by the world as it has numerous advantages like high profitability, the supply of the right amount of nutrients and essential chemicals to the crops and reduced labor cost, etc. (Miller et al., 2017). This technology is transforming farming-related data into useful information which is helpful for decision-making in agriculture (Liu et al., 2017). The need for precision agriculture was sensed when the problem of food security and agricultural soil productivity emerged as an issue of concern worldwide. Its emergence may be the result of climate change phenomena followed by excessive emission of greenhouse gasses (Yohannes, 2016). Many factors contribute in worsening the situation like households, and their household size (Oluyole et al., 2009), farm size (Sikwela, 2008), low annual production (Alem, 2007), age of household head, livestock ownership (Bogale & Shimelis, 2009), and agricultural practices for conserving natural resources (Beyene & Muche, 2010). Moreover, extreme weather conditions, insect-pest attacks, and rapid population growth are also among the common causes of food insecurity in third world countries (AFI, 2012).

Precision agriculture involves the use of hi-tech and most modern technology, agricultural equipment and implements for the improvement of agricultural productivity, yield and optimization of soil nutrients, moisture, and other agronomic practices (Chivenge & Sharma, 2019). The most common practices used in this technique are minimum or zero tillage which also gives rise to a new idea of organic agriculture, a very profitable business. There are many advantages of zero tillage like an organic matter of the soils under zero tillage is significantly high as compared to the soil receiving tillage regularly (Landers, de Freitas & Boddey, 2017) as well as improve soil health and productivity (El-Shater et al., 2016). Integrated nutrient management (INM) is also practiced in precision agriculture, it also has the advantages of improved soil as soil undergoing INM practices has fewer weeds and require fewer nutrients than those without INM (Singh & Prasad, 2016). Integrated pest management (IPM) is also associated with integrated nutrient management (INM). The supply of the right amount of nutrients also interferes with weed growth (Méndez-Vázquez et al., 2019). Other activities included in PA involve practices like laser land leveling, hoeing, water, and nutrient application and management. The main theme of precision agriculture is the site-specific allocation of all the available resources to ensure their optimum use (Chivenge & Sharma, 2019).

Arable lands are the soils that have the potential to grow crops but left fallow or not used for crop production permanently (Han et al., 2017). Arable lands can be used for crop production and other agricultural uses but nowadays facing several problems - (i) soil salinity due to the use of brackish water, excessive fertilizers application, etc., (ii) high temperatures induced land degradation, erosion, excessive tillage practices, and waterlogging, (iii) exhaustion of soil fertility due to continuous crop cultivation and other organic, inorganic pollutants (Baude et al., 2019; Sharma & Shehrawat, 2019). The practices in PA can help tackle these issues as adopting precision agriculture helps boast soil physical, chemical, and biological properties. This improvement in soil properties happens because of the microbial diversity and population improvement, soil aggregation, and nutrient holding capacity (Wallor et al., 2018). Nowadays, GPS, GIS, GNSS, remote sensing, satellite imagery, and drones are also used for the improvement of crop productivity and soil health as well as monitoring the soil fertility and application of pesticides, fertilizers, and irrigations (Higgins et al., 2019).

Arable lands can be, salt-affected soils, eroded soils, and contaminated soils with heavy metals, pesticides, or fertilizers (Ahamer, 2017). In Pakistan, a wide range of soils are affected by salinity (Qasim et al., 2017), fertilizers, pesticides, and heavy metals contamination (Salam et al., 2018), and some area is rangeland (Mansoor et al., 2018). These soils which are affected by different types of contamination and deterioration can potentially be used for productive purposes. Salt-affected soils can be reclaimed and used for crop cultivation (Al-Saedi et al., 2018) or for sub-surface carbon sequestration to mitigate climate change (Lim et al., 2020), and mitigation of food security problems by crop cultivation on these soils (Saqib et al., 2017). Pesticides, heavy metals, and nutrients polluted soils can be remediated by different physical (soil scraping, excavation, washing, and encapsulation), chemical (solidification, precipitation, and ion exchange) and biological (bioremediation, bio-membranes) methods and transformed into productive soils (Liu et al., 2018). Rangelands can be used as pastures and grazing of livestock animals (Bauer et al., 2017). This chapter discusses all the advances, benefits, and techniques used in precision agriculture for sustainable arable land-use with necessary prospects and recommendations.

The prime objectives of this chapter are:

i. Acknowledge the reader about various beneficial aspects of precision agriculture
ii. Discuss the future needs to sustain this beneficial approach.

THREATS TO SUSTAINABLE AGRICULTURE AND ARALE LANDS

The world's agriculture is facing different types of challenges for its sustainability. Some of the challenges are explained as follows:

Soil Salinity and Contamination

With an increased world population, more food is needed to meet the food requirements of the people, but due to different agricultural constraints, the existing soil's productivity is also decreasing, and hence, the problem of food security arises (Islam & Wong, 2017).

Soil Degradation

The decomposition of soil organic matter at high temperature leads to soil degradation and soil particles are dispersed as organic matter binds the soil particles (Moinet et al., 2018). As stable soil structure is necessary for plant growth, nutrient supply, and water holding capacity, so, the ability of the soil to support plant growth is reduced (Johannes et al., 2017).

Soil Fertility Loss

Due to the continuous cultivation of nutrient exhaustive crops, nutrients in soil starts depleting. Crops like sugarcane and other long-seasoned crops extensively use soil nutrients and cause nutrients deficiency in soil (Yadav et al., 2019). One of the main factors in soil fertility loss is the loss of soil organic matter due to high temperature (Moinet et al., 2018).

Rangelands

These are the lands with compact structure and the least amount of nutrients which can support plant life (only grasses can be cultivated on them) (Tuffa, Hoag & Treydte, 2017). These soils have multiple uses as these soils can be used as pastures for livestock grazing or used as residential or commercial areas and for fish farms etc. (Favretto et al., 2016; Farley, Walsh & Levine, 2017).

Impacts of Urban Land Use

Soils are directly or indirectly exposed to human interferences to varying degrees which pose serious effects on soil health as well as agricultural outputs. This includes land-use change, land degradation (salinization, compaction, sealing, and erosion (Smith et al., 2016). Intensive land use as a part of human activities may exert enormous pressure on soil quality, such as heavy metal contamination of soil and acid deposition (nitrogen and sulfur). Excessive human impacts on the soil are attributed to increased demand for food, feed, and fiber for an ever-growing population which is expected to reach up to nine billion by the end of 2050 (FAO, 2013). Consistent rise in population leads to alterations in the land use mainly due to i) demand of food for growing population, ii) housing requirements for accommodation, iii) development of infrastructure as a result, agricultural practices and urbanization are hastened (Giri & Qiu, 2016). Urbanization leads to an increased impermeability of surface e.g., rooftop, parking lots, sidewalks, and roads. As a result, runoff is accelerated, and ultimately transportation of various hazardous pollutants to the water bodies and subsoil occurs (Wilson & Weng, 2010).

Change in the land use results in the removal of biomass, shifts in the vegetation, and disturbance of the soil. Consequently, it causes a reduction in soil carbon (C) fluxes and dynamics of other important nutrients and alterations in the physicochemical properties of soil and its biodiversity. Different land management practices that do not result in land cover change, potentially cause degradation of different soil characteristics such as harvest as well as regrowth of forests, intensive grazing and crop production (Smith et al., 2016). An acceleration in the land-use changes has been observed lately as a result of population increase and migration of people which puts pressure on limited available resources such as food and shelter etc. Research has shown that humans have induced modification of nearly 70 Mkm^2 or >50% of the ice-free land area of the earth (Hooke & Martin-Duque, 2012). The new global land cover share database exhibits major land-cover divisions identified by FAO (Latham, Cumani, Rosati & Bloise, 2014). Grassland and croplands (consisting of both the natural as well as managed grazing lands) both cover almost 13% area. Areas covered by trees occupy nearly 28% and similarly, the shrub-occupied area is 9.5%. Moreover, artificial surfaces cover only 1% which includes urbanized areas. Globally, degraded lands occupy nearly 24% of the total land area (35 Mkm^2). Moreover, out of the degraded lands, 23% is covered with broad-leaves forest, whereas, 19% under the needle-leaved canopy and 20-25% under rangelands (Bai et al., 2008). Among land-use practices, deforestation imparts the greatest impact on the historical soil carbon change and as a result, nearly 25% of the total soil carbon is lost (Murty et al., 2002). This loss of soil carbon is mainly attributed to oxidation of organic matter and soil erosion. According to estimates of FAO, deforestation caused a net forest loss of 5.32 million hectares per year from 2000 to 2010 (FAO, 2010). Among these, most of the deforestation occurs in tropical countries (Hansen et al., 2013).

SOIL DEGRADATION: CAUSES AND EXTENT

The global population is expected to reach ~10 billion in 2050, which will put pressure on the food supply and health conditions and will lead to agricultural intensification. As a result, soil degradation and exhaustion will likely occur (Gerland et al., 2014; United Nations, 2015). Since soil degradation is a global issue, so sometimes, it is also identified as a global pandemic (Delong et al., 2015). Soil degradation involves soil erosion, loss of soil cover, acidification, salinization, and compaction, etc. Soil erosion and salinization are the most important as these two factors compel the farmers to either abandon the land or adopt costly management practices to continue farming the same land. It has become a serious global threat in densely populated areas (Gomiero, 2016). Soil degradation due to different factors not only causes a decline in crop production but also causes enormous economic losses, and as a result, food security, as well as the livelihood of farmers, are seriously threatened (Bhattacharyya et al., 2015). Nutrient depletion is the primary form of soil degradation in sub-Saharan Africa and has resulted in tremendous loss of crop productivity and has further added to hunger and poverty (Tully et al., 2015).

Global assessment of soil degradation (GLASOD) designates soil degradation as a "human-induced phenomenon" and in a general sense, it can be described as "deterioration of soil quality" i.e., complete or partial loss of whole soil functions. In general, soil degradation involves broad-spectrum changes in the properties of soil as a result of natural or anthropogenic activities altering its quality and structure. Also, it includes different processes like deforestation, agricultural activities, overgrazing, industrial activities and removal of natural vegetation, etc. (Lal, 2015). It compels the farmers to abandon their land and look for new marginal areas which are generally, not suitable regarding agricultural uses, and their transformation towards high productiveness requires huge costs (Lambin et al., 2013; Tully et al., 2015). According to an estimation of FAO, approximately 25% of the land is highly degraded (FAO, 2015). These estimates are highly variable, and their overall effects pose threats to food security, particularly in developing economies. FAO (2015) highlights a strong relationship between poverty and land degradation and hence, it is necessary to halt land degradation and adopt suitable management practices to improve soil health. There are different processes through which soil degradation takes place, such as physical (compaction, erosion), chemical (salinization, acidification), and biological (loss of biodiversity and organic matter). Various factors influence degradation types such as physicochemical properties of soil, climate (temperature, precipitation), terrain characteristics (drainage, slope), and the vegetation type (biodiversity, biomass) (Lal, 2015). Different causes that result in soil degradation are very complex and they may be different such as socioeconomic (markets, institutions, poverty), political (conflicts, policies) and biophysical (cropping systems, land use, deforestation, and farming practices) (Barrett & Bevis, 2015).

ESTIMATES OF SOIL DEGRADATION

It is a difficult task to assess the amount of degraded land and soils and great differences exist among various models regarding the estimation of intensity and extent of land degradation (Gibbs & Salmon,

2015). In the last two decades, different assessments in this regard were done and their figures indicated that nearly 15-80% of the agricultural land globally, is degraded as a result of different factors (Bai et al., 2008; Pimentel & Burgess, 2013; Hurni et al., 2015). However, later assessments in this context exhibited that almost 25% of the present agricultural lands are highly degraded, 44% are exposed to slight degradation and nearly 10% are recovering from degradation (FAO, 2015). Moreover, estimated reports of FAO-UNDP project "Land Degradation Assessment in Drylands" indicated the categorization of global land status in order of importance as highly degraded soils comprise of 25% land area, 36% area is moderately or slightly degraded, 8% comes under improving lands and 18% area is bare (Bindraban et al., 2012). Different types of soil degradation are:

1. Soil Salinization

Soil salinization is a relative term, which comprises saline, sodic and alkaline soils, defined based on high exchangeable salt concentration, high soluble sodium (Na^+) concentration, and high pH respectively. Soil salinization often results in alterations in the natural biological (Smith et al., 2016), hydrological (Keesstra et al., 2012), erosional (Berendse, van Ruijven, Jongejans & Keesstra, 2015) and biochemical (Decock et al., 2015) cycles. Soil salinization is one of the major global phenomena that affects more than 10% of irrigated lands worldwide (Aquastat, 2016). The evidence says that 30.7 mha of saline and sodic soils evident in Europe which 3.3% of the global land availability (Daliakopoulos, 2016). Due to growing concern irrigation mismanagement (Young et al., 2015), organic (Singh, 2015; Drakeet al., 2016) and inorganic amendments selection and quantification (Ahmad et al., 2016) in the soil reclamation process, this threat has attained much attention worldwide. Soil salinization has two types; primary and secondary salinization.

Primary salinization occurs as a result of natural processes that involve chemical as well as physical weathering of parent material, groundwater, or geological deposits. Soils originating from parent rock containing carbonate minerals and/or feldspar may be rich in salt contents. Naturally, saline soil occurs in various parts of the world, such as Hungary, Austria, Ukraine, Bulgaria, and in the Caspian Basin, etc. (Trnka et al., 2013; Van Beek & Tóth, 2013). In addition to long-term accumulation of salts in the soil profile, salinization can also naturally occur in those soils which were once submerged under seawater. During the submergence period, seawater enters the voids present in the soil sediments and stays there even after the incursion of seawater. Moreover, eventual rise in the sea level can result in the flooding of coastal lands either for longer or shorter periods. Apart from this, a rise in the sea level can enhance lateral intrusion of seawater towards coastal areas and consequently, cause huge problems across the coastal regions. This situation has already been observed in Denmark, North-eastern France, Belgium, and Netherland (Raats, 2015).

In contrast to primary salinization, secondary salinization usually results from anthropogenic activities such as using saline water for irrigation purposes and various irrigation practices coupled with poor drainage conditions of the soil (Fan et al., 2012). Arid lands are assumed to be prominent salinization hotspots due to less rainfall, more evapotranspiration rates, and land properties that limit salt leaching. In addition to that, human interventions that restrict sufficient drainage through an increased time of ponding also result in salinization. Moreover, increased groundwater table as a result of lateral water movement in the soil through unlined canals and reservoirs (Barros et al., 2012), land clearing, unevenness in the distribution of irrigation water and poor drainage may lead to the mobilization of salts that are accumulated in the soil profile (Chesworth, 2007). Groundwater containing high salt contents may reach the root zone of the plants and supply salts to the roots. In arid zones, poor drainage also results in much evaporation, and salt residues are left behind on soil surface (Mateo-Sagasta & Burke, 2011). Extensive and non-judicious use of chemical fertilizers and other agricultural inputs (Moreira et al., 2015) linked with irrigation practices and poor drainage result in soil salinization.

Precision agriculture has been extensively applied to evaluate the extent of soil salinity as an assessment of soil salinization followed by mapping can be a useful tool to mitigate soil salinity and resultant increment in crop production. Castrignano et al. (2008) modeled the spatial variation of soil salinization for delineating the areas that were at high risk. They employed a probabilistic approach that was based on multivariate geostatistics. The main purpose of the study was to divide an area into different zones based upon the degree of soil salinization. The binary transformation of soil samples demonstrated that nearly 51% were above the critical level of ECe that was set to be 4 dSm^{-1}, 31% samples indicated increased ESP against a critical level of 10%, and 73% samples showed high pH which was set to be 8. The application of precision agriculture was helpful in this regard to alert those farmers whose lands lie in the potentially salt-affected areas. In this way, farmers were advised to apply the best management practices for preventing soil salinization. Also, precision agriculture enabled the researchers to find out the problems responsible for soil degradation.

2. Poor Nutrition

Excessive cultivation leads to a decline in soil nutrients (nutrient mining). Mineral nutrition is a prerequisite for plant growth and sustainable soil health, whether it is from natural or anthropogenic sources. Balanced nutrition not only improves plant growth rather but also adds organic matter to the soil and as a result, improves soil quality. So, balanced nutrition is inevitable as far as soil health is concerned. Mineral depletion in the soil is also another form of soil degradation which mainly occurs due to long-term cultivation practices in the soils and as a result, soil organic matter contents are depleted. Also, a decrease in the organic matter contents causes a decline in the aggregate stability of the soil (Annabi et al., 2011). Reduction in the soil organic matter contents can be revealed in numerous ways and all of these are related to soil degradation. Since organic matter is an ample source of readily mineralizable nutrients such as nitrogen (N), phosphorous (P), sulfur (S), and other important nutrients (Baldock & Broos, 2011). Well-structured soils have properly arranged soil aggregates that not only ensure well-structured soils but also enhance the physicochemical properties of soils and as a result, the porosity of the soil is increased thereby, increasing its nutrient and water retention abilities. Also, it adds organic matter to the soil. Also, soil compaction interferes with the available nutrient status of soil because of its direct impact on the soil porosity through an increase in the bulk density of the soil and concomitant decrease in the porosity of the soil. Compaction of sub-soil can deteriorate nutrient flows and in turn, leads to crop yields, poor crop quality, and a simultaneous increase in the green-house gases (GHG) emissions, nutrient run-off, reduced biodiversity, and erosion (Batey, 2009).

Hummel et al. (2001) experimented to document the ability of near-infrared spectroscopy (NIR) for predicting soil organic matter. They collected three soil cores and wetted them to six different moisture levels that were ranging from air-dry to saturated. In the laboratory, spectral reference data (1603-2598 nm) was obtained on undisturbed soil samples. Data were collected on a 6.6 nm spacing with each reflectance value having a 45 nm bandpass. Multilinear regression was used for analyzing the data. The standard error of prediction for the organic matter was 0.62. their results described that soil C was ranging from 0.15-5.35% (0.27-9.20 SOM).

Ramane et al. (2015) used a fiber optic-based color sensor for the evaluation of primary macronutrients (NPK) in the soil samples. They performed the colorimetric measurement of an aqueous solution of soil samples. This color sensor works based on color absorption by the solution. It determines the NPK amounts in soil solution as low, medium, or high. Based on this technique, they were able to differentiate the soil samples based on different NPK concentrations. This could be an efficient tool to avoid the unnecessary and excessive use of chemical fertilizers and reduce the cost of production. Moreover, assessment of the nutritional status of the soil may also limit the probability of environmental degradation which usually occurs because of non-judicious fertilizer application.

3. Organic and Inorganic Pollution

Continuous loading of various pollutants (organic as well as inorganic) in agricultural soils may cause serious concerns to the ecological soil functioning, plant growth, and survival, and ultimately human health. Extensive use of agrochemicals and plastic films are the most common contaminants (Sun et al., 2017). The non-biodegradability and persistent nature of these contaminants in the soil atmosphere pose severe threats to the physicochemical properties of soil and affect agricultural sustainability. Several organic contaminants (OCs) have been characterized by their high persistence, toxicity, and accumulation in the environment such as polychlorinated biphenyls (PCBs), polyaromatic hydrocarbons (PAHs) and phthalate esters (PAEs) (Sun et al., 2017). Wide areas of farmland soils are major sources of organic carbons (Zhong et al., 2014). Most of these organic carbons are resistant to biological degradation under normal circumstances. Their residues can also enter the food chain and move to higher trophic levels and ultimately exhibit a potential threat to human health (Liu, Langemeier, Small, Joseph & Fry, 2017). Soil pollution by organic pollutants is usually dynamic, cumulative, irreversible, and hidden and the majority of the organic pollutants are mutagenic, low soluble, carcinogenic, and ecotoxic (Zhou et al., 2019). These organic chemicals can affect the soil properties through their direct effects on the fauna, flora and can interfere with the normal human activities through amplification and enrichment effect of the food chains.

Most of these persistent organic pollutants (POPs) are toxic even at lower concentrations (Deng et al., 2017). Moreover, the sorption of these pollutants on soil surface decreases their availability for microbial actions and hence, is recalcitrant towards microbial-based degradation and remains in the soil for a relatively long period (Wu et al., 2014). This group of POPs comprises industry-based chemicals, pesticides, and by-products of different industrial processes (e.g., furans and dioxins) (EU, 2016). In 2015, almost 26 compounds were identified which causes serious adverse impacts on human health and the ecosystem. Even though most of these chemicals are banned nowadays, enormous quantities of these contaminants still prevail in the soil.

Major inorganic contaminants that degrade soil quality are metals (Cr, Cd, Cu, Ni, Mn, Pb, Hg, Zn, and V), metalloids (Bo, Sb, and As) and nonmetals (Se), etc. All these elements are ubiquitous in the environment and their concentrations are mostly less than 100 mg kg^{-1}. Soil is the ultimate sink for various inorganic pollutants such as heavy metals Among various anthropogenic activities responsible for the discharge of these trace elements in the urban environment are traffic emissions, industrial effluents, mining and smelting of ores and coal power generation processes, etc. (Li et al., 2018). Over-use of inorganic fertilizers is a common practice in the developing nations and as a result, various problems such as water pollution due to nutrient leaching occur. Moreover, soil alkalization or acidification may also occur which leads to a decline in the ability of soil to supply essential nutrients for plant uptake.

Also, the application of chemical fertilizers encourages the degradation of organic matter and as a result, soil structure is degraded with concomitant inhibition in soil aggregation. Hence, nutrients loss from soil occurs through leaching, gas emission, and fixation (Savci, 2012). In addition to decreasing the soil fertility, non-judicious use of chemical inorganic fertilizers can also destroy microbial biota as well as other populations of the soil organisms, inhibit biological nitrogen fixation (BNF) by rhizobia due to more availability of nitrogen (N) and also cause a decline in the mycorrhizal colonization of plant roots (Abedi et al., 2010).

4. Fertilizers and Pesticides Misuse

Extensive use of agricultural inputs such as chemical fertilizers and pesticides to enhance crop production and maximize agricultural output as well as profits is a common practice adopted by farmers' community and as a result, nutrient fixation and leaching occur which deteriorates soil quality as was observed in Latin America. In recent times, extensive use of nano-fertilizers and nano-pesticides is an emerging trend. According to a survey, almost a 40% increase in grain products has been attributed to the application of chemical fertilizers worldwide (MOA, 2015). Fertilizers and pesticides utilized substances in today's agriculture. Though, their over-use results in increased productivity but this increase is concomitant with serious unwanted drawbacks such as non-point source pollution. The use of pesticides and fertilizers on larger scales in combination with low efficiency as well as unscientific application techniques cause an increment in the agricultural costs, followed by a decline in the soil fertility and pesticide residues.

The use of agrochemicals such as fertilizers and pesticides etc. are aimed to maximize profits and economic returns. Though, the use of these agriculture-based chemicals enhances crop production up to a certain extent, however, their intensive and continuous use also deteriorates soil quality. In most intensive agricultural systems, these chemicals cause severe environmental degradation, especially vegetation, water, and soil resources. Soil is considered as a potential pathway for the transfer of contaminants to the water, air, plants, and ultimately to humans through runoff, leaching, sub-surface drainage, and final transfer to the human body food chain. The ability of soil to buffer and detoxify these agrochemicals is a function of soil quality. The use of fertilizers on a prolonged basis can result in soil acidification which in turn, affects the ability of soil to support plant growth on a sustainable basis. Many chemicals used in pesticides persist in the soils for a longer period which may endure there for even decades and adversely affect soil conservation. Environmental risk as a result of soil pollution with these contaminants is of prime concern for agricultural areas as enough reliance on the different agrochemicals have significantly resulted in the accumulation of various harmful heavy metals in the soil (Patle et al., 2020).

Besides the effects of agrochemicals on the physicochemical properties of soils, soil biota is also disturbed due to the excessive application of different chemicals. As these inputs are applied to overcome yield losses due to several factors but still, their effects on the biological properties of soil are often neglected. Over-use of pesticides has declined the population of beneficial bacteria to such an extent that a nutrient pool of essential plant nutrients such as NPK has been adversely affected (Sardar & Kole, 2005). Important soil processes such as mineralization, phosphorus cycles, and nitrification, etc. are dependent upon the equilibrium that exists between different microbial groups in soil. Some studies on the effect of different pesticides on the health of the microbial population have stated that some organophosphorus and organochlorine pesticides inhibit the symbiotic fixation of atmospheric nitrogen by bacteria and consequently, cause a decline in crop yields (Fox et al., 2007).

PRECISION AGRICULTURE

Extent, Domains, and Current Status

Food security and sustainability is a major concern for the world. The increasing human population needs more food and sustainable supplies of food for the present and future which needs sophisticated agricultural practices as well as modern technologies to be adopted for increased food production and increased shelf life of food. Increasing human pressure on earth results in accelerated soil degradation, overexploitation of natural resources increased per acre requirements of agricultural production and increased cost of food production (Glick, 2014) which ultimately posed a threat to future food security due to decreased agricultural production caused by above-mentioned factors (Carmen & Roberto, 2011). Food production needs to be increased by up to 70% to meet the demand of the projected population growth in 2050. In recent years, agriculture and food production have become unsustainable due to the increased demand of fertilizer, pesticide, and labor efficiency which ultimately affects the natural resources, environmental sustainability, human health and more importantly cost-benefit ratio of food production (Dong et al., 2018).

Site-specific management of crops coupled with the suit of information technology providing spatial and temporal information to ensure optimized field management, decision-making practices in terms of reducing input cost, and gaining more output is called Precision agriculture (National Research Council, 1997). Fertilizer and pesticide use history, climatic data and numerous predictive tools to optimize the crop management for getting maximum outputs under defined resources in precision agriculture are vital to get it linked with technology. agricultural systems (Bujang & Bakar, 2019).

Crop yield mapping or yield monitoring is the most adaptive technique of precision agriculture. Crop yield history, soil history concerning crop, automated steering systems, and crop location information enable the farmer to better cope with site-specific resource utilization and precise control over maintenance and production cost as well as repetitive field operations. It is adopted 61.4% among the precision agriculture techniques overall (Vuran et al., 2018). Yield mapping or crop history leads to the effective use of resources and labor for site-specific crop management for retrieving maximum crop yield under the umbrella of limited or defined resources. It involves the wise use of chemical fertilizers and pesticides to the sites according to their need and smartly increasing labor efficiency. Decision support software and models can be linked with yield maps for automatic and site-specific control of farm machinery.

Fertilizers and pesticides have revolutionized the agricultural system since the green revolution and yield increased manifolds due to these synthetic agrochemicals. Cost of production and environmental damage has also been increased by the haphazard agrochemical use. Nanotechnology (nano-fertilizers, nano-herbicides, nano-fungicides, nano- pesticides and nano-biomolecules) is another useful precision agriculture technique for reducing the cost of production and efficient resource use. Nano-fertilizers are more stable and slow-releasing nutrients with more chances of uptake by plants while nano-agrochemicals have more effectiveness and penetration characteristics than the common ones (Duhan et al. 2017). Nano-fertilizers can be proven more efficient source of nutrients for plants due to their stability and long term availability in the soil as slow-release fertilizers. Nano-fungicides and nano-pesticides can effectively reduce the damage to crops by more penetrating power due to the smaller nano size of the active ingredient. Moreover, the application rate can be reduced by decreasing the size and increasing the efficiency of agrochemicals. Soils are the direct or indirect source of 95% global food production. Exact knowledge of soil nutrients and soil fertility status is the prerequisite of precision agriculture Digital mapping of soil has been introduced from the 1990s and it is improved over the years. Precise and accurate soil nutrients mapping is the way of efficient land and resource management. Various nutrient management tools and decision support models have been introduced to better understand the need for agricultural crop production systems (Dong et al., 2018).

Precision agriculture is a beneficial technique to tackle the current food requirement without wastage of natural resources. Future food requirements can not be fulfilled with current or conventional agricultural production technologies. Its a need for time to adopt advanced techniques and technologies to maximize the efficiency of agricultural production systems. Precision agriculture with variable rate input can be proved more beneficial in larger areas as well as small land holding agricultural systems. Variable-rate technology (VRT) for irrigation, pesticides, and fertilizers demands timely and accurate information from the field. Small land holding farmers can increase the profitability of their crops by reducing the cost of crop production by adopting VRT. It is cleared that exact and timely knowledge of the field is a prerequisite of adopting VRT. Precision agriculture has been proved to be beneficial and synchronized with future food demands, but, much work is still needed for the adoption of precision agriculture by farmer's communities and the relation of latest technologies with agricultural operations must be further exploited to reduce the operational cost and enhance the input efficiency for higher yields and crop productivity. Precision agriculture emphasizes the use of modern techniques in agricultural systems and optimizes agricultural productivity without any deterrent effects on environmental quality. This is also related to the landholding of the farmers as the majority of the farming community in the developing countries live below the poverty line. They can not afford to sacrifice their outputs for ensuring soil health. Their sole income source is based upon agricultural outputs and hence, they are forced to apply conventional agricultural practices which affect land quality in the long run. This, in turn, uplifts their cost of production with a concomitant decline in the profits. Precision agriculture in this regard offers a sustainable way of enhancing agricultural productivity with site-specific application of all the inputs to avoid their unnecessary use and hence, the cost of production is also reduced.

Modern agricultural practices such as minimum or zero tillage, integrated use of organic, inorganic and biofertilizers, latest irrigation techniques such as a sprinkler or drip irrigation, use of cover crops, proper crop rotation with the inclusion of green manures, etc. are the major pillars of conservational agriculture which is an important milestone towards achieving the goal of precision agriculture. Precision agriculture requires the site-specific allocation of all the inputs to ensure its judicious use and sustainable environmental quality protection. The adoption of conservational agricultural techniques can be a suitable alternative to ensure sustainable food production at a lower cost with minimal risk impact on the environment. It may also avoid the unnecessary wastage of nutrients caused by their excessive application in the form of commercial fertilizers. Moreover, suitable irrigation techniques may substantially avoid water loss which is a limiting factor in agriculture.

PRECISION AGRICULTURE TO STOP AND REVERSE SOIL DEGRADATION

The management of farms to utilize all the resources like best sowing time, proper application of inputs, fertilizers, irrigations, and pesticides application using digital technology like remote sensing is called precision agriculture.

There is a need to save and conserve natural resources for future generations. Sustainable agriculture is a good practice that helps to conserve natural resources using them at the minimal exploiting rate and gaining benefits to the optimum levels. The population is increasing at an exponential rate owing to this a lot of food is required for them. Due to progress in industrialization and urbanization, agricultural land is shrinking, and it is a threat to the future to meet the food requirement using small natural resources. It is an alarming situation for the future to save natural resources on a sustainable basis. Sustainable agriculture is a practice which aids to conserve and save the natural resources for sustainable planning.

1. ROLE OF PRECISION AGRICULTURE IN LAND PRESERVATION

a. Proper Management of Nutrients

The essential nutrients for crop plants must be applied at the proper rate according to the crop needs and other climatic conditions. Most of the nutrients lost due to improper management practices. In the case of primary macronutrients (N, P, and K) these should have to be applied according to crop needs using best management practices. It has been estimated that about 50% N is lost in crops after application in different ways including volatilization, leaching, and denitrification. Gaseous loss of N accelerates the phenomenon of climate change. Similarly, P and K are transformed into non-volatilized forms and caused eutrophication which ultimately affects aquatic life. Precision agriculture restores the soil's physical, chemical, and biological properties which help in plant growth promotion. So, the nutrient application must be done considering 4R (right source, right rate, right time, and right place) strategy for fertilizer application (Osmond & Line 2017).

b. Restore the Organic Residues

The organic matter is considered as the "heart of soil''. It plays an important role in sustainable crop production and maintaining soil health. As a result of organic matter decomposition organic acids released which can maintain the soil pH, this ability of organic matter to buffer the pH increase the nutrient availability to plants. This can only be done by the application of organic residues in the soil and maintaining maintain soil properties and promote plant growth. Apart from that organic matter also plays an important role in maintaining the soil moisture level. Sequestration of carbon in the soil is a win-win strategy for sustainable agricultural production. This can only be achieved by adopting precision management practices by using innovative and modern technologies based on proper irrigation applications (Blanco-Canqui & Lal 2009).

c. Encouraging Cover Crop Practices

Land degradation is a major issue owing to salinization, water scarcity, and soil erosion. To overcome these problems, cover crops must be grown on a sustainable basis. Cover crops enhance the nutrient status of the soil and enable the soil to cope with the above-mentioned future challenges against further deterioration. Major cover crops include clover, oats, oilseed crops, and annual ryegrass, etc. As mentioned earlier, precision agriculture restores the soil physical (pH, EC, and aggregation, etc.), chemical (CEC), and biological properties (soil microbiota, enzymes) which helps in plant growth promotion. Cover crops can also overcome the problems of soil compaction and erosion. It also has been reported that the growing of cruciferous plants improves the nutrient status, reducing the erodibility of soil, and protecting the soil water (Ugrenović et al., 2019).

2. PRECISION AGRICULTURE AND LAND RESTORATION

Several factors were involved in the degradation of land and reduced crop production. Soil erosion, salinity, waterlogging, and structure loss are the key factors that cause the deterioration of land as compared to the other factors. Management practices based on precision agriculture must be adapted to restore the degraded land. Crop management, intercropping, crop selection, crop rotation, cover cropping shelterbelts, and strip cropping are the practices adopted for the preservation of agriculture. Similarly, the use of appropriate tillage practices, organic manures, fertilizer application, crop residues management, mulching, agroforestry, contour farming is some measures which must be done for the restoration of saline soils (Alex, 2018). However, croplands must be converted into agroforest lands without considering the reduction of crop yield for sustainable agriculture. All these practices can be adopted only by practicing precision agriculture management at the farm level.

3. PRECISION AGRICULTURE AND LAND USE PRESSURE

In this modern era, the land for agriculture is squeezing and converting into industrialized cities for buildings and other infrastructure. The relationship between the growing population is directly proportional to the change in land use. So, actions should be taken to cope with these problems. There are two options for feeding the growing population, either increase the land-use area for cultivation of more crops to meet the food requirement of the world or use the innovative and modern technologies for more yield production. The second strategy is more suitable to enhance crop production owing to the increment of population exerts the pressure on squeezing land use for feeding the people. However, precision agriculture is an option in which modern technologies are used to improve production considering the available natural resources.

CONCLUSION

Precision agriculture focuses on site-specific activities to meet the requirements of plants and soils. It can restore degraded soils e.g., the use of cover crops or mulching can control soil erosion. It also helps in the mitigation of food insecurity and climate change by carbon sequestration and production of food crops at the same time. Therefore, to meet the food requirement of the growing population and ensure environmental quality, larger-scale adoption of precision agriculture is inevitable so that agricultural output can be optimized and a better environmental quality may be ensured on a sustainable basis.

With the increase in the dietary demands of ever-growing populations and depleted the natural resources to a greater extent. Increment in the global cultivated lands and intensification in agriculture has accelerated the loss of soil fertility, induced salinity, fertilizers, and pesticide pollution, increased soil degradation, and food insecurity problems.

REFERENCES

Abedi, T., Alemzadeh, A., & Kazemeini, S. (2010). Effect of Organic and Inorganic Fertilizers on Grain Yield and Protein Banding Pattern of Wheat. *Australian Journal of Crop Science, 4*, 384–389.

Ahamer, G. (2017). Mapping Global Dynamics. Springer.

Ahmad, P., Abdel Latef, A. A., & Hashem, A. Abd_Allah, E. F., Gucel, S., & Tran, L. S. P. (2016). Nitric oxide mitigates salt stress by regulating levels of osmolytes and antioxidant enzymes in chickpea. *Frontiers in Plant Science, 7*, 347.

Al-Saedi, S. A., Al-Ameri, B. H., & Rasheed, A. G. (2018). Sulfuric acid as a chemical amendment for increasing efficiency of reclamation process of salt affected soils of Iraq. *Net Journal of Agricultural Science, 6*(3), 49–52. doi:10.30918/NJAS.63.18.022

Annabi, M., Le Bissonnais, Y., Le Villio-Poitrenaud, M., & Houot, S. (2011). Improvement of soil aggregate stability by repeated applications of organic amendments to a cultivated silty loam soil. *Agriculture, Ecosystems & Environment, 144*(1), 382–389. doi:10.1016/j.agee.2011.07.005

Aquastat. (2016). Available at: www.fao.org/nr/water/aquastat/main/index.stm

Bai, Z. G., Dent, D. L., Olsson, L., & Schaepman, M. E. (2008). Proxy global assessment of land degradation. *Soil Use and Management, 24*(3), 223–234. doi:10.1111/j.1475-2743.2008.00169.x

Baldock, J. A., & Broos, K. (2011). Soil organic matter. In P. Huang (Ed.), *Handbook of soil science* (2nd ed., pp. 11.1–11.52).

Barrett, C. B., & Bevis, L. E. (2015). The self-reinforcing feedback between low soil fertility and chronic poverty. *Nature Geoscience, 8*(12), 907–912. doi:10.1038/ngeo2591

Barros, R., Isidoro, D., & Aragüés, R. (2012). Three study decades on irrigation performance and salt concentrations and loads in the irrigation return flows of La Violada irrigation district (Spain). *Agriculture, Ecosystems & Environment, 151*, 44–52. doi:10.1016/j.agee.2012.02.003

Batey, T. (2009). Soil compaction and soil management–a review. *Soil Use and Management, 25*(4), 335–345. doi:10.1111/j.1475-2743.2009.00236.x

Baude, M., Meyer, B. C., & Schindewolf, M. (2019). Land use change in an agricultural landscape causing degradation of soil based ecosystem services. *The Science of the Total Environment, 659*, 1526–1536. doi:10.1016/j.scitotenv.2018.12.455 PMID:31096362

Bauer, H., Müller, L., Van Der Goes, D., & Sillero-Zubiri, C. (2017). Financial compensation for damage to livestock by lions Panthera leo on community rangelands in Kenya. *Oryx, 51*(1), 106–114. doi:10.1017/S003060531500068X

Berendse, F., van Ruijven, J., Jongejans, E., & Keesstra, S. (2015). Loss of plant species diversity reduces soil erosion resistance. *Ecosystems (New York, N.Y.), 18*(5), 881–888. doi:10.100710021-015-9869-6

Bhattacharyya, R., Ghosh, B. N., Mishra, P. K., Mandal, B., Rao, C. S., Sarkar, D., Das, K., Anil, K., Lalitha, M., Hati, K., & Franzluebbers, A. (2015). Soil degradation in India: Challenges and potential solutions. *Sustainability*, *7*(4), 3528–3570. doi:10.3390u7043528

Bindraban, P. S., van der Velde, M., Ye, L., Van den Berg, M., Materechera, S., Kiba, D. I., ... Hoogmoed, W. (2012). Assessing the impact of soil degradation on food production. *Current Opinion in Environmental Sustainability*, *4*(5), 478–488. doi:10.1016/j.cosust.2012.09.015

Blanco-Canqui, H., & Lal, R. (2009). Crop residue management and soil carbon dynamics. *Soil Carbon Sequestration and the Greenhouse Effect, 57*, 291-309.

Bujang, A. S., & Bakar, B. H. A. (2019). Precision Agriculture in Malaysia. *International Workshop on ICTs for Precision Agriculture*, 91–104.

Carmen, B., & Roberto, D. (2011). Soil bacteria support and protect plants against abiotic stresses. Abiotic stress in plants-Mechanisms and daptations, 143-170. doi:10.5772/23310

Carolan, M. (2017). Publicising food: Big data, precision agriculture, and co-experimental techniques of addition. *Sociologia Ruralis*, *57*(2), 135–154. doi:10.1111oru.12120

Castrignano, A., Buttafuoco, G., & Puddu, R. (2008). Multi-scale assessment of the risk of soil salinization in an area of south-eastern Sardinia (Italy). *Precision Agriculture*, *9*(1-2), 17–31. doi:10.100711119-008-9054-4

Chesworth, W. (Ed.). (2007). *Encyclopedia of soil science*. Springer Science & Business Media.

Chivenge, P., & Sharma, S. (2019). Precision Agriculture in Food Production: Nutrient Management. *International Workshop on ICTs for Precision Agriculture*, 12.

Daliakopoulos, I. N., Tsanis, I. K., Koutroulis, A., Kourgialas, N. N., Varouchakis, A. E., Karatzas, G. P., & Ritsema, C. J. (2016). The threat of soil salinity: A European scale review. *The Science of the Total Environment*, *573*, 727–739. doi:10.1016/j.scitotenv.2016.08.177 PMID:27591523

Decock, C., Lee, J., Necpalova, M., Pujol Pereira, E. I., Tendall, D. M., & Six, J. (2015). Mitigating N2O emissions from soil: From patching leaks to transformative action. *Soil (Göttingen)*, *1*(2), 687–694. doi:10.5194oil-1-687-2015

DeLong, C., Cruse, R., & Wiener, J. (2015). The soil degradation paradox: Compromising our resources when we need them the most. *Sustainability*, *7*(1), 866–879. doi:10.3390u7010866

Deng, R., Lin, D., Zhu, L., Majumdar, S., White, J. C., Gardea-Torresdey, J. L., & Xing, B. (2017). Nanoparticle interactions with co-existing contaminants: Joint toxicity, bioaccumulation and risk. *Nanotoxicology*, *11*(5), 591–612. doi:10.1080/17435390.2017.1343404 PMID:28627273

Dong, W., Wu, T., Sun, Y., & Luo, J. (2018). Digital mapping of soil available phosphorus supported by AI Technology for precision agriculture. *2018 7th International Conference on Agro-Geoinformatics (Agro-Geoinformatics),* 1–5.

Drake, J. A., Cavagnaro, T. R., Cunningham, S. C., Jackson, W. R., & Patti, A. F. (2016). Does biochar improve establishment of tree seedlings in saline sodic soils? *Land Degradation & Development*, *27*(1), 52–59. doi:10.1002/ldr.2374

Duhan, J. S., Kumar, R., Kumar, N., Kaur, P., Nehra, K., & Duhan, S. (2017). Nanotechnology: The new perspective in precision agriculture. *Biotechnology Reports (Amsterdam, Netherlands)*, *15*, 11–23. doi:10.1016/j.btre.2017.03.002 PMID:28603692

El-Shater, T., Yigezu, Y. A., Mugera, A., Piggin, C., Haddad, A., Khalil, Y., Loss, S., & Aw-Hassan, A. (2016). Does zero tillage improve the livelihoods of smallholder cropping farmers? *Journal of Agricultural Economics*, *67*(1), 154–172. doi:10.1111/1477-9552.12133

EU. (2016). *Persistant organic pollutants—environment—European Commission.* http://ec.europa.eu/environment/chemicals/international_conventions/index _en.htm

Fan, X., Pedroli, B., Liu, G., Liu, Q., Liu, H., & Shu, L. (2012). Soil salinity development in the yellow river delta in relation to groundwater dynamics. *Land Degradation & Development*, *23*(2), 175–189. doi:10.1002/ldr.1071

FAO. (2010). *Global Forest Resources Assessment (FRA).* FAO. Available at: http://www.fao.org/forestry/fra/fra2010/en/

FAO. (2013). *High level expert forum. – how to feed the world in 2050.* Economic and Social Development Department, Food and Agricultural Organization of the United Nations.

FAO. (2015). *The Food and agriculture organization of the united nations. climate change and food systems: global assessments and implications for food security and trade.* FAO. Available online: http://www.fao.org/3/a-i4332e.pdf

Farley, K. A., Walsh, K. C., & Levine, A. S. (2017). Opportunities and obstacles for rangeland conservation in San Diego County, California, USA. *Ecology and Society*, *22*(1), art38. doi:10.5751/ES-09077-220138

Favretto, N., Stringer, L. C., Dougill, A. J., Dallimer, M., Perkins, J. S., Reed, M. S., Atlhopheng, J. R., & Mulale, K. (2016). Multi-criteria decision analysis to identify dryland ecosystem service trade-offs under different rangeland land uses. *Ecosystem Services*, *17*, 142–151. doi:10.1016/j.ecoser.2015.12.005

Fox, J. E., Gulledge, J., Engelhaupt, E., Burow, M. E., & McLachlan, J. A. (2007). Pesticides reduce symbiotic efficiency of nitrogen-fixing rhizobia and host plants. *Proceedings of the National Academy of Sciences of the United States of America*, *104*(24), 10282–10287. doi:10.1073/pnas.0611710104 PMID:17548832

Gerland, P., Raftery, A. E., Sevčíková, H., Li, N., Gu, D., Spoorenberg, T., Alkema, L., Fosdick, B. K., Chunn, J., & Lalic, N. (2014). World population stabilization unlikely this century. *Science*, *346*(6206), 234–327. doi:10.1126cience.1257469 PMID:25301627

Gibbs, H. K., & Salmon, J. M. (2015). Mapping the world's degraded lands. *Applied Geography (Sevenoaks, England)*, *57*, 12–21. doi:10.1016/j.apgeog.2014.11.024

Giri, S., & Qiu, Z. (2016). Understanding the relationship of land uses and water quality in Twenty First Century: A review. *Journal of Environmental Management, 173*, 41–48. doi:10.1016/j.jenvman.2016.02.029 PMID:26967657

Glick, B. R. (2014). Bacteria with ACC deaminase can promote plant growth and help to feed the world. *Microbiological Research, 169*(1), 30–39. doi:10.1016/j.micres.2013.09.009 PMID:24095256

Gomiero, T. (2016). Soil degradation, land scarcity and food security: Reviewing a complex challenge. *Sustainability, 8*(3), 281. doi:10.3390u8030281

Han, X., Zhao, F., Tong, X., Deng, J., Yang, G., Chen, L., & Kang, D. (2017). Understanding soil carbon sequestration following the afforestation of former arable land by physical fractionation. *Catena, 150*, 317–327. doi:10.1016/j.catena.2016.11.027

Hansen, M. C., Potapov, P. V., Moore, R., Hancher, M., Turubanova, S. A., Tyukavina, A., Thau, D., Stehman, S. V., Goetz, S. J., Loveland, T. R., Kommareddy, A., Egorov, A., Chini, L., Justice, C. O., & Townshend, J. R. G. (2013). High-resolution global maps of 21st-century forest cover change. *Science, 342*(6160), 850–853. doi:10.1126cience.1244693 PMID:24233722

Higgins, S., Schellberg, J., & Bailey, J. S. (2019). Improving productivity and increasing the efficiency of soil nutrient management on grassland farms in the UK and Ireland using precision agriculture technology. *European Journal of Agronomy, 106*, 67–74. doi:10.1016/j.eja.2019.04.001

Hooke, R. L., Martín-Duque, J. F., & Pedraza, J. (2012). Land transformation by humans: A review. *GSA Today, 22*(12), 4–10. doi:10.1130/GSAT151A.1

Hummel, J. W., Sudduth, K. A., & Hollinger, S. E. (2001). Soil moisture and organic matter prediction of surface and subsurface soils using an NIR soil sensor. *Computers and Electronics in Agriculture, 32*(2), 149–165. doi:10.1016/S0168-1699(01)00163-6

Hurni, K., Zeleke, G., Kassie, M., Tegegne, B., Kassawmar, T., Teferi, E., ... Kebebew, Z. (2015). *Economics of Land Degradation (ELD) Ethiopia Case Study: Soil degradation and sustainable land management in the rainfed agricultural areas of Ethiopia: An assessment of the economic implications.* Academic Press.

Islam, M. S., & Wong, A. T. (2017). Climate change and food in/security: A critical nexus. *Environments, 4*(2), 38. doi:10.3390/environments4020038

Johannes, A., Matter, A., Schulin, R., Weisskopf, P., Baveye, P. C., & Boivin, P. (2017). Optimal organic carbon values for soil structure quality of arable soils. Does clay content matter? *Geoderma, 302*, 14–21. doi:10.1016/j.geoderma.2017.04.021

Keesstra, S. D., Geissen, V., Mosse, K., Piiranen, S., Scudiero, E., Leistra, M., & van Schaik, L. (2012). Soil as a filter for groundwater quality. *Current Opinion in Environmental Sustainability, 4*(5), 507–516. doi:10.1016/j.cosust.2012.10.007

Lal, R. (2015). Restoring soil quality to mitigate soil degradation. *Sustainability, 7*(5), 5875–5895. doi:10.3390u7055875

Lambin, E. F., Gibbs, H. K., Ferreira, L., Grau, R., Mayaux, P., Meyfroidt, P., Morton, D. C., Rudel, T. K., Gasparri, I., & Munger, J. (2013). Estimating the world's potentially available cropland using a bottom-up approach. *Global Environmental Change, 23*(5), 892–901. doi:10.1016/j.gloenvcha.2013.05.005

Landers, J. N., de Freitas, P. L., & Boddey, R. M. (2017). Potential for mitigation of deforestation and negative off-farm impacts with conservation agriculture: employing Zero Tillage farming in the Brazilian Cerrado. In *Savannas and Dry Forests* (pp. 253–276). Routledge. doi:10.4324/9781315243788-10

Latham, J., Cumani, R., Rosati, I., & Bloise, M. (2014). *Global land cover share (GLC-SHARE) database beta-release version 1.0-2014*. FAO.

Li, X., Li, Z., Lin, C. J., Bi, X., Liu, J., Feng, X., Zhang, H., Chen, J., & Wu, T. (2018). Health risks of heavy metal exposure through vegetable consumption near a large-scale Pb/Zn smelter in central China. *Ecotoxicology and Environmental Safety, 161*, 99–110. doi:10.1016/j.ecoenv.2018.05.080 PMID:29879579

Lim, S. S., Yang, H. I., Park, H. J., Park, S. I., Seo, B. S., Lee, K. S., ... Kwak, J. H. (2020). Land-use management for sustainable rice production and carbon sequestration in reclaimed coastal tideland soils of South Korea: A review. *Soil Science and Plant Nutrition, 66*(1), 60–75. doi:10.1080/00380768.2019.1674121

Liu, Y., Langemeier, M. R., Small, I. M., Joseph, L., & Fry, W. E. (2017). Risk management strategies using precision agriculture technology to manage potato late blight. *Agronomy Journal, 109*(2), 562–575. doi:10.2134/agronj2016.07.0418

Liu, L., Li, W., Song, W., & Guo, M. (2018). Remediation techniques for heavy metal-contaminated soils: Principles and applicability. *The Science of the Total Environment, 633*, 206–219. doi:10.1016/j.scitotenv.2018.03.161 PMID:29573687

Liu, S. H., Zeng, G. M., Niu, Q. Y., Liu, Y., Zhou, L., Jiang, L. H., Tan, X., Xu, P., Zhang, C., & Cheng, M. (2017). Bioremediation mechanisms of combined pollution of PAHs and heavy metals by bacteria and fungi: A mini review. *Bioresource Technology, 224*, 25–33. doi:10.1016/j.biortech.2016.11.095 PMID:27916498

Mansoor, M., Jamil, M., Anwar, F., Awan, A. A., & Muhammad, S. (2018). Review A Review on Rangeland Management in Pakistan, Bottlenecks and Recommendations. *Biological Sciences- PJSIR, 61*(2), 115-120.

Mateo-Sagasta, J., & Burke, J. (2011). Agriculture and water quality interactions: A global overview. *SOLAW Background Thematic Report-T, R08*, 46.

Méndez-Vázquez, L. J., Lira-Noriega, A., Lasa-Covarrubias, R., & Cerdeira-Estrada, S. (2019). Delineation of site-specific management zones for pest control purposes: Exploring precision agriculture and species distribution modeling approaches. *Computers and Electronics in Agriculture, 167*, 105101. doi:10.1016/j.compag.2019.105101

Miller, N., Griffin, T., Bergtold, J., Ciampitti, I., & Sharda, A. (2017). Farmers' adoption path of precision agriculture technology. *Advances in Animal Biosciences, 8*(2), 708–712. doi:10.1017/S2040470017000528

Ministry of Agriculture. (2015). *Circular of the Ministry of Agriculture on printing and distributing the Action Plan for Zero Growth in the Application of Fertilizer by 2020 and the Action Plan for Zero Growth in the Application of Pesticide by 2020.* http://jiuban.moa.gov.cn/zwllm/ tzgg/tz/201503/t20150318_4444765.htm

Moinet, G. Y., Hunt, J. E., Kirschbaum, M. U., Morcom, C. P., Midwood, A. J., & Millard, P. (2018). The temperature sensitivity of soil organic matter decomposition is constrained by microbial access to substrates. *Soil Biology & Biochemistry*, *116*, 333–339. doi:10.1016/j.soilbio.2017.10.031

Moreira Barradas, J. M., Abdelfattah, A., Matula, S., & Dolezal, F. (2015). Effect of fertigation on soil salinization and aggregate stability. *Journal of Irrigation and Drainage Engineering*, *141*(4), 05014010. doi:10.1061/(ASCE)IR.1943-4774.0000806

Murty, D., Kirschbaum, M. U. F., McMurtrie, R. E., & McGilvray, H. (2002). Does conversion of forest to agricultural land change soil carbon and nitrogen? A review of the literature. *Global Change Biology*, *8*(2), 105–123. doi:10.1046/j.1354-1013.2001.00459.x

National Research Council. (1997). *Precision Agriculture in the 21st Century: Geospatial and Information Technologies in Crop Management.* Washington, DC: The National Academies Press; doi:10.17226/5491

Osmond & Line. (2017). *Best Management Practices for Agricultural Nutrients.* Academic Press.

Patle, P. N., Kadu, P. R., Gabhane, A. R., Pharande, A. L., Bhagat, A. P., Bhoyar, S. M., Konde, N. M., & Rahangdale, M. K. (2020). Consequences provoked due to excess application of agrochemical on soil health deterioration–A review for Sustainable Agriculture. *Journal of Pharmacognosy and Phytochemistry*, *9*(1), 63–66.

Pimentel, D., & Burgess, M. (2013). Soil erosion threatens food production. *Agriculture*, *3*(3), 443–463. doi:10.3390/agriculture3030443

Qasim, S., Shrestha, R. P., & Qasim, M. (2017). A National Review of Land Degradation in Pakistan. *Current Politics and Economics of South, Southeastern, and Central Asia*, *26*(1), 91–108.

Raats, P. A. (2015). Salinity management in the coastal region of the Netherlands: A historical perspective. *Agricultural Water Management*, *157*, 12–30. doi:10.1016/j.agwat.2014.08.022

Ramane, D. V., Patil, S. S., & Shaligram, A. D. (2015, February). Detection of NPK nutrients of soil using Fiber Optic Sensor. In *International Journal of Research in Advent Technology Special Issue National Conference ACGT 2015* (pp. 13-14). Academic Press.

Salam, A., Bashir, S., Khan, I., Shahid Rizwan, M., Afzal Chhajro, M., Feng, X., Zhu, J., & Hu, H. (2018). Biochars immobilize lead and copper in naturally contaminated soil. *Environmental Engineering Science*, *35*(12), 1349–1360. doi:10.1089/ees.2018.0086

Saqib, A. I., Ahmed, K., Qadir, G., Nawaz, M. Q., Rizwan, M., Zaka, M. A., & Warraich, I. A. (2017). Comparison the Efficient Reclamation of Different Inorganic Materials with Organic Amendments to Rice-Wheat Crop Sustainable Production in Salt-Affected Soils. *Cercetari Agronomice În Moldova*, *50*(1), 19–29. doi:10.1515/cerce-2017-0002

Sardar, D., & Kole, R. K. (2005). Metabolism of chlorpyrifos in relation to its effect on the availability of some plant nutrients in soil. *Chemosphere, 61*(9), 1273–1280. doi:10.1016/j.chemosphere.2005.03.078 PMID:15894348

Alex, S. (2018). *Restoration of Degraded Agricultural Land.* Academic Press.

Savci, S. (2012). Investigation of Effect of Chemical Fertilizers on Environment. *APCBEE Procedia, 1*, 287–292. doi:10.1016/j.apcbee.2012.03.047

Sharma, N., & Shehrawat, P. S. (2019). Judging causes of soil degradation and remedial measures for reclamation in Kaithal district of Haryana state. *Journal of Applied and Natural Science, 11*(4), 802–805. doi:10.31018/jans.v11i4.2183

Singh, A. (2015). Soil salinization and waterlogging: A threat to environment and agricultural sustainability. *Ecological Indicators, 57*, 128–130. doi:10.1016/j.ecolind.2015.04.027

Singh, A. U., & Prasad, D. (2016). Integrated Pest Management with Reference to INM. *Advances in Crop Science and Technology, 4*(220), 2. doi:10.4172/2329-8863.1000220

Smith, P., House, J. I., Bustamante, M., Sobocká, J., Harper, R., Pan, G., West, P. C., Clark, J. M., Adhya, T., Rumpel, C., Paustian, K., Kuikman, P., Cotrufo, M. F., Elliott, J. A., McDowell, R., Griffiths, R. I., Asakawa, S., Bondeau, A., Jain, A. K., ... Pugh, T. A. M. (2016). Global change pressures on soils from land use and management. *Global Change Biology, 22*(3), 1008–1028. doi:10.1111/gcb.13068 PMID:26301476

Sun, H., Lu, H., Chu, L., Shao, H., & Shi, W. (2017). Biochar applied with appropriate rates can reduce N leaching, keep N retention and not increase NH3 volatilization in a coastal saline soil. *The Science of the Total Environment, 575*, 820–825. doi:10.1016/j.scitotenv.2016.09.137 PMID:27693153

Trnka, M., Kersebaum, K. C., Eitzinger, J., Hayes, M., Hlavinka, P., Svoboda, M., ... Možný, M. (2013). Consequences of climate change for the soil climate in Central Europe and the central plains of the United States. *Climatic Change, 120*(1-2), 405–418. doi:10.100710584-013-0786-4

Tuffa, S., Hoag, D., & Treydte, A. C. (2017). Clipping and irrigation enhance grass biomass and nutrients: Implications for rangeland management. *Acta Oecologica, 81*, 32–39. doi:10.1016/j.actao.2017.05.001

Tully, K., Sullivan, C., Weil, R., & Sanchez, P. (2015). The state of soil degradation in Sub-Saharan Africa: Baselines, trajectories, and solutions. *Sustainability, 7*(6), 6523–6552. doi:10.3390u7066523

Ugrenović, V., Filipović, V., Jevremović, S., Marjanović-Jeromela, A., Popović, V., Buntić, A., & Delić, D. (2019). Effect of Brassicaceae as cover crops. *Selekcija i semenarstvo, 25*(2), 1-8.

UN (United Nations). (2015). *World Population Prospects—The 2015 Revision: Key Findings and Advance Tables; Working Paper No. ESA/P/WP.241*. Department of Economic and Social Affairs—Population Division, United Nations. Available online: https://esa.un.org/unpd/wpp/publications/files/key_findings_wpp_2015.pdf

Van Beek, C. L., & Tóth, G. (2012). *Risk assessment methodologies of soil threats in Europe*. JRC Scientific and Policy Reports EUR, 24097.

Vernekar, K. G., Sinha, S., Sadani, L. K., Sivaramakrishnan, S., Parasnis, S. S., Mohan, B., ... Debaje, S. B. (2003). An overview of the land surface processes experiment (LASPEX) over a semi-arid region of India. *Boundary-Layer Meteorology*, *106*(3), 561–572. doi:10.1023/A:1021283503661

Vuran, M. C., Salam, A., Wong, R., & Irmak, S. (2018). Internet of underground things in precision agriculture: Architecture and technology aspects. *Ad Hoc Networks*, *81*, 160–173. doi:10.1016/j.adhoc.2018.07.017

Wallor, E., Kersebaum, K. C., Lorenz, K., & Gebbers, R. (2018). A comprehensive data set demonstrating the spatial variability of soil properties and crop growth conditions at field scale. *Open Data Journal for Agricultural Research*, *5*, 1–10. doi:10.18174/odjar.v5i0.15888

Wilson, C., & Weng, Q. (2010). Assessing surface water quality and its relations with urban land cover changes in the Lake Calumet Area, Greater Chicago. *Environmental Management*, *45*(5), 1096–1111. doi:10.100700267-010-9482-6 PMID:20364379

Wu, Y., Luo, H., Wang, H., Zhang, L., Liu, P., & Feng, L. (2014). Fast adsorption of nickel ions by porous graphene oxide/sawdust composite and reuse for phenol degradation from aqueous solutions. *Journal of Colloid and Interface Science*, *436*, 90–98. doi:10.1016/j.jcis.2014.08.068 PMID:25265590

Yadav, S. K., Benbi, D. K., & Prasad, R. (2019). Effect of Continuous Application of Organic and Inorganic Sources of Nutrients on Chemical Properties of Soil. *International Journal of Current Microbiology and Applied Sciences*, *8*(4), 2455–2463. doi:10.20546/ijcmas.2019.804.286

Yohannes, H. (2016). *A review on relationship between climate change and agriculture*. Academic Press.

Young, J., Udeigwe, T. K., Weindorf, D. C., Kandakji, T., Gautam, P., & Mahmoud, M. A. (2015). Evaluating management-induced soil salinization in golf courses in semi-arid landscapes. *Solid Earth*, *6*(2), 393–402. doi:10.5194e-6-393-2015

Zhong, L., Cantrell, K. J., Bacon, D. H., & Shewell, J. (2014). Transport of organic contaminants mobilized from coal through sandstone overlying a geological carbon sequestration reservoir. *International Journal of Greenhouse Gas Control*, *21*, 158–164. doi:10.1016/j.ijggc.2013.12.014

Zhou, Z., Liu, X., Sun, K., Lin, C., Ma, J., He, M., & Ouyang, W. (2019). Persulfate-based advanced oxidation processes (AOPs) for organic-contaminated soil remediation: A review. *Chemical Engineering Journal*, *372*, 836–851. doi:10.1016/j.cej.2019.04.213

Chapter 12
Role of Urban Vegetation:
Urban Forestry in Micro-Climate Pollution Management

Muhammad Ashar Ayub
https://orcid.org/0000-0003-1276-9979
University of Agriculture Faisalabad, Pakistan

Zia Ur Rahman Farooqi
https://orcid.org/0000-0003-2398-1895
Institute of Soil and Environmental Sciences, University of Agriculture Faisalabad, Pakistan

Wajid Umar
Szent Istvan University, Gödöllő, Hungary

Muhammad Nadeem
Institute of Soil and Environmental Sciences, University of Agriculture Faisalabad, Pakistan

Zahoor Ahmad
Department of Field Crops, Faculty of Agriculture, University of Cukurova, Adana, Turkey

Hina Fatima
School of Applied Biosciences, Kyungpook National University, South Korea

Irfan Iftikhar
Institute of Soil and Environmental Sciences, University of Agriculture Faisalabad, Pakistan

Muhammad Zohaib Anjum
Department of Forestry and Range Management, University of Agriculture Faisalabad, Pakistan

ABSTRACT

Increasing world population is the main reason behind rapid urbanization which is coupled with environmental pollutions (i.e., air, water, soil, noise, and atmospheric pollution). Urbanization is responsible for deteriorating living standards and quality of life for humans in major metropolitan cities around the world. The urban ecosystem leaves a major impact on world renewable resources and carbon footprint. Urban vegetation and forests can help in net balancing and buffering of immense pollutant surge intro urban ecosystems being done due to urbanization. Extensive urbanization is responsible for more and more wastewater and gaseous pollutant release in the environment which urban forests can help tackle effectively. Moreover, city vegetation also plays a critical role in decreasing city surface temperatures thus helping shrinkage of the urban heat island. The present draft presents the role of urban vegetation in effective management and buffering of urban microclimate.

DOI: 10.4018/978-1-7998-4372-6.ch012

INTRODUCTION

Urbanization of global cities has put enormous pressure on natural resources and is always coupled with pollution and land resource depletion. Among all problems, urbanization is responsible for the creation of more bare land responsible for urban heat island (UHI) generation (Orlandini et al., 2017). The development of UHI has a very negative effect on people's lives as it affects the thermal comfort of people (Petralli et al., 2012; Vanos, 2015; Brandani et al., 2016).

Urban vegetation is very much involved in controlling land surface temperature (LST) and ultimately UHI via controlling air humidity and sunlight influx. Trees can also reduce the environmental pollution by their cooling effect which reduces the need for air-conditioning, playing role in decreasing carbon footprint via energy consumption using fossil fuel (Chang et al., 2007; Escobedo et al., 2008). Besides this, urban land surface temperature, another problem associated with urbanization is soil, water, and air pollution. The urban plantation can help manage this issue as according to Denman et al. (2016) tree plantation in urban areas should be according to the promising traits of the species which can help in the removal of pollutants from soil and water. Various forms of organic and inorganic pollutants are being added into urban water streams causing direct water and indirect soil and air pollution which can be managed via supporting urban forestry (Livesley et al., 2016). The urban environment is always facing issues of pollution like ozone (Chameides et al., 1992; Calfapietra et al., 2013; Livesley et al., 2016), air pollutants (Pataki et al., 2011) and pollens (Carinanos et al., 2016) causing an allergic reaction in human which can be effectively managed by growing urban plantation. Besides, directly controlling urban pollution, vegetation is also a source of very much needed oxygen and absorber of tremendously produced CO_2.

The microclimate is defined as a set of climatic conditions that are assessed near the earth's surface in a localized space. This term is usually used for climatic conditions prevailing within few meters above and below earth surfaces, usually in relatively small areas or within the canopies of the trees (Rafferty, 2020). The microclimate of any specific area depends on several variables/components including temperature, humidity, light, wind, and turbulence which in turn play a crucial role in habitat selection and other ecological activities (Barry & Blanken, 2016). Further, microclimate not only has a significant role in determining the ecological patterns but also drive various processes like growth and mortality in both plant and animal communities (Naiman et al., 2010). However, it is not easy to analyze the relationship between the microclimate and the biological processes since they are often complex and nonlinear. These associations can be evaluated only when considering the effect of various variables (light, heat, and humidity) on the plant's biological functions including photosynthesis, seed germination, and mortality. In short, it will be true to write that various ecosystem processes i.e., nutrient movement, yield, succession, and decomposition are to some extent dependent on microclimate variables. For instance, change in the wind speed, temperature, and humidity of a specific area can cause the dispersal of the animal communities which were adapted to certain microclimate (Naiman et al., 2005).

Numerous models have been proposed for assessing the impacts of urban vegetation on the microclimate i.e., "plant evaluation model (Yang et al., 2019), "VTUF-3D v1.0 urban micro-climate model" (Nice et al., 2018), "ENVI-met microclimate model" (Tsoka et al., 2018; Roth & Lim, 2017; Simon et al., 2018) "Species distribution model" (Lembrechts et al., 2019), "drone-assisted infrared thermography" (Fabbri & Costanzo, 2020). Furthermore, this chapter will cast a light on the role of urban forestry/woodlands on microclimate with special focus on the components of microclimate affected by urban vegetation/forestry and the pollution management of urban regions in later part of the chapter.

URBANIZATION AND URBAN CLIMATE

Impacts of rapid urbanization on urban climate has been investigated by several researchers in the recent past (Unkasevic et al., 2001; Mahmoud & Gan, 2018). Findings on the impact of urbanization on urban climate and atmospheric components are discussed below.

a. Urban Growth and Heat Island

An island where hot surface air is accumulated in urban areas and spatially cools down progressively to the surrounding rural areas are called urban heat island (UHI) (Ningrum, 2018). One of the major factors on which air temperature depends is relative humidity which affects the local environment significantly (Wypych, 2010). According to the investigations, urban growth reduces the relative humidity (Liu et al., 2015; Fu & Weng, 2016), but increases the temperature of the air (Liu et al., 2015). Also, air temperature and relative humidity are the most important components of any climate because they have a significant impact on the physiological comfort of humans (Wypych, 2010). Liu et al., (2015) conducted a study to analyze the temperature differences and rural-urban humidity in Beijing, China. Results showed that urbanization/urban growth significantly increased the temperature of air and reduced humidity. Shaharuddin et al. (2014) and Li et al. (2018) conducted studies to evaluate the effect of urbanization on urban heat island with a special focus on human comfort. Findings stated that energy consumption and heat stress was increased with the increase in air temperature in cities which enhanced the greenhouse gas emission. Kloustian and Diab, (2015) researched to evaluate the effect of urban growth on UHI in Beirut. Findings stated that the areas which have dense vegetation had about 6°C lower temperature as compared to barren areas. Release of heat from anthropogenic sources such as building climate control, humans, and traffic also plays a significant role in urban heat island as it is reported higher in urban areas as compared to rural areas (Allen et al., 2011). The UHI is considered as the best example of how the land cover changes and affects the regional and local climate (Chun and Guldmann, 2014). The effect of UHI on average is 2°C (Chang et al., 2007), but can reach up to 10°C depending on the location of the place and weather conditions (Sharifi & Lehmann, 2014). Wang et al., (2016) reported that the expansion of UHI is closely correlated with urbanization and urban vegetation. An effective way of controlling micro-climate temperature and reduction in UHI expansion is via supporting urban vegetation (Emmanuel & Loconsole, 2015; Masson et al., 2013). According to Masson et al. (2013), a 2-3°C fall in temperature was recorded in Paris with an increase in reflective surfaces and green areas. Similarly, increasing vegetation cover reduced the UHI by 1°C in Stuttgart (Fallmann, et al., 2013).

b. Urbanization and Atmospheric Quality

One of the major problems which the developing and developed world is facing is urban air pollution (UAP). A drastic increase in the population in cities and the increase in vehicular transportation cause severe air pollution which is affecting human and environmental health (Gulia et al., 2015). The World Health Organization (WHO) has reported that around two million deaths annually are being directly or indirectly caused by UAP (WHO, 2014). Vehicular transportation is one of the major sources of UAP. Apart from that, industrial, commercial, and domestic activities also contribute to air pollution. But it is reported that about 70-80% emission of pollutants in big cities in the developing world is by vehicular sources including, many old vehicles, poor maintenance, poor quality of fuels, and poor road infrastructures (Singh et al., 2007). Major pollutants that are responsible for UAP are particulate matter (PM), sulfur dioxide (SO_2), nitrogen (NOx), volatile organic compounds (VOCs) and carbon monoxide (CO) (Gulia et al., 2015). Another source of PM generation in an urban environment is vehicle tires wear and tear (Amato et al., 2014). In 20 European cities, the UAP is increased at hotspot zones in cities as compared to background concentrations due to an increase in vehicular transportation (Moussiopoulos et al., 2005). In urban areas air pollution can be generated by different activities such as NO_2 mainly generated by vehicular transportation on roads, electricity generation is responsible for SO_2 production and industrial processes, household heating and transportation on roads mainly generate particulate matter PM_{10} (Rodriguez et al., 2015). Due to variations in the generation processes of air pollutants, different urban areas have different concentrations of air pollutants. At the initial stage of the twenty-first century, a noticeable change in urbanization (about 50%) has been achieved throughout the world. Population statistics have been increased from 1.52 billion in 1970 to 4.6 billion in 2030 and all this because of rapid urbanization (Acaravci & Ozturk, 2010). More than 50% of energy has been consumed by half of the world population which is living in urban areas and emit more than 60% CO_2 which contributes massively to global warming (Shahbaz et al., 2015). It is reported that since 2001, emission of CO_2 has increased in developing countries like India, China, South, and Southeast Asian regions, which accounts for about 50% of the CO_2 released all over the world (Behera & Dash, 2017). This bitter reality forced the countries towards sustainable urbanization also known as smart city or green city development to overcome the negative effects of rapid urbanization. Guttikunda et al. (2003) reported that the most prominent cities in Asia like Karachi, New Delhi, Mumbai, Dhaka, Kolkata, Bangkok, Singapore, Jakarta, Kuala Lampur only contain 2% of the total landmass but released about 30% of SO_2 to the world from 1975 to 2000 due to rapid urbanization. A layer of pollution commonly known as Asian brown cloud affects different countries like some parts of India, China, South East Asia, Bangladesh, Pakistan, Sri Lanka, and Bhutan (Pandve, 2008).

One of the major air pollutants in urban areas is the particulate matter (PM) (Complex mixture of small-sized particles suspended in the air) (Ite et al.,2017). Particulate matter has been divided into different categories based on the particle size, the most common and most hazardous types are $PM_{2.5}$ and PM_{10} (Maricq, 2007). Particle size less than 2.5 microns comes under $PM_{2.5}$ while the particles which have a size less than 10 microns are categorized as PM_{10} (Ezeah et al., 2015). These two categories $PM_{2.5}$ and PM_{10} can diffuse to the bloodstream through the lungs (Krzyzanowski et al., 2005). According to reports, particulate matter is responsible for about 40000 premature deaths annually (Ezeah et al., 2015). The concentration of $PM_{2.5}$ directly depends on human activity and the surrounding environment (Han et al., 2014), while vehicular transport is the major cause of PM_{10} in the atmosphere (Krzyzanowski et al., 2005). It is reported that the production of $PM_{2.5}$ is higher in urban areas as compared to rural areas because of higher human activities which generate higher amounts of air pollutants (von Bismarck-Osten et al., 2013). According to Lai et al. (2004) a higher concentration of $PM_{2.5}$ has been recorded for 37 metals in Oxford city UK. Liu et al. (2015) conducted a study to evaluate the effect of urbanization on metrological parameters and diffusion of pollutants in Hangzhou. Results showed that the increase in fine particulate matter ($PM_{2.5}$) concentration up to 30 μg m^{-3} was recorded in highly urbanized areas and reduced the average visibility up to 2.2 km. According to Ite et al. (2019) air quality in schools located in urban and industrial regions of Nigeria was analyzed and significantly higher concentrations of PM_1, PM_2, $PM_{5,}$ and PM_{10} were recorded.

TYPES OF POLLUTION IN URBAN AREAS

a. Air Pollution

Our planet earth is surrounded by an envelope held firmly by the force of gravity containing a mixture of gases i.e., nitrogen, oxygen, argon, and carbon dioxide 78%, 21%, 0.97%, and 0.04% respectively (Sharp, 2017). This uniquely gifted envelope of chemicals is known as air which is essential to sustain life on earth. Air pollution is the presence of toxic materials either in the form of solid, liquid, and gases which have detrimental effects on human, animal, and plant life (National Institute of Environmental Health Sciences, 2019). Moreover, "air pollutants" are undesired adverse substances whose concentration in air is greater than a safe level or specifically those adverse substances which cause detrimental effects on the human health and environment. There are generally two types of pollutants primary pollutants and secondary pollutants. Primary pollutants are directly emitted from sources and pollute the air for example emission of carbon monoxide from motor vehicle exhaust while secondary pollutants are formed after an interaction in the air for example ground-level O3 (Lioy, 2017). There are two well-known sources of air pollution: (1) Natural sources/biogenic sources (when nature of origin is animals & plants) (2) Anthropogenic sources/ man-made sources (when the cause of origin is human beings). Urban pollution is primarily owing to anthropogenic activities i.e., burning of fossil fuels for energy generation, smoke from the vehicles, and toxic gasses released into the air from the production points (Tiwary & Williams, 2018).

Worldwide air pollution has become a threat to several adverse effects on the environment and human health. For example, recently a group of American researchers conducted a study to emphasize that GHGs are the primary source of global warming (Herndon, 2018). Another study by Lu et al. (2018) unveiled the severe effects of ozone air pollution on the air quality, human health, and plants of China, Japan & South Korea, USA, and Europe. It was observed that pollution of 93.5% air of China and 5.5% air of Japan & Korea was due to ozone pollution. Ozone pollution affected the human health of China 82% and the USA 15.5%. Further effects of ozone pollution on plant damage, attributed to China and the USA were 79.5% and 17.5% respectively. It is obvious from the above-mentioned findings that ozone pollutants have a severe impact on the air quality of China compared to the rest of the industrialized regions (Lu et al., 2018). Not only this, but air pollution is also responsible for causing several respiratory, cardiovascular diseases, stroke, skin cancer, lung cancer, and diabetes (World Health Organization, 2014). An increased concentration of air pollutant PM2.5 approximately10 $\mu g/m^3$ was associated with an increased risk of diabetes. Worldwide out of 8.2 million, 206105 deaths caused by diabetes were ascribed to PM2.5. Therefore, reduced exposure to the PM2.5 pollutant will be helpful for the human wellbeing (Bowe et al., 2018). Worldwide several strategies are being followed to combat this emerging menace which can play havoc in the future.

Several preventive measures have been reported i.e. use of more public transport instead of personal vehicles, use of less sulfur petrol, moving industries from urban to rural areas, using eco-friendly methods and machines, finding the alternatives of fossil fuel burning, no more burning of crop residues, use of bio-friendly fuels, use of personal vehicles on odd or even days and cultivation of more vegetation especially in urban areas (Puri et al., 2017). Apart from that, various studies have been conducted emphasizing the ecological services provided by urban vegetation. For instance, a study was conducted to analyze the role of urban parks in the abatement of air pollutants and also their mode of abatement. It was reported that the dispersion of air pollutants by urban parks was a more effective way of removal compared to deposition. However, overall urban parks had a small contribution toward air pollution control (Xing & Brimblecombe, 2019). Another study, cast a light on the dual role of the vegetation both in air pollution removal and augmentation of air pollution under the warm season. For instance, volatile organic compounds (VOCs) released from the urban green space in combination with anthropogenic activities especially under warm season has a role in ozone pollution. Therefore, to make urban vegetation beneficial it is imperative to reduce the use of motor vehicles (source of NOx, VOCs, and particulate matters) along with the cultivation of trees on the roadside (Churkina et al., 2017).

b. Water Pollution

Water is an important renewable resource for the sustenance of life on earth after the air. Contamination of water bodies i.e., rivers, lakes, streams, and oceans by the addition of excessive amounts of harmful substances render water unsuitable for human, animal, and plant use (Woodford, 2019). As per water pollution statics of 2018-2019 70% of the world population will struggle for drinking water by 2050 (Globewater, 2018). There are two main types of water pollution, surface water pollution, and groundwater pollution. Apart from this, water pollution is sometimes also classified on the bases of its source of origin i.e., point source pollution (from a single source), nonpoint source pollution (from more than one source), and trans-boundary pollution.

Pollutants that enter the water bodies are broadly divided into two major groups inorganic and organic pollutants. Inorganic pollutants are usually present in water in the form of cations and anions, for example, lead, copper, zinc, cadmium, arsenic, antimony, radium, and cesium are common heavy metals found in effluents. However, heavy metals are toxic and detrimental for both humans and the environment (Burakove et al., 2018). Among non-metal pollutants, the interconversion of toxic to non-toxic forms is visible. For example, NO_3 or ammonia NH_4^+ can be degraded into N_2 and N_2O. Heavy metals can cause lung cancer, liver cancer and kidney failure especially high levels of arsenic in water are carcinogenic (Goldscheider, 2010). On the other hand, the second type of harmful pollutants in water is organic pollutants which include dyes, organic pesticide residues, petroleum products, and products from the cosmetic industry. These organic pollutants are involved in the disruption of normal activities, which are carcinogenic and mutagenic. Hence the effluents from the industries containing both organic and inorganic pollutants must be treated before their discharge to the water bodies (Inyinbor Adejumoke et al., 2018).

Several approaches have been reported for the remediation of polluted waters. Heavy metals have been removed by chemical precipitation (Chen et al., 2018), ion exchange (Chen et al., 2017), coagulation (Yao et al., 2017), membrane filtration (Efome et al., 2018), solvent extraction (Li et al., 2017) and adsorption. For instance, Wang and colleagues unveiled the high adsorption efficiency of a novel adsorbent made with sugarcane cellulose. Novel sugarcane-based adsorbent adsorbed 558.9, 446.2, and 363.3 mg^{-1} of Pb^{+2}, Cu^{+2}, and Zn^{+2} respectively in a single adsorption system. However, in binary competitive adsorption system lead was preferably adsorbed compared to copper (Wang et al., 2017). Not only heavy metals excessive amounts of nitrogen and phosphorus in the city's water are also problematic and pose adverse effects on human health and the environment. Moreover, vegetation not only intercepts the runoff but also has a role in improving the quality of the runoff water. Muerdter et al. (2018) compiled a review describing various mechanisms involved for removing pollutants from stormwater including phytoextraction, phytodegradation, Rhizosphere mechanisms. Various suitable strategies as well as suitable urban species for water pollution control have been reported. For instance, Pinus nigra J.F showed a significant potential to translocate heavy metals like As, Cd, and Pb in turn showing substantial potential to provide ecological services (Petrova et al., 2020). Hence, to clean urban waters urban vegetation can be used as a cheap and eco-friendly approach providing multiple services to the ecosystem.

c. Noise Pollution

In simple words, noise pollution is "long-term exposure to substantially higher sound levels posing detrimental effects on living organisms". Sound waves are detected in decibels (dB) units. A normal ear can detect from 0-140 dB however, sound waves from 120-140 dB hurt the ears. Since sound waves, less than 70dB are safe for hearing regardless of exposure duration. Further, constant 8-hour exposure of sound waves of >85dB is harmful (National Geographic Society, 2019). Causes of noise pollution are diverse ranging from traffic horns, construction sounds including drilling & machinery sounds, workplace noise, loud music in concerts, train stations sounds, airport noise of plane landing and taking off, industrial noise, fireworks, and firecrackers sound to household sounds especially from the washing machine, lawnmowers and vacuum cleaners (Bello et al., 2018). Noise pollution comparatively gets less attention in terms of being detrimental to human health. However, surprisingly recent research revealed the death of 356,000 Britain people by roadside traffic noise. Since long term exposure to the traffic, noise poses serious effects on our blood chemistry, far greater than an exhaust fume does (Hansell et al., 2017). Another study displayed an association between traffic noise and diabetes type II (Clark et al., 2017). Health hazards from noise pollution can be broadly divided into pathological effects (hear loss, acoustic trauma, and auditory fatigue), physiological effects (change in blood pressure, cholesterol level and dilation of the pupil) Psychological effects (fatigue, irritation, discomfort, neurological disorders and interrupted sleep) (Kumar & Kumar, 2018).

Physical abatement of noise pollution is not always effective. Hence, urban vegetation can be used as a cheap and eco-friendly strategy to ameliorate the effect of noise pollution on the richness, habitation, and breeding of urban wildlife. Living near the green spaces in urban areas can reduce noise annoyance (Dzhambov & Dimitrova, 2015). Likewise, another study reported similar findings. The Goal of the study was to identify an association between urban green spaces, resident's satisfaction levels, and noise perception. It was observed that noise annoyance was lower in green spaces compared to other urban areas. Further, the reported decline in a noise level was attributed to an increase in relaxation and walking activities (Gozalo et al., 2018). However, it is also imperative to know "at which location" and "what intensity" of vegetation is effective to ameliorate the effects of traffic noise. Vegetation along the roadside with minimum to moderate intensity was effective in removing 50% of traffic noise. Vegetation barriers with 5m depth were ideal for ameliorating traffic noise. Further, moderate to dense vegetation was found to reduce 9-11dB while the average recorded noise level was 78dB without vegetation (Ow & Ghosh, 2017). Further, a case study conducted in Gothenburg, Sweden revealed that urban vegetation has a significant role in the abatement of NO_2 and benzo(a) pyrene along busy traffic roads. Also, significantly lower levels of NO_2 and polyaromatic hydrocarbons were detected in parks compared to areas near traffic suggesting the positive role of urban vegetation in noise pollution control (Klingberg et al., 2017).

4. URBAN FORESTRY STATUS

a. Causes

Deforestation is the cutting of forests for various objectives other than forestry. The objectives may include clearing land for agriculture, ranching, urbanization, pasture, construction, fuel, and timber (Derouin, 2019). Data by the University of Maryland revealed that 2017 was the 2nd worst year for deforestation with a tree cover loss of 15.8 million hectares, an area equal to the size of Bangladesh (Weisse & Goldman, 2018). On the other hand, the World Bank reported a loss of 1.3 million square Km since 1990, an area equal to the size of South Africa (Khokhar & Tabar, 2016). However, urban forestry is slightly different from the agroforestry as the purpose of the urban forestry is chiefly the maintenance of the urban environment and aesthetic beauty.

To improve the standards of living, people move from rural to urban areas (Ritchie & Roser, 2020). To provide shelter to the increasing number of urban inhabitants, more and more hospital schools, industries, and residential apartments are being constructed at the cost of urban forestry. For instance, according to the European Environmental Agency, 25% of land intended to be used for urban greenery was used for other objectives (Cobbinah & Darkwah, 2016). Similarly, McDonald and coworkers unveiled that $1.4x10^6$ hectares of urban forestry land in the USA were used for other land uses in 274 cities from 1990-2000 (McDonald, et al., 2010). Overpopulation and industrialization are other big reasons for the degradation of the urban environment. Industrialization leads towards the use of more urban land for constructing industries and business hubs to cope with the increasing demand for commodities. Industries cause further damage to the urban environment by emitting toxic gasses (NO_2, SO_2, CO) to the air and toxic effluents containing heavy metals to the water (Aroh, 2018; Chopra, 2016). Bad urban green space policies and governance could be another reason for the decline in urban forestry. Since urban forestry is beneficial for the public health, for protecting the urban biodiversity and for providing a natural habitat for native and non-native species. Therefore, policymakers and stakeholders should pay special attention to urban vegetation management.

b. Requirements

The urban environment is becoming more diverse and complex with every passing day. Therefore, worldwide municipalities, urban green space policymaker, concerned stakeholders, and urban inhabitants are diverting their focus to conserve and improve the urban forest ecosystem to get a continuous supply of beneficial services which they offer. Urban green space, urban trees, urban forests, grasses are an essential factor for the sustainability of the urban ecosystem. Unfortunately, urban green spaces are rapidly being converted to residential areas worldwide. In short, the sustainability of the urban natural ecosystem is a vital factor to consider for the safe future of mankind.

In this regard, a study conducted by Barron et al. (2016) suggested some indicators guide, design, and plan the urban forestry. This study gave prime importance to "social indicators" i.e. those about human health and wellbeing while planning. However, these values were not part of the urban forestry valuation for a long time (Peckham et al., 2013). Once added they were highly valued by the participants. They were further divided into structural (diversity, distribution, and density indicators) and functional indicators (stormwater management, habitat provision, improvement in air quality, and GHGs sequestration and storage) (McPherson et al., 1997). Among structural indicators "urban diversity indicator" was highly rated which means to grow plants of various species and ages which can aid more diverse benefits for a longer period (Kenney et al., 2011). Distribution indicator meant; urban forests should be located at places where they are in easy access to all the citizens. Finally, the "density indicator" pointed toward the amount of space that should be assigned for the urban forests (Barron et al., 2016). Moreover, another study suggested an opportunity to improve urban forestry. According to this study linking urban forestry with ecological engineering will help conserve the urban ecosystem. For instance, growing the vertical forests on multi-story can provide the best services to the occupants and can also keep the air clean by capturing pollutants (Endreny, 2018). On the other hand, an Egyptian study suggested "Greening the City" strategy for a sustainable urban future. This approach can include greening public parks, restoration of open spaces, the greening of concrete sidewalks, private outdoor spaces, development of urban agriculture, backing local economy by local produce sales protection, and restoration of abandoned streams, swamps, and beaches (Mersal, 2016).

c. Suitable Urban Vegetation

Researchers globally are putting their efforts into maintaining and improving the urban environment. For instance, Chalker-Scott, (2015) compiled a review paper to display the importance of non-native and non-invasive species in improving the biodiversity of the urban ecosystem. while planning for urban vegetation (1) both native and non-invasive tree and shrub species should be considered to increase biodiversity (2) To benefit both human and animal's, fruit-bearing trees, shrubs should be planted (3) open lawns should be replaced by vertically diverse vegetation (4) water supply should be provided when available (Chalker-Scott, 2015). Moreover, another study reported some suitable plants for drought-stressed urban areas. Seven different species of Acer i.e., Acer *carpinifolium*, Acer *rubrum*, Acer x *freemanii,* Acer *spicatum*, Acer *monspessulanum*, A. *rubrum,* and Acer s*accharum* were analyzed for their suitability. Overall, Acer displayed high potential to survive in the drought-stressed urban areas. The osmotic adjustment was observed as the main driving force which kept Acer alive in summer (Sjöman et al., 2015). On the other hand, a study was conducted to identify the effect of 3 common functional plant groups (evergreen trees, deciduous trees, grass) on the physicochemical properties of the different aged park soil. It was observed that soils with evergreen forests had a greater tendency to sequester both carbon and nitrogen with low pH and higher organic matter contents. This could be because of the leaf characteristic and root exudates of evergreen plants. Another approach to protecting the urban environment from destruction is green roofing. Plant selection for green roofing needs wise consideration. For the survival of the plant, it must tend to survive in an artificial environment. The perfect plant for green roofing should be heat, cold, climate change, disease, pest resistance, and must have high water and nutrient use efficiency. Not all but most of the shrubs are suitable for this purpose.

ROLE OF URBAN FORESTS

a. Air Quality Improvement

Urban forests can improve air quality by reducing air pollution and particulate matter as well as by the provision of other ecological services i.e. decreasing air temperature. Although, urban forestry is involved in the reduction of air pollution to the extent of 1% only this can be fruitful for human health across the city to varying degrees. By understanding different social and environmental variables contributing air quality and affecting human health directly or indirectly, Urban Forests can be designed in such a way to maximize their efficacy in managing air pollution and other ecological services (Nowak et al.,2018).

Air pollutants including Nitrogen dioxide (NO_2), Carbon monoxide (CO), Sulfur dioxide (SO_2), Ozone (O_3) and particulate matter ranging 2.5 µm ($PM_{2.5}$) to 10 µm (PM_{10}) in diameter are the major threat to human respiratory and pulmonary health as well as vascular, cardiac and neurological health Pope et al. (2002). Retention of particles on leaf surfaces can cause a reduction in photosynthetic efficiency hence reducing the pollutants removal by trees. Vegetation is therefore only a temporary site of retention for suspended air particles as they are removed by washing off rain and adds to the ground surface about a threat to re-include in the atmosphere. Annually 0.655 m tons of air pollution is removed only by urban trees in the USA (Nowak et al., 2014). Suspended particulate matter and gaseous pollutants are primarily removed from the air by stomata of trees. Once these particles are absorbed, these are diffused in intercellular spaces and subjected to water columns in plants to form acidic compounds or to that adhere to the inner leaf surface. Most of the particulate matter adheres to the leaf surface is washed off by rain, absorbed by plants, or falls to the ground with leaves and twigs (Smith, 1990).

Only park vegetation in urban areas may remove the three main air pollutants i.e. 2% of PM_{10}, 1% of $O_{3,}$ and 0.02% of CO emphasizing the role of park trees, shrubs, and grasses in urban air quality improvement (Baumgardner et al., 2012). Living quality and air quality improvement is being advocated worldwide by urban forestry. Urban trees and shrubs removed 0.238 million tonnes of air pollutants as simulated by the i-Tree model improving the city air quality of Tabriz, Iran (Amini et al., 2019). Pollutant removal by the trees directly affects the air pollution concentration which can be measured in terms of percent air quality improvement. As simulated by the i-Tree model, a total of 16,500 tones of air pollutants removed by urban forests in 86 cities of Canada with average annual percent air quality improvement of as low as 0.001% and as high as 0.237% for CO and SO_2 respectively (Nowak et al., 2018). A total of 738 tons of air pollution was removed by approximately 2.5 million planted trees in Bangkok, Thailand Intasen et al. (2017) whereas 88.23 tons of air pollution was removed by 0.58 million trees in Strasbourg, France yearly (Selmi et al., 2016).

b. Land Surface Temperature

Due to increased urbanization and air pollution, temperature over the city is a bit higher than the surrounding areas (Kang et al., 2010). The urban forest canopy is proved to decrease the land surface temperature as compared to surroundings as trees lower down the atmospheric and ground temperature by shading and transpiration processes (Ren et al., 2016). Urban forests have an obvious cooling effect on Land Surface Temperature (LST) as compared to surrounding areas. This cooling effect is directly related to spatial characteristics of urban forest (i.e. area and shape) and type of Urban forest (i.e. forest canopy, forest age, and tree species) (Zhao, et al., 2016). These forests are the main productivity source of urban areas (Cetin, 2015). Conversion of vegetation and farmland area into asphalt and concrete impervious areas cause an increase in the urban heat island phenomenon (Buyantuyev & Wu, 2010).

Urban temperature is decreased by increasing the green area ratio in the cities while land to building ratio has an opposite effect on LST. Shades of leaves and branches in the urban forest play an important role in reflecting the direct radiations from the sun and also reflected radiations from the buildings, pavements, and other objects in urban areas. Moreover, the transpiration process of plants causes a cooling effect which is also important in reducing LST. Urban forests are not only important for the UHI phenomenon but also plays an important role in climate change by carbon sequestration and adjustment of urban climate (Kong et al., 2014). Change in land surface temperature increases the sustainability of the urban area by reducing energy and water consumption, climate change, and also affecting public health.

The LST of different scenes was recorded in the years 2005-2011. Coolest LST was recorded in water bodies with an average temperature of 14.9°C followed by the green areas with LST 10.9°C more than these water bodies in Colorado, while mean LST of buildings and commercial areas was maximum in all the landscapes (Gage & Cooper, 2017). During ten years of the study period in diverse cities of Europe, the relationship of land use and Urban Heat Island Magnitude (UHIM) was determined. A high proportion of forest land had a significant influence on reduced UHIM as compared to agricultural lands. Grey structures and green areas of cities had elevated UHIM as compared to those forests and agricultural lands (Nastranet al., 2019).

Urban forests and urban green areas i.e. parks, vegetation is crucial for decreasing the LST of urban soils. These are proved to be the main factors for decreasing UHIM in urban areas with additional benefits of carbon sequestration, air quality improvement, and resource provision. Urban forests are important not only for decreasing LST but also for decreased air temperature in summers in urban areas. Landsat images and remote sensing are used to compare LST in different years in different land types. Many factors influencing the LST of urban areas and components of urban forests affecting the LST can be studied and managed through these techniques.

c. Vertical Plantation Under Bridges to Harvest Rainwater

Rainwater in cities is mostly disposed of in the sewerage system and by runoff from the roads and houses. It can be useful in numerous ways if we harvest rainwater through the vertical plantation and store it. Ponds and water reservoirs may store the rainwater and it can be further used for many purposes i.e. irrigation for the agricultural crop, washing, industrial use, and household use after filtering and recycling. The harvesting of rainwater is very important especially for farmers of arid and semi-arid regions because of the financial status of farmers of these areas depending on the high yield of crops. Most of the water wasted by runoff can be saved through harvesting it by increasing the plantation in urban areas n and conserving it for long period. Moreover, vertical plantations and vegetation in urban areas will harvest more rainwater and reduce its wastage in the sewerage system. The wastage of rainwater caused the water scarcity and increased the level of water in seas.

Water shortage or drought conditions are destructive for vegetation and daily life is also disturbed by it. Approximately 30% of the world is exposed to water shortage (Bodner et al., 2015). It is a need of time to enhance the storing capacity of rainwater. Vertical plantation under bridges is very effective in harvesting the rainwater in dense and populated areas where there is no more space for afforestation. Rainwater will be stored in the soil and used by the plants for their metabolic processes and life cycle. This plantation can be a useful tool for rainwater harvesting but it can also enhance the beauty of the cities and reduced the negative impact of environmental pollution and water scarcity. It is also helpful in the maintenance of road infrastructure which can be damaged by the force of rainwater. The vertical plantation under the bridge depends upon the climatic and environmental conditions of a specific region.

CONCLUSION

In the era of urbanization, nowadays we are facing several issues regarding environmental pollution affecting the health of the biosphere in various ways (Figure 1). The shortage of water has been a very severe issue and increasing day by day due to higher air temperature and a decrease in the annual rainfall. Urban vegetation is very much effective in managing urban environment quality, water scarcity, and the health of another biota. Smart building structures should be made with significant space for vegetation and all barren lands in cities must be covered with some vegetation to minimize the anthropogenic effect on the urban environment.

Figure 1. Role of urban forestry

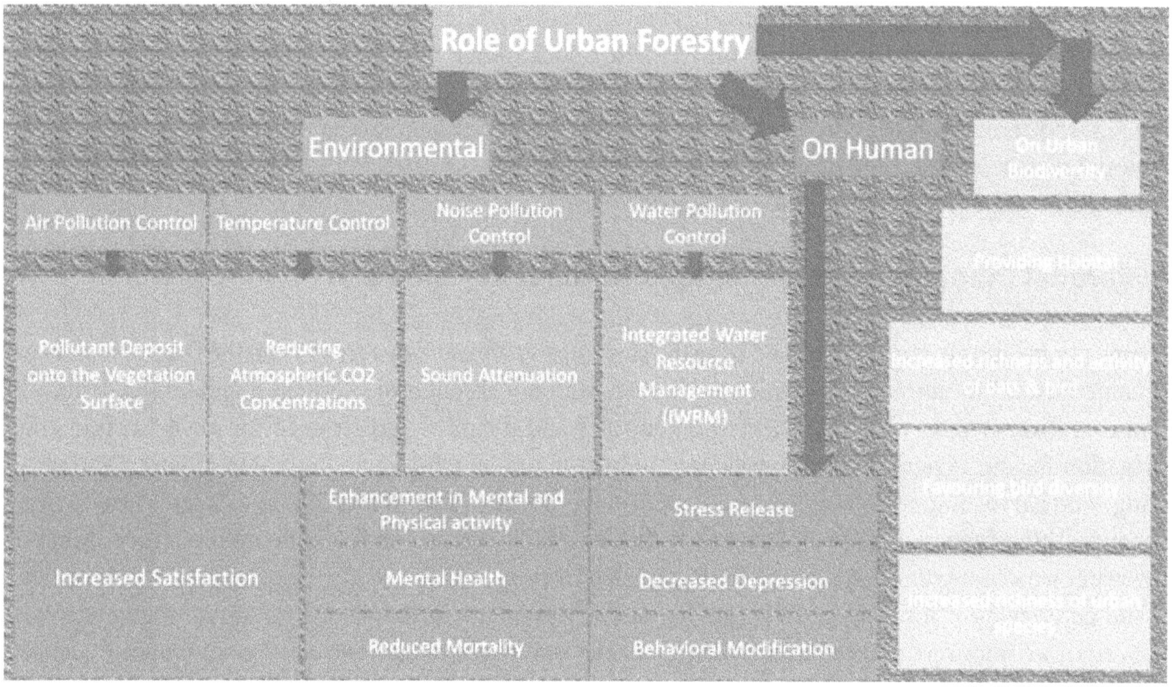

REFERENCES

Acaravci, A., & Ozturk, I. (2010). On the relationship between energy consumption, CO2 emissions and economic growth in Europe. *Energy*, *35*(12), 5412–5420. doi:10.1016/j.energy.2010.07.009

Allen, L., Lindberg, F., & Grimmond, C. S. B. (2011). Global to city scale urban anthropogenic heat flux: Model and variability. *International Journal of Climatology*, *31*(13), 1990–2005. doi:10.1002/joc.2210

Amato, F., Cassee, F. R., van der Gon, H. A. D., Gehrig, R., Gustafsson, M., Hafner, W., Harrison, R. M., Jozwicka, M., Kelly, F. J., Moreno, T., & Prevot, A. S. (2014). Urban air quality: The challenge of traffic non-exhaust emissions. *Journal of Hazardous Materials*, *275*, 31–36. doi:10.1016/j.jhazmat.2014.04.053 PMID:24837462

Aroh, K. (2018). *Globalization, Industralization and Population Growth the Fundamental Drivers of Pollution in a Given Society (India).* Available at SSRN 3453740

Barron, S., Sheppard, S. R., & Condon, P. M. (2016). Urban forest indicators for planning and designing future forests. *Forests*, *7*(9), 208. doi:10.3390/f7090208

Barry, R. G., & Blanken, P. D. (2016). *Microclimate and local climate.* Cambridge University Press. doi:10.1017/CBO9781316535981

Baumgardner, D., Varela, S., Escobedo, F. J., Chacalo, A., & Ochoa, C. (2012). The role of a peri-urban forest on air quality improvement in the Mexico City megalopolis. *Environmental Pollution*, *163*, 74–183. doi:10.1016/j.envpol.2011.12.016 PMID:22245735

Behera, S. R., & Dash, D. P. (2017). The effect of urbanization, energy consumption, and foreign direct investment on the carbon dioxide emission in the SSEA (South and Southeast Asian) region. *Renewable & Sustainable Energy Reviews*, *70*, 96–106. doi:10.1016/j.rser.2016.11.201

Bello, J. P., Silva, C., Nov, O., DuBois, R. L., Arora, A., Salamon, J., Mydlarz, C., & Doraiswamy, H. (2018). *SONYC: A system for the monitoring, analysis and mitigation of urban noise pollution.* arXiv preprint arXiv:1805.00889

Bodner, G., Nakhforoosh, A., & Kaul, H. P. (2015). Management of crop water under drought: A review. *Agronomy for Sustainable Development*, *35*(2), 401–442. doi:10.100713593-015-0283-4

Bowe, B., Xie, Y., Li, T., Yan, Y., Xian, H., & Al-Aly, Z. (2018). The global and national burden of diabetes mellitus attributable to PM2· 5 air pollution. *The Lancet Planetary Health*, *2*(7), e301–e312. doi:10.1016/S2542-5196(18)30140-2 PMID:30074893

Brandani, G., Napoli, M., Massetti, L., Petralli, M., & Orlandini, S. (2016). Urban soil: Assessing ground cover impact on surface temperature and thermal comfort. *Journal of Environmental Quality*, *45*(1), 90–97. doi:10.2134/jeq2014.12.0521 PMID:26828164

Burakov, A. E., Galunin, E. V., Burakova, I. V., Kucherova, A. E., Agarwal, S., Tkachev, A. G., & Gupta, V. K. (2018). Adsorption of heavy metals on conventional and nanostructured materials for wastewater treatment purposes: A review. *Ecotoxicology and Environmental Safety*, *148*, 702–712. doi:10.1016/j.ecoenv.2017.11.034 PMID:29174989

Buyantuyev, A., & Wu, J. (2010). Urban heat islands and landscape heterogeneity: Linking spatiotemporal variations in surface temperatures to land-cover and socioeconomic patterns. *Landscape Ecology*, *25*(1), 17–33. doi:10.100710980-009-9402-4

Calfapietra, C., Fares, S., Manes, F., Morani, A., Sgrigna, G., & Loreto, F. (2013). Role of Biogenic Volatile Organic Compounds (BVOC) emitted by urban trees on ozone concentration in cities: A review. *Environmental Pollution*, *183*, 71–80. doi:10.1016/j.envpol.2013.03.012 PMID:23597803

Cariñanos, P., Adinolfi, C., Diaz de la Guardia, C., De Linares, C., & Casares-Porcel, M. (2016). Characterization of allergen emission sources in urban areas. *Journal of Environmental Quality*, *45*(1), 244–252. doi:10.2134/jeq2015.02.0075 PMID:26828180

Cetin, M. (2015). Using GIS analysis to assess urban green space in terms of accessibility: Case study in Kutahya. *International Journal of Sustainable Development and World Ecology*, *22*(5), 420–424.

Chalker-Scott, L. (2015). Nonnative, noninvasive woody species can enhance urban landscape biodiversity. *Arboriculture & Urban Forestry*, *41*(4), 173–185.

Chameides, W. L., Fehsenfeld, F., Rodgers, M. O., Cardelino, C., Martinez, J., Parrish, D., Lonneman, W., Lawson, D. R., Rasmussen, R. A., Zimmerman, P., Greenberg, J., Mlddleton, P., & Wang, T. (1992). Ozone precursor relationships in the ambient atmosphere. *Journal of Geophysical Research, D, Atmospheres*, *97*(D5), 6037–6055. doi:10.1029/91JD03014

Chang, C. R., Li, M. H., & Chang, S. D. (2007). A preliminary study on the local cool-island intensity of Taipei city parks. *Landscape and Urban Planning*, *80*(4), 386–395. doi:10.1016/j.landurbplan.2006.09.005

Chen, Q., Yao, Y., Li, X., Lu, J., Zhou, J. and Huang, Z. (2018). Comparison of heavy metal removals from aqueous solutions by chemical precipitation and characteristics of precipitates. *Journal of Water Process Engineering*, *26*, 289-300.

Chen, Z., Liang, Y., Jia, D., Chen, W., Cui, Z., & Wang, X. (2017). Layered silicate RUB-15 for efficient removal of UO 2 2+ and heavy metal ions by ion-exchange. *Environmental Science. Nano*, *4*(9), 1851–1858. doi:10.1039/C7EN00366H

Chopra, R. (2016). Environmental degradation in India: Causes and consequences. *International Journal of Applied Environmental Sciences*, *11*(6), 1593–1601.

Chun, B., & Guldmann, J. M. (2014). Spatial statistical analysis and simulation of the urban heat island in high-density central cities. *Landscape and Urban Planning*, *125*, 76–88. doi:10.1016/j.landurbplan.2014.01.016

Churkina, G., Kuik, F., Bonn, B., Lauer, A., Grote, R., Tomiak, K., & Butler, T. M. (2017). Effect of VOC emissions from vegetation on air quality in Berlin during a heatwave. *Environmental Science & Technology*, *51*(11), 6120–6130. doi:10.1021/acs.est.6b06514 PMID:28513175

Clark, C., Sbihi, H., Tamburic, L., Brauer, M., Frank, L. D., & Davies, H. W. (2017). Association of long-term exposure to transportation noise and traffic-related air pollution with the incidence of diabetes: A prospective cohort study. *Environmental Health Perspectives*, *125*(8), 087025. doi:10.1289/EHP1279 PMID:28934721

Cobbinah, P. B., & Darkwah, R. M. (2016), June. African urbanism: the geography of urban greenery. In *Urban Forum* (Vol. 27, No. 2, 149-165). Springer Netherlands.

Denman, E. C., May, P. B., & Moore, G. M. (2016). The potential role of urban forests in removing nutrients from stormwater. *Journal of Environmental Quality*, *45*(1), 207–214. doi:10.2134/jeq2015.01.0047 PMID:26828176

Derouin, S. (2019). *Deforestation: Facts, Causes & Effects.* Accessed 20 February 2020, https://www.livescience.com/27692-deforestation.html

Dzhambov, A. M., & Dimitrova, D. D. (2015). Green spaces and environmental noise perception. *Urban Forestry & Urban Greening*, *14*(4), 1000–1008. doi:10.1016/j.ufug.2015.09.006

Efome, J. E., Rana, D., Matsuura, T., & Lan, C. Q. (2018). Experiment and modeling for flux and permeate concentration of heavy metal ion in adsorptive membrane filtration using a metal-organic framework incorporated nanofibrous membrane. *Chemical Engineering Journal, 352*, 737–744. doi:10.1016/j.cej.2018.07.077

Emmanuel, R., & Loconsole, A. (2015). Green infrastructure as an adaptation approach to tackling urban overheating in the Glasgow Clyde Valley Region, UK. *Landscape and Urban Planning, 138*, 71–86. doi:10.1016/j.landurbplan.2015.02.012

Endreny, T. A. (2018). Strategically growing the urban forest will improve our world. *Nature Communications, 9*(1), 1160. doi:10.103841467-018-03622-0 PMID:29563541

Escobedo, F. J., Wagner, J. E., Nowak, D. J., De la Maza, C. L., Rodriguez, M., & Crane, D. E. (2008). Analyzing the cost effectiveness of Santiago, Chile's policy of using urban forests to improve air quality. *Journal of Environmental Management, 86*(1), 148–157. doi:10.1016/j.jenvman.2006.11.029 PMID:17275162

Ezeah, C., Finney, K., & Nnajide, C. (2015). A critical review of the effectiveness of low emission zones (LEZ) as a strategy for the management of air quality in major European cities. *Journal of Multidisciplinary Engineering Science and Technology, 2*(7), 1860–1868.

Fabbri, K., & Costanzo, V. (2020). Drone-assisted infrared thermography for calibration of outdoor microclimate simulation models. *Sustainable Cities and Society, 52*, 101855. doi:10.1016/j.scs.2019.101855

Fallmann, J., Emeis, S., & Suppan, P. (2013). Mitigation of urban heat stress–a modelling case study for the area of Stuttgart. *DIE ERDE–Journal of the Geographical Society of Berlin, 144*(3-4), 202–216.

Ferrini, F., van den Bosch, C. C. K., & Fini, A. (Eds.). (2017). *Routledge handbook of urban forestry*. Taylor & Francis. doi:10.4324/9781315627106

Fu, P., & Weng, Q. (2016). A time series analysis of urbanization induced land use and land cover change and its impact on land surface temperature with Landsat imagery. *Remote Sensing of Environment, 175*, 205–214. doi:10.1016/j.rse.2015.12.040

Gage, E. A., & Cooper, D. J. (2017). Urban forest structure and land cover composition effects on land surface temperature in a semi-arid suburban area. *Urban Forestry & Urban Greening, 28*, 28–35. doi:10.1016/j.ufug.2017.10.003

Globe Water. (2018). *Water pollution statistics 2018-2019*. Accessed 24 February 2020, https://www.globewater.org/facts/water-pollution-statistics/

Goldscheider, N. (2010). Delineation of spring protection zones. In Groundwater hydrology of springs (pp. 305-338). Butterworth-Heinemann. doi:10.1016/B978-1-85617-502-9.00008-6

Gozalo, G. R., Morillas, J. M. B., González, D. M., & Moraga, P. A. (2018). Relationships among satisfaction, noise perception, and use of urban green spaces. *The Science of the Total Environment, 624*, 438–450. doi:10.1016/j.scitotenv.2017.12.148 PMID:29268216

Gulia, S., Nagendra, S. S., Khare, M., & Khanna, I. (2015). Urban air quality management-A review. *Atmospheric Pollution Research, 6*(2), 286–304. doi:10.5094/APR.2015.033

Guttikunda, S. K., Carmichael, G. R., Calori, G., Eck, C., & Woo, J. H. (2003). The contribution of megacities to regional sulfur pollution in Asia. *Atmospheric Environment, 37*(1), 11–22. doi:10.1016/S1352-2310(02)00821-X

Han, L., Zhou, W., Li, W., & Li, L. (2014). Impact of urbanization level on urban air quality: A case of fine particles (PM2. 5) in Chinese cities. *Environmental Pollution, 194*, 163–170. doi:10.1016/j.envpol.2014.07.022 PMID:25113968

Hansell, A., Cai, Y. S., & Gulliver, J. (2017). Cardiovascular Health Effects of Road Traffic Noise. In Environmental Impacts of Road Vehicles (pp. 107-132). doi:10.1039/9781788010221-00107

Herndon, J. M. (2018). Air pollution, not greenhouse gases: The principal cause of global warming. *J Geog Environ Earth Sci Intn, 17*(2), 1–8.

Intasen, M., Hauer, R. J., Werner, L. P., & Larsen, E. (2017). Urban forest assessment in Bangkok, Thailand. *Journal of Sustainable Forestry, 36*(2), 148–163. doi:10.1080/10549811.2016.1265455

Inyinbor Adejumoke, A., Adebesin Babatunde, O., Oluyori Abimbola, P., Adelani Akande Tabitha, A., Dada Adewumi, O., & Oreofe Toyin, A. (2018). Water pollution: effects, prevention, and climatic impact. *Water Challenges of an Urbanizing World, 33*.

Ite, A. E., Harry, T. A., Obadimu, C. O., & Ekwere, I. O. (2019). Comparison of Indoor Air Quality in Schools: Urban vs. Industrial'Oil & Gas' Zones in Akwa Ibom State–Nigeria. *Journal of Environment Pollution and Human Health, 7*(1), 15–26. doi:10.12691/jephh-7-1-3

Ite, A. E., Ogunkunle, C. O., Obadimu, C. O., Asuaiko, E. R., & Ibok, U. J. (2017). Particulate matter and staff exposure in an air-conditioned office in Akwa Ibom State University–Nigeria. *Journal of Atmospheric Pollution, 5*(1), 24–32. doi:10.12691/jap-5-1-4

Kaloustian, N., & Diab, Y. (2015). Effects of urbanization on the urban heat island in Beirut. *Urban Climate, 14*, 154–165. doi:10.1016/j.uclim.2015.06.004

Kang, T. J., Park, H. J., Chae, B. G., Jeong, N. S., & You, K. H. (2010). Analysis of landslide susceptibility in Pyeong-Chang area using fuzzy relation method. *The Journal of Engineering Geology, 20*, 217–222.

Kenney, W. A., van Wassenaer, P. J., & Satel, A. L. (2011). Criteria and indicators for strategic urban forest planning and management. *Arboriculture & Urban Forestry, 37*(3), 108–117.

Khokhar, T., & Tabary, M. E. (2016). *Five forest figures for the international day of forests*. The World Bank the Data Blog.

Klingberg, J., Broberg, M., Strandberg, B., Thorsson, P., & Pleijel, H. (2017). Influence of urban vegetation on air pollution and noise exposure–a case study in Gothenburg, Sweden. *The Science of the Total Environment, 599*, 1728–1739. doi:10.1016/j.scitotenv.2017.05.051 PMID:28545203

Kong, F., Yin, H., James, P., Hutyra, L. R., & He, H. S. (2014). Effects of spatial pattern of greenspace on urban cooling in a large metropolitan area of eastern China. *Landscape and Urban Planning, 128*, 35–47. doi:10.1016/j.landurbplan.2014.04.018

Krzyżanowski, M., Kuna-Dibbert, B., & Schneider, J. (Eds.). (2005). *Health effects of transport-related air pollution*. WHO Regional Office Europe.

Kumar, D., & Kumar, D. (2018). *Sustainable Management of Coal Preparation*. Woodhead Publishing.

Lai, H. K., Kendall, M., Ferrier, H., Lindup, I., Alm, S., Hänninen, O., Jantunen, M., Mathys, P., Colvile, R., Ashmore, M. R., Cullinan, P., & Nieuwenhuijsen, M. J. (2004). Personal exposures and microenvironment concentrations of PM2. 5, VOC, NO2 and CO in Oxford, UK. *Atmospheric Environment*, *38*(37), 6399–6410. doi:10.1016/j.atmosenv.2004.07.013

Lembrechts, J. J., Nijs, I., & Lenoir, J. (2019). Incorporating microclimate into species distribution models. *Ecography*, *42*(7), 1267–1279. doi:10.1111/ecog.03947

Li, Y., Yang, L., Xu, Z., & Sun, Q. (2017). January. Separation and recovery of heavy metals from wastewater using synergistic solvent extraction. *IOP Conference Series. Materials Science and Engineering*, *167*(1), 012005.

Lioy, P. J. (2017). *Toxic Air Pollution: A Comprehensive Study Non-Criteria Air Pollutants*. CRC Press.

Liu, H., Ma, W., Qian, J., Cai, J., Ye, X., Li, J., & Wang, X. (2015). Effect of urbanization on the urban meteorology and air pollution in Hangzhou. *Journal of Meteorological Research*, *29*(6), 950–965. doi:10.100713351-015-5013-y

Livesley, S. J., McPherson, E. G., & Calfapietra, C. (2016). The urban forest and ecosystem services: Impacts on urban water, heat, and pollution cycles at the tree, street, and city scale. *Journal of Environmental Quality*, *45*(1), 119–124. doi:10.2134/jeq2015.11.0567 PMID:26828167

Lu, X., Hong, J., Zhang, L., Cooper, O. R., Schultz, M. G., Xu, X., Wang, T., Gao, M., Zhao, Y., & Zhang, Y. (2018). Severe surface ozone pollution in China: A global perspective. *Environmental Science & Technology Letters*, *5*(8), 487–494. doi:10.1021/acs.estlett.8b00366

Mahmoud, S. H., & Gan, T. Y. (2018). Urbanization and climate change implications in flood risk management: Developing an efficient decision support system for flood susceptibility mapping. *The Science of the Total Environment*, *636*, 152–167. doi:10.1016/j.scitotenv.2018.04.282 PMID:29705434

Maricq, M. M. (2007). Chemical characterization of particulate emissions from diesel engines: A review. *Journal of Aerosol Science*, *38*(11), 1079–1118. doi:10.1016/j.jaerosci.2007.08.001

Masson, V., Lion, Y., Peter, A., Pigeon, G., Buyck, J., & Brun, E. (2013). "Grand Paris": Regional landscape change to adapt city to climate warming. *Climatic Change*, *117*(4), 769–782. doi:10.100710584-012-0579-1

McDonald, R. I., Forman, R. T., & Kareiva, P. (2010). Open space loss and land inequality in United States' cities, 1990–2000. *PLoS One*, *5*(3), e9509. doi:10.1371/journal.pone.0009509 PMID:20209082

McPherson, E. G., Nowak, D., Heisler, G., Grimmond, S., Souch, C., Grant, R., & Rowntree, R. (1997). Quantifying urban forest structure, function, and value: The Chicago Urban Forest Climate Project. *Urban Ecosystems*, *1*(1), 49–61. doi:10.1023/A:1014350822458

Mersal, A. (2016). Sustainable urban futures: Environmental planning for sustainable urban development. *Procedia Environmental Sciences*, *34*, 49–61. doi:10.1016/j.proenv.2016.04.005

Moussiopoulos, N., Kalognomou, E. A., Douros, I., Samaras, Z., Gionnouli, M., & Mellios, G. (2005). Air pollution level at hotspot areas of selected European cities. In *Proceeding of 10th Conference on Harmonization within Atmospheric Dispersion Modelling for Regulatory Purposes* (pp. 283-287). Academic Press.

Muerdter, C. P., Wong, C. K., & LeFevre, G. H. (2018). Emerging investigator series: The role of vegetation in bioretention for stormwater treatment in the built environment: Pollutant removal, hydrologic function, and ancillary benefits. *Environmental Science. Water Research & Technology*, *4*(5), 592–612. doi:10.1039/C7EW00511C

Naiman, R. J., Decamps, H., & McClain, M. E. (2010). *Riparia: ecology, conservation, and management of streamside communities*. Elsevier.

Naiman, R. J., Décamps, H., McClain, M. E., & Likens, G. E. (2005). Biotic Functions of Riparia. In N. Maragioglio (Ed.), Riparia: Ecology, Conservation and Management of Streamside Communities. Elsevier. doi:10.1016/B978-012663315-3/50006-X

Nastran, M., Kobal, M., & Eler, K. (2019). Urban heat islands in relation to green land use in European cities. *Urban Forestry & Urban Greening*, *37*, 33–41. doi:10.1016/j.ufug.2018.01.008

National Geographic Society. (2019). *Noise Pollution*. Accessed 25 February 2020, https://www.nationalgeographic.org/encyclopedia/noise-pollution/

National Institute of Environmental Health Sciences. (2019). *USA.gov*. Accessed 23 February 2020, https://www.niehs.nih.gov/health/topics/agents/air-pollution/

Nice, K. A., Coutts, A. M., & Tapper, N. J. (2018). Development of the VTUF-3D v1. 0 urban microclimate model to support assessment of urban vegetation influences on human thermal comfort. *Urban Climate*, *24*, 1052-1076.

Ningrum, W. (2018). February. Urban heat island towards urban climate. In *IOP Conference Series: Earth and Environmental Science* (*Vol. 118*, No. 1, 012048). IOP Publishing.

Nowak, D. J., Hirabayashi, S., Bodine, A., & Greenfield, E. (2014). Tree and forest effects on air quality and human health in the United States. *Environmental Pollution*, *193*, 119–129. doi:10.1016/j.envpol.2014.05.028 PMID:25016465

Nowak-Sliwinska, P., Alitalo, K., Allen, E., Anisimov, A., Aplin, A. C., Auerbach, R., Augustin, H. G., Bates, D. O., van Beijnum, J. R., Bender, R. H. F., Bergers, G., Bikfalvi, A., Bischoff, J., Böck, B. C., Brooks, P. C., Bussolino, F., Cakir, B., Carmeliet, P., Castranova, D., ... Griffioen, A. W. (2018). Consensus guidelines for the use and interpretation of angiogenesis assays. *Angiogenesis*, *21*(3), 425–532. doi:10.100710456-018-9613-x PMID:29766399

Ow, L. F., & Ghosh, S. (2017). Urban cities and road traffic noise: Reduction through vegetation. *Applied Acoustics*, *120*, 15–20. doi:10.1016/j.apacoust.2017.01.007

Pandve, H. T. (2008). The Asian brown cloud. *Indian Journal of Occupational and Environmental Medicine*, *12*(2), 93. doi:10.4103/0019-5278.43269 PMID:20040987

Parsa, V. A., Salehi, E., Yavari, A. R., & van Bodegom, P. M. (2019). Analyzing temporal changes in urban forest structure and the effect on air quality improvement. *Sustainable Cities and Society*, *48*, 101548. doi:10.1016/j.scs.2019.101548

Pataki, D. E., Carreiro, M. M., Cherrier, J., Grulke, N. E., Jennings, V., Pincetl, S., Pouyat, R. V., Whitlow, T. H., & Zipperer, W. C. (2011). Coupling biogeochemical cycles in urban environments: Ecosystem services, green solutions, and misconceptions. *Frontiers in Ecology and the Environment*, *9*(1), 27–36. doi:10.1890/090220

Peckham, S. C., Duinker, P. N., & Ordóñez, C. (2013). Urban forest values in Canada: Views of citizens in Calgary and Halifax. *Urban Forestry & Urban Greening*, *12*(2), 154–162. doi:10.1016/j.ufug.2013.01.001

Petralli, M., Morabito, M., Cecchi, L., Crisci, A., & Orlandini, S. (2012). Urban morbidity in summer: Ambulance dispatch data, periodicity and weather. *Central European Journal of Medicine*, *7*(6), 775–782.

Petrova, S. T. (2020). Efficiency of Pinus nigra JF Arnold in removing pollutants from urban environment (Plovdiv, Bulgaria). *Environmental Science and Pollution Research International*, 1–17. PMID:32648225

Pope Iii, C. A., Burnett, R. T., Thun, M. J., Calle, E. E., Krewski, D., Ito, K., & Thurston, G. D. (2002). Lung cancer, cardiopulmonary mortality, and long-term exposure to fine particulate air pollution. *Journal of the American Medical Association*, *287*(9), 1132–1141. doi:10.1001/jama.287.9.1132 PMID:11879110

Puri, P., Nandar, S. K., Kathuria, S., & Ramesh, V. (2017). Effects of air pollution on the skin: A review. *Indian Journal of Dermatology, Venereology and Leprology*, *83*(4), 415. doi:10.4103/0378-6323.199579 PMID:28195077

Rafferty, P. J. (2020). *Microclimate*. Britannica. Accessed 23 august 2020, https://www.britannica.com/science/microclimate

Ren, Y., Deng, L. Y., Zuo, S. D., Song, X. D., Liao, Y. L., Xu, C. D., Chen, Q., Hua, L. Z., & Li, Z. W. (2016). Quantifying the influences of various ecological factors on land surface temperature of urban forests. *Environmental Pollution*, *216*, 519–529. doi:10.1016/j.envpol.2016.06.004 PMID:27321883

RitchieH.RoserM. (2020). *Urbanization*. https://ourworldindata.org/urbanization

Rodríguez, M.C., Dupont-Courtade, L. and Oueslati, W. (2015). Air Pollution and Urban Structure Linkages.

Roth, M., & Lim, V. H. (2017). Evaluation of canopy-layer air and mean radiant temperature simulations by a microclimate model over a tropical residential neighbourhood. *Building and Environment*, *112*, 177–189. doi:10.1016/j.buildenv.2016.11.026

Selmi, W., Weber, C., Rivière, E., Blond, N., Mehdi, L., & Nowak, D. (2016). Air pollution removal by trees in public green spaces in Strasbourg city, France. *Urban Forestry & Urban Greening*, *17*, 192–201. doi:10.1016/j.ufug.2016.04.010

Shaharuddin, A., Noorazuan, M.H., Takeuchi, W., & Noraziah, A. (2014). The effects of urban heat islands on human comfort: A case of Klang Valley Malaysia. *Global Journal on Advances Pure and Applied Sciences, 2*.

Shahbaz, M., Loganathan, N., Sbia, R., & Afza, T. (2015). The effect of urbanization, affluence and trade openness on energy consumption: A time series analysis in Malaysia. *Renewable & Sustainable Energy Reviews*, *47*, 683–693. doi:10.1016/j.rser.2015.03.044

Sharifi, E. & Lehmann, S. (2014). *Comparative analysis of surface urban heat island effect in central Sydney*. Academic Press.

Sharp, T. (2017). *Earth's Atmosphere: Composition, Climate & Weather.* https://www. space. com/17683-earth-atmosphere. html

Simon, H., Lindén, J., Hoffmann, D., Braun, P., Bruse, M., & Esper, J. (2018). Modeling transpiration and leaf temperature of urban trees–a case study evaluating the microclimate model ENVI-met against measurement data. *Landscape and Urban Planning*, *174*, 33–40. doi:10.1016/j.landurbplan.2018.03.003

Singh, A. K., Gupta, H. K., Gupta, K., Singh, P., Gupta, V. B., & Sharma, R. C. (2007). A comparative study of air pollution in Indian cities. *Bulletin of Environmental Contamination and Toxicology*, *78*(5), 411–416. doi:10.100700128-007-9220-9 PMID:17599225

Sjöman, H., Hirons, A. D., & Bassuk, N. L. (2015). Urban forest resilience through tree selection—Variation in drought tolerance in Acer. *Urban Forestry & Urban Greening*, *14*(4), 858–865. doi:10.1016/j.ufug.2015.08.004

Smith, S. J., Schepers, J. S., & Porter, L. K. (1990). Assessing and managing agricultural nitrogen losses to the environment. In Advances in soil science (1-43). Springer. doi:10.1007/978-1-4612-3356-5_1

Tiwary, A., & Williams, I. (2018). *Air pollution: measurement, modelling and mitigation*. CRC Press. doi:10.1201/9780429469985

Tsoka, S., Tsikaloudaki, A., & Theodosiou, T. (2018). Analyzing the ENVI-met microclimate model's performance and assessing cool materials and urban vegetation applications–A review. *Sustainable Cities and Society*, *43*, 55-76.

Unkašević, M., Jovanović, O., & Popović, T. (2001). Urban-suburban/rural vapour pressure and relative humidity differences at fixed hours over the area of Belgrade city. *Theoretical and Applied Climatology*, *68*(1-2), 67–73. doi:10.1007007040170054

Vanos, J. K. (2015). Children's health and vulnerability in outdoor microclimates: A comprehensive review. *Environment International*, *76*, 1–15. doi:10.1016/j.envint.2014.11.016 PMID:25497108

von Bismarck-Osten, C., Birmili, W., Ketzel, M., Massling, A., Petäjä, T., & Weber, S. (2013). Characterization of parameters influencing the spatio-temporal variability of urban particle number size distributions in four European cities. *Atmospheric Environment*, *77*, 415–429. doi:10.1016/j.atmosenv.2013.05.029

Wang, F., Pan, Y., Cai, P., Guo, T., & Xiao, H. (2017). Single and binary adsorption of heavy metal ions from aqueous solutions using sugarcane cellulose-based adsorbent. *Bioresource Technology*, *241*, 482–490. doi:10.1016/j.biortech.2017.05.162 PMID:28600942

Wang, J., Huang, B., Fu, D., Atkinson, P. M., & Zhang, X. (2016). Response of urban heat island to future urban expansion over the Beijing–Tianjin–Hebei metropolitan area. *Applied Geography (Sevenoaks, England), 70*, 26–36. doi:10.1016/j.apgeog.2016.02.010

Weisse, M., & Goldman, E. D. (2017). *Was the Second-Worst Year on Record for Tropical Tree Cover Loss*. Global Forest Watch Blog.

WHO. (2014). https://www.who.int/mediacentre/news/releases/2014/air-pollution/en/

Woodford, M. (2019). Monetary policy analysis when planning horizons are finite. *NBER Macroeconomics Annual, 33*(1), 1–50. doi:10.1086/700892

World Health Organization. (2014). *7 million premature deaths annually linked to air pollution*. Accessed 23 February 2020, https://www.who.int/mediacentre/news/releases/2014/airpollution/en/

Wypych, A. (2010). Twentieth century variability of surface humidity as the climate change indicator in Kraków (Southern Poland). *Theoretical and Applied Climatology, 101*(3-4), 475–482. doi:10.100700704-009-0221-y

Xing, Y., & Brimblecombe, P. (2019). Role of vegetation in deposition and dispersion of air pollution in urban parks. *Atmospheric Environment, 201*, 73–83. doi:10.1016/j.atmosenv.2018.12.027

Yang, Y., Gatto, E., Gao, Z., Buccolieri, R., Morakinyo, T. E., & Lan, H. (2019). The "plant evaluation model" for the assessment of the impact of vegetation on outdoor microclimate in the urban environment. *Building and Environment, 159*, 106151. doi:10.1016/j.buildenv.2019.05.029

Yao, W., Wang, J., Wang, P., Wang, X., Yu, S., Zou, Y., Hou, J., Hayat, T., Alsaedi, A., & Wang, X. (2017). Synergistic coagulation of GO and secondary adsorption of heavy metal ions on Ca/Al layered double hydroxides. *Environmental Pollution, 229*, 827–836. doi:10.1016/j.envpol.2017.06.084 PMID:28760526

Zhao, S., Zhou, D., & Liu, S. (2016). Data concurrency is required for estimating urban heat island intensity. *Environmental Pollution, 208*, 118–124. doi:10.1016/j.envpol.2015.07.037 PMID:26243476

Chapter 13
Urban Forestry in Sabah, Malaysia: A Perspective Review

Andy Russel Mojiol
University Malaysia Sabah, Malaysia

Wing Shen Lim
https://orcid.org/0000-0003-1749-2120
Universiti Malaysia Sabah, Malaysia

ABSTRACT

This chapter provides a holistic understanding of the existing conditions of urban green spaces in Sabah by reviewing relevant past studies and publications. Nature serves as the foundation in the establishment of pocket parks, urban parks, and forest protected areas that are made available for public access within and outside of the major urban areas in Sabah. Presently, both native and exotic flora and fauna species are coexisting at the local urban green spaces, although some invasive exotic species have developed into urban pests of Sabah. Moreover, the importance and functions of urban green spaces in maintaining the well-being of mankind and ensuring the survival of indigenous wildlife species are acknowledged by society. Nevertheless, much research is required to fill up the research gaps of urban forestry, and also to provide solutions to the existing problems that happened at the urban green spaces in Sabah.

URBANIZATION PRESSURE FROM RAPID URBAN GROWTH

Sabah is the second largest Federal State of Malaysia, as well as one of the two Federal States that are located at Borneo Island. According to the statistic provided by the Department of Statistics Malaysia (2019), the human population in Sabah reached approximately 3.9 million in 2018, which was estimated to increase by 0.06 million populations per year since 2015. Three major urban areas in Sabah were enlisted as top 20 cities by population in Malaysia, with Kota Kinabalu ranked in 10th place (457,326 population), followed by Sandakan in 11th place (392,288 population) and Tawau in 15th place (306,462

DOI: 10.4018/978-1-7998-4372-6.ch013

population) in 2019. In other words, the urban population continues to rise every year in Sabah, hence rapid urbanization has occurred to provide sufficient living spaces for accommodating the increase in the local urban human population. Nevertheless, urban development and growth indicate the loss of the natural environment, which can subsequently reduce public access to nature in these urban regions (Chaudhry & Tewari, 2011). Therefore, the Federal Government of Malaysia included the concept of "Urban Forestry" in urban landscape development and management in 1995. Today, Sabah is rich in green cities and towns that successfully mix nature into the urban landscape, thanks to the preferences of the Sabah community in living harmoniously with Mother Nature (Lee et al., 2004).

Urban forestry involves the planning, caring, and managing of the urban environment, by using urban plants to maintain environmental and social benefits that are crucial to the well-being of urban dwellers. Then, a greener urban landscape that is established for non-priced benefit is regarded as an urban green space (Chaudhry & Tewari, 2011). Presently, various urban green spaces are available for public access within or outside of the major cities in Sabah, and then they share common functions in providing ecosystem services to the surrounding urban environment. Costanza et al. (2017) highlighted that ecosystem services were categorized into provisioning, regulating, supporting, and cultural services, and then urban forests could provide similar ecosystem services as the natural forests to their surrounding environments. Besides that, Mojiol (2001) revealed that urban forests could enhance aesthetic value, provide a sense of serenity to urban dwellers, regulate urban environmental condition, reduce the disturbance and pollution impacts, house urban biodiversity, maintain the urban nutrient cycle and hydrological cycle, and lastly provide recreational, tourism, research and education opportunities in an urban area, as shown in below Table 1. In sum, urban green spaces serve as a replacement to natural forests in providing ecosystem services to the urban regions of Sabah, and also to the urban dwellers, flora, and fauna that reside within the given areas.

However, the current conditions of the urban environments in Sabah are rarely being assessed by researchers. Urban forestry is considered to be a rather new field of a research study in Sabah because the oldest publication was found written by Mojiol (2001). Although the number of studies conducted onto urban green spaces in Sabah was increased in recent years (e.g.: Lee et al., 2004; Mojiol et al., 2008; Mojiol and Bürger-Arndt, 2012; Wells, et al., 2014; Nair et al., 2018; Lim et al., 2019; and Lim & Mojiol, 2019), still each of these past studies mainly focused onto a specific component of the local urban forestry. Because of that, there is a lacking of information to understand the local urban forestry as a whole at this moment. Therefore, this chapter aims to provide a comprehensive understanding of the urban forestry that has been implemented in Sabah by reviewing relevant past research articles and publications. In this chapter, accessibilities and functionalities of different urban green spaces will be discussed in detail and followed by the existing species compositions and diversities of urban flora and fauna communities, existing urban trail condition, public perceptions on urban green spaces, and the application of geographical information system in urban forestry of Sabah.

A PERSPECTIVE REVIEW ON URBAN FORESTRY IN SABAH

Variation in Urban Green Spaces of Sabah

Various type of urban green spaces is established within and outside of the three major cities in Sabah, which are the pocket parks, urban parks and forest protected areas (Mojiol et al., 2017; Mojiol, 2018a;

and Nair et al., 2018). These urban green spaces incorporated both naturally-grown and human-planted plants into the landscape, thus including both natural woodlands and planted forests (Konijnendjik et al., 2013). At the same time, the provided facilities, infrastructures, and outdoor recreational activities can be different between one urban green space and another, due to the differences in size, setting, and location. Due to that, each urban green space has its uniqueness and importance to the surrounding urban environment. To date, Kota Kinabalu has the highest number of urban green spaces provided for public uses, when compared to Sandakan and Tawau, and also with the other urban regions in Sabah.

Table 1. Ecosystem services provided by an urban green space to the surrounding urban environment.

Category	Ecosystem Service	Example
Provisioning	Consumable Food Tangible Resource Genetic Resource	Providing edible fruits or plants to the urban inhabitants. Provisioning of clean water, fuel, lumber, fodder, and sources of medicinal and ornamental plants to the urban inhabitants. Sources of a wide range of biological materials and products in the urban environment.
Regulating	Pollution Control Climate Control Air Purification Carbon Sequestration Shading Effect Disturbance Regulation Natural Pollination Biological Control Erosion Control and Sediment Retention	Regulating air, water, noise, and light pollutions in urban areas. Regulating surrounding solar radiation, ambient temperature, and humidity of the urban environment. Absorbing air pollutants and releasing clean oxygen supply to the urban environment. Serving as carbon sinks for the surrounding urban environment. Providing shade to the urban inhabitants during the daytime. Providing windbreak and protecting the urban environment against the storm, flood, landslide, and other disturbance. Providing pollinators that are crucial for the reproduction of urban plant populations. Providing prey or predator individuals to regulate the prey-predator abundances in urban areas. Retaining sediments and protecting coastal and soil erosions in urban areas.
Supporting	Habitat Provisioning Nutrient Cycling Soil Formation	Serving as habitat for indigenous and exotic plant species, as well as for resident and migration wildlife species in urban areas. Maintaining equilibrium in nutrient cycling in urban areas. Accumulating organic matters as nutrients for urban plants.
Cultural	Recreation Opportunity Intangible Resource	Providing greenery landscapes with suitable natural resources for conducting outdoor recreation and tourism activities. Providing intangible products (e.g.: aesthetic, spiritual, scientific, and/or educational values), which are beneficial to the well-being of urban inhabitants.

Sources: (Mojiol, 2001; Costanza et al., 2017; and Nair et al., 2018)

Through the reviewing of several relevant past studies and publications, a summary of the pocket parks, urban parks, and forest protected areas at the three major urban regions in Sabah is obtained and tabulated as shown in Table 2. Based on Table 2, an urban green space that has a size of less than 0.5 ha is known as a pocket park, whereas an urban park has a size of more than 0.5 ha (Endreny, 2018). Both parks are managed by the City Council Municipalities (i.e Kota Kinabalu City Hall, Sandakan Municipal Council, and Tawau Municipal Council). Pocket parks are often established as replacements to the larger-sized urban parks, especially in the highly-developed city centers with limited free spaces. Because of its confined space, pocket park mainly serves as a safe area for urban dwellers to rest, walk to other places and, socialize with others (Peschardt et al., 2012). Aesthetic value is determined to be the main contribution of a pocket park, while the urban park mainly provides outdoor activity opportunity to urban inhabitants in Sabah (Mojiol, 2018a), although both parks provide recreation and education opportunities, have high aesthetic values, function as wildlife habitat and wind barrier, and help in soil erosion control and pollution reduction. At most, trees and seats are provided for urban dwellers to rest under shading during daytime (Mojiol, 2018a). On the other hand, a wide range of infrastructures and facilities are provided to enable different types of outdoor recreation activities to be conducted at the urban park, and by many people at the same time.

Apart from the pocket the park and urban park, forest protected areas also play a vital role as urban green spaces in Sabah. Generally, forest protected areas are conserved by government agencies (Sabah Park and Sabah Forestry Department) to provide various ecosystem services to the surrounding environments, and also to the state, country, and world in long-term (Costanza et al., 2017; and Nair et al., 2018), unlike the urban parks and pocket parks that mainly focus on providing cultural services to urban dwellers in Sabah (Mojiol, 2018a). Still, the public is allowed to access and enjoy the ecosystem services supplied by the forest protected area (Sugau et al., 2017). Besides that, forest protected area is the largest type of urban green space, at the same time it is located outside of city border, when compared to the local urban parks and pocket parks (Lee et al., 2004; Gobilik & Limbawang, 2010; and Nair et al., 2018). In a nutshell, forest protected areas provide a wider range and higher quality of ecosystem services, but less accessible than urban parks and pocket parks by the urban dwellers. The quality and quantity of ecosystem services that can be provided at a given urban green space are somewhat connected inversely with its accessibility to the urban inhabitants of Sabah, Malaysia.

Wildlife Community at Urban Green Spaces of Sabah

Urban green spaces function as habitats to native, migratory and introduced wildlife species, and then the presences of rich wildlife diversity can attract visitations of urban dwellers to conduct recreation activities there as well (Wells et al., 2014; Endreny, 2018; and Nair et al., 2018). To date, a wide range of species of bird (143 species) and mammal (21 species) are observed at various urban green spaces in Kota Kinabalu, Tawau and Sandakan (Mojiol et al., 2008; Salfinas, 2008; Damit, 2009; Wells et al., 2014; Ten, 2018; and Lim & Mojiol, 2019), and then a list of wildlife species that are viewable at the local urban green spaces is tabulated as shown in Table 3 (refer to Appendix 1). According to the information provided in Table 3, urban inland forests are inhabited and visited by more avifauna species (95 species or 66.4%) than urban mangrove forest (79 species or 55.2%), and then 21.0% of the recorded species can be observed at both types of urban forests in Sabah (30 species). However, migratory avifauna species at the urban mangrove forests are more diverse (16 species or 66.7%) than those at the urban inland forests (12 species or 50.0%), and vice versa for the native species (Inland: 83 species or 69.7%; Mangrove: 63 species or 52.9%).

This shows that native species are more dependent on inland forests for survival while migratory species prefer over mangrove forests as their seasonal breeding sites, in the urban regions of Sabah.

Table 2. Descriptions, main functions, and examples for different types of urban green spaces in Sabah.

Urban Forest	Description	Main Function	Example	Management
Pocket Park	Urban green space that is smaller than 0.5 ha and often being established in the city center. It is highly accessible to urban inhabitants through walking.	Provide a safe zone for walking, jogging, resting, and other socializing activity with others.	Lintasan Deasoka Pocket Park (KK), Ujana Rimba Tropika Park (KK), Tun Abdul Razak Park (SDK), Muhibbah Public Park (TWU).	Kota Kinabalu City Hall; Sandakan Municipal Council; Tawau Municipal Council.
Urban Park	Urban green space that is larger than 0.5 ha and often established in the suburban area. It is more accessible to urban dwellers with transportation.	Allowing numerous people to do outdoor recreation activities together at the same time (e.g.: hiking and hill-climbing).	Tun Fuad Stephens Public Park (KK); Sandakan Memorial Park (SDK); & Tinagat Bukit Panchang (TWU).	Kota Kinabalu City Hall; Sandakan Municipal Council; Tawau Municipal Council.
Forest Protected Area	A total protected forest that is managed to provide the ecosystem services, at the same time open for public use. It is accessible only to the urban inhabitants with suitable transportation.	Provide supporting, regulating, cultural, and provisioning services towards the surrounding area.	Kawang Recreation Centre (KK); Sandakan Rainforest Park (SDK); & Tawau Hill Park (TWU).	Sabah Forestry Department; Sabah Park.

Note: KK = Kota Kinabalu; SDK = Sandakan, and; TWU = Tawau.

Sources: (Lee et al., 2004; Damit, 2009; Gobilik & Limbawang, 2010; Peschardt et al., 2012; Sugau et al., 2017; Endreny, 2018; Mojiol, 2018a; and Nair et al., 2018)

Nonetheless, the increase in the human population at urban regions has accelerated the shrinking of these urban green space (Chaudhry & Tewari, 2011), which can have threatened the survival of native avifauna species, and also resulted in migratory species avoid using urban green spaces as their seasonal breeding sites (Lim & Mojiol, 2019). In a long-term sense, the impact can be detrimental towards the threatened species that inhabit or visit the pocket parks and urban parks of Sabah, such as the Large Green Pigeon (*Treron capellei*), Straw-headed Bulbul (*Pycnonotus zeylanicus*), Greater Green Leaf Bird (*Chloropsis sonnerati*), Wallace's Hawk Eagle (*Nisaetus nanus*), Hook-billed Bulbul (*Setornis criniger*), Chinese Egret (*Egretta eulophotas*), Lesser Adjutant (*Leptoptilos javanicus*), and), if the given matter is not managed properly from now on (Mojiol et al., 2008; Damit, 2009; and Lim & Mojiol, 2019).

Moving on, the critically-endangered Sunda Pangolin (*Manis javanica*), as well as the vulnerable Rajah Spiny Rat (*Maxomys rajah*), Sambar Deer (*Cervus unicolor*) and Red Leaf Monkey (*Presbytis rubicunda*) are presented, yet hardly be encountered, at the urban areas in Sabah nowadays (Damit, 2009; and Wells et al., 2014). Although Sunda Pangolin and Sambar Deer can survive outside of pristine and secondary forests, still the increase in illegal poaching and hunting have accelerated the decreasing in their local population, especially at urban green spaces that are surrounded by high human populations or highly accessible by a human (Timmins et al., 2016; and Challender et al., 2019). Besides that, Red Leaf Monkey and Rajah Spiny Rat mainly depend on primary and undisturbed inland forests for survival, therefore illegal hunting and habitat loss have threatened their survival, not only at urban regions but also the entire Sabah and Borneo (Reudas, 2016; and Cheyne et al., 2020). Most of the native small mammal species mainly inhabit the inland forests that surround the urban landscapes of Kota Kinabalu, except for Müller's Sundamys (*Sundamys muelleri*) that can survive within the local residential areas in small population size (Wells et al., 2014). However, rapid urbanization has resulted in three exotic species being introduced and spread as urban pests across Kota Kinabalu. Wells et al. (2014) discovered that the Norway Rat (*Rattus norvegicus*) was presented only within the urban region, while House Rat (*Rattas rattus*) and House Shrew (*Suncus murinus*) exhibited the tendencies to invade and compete with indigenous small mammal species for the suburban forest habitats of Kota Kinabalu. The given findings highlight that the lacking in the proper management of urban green spaces have exposed the native mammal species to extinctions risks, and also accelerated the spreading of urban pests across the urban landscape of Sabah. If this issue is left unsolved from now on, these native wildlife species may ultimately be replaced entirely by exotic wildlife species in the coming future (Wells et al., 2014).

A majority of the past studies mentioned in previous contexts are conducted mainly on species composition and abundance, and also habitat preference of avian community at the urban green spaces of Kota Kinabalu (e.g.: Mojiol et al., 2008; and Lim & Mojiol, 2019), except Wells et al. (2014) that focused onto small mammal species at the local urban landscape. On the contrary, related studies are seldom being conducted at Sandakan and Tawau, as well as onto non-avian communities liked mammal, amphibian, and reptile. The native urban mammalian, reptilian and amphibian species are facing extinction risks as much as the urban avifauna species in Sabah, as well as throughout the world (Bishop et al., 2012; Wells et al., 2014; and Davis & Doherty, 2015). Nevertheless, their respective existing population sizes are difficult to be investigated in the urban areas of Sabah, therefore their respective existing composition, diversity, and abundance remain uncertain, in which there is a need to conduct further research on this matter in the future.

Plant Community at Urban Green Spaces of Sabah

The urban landscape of Sabah is inhabited by both indigenous and introduced plant species, and then the composition and diversity of urban plant species are varied between the pocket park, urban park, and forest protected area (Mojiol, 2001; Damit, 2009; Mojiol et al., 2016; Sugau et al., 2017; and Majuakim et al., 2018). Since each plant species has its uniqueness, in terms of physical and functional traits, thus the cultivation of different combinations of plant species can dictate the ecosystem service that is provided at a given urban green space (National Landscape Department, 2008). The presences of different types of urban forest habitats at Sabah are proof that a wide range of indigenous and exotic plant species remain viewable at the local urban landscapes for the time being In Kota Kinabalu, the urban mangrove plant species is mainly comprised of Bakau Minyak (*Rhizophora apiculata*) and Bakau Kurap (*R. mucronata*), whereas the Manila Palm (*Veitchia merillii*) and Angsana (*Pterocarpus indicus*) are distributed across the entire town area, same goes for the Mango (*Mangifera indica*) and Coconut (*Cocos nucifera*) trees in the local mixed horticulture areas (Mojiol & Bürger-Arndt, 2012; and Mojiol et al., 2016). Then, native dipterocarp and nepenthes species are conserved, along with other pristine and disturbed forest species, as part of the urban landscapes in Sandakan (Damit, 2009; and Sugau et al., 2017). Since the information on species diversity and composition of urban plant community of Tawau city remain scarce at this moment, thus there isn't much that can be discussed for the given city in this chapter.

Then again, certain native and exotic species are widely being cultivated in urban landscaping at Sabah, due to their capabilities to provide a wide variety of ecosystem services at a time, and also the low consumptions of time and cost for their long-term maintenances (Mojiol and Bürger-Arndt, 2012; and Mojiol, 2018b). These urban plant species include the Cemetery Tree (*Polyalthia longifolia*), Poui (*Tabebuia pallida*), Payung Indonesia (*Hura crepitans*), Semarak Api (*Delonix regia*), Hujan-hujan (*Samanea saman*), Pong-pong (*Cerbera* spp.), Cengkih (*Syzagium aromaticum*), Royal Palm (*Roystonea regia*), Aru (*Casuarina equsetifolia*), Tapak Kuda (*Bauhinia* spp.), Banyan (*Ficus microcarpa*), Tanjung (*Mimusop elengi*), Kayu Manis (*Cinnamomum iners*), Golden Shower (*Cassia fistula*), Batai Laut (*Peltophorum pterocarpum*), Talisai Ketapang (*Terminalia cattapa*), Pulai Bukit (*Alstonia angustiloba*), Bungur (*Lagerstroemia* spp.), Angsana (*Pterocarpus indicus*), and Coconut (*Cocos nucifera*). Moreover, urban tree stands were evaluated and verified as generally healthy, in the sense that they exhibited moderate growth performance, and then infection issues for the given tree stands were still under control (Mojiol, 2018b).

On the contrary, long-term maintenance of certain introduced species liked the Ear-leaf Acacia (*Acacia auriculiformis*) and Mangium (*A. mangium*) are proven to be difficult, to the extent that these two exotic species are determined as unsuitable for urban landscaping in Sabah (Mojiol, 2001). This is because these exotic plant species can constantly shed leaves and create leaf debris, which requires frequent maintenance effort to clean up the mass of leaf debris created by these two species throughout the day and year if they are introduced into the local urban landscapes (Mojiol & Bürger-Arndt, 2012). Besides that, these two species are known to invade and replace the native tree stands at various urban green spaces of Sabah, thanks to the lacking in natural predators that can control their population and distribution in the state (Mojiol & Bürger-Arndt, 2012; and Majuakim et al., 2018). The given two species are considered as urban invasive tree species to Sabah as well, due to their capabilities to threaten the survival of native plant species that inhabit the local urban green spaces. Olejniczak et al. (2018) highlighted that invasive species were more likely to spread and dominate the isolated urban green spaces when compared to the large natural forest landscape, although further study should be conducted to evaluate the extent of invasion of these two exotic species across Kota Kinabalu and other urban landscapes in Sabah. Then again, information on urban plant community in Sabah is mainly based on the past studies conducted at Kota Kinabalu, because this piece of information is more available for the urban landscape of Kota Kinabalu (e.g.: Sugawara et al., 2009; Mojiol & Bürger-Arndt, 2012; Mojiol et al., 2016; and Majuakim et al., 2018) than Sandakan (e.g.: Damit, 2009; Chin et al., 2014; and Sugau et al., 2017) and Tawau (e.g.: Gobilik & Limbawang, 2010). Henceforth, information on the urban tree stand condition at Kota Kinabalu is well-defined than those at Sandakan and Tawau at this moment, where further research studies are required to obtain a comprehensive understanding onto the urban plant community in urban green spaces of Sandakan and Tawau, as well as in Sabah as a whole in future.

Existing Conditions of the Natural Trails in Urban Green Space of Sabah

To date, a wide range of nature trails, both formal and informal trails, are established in different parts of the urban regions in Sabah. Nonetheless, only the natural trails at UMS Peak (Universiti Malaysia Sabah, Kota Kinabalu are evaluated by local experts' art this moment. Although Lim et al. (2019) only conducted preliminary assessment onto the condition of natural trails at the given site, still the results indicated that high visibility and aesthetic value (scenic beauty) can result in high usage of a natural trail by the public. The clear view of a wide variety of natural features (e.g.: flora, mountain, ocean, and island) can result in high usage by visitors, which can subsequently trigger the degradation to local biological, physical, and cultural aspects, especially at the interior segments of these nature trails. This is because the given trails aren't maintained frequently, and then there is lacking in the management on the carrying capacities of the given trails at a particular time and day. Since the interior segments of these trails have wider widths, steeper slopes, and without ground cover protection, hence more susceptible to ecological degradation liked soil erosion and soil compaction, when compared to their counterparts (Wimpey & Marion, 2011). Likewise, the increase in visiting frequency by the public can further worsen the recreational impact imposed onto the fragile interior segments of these trails if left alone and without proper maintenance and management in the long-term (Monz et al., 2010; and Ólafsdóttir & Runnström, 2013). This only covers the natural trails at one particular urban green space in Kota Kinabalu, and then there are more natural trails in urban green spaces of Sabah that are yet to be properly examined, in terms of the existing trail condition, by both local and international experts. In sum, future research is required to investigate the existing conditions of these trails, and then determine if maintenance and management efforts are required for the given trails.

Public Perceptions on the Urban Green Space in Sabah

Public perceptions of the functions and importance of urban green spaces are conducted by local experts, mainly at Kota Kinabalu of Sabah as well at this moment. The findings of past studies highlighted that a majority of urban inhabitants in Kota Kinabalu accept the fact that different urban green spaces provided different ecosystem services and functions, and also the importance of urban forestry in the management of local urban tree stands (Mojiol & Bürger-Arndt, 2012; Mojiol et al., 2017; and Mojiol, 2018a). The main functions of the local urban green spaces and tree stands are for climate and erosion controls, shading, aesthetic value, providing recreation and education opportunities, serving as wildlife habitat (flora and fauna), pollution reduction, and acting as a coastal wind barrier. On the other hand, villagers that live at the surrounding rural and suburban regions of Kota Kinabalu revealed that their livelihoods are dependent to the urban green spaces, especially for obtaining clean air and water, food sources, wooden and non-forest timber products (Mojiol et al., 2013; and Nair et al., 2018). Although they acknowledged the importance of conserving these urban green spaces, still many villagers revealed their concerns over their surrounding urban green spaces as the breeding sites for mosquitoes and dangerous wildlife (e.g.: snakes and wasps), waste disposal sites, and red zones for crime and drug turnover (Mojiol & Bürger-Arndt, 2012). Besides that, they realized that their actions in land clearing for domestic agricultural use, and also river pollution caused by forest clearing at upstream, mainly threatened their surrounding urban green spaces. Urban dwellers have different opinions with the villagers regarding this matter, which is mainly due to the difference in independence towards forest resources, although both parties accept the importance of conserving these urban green spaces to their well-being in the long-term.

Moving on, willingness to pay (WTP) is often used as a tool in quantifying the ecosystem service values provide perceived by the public for the urban green spaces in Sabah (e.g.: Hilmi & Mojiol, 2017; Mojiol et al., 2017; and Nair et al., 2018). Then, differences in gender and age, as well as distance traveled to an urban green space, can affect the ecosystem service values perceived by an individual, therefore can ultimately dictate the overall ecosystem service values perceived by the public. However, soil fertility, erosion control, provisioning of clean water, recreational opportunities, and aesthetic value, were regarded by the public to be vital (Mojiol et al., 2017; and Nair et al., 2018), and then the public was determined to willing to provide funding for the conservation of these biological assets, in which the present value of the urban tree stands at Kota Kinabalu city was approximately RM 1,086,373.87 at 2017 (Hilmi & Mojiol, 2017). On the contrary, both public perceptions and their willingness to pay for ecosystem services provided at the urban green spaces in Sandakan and Tawau remain unknown at this point, due to the lacking of past studies conducted at these two major urban areas of Sabah. Nonetheless, the presence of recreation opportunities at the urban green spaces further attract visitors to conduct recreational activities there, hence suitable to be promoted as tourism destinations for attracting both domestic and international tourists (Lee et al., 2004). In other words, there is a need to conduct further studies on the given matters at Sandakan and Tawau in the future.

Application of Geographical Information System in the Urban Forestry of Sabah

The application of geographical information system (GIS) can be both effective and efficient, in terms of time and cost consumptions, especially in assessing the existing condition and predicting the future condition of urban green space in Sabah. In recent years, Mojiol and Bürger-Arndt (2012) mapped out the existing conditions and functions of different urban green spaces at Kota Kinabalu through GIS and using various secondary data (e.g.: digitized Sabah Soil Map, high-resolution aerial photography and satellite images). Several parameters were taken into account during the categorization of urban green spaces, including landform characteristics, vegetation zones, agriculture capabilities, land use, and biotope classification. In the end, boundaries of different urban green spaces with different functions (e.g.: wildlife habitat, nature conservation, protection, recreation, and utility) were determined throughout the urban landscape of Kota Kinabalu. The given findings can be beneficial to the state government in monitoring urban green spaces that have contributed important ecosystem services and sensitive towards the anthropogenic disturbance.

This is the only urban-forestry-related study that applies GIS, despite that GIS is widely used in urban green space monitoring and management by researchers in recent years (e.g.: Weber & Puissant, 2003; Liang et al., 2008; and Kanniah, 2017). Spatial-temporal change in the size and type of urban green spaces across different periods can be modeled by using GIS, which can vividly show the outcome of a given management plan imposed onto the given urban green spaces. This type of research was already conducted by Kanniah (2017), in which the results pictured the loss of urban green space at Kuala Lumpur (Malaysia) within two years (2014 – 2016). Besides that, the future trend of urban green space at a particular city can also be predicted, based on the prediction model created from the comparison data between different periods (e.g.: Weber & Puissant, 2003). In fact, through the applications of both forest mensuration survey and GIS, spatial-temporal variation in the species composition and diversity of the urban plant community across different periods can be determined with high accuracy and precision as well (e.g.: Liang et al., 2008). This shows that various research opportunities remain available for local experts to expand their horizons through the application of GIS in urban forestry at Sabah in the future.

SOLUTIONS AND RECOMMENDATIONS

Rapid urbanization has become a potential threat to the survival of certain native wildlife species at the urban landscapes of Sabah (Chaudhry & Tewari, 2011). Habitat loss can result in certain native avifauna and mammal species to face extinction risks locally and globally, and also trigger the migratory avian species to select other locations as their seasonal breeding sites in the state (Mojiol et al., 2008; Wells et al., 2014; Reudas, 2016; and Cheyne et al., 2020). Moreover, illegal hunting and poaching activities can further threaten the survival of native species in urban green spaces (Timmins et al., 2016; and Challender et al., 2019). All of these continue to happen throughout Sabah because of the lacking of proper planning and management over the local urbanization, and also the difficulties in tracking the movements of illegal poachers and hunters throughout the urban regions of the state. When the diversity and abundance of native species are decreased, invasive species are more likely to take over and spread across the urban landscapes, such as the Norway Rat, House Shrew, and House Rat at Kota Kinabalu (Wells et al., 2014). This also applies to the outbreak of Ear-leaf Acacia and Mangium across the suburban regions of this city in recent years (Mojiol & Bürger-Arndt, 2012). Since these exotic species lack natural predators to control their population sizes, therefore they are more likely to thrive and dominate the urban landscapes of Sabah if no actions are taken right now. In sum, certain countermeasures are in need to turn the table around, where law enforcement is a good start to help to conserve and protecting sensitive urban green spaces from being converted into other land cover uses, and also control the illegal poaching and hunting activities at these urban green spaces. Then, the State Government of Sabah should cooperate with non-government agencies (NGOs), to conduct activities that allow both urban inhabitants and villagers to interact with one another. This can serve as an opportunity for both parties to share their collective views on the functions and importance of urban green spaces because their current mindsets on this matter are shaped by their surrounding living environments (Mojiol & Bürger-Arndt, 2012). When the urban inhabitants and villagers, as well as the local State Government and NGOs, can work together, it will be much easier to thin out the existing population sizes of these invasive tree and wildlife species, before these species have replaced the native species entirely and spread across the local urban landscapes.

Moving on, natural trails are highly susceptible to ecological degradation, especially at sensitive segments of the trails, when the visitor number and usage have exceeded the carrying capacities, plus maintenance works are not applied frequently to the given trails from time-to-time (Wimpey & Marion, 2013). In the long-term, not only that it can post potential hazards to visitors, but also the trails can be rendered inaccessible to visitors in the future (Lim et al., 2019). Therefore, the strengthening in management can be a solution to this matter, in which a limited number of allowed visitors and usage per day must be implemented for each trail, according to the carrying capacity of the given trail. Not only that it can minimize the recreational impact, at the same time reduce the time and cost needed to maintain the given trail from time-to-time (Monz et al., 2010; and Ólafsdóttir & Runnström, 2013). Besides that, sensitive urban green spaces have been successfully identified by using GIS (Mojiol & Bürger-Arndt, 2012). Thanks to the efforts of local experts, the approximated locations, sizes, boundaries, and conditions of these urban green spaces become known to both the State Government, NGOs, and researchers. Since these urban green spaces are critical to the well-being of urban dwellers and survival of wildlife, hence field demarcation can be done to ease the process of conserving and protecting these regions, and then field monitoring can be conducted from time-to-time, through joint efforts of various relevant parties. This can be another way of securing the survival of native wildlife species in the urban landscapes of Sabah in the long-term.

FUTURE RESEARCH DIRECTIONS

First of all, a majority of the previously mentioned past studies are conducted at Kota Kinabalu, in which information on the existing conditions of urban green spaces at Sandakan and Tawau remain scarce at this moment. Therefore, future research is in dire need to be conducted at the urban green spaces of these two major urban regions of Sabah, in terms of the species composition and ecology of urban flora and fauna, existing conditions of urban trails and tree stand, potentials and functions of urban green spaces, public perception towards urban green spaces, and application of GIS in urban green space management and monitoring. As for Kota Kinabalu, there are certain aspects of urban forestry that require further research in the future. Firstly, assessment of the species composition, diversity, and abundance of mammal, amphibian, and reptile are very limited, as the major concerns of past studies are mainly towards the local avifauna community (e.g.: Mojiol et al., 2008; and Lim & Mojiol, 2019). Since the local mammalian, reptilian and amphibian species are threatened by rapid urbanization (Bishop et al., 2012; Wells et al., 2014; and Davis & Doherty, 2015), hence it is urgent to conduct further research onto their existing species compositions, diversities and abundances across different urban green spaces in Kota Kinabalu, as well as at Sandakan and Tawau of Sabah, Malaysia.

Next, information on the urban plant community in Tawau is mainly for the forest protected area (Tawau Hill Park) that is located outside of this urban area (e.g.: Gobilik & Limbawang, 2010). As for Sandakan, plant species composition and diversity are determined mainly for forest protected areas and urban park (e.g.: Damit, 2009; Chin et al., 2014; and Sugau et al., 2017), unlike for Kota Kinabalu this information is readily available for every type of urban green space at this moment (e.g.: Sugawara et al., 2009; Mojiol & Bürger-Arndt, 2012; Majuakim et al., 2018; and Mojiol, 2018b). This highlights that further research on the urban plant community at Sandakan and Tawau is in dire need to be conducted by future researchers. Besides that, fragmented and isolated urban green spaces are more likely to be invaded by exotic species, plus have lower species diversity, when compared to large natural forest habitats (Olejniczak et al., 2018). Especially the Ear-leaf Acacia and Mangium, their distributions and abundances, as well as the severity of their invasions onto the survival of native plant species, are yet to be properly examined by researchers at this moment. In sum, this serves as a new research gap for the field of urban forestry in Sabah.

Moving on, most of the established natural trails at urban landscapes of Sabah, may it be an informal or formal trail, require detailed assessment onto their respective existing conditions and carrying capacities. These two pieces of information are crucial to the long-term management and conservation of urban trails (Monz et al., 2010; Wimpey & Marion, 2013; and Lim et al., 2019), and then further studies are required for most of the urban trails presented at urban landscapes of Sabah. On the other hand, public perception onto urban green spaces is well-assessed for Kota Kinabalu, in terms of their willingness to pay for the ecosystem services (e.g.: e.g.: Hilmi & Mojiol, 2017; Mojiol et al., 2017; and Nair et al., 2018), plus their perceptions on potentials, threats and functions (e.g.: Mojiol & Bürger-Arndt, 2012; Mojiol et al., 2017; and Mojiol, 2018a) of the given urban green spaces. Once again, similar studies are yet to be conducted at Sandakan and Tawau, indicating that this research gap is required to be fill-up as soon as possible now.

Last but not least, the application of GIS in urban green space monitoring and management is considered to be a new approach in the field of urban forestry at Sabah, which is started by Mojiol and Bürger-Arndt (2012). It allows the assessment of a large study area under different periods with minimal cost and time consumptions, and yet its application in the local urban green spaces remain minimal at this moment. Not only that it can provide critical information on locating and demarcating sensitive urban green spaces at the field (Mojiol & Bürger-Arndt, 2012), but also the spatial-temporal variations in urban plant composition and diversity (Liang et al., 2008), land cover type and coverage of urban green spaces (Weber & Puissant, 2003; and Kanniah, 2017) across different times periods. Prediction of the future trend of urban green spaces at Sabah can be done through the application of GIS (Weber & Puissant, 2003). In other words, it is essential to apply GIS in future studies, especially for urban green space monitoring and management at Kota Kinabalu, Sandakan, and Tawau.

CONCLUSION

Rapid urbanization has occurred to Sabah in recent years, which transforms Kota Kinabalu, Sandakan, and Tawau into major urban areas, and then pocket park, urban park, and forest protected area are established as the urban green spaces of these major cities. These urban green spaces are available for public access, and then they provide different ecosystem services to maintain the well-being of urban inhabitants and the survival of native urban wildlife. Presently, native plant species remain dominating the urban landscape of Sabah, although certain exotic species are cultivated to enhance the ecosystem services provided at a particular urban green space. Both the native and migratory bird species can be observed at certain urban green spaces of Sabah, whereas the native mammalian species is slowly being replaced by invasive rodent species liked the Norway Rat, House Rat, and House Shrew. Ear-leaf Acacia and Mangium are invading and spreading across the urban landscape of Kota Kinabalu, which makes them urban invasive species as well, along with the three mentioned rodent species. Moving on, both urban inhabitants and surrounding villagers of the major cities generally acknowledge the importance and function of urban green space towards their well-being in the long-term. Nonetheless, most of the past studies of urban forestry in Sabah are mainly conducted at Kota Kinabalu, and then information related to the urban flora and fauna community, existing conditions of urban trails and tree stands, public perceptions and satisfactions onto urban green spaces, and the application of GIS in urban green space monitoring and management, remain scarce for Sandakan and Tawau. Therefore, there is a need to conduct further research to fill up these research gaps for the urban forestry in Sabah. At the same time, further efforts are in dire need to prevent the invasive species from colonizing the local urban landscapes, plus conserving the urban trails and their native inhabitants from being facing extinctions locally and globally in the future. In sum, this chapter manages to achieve its objectives and covering all of the necessary topics.

ACKNOWLEDGMENT

The given research is conducted and completed without receiving a grant and financial support from any funding agency in the public, commercial, or not-for-profit sectors.

REFERENCES

Bishop, J. P., Angulo, A., Lewis, J. P., Moore, R.D., Rabb G. B., & Garcia Moreno, J. (2012). The Amphibian Extinction Crisis - What will it take to put the action into the Amphibian Conservation Action Plan? *S.A.P.I.EN.S, 5*(2), 97–111.

Challender, D., Willcox, D.H.A., Panjang, E., Lim, N., Nash, H., Heinrich, S. & Chong, J. (2019). *Manis javanica. The IUCN Red List of Threatened Species 2019: e.T12763A123584856.* doi:10.2305/IUCN.UK.2019-3.RLTS.T12763A123584856.en

Chaudhry, P., & Tewari, V. P. (2011). Urban forestry in India: Development and research scenario. *Interdisciplinary Environmental Review, 12*(1), 80–93. doi:10.1504/IER.2011.038881

Cheyne, S., Ehlers-Smith, D.A., Nijman, V. & Traeholt, C. (2020). *Presbytis rubicunda. The IUCN Red List of Threatened Species 2020: e.T18131A17953935.* doi:10.2305/IUCN.UK.2020-2.RLTS.T18131A17953935.en

Chin, L., Chung, A. Y. C., & Clarke, C. (2014). Interspecific variation in prey capture behavior by co-occurring nepenthes pitcher plants: Evidence for resource partitioning or sampling-scheme artifacts? *Plant Signaling & Behavior*, *9*(1), 1–16. doi:10.4161/psb.27930 PMID:24481246

Costanza, R., de Groot, R., Braat, L., Kubiszewski, I., Fioramonti, L., Sutton, P., Farber, S., & Grasso, M. (2017). Twenty years of ecosystem services: How far have we come and how far do we still need to go? *Ecosystem Services*, *28*, 1–16. doi:10.1016/j.ecoser.2017.09.008

Damit, A. (2009). *Sandakan Rainforest Park: A Scientifically & Historically Important Forest*. Forest Research Centre.

Davis, R. A., & Doherty, T. S. (2015). Rapid recovery of an urban remnant reptile community following summer wildfire. *PLoS One*, *10*(5), 1–15. doi:10.1371/journal.pone.0127925 PMID:25992802

Department of Statistics Malaysia. (2019). *Department of Statistics Malaysia, Official Portal*. https://www.dosm.gov.my/v1/

Endreny, T. A. (2018). Strategically growing the urban forest will improve our world. *Nature Communications*, *9*(1), 10–12. doi:10.103841467-018-03622-0 PMID:29563541

Gobilik, J., & Limbawang, S. (2010). Notes on species composition and ornamental gingers in Tawau Hills Park, Sabah. *Journal of Tropical Biology & Conservation*, *7*(1), 31–48.

Hilmi, M. A., & Andy, R. M. (2017). Contingent Valuation on Urban Trees in City of Kota Kinabalu, Sabah. *Transactions on Science and Technology*, *4*(2), 166–173.

Kanniah, K. D. (2017). Quantifying green cover change for sustainable urban planning: A case of Kuala Lumpur, Malaysia. *MIT-UTM Malaysia Sustainable Cities Program* (Working Paper Series 1). Universiti Teknologi Malaysia.

Konijnendijk, C. C., Annerstedt, M., Nielsen, A. B., & Maruthaveeran, S. (2013). *Benefits of Urban Parks – A systematic review*. World Urban Parks.

Lee, Y. F., Ligunjang, J., & Yong, S. C. (2004). *Urban forestry and its relevance to tourism development in Sabah* [Paper presentation]. The Asia Europe Meeting (ASEM) *Symposium on Urban Forestry*, Suzhou & Beijing, China.

Liang, Y. Q., Li, J. W., Lee, J., & Valimaki, S. K. (2008). Impact of urbanization on plant diversity: A case study in built-up areas of Beijing. *Forestry Studies in China*, *10*(3), 179–188. doi:10.100711632-008-0036-4

Lim, W. S., Nisa, S., & Mojiol, A. R. (2019). Rapid observational assessment on urban forest trails established at UMS Peak of Universiti Malaysia Sabah. *Tropical Forest Journal*, *14*(1), 18–31.

Lim, W. S., & Mojiol, A. R. (2019). A Preliminary Assessment on Avian Community in the Urban Forest of Universiti Malaysia Sabah. *Transactions on Science and Technology*, *6*(3), 292–297.

Majuakim, L., Lee, A. M. L., & Gisil, J. (2018). An Inventory of Flora in Urban Forests of Universiti Malaysia Sabah Campus, Sabah, Malaysia. *Journal of Tropical Biology & Conservation*, *15*, 173–188.

Mojiol, A. R. (2001). *Pokok-Pokok Hiasan Bandar*. Penerbit Universiti Malaysia Sabah.

Mojiol, A. R. (2018a). Public awareness on the importance of urban forest parks in Kota Kinabalu City, Sabah. *Borneo Science*, *39*(1), 39–47.

Mojiol, A. R. (2018b). Tree Health Assessment for Roadside Tree in Kota Kinabalu City Centre, Sabah. *Borneo Science*, *39*(2), 104–113.

Mojiol, A. R., & Bürger-Arndt, R. (2012). Urban Green Areas Management in Kota Kinabalu, Sabah-Malaysia: Concept and Sustainability. Lambert Academic Publishing.

Mojiol, A. R., Hassan, A., Maluda, J., & Immit, S. (2008). Rapid assessment on the abundance of bird species utilizing the Kota Kinabalu Wetland Centre mangroves. *Journal of Tropical Biology & Conservation*, *4*(1), 99–107.

Mojiol, A. R., Lo, M. W., Lintangah, W., & Amat, R. (2016). *A Guide to the Plants of Kota Kinabalu Wetlands*. Sabah Wetland Conservation Society.

Mojiol, A. R., Zamri, Z., Hilmi, M. A., & Gitom, M. (2017). Visitors' Willingness To Pay (WTP) at Kionsom Recreation Centre, Inanam, Kota Kinabalu, Sabah. *Transactions on Science and Technology*, *4*(42), 174–182.

Monz, C. A., Goonan, K. A., Carr, C., Wimpey, J., Marion, J. L., & Manning, R. E. (2010). Assessment and Monitoring of Recreation Impacts and Resource Conditions on Mountain Summits: Examples from the Northern Forest, USA. *Mountain Research and Development*, *30*(4), 332–343. doi:10.1659/MRD-JOURNAL-D-09-00078.1

Nair, G. V. G., Mojiol, A. R., Kamlun, K. U., & Lintangah, W. (2018). The Contribution of forest ecosystem services toward the local community living vicinity to the forest protected area : The case of Kawang Forest Reserve, Sabah, Malaysia. *Transactions on Science and Technology*, *5*(1), 25–30.

National Landscape Department. (2008). *National Landscape Guideline* (2nd ed.). National Landscape Department.

Ólafsdóttir, R., & Runnström, M. C. (2013). Assessing hiking trails condition in two popular tourist destinations in the Icelandic highlands. *Journal of Outdoor Recreation and Tourism*, *3–4*, 57–67. doi:10.1016/j.jort.2013.09.004

Olejniczak, M. J., Spiering, D. J., Potts, D. L., & Warren, R. J. (2018). Urban forests form isolated archipelagos. *Journal of Urban Economics*, *4*(1), 1–8.

Peschardt, K. K., Schipperijn, J., & Stigsdotter, U. K. (2012). Use of small public urban green spaces (SPUGS). *Urban Forestry & Urban Greening*, *11*(3), 235–244. doi:10.1016/j.ufug.2012.04.002

Ruedas, L. (2016). *Maxomys rajah. The IUCN Red List of Threatened Species 2016: e.T12904A22455724*. doi:10.2305/IUCN.UK.2016-2.RLTS.T12904A22455724.en

Salfinas, N. (2008). *The Study of Bird Species Composition in Forest Plantation and Domestic Forest Areas at Kinarut, Papar, Sabah* [Unpublished Bachelor Dissertation]. Universiti Malaysia Sabah, Sabah, Malaysia.

Sugau, J. B., Pereira, J. T., & Damit, A. (2017). A Guide to the Trees in Heritage Amenity Forest Reserve (HQ), Sandakan: A Revised and Expanded Edition. Sabah Forestry Department.

Sugawara, Sudin, Said, Suleiman,Gisil, & Sundaling. (2009). *Buku Panduan Hutan Bukit UMS: Tumbuh-tumbuhan*. Pernebit Universiti Malaysia Sabah.

Ten, W. L. (2018). *Distribution of bird species and their role as ecotourism attraction in Tawau Hill Park, Sabah* [Unpublished Bachelor Dissertation]. Universiti Malaysia Sabah, Sabah, Malaysia.

Timmins, R., Kawanishi, K., Giman, B, Lynam, A., Chan, B., Steinmetz, R., Sagar Baral, H. & Samba Kumar, N. (2015). *Rusa unicolor. The IUCN Red List of Threatened Species 2015: e.T41790A85628124.* doi:10.2305/IUCN.UK.2015-2.RLTS.T41790A22156247.en

Weber, C., & Puissant, A. (2003). Urbanization pressure and modeling of urban growth: Example of the Tunis Metropolitan Area. *Remote Sensing of Environment*, *86*(3), 341–352. doi:10.1016/S0034-4257(03)00077-4

Wells, K., Lakim, M. B., & O'Hara, R. B. (2014). Shifts from native to invasive small mammals across gradients from tropical forest to urban habitat in Borneo. *Biodiversity and Conservation*, *23*(9), 2289–2303. doi:10.100710531-014-0723-5

Wimpey, J., & Marion, J. L. (2011). *Formal and Informal Trail Monitoring Protocols and Baseline Conditions: Great Falls Park and Potomac Gorge* (Final Report). Virginia Tech, College of Natural Resources & Environmental.

ADDITIONAL READING

Lim, W. S., Syazwani Nisa, & Mojiol, A. R. (2019). Rapid observational assessment on urban forest trails established at UMS Peak of Universiti Malaysia Sabah. *Tropical Forest Journal*, *14*(1), 18–31.

Lim, W. S., & Mojiol, A. R. (2019). A Preliminary Assessment on Avian Community in the Urban Forest of Universiti Malaysia Sabah. *Transactions on Science and Technology*, *6*(3), 292–297.

Mojiol, A. R. (2001). *Pokok-Pokok Hiasan Bandar*. Penerbit Universiti Malaysia Sabah.

Mojiol, A. R. (2018a). Public awareness on the importance of urban forest parks in Kota Kinabalu City, Sabah. *Borneo Science*, *39*(1), 39–47.

Mojiol, A. R. (2018b). Tree Health Assessment for Roadside Tree in Kota Kinabalu City Centre, Sabah. *Borneo Science*, *39*(2), 104–113.

Mojiol, A. R., & Bürger-Arndt, R. (2012). Urban Green Areas Management in Kota Kinabalu, Sabah-Malaysia: Concept and Sustainability. Lambert Academic Publishing.

Mojiol, A. R., Hassan, A., Maluda, J., & Immit, S. (2008). Rapid assessment on the abundance of bird species utilizing the Kota Kinabalu Wetland Centre mangroves. *Journal of Tropical Biology & Conservation*, *4*(1), 99–107.

Mojiol, A. R., Lo, M. W., Lintangah, W., & Amat, R. (2016). *A Guide to the Plants of Kota Kinabalu Wetlands*. Sabah Wetland Conservation Society.

Mojiol, A. R., Zamri, Z., Hilmi, M. A., & Gitom, M. (2017). Visitors' Willingness to Pay (WTP) at Kionsom Recreation Centre, Inanam, Kota Kinabalu, Sabah. *Transactions on Science and Technology*, *4*(42), 174–182.

Nair, G. V. G., Mojiol, A. R., Kamlun, K. U., & Lintangah, W. (2018). The Contribution of forest ecosystem services toward the local community living vicinity to the forest protected area: The case of Kawang Forest Reserve, Sabah, Malaysia. *Transactions on Science and Technology*, *5*(1), 25–30.

KEY TERMS AND DEFINITIONS

Ecosystem Service: A direct and indirect contribution of the ecosystem towards the well-being of human beings.

Exotic Species: A species that is known to be non-native to a specific location, region, country, or continent. An exotic species is regarded as invasive and introduced species as well.

Forest Protected Area: A total protected forest that is managed mainly to provide ecosystem services, yet at the same time open for public use. A forest protected area is accessible only to urban inhabitants with transportation.

Formal Trail: An urban trail that is designed by the local management authority. A formal trail is under management and equipped with basic facilities and infrastructures.

Informal Trail: An urban trail that is established by visitors. An informal trail is mostly poorly designed and maintained by visitors, thus lacking in basic facilities and infrastructures.

Native Species: A species that is known to be indigenous to a specific location, region, country, or continent. A native species is also known as an indigenous species.

Pocket Park: An urban green space that is smaller than 0.5 ha and established at the city center with limited free space. A pocket park is highly accessible to urban inhabitants through walking.

Urban Green Space: A greenery urban landscape that is established for providing non-priced benefits to the urban inhabitants and environments.

Urban Park: An urban green space that is larger than 0.5 ha and established outside of the city center. An urban park is still located within the city border, and then it is more accessible to urban inhabitants with transportation.

Urban Pest: An invasive species that has the tendency to spread and cause damage towards the economic, healthy, and living environment of human society in an urban region.

APPENDIX 1

Table 3. List of wildlife species that are viewable at different urban green spaces in Sabah

Family	Species	Common Name	Habitat
AVES			
Accipitridae	*Accipiter trivirgatus*	Crested Goshawk	Forest
	Haliaeetus leucogastor	White-bellied Sea Eagle	Forest, Mangrove
	Haliastur indus	Brahminy Kite	Forest, Mangrove
	Nisaetus nanus	Wallace's Hawk Eagle	Forest
	Pandion haliaetus	Osprey	Mangrove
	Spilornis cheela	Crested Serpent Eagle	Forest, Mangrove
Bucerotidae	*Buceros rhinoceros*	Rhinoceros Hornbill	Forest
	Rhyticeros undulatus	Wreathed hornbill	Forest
Apodidae	*Aerodramus fuciphagus*	Edible-Nest Swiftlet	Forest
	Aerodramus maximus	Black Nest Swiftlet	Forest
	Apus affinis	**Little Swift**[*a]	Mangrove
	Apus nipalensis	House Swift	Forest
	Apus unicolor	**Plain Swift**[*a]	Forest
	Collocalia esculenta	Glossy Swiftlet	Forest, Mangrove
Caprimulgidae	*Caprimulgus macrurus*	Large-tailed Nightjar	Mangrove
Hemiprocnidae	*Hemiprocne longipennis*	Grey-rumped Treeswift	Forest
Charadriidae	***Pluvialis fulva***	**Pacific Golden Plover**[*a]	Mangrove
Recurvirostridae	***Himantopus himantopus***	**Black-winged Stilt**[*a]	Mangrove
Scolopacidae	***Actitis hypoleucos***	**Common Sandpiper**[*a]	Mangrove
	Gallinago megala	**Swinhoe's Snipe**[*a]	Mangrove
	Tringa brevipes	**Grey-tailed Tattle**[*a] **r**	Mangrove
	Tringa glareola	**Wood Sandpiper**[*a]	Mangrove
	Tringa nebularia	**Common Greenshank**[*a]	Mangrove
	Tringa stagnatilis	**Marsh Sandpiper**[*a]	Mangrove
	Tringa totanus	**Common Redshank**[*a]	Mangrove
Ciconiidae	*Leptoptilos javanicus*	Lesser Adjutant	Mangrove
Columbidae	*Caloenas nicobarica*	Nicobar Pigeon	Forest
	Chalcophaps indica	Grey-capped Emerald Dove	Forest, Mangrove
	Columba livia	Rock Dove	Forest, Mangrove
	Ducula aenea	Green Imperial-pigeon	Mangrove
	Geopelia striata	Zebra Dove	Forest, Mangrove
	Spilopelia chinensis	Eastern Spotted Dove	Mangrove
	Treron capellei	Large Green Pigeon	Forest
	Treron olax	Little Green-pigeon	Mangrove
	Treron vernans	Pink-necked Green-pigeon	Mangrove
Rallidae	*Amaurornis phoenicurus*	White-breasted Waterhen	Mangrove
	Gallinula chloropus	Common Moorhen	Mangrove
	Lewinia striata	Slaty-breasted Rail	Mangrove
Alcediniidae	*Alcedo atthis*	Eurasian Kingfisher	Forest, Mangrove
	Alcedo meninting	Blue-earded Kingfisher	Mangrove
	Ceyx erithaca	Oriental Dwarf-kingfisher	Forest
	Halycon pileata	Black-capped Kingfisher	Forest, Mangrove
	Pelargopsis capensis	Stork-billed Kingfisher	Mangrove
	Todiramphus chloris	Collared Kingfisher	Forest, Mangrove
Coraciidae	*Eurystomus orientalis*	Oriental Dollarbird	Forest
Meropidae	*Merops viridis*	Blue-throated Bee-eater	Forest, Mangrove
Cuculidae	*Cacomantis merulinus*	Plaintive Cuckoo	Mangrove
	Centropus bengalensis	Lesser Coucal	Mangrove
	Centropus rectunguis	Short-toead Coucal	Forest
	Centropus sinensis	Greater Coucal	Mangrove
	Phaenicophaeus curvirostris	Chestnut Breasted Malkoha	Forest

continued on following page

Table 3. Continued

Family	Species	Common Name	Habitat
	Zancostomus javanicus	Red-billed Malkoha	Forest
Acanthizidae	*Gerygone sulphurea*	Golden-bellied Gerygone	Forest
Acrocephalidae	***Acrocephalus schoenobaenus***	**Sedge Warbler**[*a]	Forest
Aegithinidae	*Aegithina tiphia*	Common Iora	Forest, Mangrove
	Aegithina viridissima	Green Iora	Mangrove
Artamidae	*Artamus leucoryn*	White-breasted Woodswallow	Forest, Mangrove
Calyptomenidae	*Calyptomena viridis*	Green Broadbill	Forest
	Calyptomena whiteheadi	Whitehead's Broadbill	Forest
Campephagidae	*Coracina fimbriata*	Lesser Cuckooshrike	Forest
	Lalage nigra	Pied Triller	Forest, Mangrove
Chloropseidae	*Chloropsis cyanopogon*	Lesser Green Leafbird	Forest
	Chloropsis moluccensis	Blue-winged Leafbird	Forest
	Chloropsis sonnerati	Greater Green Leafbird	Mangrove
Cisticolidae	*Orthotomus ruficeps*	Ashy Tailorbird	Forest, Mangrove
	Orthotomus sericeus	Rufous-tailed Tailorbird	Mangrove
	Prinia flaviventris	Yellow-bellied Prinia	Forest, Mangrove
Corvidae	*Corvus macrorhynchos*	Large-billed Crow	Forest
Dicaeidae	*Dicaeum trigonostigma*	Orange-bellied Flowepecker	Forest
	Dicaeum trochileum	Scarlet-headed Flowerpecker	Forest
	Prionochilus percussus	Crimson-breasted Flowerpecker	Mangrove
	Prionochilus xanthopygius	Yellow-rumped Flowerpecker	Forest
Emberizidae	***Emberiza pusilla***	**Little Bunting**[*a]	Forest
Estrildidae	*Lonchura atricapilla*	Chestnut Munia	Forest
	Lonchura fuscans	Dusky Munia	Forest, Mangrove
	Lonchura malacca	**Black-headed Munia**[*a]	Forest, Mangrove
Eurylaimidae	*Cymbirhynchus macrorhynchos*	Black-and-Red Broadbill	Forest
	Eurylaimus ochromalus	Black-and-yellow Broadbill	Forest
Hirundinidae	***Hirundo rustica***	**Barn Swallow**[*a]	Forest, Mangrove
	Hirundo tahitica	**Pacific Swallow**[*a]	Forest, Mangrove
Laniidae	***Lanius cristatus***	**Brown Shrike**[*a]	Forest, Mangrove
Locustellidae	*Megalurus palustris*	Striated Grassbird	Mangrove
Motacillidae	***Anthus richardii***	**Richard's Pipit**[*a]	Forest
	Anthus rufulus	Paddyfield Pipit	Forest, Mangrove
Muscicapidae	*Copsychus saularis*	Oriental Magpie-Robin	Forest, Mangrove
	Cyornis caerulatus	Large-billed Blue-flycatcher	Forest
	Cyornis superbus	Bornean Blue-flycatcher	Forest
	Cyornis turcocus	Malaysian Blue Flycatcher	Forest
	Ficedula westermanni	Little Pied Flycatcher	Forest
	Kittacincla malabarica	White-rumped Shama	Forest
	Larvivora cyane	**Siberian Blue Robin**[*a]	Forest
	Muscicapa dauurica	**Asian Brown Flycatcher**[*a]	Forest
	Vauriella gularis	Eye-browed Jungle-flycatcher	Forest
Nectariniidae	*Aethopyga siparaja*	Crimson Sunbird	Forest
	Aethopyga temminckii	Temminck's Sunbird	Forest
	Anthreptes malacensis	Brown-Throated Sunbird	Forest, Mangrove
	Arachnothera juliae	Whitehead's Spiderhunter	Forest
	Arachnothera longirostra	Little Spiderhunter	Forest, Mangrove
	Cinnyris jugularis	Olive-backed Sunbird	Forest, Mangrove
	Hypogramma hypogrammicum	Purple-napped Spiderhunter	Mangrove
Passeridae	*Passer domesticus*	House Sparrow	Forest
	Passer montanus	Eurasian Tree Sparrow	Forest, Mangrove
Pellorneidae	*Malacocincla perspicillata*	Black-browned Babbler	Forest
	Trichastoma bicolor	Ferruginous Babbler	Mangrove
Phylloscopidae	***Phylloscopus borealis***	**Arctic Warbler**[*a]	Forest
Pycnonotidae	*Ixos malaccensis*	Streaked Bulbul	Forest
	Pycnonotus brunneus	Red-eyed Bulbul	Mangrove

continued on following page

Table 3. Continued

Family	Species	Common Name	Habitat
	Pycnonotus goiavier	Yellow-vented Bulbul	Forest, Mangrove
	Pycnonotus plumosus	Olive-winged Bulbul	Mangrove
	Pycnonotus simplex	Cream-vented Bulbul	Forest
	Pycnonotus zeylanicus	Straw-headed Bulbul	Mangrove
	Setornis criniger	Hook-billed Bulbul	Forest
Rhipiduridae	*Rhipidura javanica*	Pied Fantail	Forest Mangrove
Sittidae	*Sitta frontalis*	Velvet-fronted Nuthatch	Forest
Sturnidae	*Aplonis payanensis*	Asian Glossy Starling	Forest, Mangrove
	Gracula religiosa	Common Hill Myna	Forest
Timaliidae	*Mixornis bornensis*	Bold-striped Tit Babbler	Forest
	Stachyris maculata	Chestnut-rumped Babbler	Forest
	Stachyris poliocephala	Grey-headed Bulbul	Forest
Vangidae	*Hemipus picatus*	Bar-winged Flycatcher-shrike	Forest
Zosteropidae	*Zosterops atricapilla*	Black-capped White-eye	Forest
Ardeidae	*Ardea alba*	Great White Egret	Mangrove
	Ardea cinerea	Dusky-grey Heron	Mangrove
	Ardea intermedia	Intermediate Egret	Mangrove
	Ardea purpurea	Purple Heron	Mangrove
	Bubulcus ibis	**Cattle Egret**[*a]	Forest
	Butorides striata	Green-backed Heron	Mangrove
	Egretta eulophotas	**Chinese Egret**[*a]	Mangrove
	Egretta garzetta	Little Egret	Mangrove
	Egretta sacra	Pacific Reef-egret	Mangrove
	Gorsachius melanolophus	**Malay Night-heron**[*a]	Mangrove
	Ixobrychus cinnamomeus	Cinnamon Bittern	Mangrove
	Ixobrychus sinensis	Yellow Bittern	Mangrove
	Nycticorax caledonicus	Rufous Night-heron	Mangrove
	Nycticorax nycticorax	Black-crowned Night-heron	Mangrove
Megalaimidae	*Calorhamphus fuliginosus*	Bornean Brown Barbet	Forest
	Psilopogon haemacephalus	Coppersmith Barbet	Forest
	Psilopogon rafflesii	Red-crowned Barbet	Forest
Picidae	*Meiglyptes grammithorax*	Buff-rumped Woodpecker	Forest
	Picoides moluccensis	Brown-capped Woodpecker	Forest, Mangrove
	Hemicircus sordidus	Grey-and-buff Woodpecker	Forest
Anhingidae	*Anhinga melanogester*	Oriental Darter	Forest
Trogonidae	*Harpactes duvaucelii*	Scarlet-rumped Trogon	Forest
MAMMALIA			
Cervidae	*Muntiacus muntjak*	Southern Red Muntjac	Forest
	Rusa unicolor	Sambar Deer	Forest
Tragulidae	*Tragulus kanchil*	Lesser Mousedeer	Forest
	Tragulus napu	Greater Mousedeer	Forest
Viverridae	*Paradoxurus hermaphroditus*	Common Palm Civet	Forest
Soricidae	***Suncus murinus***	**House Shrew**[*b]	Forest
Manidae	*Manis javanica*	Sunda Pangolin	Forest
Cercopithecidae	*Presbytis rubicunda*	Red Leaf Monkey	Forest
Muridae	*Leopoldamys sabanus*	Long-tailed Giant Rat	Forest
	Maxomys rajah	Rajah Sundaic Maxomys	Forest
	Maxomys surifer	Indomalayan Maxomys	Forest
	Maxomys whiteheadi	Whitehead's Sundaic Maxomys	Forest
	Niviventer cremoriventer	Sundaic Arboreal Niviventer	Forest
	Rattus norvegicus	**Norway Rat**[*b]	Urban
	Rattus rattus	**House Rat**[*b]	Urban
	Sundamys muelleri	Müller's Sundamys	Forest
Sciuridae	*Callosciurus notatus*	Plantain Squirrel	Forest
	Callosciurus prevostii	Prevost's Squirrel	Forest
	Ratufa affinis	Pale Giant Squirrel	Forest
	Sundasciurus lowii	Low's Squirrel	Forest
	Tupaia tana	Large Treeshrew	Forest

Note: [*a] = Migratory avifauna species to Sabah; [*b] = Invasive mammal species from foreign countries in Sabah.
Sources: (Mojiol et al., 2008; Damit, 2009; Wells et al., 2014; Ten, 2018; and Lim & Mojiol, 2019).

APPENDIX 2

Table 4. List of urban tree species that are frequently grown and planted in the urban landscapes of Sabah

Family	Scientific name	Common Name
Annonaceae	*Polyalthia longifolia**	Cemetery tree
Apocynaceae	*Cerbera manghas*	Pong-pong
Apocynaceae	*Cerbera odollam*	Pong-pong
Bignoniaceae	*Tabebuia pallida**	Pink trumpet tree
Bignoniaceae	*Tabebuia rosea**	Poui
Burseraceae	*Canarium dacryodes*	Kodondong
Casuarinaceae	*Casuarina equisetifolia*	Aru
Combretaceae	*Terminalia catappa*	Talisai Ketapang
Dilleniaceae	*Dillenia suffruticosa*	Simpor
Elaeocarpaceae	*Muntingia calabura*	Kerukup siam
Euphorbiaceae	*Hura creptans**	Payung indonesia
Euphorbiaceae	*Macaranga sp*	Mahang
Fabaceae	*Erythrina crista-galli**	Coral tree
Fabaceae	*Pithecellobium dulce**	Manila tamarind
Guttiferae	*Callophylum innophylum*	Penaga laut
Leguminosae	*Acacia auriculiformis**	Akasia kuning
Leguminosae	*Acacia mangium**	Mangium
Leguminosae	*Andira surinamensis**	Kedondong
Leguminosae	*Bauhinia blakeanna*	Tapak kuda
Leguminosae	*Bauhinia purpurea*	Tapak kuda
Leguminosae	*Cassia biflora**	Twin flowered cassia
Leguminosae	*Cassia fistula*	Golden shower
Leguminosae	*Cassia siamea**	Kassod tree
Leguminosae	*Cassia spectabilis*	Sena
Leguminosae	*Delonix regia**	Semarak api
Leguminosae	*Leucaena leucocephala**	Ipil-ipil
Leguminosae	*Peltophorum pterocarpum*	Batai laut
Leguminosae	*Pongamia pinnata*	Marabahai
Leguminosae	*Pterocarpus indicus*	Angsana
Leguminosae	*Samanea saman**	Hujan hujan
Lythraceae	*Lagerstroemia speciosa*	Bungur
Malvaceae	*Hibiscus tiliaceus*	Baru
Malvaceae	*Thespesia populnea*	Baru laut
Meliaceae	*Azadirachta sp*	Limpaga
Meliaceae	*Xylocarpus granatum*	Nyirih
Moraceae	*Ficus benjamina*	Beringin
Moraceae	*Ficus elastica**	Indian rubber
Moraceae	*Ficus speciosa*	Ara
Musaceae	*Musa speciosa*	Pisang
Myrtaceae	*Eugenia grandis*	Kelat jambu
Palmae	*Cocos nucifera*	Kelapa
Palmae	*Cryfostachys lakka*	Pinang raja
Palmae	*Nypa fruticans*	Nipah
Palmae	*Ptychosperma macarthurii*	Macartur palm
Palmae	*Roystonea regia*	Royal palm
Palmae	*Veitchia merrillii*	Christmas palm
Rhizophoraceae	*Bruguiera cylindrica*	Beus
Rhizophoraceae	*Bruguiera parviflora*	Lenggadai
Rhizophoraceae	*Rhizophora apiculata*	Bakau minyak
Rhizophoraceae	*Rhizophora mucronata*	Bakau kurap
Sapotaceae	*Mimusops elengi*	Tanjong
Ulamaceae	*Trema virgata*	Randangong
Verbenaceae	*Avicennia sp*	Api-api
Verbenaceae	*Tectona grandis**	Jati

Note: Exotic tree species marked with *
Sources: (Mojiol and Bürger-Arndt, 2012; and Mojiol, 2018)

Chapter 14
Socio-Economic Aspects of Mangrove Degradation in an Urban Setting:
A Case Study of Muanivatu Settlement, Suva, Fiji

Eberhard Heinrich Weber
The University of the South Pacific, Fiji

ABSTRACT

In Pacific Small Island Developing States (PSIDS), the degradation of mangroves advances at a fast pace, especially in urban places. Rural to urban migration let urban settlements grow tremendously in the past 60 years. People built many informal settlements straight into mangrove forests. Health implications are severe, but settlements in mangrove forests provide protection against eviction. The case study provides insight into people's lives, perception and actions in a degraded mangrove forest in the eastern part of Suva, the capital of Fiji. The major question is why people are exposing themselves to serious environmental health hazards. Based on recent changes, the chapter also looks at development efforts that threaten residents of informal settlement to get evicted from the locations they right now reside. Investigations concentrate on people's actions in space, particularly, the role degraded urban mangroves play in their decision to reside in a particular place. A major explanation is that people want to reduce risk and enhance security: security from eviction.

URBANIZATION AND THE DESTRUCTION OF MANGROVE FORESTS

Mangrove forests play a crucial role in coastal ecosystems and coastal protection. They provide multiple benefits to people such as filtering and moistening the air, regulating micro-climate, acting as buffer zones against flooding, allowing rivers to spread, protecting against sea surges and tsunamis, providing food, fire and construction timber, and traditional medicines to poorer sections of societies (Wang, Jia,

DOI: 10.4018/978-1-7998-4372-6.ch014

Yin, & Tian, 2019). These functions and services also apply to urban mangrove forests. Still, for many decades, urban planners and politicians have ignored the importance of mangrove forests. Mangrove destruction often happened unnoticed and unopposed. In the question of analyzing the opportunity cost, these resources were paid less importance than economically valuable agriculture, aquaculture, industrial and urban development. Thus mangroves were destroyed and degraded for other economic conversions.

By the beginning of the 21st century, an estimated one third of global mangrove forests had been lost within the past 50 years (Alogni, 2002; Wang et al., 2019). In 2007, scientists feared that within 100 years mangrove deforestation and destruction would be so extensive that most of their functions disappeared (Friess et al., 2019). Scientists estimate that annually 1-2% of global mangroves did disappear and the deforestation rate is higher than for tropical rainforests (Rodríguez, 2018). Confirmed and up-to-date figures on the global extension of mangrove forests are difficult to get. For the beginning of the third millennium Spalding, Kainuma, & Collins (2010) put the global size of mangrove forests at "just over 150,000 km^2". Fries et al. (2019) gave a figure of 137,600 km^2 for the year 2010. The latest figures are available for 2015 from the FAO database on Global Forest Resources Assessments (2015). According to this assessment, there were 117,000 km^2 of mangrove forests worldwide.

In Asia and the Pacific, mangrove forests have been particularly exposed to human activities. The region, which has almost half of global mangrove forests, loses them much faster than any other place in the world (DasGupta & Shaw, 2017). In some countries, the decline in mangrove forest cover has been spectacular. Within eight years (1992-2000), the mangrove cover along the Pakistan coastline has decreased from 122,000 ha to 73,000 ha (Rahman & Shaw, 2017). In Myanmar mangrove cover shrank by 52% between 1996 and 2007 (De Alban, Jamaludin, de Wen, Than, & Webb, 2020). It was possible to mitigate severe dangers of degradation in the Sundarbans of West Bengal in India, and Bangladesh through community-based Joint Forest Management Programs. Sundarbans of West Bengal and Bangladesh comprise the world's largest contiguous mangrove forests. High population densities and people's poverty continue to be a major threat to these forests (DasGupta & Shaw, 2017). Also, in Africa and Latin America, vast areas of mangrove forests disappeared in the past few decades. This process continues unabated.

Among the many causes of mangrove degradation, urban development does not figure on top of lists (see below). Still, it has contributed much to the disappearance of mangrove forests in locations where a high density of people live. But, the forests compromise the protection of settlements against hazards that come from the sea, such as tsunamis (Kathiresan & Rajendran, 2005) and tropical cyclones (Das & Vincent, 2009).

In many urban areas, mangrove forests today exist only as tiny, highly fragmented patches. Remaining mangroves are often heavily polluted from liquid effluents of industrial complexes and untreated sewerage. Solid waste, in particular ever-increasing plastic waste, let mangrove forests appear like rubbish dumps rather than recreational places they actually could be.

Bunt (1992) highlighted that in the early 1990s irreversible damage was caused by reclamation of urban mangrove forests throughout the tropic. It comes therefore as a surprise that relevant literature rarely covers urban mangroves. 30 and more years ago publications about mangrove forests missed the word 'urban' entirely (e.g. Jaccarini & Martens, 1990; Wong & Tam, 1995). Even an edited book in 2009 dedicated to the ecology, planning, and management of urban forests from international perspectives (Carreiro, Song, & Wu, 2007) does not contain the word 'mangrove'.

In some publications, urbanization is mentioned among many other reasons for mangrove destruction. Details remain sketchy (DasGupta & Shaw, 2017; Faridah-Hanum, Latiff, Hakeem, & Ozturk; 2014;

Rivera-Monroy, Lee, Kristensen, & Twilley, 2017; Saint-Paul & Schneider, 2010). In a recent edited volume by Makowski & Finkl (2018), however, urbanization processes and their impacts on mangrove forests take great emphasis. A chapter is on tropical urban mangrove forests in general (Branoff, 2018). Other chapters cover mangrove forests in major areas of South America (Gorman, 2018), Brazil (Mounier, Marins, & de Lacerda, 2018), the Niger River Delta (Numbere, 2018), Singapore (Ramos & Hesp, 2018), and all major cities in Australia (Semeniuk & Cresswell, 2018).

Mangroves are crucial resources in PSIDS and people are aware of the huge diversity of functions that mangrove forests provide. The Pacific Islands region cover about 3.8% of global mangrove forests (Spalding, 2010). This relatively small share undervalues the importance mangrove forests have in this part of the world: with some 550,000 km^2 the Pacific Island Countries and Territories (PICT) comprise an area that is smaller than Kenya. This is an area that is scattered in an ocean of more than 165 million km^2, almost 1/3 of the extension of Planet Earth.

In most Pacific Island countries (a notable exemption is PNG) major parts of the population live in coastal areas. With roughly 43,000 ha (430 km^2) Fiji stands third in the total size of mangrove forests in the Pacific Islands (Mangrove Management Committee, 2013). Precise numbers, however, are difficult to get. The Fiji State of the Environment Report (Government of Fiji, 1992) writes of a mangrove cover between 19,700 ha and 49,777 ha. The Forest Department estimates the country's mangrove forests at 18,000 ha (Government of Fiji, 1992). Exact and conclusive numbers are still not available. Similar applies to Papua New Guinea (372,770 ha) and the Solomon Islands (64,200 ha) which are the two countries with a mangrove forest area bigger than that of Fiji (Gilman et al., 2006).

In a time of climate change the needs for intact mangrove forests will increase. At the same time there is an incrwase danger that mangrove destruction/degradation will worsen. When the intensity of tropical cyclones increases, when average sea-levels get higher, coastal areas are more at risk. This leads to severe impacts on food production and environmental security (Weber 2011, 2012, 2014a). In such situations urban mangrove forests play an even bigger role in the Pacific Islands region.

Figures on mangrove destruction in Suva and other urban areas in Fiji are not available. It is not possible to quantify changes in mangrove forest cover for the past 140 years, the period Suva exists. Some qualitative remarks, however, are possible, indicating that huge sections of the mangrove forests on Suva peninsula have disappeared in the past 140 years. Those that still exist are highly degraded and fragmented. They are located at the northwestern and northeastern rim of Suva peninsula.

URBANIZATION IN THE PACIFIC ISLANDS WITH SPECIAL REFERENCE TO SUVA

Known to Europe since the early 16th century, it took until the final decades of the 18th century before Pacific islands were slowly integrated in a colonial system. It started, when a few whaling stations came up serving US, British and Australian whaling vessels. A tiny few Europeans settled at these stations, which lacked much of what today we would describe as urban functionality. Urbanization as a more comprehensive process set in slowly when in the second half of the 19th century European settlers arrived to start colonial plantation agriculture. Still urban centers were few and tiny.

When European settlers chose Fiji as their new homes, they cultivated coconuts to produce copra/ coconut oil. In the 1860s, cotton became an important colonial commodity for a few years when cotton production in the USA was severely affected by the American Civil War. Not much later, sugar cane production started as the most important colonial economic activity in Fiji and a few other Pacific Islands (Weber, 2005, 2009). Colonial structures kept urbanization processes small. Most commercial activities happened in rural areas, where coconut and sugar cane plantations were located. Traditional chiefs even disallowed their subjects to live in the small cities that had come up.

Until today urban settlements in the Pacific Islands are tiny compared to global standards (Cocklin & Keen, 2000; Jones, 2016a, 2016b). Urban areas in the Pacific Islands are young by any measure. Pre-colonial societies in the Pacific islands were decentrally organized. In Fiji where agriculture and related activities were the main sources of livelihoods of the population, the political structure consisted of many tiny chiefdoms.

When Suva became Fiji's colonial capital in 1882, a Central Business District (CBD) slowly emerged at the western side of Suva peninsula. Here the protected bay became the starting point for commercial and residential development. Except a few indigenous villages, no human settlement was on the entire peninsula, which today is one of the biggest urban conglomerations in the Pacific Islands.

As major trading center Suva received the Queens Wharf in 1883. During World War I, the Kings Wharf was established north of the Queens Wharf. For the construction of both wharfs, extensive areas of mangroves were removed and land was reclaimed. The same happened to much of Suva's waterfront. Most areas on the seaward side of Victoria Parade are on reclaimed land. Victoria Parade is Suva's main road along the city's Central Business District (CBD) and the government/administrative area. The road stretches from Nabukalou Creek in the north and Albert Park in the south. Here large areas of mangroves were removed, a sea wall was built and the area filled to gain land for development activities (Figure 1).

The 1960s mark the beginning of independence in the Pacific Islands. Colonialism ended first in Samoa (1982), Nauru (1968), and then Fiji (1970). When countries became the masters of their own affairs modernization optimism prevailed. Politicians and planners considered urban areas as the centers of economic and social innovation and development. The urban centers triggered large-scale rural to urban migration. Major urban areas spread quickly. Developments in housing, infrastructure and economic activities put much pressure on existing resources and ecosystems, including mangrove forests.

Since then, urbanization picked up considerably. In the census of 1911, Fiji's urban population was some 4%. In 1966, a third of the country's population lived in urban areas (Chandra, 1985). In 2004, Fiji's urban population overtook its rural for the first time. According to the census of 2017, Fiji then had an urban population of 57% (Fiji Bureau of Statistics, 2020), living in 19 urban centers with two cities, Suva and Lautoka, with 93,870 and 71,103 residents respectively. A concentration of urban population is in the southeast of Viti Levu, Fiji's main island. About 270,000 people are living in the so-called Lami-Suva-Nasinu-Nausori corridor (Greater Suva). This is more than half of the country's urban population.

EMERGING INFORMAL SETTLEMENTS IN SUVA

It did not take too long before it became evident that modernization had its downsides. A fast increasing urban population brought many challenges that were difficult to resolve. The huge influx of people from rural areas became unmanageable. The provision of social infrastructures like schools, health centers and first of all affordable housing was inadequate. People started to live in informal settlements. In Fiji, they are called squatter settlements as those who stay there have no right to occupy the space.

Fiji's land tenure system allocates some 90% of the land to clans, called Mataqali. There are thousands of such landowning units. Mataqali land cannot be sold or purchased. Usually, the chief of a Mataqali assigns land to individual families of the clan for their usage. Such use rights usually can be carried on over generations. Some 6% of the land is private (freehold) land. Most of the land alienation happened in a few decades before Fiji became a British colony in 1874. The third category of land is state (crown) land, which is some 4% of the land in the country. In urban areas, particularly in Suva, the picture is quite different. Here no native land is left; around 52% of the land is owned by various sections of the state (including Suva City Council) and the remaining 48% is private (freehold) land (Walsh, 1978, p. 132, Table 7.1).

For long, it was rather easy to evict people who illegally had occupied land. With the National Housing Policy (2011), it is acknowledged that past policies "have failed to meet growing needs of housing of people resulting in a rapid growth of squatter settlements" (p.4). Now the expressed commitment is "to assist all [of Fiji's] population to be adequately housed" (p.4). Central issues relevant to informal settlements are "to improve tenure of the poor" (p. 18), and to provide basic infrastructure (p. 20/21).

Many informal settlements in Suva exist for decades. They were established in sub-urban places in Suva's periphery. In the meanwhile, a rapidly expanding city has engulfed them. Many informal settlements are now located on or around prime real estate properties.

During the modernization haste, severe environmental and ecological challenges did hardly play a role when urban areas expanded. Planers considered the disappearance of mangrove forests an unavoidable side effect of modernization and development. The biggest informal settlements of 2020 have their origin in the first years following independence. Authorities tolerated the establishment and growth of settlements, especially when they were near to industrial and commercial areas. This helped to maintain a workforce near to factories, keeping transportation costs and costs for accommodation low. Low costs of living helped to legitimate low wages.

Initially, informal settlements came up in locations where competition with alternative uses was small or missing. As long as sufficient land of good quality was available, the settlements remain. Nobody wanted to use these locations at the rim of urban areas, inferior in quality. Development activities in such areas require considerable additional investment for mangrove conversion, earth filling, waterproofing of buildings, and the establishment of extensive drainage systems. Residents of informal settlements 'benefitted' from extremely adverse environmental conditions of the settlements (Weber, Kissoon, & Koto, 2019).

SUVA'S EASTERN PERIPHERY

A fast-growing area of Suva city lies in its eastern part between Grantham and Fletcher Road, two major arterial roads that run parallel from south to north (Figure 1). In the 1950s, the area was in the very periphery of Suva peninsula with no major settlements. Grantham Road did not even exist then. The major landmark at the eastern side of Suva peninsula was the Laucala Bay Airport for seaplanes (flying boats). The airport and adjunct military barracks had been established by the Royal New Zealand Air Force (RNZAF) in 1941. In 1967, the RNZAF left, and a year later, the locality became the campus of The University of the South Pacific established in the same year.

Figure 1. The south-eastern part of Suva (Source: Weber, 2020)

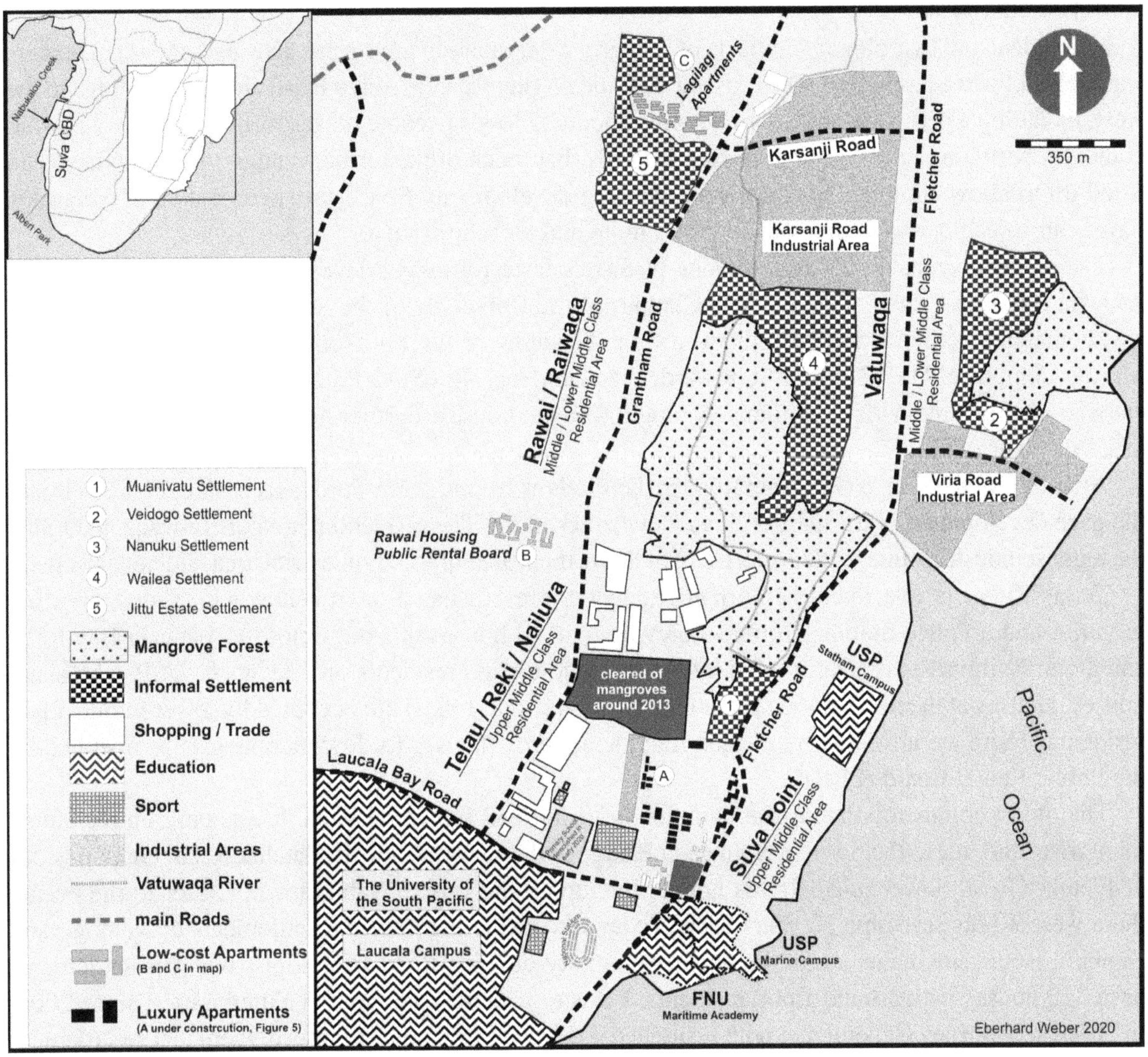

An important natural feature of the area is the Vatuwaqa river, a small waterway with a length of about 6 km. In its lower 3 km extensive mangrove forests once were on both sides of the river. The empirical part of this chapter provides insight into people's lives in one of the informal settlements built into a degraded mangrove forest in the eastern part of Suva.

People established settlements where once mangrove forests have been. The settlements contributed to mangrove degradation and destruction. Timber from mangroves is used for house construction; firewood from mangroves is an important source of energy. More important, however, is the pace of development in the eastern part of Suva peninsula over the past 60 years. An aerial image from 1957 shows the extension of mangrove forests in this part of Suva peninsula. It is possible to verify the progression of mangrove destruction with time series of aerial images.

In just over 60 years, the lower Vatuwaqa river has lost much of its mangrove forest to urban development. Small, fragmented and heavily degraded patches remain. The inter-tidal zone along the coast also had extended mangrove forests. Rice fields existed adjacent to the watershed of the Vatuwaqa river until the mid-1940s.

Ecological and hydrological impacts of mangrove degradation are severe. During heavy rain, excess water cannot spread as before. The crossing at Laucala Bay Road/Fletcher Road and the buildings to the west, including a petrol station, are frequently flooded. Floods become most severe when heavy rainfall coincides with king tides. An aggravating factor is that much of the former mangrove swamp has been filled up to allow commercial and formal housing development. Space to where waters of Vatawaqa River can spread during heavy rain becomes more and more restricted.

The eastern peninsula has become one of Suva's fastest-growing development areas. Along lower Laucala Bay Road, there is the Laucala Campus of the University of the South Pacific (USP). Further east comes the National Stadium, the Maritime Academy of the Fiji National University (FNU), the Marine Campus of USP. North of it, towards the waterfront, lies Suva Point, a colonial higher middle-class residential area with predominately single wooden houses. Further north is the Statham Campus of USP (Figure 1).

After the completion of Grantham Road in the 1960s as second south-north axis besides Fletcher Road, the pace development in this part of Suva slowly picked up. The residential area of Raiwaqa and today the biggest industrial area in the eastern rim of Suva, the Karsanji Road Industrial area, did not exist then.

Today Raiwaqa is a major sub-urban residential area. It has a town center with shops, sporting grounds, and a Police Station. Double-storey, individual houses in streets close to Laucala Bay Road and along Nailuva Road are occupied by higher middle-class residents or students of USP, who share houses. Houses at the north (along Grantham Road and side-roads) are occupied by lower middle class residents. There are also clusters of individual houses/row houses for low-income groups operated by the Public Rental Board (PRB).

The oldest commercial/industrial complex is Viria Road Industrial Area. It was built on reclaimed mangrove land just to the north of Vatuwaqa Bridge to the seaward side of Fletcher Road. On both sides of Fletcher Road, lower middle-class houses line up all the way to Nabua town. Closer to the ocean, there were 30 houses some 50 years back. Today the area is the informal settlements of Veidogo and Nanuku. Both settlements are in the northern vicinity of Viria Road Industrial Area. The settlements have 350 houses with around 1,600 residents. Plans to resettle Veidogo and Nunuku exist since 2006. In 2016 the Attorney General met with residents of the two settlements to inform them that resettlement will be carried out soon (Rainima, 2016; Vakasukawaqa, 2016). Residents of Nanuku and Veidogo are to receive a parcel of land on a 99-years lease to construct their houses. The new location is some 10 km to the north. Each plot has water and electricity supply and is connected to the sewerage system. The government promised to provide FJD 1,000 to each household for their relocation. People themselves need to spend between FJD 10,000-20,000 for house construction. With a lease title, residents should be able to raise this amount as mortgage loans from banks. By September 2020, resettlement has yet to start.

Other informal settlements of the area are Wailea, one of the oldest and biggest informal settlements in Fiji with about 400 houses and 2,000 residents along west of Fletcher Road. Jittu Estate is even bigger. It has 640 households and almost 3,000 residents. It stretches along Grantham Road at the northern end of Raiwaqa (Government of Fiji, 2006).

MUANIVATU: AN INFORMAL SETTLEMENT AT THE EASTERN RIM OF SUVA

There are 85-90 informal settlements in Greater Suva. Residents or their parents have moved to these informal settlements when they migrated to Suva. They have no own properties in Suva. To live in an informal settlement is much cheaper than renting a house or a flat in the formal housing market. In Greater Suva, rents are very high and usually out of reach of migrants from rural areas. Most of the migrants are unskilled, semi-skilled, without advanced school degrees. They work as low paid workers, or in informal activities.

The author's research on informal settlement in the eastern part of Suva peninsula has started almost 20 years ago. Since then, research enhanced knowledge regarding people's sources of livelihoods and their reasons to leave their villages and come to Suva. A crucial question, however, remained largely open. Why do people settle in places that obviously cause severe environmental health risks? A major round of fieldwork ended in mid-2016 looking into environmental health risks in some informal settlements in the eastern part of Suva peninsula. Open-ended interviews with one participant from 50 randomly selected households revealed that in informal settlements people's environmental health is severely compromised, that residents are well aware that they expose themselves to substantial health risks. During this round of fieldwork, people mentioned that they take these risks to reduce another risk. It is the risk of being evicted from the places they have settled (see Weber, Kission, & Koto, 2019). This question was in the center of fieldwork carried out later in 2016 and early 2017. Much information for this chapter comes from this fieldwork. Observations on-site, talks with many residents of Muanivatu, as well as investigations into the progression of degradation of mangrove forests in the vicinity have been carried out during these two years. In addition aerial images, old maps, and recent satellite imaginary were obtained and analyzed. Research methods were mainly qualitative to get a deeper understanding of people's perception of their settlement's environment, and reasons why people are willing to live under adverse environmental conditions. In 2018, 2019, and 2020 frequent visits to Muanivatu and its environment continued. During the last visit on May 31, 2020 additional information was collected to include in Figure 1.

Muanivatu is an informal settlement along Fletcher Road. It occupies land where once mangrove forests had been. Vatuwaqa river comes from the north, flows along the northern boundary of Muanivatu, then makes a 180° bend to the north to flow into the Pacific Ocean about 500 m north of Muanivatu. The settlement was once in Suva's periphery, but today Muanivatu is on prime real estate property. Compared to other informal settlements in the area, Muanivatu is the smallest and also the youngest. Within one kilometer to Muanuvatu, there are many manufacturing plants, repair shops and trading companies. There are also major facilities of the Fiji Sports Council, which include the National Stadium, a field-hockey stadium, a swimming complex, and the biggest in-door sports arena of Fiji. The area also houses three campuses of the University of the South Pacific, a McDonald's and a number of major shopping centers. Right opposite of Muanivatu, to the east towards the ocean, there is an old higher middle-class residential area called Suva Point. Directly adjunct south to Muanivatu there is a recently built apartment complex for higher income earners known as Suva Point Appartments. Commercial development is very dynamic around Muanivatu. New facilities are added frequently. At the corner of Fletcher Road/ Laucala Bay Road right now, land is prepared for the construction of a major large retailer of homeware, including furniture, clothing, hardware, and electrical goods. Immediately north of this area, some 20 multi-story buildings were completed in 2019 or are still under construction. They are apartment buildings for long- and short-term rent and ownership (Figure 1).

Figure 2. Muanivatu Informal settlement and surroundings in 2005. (Source: Google Earth 16.04.2005)

Muanivatu is built into the mangrove forests. Although it appears that the settlement is at the southern rim of the mangrove forest, it occupies land earlier completely covered by mangrove forests. The land was not filled up to improve land quality and to make the settlement better fit for residential purposes. The natural features of the mangrove swamp had a significant impact on the settlement. The area covered by mangroves shrank a lot over time in near-by locations too (Figures 2 and 3). When development activities started close to Munaivatu land near to the settlement was filled up and a drainage system created.

TO MOVE TO MUANIVATU

Information on the history of Muanivatu are sketchy. Aerial images suggest that the settlement did not exist much longer than 25 years. Aerial images of 2002 show less than 10 houses. By 2020 the number has increased to more than 100. During its rather short existence, local authorities asked the people of Munaivatu several times to vacate the land. The Suva City Council served at least five eviction notices to the resients of Muanivatu (Asian Coalition For Housing Rights in Suva, Fiji [n.d.]). In 2018 people's prospects changed considerably when Muanivatu was included in the *Revitalising Informal Settlements and their Environments (RISE)* program. Led by Monash-University from Melbourne, Australia, 12 informal settlements in Suva and another 12 in Makassar, Indonesia, are upgraded using an "environmentally sustainable and socially inclusive design with management of the water cycle, benefiting human health and urban ecosystems" (Brown et al., 2018, p. 29).

The settlement has a mixed ethnic composition. Native Fijians (iTaukei) form the majority with around 60% of the people. Some 35% are Fijians of Indian ancestry and about 5% belong to other ethnic groups. Most of the settlers are Pacific Islanders. Almost all participants in interviews responded that they would not be able to live in Suva, if there were no informal settlements. Still a considerable share of those interviewed, almost 10%, had purchased their house in Muanivatu rather than built it themselves.

Figure 3 Muanivatu Informal settlement and surroundings in 2020. (Source: Google Earth 28.01.2020)

An important factor for people to move to a particular settlement is when already relatives or other people from their village live there. Social capital, people being part of social networks such as family and village networks, give them orientation, which of the many settlements to select. Around 70% of migrants to Muanivatu knew people in this settlement already when they made their choice to move to this settlement. More information still needs to come up, why the first settlers selected Muanivatu to live there. One reason is the proximity to locations where people earn their livelihood. Inner-city travel is costly and time consuming. People prefer to live close to their workplaces. It still makes a difference, if one has to pay some FJD 2 a day to reach distant workplaces and return home after work. It would mean to work for about an hour just to earn enough to cover transportation costs.

ENVIRONMENTAL HEALTH AND THE DANGER OF EVICTION

Living in Muanivatu is a serious health hazard. Being built into a mangrove forest leads to a continuously moist surface around the houses. The houses rest on stilts and are rarely flooded. The outside area, however, is swampy and often exposed to floodwaters. In that case floodwaters and sewerage from improvised septic tanks can mix and expose people to pathogens. Stagnant water, which is omnipresent, expose people to vectors such as mosquitoes transmitting dengue fever.

Well over 80% of people interviewed are aware of adverse environmental conditions. Many indicated that these conditions had shown negative consequences to their health. Well over 70% are aware of these health risks. They particularly worry about diseases their children can get from the adverse environment. More than 50% of environmental concerns mentioned relate to water, which includes flooding, high tide, and waterlogging. Although houses rarely get flooded, the grounds do. During floods, people face great difficulties to leave their houses and walk to the street. Residents in the northern parts of Muanivatu, closest to the river and the remaining mangrove forest, face the biggest challenges. A couple of times in a year flooding becomes extreme. Then the improvised septic tanks overflow and mix with rain and floodwater. This mix of water and sewage is a severe health hazard.

Next to water-related issues, participants in interviews consider sanitation the second severe challenge. Between 15-20% mentioned that overflowing septic tanks during floods cause even bigger challenges than the flooding itself. Some people stated about garbage collection and littering in the settlement as serious environmental challenges. This not only looks scruffy but blocks drainages and makes flooding more severe.

Talks to doctors and nurses in near-by health centers confirm that people from Muanivatu often consult them because of diseases that relate to an unsafe environment. To due ethical considerations doctors were not able to provide exact statistical information. In their professional opinion they confirmed that the adverse environmental situation is indeed showing impacts on people's health. Most frequent are skin rashes especially among children.

On the other hand, many people feel that the adverse environmental situation has positive sides as well. The unhealthy eonvironment protects people against eviction. Quite a number of people had negative experiences with evictions. The matter was mentioned again and again during the study. At least 60% of people interviewed have eviction experiences by themselves, or by their family members, friends and neighbors . People had to leave settlements near Raiwaqa when the Karsaji Road Industrial Area came up in the 1970s. The owner of the land brought people to Veidogo informal settlement, others moved on their own some later to Muanivatu. Here they felt safe from eviction. Over time, people made the experience that adverse environmental conditions protect them from being chased away.

Some 20 years ago, Muanivatu became an ideal location to establish residence. Industrial areas nearby extended a lot, transport facilities became excellent, schools for children, sports facilities and shopping centers mushroomed just around the corner. Infrastructure has further improved in the past 20 years. For long informal settlers remained the only ones who showed interest to live in the environmentally disadvantaged location. Although the area was already fast-growing, a dynamic area, plenty of much better sites near-by were still available for investors.

As highlighted above, people know well that living under such conditions is unhealthy. They express concerns that they have little choices to live elsewhere. "We know that it is not good for our children to live here being exposed to all the mud and dirty water. However, we cannot afford to live in a better place. At least nobody else wants to live here, and therefore we are not asked to move away" (Jone, 35, resident).

People taking efforts to protect them and their children from dirty water, human and animal feces, and contaminated mud as good as possible (Weber, 2020). They create walkways that keep them at least at some distance from the unhealthy ground. In Veidogo settlement, residents even found support from a church group from Northern Texas. The group helped them to construct a wooden walkway, which keeps them some 50 cm away from the ground (see Figure 5). Many residents of Muanivatu hope that the RISE Project will improve their environmental health situation and better protect them against eviction.

Figure 4. Adaptation to flooding in an informal settlement (Source: author, January 2015)

ENVIRONMENTAL CHANGE, HUMAN SECURITY AND INFORMAL SETTLEMENTS

For many years people of Muanivatu have settled in 'dangerous places' to enhance security from being evicted. Such a strategy worked well as long as sufficient land was available for development purposes. More recently, the eastern rim of Suva peninsula, in particular the area between Fletcher Road and Grantham Road, became a rapidly developing prime location. Land prices have increased a lot. Land that nobody wanted to use earlier now is in high demand for commercial activities (shopping centers, wholesale trade, manufacturing), and residential purposes (high-end apartment blocks, individual housing for the higher middle class). Although development costs are high, environmentally marginal lands today attract many investors.

Informal settlers face severe challenges to survive amidst commercial and real estate interests. In the past two decades, there have been many attempts to resettle informal settlements and bring their residents to locations at the rim of Greater Suva. Informal settlements occupy land that has become very expensive. Many planners also feel that informal settlements and their residents disfigure the character of this increasingly posh location.

The future of the people of Muanivatu right now looks bright as the settlement has been included in a list of 12 informal settlements in Greater Suva, which should be upgraded until 2023. The RISE project aims to improve health of the residents of informal settlement through water sensitive approaches.

Figure 5. Luxury apartment development near to Muanivatu (Source: author, May 31, 2020)

There are plans to improve water supply, sanitation and quality of people's houses. A crucial emphasis is given to plan all interventions with the active participation of residents of settlements. This includes the participation of settlers in the decision-making and implementation of activities. People's ideas, commitment and participation help to achieve that they take ownership of the project. To support such participation, RISE has established committees in all 12 settlements. Frequent meetings and trainings of community organizers aim to strengthen participation and bottom-up approaches in urban planning. Muanivatu is an ideal location for such a challenge. People repeatedly have expressed their eagerness to contribute to the RISE effort. They are aware of the difficult environmental situation that they are facing. Even if it is not possible to restore the mangrove ecosystem, it is essential to find solutions to cope with the destruction of mangroves have created to the residents of Munaivatu.

INFORMAL SETTLEMENT UPGRADE AND THE DANGER OF 'GENTRIFICATION"

Experience from other efforts to upgrade informal settlements in Suva show that often better-off people move in once standards in informal settlements improve. Then others benefit from efforts carried out to serve poorer sections of Suva's society. The danger that this happens also in Muanivatu is great. The economically very dynamic environment has become attractive to higher middle-class people. They are eager to live in this area. They have the money power to crowd out poorer sections of the community. A danger exists that once the RISE project finishes, better-off people will substitute the erstwhile residents of "old" Muanivatu.

Such special form of 'gentrification' happened in the past in Suva. Apartment blocks built in the early 1970s by the Public Rental Board (PRB) at Raiwai and Raiwaqa were demolished in 2008. Six years later, new apartment blocks of the PRB were inaugurated. Similar happened to the people of the Lagilagi Housing Project at the northern end of GranthamRoad. The People's Community Network (PCN), an NGO, which has worked in informal settlements for many years, took the initiative to prevent the resettlement of Jittu Estate informal settlement.

The PRB apartments and those of PCN in Lagilagi are for poorer sections of Suva's society. When the apartments were completed interest to move in was huge. It could take some time before a family was able to get a flat allocated. In the Lagilagi project, people need to pay regular installments over a period of up to 15 years before the flat becomes their property. End of 2018, public media reported that many occupants of Lagilagi apartments never lived in informal settlements. Allegations surfaced that many illegally occupy flats. It seems that preference was given to people who actually did not qualify to live in the flat. Many on waiting lists, who regularly had paid their installments and for whom the apartments actually had been built, were sidelined. Accusations of fraud and corruption came up (Bia, 2018; Chand, 2019a). In May 2019, the Fiji Government took over Lagilagi Housing Project (Chand, 2019b; see also Walsh, 2019). Later in the same year, similar allegations surfaced with regards to the PRB apartments in Raiwai. About two-thirds of the tenants (140 out of 210) were given notices to leave the apartments because their incomes were too high to be eligible to live there (Chand, 2019c).

Vulnerable people put much emphasis on security. It is insecure to live in an environment that causes many health hazards. It is also insecure to live in a place from which one easily is driven away, evited. People know about health risks and about eviction. This has been part of their daily experience. At the end of the day they need to choose between one of the risks: it appears that they decide to accept the health risk to minimize the risk of being evicted. Migration to urban areas and even overseas (Weber 2014b, 2014c, 2015, 2016, 2019) is a requirement for such strategy. Households remain connected, flows of goods and remittances between different sections of the same households enhance security and well-being.

Above are just two examples where the upgrade of informal settlements led to changes in the social composition in the area. Another reported case is the Namadai settlement. Similar processes of crowding-out happened there already in the late 1990s (Koto, 2020).

CONCLUSION

The destruction and degradation of urban mangrove forests has created many challenges. Well maintained they can provide valuable recreational functions in urban areas. This is in addition to the big numbers of positive uses they have anyway. When getting degraded they easily can become a major health hazard. Where earlier forests have been there are now houses, factories, roads, and other immobile structures. Technical considerations make it difficult to bring back the forests to their original status. The biggest challenge, however, is the scarcity of land, urban areas often face. Before such background nobody wants to restore mangrove forest to their original status, even if it would be technically possible.

People who settle in mangrove forests know that they live in 'dangerous places'. They are aware of the risks, but they they have limited choices. An active planning strategy thus is to reduce risks to people's lives. For informal settlements, this would mean to formalize residency, to give land titles or at least long term leases. It also would mean to create strong safeguards that people are not driven out of settlements improved for them. Safeguards that enable residents of informal settlements to enjoy the enhanced quality of their places. Otherwise, it can easily happen that environmental improvements become a thread to those for whom and with whom environmental situations have enhanced.

REFERENCES

Alongi, D. M. (2002). Present state and future of the world's mangrove forests. *Environmental Conservation, 29*(3), 331–349. doi:10.1017/S0376892902000231

Bia, A. (2018, November 19). PCN needs $1.2M to complete Lagilagi Housing Project. *Fiji Broadcasting Corporation*. Retrieved from https://www.fbcnews. com.fj/news/pcn-needs-1-2m-to-complete-lagilagi-housing-project/

Brown, R., Leder, K., Wong, T., French, M., Chown, S. L., Luby, S., ... Forbes, A. (2018). Improving human and environmental health in urban informal settlements: The Revitalising Informal Settlements and their Environments (RISE) programme. *The Lancet Planetary Health, 2*, S29. doi:10.1016/S2542-5196(18)30114-1

Bryant-Tokalau, J. (2010). *The Fijian Qoliqoli and urban squatting in Fiji: Righting an historical wrong?* Alfred Deakin Research Institute, Deakin University.

Bryant-Tokalau, J. (2014). Urban squatter and the poor in Fiji: Issues of land and investment in coastal areas. *Asia Pacific Viewpoint, 55*(1), 54–66. doi:10.1111/apv.12043

Bryant-Tokalau, J., & Campbell, J. (2014). Coping with floods in urban Fiji: responses and resilience of the poor. In M. Sakai, E. Jurriëns, J. Zhang, & A. Thornton (Eds.), *Disaster Relief in the Asia Pacific* (pp. 150–164). Routledge.

Bunt, J. S., Robertson, A. I., & Alongi, D. M. (1992). Introduction. In D. M. Alongi & A. I. Robertson (Eds.), *Tropical mangrove ecosystems* (pp. 1–6). American Geophysical Union. doi:10.1029/CE041p0001

Carreiro, M. M., Song, Y. C., & Wu, J. (Eds.). (2007). *Ecology, planning, and management of urban forests: International perspective*. Springer.

Chand, S. (2019a, May 31). Government takes over Lagilagi project after alleged abuse of funds. *Fiji Sun*. Retrieved from https://fijisun.com.fj/2019/05/31/

Chand, S. (2019b, June 25). Father Barr Breaks Silence On Lagilagi Housing Project. *Fiji Sun*. Retrieved from https://fijisun.com.fj/2019/06/25/

Chand, S. (2019c, September 19). 140 tenants of Raiwai flats issued eviction notice, no longer eligible to occupy flats. *Fiji Sun*. Retrieved from https://fijisun. com.fj/2019/09/19/

Chandra, R. (1985). *Industrialization in Fiji* (Doctoral dissertation). University of British Columbia, Vancouver.

Cocklin, C., & Keen, M. (2000). Urbanization in the Pacific: Environmental change, vulnerability and human security. *Environmental Conservation*, *27*(4), 392–403. doi:10.1017/S0376892900000448

Das, S., & Vincent, J. R. (2009). Mangroves protected villages and reduced death toll during Indian super cyclone. *Proceedings of the National Academy of Sciences of the United States of America*, *106*(18), 7357–7360. doi:10.1073/pnas.0810440106 PMID:19380735

DasGupta, R., & Shaw, R. (2017). Mangroves in Asia-Pacific: a review of threats and responses. In R. DasGupta & R. Shaw (Eds.), *Participatory Mangrove Management in a Changing Climate* (pp. 1–16). Springer. doi:10.1007/978-4-431-56481-2_1

DasGupta, R., & Shaw, R. (2017). Retrofitting Joint Forest Management (JFM) in Protected Areas of Indian Sundarbans: How Sustainable It Is? In R. DasGupta & R. Shaw (Eds.), *Participatory Mangrove Management in a Changing Climate* (pp. 59–71). Springer. doi:10.1007/978-4-431-56481-2_4

DasGupta, R., & Shaw, R. (Eds.). (2017). *Participatory Mangrove Management in a Changing Climate: Perspectives from the Asia-Pacific*. Springer. doi:10.1007/978-4-431-56481-2

De Alban, J. D. T., Jamaludin, J., de Wen, D. W., Than, M. M., & Webb, E. L. (2020). Improved estimates of mangrove cover and change reveal catastrophic deforestation in Myanmar. *Environmental Research Letters*, *15*(034034), 1–14.

Ellison, J. (2010). *Vulnerability of Fiji's mangroves and associated coral reefs to climate change. A Review*. WWF South Pacific Office.

Faridah-Hanum, I., Latiff, A., Hakeem, K. R., & Ozturk, M. (Eds.). (2014). *Mangrove ecosystems of Asia: status, challenges and management strategies*. Springer. doi:10.1007/978-1-4614-8582-7

Fiji Bureau of Statistics. (2020). Data available on FBS website: https://www.statsfiji.gov.fj/index.php

Food and Agricultural Organization (FAO). (2015). *Global Forest Resources Assessments 2015*. Available from: http://www.fao.org/forest-resources-assessment/past-assessments/fra-2015/en/

Friess, D. A., Rogers, K., Lovelock, C. E., Krauss, K. W., Hamilton, S. E., Lee, S. Y., Lucas, R., Primavera, J., Rajkaran, A., & Shi, S. (2019). The State of the World's Mangrove Forests: Past, Present, and Future. *Annual Review of Environment and Resources*, *44*(1), 89–115. doi:10.1146/annurev-environ-101718-033302

Gilman, E., Van Lavieren, H., Ellison, J., Jungblut, V., Wilson, L., & Areki, F. Yuknavage. (2006). Pacific Island Mangroves in a Changing Climate and Rising Sea. UNEP Regional Seas Reports and Studies No. 179. Nairobi, Kenya: United Nations Environment Programme, Regional Seas Programme.

Gorman, D. (2018). Historical Losses of Mangrove Systems in South America from Human-Induced and Natural Impacts. In C. Makowski, & C.W. Finkl (Eds.), Threats to Mangrove Forests: Hazards, Vulnerability, and Management (pp. 155-171). Cham: Springer. doi:10.1007/978-3-319-73016-5_8

Government of Fiji. (2006).Department of Statistics. Census 2007. Author.

Government of Fiji / IUCN. (1992). *Fiji State of the Environment Report 1992*. Author.

V. Jaccarini, & E. Martens (Eds.). (1990). The Ecology of Mangrove and Related Ecosystems*: Proceedings of the International Symposium held at Mombasa*. Dordrecht: Springer.

Jones, P. (2016a). Informal urbanism as a product of socio-cultural expression: Insights from the Island Pacific. In S. Attia, S. Shabka, Z. Shafik, & A. Ibrahim (Eds.), *Dynamics and Resilience of Informal Areas: International Perspectives* (pp. 165–181). Springer. doi:10.1007/978-3-319-29948-8_10

Jones, P. (2016b). *The Emergence of Pacific Urban Villages: Urbanization Trends in the Pacific Islands*. Asian Development Bank.

Kathiresan, K., & Rajendran, N. (2005). Coastal mangrove forests mitigated tsunami. *Estuarine, Coastal and Shelf Science*, *65*(3), 601–606. doi:10.1016/j.ecss.2005.06.022

Koto, C. W. (2008). *Coping strategies of Fiji's urban poor: A case study of Namadai settlement, Suva, Fiji Islands* (Master's thesis). The University of the South Pacific, Suva.

Makowski, C., & Finkl, C. W. (Eds.). (2018). *Threats to Mangrove Forests: Hazards, Vulnerability, and Management*. Springer. doi:10.1007/978-3-319-73016-5

Mangrove Management Committee. (2013). Mangrove Management Plan 2013. Author.

Mounier, S. J. L., Marins, R. V., & de Lacerda, L. D. (2018). Determining the Influence of Urbanization on Mangrove Zones of Northeastern Brazil: Characterization of Ceará State Coastal Zone Organic Matter Inputs. In C. Makowski & C. W. Finkl (Eds.), *Threats to Mangrove Forests: Hazards, Vulnerability, and Management* (pp. 199–222). Springer. doi:10.1007/978-3-319-73016-5_10

Numbere, A. O. (2018). The impact of oil and gas exploration: invasive nypa palm species and urbanization on mangroves in the Niger River Delta, Nigeria. In C. Makowski & C. W. Finkl (Eds.), *Threats to Mangrove Forests: Hazards, Vulnerability, and Management* (pp. 247–266). Springer. doi:10.1007/978-3-319-73016-5_12

Ragg, A. A. (1934). The port of Suva, Fiji; its history and development. *Selected Engineering Papers*, *1*(171), 3–24. doi:10.1680/isenp.1934.13635

Rahman, A. U., & Shaw, R. (2017). Fragile Mangroves and Increasing Susceptibility to Coastal Hazards in Pakistan. In R. DasGupta & R. Shaw (Eds.), *Participatory Mangrove Management in a Changing Climate* (pp. 17–30). Springer. doi:10.1007/978-4-431-56481-2_2

Rainima, T. (2016, July 24). Vatuwaqa squatters accept relocation to Makoi. *Fiji Broadcasting Corporation*. Retrieved from https://www.fbcnews.com.fj/news/ vatuwaqa-squatters-accept-relocation-to-makoi/

Ramos, S., & Hesp, P. A. (2018). Mangrove Establishment in an Artificially Constructed Estuarine Channel, Sungei Api-Api, Singapore. In C. Makowski & C. W. Finkl (Eds.), *Threats to Mangrove Forests: Hazards, Vulnerability, and Management* (pp. 419–427). Springer. doi:10.1007/978-3-319-73016-5_19

Rivera-Monroy, V. H., Lee, S. Y., Kristensen, E., & Twilley, R. R. (2017). *Mangrove ecosystems: a global biogeographic perspective*. Springer. doi:10.1007/978-3-319-62206-4

Rodríguez, F. V. L. (2018). Mangrove Concessions: An Innovative Strategy for Community Mangrove Conservation in Ecuador. In C. Makowski & C.W. (Eds.), Threats to Mangrove Forests: Hazards, Vulnerability, and Management (p. 557-578). Cham: Springer.

Saint-Paul, U., & Schneider, H. (Eds.). (2010). *Mangrove dynamics and management in North Brazil*. Springer. doi:10.1007/978-3-642-13457-9

Secretariat of the Pacific Regional Environment Programme. (2013). Fiji State of Environment Report 2013. Author.

Semeniuk, V., & Cresswell, I. D. (2018). Australian mangroves: Anthropogenic impacts by industry, agriculture, ports, and urbanisation. In C. Makowski & C. W. Finkl (Eds.), *Threats to Mangrove Forests: Hazards, Vulnerability, and Management* (pp. 173–197). Springer. doi:10.1007/978-3-319-73016-5_9

Spalding, M., Kainuma, M., & Collins, L. (2010). *World atlas of mangroves*. Earthscan. doi:10.4324/9781849776608

Vakasukawaqa, A. (2016, July 13). You're Not Forgotten: A-G Assures Squatters. *Fiji Sun*. Retrieved from https://fijisun.com.fj/2016/07/13/youre-not-forgotten-a-g-assures-squatters/

Veitayaki, J., Waqalevu, V., Varea, R., & Rollings, N. (2017). Mangroves in small island development states in the Pacific: An overview of a highly important and seriously threatened resource. In R. DasGupta & R. Shaw (Eds.), *Participatory Mangrove Management in a Changing Climate* (pp. 303–327). Springer. doi:10.1007/978-4-431-56481-2_19

Walsh, C. (2019). *The Lagilagi controversy. Government and the People's Community Network, Part I, II and other information.* Coz Walsh's blog. Retrieved from https://crosbiew.blogspot.com/search?q=lagilagi

Wang, L., Jia, M., Yin, D., & Tian, J. (2019). A review of remote sensing for mangrove forests: 1956–2018. *Remote Sensing of Environment, 231*, 111223. doi:10.1016/j.rse.2019.111223

Weber, E. (2005). Sugar in Fiji – a dying sector? *The Indian Geographical Journal, 80*(2), 71–86.

Weber, E. (2007). Gewalt und Staatsversagen in Fidschi. *Zeitschrift für Wirtschaftsgeographie / The German. Journal of Economic Geography, 3-4*, 206–220.

Weber, E. (2011). Climate change and food security – some conceptual considerations. *Journal of South Pacific Agriculture, 15*(1 & 2), 85–97.

Weber, E. (2012). Climate and environmental change and food security. *Journal of Pacific Studies, 32*, 99–110.

Weber, E. (2014a). Climate change, agriculture and food security in the Pacific Islands. *Journal of South Pacific Agriculture, 17*(1&2), 20–35.

Weber, E. (2014b). Environmental change and (im)mobility in the South. In R. Anich, J. Crush, S. Melde, & J.O. Oucho (Eds.), A new perspective on human mobility in the South (pp.119-148). Dordrecht: Springer.

Weber, E. (2015). Envisioning South-South relations in the fields of environmental change and migration in the Pacific Islands-past, present and futures. *Bandung. Journal of the Global South, 2*(1), 1–21. doi:10.118640728-014-0009-z

Weber, E. (2016). Only a pawn in their games? environmental (?) migration in Kiribati – past, present and future. *Die Erde*, *147*(2), 153–164.

Weber, E. (2017). Trade agreements, labour mobility and climate change in the Pacific Islands. *Regional Environmental Change*, *17*(4), 1089–1101. doi:10.100710113-016-1047-7 PMID:31258413

Weber, E. (2020). Zur Trinkwasserproblematik im Südpazifik. In M. Dickel & M. Kowasch (Eds.), Geographien Ozeaniens - Annäherungen an das Fremde. Praxis Neue Kulturgeographie. LIT Verlag: Berlin, Münster, Wien, waterZürich (pp. 77–96). Academic Press.

Weber, E., Kissoon, P., & Koto, C. (2019). Moving to dangerous places. In C. Klöck & M. Fink (Eds.), *Dealing with climate change on small islands: towards effective and sustainable adaptation?* (pp. 267–293). Göttingen University Press. doi:10.17875/gup2019-1220

Wong, Y. S., & Tam, N. F. (Eds.). (1995). *Asia-Pacific Symposium on Mangrove Ecosystems: Proceedings of the International Conference held at The Hong Kong University of Science & Technology, September 1–3, 1993*. Dordrecht: Springer.

Chapter 15
Diversifying Urbanization in the Context of Sustainable Urban Development:
A Case of Haryana Sub-Region, National Capital Region (Delhi), India

Krishan Kumar Yadav
Independent Researcher, India

Kumud Dhanwantri
https://orcid.org/0000-0002-1616-2480
Amity University, Gurugram, India

ABSTRACT

The world is experiencing a phenomenal pattern of urbanization with diverse spatial, social, economic, political, and environmental consequences. Its diversity and dynamism are more apparent in developing economies like India. Urban settlements present two distinct features of urbanization – opportunities and challenges. Opportunities in terms of being 'Engines of Growth', 'Center of Knowledge', and 'Concentration of socio-economic activities', while challenges are faced in terms of social, economic, and environmental consequences. Haryana sub-region is no exception to this trend. Theoretical framework using data and information forms the basis while examining critical arguments in pursuit to minimize these challenges. This chapter results in a sustainable development of a framework, channelizing the opportunities in the urbanization process.

INTRODUCTION

Development triggers urbanization. Whether it is social, economic, or physical development, it gives impetus to the urbanization process. In general, urbanization refers to a proportion of urban dwellers

DOI: 10.4018/978-1-7998-4372-6.ch015

to the total population in an area. Simple or absolute growth in the number of urban dwellers would mean urban growth while the characteristic way of life of urban dwellers would refer to urbanism. Swift urbanization develops challenges and opportunities for sustainable development. Complexities of the social-ecological-technical system pose challenges to the policy and decision-makers. Opportunities remain in the form of developing integrated strategies to solve the mentioned complexities by involving researchers, practitioners, and other stakeholders (Webb et al, 2018). Industrialization and urbanization have been the major forces in the 20th century that shaped the present face of cities in the world. Many cities in developing countries in their peri-urban areas witness informal settlements of low-income groups with limited access to clean water, roads, electricity, and other urban facilities. Most urban settlements in developing nations are yet not capable of coping with infrastructural problems. The dynamic interactions between environmental, social, and economic values as well as their corresponding institutional arrangements describe the distinctive nature of sustainable development (Fred Langeweg et al, 2000).

A sustainable city needs to be economically competitive, socially acceptable, environmentally resource conservative, and eco-friendly. While assessing social sustainable urban development in India, Panda, Chakraborty & Misra, in 2016, mentioned that sustainability cannot be developed in isolation. Urban sustainability mainly has four dimensions i.e. social, economic, environmental, and institutional. The cities in developing economies exhibit a dilemma of growth–in terms of economic development with modern technologies on the one hand and environmental and social sufferings in terms of inadequate infrastructure facilities, services, and environmental degradation on the other. As per "Limits to Growth", it was observed that exponential growth in a closed system may not be sustainable as natural limits pose a barrier for the same (Meadows et al,1972). Though some researchers hold that overall higher economic growth does not necessarily mean high inequality (Lucas Chancel, 2017), yet in the case of urban dwellers in developing economies access to quality health and education remains a dream. Therefore, the government's role becomes crucial in provisioning and delivering public facilities and services for vulnerable sections of society.

Urbanization on various accounts plays a vital role in the physical expansion (size) of the city, its morphology, or form varying from region to region. A high level of urbanization began in the developed nations before less-developed nations. The world is transforming into highly urbanized and 55% percent of its population is residing in cities. This proportion is projected to rise by 60 percent in 2030 (United Nations, 2020). The urban population growth in developing nations has been more rapid with an average rate of 2.4% per year. The world's 33 megacities are located in the developing regions (Fig.2). The studies on urbanization in the developed and developing nations indicated that Asia experienced the largest increase in the urban population followed by Africa, Latin America, and Europe (Fig.1). In addition to this, research also supports the world's fastest-growing cities emerging in Asia and Africa (The World Cities, 2018).

Figure 1. Global Pattern of Urbanization
Source: The World Cities, 2018

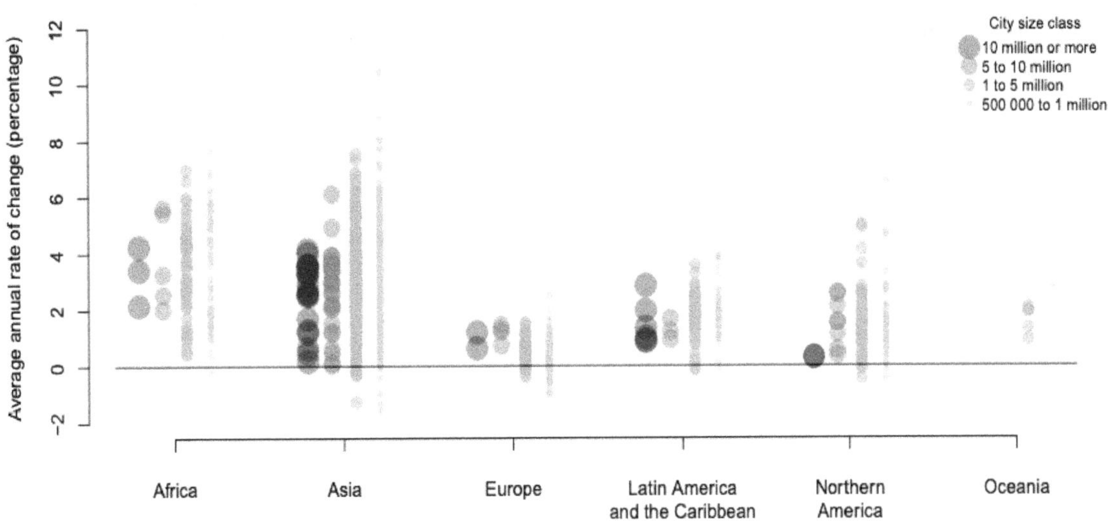

Courageous and robust transformative actions are imperatively required to progress the world towards a sustainable and resilient future. Sustainable development goals sincerely emphasized the integrated, inclusive, and balanced planning of economic, social, and environmental sectors (Sustainable Development, 2018).

This chapter especially, explores settlement patterns, their size, growth, and trend because of the problems they pose and the opportunities they offer. It analyzes the challenges and opportunities for sustainable urban development in the Haryana Sub-Region of National Capital Region (NCR), Delhi, India. Hence, the chapter starts with characteristics of urbanization in India and then discusses urbanization and development trends in Haryana Sub-Region. This part of the study critically covers the challenges of sustainable urban development in the region. Finally, it discusses rational and diverse opportunities as well as their channelization in the urbanization process towards a sustainable urban future. It further concludes and proposes with a conceptual development framework to be the part of the Sustainable Urbanization Process.

RESEARCH METHODOLOGY

The present study is an attempt to examine the relationship between urbanization and sustainable development. It has been supported by field practices and evidence-based researches, studies, and approaches. A conceptual and theoretical framework has been adopted as tools for analyzing the urban pattern, size, growth, development, hierarchy, and relationship with sustainable development. The study mainly relies on available literature and secondary data from the Census of India, government reports and books, research papers, newspaper articles as well as website-based information. The study area of the Haryana Sub-Region of NCR is limited to the nine districts namely; Panipat, Sonipat, Rohtak, Jhajjar, Rewari, Gurgaon, Mewat, Faridabad, and Palwal. The study does not include the districts of Karnal, Jind, Bhiwani, Charkhi Dadri, and Mahendragarh which were recently added to extend the Haryana Sub-Region of NCR. Opportunities and strategies proposed for sustainable urban development in the region are based on the Authors' observation and knowledge about the ground realities and government's policies. Besides, discussions and exchange of views with different experts in planning and social sciences also form the base for describing the challenges and developing the strategies.

Figure 2. Change in Urban Population by Major Regions in the World
Source: The World Cities, 2018

CHARACTERISTICS OF URBANIZATION IN INDIA

Before identifying characteristics of urbanization, it is significant to define as to what a settlement is considered a town in India. To consider a settlement as urban, the Census of India (2011) adopted two sets of criteria:

1. Statutory Towns (STs) are towns with a municipal status and fulfill the criteria of size, density, employment, economy, and revenue[1].

2. Census Towns (CTs) are towns which fulfill three conditions (size, density, and workforce);
   i) Should have a population of 5000 or more,
   ii) Should have density not less than 400 persons per sq.km,
   iii) Should have male work-force in the non-agricultural sector not less than 75% (Census of India, 2011).

Since Census Town is not governed by municipal bodies in India, therefore, a large proportion of the urban population remains unserved by urban services. As per the state government records, this population is considered as the residents of a rural settlement, hence indeed it is governed by a Panchayati Raj institution. There were a total of 5161 towns in India in 2001 which increased to 7935 in the year 2011. This period witnessed an increase of 2772 towns in a decade (Census of India 2011). The total number of towns was further divided into the 3799 Statutory Towns and 1362 Census Towns in 2001. This further increased to 4041 Statutory towns and 3894 Census Towns in 2011. These figures show a phenomenal increase of 2532 towns in the number of total Census Towns from 2001 to 2011. Among these, metropolitan and megacities have witnessed a large number of people settling in their fringes, also referred to as peri-urban areas with limited excess to basic urban facilities and services. This phenomenon has become one of the biggest challenges for sustainable urban development planning and decision making.

An equally significant aspect is the addition in the numbers of million-plus cities from 35 to 53 in a decade (2001 to 2011) and accounts for about 43% increase in the total urban population (Census 2011). Class-I cities (including million-plus cities) together constitute about 70% of the total urban population of India (P. Jayapal, 2016). Delhi and Mumbai have been observed among World's largest cities by securing second and seventh positions respectively in the global ranking of cities. Moreover, Delhi has been projected as the largest city in the entire world by 2030 (The World Cities, 2018). Considering the potential challenges of this huge concentration of urban population in Class-I cities, the role of planners and policymakers becomes more crucial to attaining sustainable development in their regional context. The continuous growth of the urban population in metropolises is one of the characteristics of urbanization, which compels the planners and policy decision-makers to bring out a paradigm shift in the perception, policies, and planning process of regional development in India. By developing poly-nucleated growth centers in a wider region, it was conceptualized that these polycentric metropolitan regions will regulate future urban growth (Sub-Regional Plan for Extended Haryana Sub-Region, 2014).

There could be four types of developmental dynamics that need to be considered while formulating policies. These are city-specific, city-region specific, sub-state/state-specific and national/international-specific. i) City-specific dynamics involve features of historic, cultural, religious, and administrative components. It may also have a function/centrality feature of linkages radiating in all directions. ii) City-region specific dynamics include features of importance such as a river/stream passing through or in its vicinity or it may have some natural resources/features in its areas of influence such as hills, forests, sources of water, natural conservation zones, recreational centers, tourist spots, industrial estate/hubs or educational institutions. iii) Sub-state/State specific dynamics may have an administrative function such as a capital city, besides, it may be agriculturally, industrially, or historically very potential region. National/International Specific dynamics include a metropolitan megacity, a financial city, or a tourist destination such as Delhi, Mumbai, and Agra respectively. It may also have a concentration of a particular function such as IT and its enabled activities. The best example of this is the Bengaluru and Gurugram cities in India.

URBANIZATION AND DEVELOPMENT TRENDS IN HARYANA SUB-REGION

After attaining statehood in 1966, the state of Haryana has recorded impressive overall development. This development has mobilized human, spatial, and natural resources especially, at the sub-state level. The state has shown a high rate of industrial growth triggering urbanization with a share of 35%. And it is further projected to grow at an accelerated rate especially, in the towns and cities of Gurugram, Faridabad, Sonipat, Rewari, Panipat, and Rohtak (Haryana Sub-Regional Plan, 2014). All of these districts form part of the Haryana Sub-Region of NCR. Comprising of NCT Delhi in the middle, the NCR is sprawled over an area of 58332 sq km. including areas of its other surrounding constituent states of Haryana, Rajasthan, and Uttar Pradesh. The urbanization level of NCR in the year 2001 with 56% jumped to 63% in 2011, recording a 6.5% increase within a decade. While comparing GDP and per capita income in the NCR, it has been noticed that NCR has contributed about 7% of the overall Indian GDP in the financial year 2009-10 at 2004-05 constant prices. The per capita income and the urbanization level in various Sub-Regions of NCR are given in Table 1.

Table 1. Development Statistics in NCR and Different Sub-Regions of NCR

Sl. No.	Development Indicators	Development Statistics in NCR and its Sub-Regions				
		Overall NCR	NCT of Delhi	Haryana Sub-Region	U.P. Sub-Region	Rajasthan Sub-Region
1	Urban Settlement Level	62.5%	97.5%	43.1%	48.3%	17.8%
2	Per Capita Income in Rs.	59264	98262	74457	35036	29300
3	GDP (2009-10)	100%	53%	27%	16%	4%

Source: Final Report Economic Profile of NCR, 2015

The Sub-Region of Haryana at the urbanization level of 43% contributes 27% of GDP next only to NCT of Delhi. Even, its per capita income (74457) falls next to NCT Delhi (98262) which is much higher than the overall NCR per capita income (refer Table 1). It has been revealed (Table 2) that Haryana has a total population of 25.37 million out of which 34.86% is the share of Urban Population. In addition to this, Haryana Sub-Region has 43% urban population out of 1.1 million total population. Hence the share of the urban population in the Sub-Region is higher even than the state urban population. District wise figures disclose that the share of urban population is highest in the district of Faridabad and subsequently followed by Gurugram, Panipat, and Rohtak. This is mainly due to the proximity of the Delhi metropolis and the radiation of National highways through these districts.

Table 2. Urban Population share in the districts of Haryana Sub-Region, as per Census 2011

Sr. No.	District	Total Population	Urban Population	Urban Share
1	Panipat	12,05,437	5,55,085	46.05
2	Sonipat	14,50,001	4,53,364	31.27
3	Rohtak	10,61,204	4,46,164	42.04
4	Jhajjar	9,58,405	2,43,339	25.39
5	Rewari	9,00,332	2,33,430	25.93
6	Gurugram	15,14,432	10,42,253	68.82
7	Mewat	10,89,263	1,24,106	11.39
8	Palwal	10,42,708	2,36,544	22.69
9	Faridabad	18,09,733	14,38,855	79.51
Sub-Region Total		**1,10,31,515**	**47,73,140**	**43.19**
State Total		**25371262**	**88,42,103**	**34.85**

Source: Based on the Sub-Regional Plan for Extended Haryana Sub-Region of NCR

Four National Highways radiating from the National Capital of Delhi and two other National Highways passing through the Sub-Region have attracted a large population in the nearby cities in this region. Likewise, the Western Peripheral Expressway (Kundli-Manesar-Palwal) (Fig.3) was proposed by the government in 2006 and decided to be made operational by the year of 2009. It has been completed and made operational last year in 2019. It is a 135 km long expressway passing through five districts of Haryana and encompassing about ten existing towns/cities in its proximity. Kundli and Kharkoda in district Sonipat, Bahadurgarh, and Badli in district Jhajjar, Farukhnagar, Manesar, Pachgaon, and Sohna in district Gurugram, Tauru in district Mewat, Palwal town in Palwal district are the existing progressing settlements close to the KMP expressway. This expressway was conceptualized and executed to divert and decongest the traffic pressure of the National Capital of Delhi. But the state government has plans to develop this as a world-class industrial and commercial corridor. It will play a magnetic role in attracting the urban population soon. Further, the proposal of five new townships (industrial and commercial) along the Western Peripheral Expressway will invite much more population which would be added towards urban components. These five townships have been called as greenfield cities by the state government. Though the initial intention of the government was to reduce the pressure of Delhi and Gurugram metropolises with the establishment of these new towns yet, cities with a high concentration of population will be far beyond imagination. This entire stretch of KMP expressway is already encompassing about ten existing towns and cities in its proximity. The population range of these towns is between 20,000 to 1,00,000. Four of the towns such as Kundli, Bahadurgarh, Manesar, and Palwal are having a population of about one lac, and rest six settlements are covering a population between 20,000 to 50,000 (Census of India, 201,1 and newspaper articles). Moreover, Central Ground Water Board (CGWB), India has categorized the said towns of Gurugram, Nuh, and Palwal as 'overexploited', the town of Jhajjar as 'critical' and Sonipat as 'critical and semi-critical'(Haryana Sub-Regional Plan, 2021). The introduction of new towns and adding new urban populations is surely going to place this region in the worst situation in terms of groundwater shortly.

Figure 3. Proposed New Green-Field Towns along KMP Expressway, Haryana, India
Source: Based on Indian Express, June 2018 and Wikimedia Map

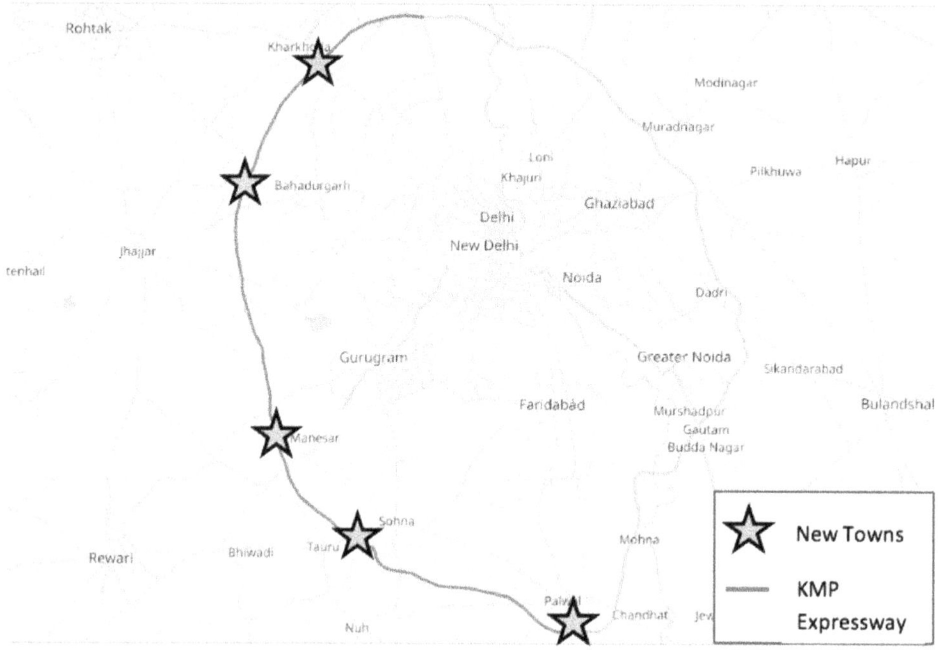

Table 3. District-wise distribution of towns in the Haryana Sub-Region, as per Census 2011

Sl. No.	District	Class-wise Statutory Towns (ST)[3]						Census Towns (CT)	Total (ST & CT)
		I	II	III	IV	V	Total		
1	Panipat	1	-	1	-	-	2	10	12
2	Sonipat	1	1	2	-	-	4	4	8
3	Rohtak	1	-	3	-	-	4	1	5
4	Jhajjar	1	-	1	1	-	3	2	5
5	Rewari	1	-	1	1	-	3	6	9
6	Gurugram	1	-	3	1	-	5	4	9
7	Mewat	-	-	3	1	-	4	4	8
8	Palwal	1	1	-	2	-	4	2	6
9	Faridabad	1	-	-	-	-	1	2	3
Sub-Region		**8**	**2**	**14**	**6**	**-**	**30**	**35**	**65**
State Total		**20**	**10**	**32**	**16**	**2**	**80**	**74**	**154**

Source: Based on the Sub-Regional Plan for Extended Haryana Sub-Region of NCR

This entire scenario poses a sustainability question to the planners and decision-makers. Besides, thinking about the up-gradation of the existing towns/cities along the KMP expressway, will the development policy of five new towns on a small stretch be a mindful move towards sustainable urban management?

Lessons can be learned from the development of industrial model townships of Manesar, Dharuhera, and Bawal, where actual industrial's occupancy and functional working are hardly 50-60% of the units[2]. Is Haryana Sub-Region moving towards sustainable urban development or creating another room for land speculators? In the future, this will further lead to a polarization of socio-economic activities and consequent congestion between the Haryana-Delhi border and the KMP expressway.

As per the census 2011, Haryana has a total of 154 towns including both Statutory and Census towns. Besides, the Sub-Region constitutes 42% of the total towns with 65 Statutory and Census towns. Statutory towns of the Class-III category are comparatively higher in the Sub-Region than any other category of towns. These are mainly concentrated in three districts of the Sub-Region – Rohtak, Gurugram, and Mewat. On the contrary, Census towns are concentrated more in Panipat and Rewari districts as evident in Table 3. The analysis of district wise urbanization level in the state of Haryana shows that the districts falling in the Sub-Region are much more urbanized than the districts lie outside. Besides, the high urban population also follows the transport routes especially the road network i.e. the National Highways and State Highways. Earlier, in the year 1981, 25% of the total urban population of Haryana was found to be settled along National Highway No.1. However, gradually the situation has changed with the improved road transport network not only in the entire Sub-Region of Haryana except Mewat district but also in the state. Hence Haryana Sub-Region has now become the preferred destination for urban dwellers.

Another relevant issue is often left out, not only by the decision-makers and planners but also by other experts and researchers. It is the urban population of Census Towns which is counted towards the urban population but not governed by any urban local body or other urban agency. Census Towns are governed by Panchayati Raj institutions in India which are already characterized by meager resources. Hence, Census Towns remain devoid of the provision of urban facilities, services, and physical infrastructure such as sewage, water supply, solid waste disposal, electricity, and drainage, etc. There are 35 Census Towns (2011) in Haryana Sub-Region which are struggling to receive urban facilities, services, and physical infrastructure. This situation presents a lop-sided and distorted development impacting the sustainability of not only the urban development but also of the rural hinterland. The scenario referred above presenting urban settlement size, pattern and growth needs to be planned with a regional context in view.

Figure 4. Proposed Settlement Hierarchy in Haryana Sub-Region, 2021
Source: Sub-Regional Plan for Haryana Sub-Region of NCR-2021

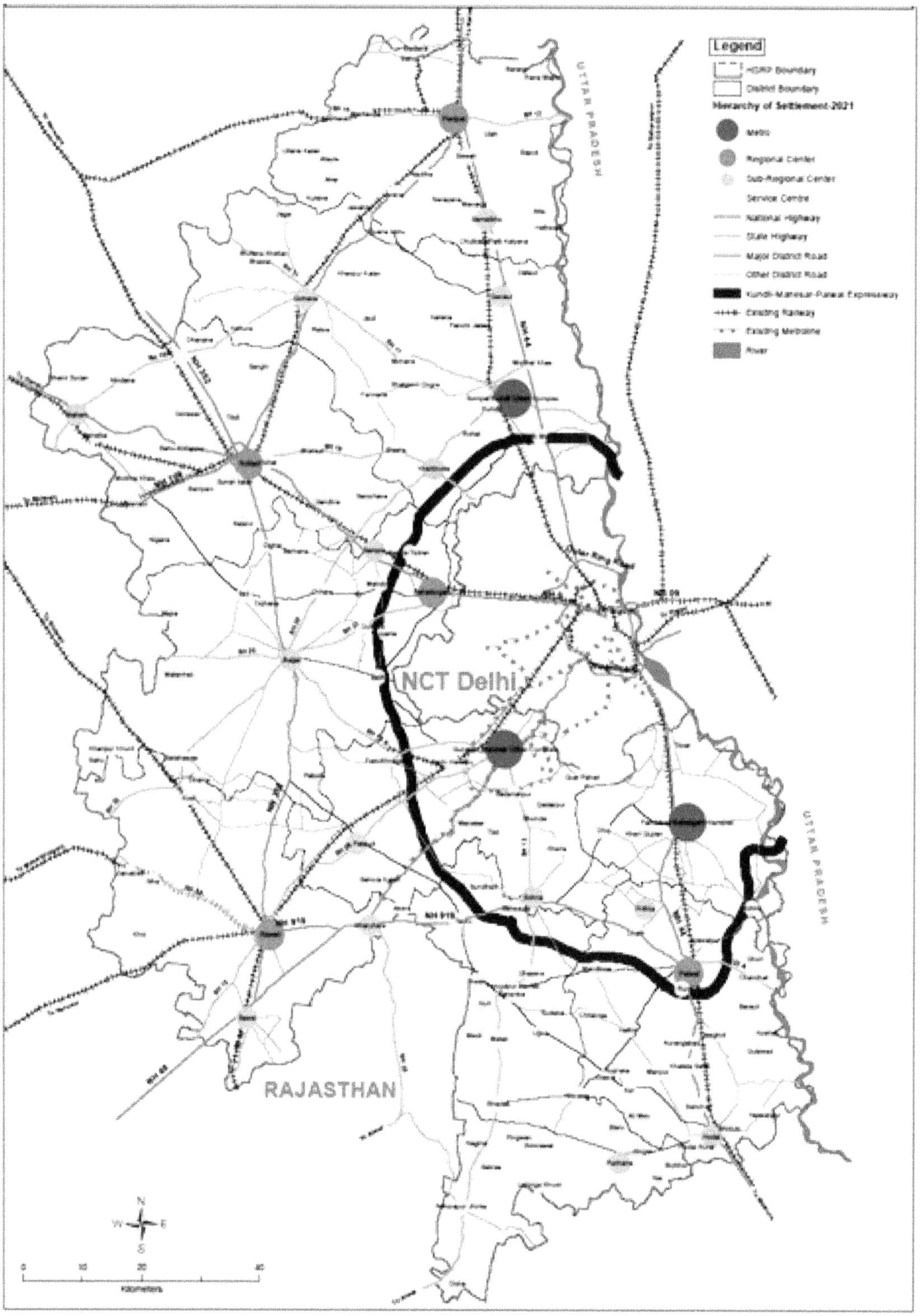

CHALLENGES FOR SUSTAINABLE URBAN DEVELOPMENT IN THE SUB-REGION

As per the RIVM[4] report, globalization created pressure on cities to compete with each other on their economic, social, and ecological attractiveness. Competitive mega-cities will continue to grow, while other ones may stagnate or decline (Fred Langeweg et. al., 2000). Megacity regions in Asia are experiencing severe environmental problems and resource depletion. Research questions urban sustainability in Asian cities and presents a strong critique of government failure to address sustainability in the urban development policy framework and its implementation in Asian countries (Ooi, 2009). Sustainable development of cities is a faraway dream for many of the developing countries. A mindful urbanization and poverty management is essential to achieve sustainable urban development (Cobbinah, et al, 2015). Cities are prone to huge intra-urban social inequalities. Economic inefficiency and the environmental side effects of rapid urbanization remained the unaccountable style of urban governance and management. Institutional factors and land market processes have created unequal urban development patterns in cities and their hinterlands (Ramin Keivani, 2010). Cities in Haryana Sub-Region are weighing down the natural resources especially in their hinterlands in 'the name of development'. The Sub-region of Haryana is still far away from the path of sustainable urban development. The key challenges which are acting as barriers in the path of sustainable development are as follows:

1. Uncontrolled Urbanization

The boom in the real estate market and the consequent transformation of urban society have given the biggest challenges to sustainable urban development. The market-oriented integration of the settlement network has increased social disparity in urban areas. The transformation of the urban economy towards industrialization acted as a growth trigger and has become one of the threats towards sustainable development. The transformation of the built-up landscape from horizontal to vertical development without understanding the importance and the availability of most crucial natural resources like forest, land and, water have compelled the urban and rural communities to struggle for their sustenance. Extended use of rich agricultural land for speculation and other urban purposes has threatened the surrounding ecosystems of cities. For instance, the area for Industrial Model Township (IMT) of Manesar was acquired way back in 1994, but even at present, the functional industries at IMT are only 50-60%. Consequently, there has been a loss in agricultural production associated with the acquired area, and simultaneously, the loss of industrial production is also evident as the function occupancy of industries remained very low in the acquired area. Moreover, the conversion of fertile agricultural land into urbanized lands lead to the loss of the scarce land resources, meant for primary production. While analyzing the land use pattern in Gurgaon-Manesar Urban Complex it has been noted that i) non-agricultural lands are increasing i.e. 15.20% in 1981, 26.78% in 1991 and 35.21% in 2001 whereas agricultural lands are decreasing i.e. 78.03% in 1981, 68.72% in 1991 and 62.32% in 2001 (Haryana Sub-Regional Plan, 2021). The continuous increase of urbanization in the Haryana Sub-Region of NCR indicated that the situation of cities will be even more critical in near future; if an appropriate population distribution and urbanization policy are not brought out soon by the state government.

2. The Pressure of Urbanization on Ecology and Environment

The pressure of increased urbanization on the environment has become the biggest challenge against the protection of the environment as well as on human sustenance. The unprecedented increase in water, air, and noise pollution in cities of the Sub-Region are the results of urbanization. For centuries, the Aravalis in the Sub-Region has been playing an important role in sustaining the rural and urban settlements, including the megacity of Delhi. Increasing urbanization is encroaching the Aravalis and thus degrading and destroying the life-supporting-system that have been preserving for ages by the pristine Aravalis. Over-exploitation of eco-system services from this natural endowment has disturbed and destabilized the right balance between development and environment in the region. However, Aravalli provides the Sub-Region of Haryana a great opportunity in balancing the symbiotic relationship between man and nature.

3. Infrastructure Deficit

Haryana as a whole has shown an impressive achievement in physical, social, and environmental infrastructure. It has already built an integrated road network of more than 27000 km including National and State highways. The metro connectivity from Delhi to Faridabad and Gurugram along with the rapid metro within Gurugram with its proposed connectivity to Manesar and Bawal are milestone projects of the transport network in the region. The state has also improved power generation capacity and installed capacity of more than 9500 MW within the last five years. Its industrial production has also doubled over the last decade. Similarly, the state has also shown noticeable progress in education, health, and IT infrastructures. Yet the fact remains that the development of infrastructure could not keep pace with the growth rate of the population especially, in the urban settlements. Traffic congestion and jams, increasing air and water pollution, water and power shortage, exclusion of an economically weaker section of society, a crime against women, children, and the elderly people, loss of green cover and bio-diversity pose serious problems for sustainable development. The transformation of cities into smart cities through the flagship program of Smart City Mission does not seem to have appreciated fully by integrating the ecosystem services components with the development of infrastructure.

4. Policy, Planning and Governance Deficits

Government policies and planning remain the major factor behind the attainment of sustainable development. However, in the case of the Haryana Sub-Region, a deficit of such factors has largely been observed. The land use and land management policy framework has been designed keeping in view only the economic viability that supports the powerful and the rich strata of the society. In such circumstances where indiscriminate exploitation of natural resources supported by the policies and programs designed keeping in view only a particular section of society. The deficit in the appropriate conceptual framework added with lack in exploring local and regional dynamics in the planning approach is greatly responsible for creating un-sustainability in urban patterns and development in the Sub-Region of Haryana. Restructuring is required in the role of development authorities to provide effective and more responsive governance to the Sub-Region. A periodic capacity assessment is essential to be done for the local bodies. The policy and governance deficit furthermore support the demand to set up a high-powered task force.

URBANIZATION AND SUSTAINABLE DEVELOPMENT STRATEGIES

The urbanization process a great significance from a sustainable perspective. Sustainable development requires economic efficacy, social equity, human well-being, security to human life, a better environment, and ecological strength as well as recovery. There could be different ways and means to attain human developmental parameters. Every human activity is originated and taken place on land. Therefore, it is the land that matters the most for urbanization and development planning. Since the development expansion and decentralization go hand in hand for balanced and need-based urbanization, it is very important to locate and distribute the urban population over an area/region in such a manner that it becomes resilient reaping its optimal benefits at the same time.

1. A Sensible Land Use Policy to Maintain the Equilibrium of the Settlement Pattern

Haryana Sub-Region is traversed by various National Highways such as NH-9, 44, 48, 148, 352, 709, 919, and 3348. However, urban sprawl has been noticed especially along NH-48 and 44. The urban sprawl along these highways allowed by the state government has resulted in some problems. The major one among those is the conversion of fertile agricultural lands into non-agricultural lands. The newly constructed Western Peripheral Expressway (WPE) is being preferred by the state government to locate five new greenfield towns along its total length of 135 km. from Kundli to Palwal. The short distance between already over-congested towns and cities of Faridabad, Gurugram, and Sonipat and the proposed new towns along WPE will not only require more fertile land but also prove to be spatially unviable. Strict Spatial planning tools need to be developed and adopted to optimize land uses of Urban as well as Rural especially in the new areas proposed for development. Protection of landscapes, naturally rich regions, and forests are also very crucial in the development process. To balance economic, social, and environmental development, a comprehensive urban and infrastructure planning is essentially required. A detailed survey of physical, social, economic, cultural, and environmental elements in a scientific manner is a pre-requisite to achieve success in planning any small area, city, or region. Especially, while planning a city or a township, city planners usually keep the city limits in their minds while regional context is of paramount importance in its ecosystem services and socio-economic delivery stream.

2. Policy Interventions in Settlements and Transportation

The Haryana state government has come out with certain policies and programs which have a direct bearing on the Sub-Region of Haryana. One such scheme is the Mass Rapid Transport System (MRTS) proposed linking both the residential and industrial hubs of Gurugram and Manesar. It has also been decided that this metro link will be extended up to Bawal and the Neemrana in Rajasthan as a project under Delhi-Mumbai Industrial Corridor Development Corporation (DMICDC) with the aid and guidance of Japan International Cooperation Agency (JICA). Northern Peripheral Road (NPR) and Southern Peripheral Road (SPR) and a small portion of Central Peripheral Road (CPR) have also been proposed. About 80% of NPR and SPR lengths have been fully constructed leaving only a small part of NPR and complete CPR due to legal hurdles. The peripheral expressway of KMP and KGP[5] around the Delhi megacity is a good example of segregation of traffic in Delhi and Gurugram for decongestion. However, the development of the five new towns along with KMP would prove to be unsustainable in its entirety.

Besides, V1 (e) (90-meter-wide) road has been provided in the east and south-east outside the urbanizable area of the Gurgaon-Manesar Urban Complex. If this link is developed soon, the congestion on the NH-48 within the Gurgaon-Manesar Urban Complex will be reduced considerably.

3. Equilibrium in the Spatial Distribution of Livelihood Facilities and Services to All

Equity in a city society lacking largely in our towns and cities cannot make our cities balanced and sustainable unless a specific policy framework for economically and socially vulnerable society is put in place. Therefore, it emphasizes the fact that this equilibrium must reflect in spatial distribution with access to livelihood facilities and services to all especially the economically weaker sections of society, and other vulnerable people such as the aged population, women, and children in city planning and its implementation. It has been noticed during the COVID-19 pandemic, a large number of daily wage workers have to leave to their far-flung native places due to lack of assured livelihood and other basic services like housing, water, and sanitation. Had they been provided these basic services they would not have left their working areas. This, therefore calls for making provision of these basic services in the masterplan.

Figure 5. Constitution of a Task Force
Source: Author

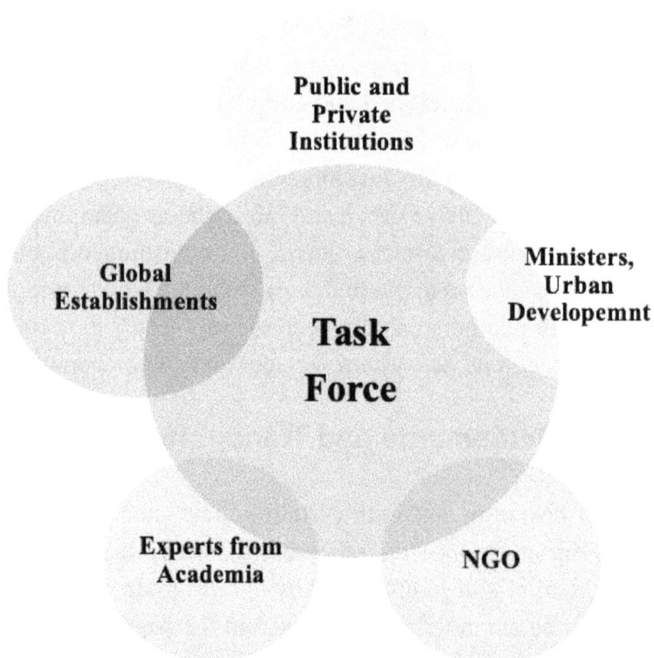

Table 4. Sub-Regional Plan - Hierarchy of Settlement

Sr. No.	Hierarchy of Settlement	Population	Haryana Sub-Region	
			Total Number	Cities/Towns/Villages
1	Metro Centre/Growth Pole	> 10 lakhs	3	Gurgaon-Manesar Complex and Faridabad
2	Regional Centre/ Growth Centres	3 to 10 lakhs	5	Panipat, Rohtak, Sonipat-Kundli, Rewari
3	Sub-Regional Centre/Mandi Towns	0.5 to 3 lakhs	14	Jhajjar, Gohana, Palwal, Hodal, Bahadurgarh, Pataudi and Helimandi
4	Agro Service Centre	10,000 to 50,000	157	Badli, Bhondsi, Badshahpur, Nuh, Bhorakalan, Sohna, Kalanaur, Chhara, Beri, Gannur, Hasanpur, and Firozpur Jhirka, etc.
5	Central village	5000 to 10,000	327	Sidhraawali, Kasan, Shikohpur, Khoh, Pathrari, Mohna, Badoli, etc.
6	Basic Village	< 5000	1331	Faizabad, Fazalpur, Walipur, Chandpur

Source: Conceptualized by the author based on Haryana Sub-Regional Plan
(*Note: Refer Annexure-I for more information on Central and Basic villages in Haryana Sub-Region)

4. Strengthening of Governance and Public Institutions

Haryana Sub-Region is a mandated constituent unit of the National Capital Region (NCR), Delhi like the other three Sub-Regions and it is managed by National Capital Regional Planning Board (NCRPB), Delhi. It is mainly for planning and its implementation. But the fact is that all the states of their constituent Sub-Regions do not carefully incorporate the planning proposals envisaged by NCRPB. Hence, NCRPB is left with merely an unarmed spectator. The fact that the public institutions, such as the line department of town and country planning along with other development departments, parastatal development authorities, local municipal bodies, and even the separate wing of NCR planning board at the state level are in place, they are inefficient and abysmally inadequate to tackle the planning and management of urban settlements in the Sub-Region. Therefore, there is an urgent need to strengthen them with strong capacity building and legislative provisions. A high powered task force is required to be constituted at the Regional level including identified public and private institutions, concerned ministers of urban development/town and country planning, NGOs, experts from academia, experts from global establishments. This will bridge the gap between research (based on ground realities) and development-related policies/programs. It is also strongly emphasized that any planning/resource region involving more than one state should be brought into the ambit of the federal government. The issues augmented by the accelerated development of urban centers and their respective potential solutions in the light of sustainable development should be the prime agenda of the proposed task force. This task force will facilitate coordination and build synergy among the National, Regional and Sub-Regional levels.

5. Municipal Finance and Mobilisation of Resources

This is highly important to mobilize municipal finances through direct and indirect methods to achieve the goal of sustainable cities. Municipal revenues should be raised through targeted capital projects to support economic activities and thus increased finances can be utilized for the provision of essential urban services. Utilization of corporate social responsibility (CSR), municipal equity bonds and participatory budgeting can also fund the municipalities after targeting what is needed on the ground.

6. Identification and Integration of Physical, Social, Economic and Environmental Resources

Towns/cities/metro/megacities are not independent entities. These towns and cities draw their resources from their area of influence in their surroundings. They also provide several urban services to the region in return. Therefore, it becomes obvious to prepare a detailed inventory of their surroundings in terms of natural landscape and resources, demographic and other social and economic indicators of the settlements in both rural and urban areas. This inventory would provide a clear idea about the relationship between the urban and rural settlements which would help in integrating the rural and urban planning with an emphasis on sustainable development. Having detailed information and knowledge about the town/city planning in its regional context, the planner would be in a position to make decisions with the positive inputs from other decision-makers, as to what should be the overall settlement pattern, especially in the metro/mega-city region. In the Indian context, urban settlements in the plains, to a larger extent has shown an equidistributional pattern. The polycentric model of development would prove to be an efficient and viable with sustainability not only to the individual city but also be viable to its surrounding region. The hierarchy of settlements could be devised depending upon local conditions and regional context. In the case of the Haryana Sub-Region, a tentative hierarchy of settlements is suggested in Table 4.

7. Adoption of Sustainable Lifestyle by the Urban Residents and Consumers

Strategic planning should be done to influence the urban residents cum consumers for the adoption of sustainable lifestyles. The COVID-19 lockdown has already gave lessons on differentiating between actual necessities and unnecessary consumptions. There should be a focus to sensitize urban dwellers for the optimal use of resources, energy, and other materials. Technological optimization can be a great asset to the reduction of material and energy losses. Moreover, the use of renewable resources should be promoted more and more in the Sub-Region to achieve energy sustainability in its cities. The need for local actions matching the national as well as Sustainable Development Goals (SDG) would make cities and regions sustainable. The role of civil society and the resident's welfare association (RWAs) should not be ignored while planning and management of a city or region. Besides, the cultural and social institutions/entities may become partners with the local authorities in overall development of not only towns and cities but also of rural settlements.

With the contextual presentation of challenges and potentials in the patterns of urbanization in India in general and in the Sub-Region of Haryana in particular, it becomes obvious as to how to minimize the challenge and channelize the potentials in a manner that leads to sustainable urban development. Furthermore, a conceptual framework has been suggested for sustainable development in the urbanization process as follows.

Table 5. A Conceptual Framework for Sustainable Development in the Urbanization Process

Planning Spheres	Parameters	Indices for Performance	Possible Outcome
Spatial Planning	· Regional Context · Natural Resources · Physical, Social and Cultural relations	· Equity · Economically Viable · Environmentally Sustaining	· Polycentric development in a region – Equity, environment, and economy
Infrastructure	· Provisioning of Infrastructure	· Matching with population distribution and mobility	· Synchronizing planning and development
Economic Base	· Assigning functions based on Regional, local and Traditional consideration	· Mapping of Economic activities · Trade and Commercial activities	· Efficiency · Viability · Competitiveness
Environment	· Sustainability	· City ecosystem · Biotic and abiotic	· Symbiotic relationship – Man and Nature
Governance	· Participatory · Public institution · Stakeholders' role	· Community participation · Operations efficiency · Evaluation of Cities' Performance · Citizen Charters	· Transparent administration · Responsive · Accountable · Citizen centric Solutions

Source: Author

CONCLUSION

Finally, the chapter summarizes the characteristics and developmental dynamics of urbanization mainly for the Haryana Sub-Region. It documents a realistic settlement hierarchy and aspires to achieve balanced regional development. However, census towns along with class-III statutory towns in the Sub-Region remained ignored in the developmental policies and practices of the state. Though the Haryana Sub-Region has recorded the highest per-capital income and GDP after NCT Delhi, yet its progress to this end should not be at the cost of social and environmental sustainability. State government's development policies are caught in the whirls of globalization. Hence these are resulting in irrational spatial planning misusing the scares land resources. These are lop-sided developmental policies supported by political expediency only. This is reflected in the proposal of five new greenfield cities on the KMP expressway.

For achieving sustainable urban development, this chapter advocates the adoption of a synergetic relationship between a city and its region with a polycentric approach--Delhi being the mother city. It largely emphasized on the development of smaller towns while giving due considerations to the newly emerging census towns. Bipolar characteristics of rural and urban development schemes and policies in the present planning practices need to be seen in a holistic perspective. In such a case, both settlement entities complement and supplement each other within an integrated approach. This integration is a hierarchical set up - hamlet, village, small town, large town, city, metro city, a megacity with their varied size and functions. Furthermore, the chapter also suggests practicing the right assessment of the needs of existing cities and avoiding misuse of land in the name of sustainable development. Sustainability in urban development, therefore, entails four key areas of concern. First is the assessment and application of the developmental dynamics of cities and their respective regions. Second is the inter and intra-city flow of energy and its management involving men, money, material, services, and information. Their mapping and sectoral network would make the cities not only liveable but adequately functional also. Third, the symbiotic relationship between rural and urban settlements would improve the delivery system and its competitiveness. Fourth, usually, lightly appreciated is the urban governance and institutional set-up. Decentralization of funds, functions, and functionaries and strengthening of urban local bodies has a high correlation with the sustainability of urban and territorial planning.

REFERENCES

Chancel, L. (2017). High growth does not necessarily mean high inequality, World inequality lab, and WID. *The Hindu*. Available at, https://www.thehindu.com/business/Economy/high-growth-does-not-necessarily-mean-high-inequality-says-lucas-chancel/article21653028.ece

Cobbinah, P. B., Erdiaw-Kwasie, M. O., & Amoateng, P. (2015). Rethinking sustainable development within the framework of poverty and urbanization in developing countries. *Environmental Development, 13*, 18–32. doi:10.1016/j.envdev.2014.11.001

Economic Profile of NCR. (2015). *Final Report, National Capital Region Planning Board*. Available at http://ncrpb.nic.in/pdf_files/Final%20Report%20of%20study%20of%20economic%20profile_17122015.pdf

Indian Express. (2018). Five new cities to up along the KMP Expressway. *The New Indian Express*. Available at https://www.newindianexpress.com/nation/2018/jun/29/five-new-cities-to-be-developed-along-the-kundli-manesar-palwal-expressway-1835666.html

Jaypal, P. (2016). *Implementation of the 74th Constitution Amendment Act and Spatial Implications, Indian Urbanisation and Sustainable Development: Spatial Perspectives*. Available at https://www.tandfonline.com/doi/full/10.1080/19463131003704213

Langeweg, F., Hilderink, H., & Maas, R. (2000). *Urbanisation, Industrialisation and Sustainable Development*. National Institute of Public Health and the Environment, Bilthoven (RIVM report 402001015). Available at https://www.pbl.nl/sites/default/files/cms/publicaties/402001015.pdf

Meadows, D. H., Meadows, D. L., Randers, J., & Behrens, W. W. III. (1972). *The Limits to Growth*. Universe Books. Available at http://www.donellameadows.org/wp-content/userfiles/Limits-to-Growth-digital-scan-version.pdf

Ooi, G. L. (2009, December). Challenges of sustainability for Asian urbanization. *Current Opinion in Environmental Sustainability, 1*(2), 187–191. Advance online publication. doi:10.1016/j.cosust.2009.09.001

Panda, S., Chakraborty, M., & Misra, S. K. (2016). Assessment of socially sustainable development in urban India by a composite index. *International Journal of Sustainable Built Environment, 5*(2), 435–450. doi:10.1016/j.ijsbe.2016.08.001

Phuttharak & Dhiravisit. (2014), Rapid Urbanization-Its Impact on Sustainable Development: A Case Study of Udon Thani, Thailand. *Asian Social Science, 10*(22). Available at, http://citeseerx.ist.psu.edu/viewdoc/download?doi=10.1.1.828.637&rep=rep1&type=pdf

Report, U. M. (2001). *Special Session of the General Assembly for an Overall Review and Appraisal of the Implementation of the Habitat Agenda*. Available at, https://www.un.org/ga/Istanbul+5/booklet4.pdf

Sharma & Sen. (2015). Gurgaon-Manesar Urban Complex. *Transactions of the Institute of Indian Geographers, 37*(1), 133-146.

Sub-Regional Plan for Haryana Sub-Region of NCR-2021, Demographic Profile and Settlement Pattern, Chapter 4. (n.d.). Available at https://tcpharyana.gov.in/ncrpb/FINAL%20SRP%20FOR%20WEB-HOSTING/04_Demographic%20Profile_Settlement%20Pattern.pdf

The World Cities. (2018). *The World Cities in 2018, Data Booklet*. United Nations. Available at, https://www.un.org/en/events/citiesday/assets/pdf/the_worlds_cities_in_2018_data_booklet.pdf

Transforming Our World. (2018). The 2030 Agenda for Sustainable Development. In *A New Era in Global Health*. Springer Publishing Company. doi:10.1891/9780826190123.ap02

United Nations. (2020). *Cities-United Nations Sustainable Development*. Available at, www.un.org/sustainabledevelopment/cities/

Wcbb, R., Bai, X., Smith, M. S., Costanza, R., Griggs, D., Moglia, M., Neuman, M., Newman, P., Newton, P., Norman, B., Ryan, C., Schandl, H., Steffen, W., Tapper, N., & Thomson, G. (2018). Sustainable urban systems: Co-design and framing for transformation. *Ambio, 47*(1), 57–77. doi:10.100713280-017-0934-6 PMID:28766172

ENDNOTES

1 This information is based on the Author (Mr. Yadav)'s working experience in the state government of Haryana, India.

2 Based on the personal observation of Authors.

3 Census of India classified towns/cities/urban agglomerations of the country in six categories based on their population.

Category of Town	Population Criteria
Class I	1,00,000 and above
Class II	50,000 – 99,999
Class III	20,000 – 49,999
Class IV	10,000 – 19,999
Class V	5,000 – 9,999
Class VI	Upto 5000

4 Rijksinstituut voor Volksgezondheid en Milieu (RIVM), is a Dutch research institute that is an independent agency of the Dutch Ministry of Health, Welfare and Sport. It is also known as The Netherlands National Institute for Public Health and the Environment.

5 KGP refers to Kundli-Gaziabad-Palwal, Eastern peripheral expressway to Delhi. This passes through Uttar Pradesh Sub-Region of National Capital Region (NCR), India.

Chapter 16
Land Use Planning and Management in Tank Cascade Environment of Sri Lanka

Muditha Prasannajith Perera
University of Peradeniya, Sri Lanka

K. W. G. Rekha Nianthi
University of Peradeniya, Sri Lanka

ABSTRACT

The Tank Cascade System is one of the unique and socially accepted land-use practices in the dry zone of Sri Lanka which has evolved since 600 B.C. The small tank builders of the historical period had a profound and unified understanding of the natural resources, regional landscape, landforms, and hydrology. Tanks and irrigation canal systems, environmental zoning, forest reservations, agro-well-based land utilization, land-sharing system (Bethma), traditional soil conservation measures have been still maintaining well in some rural areas in the dry zone. Newly developed agro-well-based agro-forestry systems and some participatory techniques are also counted as few of sustainable land-use practices. This study has provided many valuable lessons of land use planning and management from the ancient hydraulic civilization and proving that the ancient system is still appropriate for the dry zone agricultural community rather than inadequately coordinated modern efforts of land use practices.

INTRODUCTION

The history of irrigation civilization in Sri Lanka goes back to over 2000 years (Brohier, 1934). Irrigation development in the country linked with paddy cultivation which is the staple food for Sri Lankans. In addition to that, the home gardens and *chena*[1] cultivations are alsopracticing using rain water. Currently the overall land use pattern has been changed with the new agricultural interventions such as agro-well practices. The historical hydraulic civilization of the dry zone of Sri Lanka which prevailed in the North Central part (*Rajarata*) of the country, is a unique place to study the indigenous techniques of land use

DOI: 10.4018/978-1-7998-4372-6.ch016

practices. It is the Northern part of the Central mountainous and the central part of the inland plain of the country. The mountainous areas covered by the forest and act as a sponge to capture rain water and release water in the dry season to the downstream. November to January is the main rainy season, and over 70% of the total rainfall receives during this period and others months remain dry. It was the major challenge of the dry zone peasant farmers to cultivate throughout the year. The rainfall pattern and the values of landscape initiate the necessity of a water-stored system and better land use practices. In the third and fifth century, advanced hydraulic structures including tanks and irrigation canal systems have been designed and constructed which would have required a sound knowledge of some of the key hydrological relationships pertaining to rainfall, runoff, storage volume and land management processes (Panabokke,2002).

The study area of this current research belongs to the dry climatic zone of the island. The most important climatological feature of the region is that receiving more rainfall from the Northeast Monsoon season. Average annual rainfall for the area is between 1250 mm - 1400 mm. The distribution pattern of rainfall shows the bi-model pattern with a maximum of rain from November to February and a minimum rainfall received from May to September. The monthly mean temperature of the area is 28°C which falls to the lowest value of 25°C in January and the highest value of 32°C in April. The wind directions are from Northeast direction between December to February and from Southwest direction between May to September. The central dry zone area mainly falls in to the 'DL 1 Agro Ecological Region' of Sri Lanka (National Atlas of Sri Lanka, 1998). The major vegetation types include as tropical moist deciduous forests and scrub lands.

The natural drainage patterns in relation to the location of individual tanks reveal an effective pattern and it is now referred to as the "small tank cascade system" (Madduma Bandara, 1985). There are some other local terms such as "*Ellangawa*" (Thennakoon,2005) and "*Wew Mandulla*"(Perera, 2010) referring that the tanks are connected series. However, these cascade systems[2] located in meso catchments make up a micro or sub-watershed and several sub watersheds make up a main watershed in the dry zone of Sri Lanka (Panabokke,2002). Thus, the entire part of the *Rajarata* consists of nine watersheds including 50 sub watersheds and all these sub watershed areas have been converted into "Tank Cascade Systems". It refers connected series of tanks with micro catchments and command areas, organized within a small valley. The tank system is integrated in to all land use systems in the vicinity of tanks. Accordingly, major land uses are tanks, streams, paddy lands, home gardens, road system, *chena* land, forests, riverine forests, tank reservations such as *gasgommana* (a dense forest patch in the immediate catchment), *kattakaduwa* (interceptor belt between tank and the paddy field), agro-wells and agro-well based lands (Figure 1).

Figure 1. Land use in selected tank cascades in Malwathu Oya Basin
Source: Modified from Geo eye 1 satellite images, 2012.

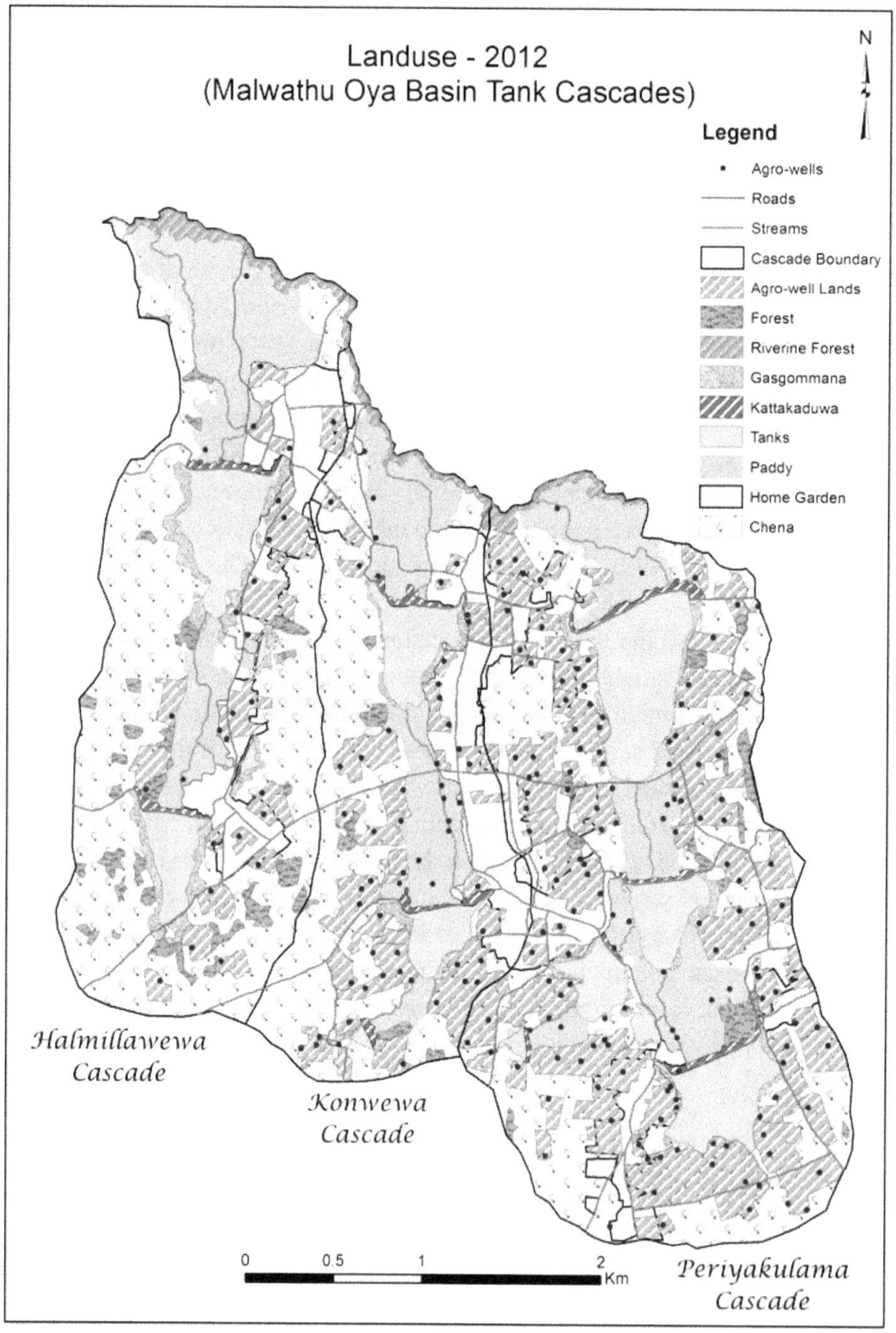

Hydrologically the tank water is inherently interlinked with groundwater and forest reservations. Such interrelation of surface and groundwater with forest systems itself drives us to conceptualize the integrated management of tank cascade systems. Further, upper tanks in a tank cascade system act as buffer reservoirs to absorb flood-generating rainfall, which would otherwise bring the risk of breaching lower tanks. Similarly, these upper tanks are buffer reservoirs to supply water to the lower tanks when they are in shortage of water to save the crops. Therefore, integrated management should be planned at the cascade scale and not for individual tanks (Dharmasena, 2002). Even in the sociological aspect, there is interlink among the entire people within a single irrigation area to apply the common practices associated with the irrigation norms and traditions.

However, this kind of unique land use types is very common throughout the dry zone of Sri Lanka and very limited in other countries except some parts of South and South-East Asian countries. The system tanks in South India and combined tanks in Eastern India are also very similar to the Cascade Systems in Sri Lanka. A significant proportion of small tanks in Eastern India, consist of a combination water sources such as rain+ river-let+ another tank+ flood water (Pant and Verma, 2010). In addition to that, individual tanks can be identified in Thailand, Myanmar, Vietnam and China.

The cascade systems in the North Central uplands in the dry zone of Sri Lanka have been maintained using certain land use management strategies since histrorical time. This context of the dry zone of Sri Lanka is a unique place to study the land use planning as well as sustainable land management practices.

HISTORICAL LANDUSE PATTERN AND RESOURCE MANAGEMENT IN TANK CASCADE AREAS

From the history, there are about 16,000 small tanks to tap the rainwater in the dry zone for paddy cultivation in addition to practicing rain-fed farming or *chena* cultivation in the small tank catchment areas (Panabokke *et al.*, 2002). Thousands of these small tanks and a few medium scales and large-scale tanks are mainly depended on the rainfall. Command area of the tank has been well conserved with land leveling and construction of ridges with the irrigation purposes. These lands do not contribute much to generate runoff. Nevertheless, spill water and irrigation return water would make a significant contribution to groundwater. The forest lands which are virtually not utilized for agriculture, but forest lands are the most important lands for the replenishment of groundwater. Forest patches confine to upper areas and micro-catchment ridges of the tank cascade areas (Dharmasena and Goodwill, 1999).

Specially, upper catchment areas of tanks are consisted of dense forest acting as a sponge to capture the rainfall to release the water gradually to the downstream. There are some *chena* lands between the dense forest and villages which are full filling the highland agricultural needs of the community. Tank based villages are the populated areas in the rural community in relation to irrigation agriculture as well as for religious practices of rituals.

Land and Water Management Practices

From the past, there are some specific land use patterns and practices in the tank cascade environments of Sri Lanka. Sustainability of the traditional tank village system had been maintained in the past, not only for structural maintenance of tanks, but also paying attention to the entire irrigation system. Every component of the ecosystem was given due consideration. The attention was paid not only on macro land uses practices such as paddy lands, settlement areas, Chena lands, tank beds etc. but also for micro land components such as *thisbambe*[3], *gasgommanan, perahana, kattakaduwa, kiulela*, etc. (Rekha and Dharmasena, 2009). The important thing is some of these features within the tank cascade environment are still practicing by proving the availability of traditional land use planning and sustainable land management practices especially in the dry zone of Sri Lanka.

It was well recognized that there were well organized land management practices in upper watershed areas in the dry zone river basins of Sri Lanka. The cascade system was a unique place to identify these practices. Different soil conservation measures have been used in the catchment areas and upper part or hilly/elevated region of the tank catchments. In the thick forest areas (*Mahamukalana*) and another three specific forest reservations were identified around the tanks. The entire paddy land had been divided either in to two or three slots as "*Purana wela" and "Akkarawela"* (old paddy strips and newly developed paddy area) or "*Mulpota"*, *Perapota* and *Akkarawela* (first, second or third paddy strips), respectively for the use of paddy cultivation depending on water availability. If they have sufficient water to feed all the command areas of the tanks, farmers used to cultivate the entire paddy command areas under the tank. However, depending on the water availability of the tank, farmers cultivate one or two parts of the paddy command areas which was the traditional practice of the paddy cultivation. It is known as "*Bethma*" cultivation which means that all farmers cultivate equally in a small part of the paddy lands when the farmers cannot cultivate the entire paddy lands due to the lack of water. "*Kurulu Paluwa*"- is a common small paddy land for feeding birds, *Chena* lands for the rain-fed cultivation, village with religious centres, were the other significant land use patterns. The tank cascade systems would have operated as ideal rainwater harvesting technologies while supporting to maintain ecological balance. A close relationship has been maintained among the irrigation tank system- village settlements - land use patterns in the dry zone of Sri Lanka (Rekha and Jayakumara, 2010).

When the stored water in the tank is limited in the dry season, farmers intended to share the remaining water in the tank among all the farmers by sharing water forcultivation. This peractice is called as "*Bethma*" the meaning *beduma* /deividing of tank irrigation area (Perera, 2010).

This practice is implemented selecting one of the methods (Figure 2).

i. Remaining water in the tank used by selecting one main irrigation area and that amount of land would share by all the farmers.
ii. Remaining water in the tank used by selecting the closest part of the command area to the tank and that amount of land would share by all the farmers.
iii. Remaining water in the tank used by selecting the most suitable alluvial parts of the command area and water distribute accordingly. The land would share by all the farmers. However this practice came in to action recently.

Figure 2. Three types of Bethma System in the dry zone of Sri Lanka
Source: Perera, 2010

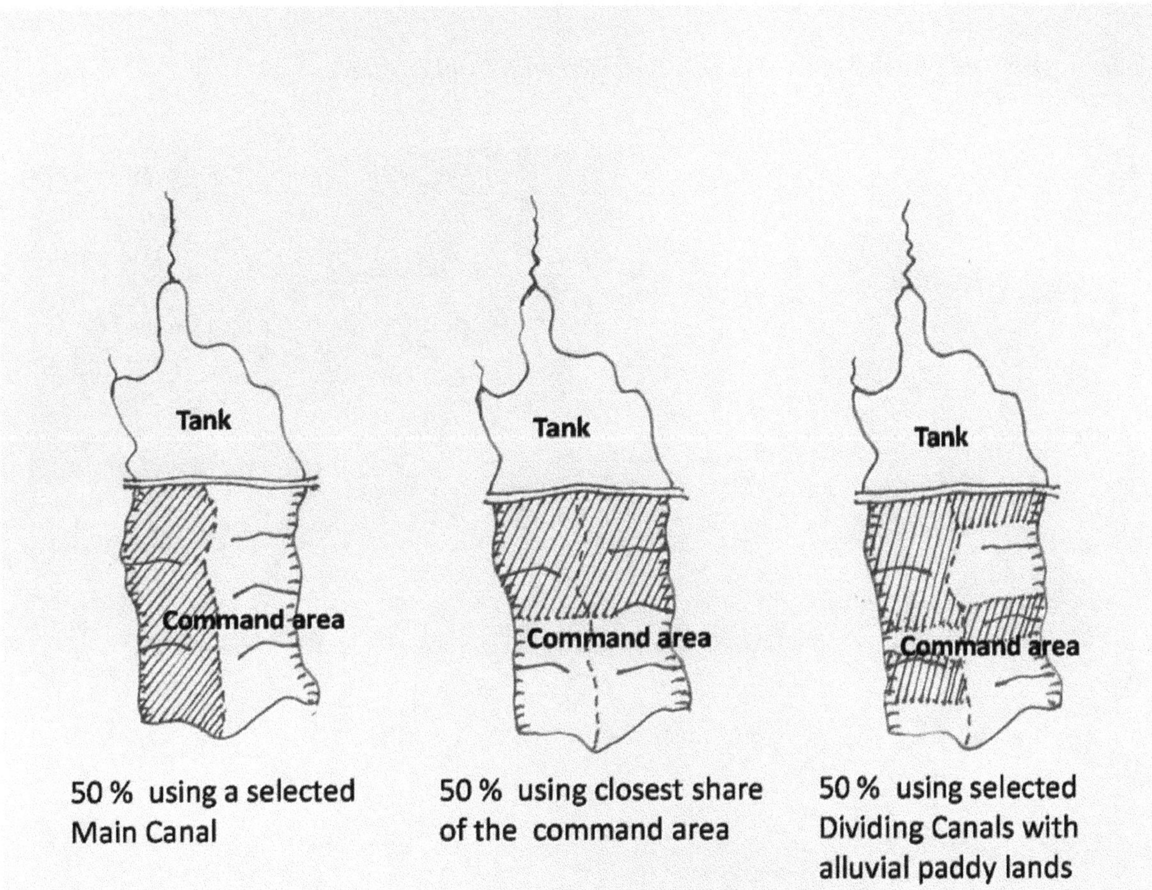

In addition to that, regarding large scale tanks there are more powerful water delivering systems through main irrigation canals, and field irrigation canals to the command areas.

Practicing Soil Conservation Measures

Controlling of the soil erosion has been achieved by using a few simple effective soil conservation measures. Much attention seems to have paid by the traditional farmers on mechanical and agronomic practices. Perera (2009) conducted a study in Malwathu oya tank cascade and found that 70% of the farmers used the Mulching system with dry grasses, paddy straws, and some material of the crops out puts. Contour Dry Grass Strips have also been used by (55%) and these dry grass strips/ridges made across the slope of up lands to reduce the soil flow with the runoff. The spacing between the ridges had been decided according to the degree of the slope which varied from 5 m to 20 m. Farmers who are living in the areas of the catchment have shown a preference of using boulders in addition to the dry grass strips. The Dry field systems are another effective method of soil conservation in the dry lands, which is very similar to dry paddy field, for trapping the soil and water in the rainy season (Figure 3). This technique helped to increase soil fertility and infiltration. About 35% low land farmers in the catchment areas have been using this method.

Figure 3. Dry field systems[4] in the Yan Oya Basin to control soil erosion
Source: Field study 2012

In addition to the traditional practices, currently using a number of soil conservation measures including, contour earth bunds, contour drains, bolder bunds and grass strips. In addition to that live fences and mulching practices are very famous in the dry zone areas to conserve the soil moisture as well managed land use practices.

Maintaining Forest Reserves

Forest reservation is one of the essential components in a watershed and it has been contributing a variety of services to the watershed processes. The mountainous and flat land areas are covered by the forest because this environment acts as a sponge to capture rainwater in the rainy season and released water in the dry season to the down streams. It is very essential to maintain the river base flow, ground water recharge at the lower areas and maintain the biodiversity.

Figure 4. Tank Reservations in the North Central dry zone of Sri Lanka
Source: Perera, 2010

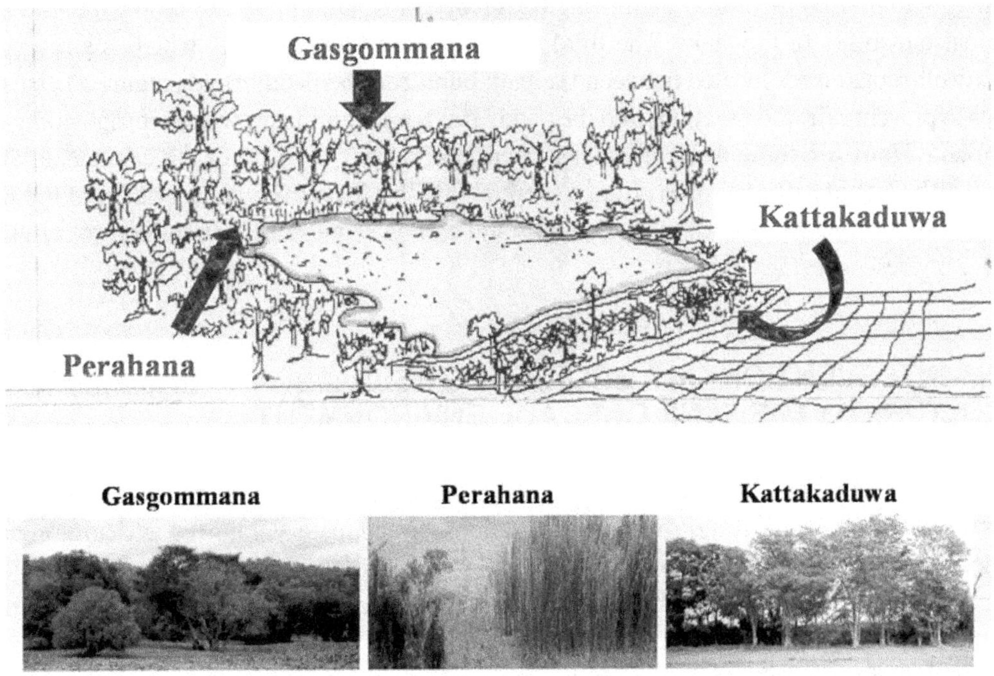

Table 1. Percentage of forest reservations within selected tank cascades

	Tank cascade / Micro or sub-watershed	Land cover % of *Mahamukalana* (dense forest)	Land cover % of tank reservations (*Gasgommana, Perahana & Kattakaduwa*)
1	Rambewewa	40	10
2	Dambagaswewa	18	04
3	Palugaswewa	32	12
4	Thirappene	22	05
5	Periyakulama	14	04

Source: (Metric maps & field survey, 2015)

Even in the history, there were large forest patches in the mountainous catchments[5] named as "*Mahamukalana*" (Dense forest) at the *Rajarata in dry zone*. It is the dense forest in the hills of the upper watershed area which has covered 25% (average) of selected cascades in this study. In addition to that there were three types of wet lands forest reservations around the tanks which are having the multiple scientific values. The first one is the "*Gasgommana*". It is a strip of large trees located in the tank catchment, (just above the water level of the tank) which serves as a windbreak, thus reducing evaporation losses. Between 10-20% of the tank water surface had been covered by this type of forest patches. These tree zones are very important in the dry and intermediate zones, as evaporation is high during the last two third of the cropping season, to have an adequate supply of water, through minimizing the evaporation. The second one is the "*Perahana*", which is a strip of bushes which acts as a filter and prevents eroded soil from agricultural lands in the catchment. These silt traps are, one of the secrets behind the long period of sustainability of the tanks. The third feature is the "*Kattakaduwa*" which is a reserved land strip with well-rooted trees located between the tank bund and the paddy field (Figure 4). This plot of land helps to prevent salt water seeping into the paddy fields and minimises water seepage going through the tank bund. However, these three plots have been representing 4 - 12% of the cascade areas (Table 1) in the North Central dry zone of Sri Lanka (Perera, 2017b). Moreover, conservation of biodiversity, supplying medicinal plants, fire woods, wild fruits and carbon sequestration in the forests, are the other advantages of these forest reserves.

RECENT INTERVENTION OF AGRO-WELL BASED AGRICULTURETO THE TANK CASCADE ENVIRONMENT

This diversified unique of tank cascade systems have been changing towards complex resource utilization with new involvements such as agro-wells constructions. In the history, rain-fed agricultural activities were practiced by farmers in their home gardens and *chena* lands in addition to the paddy cultivation under the small tank irrigation. With the shallow ground water-based agro-well practices, they cultivated throughout the year, even without rain.

Construction of agro-wells in the dry zone began in 1989, with the intervention of the Agricultural Development Authority and the Provincial Council of the North Central Province. Previously, Anuradhapura Dry Zone Agricultural Project (ADZAP) has been implemented at 12 villages, in Anuradhapura district of the dry zone (Perera 2016). The project was conducted over five years from 1981 onwards for the establishment of well-developed farming systems, including the restoration of minor tanks and encouraging agro-wells (Jayasena, 1991). However, in this project the priority was given to the restoration of minor tanks and but not to agro-wells. Although the construction of agro-wells, were started in 1989 in the area using man power, excavation of agro-wells was accelerated between 1991-1995 with the arrival of excavation machines to the area, to mitigate the hydrological issues.

The construction of agro-wells was not only determined the hydrological considerations, but also political, economic and management factors were focused towards this new development strategy, over the last few decades (Panabokke *et al.* 2002). As identified by Aheeyar and Ariyabandu (2007) about 55% of Agro-wells have been constructed with a subsidy programme in the Anuradhapura and Kurunegala districts, and the rest of the 45% have been constructed by the farmers without any external assistance. In the study area, 52% farmers have constructed agro-wells with subsidy programmes of North Central Provincial Council and The National agro-well Programme launched by the Agricultural Development Authority since 1989. In this context, the use of shallow ground water, by using agro-wells for dry land farming has become much popular (Figure 5).

Figure 5. An Agro-well in Periyakulama cascade, Malwathuoya basin
Source: Field observation - 2012

Consequently, the construction of Agro-wells was spread out throughout the low land areas of the tank cascades. Gradually farmers used to practice the agro-well based agriculture even without the external supports. However, every possible space was converted to agro-well base practices (Perera, 2017a).

Recent studies revealed that construction of agro-wells had reached the maximum level in several cascades in the dry zone. When considering the 6 tank cascades[6] in the Malwathu Oya basin, there were 102 agro-wells in 1994. But it has been doubled (212agro-wells) by the year 2000, and increased up to 404 by the year 2012 (Figure 6).

Figure 6. Availability of agro-wells in 6 tank cascades of Malwathuoya basin
Source: Aerial photos 1994, Farmer organization data, Geo Eye 1 Satellite images 2012.

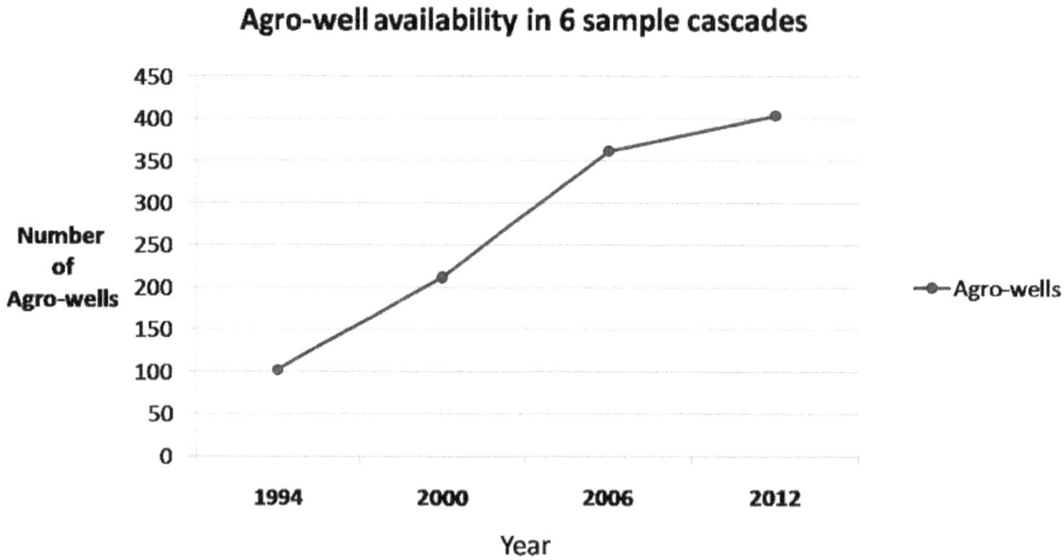

Excavating agro-wells in low land areas in tank cascades is very prominent due to the empirical knowledge of the dry zone farmers regarding the groundwater availability in these areas. Usually the ground water level is much higher in the low land areas between highlands or immediate catchment areas of small tanks. Under the agro-well practices, farmers have annually cultivated chilies, big onions, brinjals, soybeans, pumpkins, ma-beans, green gram, bitter gourd, *wetakolu, thibbatu*, okra, maize, and manioc as seasonal crops. In addition, these farmers have been cultivating perennial crops as a mixed system with seasonal crops (Perera, 2009).

Agro-well practice is an attractive model in the dry zone areas of Sri Lanka. A large number of farmers have started cultivating perennial crops such as coconut, mango, jack, cashew, lime, orange, betel beds, drumsticks, papaya and banana, in their agro-well based agricultural land. In this context, the farmers fulfilled the water requirement for both seasonal and perennial crops simultaneously. They cultivated perennial crops closer to the agro-wells or side of the agricultural land or cultivate as a mixed system. Some farmers reserved a section of their land for timber trees such as teak and halmilla for the economic purposes. Usually they reserved the tail end of the land or marginal areas for this purpose. Further these farmers have erected live fences using gliricidia, teak, and kohomba. Farmers expect to gather fuel wood and to fulfill their timber requirement through this intervention.

About 12% of farmers cultivated crops in both cultivation seasons (*Yala & Maha*) under the agro-well water in addition to rain water. A majority of the farmers have used agro-wells only in the dry season. The common cultivation season (agro-well based) is May to October. The duration was the post-harvesting period of paddy cultivation under the tank irrigation and rain-fed highland cultivation (Figure 7).

In addition, 5% of farmers in the dry zone have been engaged in animal husbandry during this seasonal and perennial cropping system (Perera, 2009). They especially like rearing cows because of the low-cost practice. The farmers use the tree shade and ground layer grasses of perennial crop lands, in their agro-well lands.

Figure 7. Agro-well based cropping in Malwathuoya basin
Source: Field study, 2014

Gradual Development of Agro-Forestry Systems in the Agro-Well Lands

The farmers have integrated trees into agro-forestry systems and they have developed their cultivation lands every year. Therefore, the number of trees has been increased in their lands. Farmers have introduced various 'food trees', 'fruit trees', 'understory crops', as well as 'woody trees' in addition to the seasonal crops. Farmers cultivate these trees around the agro-wells or around the huts (dwelling within the farmland) according to the water requirement or labor requirement. Crops requiring more water such as tempering leaves, ginger and sugarcane are placed around the well. More labor required crops such as fruit trees are placed around the hut. This practice created a new land use pattern with many diverse crops. A considerable fraction of their land allocated for timber trees such as teak. Timber trees are usually grown in the periphery of the farm lands and at the tail ends of irrigation ditches. Farmers also plant live fences using glidsiria, teak, and *kohomba* with the expectation of meeting firewood and timber. Some farmers grow timber trees in their lands for economic purposes. This was an easy income-generation activity using degraded areas of their agro-well based lands (Figure 8 and 9).

Figure 8. Land use of agro well based agro forestry in Yan Oya basin (agro-well is in the middle)
Source: Google Images (Imagery Date: 5/7/2012) and field studies, 2015

Other than crops, farmers practice animal husbandry as a part of the cropping system. They especially like rearing cows because of the low cost. A total of 15% of the farmers in the upper Malwathu Oya basin area practice rearing cows in their agro-well based farmland using tree shade and ground layer grasses in the around and closer to agro-wells. They supplement the household requirements of milk and get extra income by transporting and selling cow milk to the internal market daily. These agro-well based lands have been converted to 'seasonal and perennial cultivation system with woody trees' or 'seasonal and perennial cultivation system with woody trees and animal husbandry' within 5- 6 years. With this background, cropping pattern under these agro-wells, are being converted to 'Agroforestry systems' (Perera, 2009).

Figure 9. Land use pattern of the agro-well based agro-forestry system
Source: Perera, (2009)

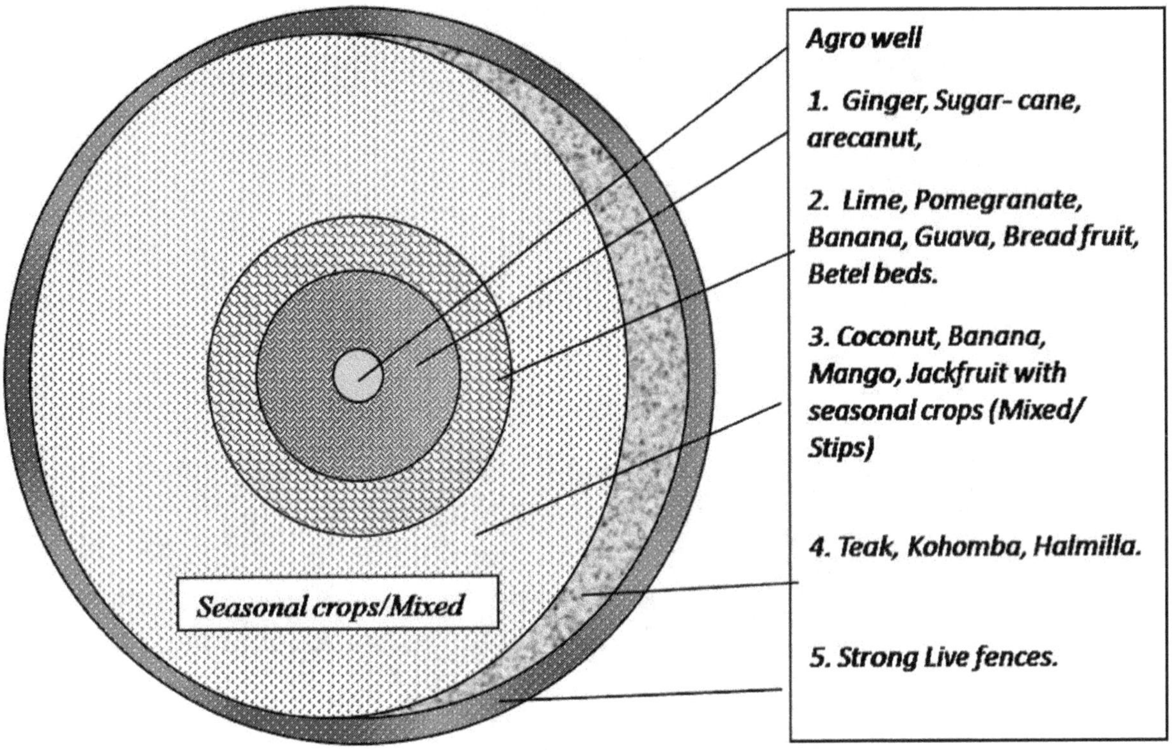

CURRENT LAND USE PATTERN AND MANAGEMENT OF THE TANK CASCADE ENVIRONMENT

The current land use patterns were based on, accessibility, fertility of lands, distribution of forests, tank system, and availability of groundwater of the area. However, a few similar land use types were noticed in 20 tank cascades during the recent studies. These are; forests, *chena*, tanks, paddy fields, agro-well lands, teak plantations, home gardens and village road networks. The forest areas consisted of Riverine forest strips, tank reservations and highland natural forest patches (Perera and Rekha, 2016). Generally, the land use pattern of the tank cascade areas is attractive. The reason was all tank cascades consists of a few tanks, paddy fields, rivulets, highland rain-fed agriculture, and home gardens in highland areas (one or both sides of the tanks). In addition to that tank reservations could be seen around the tanks too (Figure 10).

Paddy cultivation found in command areas[10] of small tanks was the typical traditional cropping system in the dry zone areas. The farmers annually cultivate paddy during the period of the North-Eastern monsoon. In general, rain-fed highland agricultural lands are the largest land use type (about 30%) and these lands emerged as a result of *chena* cultivation with other human activities during the past few decades. The *chena* cultivation was the most significant land use pattern during past few decades. But in the recent past, a lot of farmers are changing the *chena* cultivation practices into a stable cultivation system with or without agro-wells.

Figure 10. A view of the land use pattern in a tank cascade (in Malwathu oya basin)
Source: Modified from Google Images (Imagery date 05-07-2012).

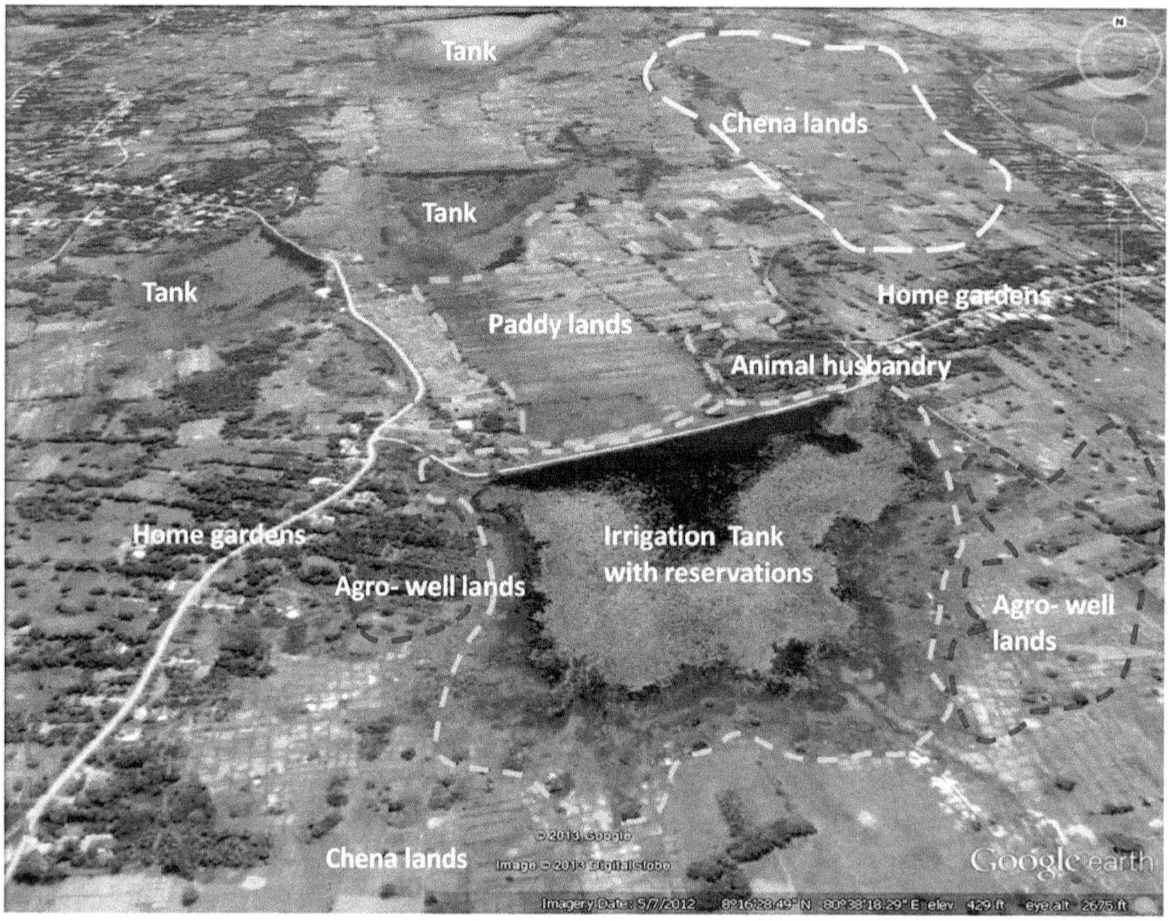

The current land use pattern of tank cascade environment was recently reported by Perera (2016) using 6 tank cascades in the North-central dry zone. Approximately 22% of the land area was covered with *chena* lands and about 20% belonged to agro-well lands. About 7% of total Agro-well lands were situated in command areas under the tanks. Paddy lands under these cascades cover about 15% of the total land area while about 10% is covered by tanks. Forest covers about 8% while about 2% of the total forest lands belong to "State or Private Teak Plantations", established in the 1960-1970 decade and in 1996-2000 under the Participatory Forestry Project of the forest department. In addition to that 6% was consisted of tank reservations. The rest 19% belong to home gardens with mixed land uses practices (Figure 11).

Figure 11. Overall land use of Selected 6 Tank cascades in Malwathu Oya and Yan oya basins
Source: Data derived from Geo eye -1 satellite images, 2012

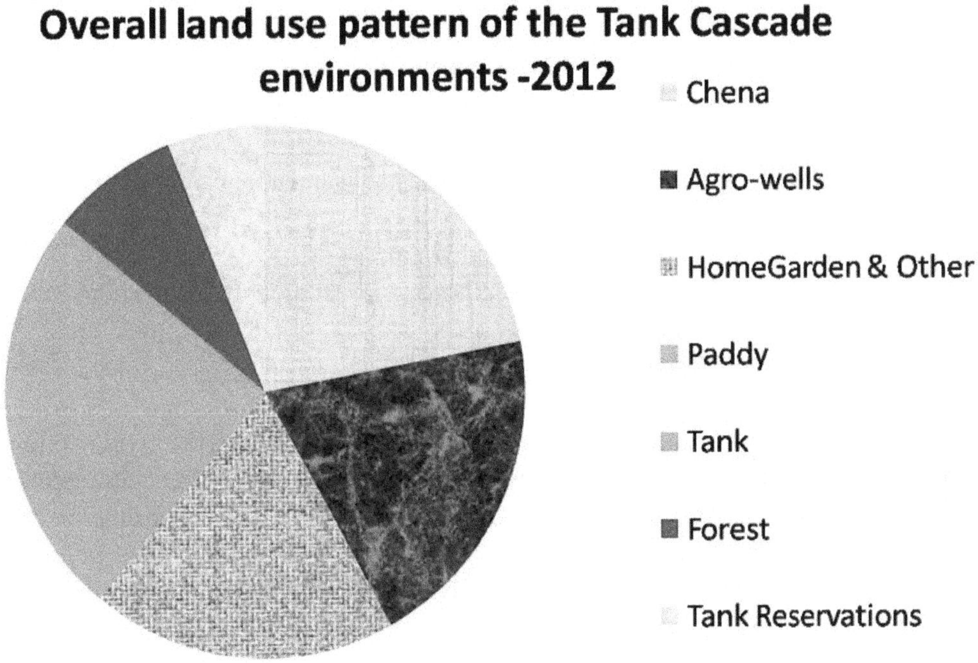

The agricultural productivity depends on a range of factors including the source of water, quantity of water, timing of water use, climatic factors, quality of soil, and overall management practices. Some of these factors may be inter-connected. The cropping pattern of the area was a mixed system. The dominant seasonal crops are paddy, chilies, big onion, maize, soybean and vegetables, while the dominant perennial crops are coconut, and various fruit tree species such as mango, cashew and banana.

In the modern period a set of hydronomic zones are identified in these areas based on hydro biological and topographic characteristics by recent scientists (IWMI, 2000). These are the Water Source Zone, Natural Recapture Zone, Regulated recapture Zone, Final Use Zone and Environmental Sensitive Zone (wet lands). However, it was revealed that there were same hydro biological and topographic zones, historically in the tank cascade environment of the Dry Zone of Sri Lanka. These are call as e "*Mahamukalana*" (dense forest with water sources), "Tanks and Anicuts" (water stores), "*Kethyaya*and *village*" (regulated zone/production zone), "*Villuwa*" (the wet or marshy land with high biodiversity at lower valley). Some of the farmers in selected tanks of the Yan Oya basin, named as*Villuwa* as '*Pan Akkaraya*' (one acre of mat grass) due to mat grasses in that marshy lands.

Planning of the cultivation of irrigation lands of the downstream area need to be considered to allocate the sufficient areas of extent for cultivation of various crops desired by the farmers, enhance the knowledge on the quantity of rainfall and water availability of tank and ground water etc. Rural farmers have the considerable knowledge of the above needs. The victory of the adoption of improved land and water management practices are mostly depending on the nature of the water source and the water users of the particular environment. It can be envisaged that the farming with groundwater through lift irrigation would have given the additional advantages and provide opportunities for farmers to adopt improved crop and water management practices, which must ultimately increase the water productivity and monitory return to the farmer. When farmers have access to groundwater, the following advantages (i-v) could be received by the dry zone farmers in tank cascades (Dharmasena,2002)

i. Land preparation can be completed in advance without waiting for seasonal rains.
ii. Limited well water available during the dry period prior to season can be utilized for raising nurseries.
iii. Soil moisture deficit; the major problem for the establishment of perennial crops can be overcome through agro-wells.
iv. High monetary return is from off season cultivation.
v. Assurance for water is high so that farmers tend to invest more on cultivation.

Participatory Intervention

This tank cascade systems could provide many lessons in participatory activities through using and exchanging natural and agricultural resources even in the present day. Many tank cascade villages have farmer organization to implement collective decisions. Each farmer is responsible for the maintenance of a section of a tank bund and canal system on the basis of land ownership of the paddy field. With the beginning of *Maha* season which is major cultivation period, all of the farmers of the village would gather to the tank bund to discuss the cultivation plan under the supervision of "*Well Vidane*" (Chief of the particular farmer organization). They have annually maintained all parts of the irrigation network on sharing basis. Sharing the seed materials and instruments are the other common practices among the villages. Further, the "*Attam System*" (exchange of labor), "*Bethma System*" (sharing of one part of the paddy land among all farmers in the dry season), are practicing by them. Seasonal water sharing with well-prepared time schedule, and sharing of agricultural instruments can be seen even today. Finally, after harvesting there is a traditional ceremonial festival with the participation of all villagers, under the respective tank.

CHALLENGES OF THE TANK CASCADE LAND USE SYSTEM

Different kinds of challenges could be noticed such as removal of the forest plots to construct the agro-wells, expansion of the agricultural area towards the reservation, physical damages, and collection of woody materials were also recorded in tank cascade areas recently (Perera,2017b). Although, 96% of lands were in the "very low soil salinity" category, soil salinity has been increased in agro-well lands with increase of cropping duration in tank cascades of the upper Malwatu Oya basin (Perera, 2016). These results indicated that, the soil salinity would be a problem, in tank cascade environment in near future. Madduma Bandara (2009), and Dharmasena (2010) have mentioned that, the various development activities, degrading biological resources, destruction of the village ecosystems, are the most distinct factors that have affected the tank cascade systems in Sri Lanka. Marambe *et al.* (2012) revealed that there has been a drastic reduction in forest cover and degrading of flora and fauna species due to various development activities in the tank cascades during the past few decades. Accordingly, the general opinion is that recent agricultural changes including village expansion, road system development, and agro-well development, have affected to decrease the floral diversity to some extent in the tank cascade systems. In addition to that, with the increases of human interventions, some of the socio-environmental challenges including Human-Elephant conflicts and other wild life impacts to agricultural areas have shown an increasing trend.

CONCLUSION

Ancient Sri Lankans in the Rajarata have practiced some land management techniques in the tank cascade environments. All these cascades have been converted in to sustainable and people friendly survival units, with surface water management, ground water development with rich biodiversity. In the 3rd and 5th centaury AD, advanced hydraulic structures including tanks and irrigation canal system have been designed and constructed with the sound traditional knowledge based on the key hydrological and land use relationship. The connected groups of tanks (as a cascade system) have become the best practice of water management in the dry season by storing water in the rainy season and release to the downstream irrigation areas during the dry period. Upper catchments of the tanks were covered by the forest, and act as a sponge to capture rain water and release to the down streams in the dry season. Traditional soil and water conservation measures and tank systems helped to maintain the groundwater level, stream base flow as well as the land productivity. Various types of effective environmental zoning systems and participatory techniques were also practiced in the system. The dry zone farmers have been engaging agro-well based agriculture in addition to the tank-based irrigation agriculture since few decades. This background has provided many valuable lessons of traditional and modern land use practices. Some traditional practices such as maintaining tank reservations with the scientific value, are still more effective than the modern efforts of integrated land and water management practices. However, with the recent interventions including village expansion and agro-well development in tank cascades, some of the challenges have been emerged, emphasizing the need of sustainable land-water management system in the dry zone of Sri Lanka.

REFERENCES

Aheeyar, M. M. M., & Ariyabandu, R. D. S. (2002).Socio-economic Issues Pertinent to Agro-well Farming in Sri Lanka. In S. Pathmarajah (Ed.), *Use of Ground Water for Agriculture in Sri Lanka -Symposium Proceedings*. Peradeniya: Agricultural Engineering Society of Sri Lanka.

Brohier, R. L. (1934). *Ancient Irrigation Works in Ceylon*. Ministry of Mahaweli Development.

Dharmasena, P. B. (2002). Integrated Management of Surface and Ground Water Resources in Tank Cascade Systems. In S. Pathmarajah (Ed.), *Use of Ground Water for Agriculture in Sri Lanka -Symposium Proceedings*. Peradeniya: Agricultural Engineering Society of Sri Lanka.

Dharmasena, P. B., & Goodwill, I. M. (1999). Use of Ground Water in Minor Tank Irrigation Schemes of Sri Lanka. *Proceedings of 17thInternational Congress on Irrigation and Drainage*, 175-194.

International Water Management Institute. (2000). *Towards Integrated Water and Land Resources Management*. International Water Management Institute.

Jayasena, W. G. (1991). *Anuradhapura Dry Zone Agricultural Project (ADZAP)-A socio economic study of project beneficiaries*. Agrarian Research & Training Institute.

Madduma Bandara, C. M. (1985). Catchment Eco-systems and Village Tank Cascades in the Dry Zone of Sri Lanka. The Geo-Journal.

Madduma Bandara, C. M. (2009). Village Tank Cascade Systems of Sri Lanka: A Traditional Technology of Water and Drought Management. *Proceedings of the third annual workshop on disaster reduction hyperbase -Asian application.*

Marambe, B., Pushpakumara, G., & Silva, P. (2012).Biodiversity and Agro biodiversity in Sri Lanka: Village Tank Systems. In Biodiversity Observation Network in the Asia-Pacific Region. Springer.

Panabokke, C. R. (2002). *The Nature and Prosperities of Small Tank Systems of the Dry Zone and Their Sustainable Production Thresholds*. International Water Management Institute.

Panabokke, C. R., Sakthivadivel, R., & Weerasinghe, A. D. (2002). *Small Tanks in Sri Lanka-Evolution, Present Status and Issues*. International Water Management Institute.

Pant, N., & Verma, R. K. (2010). *Tanks in Eastern India: A Study in Exploration*. IWMI,Hydrabad, Tata Water Policy Research Program. doi:10.5337/2010.228

Perera, M. P. (2009). Integrating Agroforestry Characteristics into Agro-well based Agricultural Lands. In *Proceedings of National Conference on Water, Food security and Climate Change in Sri Lanka*, International Water Management Institute.

Perera, M. P. (2010). *Irrigation Heritage of Sri Lanka (Sinhala Version)*. Center for Environmental Justice.

Perera, M. P. (2016). Development of Agro-well Lands and Its impact on Soil Salinity in the North Central Dry Zone of Sri Lanka. *International Journal of Scientific Research (Ahmedabad, India)*, *5*(7), 497–501. doi:10.21275/v5i7.ART2016217

Perera, M. P. (2017a). Groundwater Extraction through Agro-wells and its Impact on Groundwater Availability of Tank Cascades in the Dry Season: A Case Study in the Dry Zone of Sri Lanka. *International Journal of Scientific Research and Innovative Technology*, *4*(6), 50–62.

Perera, M. P. (2017b). Stream Reservations are at Risk?:A Case Study on the Agro-well Development in the Dry Zone of Sri Lanka. *International Journal of Scientific Research (Ahmedabad, India)*, *6*(6), 2149–2153. doi:10.21275/ART20174619

Perera, M. P., & Rekha Nianthi, K. W. G. (2016). The Impact of Agro-well Development on Floral Diversity in Tank Cascades in the Dry Zone of Sri Lanka. *International Journal of Scientific Research (Ahmedabad, India)*, *5*(6), 2061–2065. doi:10.21275/v5i6.NOV164764

Rekha Nianthi, K. W. G., & Dharmasena, P. B. (2009). Indigenous Knowledge of Farming Practices and Water Management in the Dry Zone of Sri Lanka. In R. Shaw (Ed.), *Indigenous Knowledge and Disaster Risk Reduction* (pp. 329–348). Nova Science Publishing.

Rekha Nianthi, K. W. G., & Jayakumara, M. A. S. (2010). Progress of Research on Cascade Irrigation Systems in the Dry Zone of Sri Lanka. In R. Shaw & D. Thaitakoo (Eds.), *Water Communities* (pp. 109–137). Emerald Publishing. doi:10.1108/S2040-7262(2010)0000002010

Tennakoon, M. U. A. (2005). *Ellangawa (Sinhala Version)*. Godage and Sons publishing.

KEY TERMS AND DEFINITIONS

Agro-Wells: Large diameter wells for agricultural activities.

Agroforestry Systems: Agricultural activities with woody trees.

Bethma System: Sharing of one part of the paddy land among all farmers in the dry season, due to scarcity of water.

Chena Lands: Dry zone mixed farming system, without a home garden.

Empherical Knowledge: Indigenous knowledge with practical experience.

Hydraulic Civilization: Civilized community based on irrigation activities.

Tank Cascades: Connected series of tanks with micro catchments and command areas, organized within a small valley.

Tank Reservations: Different forest reserves in the vicinity of tanks.

Woody Trees: Tree species with timber value.

ENDNOTES

1 Rain fed cultivation mainly based on seasonal crops (sometimes without proper land ownership).

2 December to February.

3 Connected series of tanks with micro catchments and command areas, organized within a small valley.

4 Land strip between the village and paddy field.

5 Combined earth bunds in the s, (similar to paddy field) to control the runoff.

6 Catchment areas in the hill country.

7 Large diameter wells for agricultural activities based on shallow groundwater.

8 Three from Malwathu Oya basin (*Halmillawewa, Koon wewa, Periyakulam*) and other three from Yan Oya basin (*Rambewewa, Dambagaswewa, BeliKulama*).

9 Irrigation area under the irrigation tank.

Chapter 17
Land Use Planning and Sustainable Development: An Overview of Remote Sensing

Mohd Nazish Khan
Aligarh Muslim University, India

Samreen Fatima
Interdisciplinary Department of Remote Sensing and GIS Applications, Aligarh Muslim University, India

ABSTRACT

This chapter explores the ability of remote sensing and GIS technology for the preparation of land use land cover plan in an effective manner. It is an established fact that remote sensing products are being widely used for land use and land cover products to facilitate their stakeholders to provide them cost effective and reproducible mechanism to extract meaningful information for the development of infrastructure in particular region at any scale. Remote sensing has produced different high resolution datasets that may be convert into fruitful products by using recently developed image processing techniques. India is vast country, having natural resources as land resources which needs reallocation as per future demands. Present legislation and regulation are hardly enough for sustainable development of land resources.

1. INTRODUCTION

A report was published by the Brunt Land Commission titled as "Our Common Future" to establish a link between economic development and environmental stability. In this way, sustainable development refers to "Development that meets the needs of present without compromising the ability of future generations to meet their own needs". It is an organized principle that delivers natural resources and ecosystem services for the economic development of human beings Rachel (2015), Brodhag & Taliere (2006) and UNGA (1987).

DOI: 10.4018/978-1-7998-4372-6.ch017

The Economist- Rene Passet (1979) proposed a three sphere framework as "ecology, economy and equity". However, some other workers regarded it as four dimensional frame work which includes politics and culture.

Figure 1. Different components of sustainable development

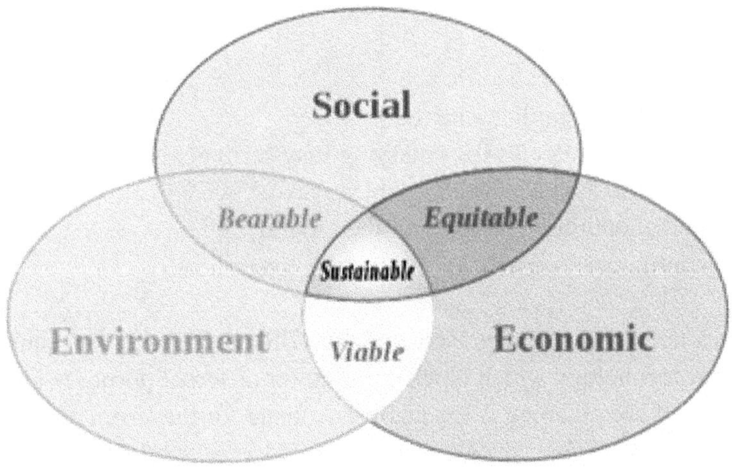

1.1 Aims and Objectives

The primary objective of land use planning is to provide an efficient mechanism for the allocation of land resources for sustainable utilization, acquisition and disposition at desired scale. Efficient land use planning fecilitates their stake holders for better decision making and sustainable utilization of resources. Further, it is aimed to demonstrate the utility of remote sensing and GIS in assessment, analysis and monitoring the land use planning and resources. For this purpose, different techniques of image analysis have been discussed in the later part of this chapter such as visual image interpretation, digital image interpretation to predict the changes as well as future directions of development in terms of land use planning and technology itself.

Land use and land cover of India has been exemplified for expressing the utility of remote sensing and GIS technology. It is evident that India is a vast country and scored second position in terms of population, contained huge diversity in the form of resources as well as their utilization for different purposes.

1.2 Land Use Planning and Its Importance

Land use planning is attributed to the reasonable rationing between environmental components and socio-economic demands to fulfill the future needs of the community. It is an important resource that is evaluated to predict the inherent capabilities of land in order to support different (specific) uses of it for a long period of time without decay (Bandyopadhyay et al., 2009). The importance of land use planning is witnessed by the frequency of analysis and evolution of analyzing techniques (conventional to remote sensing techniques) as well as the demand for land use planning to meet the future needs of human-being. For example, integrated watershed management practices have been implemented worldwide to demarcate the properties of land, the position of land categories, and its usage by many workers such as Durbude and Venkatesh (2004).

Remote sensing provides a cost effective and efficient way of land use planning at various scales. This technology can be utilized for rebuilding of an integrated land use planning policy, which will be essential for improving the methods and techniques for sustainable development and securing long-term goals.

Land use planning may be achieved through several objectives:

1. Inventory of land resources for specific use
2. Collection of information regarding change
3. Evaluation of alternative strategies for satisfying long-term goals
4. Preparation of policies to achieve different objectives
5. Implementation and adoption on policies on the ground
6. Monitoring and continuous assessment of implemented policies

For achieving objectives above, remote sensing and GIS can be used for planning at many levels. This is a state of the art technology which is widely used for different purposes including land use and land cover planning. Land use planning is the key prerequisite for the sustainable development of land resources. It has gained considerable space among stakeholders as a subject of policy discussion at the national level. Governments, communities, and other stakeholders including planners, managers, and real state players are being forced to recognize the significance of not only rationalizing the use of land. However, the progress is to slow to bridge the gap between current unscientific development and sustainable development for future generations (Lindgren, 1985; Silberstein & Maser, 2014).

2. INDIA AND DIVERSITY (LAND RESOURCES)

India is a South Asian country, having the second position in terms of population, bounded by the Bay of Bengal in the Southeast, Indian Ocean in the South and Arabian Sea in the Southwest. The country shares its boundary with Myanmar, Bangladesh, Bhutan, Nepal, China, and Pakistan. The country is expanded in 3,287,263 sq km area from Kashmir to Kanyakumari and Hindukush range to Myanmar with a population of 1.3 billion.

The major part of India is lying atop the Indian Tectonic Plate which is part of Indo-Australian Plate. Seventy-five million years ago, India was part of supercontinent Gondwana afterward, India migrated towards northeastward due to seafloor spreading to its South-west, and later South and South-east. Simultaneously, the Eurasian Plate moved towards the south to abduct over Tethyan oceanic crust, resulting uprise of Himalayan Mountain.

The forest cover of India is about 701,673 km^2 which is 21.35% of the countries total area. Further, it is divided into very dense forest (more than 70% canopy density), moderately dense forest (40-70% canopy density), and open forest (10-40% canopy density) (Table 1). The very dense forest predominates Western Ghats, Andaman Nicobar region, and the northeastern parts of India. Moderately dense forest covers the temperate parts of the Himalaya. Moreover, moderately dense forest extent to eastern central and southern India. The open forest lies in the Central Deccan and Western Gangetic plain (ISFR, 2017).

Table 1. Total forest cover in India and its concentrated regions

S. No.	Types of Forest	Total Covered Area (sq km)	Canopy Density	Concentrated Regions
01	Very Dense Forest	99,278	>70%	Western Ghats, West Bengal, Andaman Region, Arunachal Pradesh& Northeastern Areas
02	Moderately Dense Forest	3,08,472	40-70	Andhra Pradesh, Arunachal Pradesh, Chhattisgarh, Karnataka, Madhya Pradesh, Maharashtra, Meghalaya etc.
03	Open Forest	3,04,499	10-40	Andhra Pradesh, Arunachal Pradesh, Madhya Pradesh, Maharashtra, Mizoram, etc.
	Total Forest Cover	7,12,249		

(Census, 2011)

2.1 Forest Cover in India

As per census 2011, about 80% of India's population live in villages depended on the forests for their necessities. There are more than 6,500,000 villages in the country, out of which nearly 170,000 villages are located in the close proximity of forest areas. Therefore, forests play a significant role in the socio-economic as well as cultural development of inhabitants. The increasing population is posing pressure over forest resources, resulting in deforestation, cutting of wood, increasing dependency, and impaired productivity to obtain necessary items from forests (Table 2).

2.2 Land Use Planning For Sustainable Development In India

The population of India has increased by 284% (36.3 crore- 124.72 crores), and yield of food grains have increased by 386% (51- 196 million ton) (ISFR, 2019). India is conferred with important natural resources that are fulfilling the basic needs of the countries inhabitants. The country has 150-million-hectare land, used for agriculture production and contributed 24% in national Gross Domestic Production (GDP). During 1990-2000, it was estimated that India is losing 380.89 Km^2 forest cover annually. Deforestation at such a big scale is changing the natural equilibrium of the environment as well as the dependency of the social system over forest products. Although, the half of the livestock population is also dependent on the forest areas for grazing.

Modernization has imposed great pressure on the government and other stakeholders to analyze the land use pattern in the country to improve the utilization of land resources and sustainability. Remote sensing technology has provided economic and excellent avenues for land use and land cover mapping. Land use and land cover maps of an area give the insight to help their users to understand the present status of the landscape. Land use and land cover information on national resources will enable the monitoring of temporal dynamics of different ecosystems such as agriculture, forest, etc. For this purpose, the Indian Space Research Organization (ISRO) has prepared the land use and land cover map for the entire country at 1:50,000 scale by using three-season data at every five years. These maps have been prepared to deliver the land use and land cover map, land use and land cover change and identification of major change (areas). The data has been prepared for the year 2005-06, 2011-12, and 2015-16.

Table 2. Shows the total geographical area of states and area of forest cover

S. No.	Name of State	Total Geographical Area	Total Forest Area (Sq. Km)	Percentage of Forest
01	Andhra Pradesh	162968	37258	22.86
02	Arunachal Pradesh	83743	51407	61.86
03	Assam	78438	26832	34.21
04	Bihar	94163	6877	7.30
05	Chhattisgarh	135192	59772	44.21
06	Delhi	1483	102	6.88
07	Goa	3702	1225	33.09
08	Gujrat	196244	21647	11.03
09	Haryana	44212	1559	3.53
10	Himachal Pradesh	55672	37033	66.52
11	Jammu & Kashmir	222236	20230	9.10
12	Jharkhand	79716	23605	29.61
13	Karnataka	191791	38284	19.96
14	Kerala	38852	11309	29.11
15	Madhya Pradesh	308252	94689	30.72
16	Maharashtra	307713	61579	20.01
17	Manipur	22237	17418	78.01
18	Meghalaya	22429	9496	42.34
19	Mizoram	21081	5641	26.76
20	Nagaland	16579	8623	52.01
21	Odisha	155707	61204	39.31
22	Punjab	50362	3084	6.12
23	Rajasthan	342239	32737	9.57
24	Sikkim	7096	5841	82.31
25	Tamilnadu	130060	22877	17.59
26	Telangana	112077	26904	24.00
27	Tripura	10486	6294	60.02
28	Uttar Pradesh	240928	16582	6.88
29	Uttarakhand	53483	38000	71.05
30	West Bengal	88752	11879	13.38
31	A & N Islands	8249	7171	86.93
32	Chandigarh	114	35	30.70
33	Dadra & Nagar Haveli	491	204	41.55
34	Daman & Diu	111	8	7.21
35	Lakshadweep	30	0	0.00
36	Puducherry	490	13	2.65

Further, LULC maps at 1:25000 scale have been prepared to estimate the net sown area. It is also planned by the Indian Space Research Organization (ISRO) to prepare land use and land cover maps at 1:10,000 scale to provide meaningful inputs about water, land resources at the village level.

Different wasteland mapping program has also been launched at 1:50,000 and 1:25,000 scale. In this connection, the Indian Space Research Organization has launched the Natural Resource Census Programme. This program has a scope of preparation of land use and land cover maps near real-time at 1:25,000 scale. Advanced Wide Field Sensor (AWiFS) onboard Resourcesat-1, 2, and 2A is being used extensively for this project (Roy & Roy, 2010).

Although, ISRO has developed many programs that are preparing land use and land cover maps at a different scale, still needs grave concern to prepare a modern policy framework at the national level to incorporate concerns of different stakeholders. It is mandatory for the sustainability of natural resources and the optimal utilization of land resources through proper land use planning and management. For the implementation of modern policy, the framing of suitable legislation is mandatory including penalties and punishments for violation of the National Land Use Policy.

As we know that India is diverse country in terms of language, region, climate, rainfall, type of vegetation etc. Therefore, country needs a multi-region policy.

3. REMOTE SENSING

Acquisition and analysis of earth surface features to extract meaningful information without physically contact the target areas or objects, termed as Remote Sensing. This information is obtained by using the electromagnetic spectrum in the form of reflection and emission. This reflected/emitted energy is received by sensor and sensor classify this energy into the different discrete portion that are used to identify earth surface features on the basis of their characteristics. Different materials available on the surface and react to the incoming solar radiation. Further, such interactions are features dependent which means materials have a certain chemical composition that interacts with incoming solar radiation.

For extracting information via remote sensing, sensors need a wide range of sensor platforms. These platforms include hot balloons, pigeon photography, high altitude aircrafts, and earth-orbiting satellites that are used to install remote sensing sensors Lillesland et al. (2004), Khan & Suhail (2019).

Remote sensing was introduced in 1960 to replace the more traditional term "Aerial Photography" and "Aerial photointerpretation". Aerial photography is restricted to visible and thermal portion of electromagnetic spectrum while remote sensing encompassing acquisition of data from all portions of the electromagnetic spectrum including visible.

3.1 Electromagnetic Spectrum

Radiation is an energy that travels and spreads out in the form of visible light from burning candles, emission from heated objects, and radio waves from radio stations. This energy collectively termed as electromagnetic spectrum. Microwaves, infrared, ultraviolet light, X-rays, and gamma rays are also part of the electromagnetic spectrum. These electromagnetic waves have different characteristics in terms of their production and interaction with matter.

Figure 2a. High resolution imagery

Figure 2b. Colored aerial photograph

Electromagnetic spectrum consists of waves of different frequencies, invisible to human eye. Although we are enclosed by these waves, it may be significant for sensing the earth's surface features with a deep understanding of electromagnetic waves and matter. The major part of the electromagnetic spectrum is invisible to human eye. However, invisible portion of electromagnetic has a significant role on the earth surface and meaningful for information extraction.

Figure 3. Electromagnetic Spectrum

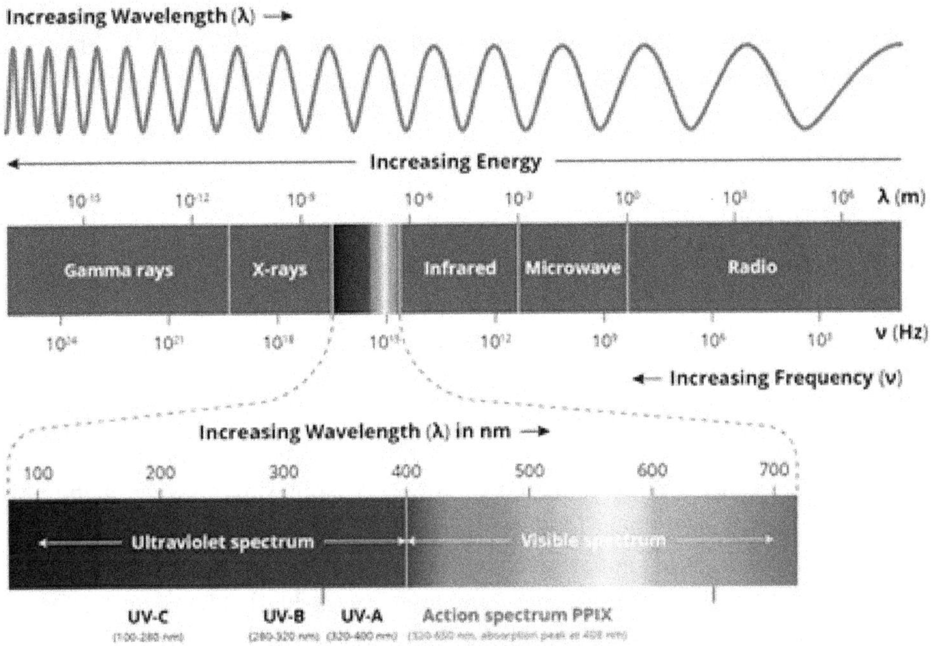

Table 3. Shows the different EM waves and the application areas

S. No.	EM Waves	Wave Length Region	Frequency	Application Areas
01	Gamma Rays	< 100 pm	> 10^{18} Hz	Cancer treatment
02	X-rays	10nm-100pm*	$3x10^{16}$ -10^{18} Hz	Radiography
03	Ultra Violet Rays	380nm-10nm	$8x10^{1}$-$3x10^{16}$ Hz	Disinfectants
04	Visible	380nm-740 nm	400-800THz	Signaling,astronomy
05	Infra-Red	740nm-380nm	30-400THz**	Thermal imaging
06	Microwave	10mm-100µm	03GHz-30THz	Radar, Communication
07	Radio-wave	1mm-1km	Upto30GHz	Communication

*pm-picometer, **THz-Terahertz

3.2 Gamma Rays

Gamma rays are part of electromagnetic spectrum as other EM waves, having smallest wavelength region. These waves are produced by the hottest and most energetic elements in the universe, can be used to treat cancer. Artificially, Gamma rays are generated by nuclear explosions. However, on Earth, it is generated by lighting and radioactive decay.

Gamma rays overlap on the hard X-rays, makes it difficult to differentiate. Although, both Gamma rays and X-rays can damage soft tissues of the flora and fauna, but cosmic origin gamma rays are blocked by the earth atmosphere (Grasty, 1976).

It was observed by Becquerel (1896) that photographic plate could be fogged by invisible and penetrating radiation, emitted from uranium. Later it was established that uranium emits three type of radiation, alpha, beta and gamma whereas gamma radiation is strongly penetrating and travel several hundred meters through air. For the study of soil resources, gammay rays remote sensing is used as substitute to acquire meaningful information of soil in the densely forested areas.Matter absorbs the gamma rays mainly by three processes:

1. The Photo-electric Effect
2. Compton Scattering
3. Pair Production

3.3 Ultra Violet Rays

Ultra violet rays are part of electromagnetic spectrum and having shorter wavelength than visible light. Therefore, these waves are invisible to human eye. However, some insects such as bumble bees can see UV radiation, similarly dog can hear low frequency waves. Ultra Violet radiation has more energy comparatively to the visible light but not as much as Gamma and X-rays, produced by the sun and man-made sources. Ultra Violet radiation have significant effect on the human being in the form of sunburn and suntan. It damages DNA and sterilizes the surfaces by contact the exposed surfaces or areas.

Ultra Violet radiation may be classified as follows:

1. Ultra Violet Radiation- A (UV-A)
2. Ultra Violet Radiation- B (UV-B)
3. Ultra Violet Radiation- C (UV-C)

Some researchers have forwarded a hypothesis that UV-A which is less harmful than UV-B, sometimes can be a cause of skin cancer. Ultra Violet A & B has capability to penetrate the Ozone layer and where UV-B is most common cause of skin cancer, Sunburn and Suntan. UV-C is most dangerous radiation that doesn't come to earth surface due to ozone layer. Therefore, it is not harmful to organisms, living on earth while it has some positive sign over health as it triggers Vitamin- D production in human beings.

3.4 Visible Spectrum

Human eyes can see very small portion of electromagnetic spectrum which is called visible spectrum (380- 740 nano meters).

Our eyes respond in different manner to different wavelength regions of visible spectrum. It is evident in the form of colours as rainbow (violet, Indigo, Blue, Green, Yellow, Orange, Red). Visibility is wavelength dependent as human cannot see the wavelength regions below than visible and above than visible.

Technically, visible spectrum falls in between infrared (IR) and ultraviolet (UV) with a frequency of about 4x1014- 8x1014 cycles per second or hertz. Its wavelength ranges from 380 nano meters to 740 nano meters.

Color is the most important characteristic of the visible light. It is an inherent property of light, also an artefact of the eye. According to Glenn Elert, the objects do not have coloursrather the reflect light that visible in the form of colours. It means colours exist in the mind of beholder.

It is also noted about the visible light that human eyes perceive colours according to the wavelength regions as longer wavelength (740 nano meter) is seen as red while shorter wavelength as 380 is seen as violet. However, human eyes perceive colours by receiving mixture of visible light and can differentiate among colours (Table 4).

Table 4. Visible Spectrum: Wavelength, Frequency and Energy Distribution

Color	Wavelength	Frequency	Photon energy
Violet	380–450 nm	680–790 THz	2.95–3.10 eV
Blue	450–485 nm	620–680 THz	2.64–2.75 eV
Cyan	485–500 nm	600–620 THz	2.48–2.52 eV
Green	500–565 nm	530–600 THz	2.25–2.34 eV
Yellow	565–590 nm	510–530 THz	2.10–2.17 eV
Orange	590–625 nm	480–510 THz	2.00–2.10 eV
Red	625–740 nm	405–480 THz	1.65–2.00 eV

3.5 Infra-Red Waves

Infrared waves are next to the visible portion of spectrum, ranges between 740 nano meters to 1,000,000 nano meters. In the 18th century, it was discovered by the William Herschel. These waves have longer wavelength region which is not visible to human eyes. It is generated by the emission of objects in the form of heat and half of received radiation from the sun is infrared.

Infrared waves can be defined into two categories as reflected infrared and thermal infrared. Reflected infrared consists of Near Infrared (NIR) and short wave infrared (SWIR) while thermal infrared consists of mid infrared (MIR), long wave infrared (LWIR) and far Infrared (FIR). Thermal infrared covers wavelength from 3- 100 micro meter.

Application of Infrared Waves:

1. Thermal Imaging
2. Cool Astronomy
3. Night Vision
4. Hyperspectral Imaging
5. Tracking of weapons
6. Communications
7. Climate Studies
8. Art and conservation Analysis

3.6 Microwaves

These wave are come next to the far infrared, ranges from 1mm to 1 meter with low frequencies due to larger wavelength. Different wavelength regions of microwaves offer wide range of applications to the scientists. Microwaves are designated as S, C,L, X, Ku, K bands, based on the frequencies.

Table 5. Shows Infrared Waves: Wavelength, Frequency and Energy Distribution

Name of Waves	Wavelength	Frequency	Photon energy
Near-infrared	0.75–1.4 µm	214–400 THz	886–1653 meV
Short-wave infrared	1.4–3 µm	100–214 THz	413–886 meV
Mid-wave infrared	3–8 µm	37–100 THz	155–413 meV
Long-wave infrared	8–15 µm	20–37 THz	83–155 meV
Far infrared	15–1000 µm	0.3–20 THz	1.2–83 meV

These waves are useful for navigation and study of earth from space due to high penetration from haze, rain, snow and clouds etc. The SeaWinds instrument which is onboardQuickSCAT satellite uses Ku band of microwaves for the measurement of direction and speed of wind near ocean surface (Adams et al., 1959).

Other Applications:

1. Cooking of food due to vibrations of molecules
2. Wifi
3. Active Remote Sensing- RADAR, Lidar etc.
4. Passive Remote Sensing- Nasa's Tropical Rainfall Measuring Mission (TRMM)
5. Communication
6. Navigation
7. Astronomy
8. Spectroscopy

3.7 Radio Waves

Radio-waves are part of electromagnetic spectrum with a frequency between 10^4 and 10^{12}, the corresponding wavelength is 01 mm and 10,000 km at 300 GHz and at 30 Hz respectively. These waves run at speed of light in the vacuum and variation in speed, may be occurred in the different medium.

Naturally radio-waves are part of electromagnetic spectrum and generated by sun light while radio-waves is generated by the artificial sources such as transmitter and detected by receiver. These waves are widely used for fixed and mobile radio-communication, broadcasting, radar and radio-navigation system and having many other applications.

4. IMAGE PROCESSING

Since the inception of Remote Sensing, the satellite imageries (products) are being classified to obtain standard products in the form of Land Use & Land Cover maps and others. Different classification schemes have been developed to classify satellite products including unsupervised, supervised and object based image analysis etc. Primary objective of classification is to divide the image into cluster of similar features.

Figure 4a. Tone

4.1 Visual Image Interpretation

Remote Sensing products viz., aerial photographs, airborne imagery and satellite imagery contain surface expressions in the form of pixels. These surface expressions may be extracted by using various image analysis techniques including visual image interpretation, evolved during few decades. Recognition of targets and associated information is based on captured differences in the aerial photograph or images. The visual elements of image interpretation are tone, shape, size, pattern, texture, shadow and association (Jansen, 2002; Dadhwal et al., 2018).

Tone: it is referred to the relative difference in the brightness of the objects in the image. Generally, tone of the objects is based on the reflectance, variation of reflectance captured in the different tones in the image. Therefore, it is used as fundamental elements for distinguishing different features.

Shape: Different objects in an image is identified on the basis of their shape or described by its boundary. For example, straight edges in a forest area, may be categorized as agriculture field while more irregular shape in the forest, may be categorized as non-cultivated area.

Size: Size of objects in an image is scale dependent. However, size can be helpful in distinguishing features on the basis of relative size of corresponding objects. Analysts generally estimate size of features approximately for quick identification.

Pattern: As it is known that certain features follow certain patterns on the surface. Therefore, pattern recognition technique is significant in the visual image interpretation to extract meaningful information from an aerial photo/image. For example, orchards with evenly spaced trees and planned colony in city and their streets.

Texture: It is referred as consistency of a surface. It means, it will reflect in the image as arrangement and frequency of tonal variation of an area or object. For example, rough texture would consist of spotted tone (change in color) where grey levels change while smooth texture would have little variation. For example, grasslands have smooth texture and natural forest would have rough texture.

Shadow: in the visual image interpretation, shadow is used to estimate relative height of object and profile. It is also useful in the identification and recognition of landscape variation in a topographic region. Shadow poses limitation to the aerial photography as it can obscure other objects that can hardly be identified.

Figure 4b. Shape

Figure 4c. Size

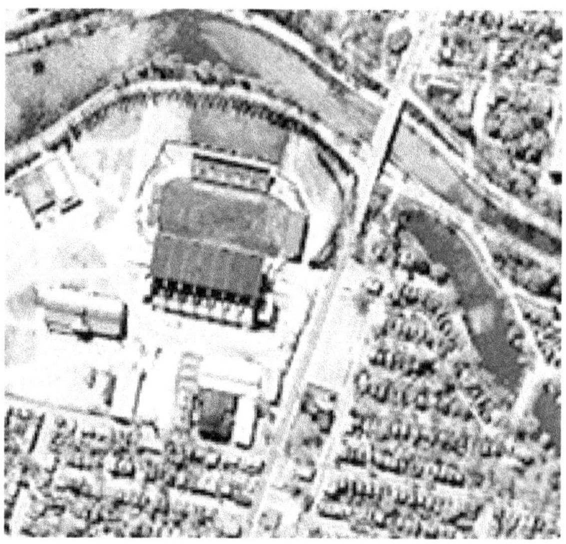

Association: it is described as how the features are organized in relation of others in image or aerial photo including slope, elevation and type of surface covers. For example, you find an activity at spatial location in the image, subsequently, you find out some associated objects/ features that are associated to the identified activity.

Figure 4d. Pattern

Figure 4e. Texture

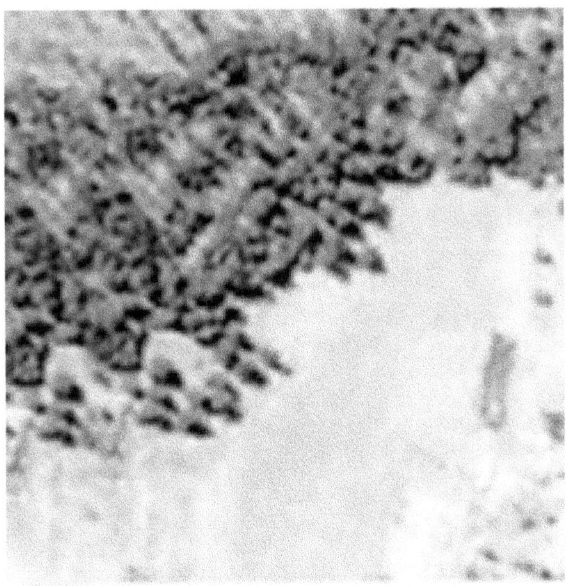

Figure 4f. Shadow

4.2 Unsupervised Image Classification

Unsupervised classification corresponds to the creation of groups/clusters in an image by using certain predefined algorithms. It doesn't require from analyst to having prior knowledge of classes. In this process, unimodal spectral classes are clustered/grouped. Generally, it is the most basic technique which convert image into number of clusters by using image clustering algorithms including K-mean and Isodata, finally assigned classes.

Figure 4g. Association of Features

4.3 Supervised Image Classification

Supervised classification is an essential process, based on the idea where analysts can select some sample pixels in the satellite image that are representative of a particular class which it belongs. In this process, analysts have sufficient knowledge about known pixels, corresponds to the type of land cover on the ground. Samples pixels are known as training sites. After extracting training pixels, the analysts prepare a signature file to input for image classification, based on the given signature file.

Finally, the signature file would be used to run a classification. There are many supervised classification techniques.

- Maximum likelihood
- Minimum-distance
- Principal Component Analysis
- Iso-Cluster
- Support Vector Machine (SVM)

Maxium likelihood is the most popular classification technique which is based on multivariate normal distribution of each spectral class. Therefore, it has advantage of both the mean vectors and multivariate analysis. However, best result of maximum likelihood depends on accurate measurement of mean vector and covariance matrix for spectral class data (Lillesland et al., 2004).

4.4 Object-based Image Classification

Object-based image analysis evolved in the early 1970s. Although due to lack of computing technology, object-based image analysis couldn't flourish. Some specialized softwares were developed in the 1980s to extract linear features. However, this idea was difficult to employ while pixel based classification was gained momentum due to development of neural networks and fuzzy sets.

After few years, advancement in the computing technology and availability of high resolution imagery launch a new avenue for object-based image analysis. Franklin et al., 2003 used this method for producing land use and land cover maps. In the present scenario, object-based image analysis has occupied considerable space and producing better result than pixel-based approach for land use and land cover mapping.

It is a simplest way of image classification which uses both spectral and spatial information of image in the form of homogenous image primitives or objects. It has many advantage over the pixel-based image analysis such as image objects are closely related to the real world objects, if derived carefully. Once, classification is done then topological relationship with other objects, statistical summaries and shape characteristics can be employed in the classification. Object-based classification is two-step process where step one is the procedure to convert image into segments and second step is to classify segmented image as follows:

1. Perform multiresolution segmentation
2. Selecting training areas
3. Define statistics
4. Classify

Image segmentation is the process by which pixel of image are clustered into segments that have similar spectral and spatial characteristics. Each group contains multiple pixel, resemble with real world features. Scale describes the number of minimum pixels into an object. After selection of training objects, further, image is classified by assigning each object to a class based on features and criteria set by analyst (Van et al., 2006).

5. Datasets (Aerial Photographs)

An aerial photograph is simply a photograph which has been captured by using airborne platform including hot balloon, flying kite, by fixing camera at the body of pigeon, helicopter, airplane and drone. The first aerial photograph was captured by Gasper Felix Tournachon (Known as Nadar) by using hot air balloon in 1858 and he patented his idea of using aerial photographs for surveying and map making. Gradually, advancement in the technology of photography as well as platforms made it easy to capture photographs in air.

Since 1855, Number of techniques have been evolved in aerial photography to capture the synoptic view of landforms, processes and events for their spatial significance. Aerial photographs have also enabled us to see stop action view and time freezing moments.

Since 1900, the aerial photography has gained momentum to be part of strategy modules of armies of different countries. Airborne photographs have replaced hand mad posters or maps to prepare efficient strategy against their enemies. For example, Wilbur Right has captured Military base at Centocelli in Rome by using airplane in 1909. During World War I, both groups had used aerial photographs atleast twice a day to capture the entire front. Significant advances have been grown in the camera technology during this time for use in air plane including thermal and infra-red photography (Paul et al., 2014).

5.1 Characteristics of Aerial Photographs

There are several significant things that look to determine the importance of

1. Three Dimensional View
2. Spectral and Spatial Resolution
3. Time Freezing Capabilities
4. Bird's Eye View
5. Availability

5.2 Types of Aerial Photographs

Aerial photographs can be classified on the basis of different parameters of aerial photography including orientation of camera axis, angle of coverage, films, filters etc. It is clear, these properties significantly influence the products.

Orientation of Camera Axis

1. Vertical Aerial Photographs (Camera Axis coincides with the vertical ground)

2. Tilted Photographs (less than 3°)
3. Oblique Photographs (more than 3°)

Angle of Coverage

1. Narrow Angle Photograph
2. Standard Angle Photograph
3. Wide Angle Photograph
4. Ultra-Wide Angle Photograph

Films and Filters

1. Panchromatic
2. Infra-Red Photographs
3. Color
4. Color and Infra-Red
5. Thermal Photographs

5.3 Optical Remote Sensing

Advancement in the computing technology has enabled humans to produce sensors that can capture visible, near infrared, far infrared, thermal and microwave radiation. Most of the radiation that reaches on the surface of the earth, reflected/ emitted back from the surface and available in the atmosphere. This reflected/ emitted energy is received by the sensor and classified into meaningful image, termed as optical remote sensing. In this way, it is interpreted that different materials reflect/emit different energy peaks, may be helpful in identification of surface features, processes and forms. Optical Imaging Systems can be classified as:

5.4 Panchromatic Imaging System

It is a single channel detector that detects and receive radiation within a broad wavelength region as black and white, commonly known as space photograph. For example, panchromatic imagery of IKONOS etc.

5.5 Multispectral Imaging System

Multispectral Imaging System are non-photographic sensors that used for object and material recognition, color analysis, remote sensing and astronomy. Multispectral imager acts on two principles as sensing of reflected/refracted/ emitted energy peaks and detection of these energy peaks into meaningful window of information at sensor. It divides the electromagnetic spectrum (for example, visible spectrum has been divided into three to fourteen bands) into few number of contiguous bands to receive energy peaks to distinguish between two closely spaced features. Multispectral imagery provides information in the form of spectral signature and in spatial extent and multispectral imaging systems improve sensitivity, control exposure and calibrate image intensity efficiently. Final output of the sensors, are received and stored by ground control units for further utilization in public domain. Different sensors are being produced different resolution imagery with different number of bands as Landsat series, IRS series, Quick bird and IKONOS etc.

Table 6. Shows the different Remote Sensing products and their Applications

S. No.	Imaging System	Bands	Characteristics	Applications
01	Aerial Photographs	No Bands	Synoptic view	Survey & Mapping
02	Panchromatic Imager	Single Band	Scene based	Discrimination between two objects
03	Multispectral Imager	03-14	Discriminate between materials	Identification of objects and classification
05	Hyperspectral Imager	> 100 Bands	Provides signature of entire spectrum at every point	Identification of materials and within the materials such as chlorophyll, minerals etc.

5.6 Hyperspectral Imaging System

It was assumed that the each and every material reflect/emit some specific region of wavelength. However, in multispectral imagers, radiation is classified into few number of bands, resulting multispectral imageries hardly provide minute details of objects. A hyperspectral imager is known as imaging spectrometer. It acquires spectral signatures of materials and surface features in more than 100 contiguous bands. The whole concept was based on the imaging spectroscopy. In this process, a data cube is generated which can be used to extract meaningful information about objects. Spectral signatures are used to identify different materials with precise details in the form of spectral reflectance curve.

Table 7. Different Hyperspectral Sensors and platforms

Space borne Sensors	Air borne Sensors	Ground based
1. MODIS 2. MERIS 3. HYPERION 4. CHRIS 5. HYSI	1. CASI 2. HYMAP 3. AVIRIS 4. HYDICE 5. DAIS 6. AIMS 7. AHySI	SPECTRORADIOMETER

To identify materials or objects, reflectance spectra of various objects/ materials of known composition are measured in the field or laboratory to prepare spectral library. Spectral Libraries are used as source information for the matching and interpretation of hyperspectral imagery (ASTER & USGS library). Hyperspectral Imager acquires images from airborne, space-borne and handheld devices (Chein, 2003; Borengasser et al., 2008).

6. CONCLUSION AND RECOMMENDATIONS

It is concluded that land use planning is the achievement of certain goals such as environmental conservation, restraint of urban sprawl, minimization of transport costs, prevention of land use conflicts and minimization of pollutants.

It was observed that during last few decade, India has witnessed unplanned and unprecedented growth in terms population, resulting pressure over the land resources. Therefore, it needs urgent attention of their stakeholders, administrators and policy makers to adopt modern innovative technology to combat with such problems for sustainable land use planning.

Remote sensing datasets are inherently capable in assessment, monitoring, management of land use and their planning for better utilization for the welfare of inhabitants. Remote sensing overcomes conventional limitations of mapping spatial phenomena efficiently and provides modern vistas for land use planning in the form of different type of acquisitions as radar, optical sensing and lidar etc.

Future land usc planning should asses the different components of the existing scenario and revision of previously done work, their objectives and policies. Future land use planning should incorporate present land use plan as agriculture land, residential, commercial, industrial, mixed use, recreational parks and open spaces etc. Future plans should be reviewed at least five years of interval to incorporate changes.

REFERENCES

Adams, J. A. S., Osmond, J. K., & Rogers, J. J. W. (1959). *Physics and Chemistry of the Earth* (Vol. 3). Pergamon Press.

Bandypadhyay, S., Jaiswal, R. K., Hegde, V. S., & Jayaraman, V. (2009). Assessment of land suitability potentials for agriculture using a remote sensing and GIS based approach. *International Journal of Remote Sensing*, *30*(4), 879–895. doi:10.1080/01431160802395235

Borengasser, M., Hungate, W. S., & Watkins, R. (2008). Hyperspectral Remote Sensing: Principles and Applications. CRC Press, Taylor & Francis Group.

Brodhag, C., & Taliere, S. (2006). Sustainable development strategies: Tools for policy coherence. *Natural Resources Forum*, *30*(2), 136–145. doi:10.1111/j.1477-8947.2006.00166.x

Chein-I Chang. (2003). *Hyperspectral Imaging: Techniques for Spectral Detection and Classification.* Springer Science & Business Media.

Dadhwal, V. K., & Kumar, S. (1553–1554). George Joseph and C. Jeganathan(2018). Fundamentals of *Remote Sensing. Photonirvachak (Dehra Dun)*, *46*. Advance online publication. doi:10.100712524-018-0834-7

Durbude, D. G., & Venkatesh, B. (2004). Site suitability analysis for soil and water conservation structures. Photonirvachak. *Photonirvachak (Dehra Dun)*, *32*(4), 399–405. doi:10.1007/BF03030865

Forest Survey of India. (2019). *India State of Forest Report*. ISFR.

Grasty, R. L. (1976). Applications of Gamma Radiation in Remote Sensing. In E. Schanda (Ed.), *Remote Sensing for Environmental Sciences. Ecological Studies (Analysis and Synthesis)* (Vol. 18). Springer. doi:10.1007/978-3-642-66236-2_7

ISFR. (2017). *Forest Survey of India (Published report).* Author.

Jensen, J. R. (2000). *Remote sensing of the environment: An earth resource perspective.* Prentice Hall.

Khan, M. N., & Suhail, M. (2019). Capacity Building: Satellites, Remote Sensing and GIS in the WANA Region. In M. Suhail & A. Rehman (Eds.), *West Asia and North Africa: Changing Paradigms* (Vol. 1). RawatPrakashan.

Lillesland, T. M., Keifer, R. W., & Chipman, J. W. (2004). *Remote Sensing and Image Interpretation* (5th ed.). John Willey and Sons.

Lindgren, D. (1985). *Land Use Planning and Remote Sensing.* doi:10.1007/978-94-017-2035-9

Passet, R. (1979). *L'Économique et le vivant.* Payot. (in French)

Paul, Wolf, Dewitt, & Wilkinson. (2014). Elementary of Photogrammetry with Applications of GIS (4th ed.). Mc Graw Hill Education.

Rachel, E. (2015), *The Concept of Sustainable Development: Definition and Defining Principles*, pp. 1-3.

Roy, P., & Roy, A. (2010). Land use and land cover change in India: A remote sensing & GIS prespective. *Journal of the Indian Institute of Science, 90*, 489–502.

Silberstein, J., & Maser, C. (Eds.). (2014). Land Use Planning for Sustainable Development (2nd ed.). CRC Press, Taylor and Francis Group.

United Nations General Assembly. (1987). Report of the world commission on environment and development: Our common future. Oslo, Norway: United Nations General Assembly, Development and International Co-operation. *Environment.*

Yan, G., Mas, J.-F., Maathuis, B. H. P., Xiangmin, Z., & Van Dijk, P. M.YAN. (2006). Comparison of pixel-based and object-oriented image classification approaches-a case study in a coal fire area, Wuda, Inner Mongolia. *China International Journal of Remote Sensing, 27*(18), 4039–4055. doi:10.1080/01431160600702632

Chapter 18
Towards Sustainable Land Management:
State-of-the-Art in Land Use Policies of Nepal

Reshma Shrestha
Department of Geomatics Engineering, School of Engineering, Kathmandu University, Nepal

Purna Bhadur Nepali
School of Management, Kathmandu University, Nepal

Tanka Prasad Dahal
Land Management Training Centre, Ministry of Land Management, Cooperatives, and Poverty Alleviation, Nepal

ABSTRACT

In the global context, land-use policies have been considered as one of the significant aspects to obtain sustainable land management. Although this is a situation, it is not always achievable. Therefore, the critical analysis of land use policies is required. This chapter aims to understand the state of the art in land-related policies in Nepal after 1951 that contribute towards SLM. The methodology applied is the desktop review approach. The analytical framework namely sustainable land management (SLM) consisting of parameters: productivity, security, protection, viability, and acceptability, is developed. Under the basis of the SLM framework, content analysis has been carried out. The results show that although the policies take into account all the components of sustainability, the lack of implementing the integrated land use policy has triggered the questions for sustainable land management. The chapter recommends innovative approaches like parcel-based land use planning to obtain sustainable land management.

DOI: 10.4018/978-1-7998-4372-6.ch018

INTRODUCTION

Land management can be understood as a process whereby land resources are utilized effectively to obtain sustainability in its use. It encompasses all the activities associated with the management of land and natural resources that are required for the achievement of sustainable development components (Enemark, 2005). According to Brundtland Report's sustainable development is defined as "that [which] meets the needs of the present without compromising the ability of future generations to meet their own needs"(WCED, 1987). and Further, the United Nations has confirmed three dimensions of sustainable development which are social, economic, and environmental (United Nations, 2005). The Agenda 21, which is an outcome from the United Nations Conference on Environment and Development (UNCED) held in 1992 in Rio de Janeiro, highlighted the importance of land use planning for achieving sustainable development (United Nations, 1992). Land use planning as defined by the United Nations Environment Programme and United Nations Food and Agriculture Organization, published in 1999, is understood as, *"Systematic and iterative procedure carried out to create an enabling environment for sustainable development of land resources that meets people's needs and demands"*. Land use planning when intact with evidence based policy (Pawson, 2006) then it brings paradigm shift in land management for obtaining sustainability in all dimensions (Enemark, 2005).

In the global context, land-use policies have been considered as one of the significant aspects to obtain sustainable land management. According to Enemark (2005), land use plan, which is one of the functions of land administration, is also a factor in the land management paradigm to obtain sustainable development. In the holistic understanding, land use policies drive the sustainable management of land and it is about integrating environmental concerns with socio-economic principles that can be achieved by combining technologies and land-use policies. The importance of land-use policies has been realized in Nepal for the sustainable management of land (Nepal et al., 2020; Sharma, 2012). National Land Use Policy 2015 is still under the implementation process due to the formulation of regulations and guidelines are under progress. The delay in the implementation had caused the consequences like encroachment on public and state lands such as forest, increment in informal settlements, and deterioration of ecosystem, food insecurity, and haphazard urban growth (Chand, 2019). To tackle the consequences the policy instruments like land-use zoning required to be enforced in order to control and to discourage unauthorized use of land, control land fragmentation and haphazard urbanization, determine land use of the specific parcel. The land use Act 2019 of Nepal has been endorsed by the apex bodies (Maharjan, 2019), and the preparation of local level land use zoning and planning for the seven provinces are planned to complete on the fiscal year 2020-21(MOF, 2020). Although, various initiatives are taken for effective use of land by the Nepal government, the management of land is still weak. Moreover, the effectiveness of land use policies should be assessed after its implementation. Since it is not possible to assess the effectiveness of Land Use Policy yet, this study proposed to analyze the existing land use policies.

The objective of this chapter is to understand, how the various sectoral policies have mentioned the dimension of sustainable land management in concerning with the integrated policy in land use. The analytical framework, namely sustainable land management (SLM) framework has been developed referring to the framework for evaluating sustainable land management (FESLM) which was initially developed by Smyth et al. (1993). The framework developed for this study is integrated also with the components of sustainable development. The content analysis based on the developed SLM framework revealed that various sectoral policies are governing the use of land. The implementation of the integrated framework for the use of land guided by specific policies related to land is of prime necessity to eliminate the conflicting situation. The implementation guideline that captures the use of land at the parcel level has been recommended.

The structure of the chapter is synchronized in a way that firstly the status of land management concerning policies and plan to control the use of land, in the various timeline, has been described in Section 2. Secondly, the methodology for the development of the analytical framework (SLM) and the process of carrying out the policy analysis has been highlighted under the section "Methodological Framework". Thirdly, the analysis of various sectoral policies concerning the sustainable use of land has been conducted under Section 3. Finally, in Section 4, the discussion regarding lapses in the current land use policy has been discussed and conclusion with a way forwards is presented in Section 5.

Status of Land Management in Nepal

The terrain of Nepal has three ecological belts extended from east to west geographically. Administratively, the country is divided into seven provinces, 77 districts and 753 local bodies (460 village municipalities, 276 municipalities, 11 sub metropolises, and 6 metropolises). The northern belt accomplishes mountainous landscape ranges in 16 districts, which contain the world's highest peak Mt. Everest. Middle hilly belt accomplish hills, valleys, and lakes and spread in 40 districts. The southern belt consists of Terai, which is a plain area, also known as grain house of the country, consisting of 21 districts (CBS, 2017). Figure 1 shows the administrative division of Nepal.

The country has a mountainous landscape with its economy dependent on agriculture, having 65.5% of the population involved. The diversity in the landscape type has a major role in the economic value of the country. Low-lying and gently sloping zones being used mainly for agricultural activities but also for residential and other purposes (Paudel et al., 2019). Therefore, proper management of these low-lying lands has been an urgent need of the country to prevent land use change from agriculture to residential. According to CBS (2017), about 28% of land out of 147, 181 square kilometers land area of Nepal consists of agricultural land, 40% is forest area.

In the past before 1950, land use was guided through royal orders. At that time, the use of land was aimed at increasing government revenue, the use of free labor for construction, and receiving favor from government servants. The different forms of land tenure before the 1950s are Birta (land granted for a livelihood by state), Guthi(land assigned to religious institutions), Kipat (communal land granted to the certain ethnic group), Raikar (land that state retains under its ownership), Jagir (land assigned to government employee as a benefit), Rakam (land is assigned as a remuneration). After 1951, when democracy was established, the traditional land tenure was abolished. The Jagir system was abolished in 1951, Birta in 1959, Rakam in 1963, and Kipat in 1968 (Nepal et al., 2020).

The regulatory practice of land management was introduced in 1962 after the formation of Land Survey and Measurement Act 1963. The Act introduced a new system of land tenure classification as shown in Figure 2. Moreover, to manage land and its resources, periodic planning began back in 1956. From 1956 to 1964, the priority area was transport, communication, and public work. The next ten-year periodic plan (1964-1974) addresses land management with a focus on agricultural development. Similarly, the periodic plans (1974-1984) emphasized in land reform to increase agricultural production including conservation of natural resources whereas the plan for (1984-1996) captured the conservation and protection of forestry and other land uses. The importance of land-use plan has been given for the Ninth Five Year Plan (1997/98-2001/02) in which the use of a piece of land has been linked with sustainable development for the preservation of ecological sectors like mountains, hills, lowlands. The Tenth Five Year Plan (2002/03-2006/07) emphasized on the service-oriented land administration for social justice and poverty alleviation. The preparation of land-use zoning regulations were mentioned in the plan of 2007-2010 whereas 2010-2013 stressed land management for socio-economic transformation (Acharya, 2011; Chand, 2019). Although the emphasis was given for the land use plan to achieve sustainable land management in the various periodic plans, the absence of a single policy related to land use was a cause for ineffective management of land for agriculture productivity and mitigation of land-induced disaster. This realization of ineffective land management led to the evolution of land use policy in Nepal (Sharma, 2012).

Figure 1. Administrative Map of Nepal (Source: Survey Department)

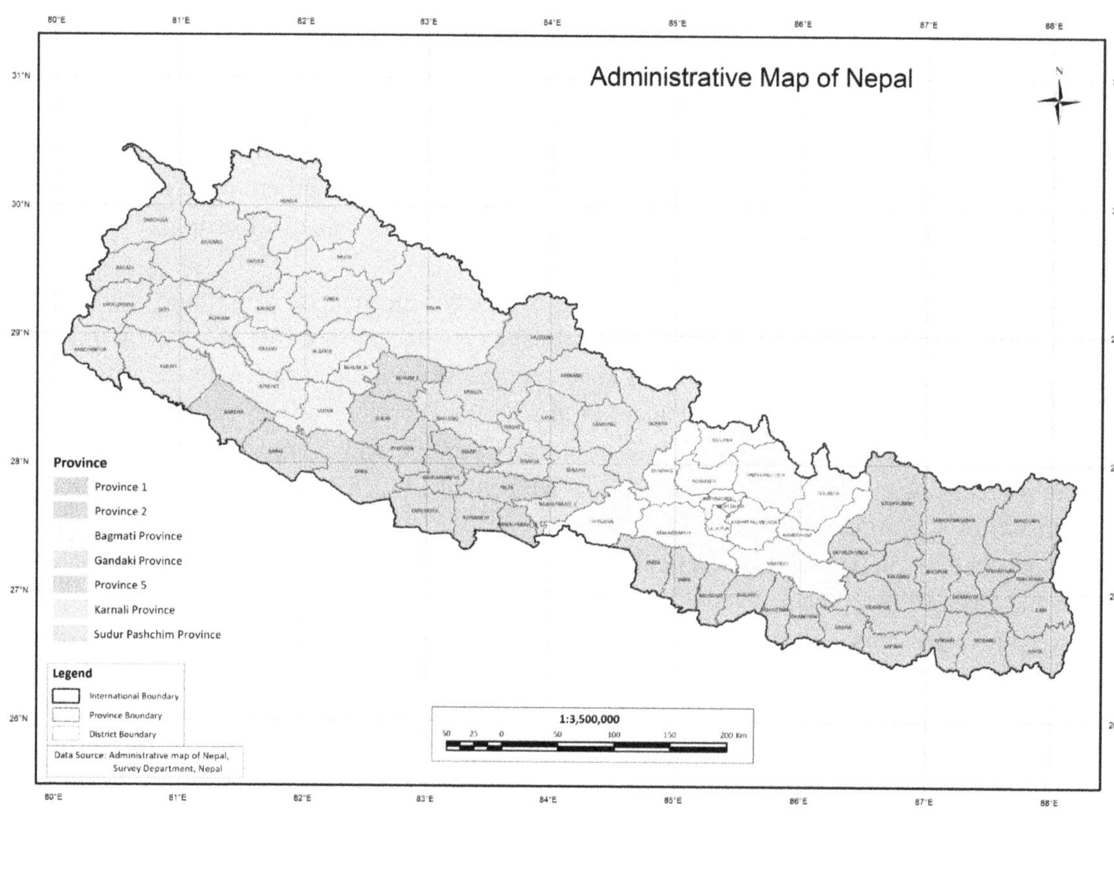

Figure 2. Existing land tenure system in Nepal (Nepal et al., 2020)

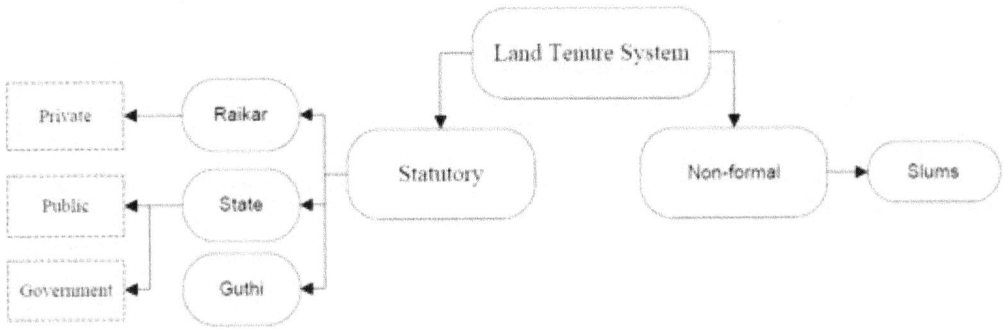

National Land Use Project was set up in 2000, with the major objectives of identifying suitability and zoning the land for agriculture, residential, industrializing, and other non-agricultural purposes. Then the National Land Use Policy (NLUP) (MoLRM, 2013) was formulated in 2013 which was amended to the new Land Use Policy in 2015 (MoLMCPA, 2015). To implement Land Use Policy 2015, the government of Nepal has approved the Land Use Act 2019 (MoLMCPA, 2019) in September 2019. The newly formulated Land Use Act 2019 mentioned about the formation of the land use Council in federal, provincial, and local levels of governments.

The Land Use Act 2019 has mentioned land zoning into nine different areas such as agricultural zone, residential zone, commercial zone, industrial zone, mines and minerals zone, forest zones, river and lake-reservoir zones, public use, and open space zone, cultural and archaeological zone. Currently, land use zoning maps at the district level are not completed but the government has an account of its completion in this fiscal year 2020/2021 (MOF, 2020). Most of the district level land use plan has been prepared but the land use plan implementation based on the Land Use Policy Act 2019 has not been exercised yet which was highlighted in the study of (Chalise et al., 2016; Sharma, 2012). In the fiscal year 2020/21, the government of Nepal has approved the implementation of an enthusiastic concept of land bank for the proper use of land to enhance productivity by discouraging it to be left as barren (MOF, 2020). This content was covered by various media [see (Poudel, 2020; ShareSansar, 2020; The Rising Nepal, 2020)].

METHODOLOGICAL FRAMEWORK

The sustainability concepts include the notion of environmental impact, economic viability, and social justice. It is dynamic because the notion of sustainability is not the same for different areas and for a different time. According to Smyth et al. (1993), although the measurement of sustainability cannot be achieved directly, its assessments can be made on the performance basis of the system applied to achieve its dimension at a specific location. The framework for evaluation of sustainable land management (FESLM) has been realized and therefore, an international working group headed by the International Board for Soil Research and Management (IBSRAM) and the Research Branch of Agriculture and Agro-Food

Canada (AAFC) in collaboration with Food and Agriculture Organization (FAO) of the United Nations has taken initiative for its development. The FESLM was developed by considering the definition of sustainable land management which refers to "enhance production and services simultaneously; reduce the level of production risk; protect the potential of natural resources; be economically viable, and be socially acceptable" (Smyth et al., 1993).

The SLM framework, consisting of five pillars namely productivity, security, protection, viability, and acceptability, is applied in the three countries (Thailand, Indonesia, and Vietnam) by Rais et al. (1999). The parameters of SLM were used by the authors to identify factors affecting all the dimensions of sustainability for agriculture. The factors are linked with expert knowledge to develop the decision support system for sustainable land management (Rais et al., 1999). Further, the work of Hurni (2000) revealed that there is a need for practical tools to execute the pillars of the SLM framework in a way that captures transdisciplinary methods by involving the social, environmental, economic dimension including the local knowledge system. While Metternicht (2018) has interlinked the concept of SLM with land use planning and highlighted that land use planning policies and its practices is a prime factor to obtain sustainable land management.

This chapter has adopted the pillars of the SLM framework and the three dimensions of sustainable development, which are social, economic, and environment. The term "sustainable land management" came as a follow up to the "sustainable development" initiated by the Brundtland commission held in Rio de Janeiro. The framework is manifested into five parameters, which are productivity to combat food security, security to mitigate risk from hazards, protection of local-level resources, viability to the local level plan, and acceptability in a local context. The framework is a modified version of FESLM (Smyth et al., 1993). Each parameter on SLM is linked with the components of sustainability namely: social, economic, and environmental. The factors on each component are developed from various literature. Based on the SLM framework, content analysis of various sectoral policies, in the context of Nepal, has been carried out. (See Annex 1 and Annex 2)

ANALYSIS BASED ON THE SLM FRAMEWORK FOR SUSTAINABLE LAND MANAGEMENT POLICIES

Productivity to Combat Food Security

One of the prime definitions of food security is about secure access to sufficient food all the time to have a healthy life (Malaysia, 2010). There are many driving factors for a decline in the food security situation in Nepal due to various causes in domestic, national, and international crises. Among them are decreasing agricultural land, poor agricultural growth, access to land for agriculture purposes are drivers that are directly related (Bista et al., 2013). Therefore, policies related to land use must capture social, economic, and environmental dimensions of productivity concerning the use of land.

Social, Economic, Environmental Dimension of Productivity

The social dimension of sustainability in productivity for food security depends upon the security of land tenure. Secure land tenure is an important institutional factor affecting investment in technologies that increases soil quality to enhance the productivity of land (Malaysia, 2010). In addition to secured tenure in terms of land ownership of marginalized farmers, it is also equally important to apply some intervention to attract the young generation in the agriculture sector (Gartaula et al., 2012). It reveals that the policies to address the use of land for food security are not governed by a single land use policy in Nepal. The Climate Change Policy 2019 mentioned that nutrition and livelihood will be improved by adopting a climate-friendly agricultural system by targeting poor, marginalized, landless, indigenous people and vulnerable households, women, and persons with disabilities for their food security (MoFE, 2019a). Besides, there is also the provision of managing pasture land for cattle farming, securing land tenure of bonded labor, and landless people for livelihood in the Local Governance Act 2017 (MoFA, 2017). The maximum ceiling for landholdings of individual households was fixed in the Land Act 1964. The land above the maximum ceiling was brought into government ownership by seizing from the individual. The Act mentions about re-distribution of the seized land to the landless people (MoLMCPA, 1964).

To obtain sustainability in the economic aspect of food security, the policies related to land should focus on the Telecoupling of global food trade and local use of land (FAO, 2017; Lange et al., 2015). The provision of proper road transportation arrangements should be developed for easy transport of agricultural products in the national market and to the international market. It has been noticed that Forest Policy, 2018 has mentioned the use of forest land for horticulture purposes for supporting income generation of the low-income people residing at the peripheral area (MoFE, 2019b). Besides, Climate change policy, 2019 mentioned about developing and promoting agroforestry with spices of multipurpose trees in uncultivated agricultural land. Another economic instrument for collecting tax based on the classification of land as residential/commercial and agriculture has been highlighted in the Land Survey and Measurement Regulation, 2001.

The balance between various land use activities for production and conservation efforts should be addressed in land-use policies. To obtain sustainability in terms of land use for food security, the environmental aspect needs to be addressed very importantly in the policies. According to Lange et al. (2015), the perception of agriculture land users regarding sustainability is about conserving land and enabling long term productivity. Land degradation, loss in soil fertility due to the use of chemical fertilizer are a major factor that triggers unsustainability in the production of agriculture. The impact on the biodiversity, greenhouse emission due to agro-forest degradation are also factors for unsustainability. Looking at sectoral policies related to the use of land, the Climate Change Policy 2019 mentioned crop diversification, protection of agricultural biodiversity, and promotion of organic farming. Besides, the existing policy focusses on redressing the risk due to climate change for agricultural land by giving priority to agroforestry, in sloppy and low-grade forests and riverbeds at climate-induced risk (MoFE, 2019a). However, one of the important components for sustainability that land-use policies should address is about preventing land degradation, soil conservation due to the use of chemical manure/ fertilizer.

Security to Mitigate Risk from Hazards

Land Use Planning (LUP) is an instrument that can be applied to reduce settlement in hazards area and obtain recovery and improve resilience after natural disasters (Roy & Ferland, 2015). The causes of disaster and vulnerability are associated to land administration issues that can be amplified through human behaviors. Those behaviors can be associated with inappropriate land tenure systems, technocratic land use planning, unsuitable distribution of land uses and uncontrolled human settlements (Baas et al., 2008; and Leanza, 2015). Solutions to sustainability should, therefore, carry on from policies and its practices like Risk Sensitive Land Use Planning (RSLP) (Sudmeier-Rieux et al., 2015). RSLP is about integrating the component of disaster risk management into traditional land use planning. In RSLP, the risk is the likelihood of a specific hazard occurring and its probable consequences for people and property (Reyes, 2005). Therefore, policies related to land use can be instrumental in the mitigation of risks that arise from the various hazards both manmade and natural hazards and termed as risk-sensitive land use planning.

Social, Economic, Environmental Dimension to Mitigate Risk

The various policies should be linked directly and indirectly with land tenure in mitigating risk from various hazards. To mitigate risk, land use policies should be capable of enforcing restrictions over an area identified as hazard zone and restriction of any new ownership and use over land-parcels located in that particular zone (Roy et al., 2015). In Land Use Policy 2015, safe human settlement by identifying secured and appropriate places at the provincial and local levels through specific zoning has been mentioned (MoLMCPA, 2015). Similarly, Land Policy 2019 mentions about mitigating risk by applying mitigation measures for using hazardous zone. The management of state and public land including open spaces for responding during a disaster like an earthquake by local ward has been highlighted in the Local Governing Act 2017. To mitigate risk, the National Policy for Disaster Risk Reduction 2018 has initiated in providing early warning system of multi-hazard and also a community-level awareness program (MoHA, 2018). Although this particular policy is not directly related to land use, the early information of disaster can be an integral part of land tenure security to reduce the vulnerability of the settlement residing in the risk zone (Caron et al., 2014).

The incentive-based policy instruments can be linked with mitigating hazards and bringing economic sustainability. Ecosystem payment service is an incentive-based policy instrument that has strong implicit links to the notion of sustainability (Abson et al., 2014). According to Burby et al. (2000), the policy instruments like impact taxes for hazardous area development, tax incentives for reducing land use intensities in hazardous areas, the financial instruments like taxation and other similar fiscal instruments can help mitigate hazards. The policies related to disaster should encourage investment of both public and private sector in disaster risk reduction such that disaster resilience can be enhanced. Similarly, arranging insurance of livelihood, crops and livestock for sharing and transfer risk of vulnerable communities have been emphasized in enhancing disaster resilience from an economic perspective. Aligning with this contextual background of policy instruments, the National Policy for Disaster Risk Reduction 2018 has made the provision of a soft loan from financial institutions and banks for risk-sharing and transfer (MoHA, 2018). However, these policies are posted in disaster mechanisms. It is important to mainstream disaster management approaches with land use planning for the mitigation of risk.

The enforcement of regulatory instruments related to risk reduction is important to restrict the settlement in the hazards prone vulnerable area. Land use zoning is a regulatory instrument that facilitates implementing the various categories of land specified in land use policies. Within disaster risk reduction intervention, the regulatory instruments like zoning can enforce restriction on uses and land development in the demarcated zones at risk thus obtaining environmental sustainability (Roy et al., 2015). The Land Use Policy 2015 seems to address disaster reduction action by land use zoning based on the environmental perspective with consideration of hazardous areas. Similarly, enhancement of adaptation capacity of the local community by incorporating best practices of watershed and landscape management in the adaptation program has been mentioned in the Climate Change Policy 2019. Further, the National Policy for Disaster Risk Reduction, 2018, spells out regarding mainstreaming disaster risk reduction in all the process of development by integrating disaster with activities on climate change adaptation.

The policy has also emphasized on multi-hazard risk assessment at the local level by formulating risk sensitive land use plan for the development and management of safer settlement. The other initiative highlighted in National Urban Policy 2007, is developing balanced towns and communities through conservation of the traditional urban structures and sustainable use of natural resources (MoUD, 2007). The study conducted by Sudmeier-Rieux et al. (2015) regarding challenges of risk sensitive land use planning including its opportunities highlighted about weakness in public policies and institutions that has allowed the expansion of informal settlements in areas exposed to hazards. Further, it was mentioned that the difficulties in providing safe relocation space and poorly regulated, controlled development in the hazardous zone are the outcome of weak land use planning and enforcement of zoning regulations.

Protection of Local Level Resources

The natural resources in terms of quality and quantity must be safeguarded for future generations. In the local context, there may be priorities for additional conservation, for instance, necessity to maintain genetic diversity, requirement to preserve individual plant or animal species (Smyth et al., 1993). The land use policies should be able to protect from all three dimensions of sustainability and have linkages with productivity and security of the SLM framework.

Social, Economic, Environmental Dimension of Protection

The protection and allocation of natural resources should also provide a secure livelihood including viable policies that support social development of the both urban and rural communities, the tribal, and the vulnerable communities (Nukala & Mutz, 2015). The policies related to use of land and land tenure security, thus, should ensure sustainability in social dimension by addressing the issues of livelihood, poverty, inclusiveness in terms of gender, low-income groups, disables. Land Use Policy 2015 and Climate Change Policy 2019 have addressed about protection and optimum use of natural heritages, tourist hubs, and historical, cultural, and religious, archaeological zones including lands belonging to the government, public and trust. This type of land use is intact with diversified social norms. Similarly, in Land Use Policy 2015 it has been mentioned about the protection of Churia Bhabhar Hill Areas and the relocation of vulnerable human settlements in these sensitive areas. It is mentioned that the process of relocation to be carried out under a "Development of Basic Infrastructure Integrated Human Settlement Programs". Besides, there is the provision of using the concept of community forest program for protection and use of forest and forest products (MoFE, 2018) and protection of land from hazards like flooding for the safety of local people (MoFA, 2017). In contrast, there is a provision of acquiring land and house inside the forest area according to the Forest Act 1993. This reveals that the land acquisition policies need to be acceptable to the affected groups.

The policies related to land are required to address the local resource available to the local populations to enhance the economic dimension of local inhabitants. Access to the market in terms of availability of transportation infrastructure, distance in input, and output market are also factors that contribute to the enhancement of the local economy (Smyth et al., 1993). In this context, analyzing from the economic dimension, the land use policy mentions the establishment of a land bank to provide access to cultivable land for the local level and provision of taxation based on the land use zone. Likewise. Conservation of the environment for tourism or conservation of tourist hubs for an economic generation (MoLMCPA, 2015). These interventions in the policy level can help in the protection of natural resources and also income-generating land use like touristic viable areas. However, the policies need to intervene more sharply for the proper trade of locally available natural resources to sustain the particular land use economically.

The policies related to land are required to spell out about preservation and conservation of land that is emphasized as important environmental functions such as national parks, wildlife reservations, conserved forests, etc. Regulating and controlling uses of land around such preserved and conserved area including the eco-sensitive zones to prevent conflicts in land use and adverse environmental impacts (Nukala et al., 2015). Aligning with this statement, Land Use Policy 2015 seems to spell out about the protection of local natural resources like "Churia Bhabhar" hill areas explicitly. The policy has emphasized the protection of soil by maintaining its natural core. Further, the policy has spelled out that "other, acts against standards of land use causing changes in the natural features shall be discouraged". In the Forest Policy 2018, it has been mentioned about the protection of the forest for a balance environmental ecosystem as well as for carbon emission reduction by preventing forest degradation (MoFE, 2018). In addition, the policy has highlighted the protection of wild animals, which means protection of land suitable for these animals. The innovative initiative to protect the bank of the river was noticed in the Local Government Act, 2017. The Act mentioned about plantation on the bank of the river, green belt formulation, and management of open spaces.

Viability and Acceptability to Local Level Plan

The viability of policies is obtained when it is compatible with local level requirements to use the particular land. If the land uses being considered are locally not viable, the land use plan will not be sustainable. Further, the implementation of land use policies can be expected to unsustainable, in time, if the social impact is unacceptable. Since, the populations most directly affected by social and economic impact are the most vulnerable, the land use policies are required to intervene towards participation of local inhabitants in such a way that fits with local systems of knowledge, values, and belief system (Smyth et al., 1993).

Social, Economic, Environmental Dimension of Viability and Acceptability

To obtain the viability and acceptability of land use at the local level, it is important to consider the social norms and its sustainability. The study of Nukala et al. (2015) has highlighted about the need to protect important cultural and historical places, religious, heritage places, archaeological sites, etc., Similarly, the requirement of social justice, equity and participation are the key ingredients necessary to be considered in policy formulation to obtain social acceptance of the policies at the implementation level. The analysis of various policies reveals that there has been an initiative to intact viability with the local level requirement for using the land. Land Use Policy 2015 includes the requirement of the careful planning and execution of level wise (federal, provincial, and local) land use plans ensuring stakeholders' participation such that gender and inclusiveness are taken into consideration to assure compatibility with local requirements. Similarly, the policies also seem to play a vital role in conserving historical, religious, cultural land (MoLMCPA, 2015).

It is revealed that there is some aspect of local level viability and acceptability in the economic dimension for sustainable land management. Since the country has an agro-based economy, the recently formulated Land Use Policy 2015 has been driven from preventing agricultural land in local level. For instance, the policy emphasis on operating incentive-oriented programs to motivate people for the use of Land and Land Resources (LLRs) and improve agricultural production. The policy spells about the establishment of land bank to develop an access mechanism to land for landless people's willingness towards agriculture (MoLMCPA, 2015). Besides, the innovative idea like "establishment of crop bank" has also been incorporated in Land Act 1964. Aligning, with economic dimension, Forest Policy 2018 seems to consider for the use of the forest by the community and the agro-forest program to create employment opportunities. Also, the protection of forest and greenery area for tourism purposes, as tourism is a major source of income for government and the local inhabitants has been emphasized. This seems to bring local level viability and acceptability of the policy from an economic perspective.

The viability and acceptability of land use policies at the local level from the environmental dimension can be obtained when there is a conservation of land with environmental functions, like national parks, wildlife sanctuaries, reserved forests, eco-sensitive zones, etc. including areas with ecosystem payment services (Nukala et al., 2015). Ecosystem payment service is an incentive-based policy instrument that has strong implicit links to the notion of sustainability (Abson et al., 2014). Therefore, it is important to address the diversity of land use structure connecting with ecosystem services to obtain acceptability and viability at the local level. The innovative initiative like the plantation on the abandoned land/ unused land and riverbank has been noticed from the Climate Change Policy 2019. Mitigating risk from the impact of climate change through land use has been mentioned in Land Use Policy, 2015. Further, there is a provision of adding required zone according to the local viability and acceptability, beyond already defined nine zones "agricultural zone, residential zone, commercial zone, industrial zone, mines and minerals zone, forest zones, river and lake-reservoir zones, public use and open space zone, cultural and archaeological zone".

DISCUSSION: UNDERLYING LAPSES FOR SUSTAINABLE LAND MANAGEMENT

The increasing pressure on use of land and its natural resources poses challenges for sustainable development via sustainable land management; the policies related to land has to take into consideration of social, economic and environmental dimension of sustainability in terms of all the pillars of SLM framework. This calls a need for doable solutions for evidence-based policies and guiding principles to practice the policies for optimal utilization of land resources.

The policies related to land should consider various interventions to increase productivity for food security by protecting land tenure security of farmers, land tillers in all dimensions of sustainability. Despite land tenure security which strengthens the social norms of the farmers, the policies should be able to intervene in the preservation of agricultural land from changing to other land uses as rapid urbanization has become the prime cause of a decrease in agricultural land (Azadi et al., 2011). The studies conducted by (Paudel et al., 2018; Paudel et al., 2017) show spatiotemporal changes in agriculture land of whole Nepal over the last 100 years (1910 to 2010). According to them, the use of land for agriculture purposes was increased in the year 2010 compared to past years, but the authors have explicitly pointed out that poor land management has led to the conversion of agriculture land to built-up areas and the abandonment of land. The authors recommended the implement suitable land use policies that are linked with the economy and lifestyle of the populations. Further, to obtain sustainability the agriculture practices that improve rural livelihoods, equity, and social well-being is important (FAO, 2017) which should be addressed through policies for the use of land. Also, protection of main elements that are related to food security like agricultural lands, catchment areas of irrigation projects, double-cropped land, and land that provides support for the livelihood of the rural population are important for sustainable agriculture (Canfora, 2016).

Relating with food security and the use of land, the driving factors for diversion from the use of land for agriculture purposes was derived by Gartaula et al. (2012) based upon the perception of farmers in Nepal. The finding of his study shows the driving factors are triggering from the lack of skilled labor force, internal and external migration, lack of interest among young people in agriculture, as they perceived the profession "undignified job", are the driving factors for diversion from use of land from agriculture purposes. Thus, the land is left barren without any use for production activity. Therefore, land use policies need to intervene by introducing an innovative mechanism in the aspect of migration, decreasing interest in agriculture/ farm activities due to less profit, and social stigma of agricultural activities as an irrespective profession. Similarly, transportation linkages between production sites to the consumption site play a vital role to bring sustainability in the agricultural sector by creating access to the market for food production trade (FAO, 2017), therefore, land use policies should be able to accommodate this holistic impact. Another important component for sustainability indicates that land use policies should spell about preventing land degradation, soil conservation due to the use of chemical manure.

The policies related to land needs incorporation of various interventions covering all three dimension of sustainability for land tenure security from disaster risk. Policies regarding the use of land should be able to capture the socially vulnerable populations such that there is necessary support during post-disaster emergency response, recovery and resettlement phase consisting of safe settlement planning (Roy et al., 2015). The study of Sudmeier-Rieux et al. (2015) has already mentioned laggings in land use policy enforcement and its practices in Nepal, particularly taking a case of Dharan Municipality. Their studies show the growing settlement in the hazardous zone like the flood-prone area because of the non-implementation of the provision that is mentioned in the policy. Similarly, the study of Rimal et al. (2015) in multi-hazards risk assessment for Pokhara city in Nepal suggested for the urgent implementation of Land Use Policy 2015. Further, the study suggested incorporating multi-hazards mapping in the policies and highlighted that sustainable hazard mitigation through land use plan must be a priority of the local and central government to minimize social and economic vulnerability. The policies that emphasized the participatory mapping for risk-sensitive land use planning adopting various types of hazards like fire, flood, health, landslide, and earthquake hazards has been argued to capture the social, economic and environmental populations given that the plan is compatible with local level requirements by various authors (Sudmeier-Rieux et al., 2015; Thapa, 2018). In this regard, there is some initiative for participatory land use planning for disaster risk reduction in some districts of Nepal (Chalise et al., 2016). However, the good practices of land use policies with the legally binding rules are important at local level for the execution of the plan prepared with the local level participation to mitigate disaster risk.

Sustainable land management requires land use policies to spells about the protection of local level resources clearly. The study conducted by Nepal et al. (2020) reveals that ownerships and accountability problems of implementing the policies to protect local level resources arises due to overlapping and conflicting provisions within legal perspective. The authors have shown how the overlapping and mis-match action plan between various policies has created confusion regarding "Chure" range protection.

Regarding local level acceptability and viability, land use planning policies should address the local economic parameters like market, income, and trade (FAO, 2017). Further, land use policies should play a vital role in translating the locally available resources and products available for the regional and national. This supports local level enhancement from an economic perspective. The results of Nepalese farmer's perception on the drivers of land use change revealed socioeconomic divers (agriculture production, new agricultural technology, high cost of agriculture, utilization of labor force), neighborhood variables (access to roads, market centers, irrigation, urbanization) are prominent (Paudel et al., 2019). Similarly, the perception-based study with farmers in Germany which was conducted by Lange et al. (2015), reflects that "*land use should be aligned with what the region has to offer in terms of site characteristic —soil quality, water supply, climate conditions—rather than narrow*". Therefore, both studies stressed the prominence of 'location-adapted' land uses as a foundation for sustainable land use in local level. Therefore, the policy should also address whether there is acceptability and adaptability in term of requirements such as availability of labor, material, proper irrigation, and financial inputs to comply with land use plans such as agricultural land derived from the land use policies.

In short, the various policies related to land in Nepal seems to capture all the dimensions of sustainability in the four pillars of sustainability, but land related policies seem to be in the shadow of various sectoral policies. Therefore, single land use policies should be implemented and synchronized with the other sectoral policies to increase productivity and secured settlement by mitigating risk of disaster, protect local level resources, and develop local level viability/ acceptability. Although there is urgent need for implementation of land use plan at different administrative units, the regulations and codes related to land use that guide for implementation of policies has not yet been endorsed. In addition, the technical capacity of local government that is required in developing a land use plan of local level does not seems sufficient and need intensive capacity-building training and courses. The National Land Use Plan 2015 has made the Ministry of land management, cooperatives, and poverty alleviation, a responsible institution, to implement land use policy. This mandate, if conducted without the horizontal coordination with other line ministries then it might be difficult to obtain holistic outcome of sustainable land management (Paudel et al., 2019).

CONCLUSION AND WAY FORWARD

In this chapter, SLM analytical framework is devised to analyze land use policies. The SLM framework adopted for this study is manifested into four parameters, which are productivity to combat food security, security to mitigate risk from hazards, protection of local level resources, viability and acceptability to the local level context.

Although, critical analysis of policies in various countries by Bonin et al. (2012) highlighted that most of the policies has considered economic components, but, this study reveals that, Nepal sectoral policies related with land use, seems to capture all the component of sustainable development. However, this study could not confirm either it has been captured equally in all the dimensions or not. The policies have emphasized all the dimensions of sustainability, which could be the strength for sustainable land management; there is a disconnection among the sectoral policies to obtain the sustainable land use plan. Therefore, decisions regarding shaping use of land through land use policy must include trade-offs between sectoral interests.

Enhanced multilevel land governance, which is more responsible for effective local and community land use planning, is key in addressing the issues and challenges of practicing land use policy. The land governance should recognize the local institutions innovation and initiatives. The responsible governance of land use should promote horizontal coordination of sectoral administration and policies vertical coordination of different administrative levels. Policymakers can play a crucial role in creating the necessary conditions for the implementation of the policy including the parameters of responsible governance. This could include making use of policy instruments to incentivize sustainable land management adoption and collaborating with land users and other relevant stakeholders to develop SLM initiatives that are adapted to the local context, bring tangible and long-term benefits, and align with national priorities.

This study suggested for the research on, firstly, development of the implementation guideline of land use at the parcel level of the unit of land considering the parameters of the SLM framework. Secondly, to conduct a critical analysis of Land Use Policy and Act from the perspective of "Suitability of land use", "Sustainability of land use" and "Stability of land use" after implementation of land use policies.

REFERENCES

Abson, D. J., Von Wehrden, H., Baumgärtner, S., Fischer, J., Hanspach, J., Härdtle, W., ... Martens, P. (2014). Ecosystem services as a boundary object for sustainability. *Ecological Economics*, *103*, 29–37. doi:10.1016/j.ecolecon.2014.04.012

Acharya, B. R. (2011). Land Use Issues in Nepal: A country in Dire Need of Solutions. *GIM International*.

Azadi, H., Ho, P., & Hasfiati, L. (2011). Agricultural land conversion drivers: A comparison between less developed, developing and developed countries. *Land Degradation & Development*, *22*(6), 596–604. doi:10.1002/ldr.1037

Bista, D., Amgain, L., & Shrestha, S. (2013). Food security scenario, challenges, and agronomic research directions of Nepal. *Agronomy Journal of Nepal*, *3*, 42–52. doi:10.3126/ajn.v3i0.8985

Bonin, M., Coudel, E., Cissé, Y., Feng, S., Gicheru, P., Novira, N., & Tonneau, J.-P. (2012). Critical analysis of land use policies. In D. M. Neill, I. Nesheim, & F. Brouwer (Eds.), *Land Use Policies for Sustainable Development* (pp. 248–281). Edward Elgar Publishing. doi:10.4337/9781781002476.00021

Burby, R. J., Deyle, R. E., Godschalk, D. R., & Olshansky, R. B. (2000). Creating hazard resilient communities through land-use planning. *Natural Hazards Review*, *1*(2), 99–106. doi:10.1061/(ASCE)1527-6988(2000)1:2(99)

Burby, R. J., Deyle, R. E., Godschalk, D. R., & Olshansky, R. B. (2000). Creating hazard resilient communities through land-use planning. *Natural Hazards Review*, *1*(2), 99–106. doi:10.1061/(ASCE)1527-6988(2000)1:2(99)

Canfora, I. (2016). Is the short food supply chain an efficient solution for sustainability in food market. *Agriculture and Agricultural Science Procedia*, *8*(1), 402–407. doi:10.1016/j.aaspro.2016.02.036

Caron, C., Menon, G., & Kuritz, L. (2014). Land Tenure & Disasters. *USAID. Issue brief.*

CBS. (2017). *Statistical Year Book*. Ramshahpath, Thapathali: Central Bureau of Statistics. https://cbs.gov.np/wp-content/upLoads/2019/02/Statistical-Year-Book-2017.pdf

Chalise, D., Joshi, A., Twanabasu, B., Rawal, N., & Amgai, S. (2016). Preparation of Land Use Zoning Maps of Chaumala VDC, Kailali. *International Journal of Applied Sciences and Biotechnology*, *4*(4), 458–463. doi:10.3126/ijasbt.v4i4.14213

Chand, B. (2019). *Land management problems in Nepal: repercussions of land use policy and implementation gaps in regional and urban planning* [Paper presention]. ISPRS Annals of Photogrammetry, Remote Sensing & Spatial Information Sciences.

Enemark, S. (2005). *Understanding the land management paradigm* [Paper presention]. FIG Commission 7, Symposium on Innovative Technologies for Land Administration, Madison, Wisconsin, USA.

FAO. (2017). Land resource planning for sustainable land management. Current and emerging needs in land resource planning for food security, sustainable livelihoods, integrated landscape management and restoration. Rome.

Gartaula, H., Niehof, A., & Visser, L. (2012). Shifting perceptions of food security and land in the context of labour out-migration in rural Nepal. *Food Security*, *4*(2), 181–194. doi:10.100712571-012-0190-3

Hurni, H. (2000). Assessing sustainable land management (SLM). *Agriculture, Ecosystems & Environment*, *81*(2), 83–92. doi:10.1016/S0167-8809(00)00182-1

Lange, A., Siebert, R., & Barkmann, T. (2015). Sustainability in land management: An analysis of stakeholder perceptions in rural northern Germany. *Sustainability*, *7*(1), 683–704. doi:10.3390u7010683

Lange, A., Siebert, R., & Barkmann, T. (2015). Sustainability in land management: An analysis of stakeholder perceptions in rural northern Germany. *Sustainability*, *7*(1), 683–704. doi:10.3390u7010683

Maharjan, U. (2019). Land Use Act 2019: An Overview. *The Rising Nepal*. Retrieved from http://therisingnepal.org.np/news/34254

Malaysia, P. (2010). Food security: Concepts and definitions. *Journal of Community Health*, *16*(2), 2.

McConnell, W. J., & Viña, A. (2018). *Interactions between food security and land use in the context of global change*. Multidisciplinary Digital Publishing Institute. doi:10.3390/land7020053

Metternicht, G. (2018). *Land use and spatial planning: Enabling sustainable management of land resources*. Springer. doi:10.1007/978-3-319-71861-3

MOF. (2020). *Budget for fiscal year 2020/2021*. Ministry of Finance.

MoFA. (2017). *Local Governing Act 2017*. Ministry of Federal Affairs and General Administration.

MoFE. (2018). *Forest Policy 2018*. Ministry of Forests and Environment.

MoFE. (2019a). *Climate Change policy 2019*. Ministry of Forests and Environment.

MoFE. (2019b). *National Forest Policy 2019*. Ministry of Forests and Environment.

MoHA. (2018). *National Policy for Disaster Risk Reduction 2018*. Ministry of Home Affairs.

MoLMCPA. (1964). *Land Act 1964*. Ministry of Land Management Cooperatives and Poverty Alleviation.

MoLMCPA. (2015). *Land use policy 2015*. Ministry of Land Management Cooperatives and Poverty Alleviation.

MoLMCPA. (2019). *Land Use Act 2019*. Ministry of Land Management Cooperatives and Poverty Alleviation.

MoLRM. (2013). *National Land Use Policy 2013*. Kathmandu Ministry of Land Reform and Management.

MoUD. (2007). *National Urban Policy 2007*. Ministry of Urban Development.

Nepal, P., Khanal, N. R., Zhang, Y., Paudel, B., & Liu, L. (2020). Land use policies in Nepal: An overview. *Land Degradation & Development*, 1–10.

Nukala, R. B., & Mutz, D. (2015). Strategic approach for sustainable land use in an emerging country – case of india [Paper presention]. Linking land tenure and use for shared prosperity, Washington, DC.

Nukala, & Mutz, D. (2015). *Strategic approach for sustainable land use in an emerging country – case of India* [Paper presention]. Linking land tenure and use for shared prosperity, Washington, DC.

Paudel, B., Zhang, Y., Li, S., & Liu, L. (2018). Spatiotemporal changes in agricultural land cover in Nepal over the last 100 years. *Journal of Geographical Sciences*, *28*(10), 1519–1537. doi:10.100711442-018-1559-9

Paudel, B., Zhang, Y., Li, S., & Wu, X. (2017). Spatiotemporal reconstruction of agricultural land cover in Nepal from 1970 to 2010. *Regional Environmental Change*, *17*(8), 2349–2357. doi:10.100710113-017-1164-y

Paudel, B., Zhang, Y., Yan, J., Rai, R., & Li, L. (2019). Farmers' perceptions of agricultural land use changes in Nepal and their major drivers. *Journal of Environmental Management*, *235*, 432–441. doi:10.1016/j.jenvman.2019.01.091 PMID:30710853

Pawson, R. (2006). *Evidence-based policy: a realist perspective*. Sage.

Poudel, U. (2020). Government preparing to set up land bank. *The Himalayan Times*. https://thehimalayantimes.com/business/government-preparing-to-set-up-land-bank/

Rais, M., Gameda, S., Craswell, E., Sajjapongse, A., & Bechstedt, H. (1999). Decision support system for sustainable land management: A South-east Asia case. In E. K. Kersten, Z. Mikolajuk, & A. Gar-On Yeh (Eds.), *Decision support systems for sustainable development: a resource book of methods and applications*. Kluwer Academic Publishers.

Reyes, M. (2005). *Risk-Sensitive Land Use Planning: Towards Reduced Seismic Disaster Vulnerability*. Kassel University Press.

Rimal, B., Baral, H., Stork, N. E., Paudyal, K., & Rijal, S. (2015). Growing city and rapid land use transition: Assessing multiple hazards and risks in the Pokhara Valley, Nepal. *Land (Basel)*, *4*(4), 957–978. doi:10.3390/land4040957

Roy, F., & Ferland, Y. (2015). Land-use planning for disaster risk management. *Land Tenure Journal*, 1.

ShareSansar. (2020). Government to establish Land Banks in 300 local level units. *ShareSansar*. https://www.sharesansar.com/newsdetail/government-to-establish-land-banks-in-300-local-level-units

Sharma, R. K. (2012). Evolution of Land Use Policy in Nepal. *Nepalese Journal of Geoinformatics*, *11*, 16–21.

Smyth, A., Dumanski, J., Spendjian, G., & Swift, M. (1993). *FESLM: An international framework for evaluating sustainable land management*. FAO Rome.

Sudmeier-Rieux, K., Paleo, U. F., Garschagen, M., Estrella, M., Renaud, F. G., & Jaboyedoff, M. (2015). Opportunities, incentives and challenges to risk sensitive land use planning: Lessons from Nepal, Spain and Vietnam. *International Journal of Disaster Risk Reduction*, *14*, 205–224. doi:10.1016/j.ijdrr.2014.09.009

Thapa, P. B. (2018). Geo-disaster and risk sensitive land use planning in Nepal. *Bulletin of Nepal Geological Society, 35*.

The Rising Nepal. (2020). Concept of land bank for utilisation of arable land: minister Aryal. *The Rising Nepal*. http://www.therisingnepal.org.np/news/33646

United Nations. (1992). *AGENDA 21* [Paper presented]. United Nations Conference on Environment & Development, Rio de Janerio, Brazil.

United Nations. (2005). *World Summit Outcome; Resolution Adopted by the General Assembly, A/RES/60/1*. https://www.un.org/en/development/desa/population/migration/generalassembly/docs/globalcompact/A_RES_60_1.pdf

WCED. (1987). *Our Common Future*. https://netzwerk-n.org/wp-content/uploads/2017/04/0_Brundtland_Report-1987-Our_Common_Future.pdf

KEY TERMS AND DEFINITIONS

Agriculture Zone: It is a zone used for agricultural production, agriculture forest products, and plants planted in private land and a zone declared by the government.

Forest Zone: It is a Zone where the land is covered fully or partially by trees and other vegetation including wildlife conservation.

Government Land: Government land can be defined as land under government ownership.

Land Tenure: Land tenure is termed as a relationship between individuals and groups of people concerning land and land-based resources.

Private Land: Private land can be defined as freehold tenure having the right to use, lease, mortgage, and transfer and build infrastructure.

Public Land: Public land can be defined as land allocated for use of the general public and mentioned in the Nepal Gazette by the government of Nepal.

Slums: According to the definition of UN-HABITAT, a slum is characterized as a contiguous settlement characterized by poor housing conditions, inadequate basic services, and insecure land tenure.

APPENDIX 1

In this appendix, the Analytical Framework namely Sustainable Land Management (SLM) Framework consisting of parameters derived in each dimension of sustainability is described

Table 1. Sustainable Land Management (SLM) framework

Dimension of Sustainability/ SLM Parameters	Social Factors	Economic Factors	Environmental Factors
Productivity to combat food security	Tenure security in terms of land holdings for productivity Protection of agricultural land resources by suitable means from land use conversions Agriculture that fails to protect and improve rural livelihoods, equity and social well-being is unsustainable	Addresses measure for food production and trade (Tele coupling global food trade and local land use)	Prevent environmental problems, such as loss of biodiversity greenhouse gas emissions, soil degradation, and alteration of hydrological cycles Sustainability requires direct action to conserve, protect and enhance natural resources
Security to mitigate risk from hazards	Provision to social justice, equity in terms of vulnerability Approaches of Participatory Land Use planning to map hazard zone participation	Taxation and fiscal policies for land use: These policies can include impact taxes for hazardous area development, tax incentives for reducing land use intensities in hazardous areas, and risk-based taxes to support emergency management services.	Risk sensitive land use planning: Zoning regulations that limit the intensity of development in hazard areas, acquisition of hazard areas with open space or environmental value Focus on location-adapted land use—especially in areas under risk of flooding Conservation of natural, productive resources,
Protection of local level resources	Existence of opportunities within and outside the resource utilization system, distribution of wealth within and between social units Protection/ Allocation of lands required to secure livelihood for tribal communities and poor	Ratio of resource availability to population's overall needs for local level economic enhancement	Biodiversity—harmful impact of current trends such as increase of energy crops Conservation of local level natural, productive resources
Viability and Acceptability to the local level plan	Protection of places/sites of religious, archaeological, scenic and tourist importance	Role of rural production for regional stability	Close-to-nature" forest management Conserve lands with environmental functions, viz. National Parks, Wild Life Sanctuaries, Reserved Forests, Eco Sensitive Zones etc. and areas with ecosystem services
	Extent of conflict, and existence of accepted conflict-resolution mechanisms, social participation in decision-making	Identifying cost benefits for certain land use plan acceptability in regard to requirements for labour, material end financial inputs	Landscape diversity; distinctiveness of regional features; ecological networks Diversity of land use structure—"cultural landscapes"

APPENDIX 2

In this appendix, the content analysis of various policies in relation to use of land has been described.

Table 2. The content analysis of sectorial policies in concern to land use

Dimension/ SLM parameter	Social	Economic	Environmental	Relates Policies/ Acts
Productivity to combat food security		Use of forest for horticulture purpose for economic income Private sector involvement for investment for economic activities		Forest Policy 2018
	Empowerment for agricultural sector with various program			Land use policy 2015
	Agriculture based intervention for vulnerable groups	Climate friendly agricultural system Agroforestry with variety of spices	Crop diversification, agricultural biodiversity, organic farming Agroforestry in risk sensitive area	Climate Change Policy 2019
		Classification of land for taxation		Land survey and measurement act 1963 Land Survey and Measurement Regulation 2001
	Provision of land ceiling for access to land for every citizen acquisition of land beyond ceiling			Land Act 1964
	Pasture land management Management of bonded labors			Local governing Act 2017
Security to mitigate risk from hazards	geologically, geographically and ecologically safe human settlement		Reduction of Disaster risk	Land use policy, 2015
			Land use plan should based on Environmental perspective	Land use Act 2019
			Protection of water and land	Forest Policy 2018
			Integrated watershed management Disaster risk management system based on federal to provincial and then in local level	Climate Change Policy 2019
				Land Act 1964
	Collection of records of open spaces and government land by local ward			Local governing Act 2017
		Compensation must be provided for acquired land and house		Forest Act 1993
	Effective response by early warning system and awareness program	Increasing resilience by investment in disaster risk reduction Arranging insurance and soft loan for risk sharing and risk transfer.	Integrating disaster risk reduction strategy with climate change adaptation activities. Formulation of risk sensitive land use plan	National Policy for Disaster Risk Reduction – 2018
			conservation of the traditional urban structures and sustainable use of natural resources	National Urban Policy 2007
Protection of local level resources	Protection of Public, Government and trust Land to conserve historical, religious, cultural activities.	Conserve tourist Hubs	Conservation of Himalaya, Hills and Churia Zone Ensure of protection and promotion of biodiversity Protection of soil by maintaining its natural core	Land Use policy, 2015
		Taxation based on land use zone.		Land Use Act 2019
	Concept of community forest for protection of forest		Protection of forest for carbon emission reduction Protection of wild animals in forest area	Forest Policy 2018
	Conservation of natural, social and cultural heritages		Build resilience ecosystem	Climate Change Policy 2019
				Land Act 1964
	Protection of land from natural hazards		Plantation on bank of the rivers	Local governing Act 2017
	Government can acquire land and house inside the forest are			Forest Act 1993
Viability and Acceptability to the local level plan	Federal/Provincial and Local level Land use Plan	Progressive tax system based on land use plan	mitigate the impact of climate change;	Land use Policy 2015
	Local land use plan should be Based on Provincial and then Federal land use plan Public, Government and trust Land to conserve historical, religious, cultural activities.	Establishment of Land Bank		Land Use Act 2019
		Employment creation Protection of forest and greenery area for tourism purpose, tourism is major source of income for government		Forest Policy 2018
	Conservation of natural, social and cultural heritages		Plantation on unused land	Climate Change Policy 2019
	Land classification			Local governing Act 2017
				Land use Act 2019
	Participatory approach	Incentive-oriented programs shall be operated in order to motivate people for the use of Land and Land Resources (LLRs)		Land Use Policy 2015
	Formation of local level land use committee Formation of land use zoning implementation committee involvement of experts of carious sectors	Establishment of crop bank	Province or Local Level can add required zone	Land Use Act 2019
			Climate change issue should be care during formulation of other policies Land use zoning based on climate change	Climate Change Policy 2019

Compilation of References

Abedi, T., Alemzadeh, A., & Kazemeini, S. (2010). Effect of Organic and Inorganic Fertilizers on Grain Yield and Protein Banding Pattern of Wheat. *Australian Journal of Crop Science*, *4*, 384–389.

Abegunawardhana & Senarathne. (2002). *Natural resources and environmental economics*. Author publication.

Abeysinghe, A. (1979). *Ancient land tenure to modern land reform in Sri Lanka*. Academic Press.

Abeywardana, N., Schütt, B., Wagalawatta, T., & Bebermeier, W. (2019). Indigenous agricultural systems in the dry zone of Sri Lanka: Management transformation assessment and sustainability. Sustainability, 11(3), 910. doi:10.3390u11030910

Abiala, M. A., Abdelrahman, M., Burritt, D. J., & Tran, L. S. P. (2018). Salt stress tolerance mechanisms and potential applications of legumes for sustainable reclamation of salt-degraded soils. *Land Degradation & Development*, *29*(10), 3812–3822. doi:10.1002/ldr.3095

Abson, D. J., Von Wehrden, H., Baumgärtner, S., Fischer, J., Hanspach, J., Härdtle, W., ... Martens, P. (2014). Ecosystem services as a boundary object for sustainability. *Ecological Economics*, *103*, 29–37. doi:10.1016/j.ecolecon.2014.04.012

Acaravci, A., & Ozturk, I. (2010). On the relationship between energy consumption, CO2 emissions and economic growth in Europe. *Energy*, *35*(12), 5412–5420. doi:10.1016/j.energy.2010.07.009

Acharya, B. R. (2011). Land Use Issues in Nepal: A country in Dire Need of Solutions. *GIM International*.

Adams, J. A. S., Osmond, J. K., & Rogers, J. J. W. (1959). *Physics and Chemistry of the Earth* (Vol. 3). Pergamon Press.

Agarwal, C., Green, G. M., Grove, J. M., Evans, T. P., & Schweik, C. M. (2002). *A review and assessment of land-use change models - Dynamics of space, time, and human choice. USDF Forest service*. North-eastern Research Station.

Aguilar, R., Zurita-Milla, R., Izquierdo-Verdiguier, E., & De By, A, R. (. (2018). A cloud-based multi-temporal ensemble classifier to map smallholder farming systems. *Remote Sensing*, *10*(5), 729. doi:10.3390/rs10050729

Ahamer, G. (2017). Mapping Global Dynamics. Springer.

Aheeyar, M. M. M., & Ariyabandu, R. D. S. (2002).Socio-economic Issues Pertinent to Agro-well Farming in Sri Lanka. In S. Pathmarajah (Ed.), *Use of Ground Water for Agriculture in Sri Lanka -Symposium Proceedings*. Peradeniya: Agricultural Engineering Society of Sri Lanka.

Ahmad, P., Abdel Latef, A. A., & Hashem, A. Abd_Allah, E. F., Gucel, S., & Tran, L. S. P. (2016). Nitric oxide mitigates salt stress by regulating levels of osmolytes and antioxidant enzymes in chickpea. *Frontiers in Plant Science*, *7*, 347.

Ahmad, I., Imran, M., Hussain, M. B., & Hussain, S. (2017). Remediation of Organic And Inorganic Pollutants From Soil: The Role Of Plant-Bacteria Partnership. In N. A. Anjum (Ed.), *Chemical Pollution Control With Microorganisms* (pp. 197–243). Nova Sci. Publisher.

Alewell, C., Borrelli, P., Meusburger, K., & Panagos, P. (2019). International Soil and Water Conservation Research. *International Soil and Water Conservation Research (ISWCR), 203.*

Alex, S. (2018). *Restoration of Degraded Agricultural Land.* Academic Press.

Allen, L., Lindberg, F., & Grimmond, C. S. B. (2011). Global to city scale urban anthropogenic heat flux: Model and variability. *International Journal of Climatology, 31*(13), 1990–2005. doi:10.1002/joc.2210

Alongi, D. M. (2002). Present state and future of the world's mangrove forests. *Environmental Conservation, 29*(3), 331–349. doi:10.1017/S0376892902000231

Al-Saedi, S. A., Al-Ameri, B. H., & Rasheed, A. G. (2018). Sulfuric acid as a chemical amendment for increasing efficiency of reclamation process of salt affected soils of Iraq. *Net Journal of Agricultural Science, 6*(3), 49–52. doi:10.30918/NJAS.63.18.022

Alsos, G. A., Carter, S., Ljunggren, E., & Welter, F. (2011). Introduction: researching entrepreneurship in agriculture and rural development. The handbook of research on entrepreneurship in agriculture and rural development, 1-18.

Alwis, J., & Wanigaratne, R. D. (2001). *Agrarian reforms and agricultural productivity: A status review of Sri Lanka's experience.* Report of the Asian Productivity Organization Meeting.

Amato, F., Cassee, F. R., van der Gon, H. A. D., Gehrig, R., Gustafsson, M., Hafner, W., Harrison, R. M., Jozwicka, M., Kelly, F. J., Moreno, T., & Prevot, A. S. (2014). Urban air quality: The challenge of traffic non-exhaust emissions. *Journal of Hazardous Materials, 275*, 31–36. doi:10.1016/j.jhazmat.2014.04.053 PMID:24837462

Amerasinghe, N. (1976). An overview of settlement schemes in Sri Lanka. *Asian Survey, 16*(7), 620–636. doi:10.2307/2643162

Amnesty International. (2014). *Thailand submission to the United Nations committee against torte (52nd session).* Amnesty International Publication. Available at: https://www.amnesty.org/download/Documents/8000/asa390032014en.pdf

Anderson, A. R., & Jack, S. L. (2002). The articulation of social capital in entrepreneurial networks: A glue or a lubricant? *Entrepreneurship and Regional Development, 14*(3), 193–210. doi:10.1080/08985620110112079

Annabi, M., Le Bissonnais, Y., Le Villio-Poitrenaud, M., & Houot, S. (2011). Improvement of soil aggregate stability by repeated applications of organic amendments to a cultivated silty loam soil. *Agriculture, Ecosystems & Environment, 144*(1), 382–389. doi:10.1016/j.agee.2011.07.005

Antonio, R. (2017). *The King and the making of modern Thailand: Routledge.* Taylor and Francis Group.

Aphornsuvan, T. (2003). *History and Politics of the Muslims in Thailand.* Bangkok: Thammasat University. Retrieved September 20, 2017, from https://seap.einaudi.cornell.edu/sites/seap/files/MuslimThailand.pdf

Aquastat. (2016). Available at: www.fao.org/nr/water/aquastat/main/index.stm

Ariyadasa, K. P. (2002). *Assessment of tree resources in the home gardens of Sri Lanka.* FAO Regional Office for Asia and the Pacific.

Ariyapala, M. B. (1956). Society in Medieval Ceylon. Academic Press.

Aroh, K. (2018). *Globalization, Industralization and Population Growth the Fundamental Drivers of Pollution in a Given Society (India).* Available at SSRN 3453740

Asia Foundation. (2013). *The Contested Corners of Asia: Subnational Conflict and International Development Assistance*. Available at: https://asiafoundation.org/publication/the-contested-corners-of-asia-subnational-conflict-and-international-development-assistance/

Auslander, M. (2017). Rose's gift: Slavery, kinship, and the fabric of memory. *Present Pasts*, *8*(1), 1. Advance online publication. doi:10.5334/pp.78

Ayipio, E., Wells, D. E., McQuilling, A., & Wilson, A. E. (2019). Comparisons between Aquaponic and Conventional Hydroponic Crop Yields: A Meta-Analysis. *Sustainability*, *11*(22), 6511. doi:10.3390u11226511

Azadi, H., Ho, P., & Hasfiati, L. (2011). Agricultural land conversion drivers: A comparison between less developed, developing and developed countries. *Land Degradation & Development*, *22*(6), 596–604. doi:10.1002/ldr.1037

B. K., A., Mahato, A., Thapa, S., Rai, A., & Devkota, N. (2019). Achieving Nepal's sustainable development goals (SDGs) by effective compliance of corporate governance. *Quest Journal of Management and Social Sciences, 1*(1), 50-72.

Baab, C. H. (2011). Heir property: A constraint for planners, an opportunity for communities—The legacy of Steve Larkin. *Planning & Environmental Law*, *63*(11), 3–11. doi:10.1080/15480755.2011.630283

Baba, A., Zabawa, R., & Zekeri, A. (2018). Utilization of property among African American heir and titled landowners in Alabama's Black Belt. *The Review of Black Political Economy*, *45*(4), 325–338. doi:10.1177/0034644619838378

Babayev, A. G. (2019). Principal Problems of Desert Land Reclamation in the USSR. In *Desertification* (pp. 203–232). CRC Press. doi:10.1201/9780429050893-9

Bairoch, P. (1991). *Cities and economic development: from the dawn of history to the present*. University of Chicago Press.

Bai, Z. G., Dent, D. L., Olsson, L., & Schaepman, M. E. (2008). Proxy global assessment of land degradation. *Soil Use and Management*, *24*(3), 223–234. doi:10.1111/j.1475-2743.2008.00169.x

Baldock, J. A., & Broos, K. (2011). Soil organic matter. In P. Huang (Ed.), *Handbook of soil science* (2nd ed., pp. 11.1–11.52).

Bandypadhyay, S., Jaiswal, R. K., Hegde, V. S., & Jayaraman, V. (2009). Assessment of land suitability potentials for agriculture using a remote sensing and GIS based approach. *International Journal of Remote Sensing*, *30*(4), 879–895. doi:10.1080/01431160802395235

Barbosa, G. L., Gadelha, F. D. A., Kublik, N., Proctor, A., Reichelm, L., Weissinger, E., Wohlleb, G. M., & Halden, R. U. (2015). Comparison of land, water, and energy requirements of lettuce grown using hydroponic vs. conventional agricultural methods. *International Journal of Environmental Research and Public Health, 12*(6), 6879–6891. doi:10.3390/ijerph120606879 PMID:26086708

Barlow, J., Lennox, G. D., Ferreira, J., Berenguer, E., Lees, A. C., Nally, R. M., & Gardner, T. A. (2016). Anthropogenic disturbance in tropical forests can double biodiversity loss from deforestation. *Nature*, *535*(7610), 144–147. doi:10.1038/nature18326 PMID:27362236

Barrett, C. B., & Bevis, L. E. (2015). The self-reinforcing feedback between low soil fertility and chronic poverty. *Nature Geoscience*, *8*(12), 907–912. doi:10.1038/ngeo2591

Barron, S., Sheppard, S. R., & Condon, P. M. (2016). Urban forest indicators for planning and designing future forests. *Forests*, *7*(9), 208. doi:10.3390/f7090208

Barros, R., Isidoro, D., & Aragüés, R. (2012). Three study decades on irrigation performance and salt concentrations and loads in the irrigation return flows of La Violada irrigation district (Spain). *Agriculture, Ecosystems & Environment*, *151*, 44–52. doi:10.1016/j.agee.2012.02.003

Barry, R. G., & Blanken, P. D. (2016). *Microclimate and local climate*. Cambridge University Press. doi:10.1017/CBO9781316535981

Bartelme, T. (2000). Heirs property tangle leads to loss of land. *The Post and Courier*. http://archives.postandcourier.com/archive/arch00/1200/arc1224276403.shtml

Bartelme, T. (2001). Families evicted from heirs' property: Deputies enforce court's directive after relative's lawsuit leads to sale order. *The Post and Courier*. http://archives.postandcourier.com/archive/arch01/0901/arc0928311298.shtml

Bartelme, T. (2002). Heirs land at risk. *The Post and Courier*. http://archives.postandcourier.com/archive/arch02/0602/arc0623648840.shtml

Bashir, S., Javed, A., Bibi, I., & Ahmad, N. (2017). *Soil and Water Conservation*. https://www.researchgate.net/publication/320729156_Soil_and_Water_Conservation

Bastian, S. (2009). The politics of land reform and land settlement in Sri Lanka. Kathmandu, Nepal: Panos South Asia.

Batey, T. (2009). Soil compaction and soil management–a review. *Soil Use and Management*, *25*(4), 335–345. doi:10.1111/j.1475-2743.2009.00236.x

Batteau, A. (1982). Mosbys and Broomsedge: The semantics of class in an Appalachian kinship system. *American Ethnologist*, *9*(3), 445–466. doi:10.1525/ae.1982.9.3.02a00010

Baude, M., Meyer, B. C., & Schindewolf, M. (2019). Land use change in an agricultural landscape causing degradation of soil based ecosystem services. *The Science of the Total Environment*, *659*, 1526–1536. doi:10.1016/j.scitotenv.2018.12.455 PMID:31096362

Bauer, H., Müller, L., Van Der Goes, D., & Sillero-Zubiri, C. (2017). Financial compensation for damage to livestock by lions Panthera leo on community rangelands in Kenya. *Oryx*, *51*(1), 106–114. doi:10.1017/S003060531500068X

Baumann, M., Kuemmerle, T., Elbakidze, M., Ozdogan, M., Radeloff, V. C., Keuler, N. S., Prishchepov, A. V., Kruhlov, I., & Hostert, P. (2011). Patterns and drivers of post-socialist farmland abandonment in Western Ukraine. *Land Use Policy*, *28*(3), 552–562. doi:10.1016/j.landusepol.2010.11.003

Baumann, M., Radeloff, V. C., Avedian, V., & Kuemmerle, T. (2015). Land-use change in the Caucasus during and after the Nagorno-Karabakh conflict. *Regional Environmental Change*, *15*(8), 1703–1716. doi:10.100710113-014-0728-3

Baumgardner, D., Varela, S., Escobedo, F. J., Chacalo, A., & Ochoa, C. (2012). The role of a peri-urban forest on air quality improvement in the Mexico City megalopolis. *Environmental Pollution*, *163*, 74–183. doi:10.1016/j.envpol.2011.12.016 PMID:22245735

Becerril-Piña, R., & Mastachi-Loza, C. A. (2019). Desertification: Causes and Countermeasures. In W. Leal Filho, A. M. Azul, L. Brandli, P. G. Özuyar, & T. Wall (Eds.), *Life on Land* (pp. 1–13). Springer International Publishing.

Begum, N., & Narayana, J., & SL, A. K. (2010). Land Use/Land Cover Changes in the Catchment of Water Bodies in and Around Davangere City, Karnataka. *International Journal of Ecology and Environmental Sciences*, *36*(4), 277–280.

Behera, S. R., & Dash, D. P. (2017). The effect of urbanization, energy consumption, and foreign direct investment on the carbon dioxide emission in the SSEA (South and Southeast Asian) region. *Renewable & Sustainable Energy Reviews*, *70*, 96–106. doi:10.1016/j.rser.2016.11.201

Bell, K. C. (2018). *Claiming freedom: Race, kinship, and land in nineteenth-century Georgia*. University of South Carolina Press. doi:10.2307/j.ctv6wghxq

Bello, J. P., Silva, C., Nov, O., DuBois, R. L., Arora, A., Salamon, J., Mydlarz, C., & Doraiswamy, H. (2018). *SONYC: A system for the monitoring, analysis and mitigation of urban noise pollution.* arXiv preprint arXiv:1805.00889

Benke, K., & Tomkins, B. (2017). Future food-production systems: vertical farming and controlled- environment agriculture. Sustainability: Science. *Practice and Policy*, *13*(1), 13–26.

Berendse, F., van Ruijven, J., Jongejans, E., & Keesstra, S. (2015). Loss of plant species diversity reduces soil erosion resistance. *Ecosystems (New York, N.Y.)*, *18*(5), 881–888. doi:10.100710021-015-9869-6

Bergin, B. (2016). Defeating an Insurgency—The Thai Effort against the Communist Party of Thailand, 1965–ca. 1982. *Studies in Intelligence*, *60*(2), 25–36.

Berkofsky, L., Faiman, D., & Gale, J. (Eds.). (2019). *Settling the desert* (Vol. 16). Routledge. doi:10.4324/9780429287886

Bhagawat, R. (2011). *Urban Growth and land use/land cover Change of Pokhara Sub-Metropolitan City, Nepal.* Retrieved from; https://docs.google.com/ viewer? A=v&q=cache

Bhat, N., Suleiman, M., & Abdal, M. (2009). Selection of crops for sustainable utilization of land and water resources in Kuwait. *World Journal of Agricultural Sciences*, *5*, 201–206.

Bhattacharyya, R., Ghosh, B. N., Mishra, P. K., Mandal, B., Rao, C. S., Sarkar, D., Das, K., Anil, K., Lalitha, M., Hati, K., & Franzluebbers, A. (2015). Soil degradation in India: Challenges and potential solutions. *Sustainability*, *7*(4), 3528–3570. doi:10.3390u7043528

Bia, A. (2018, November 19). PCN needs $1.2M to complete Lagilagi Housing Project. *Fiji Broadcasting Corporation.* Retrieved from https://www.fbcnews. com.fj/news/pcn-needs-1-2m-to-complete-lagilagi-housing-project/

Bindraban, P. S., van der Velde, M., Ye, L., Van den Berg, M., Materechera, S., Kiba, D. I., ... Hoogmoed, W. (2012). Assessing the impact of soil degradation on food production. *Current Opinion in Environmental Sustainability*, *4*(5), 478–488. doi:10.1016/j.cosust.2012.09.015

Bishop, J. P., Angulo, A., Lewis, J. P., Moore, R.D., Rabb G. B., & Garcia Moreno, J. (2012). The Amphibian Extinction Crisis - What will it take to put the action into the Amphibian Conservation Action Plan? *S.A.P.I.EN.S, 5*(2), 97–111.

Bista, D., Amgain, L., & Shrestha, S. (2013). Food security scenario, challenges, and agronomic research directions of Nepal. *Agronomy Journal of Nepal*, *3*, 42–52. doi:10.3126/ajn.v3i0.8985

Blanco, P. D., Hardtke, L. A., Rostagno, C. M., del Valle, H. F., & Metternicht, G. I. (2017). Soil Degradation in Peninsula Valdes: Causes, Factors, Processes, and Assessment Methods. In Late Cenozoic of Península Valdés, Patagonia, Argentina (pp. 191-213). Springer.

Blanco-Canqui, H., & Lal, R. (2009). Crop residue management and soil carbon dynamics. *Soil Carbon Sequestration and the Greenhouse Effect, 57*, 291-309.

Bloome, D., & Muller, C. (2015). Tenancy and African American marriage in the postbellum South. *Demography*, *52*(5), 1409–1430. doi:10.100713524-015-0414-1 PMID:26223562

Bodner, G., Nakhforoosh, A., & Kaul, H. P. (2015). Management of crop water under drought: A review. *Agronomy for Sustainable Development*, *35*(2), 401–442. doi:10.100713593-015-0283-4

Bohnet, D. (1995). Integration of Socio-economic data into GIS - a case study of the CRDA Bizerte, GTZ, Bonn, F.R. Germany. Paper presented in AfricaGIS'95. UNITAR / CNTGI / OSS / UNSO.

Boley, B. B., & Gaither, C. J. (2016). Exploring empowerment within the Gullah Geechee cultural heritage corridor: Implications for heritage tourism development in the Lowcountry. *Journal of Heritage Tourism*, *11*(2), 155–176. doi:10.1080/1743873X.2015.1080712

Bonin, M., Coudel, E., Cissé, Y., Feng, S., Gicheru, P., Novira, N., & Tonneau, J.-P. (2012). Critical analysis of land use policies. In D. M. Neill, I. Nesheim, & F. Brouwer (Eds.), *Land Use Policies for Sustainable Development* (pp. 248–281). Edward Elgar Publishing. doi:10.4337/9781781002476.00021

Borengasser, M., Hungate, W. S., & Watkins, R. (2008). Hyperspectral Remote Sensing: Principles and Applications. CRC Press, Taylor & Francis Group.

Borgman, O., & Chefetz, B. (2013). Combined effects of biosolids application and irrigation with reclaimed wastewater on transport of pharmaceutical compounds in arable soils. *Water Research*, *47*(10), 3431–3443. doi:10.1016/j.watres.2013.03.045 PMID:23591105

Borrelli, P., Paustian, K., Panagos, P., Jones, A., Schütt, B., & Lugato, E. (2016). Effect of good agricultural and environmental conditions on erosion and soil organic carbon balance: A national case study. *Land Use Policy*, *50*, 408–421. doi:10.1016/j.landusepol.2015.09.033

Bossier, P., & Ekasari, J. (2017). Biofloc technology application in aquaculture to support sustainable development goals. *Microbial Biotechnology*, *10*(5), 1012–1016. doi:10.1111/1751-7915.12836 PMID:28941177

Botwick, B. (2018). Gullah-Geechee settlement patterns from slavery to freedom: Investigation of a Georgia plantation slave quarter. *North American Archaeologist*, *39*(3), 198–228. doi:10.1177/0197693118793795

Bouma, J., Keesstra, S., & Cerdà, A. (2017). The importance of Soil Science to understand and remediate Land Degradation and Desertification processes. Paper presented at the Geophysical Research Abstracts.

Bowe, B., Xie, Y., Li, T., Yan, Y., Xian, H., & Al-Aly, Z. (2018). The global and national burden of diabetes mellitus attributable to PM2· 5 air pollution. *The Lancet Planetary Health*, *2*(7), e301–e312. doi:10.1016/S2542-5196(18)30140-2 PMID:30074893

Bradford, A. (2015). *Deforestation: facts, causes & effects.* Live Science.

Brandani, G., Napoli, M., Massetti, L., Petralli, M., & Orlandini, S. (2016). Urban soil: Assessing ground cover impact on surface temperature and thermal comfort. *Journal of Environmental Quality*, *45*(1), 90–97. doi:10.2134/jeq2014.12.0521 PMID:26828164

Briassoulis. (2006) Changes in land use and land cover: A global perspective. In *Global land use and land cover change: An overview* (pp. 3-10). Cambridge University Press.

Brodhag, C., & Taliere, S. (2006). Sustainable development strategies: Tools for policy coherence. *Natural Resources Forum*, *30*(2), 136–145. doi:10.1111/j.1477-8947.2006.00166.x

Brohier, R. L. (1934). *Ancient Irrigation Works in Ceylon.* Ministry of Mahaweli Development.

Brohier, R. L. (2000). *Seeing Ceylon.* Suriya publications.

Brooks, J. (1979). The Emergency Land Fund: A rural land retention and development model. In L. McGee & R. Boone (Eds.), *The Black Rural Landowner – Endangered Species: Social, Political, and Economic Implications* (pp. 117–134). Greenwood Press.

Brown, R., Leder, K., Wong, T., French, M., Chown, S. L., Luby, S., ... Forbes, A. (2018). Improving human and environmental health in urban informal settlements: The Revitalising Informal Settlements and their Environments (RISE) programme. *The Lancet Planetary Health*, *2*, S29. doi:10.1016/S2542-5196(18)30114-1

Bryant-Tokalau, J. (2010). *The Fijian Qoliqoli and urban squatting in Fiji: Righting an historical wrong?* Alfred Deakin Research Institute, Deakin University.

Bryant-Tokalau, J. (2014). Urban squatter and the poor in Fiji: Issues of land and investment in coastal areas. *Asia Pacific Viewpoint*, *55*(1), 54–66. doi:10.1111/apv.12043

Bryant-Tokalau, J., & Campbell, J. (2014). Coping with floods in urban Fiji: responses and resilience of the poor. In M. Sakai, E. Jurriëns, J. Zhang, & A. Thornton (Eds.), *Disaster Relief in the Asia Pacific* (pp. 150–164). Routledge.

Buckseth, T., Sharma, A. K., Pandey, K. K., Singh, B. P., & Muthuraj, R. (2016). Methods of pre- basic seed potato production with special reference to aeroponics-A review. *Scientia Horticulturae*, *204*, 79–87.

Budhathoki, P., Sapkota, B., Maharjan, R., Bista, S., & Gosain, A. (2019). Empowerment of diversity in the Nepalese corporate sector. *Quest Journal of Management and Social Sciences*, *1*(1), 96–118. doi:10.3126/qjmss.v1i1.25976

Bujang, A. S., & Bakar, B. H. A. (2019). Precision Agriculture in Malaysia. *International Workshop on ICTs for Precision Agriculture*, 91–104.

Buli, B. M., & Yesuf, W. M. (2015). Determinants of entrepreneurial intentions: Technical-vocational education and training students in Ethiopia. *Education + Training*, *57*(8/9), 57891–57907. doi:10.1108/ET-10-2014-0129

Bullard, R. D. (1993). Environmental racism and land use. *Land Use Forum: A Journal of Law. Policy & Practice*, *2*(1), 6–11.

Bullard, R. D. (1996). *Unequal protection: Environmental justice and communities of color*. Sierra Club.

Bunt, J. S., Robertson, A. I., & Alongi, D. M. (1992). Introduction. In D. M. Alongi & A. I. Robertson (Eds.), *Tropical mangrove ecosystems* (pp. 1–6). American Geophysical Union. doi:10.1029/CE041p0001

Burakov, A. E., Galunin, E. V., Burakova, I. V., Kucherova, A. E., Agarwal, S., Tkachev, A. G., & Gupta, V. K. (2018). Adsorption of heavy metals on conventional and nanostructured materials for wastewater treatment purposes: A review. *Ecotoxicology and Environmental Safety*, *148*, 702–712. doi:10.1016/j.ecoenv.2017.11.034 PMID:29174989

Burby, R. J., Deyle, R. E., Godschalk, D. R., & Olshansky, R. B. (2000). Creating hazard resilient communities through land-use planning. *Natural Hazards Review*, *1*(2), 99–106. doi:10.1061/(ASCE)1527-6988(2000)1:2(99)

Burke, A., Tweedie, P., & Phūčhārœ̄n, R. N. (2013). *The Contested Corners of Asia: Subnational Conflict and International Development Assistance: the Case of Southern Thailand*. Asia Foudation.

Burns, J. H., & Hart, H. L. A. (1970). The Collective Workers of Jeremy Bentham: An Introduction to the Principle of Morals and Legislation. University of London.

Buyantuyev, A., & Wu, J. (2010). Urban heat islands and landscape heterogeneity: Linking spatiotemporal variations in surface temperatures to land-cover and socioeconomic patterns. *Landscape Ecology*, *25*(1), 17–33. doi:10.100710980-009-9402-4

Byrd, A. (2018). Congress investigates EPA for refusing NASA's help after hurricane Harvey. *Color lines*. https://www.colorlines.com/tags/environmental-racism

Cachada, A., Rocha-Santos, T., & Duarte, A. C. (2018). Soil and pollution: an introduction to the main issues. In *Soil pollution* (pp. 1–28). Elsevier.

Calfapietra, C., Fares, S., Manes, F., Morani, A., Sgrigna, G., & Loreto, F. (2013). Role of Biogenic Volatile Organic Compounds (BVOC) emitted by urban trees on ozone concentration in cities: A review. *Environmental Pollution, 183*, 71–80. doi:10.1016/j.envpol.2013.03.012 PMID:23597803

Campbell, A. (2017, April 7). *Beyond say: Water, spirituality, and the womanist autoethnography in Beyonce's Lemonade*. The National Conference on Undergraduate Research, University of Memphis, TN. http://ncurproceedings.org/ojs/index.php/NCUR2017/article/view/2244/1264

Campos-Taberner, M., Moreno-Martínez, Á., García-Haro, F. J., Camps-Valls, G., Robinson, N. P., Kattge, J., & Running, S. W. (2018). Global estimation of biophysical variables from Google Earth Engine platform. *Remote Sensing, 10*(8), 1167. doi:10.3390/rs10081167

Canfora, I. (2016). Is the short food supply chain an efficient solution for sustainability in food market. *Agriculture and Agricultural Science Procedia, 8*(1), 402–407. doi:10.1016/j.aaspro.2016.02.036

Carastathis, A. (2016). *Intersectionality: Origins, contestations, horizons*. University of Nebraska Press. doi:10.2307/j.ctt1fzhfz8

Cariñanos, P., Adinolfi, C., Diaz de la Guardia, C., De Linares, C., & Casares-Porcel, M. (2016). Characterization of allergen emission sources in urban areas. *Journal of Environmental Quality, 45*(1), 244–252. doi:10.2134/jeq2015.02.0075 PMID:26828180

Carmen, B., & Roberto, D. (2011). Soil bacteria support and protect plants against abiotic stresses. Abiotic stress in plants-Mechanisms and daptations, 143-170. doi:10.5772/23310

Carolan, M. (2017). Publicising food: Big data, precision agriculture, and co-experimental techniques of addition. *Sociologia Ruralis, 57*(2), 135–154. doi:10.1111oru.12120

Caron, C. M. (2018). Pursuing gender-transformative change in customary tenure systems: Civil society work in Zambia. *Development in Practice, 28*(7), 872–883. doi:10.1080/09614524.2018.1480896

Caron, C., Menon, G., & Kuritz, L. (2014). Land Tenure & Disasters. *USAID. Issue brief.*

Carothers, C., Brown, C., Moerlein, K. J., López, J. A., Andersen, D. B., & Retherford, B. (2014). Measuring perceptions of climate change in northern Alaska: pairing ethnography with Glassman, M., and G. Erdem. 2014. Participatory action research and its meanings: vivencia, praxis, conscientization. *Adult Education Quarterly, 64*, 206–221. doi:10.1177/0741713614523667

Carreiro, M. M., Song, Y. C., & Wu, J. (Eds.). (2007). *Ecology, planning, and management of urban forests: International perspective*. Springer.

Carr, J. C., & Sequeira, J. M. (2007). Prior family business exposure as intergenerational influence and entrepreneurial intent: A theory of planned behavior approach. *Journal of Business Research, 60*(10), 1090–1098. doi:10.1016/j.jbusres.2006.12.016

Carter, E. D. (2018). Overpopulation. In Companion to Environmental Studies (Vol. 76, No. 80, pp. 76-80). Routledge in association with GSE Research.

Casagrande, J. G. Jr. (1986). Acquiring property through forced partitioning sales: Abuses and remedies. *Boston College Law Review, 27*(4), 755–783.

Castrignano, A., Buttafuoco, G., & Puddu, R. (2008). Multi-scale assessment of the risk of soil salinization in an area of south-eastern Sardinia (Italy). *Precision Agriculture, 9*(1-2), 17–31. doi:10.100711119-008-9054-4

CBS. (2017). *Statistical Year Book.* Ramshahpath, Thapathali: Central Bureau of Statistics. https://cbs.gov.np/wp-content/upLoads/2019/02/Statistical-Year-Book-2017.pdf

Census of India. (2011). *Provisional Population totals.* Urban Agglomerations and Cities.

Center for Heirs' Property Preservation. (2019). *Protect your land.* https://www.heirsproperty.org/

Central Bureau of Statistics (CBS). (2011). *National population and housing census 2011.* Retrieved from https://unstats.un.org/unsd/demographicsocial/census/documents/Nepal/Nepal-Census-2011-Vol1.pdf

Cetin, M. (2015). Using GIS analysis to assess urban green space in terms of accessibility: Case study in Kutahya. *International Journal of Sustainable Development and World Ecology, 22*(5), 420–424.

CFR. (2008). *The Muslim Insurgency in Southern Thailand.* Council on Foreign Relations. Available at: https://www.cfr.org/backgrounder/muslim-insurgency-southern-thailand

Chaleampong, K. (Producer). (2017). *Relationship between growth, inequality and poverty and pro-poor growth in Thailand: 1986-2011.* Retrieved from https://www.slideserve.com/pearl/relationship-between-growth-inequality-and-poverty-and-pro-poor-growth-in-thailand-1986-2011

Chalida, B. (2017). Economy and development in southernmost border provinces of Thailand: a criticized exploratory. In A decade of anthropology and sociology of southernmost border provinces study (pp. 29-68). Bangkok: O.S. Printing House.

Chalise, D., Joshi, A., Twanabasu, B., Rawal, N., & Amgai, S. (2016). Preparation of Land Use Zoning Maps of Chaumala VDC, Kailali. *International Journal of Applied Sciences and Biotechnology, 4*(4), 458–463. doi:10.3126/ijasbt.v4i4.14213

Chalker-Scott, L. (2015). Nonnative, noninvasive woody species can enhance urban landscape biodiversity. *Arboriculture & Urban Forestry, 41*(4), 173–185.

Chalk, P. (2008). *The Malay-Muslim Insurgency in Southern ThailandUnderstanding the Conflict's Evolving Dynamic.* RAND National Defense Research Institute. Available at https://www.rand.org/content/dam/rand/pubs/occasional_papers/2008/RAND_OP198.pdf

Challender, D., Willcox, D.H.A., Panjang, E., Lim, N., Nash, H., Heinrich, S. & Chong, J. (2019). *Manis javanica. The IUCN Red List of Threatened Species 2019: e.T12763A123584856.* doi:10.2305/IUCN.UK.2019-3.RLTS.T12763A123584856.en

Chameides, W. L., Fehsenfeld, F., Rodgers, M. O., Cardelino, C., Martinez, J., Parrish, D., Lonneman, W., Lawson, D. R., Rasmussen, R. A., Zimmerman, P., Greenberg, J., Mlddleton, P., & Wang, T. (1992). Ozone precursor relationships in the ambient atmosphere. *Journal of Geophysical Research, D, Atmospheres, 97*(D5), 6037–6055. doi:10.1029/91JD03014

Chancel, L. (2017). High growth does not necessarily mean high inequality, World inequality lab, and WID. *The Hindu.* Available at, https://www.thehindu.com/business/Economy/high-growth-does-not-necessarily-mean-high-inequality-says-lucas-chancel/article21653028.ece

Chand, S. (2019a, May 31). Government takes over Lagilagi project after alleged abuse of funds. *Fiji Sun.* Retrieved from https://fijisun.com.fj/2019/05/31/

Chand, S. (2019b, June 25). Father Barr Breaks Silence On Lagilagi Housing Project. *Fiji Sun.* Retrieved from https://fijisun.com.fj/2019/06/25/

Chand, S. (2019c, September 19). 140 tenants of Raiwai flats issued eviction notice, no longer eligible to occupy flats. *Fiji Sun.* Retrieved from https://fijisun. com.fj/2019/09/19/

Chand, B. (2019). *Land management problems in Nepal: repercussions of land use policy and implementation gaps in regional and urban planning* [Paper presention]. ISPRS Annals of Photogrammetry, Remote Sensing & Spatial Information Sciences.

Chandio, A. A., Jiang, Y., Rehman, A., & Rauf, A. (2020). Short and long-run impacts of climate change on agriculture: An empirical evidence from China. *International Journal Climate Change Stress., 7*, 395–402.

Chandler, A. B. (2005). "The loss in my bones": Protecting African American heirs' property with the public use doctrine. *The William and Mary Bill of Rights Journal, 14*(1), 387–414.

Chandra, R. (1985). *Industrialization in Fiji* (Doctoral dissertation). University of British Columbia, Vancouver.

Chandrasiri, J.K.M.D. (2010). *Impact of informal land transactions in settlement schemes in Sri Lanka.* HARTI-Research Report, 132.

Chandrasiri, S. (2009). Labour market trends and informal sector of the economy. *Sri Lanka Economic Journal, 2*(1), 89–106.

Chang, C. R., Li, M. H., & Chang, S. D. (2007). A preliminary study on the local cool-island intensity of Taipei city parks. *Landscape and Urban Planning, 80*(4), 386–395. doi:10.1016/j.landurbplan.2006.09.005

Chapman, S., Watson, J. E., Salazar, A., Thatcher, M., & McAlpine, C. A. (2017). The impact of urbanization and climate change on urban temperatures: A systematic review. *Landscape Ecology, 32*(10), 1921–1935. doi:10.100710980-017-0561-4

Chaudhry, P., & Tewari, V. P. (2011). Urban forestry in India: Development and research scenario. *Interdisciplinary Environmental Review, 12*(1), 80–93. doi:10.1504/IER.2011.038881

Cha-un, N., Chidthaisong, A., Yagi, K., Sudo, S., & Towprayoon, S. (2017). Greenhouse gas emissions, soil carbon sequestration and crop yields in a rain-fed rice field with crop rotation management. *Agriculture, Ecosystems & Environment, 237*, 109–120. doi:10.1016/j.agee.2016.12.025

Chein-I Chang. (2003). *Hyperspectral Imaging: Techniques for Spectral Detection and Classification*. Springer Science & Business Media.

Chen, Juan, Yuchun, & Jihua. (2009). Index system and method of agricultural land grade monitoring. *Journal of Agricultural Engineering, 25*(13), 272–276.

Chen, Q., Yao, Y., Li, X., Lu, J., Zhou, J. and Huang, Z. (2018). Comparison of heavy metal removals from aqueous solutions by chemical precipitation and characteristics of precipitates. *Journal of Water Process Engineering, 26*, 289-300.

Chen, S., Su, Y., & Hong, W. (2018). *Aquaculture of the large yellow croaker. Aquaculture in China: Success Stories and Modern Trends.* John Wiley & Sons.

Chen, S., Wang, W., Xu, W., Wang, Y., Wan, H., Chen, D., Tang, Z., Tang, X., Zhou, G., Xie, Z., Zhou, D., Shangguan, Z., Huang, J., He, J.-S., Wang, Y., Sheng, J., Tang, L., Li, X., Dong, M., ... Bai, Y. (2018). Plant diversity enhances productivity and soil carbon storage. *Proceedings of the National Academy of Sciences of the United States of America, 115*(16), 4027–4032. doi:10.1073/pnas.1700298114 PMID:29666315

Chen, Z., Liang, Y., Jia, D., Chen, W., Cui, Z., & Wang, X. (2017). Layered silicate RUB-15 for efficient removal of UO 2 2+ and heavy metal ions by ion-exchange. *Environmental Science. Nano, 4*(9), 1851–1858. doi:10.1039/C7EN00366H

Cherif, H., Marasco, R., Rolli, E., Ferjani, R., Fusi, M., Soussi, A., Mapelli, F., Blilou, I., Borin, S., Boudabous, A., Cherif, A., Daffonchio, D., & Ouzari, H. (2015). Oasis desert farming selects environment-specific date palm root endophytic communities and cultivable bacteria that promote resistance to drought. *Environmental Microbiology Reports*, *7*(4), 668–678. doi:10.1111/1758-2229.12304 PMID:26033617

Chesworth, W. (Ed.). (2007). *Encyclopedia of soil science*. Springer Science & Business Media.

Cheyne, S., Ehlers-Smith, D.A., Nijman, V. & Traeholt, C. (2020). *Presbytis rubicunda. The IUCN Red List of Threatened Species 2020: e.T18131A17953935*. doi:10.2305/IUCN.UK.2020-2.RLTS.T18131A17953935.en

Chin, L., Chung, A. Y. C., & Clarke, C. (2014). Interspecific variation in prey capture behavior by co-occurring nepenthes pitcher plants: Evidence for resource partitioning or sampling-scheme artifacts? *Plant Signaling & Behavior*, *9*(1), 1–16. doi:10.4161/psb.27930 PMID:24481246

Chivenge, P., & Sharma, S. (2019). Precision Agriculture in Food Production: Nutrient Management. *International Workshop on ICTs for Precision Agriculture*, 12.

Chlingaryan, A., Sukkarieh, S., & Whelan, B. (2018). Machine learning approaches for crop yield prediction and nitrogen status estimation in precision agriculture: A review. *Computers and Electronics in Agriculture*, *151*, 61–69. doi:10.1016/j.compag.2018.05.012

Chokkalingam, U., & Vanniarachchy, A. (2011). *Sri Lanka's REDD+ potential, myth or reality?* Forest Carbon Asia.

Chopra, R. (2016). Environmental degradation in India: Causes and consequences. *International Journal of Applied Environmental Sciences*, *11*(6), 1593–1601.

Cho, Y., Shim, W. J., Jang, M., Han, G. M., & Hong, S. H. (2019). Abundance and characteristics of microplastics in market bivalves from South Korea. *Environmental Pollution*, *245*, 1107–1116. doi:10.1016/j.envpol.2018.11.091 PMID:30682745

Chun, B., & Guldmann, J. M. (2014). Spatial statistical analysis and simulation of the urban heat island in high-density central cities. *Landscape and Urban Planning*, *125*, 76–88. doi:10.1016/j.landurbplan.2014.01.016

Churkina, G., Kuik, F., Bonn, B., Lauer, A., Grote, R., Tomiak, K., & Butler, T. M. (2017). Effect of VOC emissions from vegetation on air quality in Berlin during a heatwave. *Environmental Science & Technology*, *51*(11), 6120–6130. doi:10.1021/acs.est.6b06514 PMID:28513175

Clark, C., Sbihi, H., Tamburic, L., Brauer, M., Frank, L. D., & Davies, H. W. (2017). Association of long-term exposure to transportation noise and traffic-related air pollution with the incidence of diabetes: A prospective cohort study. *Environmental Health Perspectives*, *125*(8), 087025. doi:10.1289/EHP1279 PMID:28934721

Clarke, J., & Rhind, D. W. (1992). *A Review of Spatial Population Database Design and Modeling. Population Data and Global Environmental Change. Paper prepared for the UNEP/GRID and CGIAR, NCGIA*. Asia Population Database Documentation.

Coastal Carolina University. (2020). *International Gullah Geechee and African Diaspora Conference*. https://www.coastal.edu/joynerinstitute/conference/

Cobbinah, P. B., & Darkwah, R. M. (2016), June. African urbanism: the geography of urban greenery. In *Urban Forum* (Vol. 27, No. 2, 149-165). Springer Netherlands.

Cobbinah, P. B., Erdiaw-Kwasie, M. O., & Amoateng, P. (2015). Rethinking sustainable development within the framework of poverty and urbanization in developing countries. *Environmental Development*, *13*, 18–32. doi:10.1016/j.envdev.2014.11.001

Cocklin, C., & Keen, M. (2000). Urbanization in the Pacific: Environmental change, vulnerability and human security. *Environmental Conservation, 27*(4), 392–403. doi:10.1017/S0376892900000448

Colditz, R. R., Schmidt, M., Conrad, C., Hansen, M. C., & Dech, S. (2011). Land cover classification with coarse spatial resolution data to derive continuous and discrete maps for complex regions. *Remote Sensing of Environment, 115*(12), 3264–3275. doi:10.1016/j.rse.2011.07.010

Collier, P., & Hoeffler, A. (1998). On economic causes of civil war. *Oxford Economic Papers, 50*(4), 563–573. doi:10.1093/oep/50.4.563

Conant, R. T., Cerri, C. E., Osborne, B. B., & Paustian, K. (2017). Grassland management impacts on soil carbon stocks: A new synthesis. *Ecological Applications, 27*(2), 662–668. doi:10.1002/eap.1473 PMID:27875004

Copeland, R. W. (2015). Heir property in the African American community: From promised lands to problem lands. *Professional Agricultural Workers Journal, 2*(2), 2-9. https://tuspubs.tuskegee.edu/pawj/vol2/iss2/2

Cordesman, A. H. (2019). *Guarding the desert kingdom.* Routledge. doi:10.4324/9780429497452

Corwin, D. L., & Plant, R. E. (2005). Applications of apparent soil electrical conductivity in precision agriculture. *Computers and Electronics in Agriculture, 46*(1), 1–10. doi:10.1016/j.compag.2004.10.004

Costantini, E. A., Priori, S., Giffard, B., Fulchin, E., Tardaguila, J., Schroers, H.J., & Valboa, G. (2018). Causes of soil malfunctioning in degraded areas of European and Turkish vineyards. *EQA–Environmental Quality, 30*, 15-22.

Costanza, R., de Groot, R., Braat, L., Kubiszewski, I., Fioramonti, L., Sutton, P., Farber, S., & Grasso, M. (2017). Twenty years of ecosystem services: How far have we come and how far do we still need to go? *Ecosystem Services, 28*, 1–16. doi:10.1016/j.ecoser.2017.09.008

Crabtree, S. A., Bird, D. W., & Bird, R. B. (2019). Subsistence transitions and the simplification of ecological networks in the Western Desert of Australia. *Human Ecology, 47*(2), 165–177. doi:10.100710745-019-0053-z

Craig-Taylor, P. (2000). Through a colored looking glass: A view of judicial partition, family land loss, and rule setting. *Washington University Law Review Quarterly, 78*(3), 737–788.

Cramer, C. (2005). Violent conflict and the very poorest. *Chron Poverty Res Cent*, 4-26.

Crenshaw, K. (1998). Demarginalizing the intersection of race and sex: A Black feminist critique of antidiscrimination doctrine, feminist theory, and antiracist politics. *Feminism and Politics*, 314-343. doi:10.4324/9780429499142-5

Crenshaw, K. W. (1991). Mapping the margins: Intersectionality, identity politics, and violence against women of color. *Stanford Law Review, 43*(6), 1241–1299. doi:10.2307/1229039

Crosson, P. (2017). Degradation: Food Security and Poverty. In Encyclopedia of Soil Science (pp. 574-577). CRC Press.

CSCD. (2014). *Men and Youth in Thailand's Conflict-Affected Deep South.* Center for Conflict Studies and Cultural Diversity. Available at: https://www.deepsouthwatch.org/sites/default/files/men_and_male_youth_english_web_version.pdf

CSRC. (2012). *Land ownership and land reform in Nepal, Centre for community self-reliance, Kathmandu Nepal.* Retrieved from https://csrcnepal.org/

Cummings, R. G., & Taylor, L. O. (1999). Unbiased value estimates for environmental goods: A cheap talk design for the contingent valuation method. *The American Economic Review, 89*(3), 649–665. doi:10.1257/aer.89.3.649

D'Odorico, P., Rulli, M. C., Dell'Angelo, J., & Davis, K. F. (2017). New frontiers of land and water commodification: Socio environmental controversies of large-scale land acquisitions. *Land Degradation & Development*, *28*(7), 2234–2244. doi:10.1002/ldr.2750

Dadhwal, V. K., & Kumar, S. (1553–1554). George Joseph and C. Jeganathan(2018). Fundamentals of *Remote Sensing. Photonirvachak (Dehra Dun)*, *46*. Advance online publication. doi:10.100712524-018-0834-7

Daliakopoulos, I. N., Tsanis, I. K., Koutroulis, A., Kourgialas, N. N., Varouchakis, A. E., Karatzas, G. P., & Ritsema, C. J. (2016). The threat of soil salinity: A European scale review. *The Science of the Total Environment*, *573*, 727–739. doi:10.1016/j.scitotenv.2016.08.177 PMID:27591523

Damit, A. (2009). *Sandakan Rainforest Park: A Scientifically & Historically Important Forest*. Forest Research Centre.

Daniel, P. (2013). *Dispossession: Discrimination against African American farmers in the age of Civil Rights*. The University of North Carolina Press.

DasGupta, R., & Shaw, R. (2017). Mangroves in Asia-Pacific: a review of threats and responses. In R. DasGupta & R. Shaw (Eds.), *Participatory Mangrove Management in a Changing Climate* (pp. 1–16). Springer. doi:10.1007/978-4-431-56481-2_1

DasGupta, R., & Shaw, R. (2017). Retrofitting Joint Forest Management (JFM) in Protected Areas of Indian Sundarbans: How Sustainable It Is? In R. DasGupta & R. Shaw (Eds.), *Participatory Mangrove Management in a Changing Climate* (pp. 59–71). Springer. doi:10.1007/978-4-431-56481-2_4

DasGupta, R., & Shaw, R. (Eds.). (2017). *Participatory Mangrove Management in a Changing Climate: Perspectives from the Asia-Pacific*. Springer. doi:10.1007/978-4-431-56481-2

Das, S., & Vincent, J. R. (2009). Mangroves protected villages and reduced death toll during Indian super cyclone. *Proceedings of the National Academy of Sciences of the United States of America*, *106*(18), 7357–7360. doi:10.1073/pnas.0810440106 PMID:19380735

Davis, K. F., Yu, K., Rulli, M. C., Pichdara, L., & D'Odorico, P. (2015). Accelerated deforestation driven by large-scale land acquisitions in Cambodia. *Nature Geoscience*, *8*(10), 772–775. doi:10.1038/ngeo2540

Davis, R. A., & Doherty, T. S. (2015). Rapid recovery of an urban remnant reptile community following summer wildfire. *PLoS One*, *10*(5), 1–15. doi:10.1371/journal.pone.0127925 PMID:25992802

De Alban, J. D. T., Jamaludin, J., de Wen, D. W., Than, M. M., & Webb, E. L. (2020). Improved estimates of mangrove cover and change reveal catastrophic deforestation in Myanmar. *Environmental Research Letters*, *15*(034034), 1–14.

De Anda, J., & Shear, H. (2017). Potential of vertical hydroponic agriculture in Mexico. *Sustainability*, *9*(1), 140. doi:10.3390u9010140

De Clercq, M., Vats, A., & Biel, A. (2018). Agriculture 4.0: The future of farming technology. *Proceedings of the World Government Summit*, 11-13.

De Lauwere, C. C. (2005). The role of agricultural entrepreneurship in Dutch agriculture of today. *Agricultural Economics*, *33*(2), 229–238. doi:10.1111/j.1574-0862.2005.00373.x

De Silva, M. U. (1992). Land tenure, caste system and the rājakāriya, under foreign rule: A review of change in Sri Lanka under Western powers, 1597-1832. *Journal of the Royal Asiatic Society of Sri Lanka*, *37*, 1–57.

De Stefano, A., & Jacobson, M. G. (2018). Soil carbon sequestration in agroforestry systems: A meta-analysis. *Agroforestry Systems*, *92*(2), 285–299.

Decock, C., Lee, J., Necpalova, M., Pujol Pereira, E. I., Tendall, D. M., & Six, J. (2015). Mitigating N2O emissions from soil: From patching leaks to transformative action. *Soil (Göttingen)*, *1*(2), 687–694. doi:10.5194oil-1-687-2015

Deichmann, U. (1996). *Technical paper and digital database*. NCGIA.

Dell'Angelo, J., Rulli, M. C., & D'Odorico, P. (2018). The global water grabbing syndrome. *Ecological Economics*, *143*, 276–285. doi:10.1016/j.ecolecon.2017.06.033

DeLong, C., Cruse, R., & Wiener, J. (2015). The soil degradation paradox: Compromising our resources when we need them the most. *Sustainability*, *7*(1), 866–879. doi:10.3390u7010866

Deng, R., Lin, D., Zhu, L., Majumdar, S., White, J. C., Gardea-Torresdey, J. L., & Xing, B. (2017). Nanoparticle interactions with co-existing contaminants: Joint toxicity, bioaccumulation and risk. *Nanotoxicology*, *11*(5), 591–612. doi:10.1080/17435390.2017.1343404 PMID:28627273

Denman, E. C., May, P. B., & Moore, G. M. (2016). The potential role of urban forests in removing nutrients from stormwater. *Journal of Environmental Quality*, *45*(1), 207–214. doi:10.2134/jeq2015.01.0047 PMID:26828176

Department of Census and Statistics. (2002). *Agricultural census*. Author.

Department of Census and Statistics. (2019). *Agricultural census*. Retrieved from: http://www.statistics.gov.lk/agriculture/index.htm

Department of Statistics Malaysia. (2019). *Department of Statistics Malaysia, Official Portal*. https://www.dosm.gov.my/v1/

Deraniyagala, S. U. (1992). *The prehistory of SL, parts I, II*. Archaeological Survey Department.

Deraniyagala, S. U. (2002). A note on man and water in SL: from prehistory to history. In *Mendis DLO Water Heritage of Sri Lanka*. Sri Lanka Pugwash Group.Dharmasiri, R. K. (2009). *Land use land tenure and agricultural productivity in Sri Lanka A spatiotemporal analysis*. Retrieved from http://hdl.handle.net/10603/175107

Derickson, K. D. (2016). The assassination of Clementa Pinckney. *Southeastern Geographer*, *56*(1), 38–44. doi:10.1353go.2016.0012

Derouin, S. (2019). *Deforestation: Facts, Causes & Effects*. Accessed 20 February 2020, https://www.livescience.com/27692-deforestation.html

Devkota, N., & Phuyal, R. K. (2018). Adoption Practice of Climate Change Adaptation Options among Nepalese Rice Farmers: Role of Information and Communication Technologies (ICTs). *American Journal of Climate Change*, *7*(2), 135–152. doi:10.4236/ajcc.2018.72010

Devkota, N., Phuyal, R. K., & Shrestha, D. L. (2017). Cost and benefit analysis of adoption of climate change adaptation options among rural rice farmers in Nepal. *Asian Journal of Agriculture and Rural Development*, *7*(7), 136.

Devkota, N., Phuyal, R. K., & Shrestha, D. L. (2018). Perception, determinants and barriers for the adoption of climate change adaptation options among nepalese rice farmers. *Agricultural Sciences*, *9*(3), 272–298. doi:10.4236/as.2018.93021

Dharmasena, P. B. (2002). Integrated Management of Surface and Ground Water Resources in Tank Cascade Systems. In S. Pathmarajah (Ed.), *Use of Ground Water for Agriculture in Sri Lanka -Symposium Proceedings*. Peradeniya: Agricultural Engineering Society of Sri Lanka.

Dharmasena, P. B. (1993). Man environment interaction in-tank village home gardens: the trends in vegetations. *Proceedings of the 4th Regional Workshop on Multipurpose Trees*, 12-14.

Dharmasena, P. B. (2010). Essential components of traditional village tank systems. *Proceedings of the National Conference on Cascade Irrigation Systems for Rural Sustainability.*

Dharmasena, P. B., & Goodwill, I. M. (1999). Use of Ground Water in Minor Tank Irrigation Schemes of Sri Lanka. *Proceedings of 17thInternational Congress on Irrigation and Drainage*, 175-194.

Dhital, P. R. (2017). Agricultural extension in Nepal: Experiences and issues. *Journal of Advances in Agriculture*, *7*(3), 1071–1082. doi:10.24297/jaa.v7i3.6287

Dickens, N. (2019, March 7). *Reinventing Erzulie's past for literature's future*. Inaugural International Gullah Geechee and African Diaspora Conference, Coastal Carolina University, Conway, SC.

Dobson, A. P., Bradshaw, A., & Baker, A. Á. (1997). Hopes for the future: Restoration ecology and conservation biology. *Science*, *277*(5325), 515–522. doi:10.1126cience.277.5325.515

Dong, W., Wu, T., Sun, Y., & Luo, J. (2018). Digital mapping of soil available phosphorus supported by AI Technology for precision agriculture. *2018 7th International Conference on Agro-Geoinformatics (Agro-Geoinformatics)*, 1–5.

Dong, J., Xiao, X., Menarguez, M. A., Zhang, G., Qin, Y., Thau, D., Biradar, C., & Moore, B. III. (2016). Mapping paddy rice planting area in northeastern Asia with Landsat 8 images, phenology-based algorithm and Google Earth Engine. *Remote Sensing of Environment*, *185*, 142–154. doi:10.1016/j.rse.2016.02.016 PMID:28025586

Doran, J. W., & Parkin, T. B. (1994). Defining and assessing soil quality. *Defining soil quality for a sustainable environment, 35*, 1-21.

Drake, L., Bergström, P., & Svedsäter, H. (1999). Farmers' attitude and uptake. *Countryside Stewardship: Farmers, Policies and Markets*, 89-111.

Drake, J. A., Cavagnaro, T. R., Cunningham, S. C., Jackson, W. R., & Patti, A. F. (2016). Does biochar improve establishment of tree seedlings in saline sodic soils? *Land Degradation & Development*, *27*(1), 52–59. doi:10.1002/ldr.2374

Duffield, M. (2007). *Development, security and unending war: governing the world of peoples*. Polity Press.

Duhan, J. S., Kumar, R., Kumar, N., Kaur, P., Nehra, K., & Duhan, S. (2017). Nanotechnology: The new perspective in precision agriculture. *Biotechnology Reports (Amsterdam, Netherlands)*, *15*, 11–23. doi:10.1016/j.btre.2017.03.002 PMID:28603692

Dupuy, K., Scott, G., Håvard, M. N., Ida, R., Siri, A. S., Håvard, S., & Henrik, U. (2017). *Trends in Armed Conflict, 1946–2016*. Oslo: Peace Research Institute. Available at: https://www.prio.org/utility/DownloadFile.ashx?id=1373&type=publicationfile

Durbude, D. G., & Venkatesh, B. (2004). Site suitability analysis for soil and water conservation structures. Photonirvachak. *Photonirvachak (Dehra Dun)*, *32*(4), 399–405. doi:10.1007/BF03030865

Dyer, J. F., & Bailey, C. (2008). A place to call home: Cultural understandings of heir property among rural African Americans. *Rural Sociology*, *73*(3), 317–338. doi:10.1526/003601108785766598

Dyer, J., Bailey, C., & Tran, N. (2009). Ownership characteristics of heir property in a Black Belt county: A quantitative approach. *Southern Rural Sociology*, *24*(2), 192–217.

Dzhambov, A. M., & Dimitrova, D. D. (2015). Green spaces and environmental noise perception. *Urban Forestry & Urban Greening*, *14*(4), 1000–1008. doi:10.1016/j.ufug.2015.09.006

Economic Profile of NCR. (2015). *Final Report, National Capital Region Planning Board*. Available at http://ncrpb.nic.in/pdf_files/Final%20Report%20of%20study%20of%20economic%20profile_17122015.pdf

Efome, J. E., Rana, D., Matsuura, T., & Lan, C. Q. (2018). Experiment and modeling for flux and permeate concentration of heavy metal ion in adsorptive membrane filtration using a metal-organic framework incorporated nanofibrous membrane. *Chemical Engineering Journal, 352*, 737–744. doi:10.1016/j.cej.2018.07.077

Eklund, L., Degerald, M., Brandt, M., Prishchepov, A. V., & Pilesjö, P. (2017). How conflict affects land use: Agricultural activity in areas seized by the Islamic State. *Environmental Research Letters, 12*(5), 054004. doi:10.1088/1748-9326/aa673a

Elemike, E. E., Uzoh, I. M., Onwudiwe, D. C., & Babalola, O. O. (2019). The role of nanotechnology in the fortification of plant nutrients and improvement of crop production. *Applied Sciences, 9*(3), 499. doi:10.3390/app9030499

El-Lakany, M. (1983). A review of breeding drought resistant Casuarina for shelterbelt establishment in arid regions with special reference to Egypt. *Forest Ecology and Management, 6*(2), 129–137. doi:10.1016/0378-1127(83)90017-8

Ellison, J. (2010). *Vulnerability of Fiji's mangroves and associated coral reefs to climate change. A Review*. WWF South Pacific Office.

Ellman, A. O. (1976). *Land settlement in Sri Lanka, 1840-1975: A review of the major writings on the subject*. Academic Press.

El-Shater, T., Yigezu, Y. A., Mugera, A., Piggin, C., Haddad, A., Khalil, Y., Loss, S., & Aw-Hassan, A. (2016). Does zero tillage improve the livelihoods of smallholder cropping farmers? *Journal of Agricultural Economics, 67*(1), 154–172. doi:10.1111/1477-9552.12133

Emas, R. (2015). *The concept of sustainable development: definition and defining principles*. Florida International University.

Emergency Land Fund. (1981). *The impact of heir property on Black rural land tenure in the Southeastern region of the United States*. Report submitted to the U.S. Department of Agriculture.

Emmanuel, R., & Loconsole, A. (2015). Green infrastructure as an adaptation approach to tackling urban overheating in the Glasgow Clyde Valley Region, UK. *Landscape and Urban Planning, 138*, 71–86. doi:10.1016/j.landurbplan.2015.02.012

Emran, M., Doni, S., Macci, C., Masciandaro, G., Rashad, M., & Gispert, M. (2020). Susceptible soil organic matter, SOM, fractions to agricultural management practices in salt-affected soils. *Geoderma, 366*, 114257. doi:10.1016/j.geoderma.2020.114257

Endreny, T. A. (2018). Strategically growing the urban forest will improve our world. *Nature Communications, 9*(1), 1160. doi:10.103841467-018-03622-0 PMID:29563541

Enemark, S. (2005). *Understanding the land management paradigm* [Paper presention]. FIG Commission 7, Symposium on Innovative Technologies for Land Administration, Madison, Wisconsin, USA.

Ermida, S. L., Soares, P., Mantas, V., Göttsche, F. M., & Trigo, I. F. (2020). Google Earth Engine Open-Source Code for Land Surface Temperature Estimation from the Landsat Series. *Remote Sensing, 12*(9), 1471. doi:10.3390/rs12091471

Escobedo, F. J., Wagner, J. E., Nowak, D. J., De la Maza, C. L., Rodriguez, M., & Crane, D. E. (2008). Analyzing the cost effectiveness of Santiago, Chile's policy of using urban forests to improve air quality. *Journal of Environmental Management, 86*(1), 148–157. doi:10.1016/j.jenvman.2006.11.029 PMID:17275162

EU. (2016). *Persistant organic pollutants—environment—European Commission*. http://ec.europa.eu/environment/chemicals/international_conventions/index _en.htm

Evans, R., Collins, A. L., Foster, I. D., Rickson, R. J., Anthony, S. G., Brewer, T., & Zhang, Y. (2016). Extent, frequency and rate of water erosion of arable land in Britain-benefits and challenges for modelling. *Soil Use and Management, 32*, 149–161. doi:10.1111um.12210

Ezeah, C., Finney, K., & Nnajide, C. (2015). A critical review of the effectiveness of low emission zones (LEZ) as a strategy for the management of air quality in major European cities. *Journal of Multidisciplinary Engineering Science and Technology*, *2*(7), 1860–1868.

Fabbri, K., & Costanzo, V. (2020). Drone-assisted infrared thermography for calibration of outdoor microclimate simulation models. *Sustainable Cities and Society, 52*, 101855. doi:10.1016/j.scs.2019.101855

Falk, W. W. (2004). *Rooted in place: Family and belonging in a Southern Black community*. Rutgers University Press.

Fallmann, J., Emeis, S., & Suppan, P. (2013). Mitigation of urban heat stress–a modelling case study for the area of Stuttgart. *DIE ERDE–Journal of the Geographical Society of Berlin, 144*(3-4), 202–216.

Fan, J. L., Hu, J. W., Zhang, X., Kong, L. S., Li, F., & Mi, Z. (2020). Impacts of climate change on hydropower generation in China. *Mathematics and Computers in Simulation, 167*, 4–18. doi:10.1016/j.matcom.2018.01.002

Fan, X., Pedroli, B., Liu, G., Liu, Q., Liu, H., & Shu, L. (2012). Soil salinity development in the yellow river delta in relation to groundwater dynamics. *Land Degradation & Development, 23*(2), 175–189. doi:10.1002/ldr.1071

FAO. (2009). *Asia Pacific Forestry Sector Outlook Study II*. Working paper No APFSOS II/WP/2009/29. Sri Lanka Forestry outlook study, regional office for Asia and the Pacific. Bangkok 2009.

FAO. (2010). *Global Forest Resources Assessment (FRA)*. FAO. Available at: http://www.fao.org/forestry/fra/fra2010/en/

FAO. (2010). *Global Forest Resources Assessment 2010*. Available at: http:// foris.fao.org /static/data/fra2010/FRA2010_Report_1oct2010.pdf

FAO. (2013). *High level expert forum. – how to feed the world in 2050*. Economic and Social Development Department, Food and Agricultural Organization of the United Nations.

FAO. (2015). *The Food and agriculture organization of the united nations. climate change and food systems: global assessments and implications for food security and trade*. FAO. Available online: http://www.fao.org/3/a-i4332e.pdf

FAO. (2017). Land resource planning for sustainable land management. Current and emerging needs in land resource planning for food security, sustainable livelihoods, integrated landscape management and restoration. Rome.

FAO. (2017). *The cascade tank village system in the dry zone of Sri Lanka*. Retrieved from https:// www.fa o.org/fileadmin/templates/giahs_assets/GIAHS_test/02_GIAHS_around_the_world/01_Designated_sites/02_Asia_and_the_Pacific/07_Sri_Lanka/Mar_6th_rev_GIAHS_Proposal_Sri_Lanka_March_2017.pdf

Faridah-Hanum, I., Latiff, A., Hakeem, K. R., & Ozturk, M. (Eds.). (2014). *Mangrove ecosystems of Asia: status, challenges and management strategies*. Springer. doi:10.1007/978-1-4614-8582-7

Farley, K. A., Walsh, K. C., & Levine, A. S. (2017). Opportunities and obstacles for rangeland conservation in San Diego County, California, USA. *Ecology and Society, 22*(1), art38. doi:10.5751/ES-09077-220138

Faulkenberry, L. V., Coggeshall, J. M., Backman, K., & Backman, S. (2000). A culture of servitude: The impact of tourism and development on South Carolina's Coast. *Human Organization, 59*(1), 86–95. doi:10.17730/humo.59.1.353730461t724j02

Favretto, N., Stringer, L. C., Dougill, A. J., Dallimer, M., Perkins, J. S., Reed, M. S., Atlhopheng, J. R., & Mulale, K. (2016). Multi-criteria decision analysis to identify dryland ecosystem service trade-offs under different rangeland land uses. *Ecosystem Services, 17*, 142–151. doi:10.1016/j.ecoser.2015.12.005

Feike, T., Doluschitz, R., Chen, Q., Graeff-Hönninger, S., & Claupein, W. (2012). How to overcome the slow death of intercropping in the North China Plain. *Sustainability, 4*(10), 2550–2565. doi:10.3390u4102550

Felloni, F. &McGrenra, D. (2013). *Democratic Socialist Republic of Sri Lanka.* Academic Press.

Fernando, S., Senaratna, A., Pallewatta, N., Lokupitiya, E., Manawadu, L., Imbulana, U., … Ranwala, S. (2015). *Assessment of key policies and measures to address the drivers of deforestation and forest degradation in Sri Lanka. Final report of a consultancy awarded to the Colombo Science and Technology Cell.* Faculty of Science, University of Colombo, by United Nations Development Programme for the Sri Lanka UN-REDD Programme.

Ferrini, F., van den Bosch, C. C. K., & Fini, A. (Eds.). (2017). *Routledge handbook of urban forestry.* Taylor & Francis. doi:10.4324/9781315627106

Fiji Bureau of Statistics. (2020). Data available on FBS website: https://www.statsfiji.gov.fj/index.php

Fonseka, B., & Raheem, M. (2010). *Land in the eastern province: politics, policy and conflict.* Centre for Policy Alternatives.

Food and Agricultural Organization (FAO). (2015). *Global Forest Resources Assessments 2015.* Available from: http://www.fao.org/forest-resources-assessment/past-assessments/fra-2015/en/

Forest Survey of India. (2019). *India State of Forest Report.* ISFR.

Forouzani, M., & Karami, E. (2011). Agricultural water poverty index and sustainability. *Agronomy for Sustainable Development, 31*(2), 415–431. doi:10.1051/agro/2010026

Forstall, R. L. (1996). *Population of States and Counties of the United States: 1790 to 1990 from the Twenty-one Decennial Censuses. National Technical Information Services.* NTIS.

Fox, J. E., Gulledge, J., Engelhaupt, E., Burow, M. E., & McLachlan, J. A. (2007). Pesticides reduce symbiotic efficiency of nitrogen-fixing rhizobia and host plants. *Proceedings of the National Academy of Sciences of the United States of America, 104*(24), 10282–10287. doi:10.1073/pnas.0611710104 PMID:17548832

Franco, S., Gaetano, V., & Gianni, T. (2018). Urbanization and climate change impacts on surface water quality: Enhancing the resilience by reducing impervious surfaces. *Water Research, 144*, 491–502. doi:10.1016/j.watres.2018.07.058 PMID:30077910

Friess, D. A., Rogers, K., Lovelock, C. E., Krauss, K. W., Hamilton, S. E., Lee, S. Y., Lucas, R., Primavera, J., Rajkaran, A., & Shi, S. (2019). The State of the World's Mangrove Forests: Past, Present, and Future. *Annual Review of Environment and Resources, 44*(1), 89–115. doi:10.1146/annurev-environ-101718-033302

FSMP. (1995). Sri Lanka forestry sector master plan. Forestry Planning Unit, Forest Department, Ministry of Agriculture, Lands and Forestry, Colombo, Sri Lanka.

Fu, P., & Weng, Q. (2016). A time series analysis of urbanization induced land use and land cover change and its impact on land surface temperature with Landsat imagery. *Remote Sensing of Environment, 175*, 205–214. doi:10.1016/j.rse.2015.12.040

Gabriel, D., Sait, S. M., Hodgson, J. A., Schmutz, U., Kunin, W. E., & Benton, T. G. (2010). Scale matters: The impact of organic farming on biodiversity at different spatial scales. *Ecology Letters, 13*(7), 858–869. doi:10.1111/j.1461-0248.2010.01481.x PMID:20482572

Gage, E. A., & Cooper, D. J. (2017). Urban forest structure and land cover composition effects on land surface temperature in a semi-arid suburban area. *Urban Forestry & Urban Greening, 28*, 28–35. doi:10.1016/j.ufug.2017.10.003

Gaither, C. J. (2016). *"Have not our weary feet come to the place for which our fathers sighed?": Heirs' property in the southern United States*. https://www.treesearch.fs.fed.us/pubs/53186

Gaither, C. J., & Zarnoch, S. J. (2017). Unearthing 'dead capital': Heirs' property prediction in two US southern counties. *Land Use Policy*, *67*, 367–377. doi:10.1016/j.landusepol.2017.05.009

Gamage, D. (2000). *Little space for maneuvering: agrarian structure, land tenure regimes and agrarian development in Sri Lanka. Sri Lanka agriculture for the next decade: challenges and opportunities*. HARTI.

Ganewatta, G. & Edwards, G. W. (2000). *The Sri Lanka tea industry: economic issues and government policies*. Academic Press.

Gartaula, H., Niehof, A., & Visser, L. (2012). Shifting perceptions of food security and land in the context of labour out-migration in rural Nepal. *Food Security*, *4*(2), 181–194. doi:10.100712571-012-0190-3

Gauchan, D., & Shrestha, S. (2017). *Agricultural and rural mechanization in Nepal: status, issues and options for future*. Institute for Inclusive Finance and Development (InM).

Gebhardt, M. R., Daniel, T. C., Schweizer, E. E., & Allmaras, R. R. (1985). Conservation tillage. *Science*, *230*(4726), 625–630. doi:10.1126cience.230.4726.625 PMID:17797277

Gerland, P. (1996). *Socio-economic data and GIS: Datasets, databases, indicators and data integration issues*. UNEP/CGIAR Arendal III Workshop on the Use of GIS in Agricultural Research Management.

Gerland, P., Raftery, A. E., Sevčíková, H., Li, N., Gu, D., Spoorenberg, T., Alkema, L., Fosdick, B. K., Chunn, J., & Lalic, N. (2014). World population stabilization unlikely this century. *Science*, *346*(6206), 234–327. doi:10.1126cience.1257469 PMID:25301627

Ghosh, A., Bhattacharyya, R., Meena, M. C., Dwivedi, B. S., Singh, G., Agnihotri, R., & Sharma, C. (2018). Long-term fertilization effects on soil organic carbon sequestration in an Inceptisol. *Soil & Tillage Research*, *177*, 134–144. doi:10.1016/j.still.2017.12.006

Gibbs, H. K., & Salmon, J. M. (2015). Mapping the world's degraded lands. *Applied Geography (Sevenoaks, England)*, *57*, 12–21. doi:10.1016/j.apgeog.2014.11.024

Gilbert, J., Sharp, G., & Felin, M. S. (2002). The loss and persistence of Black-owned farms and farmland: A review of the research literature and its implications. *Southern Rural Sociology*, *18*(2), 1–30.

Gilbert, J., Wood, S. D., & Sharp, G. (2002). Who owns the land? Agricultural land ownership by race-ethnicity. *Rural America*, *17*(4), 55–62.

Gilman, E., Van Lavieren, H., Ellison, J., Jungblut, V., Wilson, L., & Areki, F. Yuknavage. (2006). Pacific Island Mangroves in a Changing Climate and Rising Sea. UNEP Regional Seas Reports and Studies No. 179. Nairobi, Kenya: United Nations Environment Programme, Regional Seas Programme.

Giri, S., & Qiu, Z. (2016). Understanding the relationship of land uses and water quality in Twenty First Century: A review. *Journal of Environmental Management*, *173*, 41–48. doi:10.1016/j.jenvman.2016.02.029 PMID:26967657

Glantz, M. H. (2019). The UN and desertification: Dealing with a global problem. In *Desertification* (pp. 1–15). CRC Press. doi:10.1201/9780429050893-1

Glick, B. R. (2014). Bacteria with ACC deaminase can promote plant growth and help to feed the world. *Microbiological Research*, *169*(1), 30–39. doi:10.1016/j.micres.2013.09.009 PMID:24095256

Globe Water. (2018). *Water pollution statistics 2018-2019.* Accessed 24 February 2020, https://www.globewater.org/facts/water-pollution-statistics/

Gobilik, J., & Limbawang, S. (2010). Notes on species composition and ornamental gingers in Tawau Hills Park, Sabah. *Journal of Tropical Biology & Conservation*, *7*(1), 31–48.

Goldblatt, R., Rivera Ballesteros, A., & Burney, J. (2017). High spatial resolution visual band imagery outperforms medium resolution spectral imagery for ecosystem assessment in the semi-arid brazilian sertão. *Remote Sensing*, *9*(12), 1336. doi:10.3390/rs9121336

Goldscheider, N. (2010). Delineation of spring protection zones. In Groundwater hydrology of springs (pp. 305-338). Butterworth-Heinemann. doi:10.1016/B978-1-85617-502-9.00008-6

Gómez, C., White, J. C., & Wulder, M. A. (2016). Optical remotely sensed time series data for land cover classification: A review. *ISPRS Journal of Photogrammetry and Remote Sensing*, *116*, 55–72. doi:10.1016/j.isprsjprs.2016.03.008

Gomiero, T. (2016). Soil degradation, land scarcity and food security: Reviewing a complex challenge. *Sustainability*, *8*(3), 281. doi:10.3390u8030281

Goodwine, M. (1997). *Gwad dun smile pun we: Beaufort Isles*. Kinship Publications.

Goonewardene, L. K. P., & Hatten, C. J. (1990). Rationalizing land use. *Economic Review*, *15*(10).

Gorelick, N., Hancher, M., Dixon, M., Ilyushchenko, S., Thau, D., & Moore, R. (2017). Google Earth Engine: Planetary-scale geospatial analysis for everyone. *Remote Sensing of Environment*, *202*, 18–27. doi:10.1016/j.rse.2017.06.031

Gorman, D. (2018). Historical Losses of Mangrove Systems in South America from Human-Induced and Natural Impacts. In C. Makowski, & C.W. Finkl (Eds.), Threats to Mangrove Forests: Hazards, Vulnerability, and Management (pp. 155-171). Cham: Springer. doi:10.1007/978-3-319-73016-5_8

GOSL. (2000). *Forest Cover Mapping 2000*. Forest Inventory Division. Forest Department.

Gould, G. (2017). The Black feminine on screen. *Sight and Sound*, *27*(6), 42–45.

Government of Fiji / IUCN. (1992). *Fiji State of the Environment Report 1992*. Author.

Government of Fiji. (2006).Department of Statistics. Census 2007. Author.

Gozalo, G. R., Morillas, J. M. B., González, D. M., & Moraga, P. A. (2018). Relationships among satisfaction, noise perception, and use of urban green spaces. *The Science of the Total Environment*, *624*, 438–450. doi:10.1016/j.scitotenv.2017.12.148 PMID:29268216

Grasty, R. L. (1976). Applications of Gamma Radiation in Remote Sensing. In E. Schanda (Ed.), *Remote Sensing for Environmental Sciences. Ecological Studies (Analysis and Synthesis)* (Vol. 18). Springer. doi:10.1007/978-3-642-66236-2_7

Gruebner, O., Rapp, M. A., Adli, M., Kluge, U., Galea, S., & Heinz, A. (2017). Cities and mental health. *Deutsches Ärzteblatt International*, *114*(8), 121. PMID:28302261

Guan, & Li. (2006). Broadening the thinking of protecting cultivated land -- the task and thinking of the investigation and evaluation of the comprehensive production capacity of agricultural land. *China Land, 0*(3), 17-18.

Guerrero, R. D., & Fernandez, P. R. (2018). Aquaculture and Water Quality Management in the Philippines. In *Water Policy in the Philippines* (pp. 143–162). Springer. doi:10.1007/978-3-319-70969-7_7

Guetté, A., Gaüzère, P., Devictor, V., Jiguet, F., & Godet, L. (2017). Measuring the synanthropy of species and communities to monitor the effects of urbanization on biodiversity. *Ecological Indicators*, *79*, 139–154. doi:10.1016/j.ecolind.2017.04.018

Guisan, A., Broennimann, O., Buri, A., Cianfrani, C., D'Amen, M., Di Cola, V., Fernandes, R., Gray, S., Mateo, R. G., Pinto, E., & Pradervand, J. N. (2019). Climate change impacts on mountain biodiversity. In *Biodiversity and Climate Change* (pp. 221–233). Yale University Press. doi:10.2307/j.ctv8jnzw1.29

Gulia, S., Nagendra, S. S., Khare, M., & Khanna, I. (2015). Urban air quality management-A review. *Atmospheric Pollution Research*, *6*(2), 286–304. doi:10.5094/APR.2015.033

Gunasena, H. P. M., & Pushpakumara, D. K. N. G. (2015). Chena cultivation in Sri Lanka: prospects for agroforestry interventions. In Shifting Cultivation and Environmental Change: Indigenous People, Agriculture and Forest Conservation. Routledge, Taylor & Francis.

Guthrie, P. (1996). *Catching sense: African American communities on a South Carolina Sea Island*. Bergin and Garvey.

Guttikunda, S. K., Carmichael, G. R., Calori, G., Eck, C., & Woo, J. H. (2003). The contribution of megacities to regional sulfur pollution in Asia. *Atmospheric Environment*, *37*(1), 11–22. doi:10.1016/S1352-2310(02)00821-X

Hall, A., Sulaiman, V. R., Clark, N., & Yoganand, B. (2003). From measuring impact to learning institutional lessons: An innovation systems perspective on improving the management of international agricultural research. *Agricultural Systems*, *78*(2), 213–241.

Han, L., Zhou, W., Li, W., & Li, L. (2014). Impact of urbanization level on urban air quality: A case of fine particles (PM2. 5) in Chinese cities. *Environmental Pollution*, *194*, 163–170. doi:10.1016/j.envpol.2014.07.022 PMID:25113968

Hansell, A., Cai, Y. S., & Gulliver, J. (2017). Cardiovascular Health Effects of Road Traffic Noise. In Environmental Impacts of Road Vehicles (pp. 107-132). doi:10.1039/9781788010221-00107

Hansen, M. C., Potapov, P. V., Moore, R., Hancher, M., Turubanova, S. A., Tyukavina, A., Thau, D., Stehman, S. V., Goetz, S. J., Loveland, T. R., Kommareddy, A., Egorov, A., Chini, L., Justice, C. O., & Townshend, J. R. G. (2013). High-resolution global maps of 21st-century forest cover change. *Science*, *342*(6160), 850–853. doi:10.1126cience.1244693 PMID:24233722

Han, X., Zhao, F., Tong, X., Deng, J., Yang, G., Chen, L., & Kang, D. (2017). Understanding soil carbon sequestration following the afforestation of former arable land by physical fractionation. *Catena*, *150*, 317–327. doi:10.1016/j.catena.2016.11.027

Harding, S. (2007). Man-made disaster and development: The case of Iraq. *International Social Work*, *50*(3), 295–306. doi:10.1177/0020872807076041

Hardy, R. D., Milligan, R. A., & Heynen, N. (2017). Racial coastal formation: The environmental injustice of colorblind adaptation planning for sea-level rise. *Geoforum*, *87*, 62–72. doi:10.1016/j.geoforum.2017.10.005

HARTI. (1998) A Study on Socio Economic Aspects of Soil Erosion for Ministry of Forestry and Environment. Hector Kobbakaduwa Agrarian Research and Training Institute, WijeramaMawatha, Colombo 7, Sri Lanka.

Hassan, M. M., & Southworth, J. (2018). Analyzing land cover change and urban growth trajectories of the mega-urban region of Dhaka using remotely sensed data and an ensemble classifier. *Sustainability*, *10*(1), 10.

He, C., Okada, N., Zhang, Q., Shi, P., & Zhang, J. (2006). Modelling urban expansion scenarios by coupling the cellular automata model and system dynamic model in Beijing. Academic Press.

Hegre, H. (2014). Democracy and armed conflict. *Journal of Peace Research, 51*(2), 159–172. doi:10.1177/0022343313512852

He, M., Kimball, J. S., Maneta, M. P., Maxwell, B. D., Moreno, A., Beguería, S., & Wu, X. (2018). Regional crop gross primary productivity and yield estimation using fused landsat-MODIS data. *Remote Sensing, 10*(3), 372. doi:10.3390/rs10030372

Herath, J. (2006). Distributional impacts of land policies in Sri Lanka. Sri Lanka n Agriculture Economics Association (SLEA) and Movement for National Land and Agricultural Reform (MONLAR), Sri Lanka.

Herath, J. (2006). *Distributional impacts of land policies in Sri Lanka. Sri Lankan Agriculture Economics Association (SLEA) and Movement for National Land and Agricultural Reform.* MONLAR.

Herndon, J. M. (2018). Air pollution, not greenhouse gases: The principal cause of global warming. *J Geog Environ Earth Sci Intn, 17*(2), 1–8.

Heymann, H., Jr. (1969). *Seminar on Development and Security in Thailand: Part 1. The Insurgency.* Rand Corp. Available at: www.dtic.mil/dtic/tr/fulltext/u2/500943.pdf

Higgins, S., Schellberg, J., & Bailey, J. S. (2019). Improving productivity and increasing the efficiency of soil nutrient management on grassland farms in the UK and Ireland using precision agriculture technology. *European Journal of Agronomy, 106*, 67–74. doi:10.1016/j.eja.2019.04.001

Hill Collins, P. (2000). *Black feminist thought: Knowledge, consciousness, and the politics of empowerment* (2nd ed.). Routledge.

Hill Collins, P. (2019). The difference that power makes: Intersectionality and participatory democracy. In *The Palgrave Handbook of Intersectionality in Public Policy* (pp. 167–192). Palgrave Macmillan. doi:10.1007/978-3-319-98473-5_7

Hill Collins, P., & Bilge, S. (2016). *Intersectionality.* Wiley.

Hilmi, M. A., & Andy, R. M. (2017). Contingent Valuation on Urban Trees in City of Kota Kinabalu, Sabah. *Transactions on Science and Technology, 4*(2), 166–173.

Hinson, W. R. (2018). Land gains, land losses: The odyssey of African Americans since Reconstruction. *American Journal of Economics and Sociology, 77*(3-4), 893–939. doi:10.1111/ajes.12233

Hitchner, S., Schelhas, J., & Gaither, C. J. (2017). "A privilege and a challenge": Valuation of heirs' property by African American landowners and implications for forest management in the Southeastern US. *Small-scale Forestry, 16*(3), 1–23. doi:10.100711842-017-9362-5

Holsinger, M. (2002). *History of Ceylon Tea.* Undergraduate thesis.

Hooke, R. L., Martín-Duque, J. F., & Pedraza, J. (2012). Land transformation by humans: A review. *GSA Today, 22*(12), 4–10. doi:10.1130/GSAT151A.1

Hotez, P. J. (2017). Global urbanization and the neglected tropical diseases. *PLoS Neglected Tropical Diseases, 11*(2), e0005308. doi:10.1371/journal.pntd.0005308 PMID:28231246

Housman, I., Tanpipat, V., Biswas, T., Clark, A., Stephen, P., Maus, P., & Megown, K. (2015). *Monitoring forest change in southeast Asia: case studies for USAID Lowering Emissions in Asia's Forests.* US Department of Agriculture, Forest Service, Remote Sensing Applications Center.

Hsiang, S., Kopp, R., Jina, A., Rising, J., Delgado, M., Mohan, S., & Larsen, K. (2017). Estimating economic damage from climate change in the United States. *Science, 356*(6345), 1362–1369. doi:10.1126cience.aal4369 PMID:28663496

Huang, Zhu, Jun, & Xin. (2013). Reflections on improving the land ticket system in Chongqing -- from the perspective of land ticket nature and function. *China Land Science*, (6), 48-52.

Hummel, J. W., Sudduth, K. A., & Hollinger, S. E. (2001). Soil moisture and organic matter prediction of surface and subsurface soils using an NIR soil sensor. *Computers and Electronics in Agriculture*, *32*(2), 149–165. doi:10.1016/S0168-1699(01)00163-6

Humphreys, M. (2005). Natural resources, conflict, and conflict resolution: Uncovering the mechanisms. *The Journal of Conflict Resolution*, *49*(4), 508–537. doi:10.1177/0022002705277545

Hurni, K., Zeleke, G., Kassie, M., Tegegne, B., Kassawmar, T., Teferi, E., ... Kebebew, Z. (2015). *Economics of Land Degradation (ELD) Ethiopia Case Study: Soil degradation and sustainable land management in the rainfed agricultural areas of Ethiopia: An assessment of the economic implications*. Academic Press.

Hurni, H. (2000). Assessing sustainable land management (SLM). *Agriculture, Ecosystems & Environment*, *81*(2), 83–92. doi:10.1016/S0167-8809(00)00182-1

Hussain, M., & Imitiyaz, I. (2018). Urbanization Concepts, Dimensions and Factors. *International Journal of Recent Scientific Research*, *9*(1), 23513–23523.

Ikejiaku, B.-V. (2009). The relationship between poverty, conflict and development. *Journal of Sustainable Development*, *2*(1), 15. doi:10.5539/jsd.v2n1p15

Indian Express. (2018). Five new cities to up along the KMP Expressway. *The New Indian Express*. Available at https://www.newindianexpress.com/nation/2018/jun/29/five-new-cities-to-be-developed-along-the-kundli-manesar-palwal-expressway-1835666.html

Intasen, M., Hauer, R. J., Werner, L. P., & Larsen, E. (2017). Urban forest assessment in Bangkok, Thailand. *Journal of Sustainable Forestry*, *36*(2), 148–163. doi:10.1080/10549811.2016.1265455

International Crisis Group. (2017). *Thailand: Malay-Muslim Insurgency and the Dangers of Intractability*. Available at: https://www.crisisgroup.org/global/8-watch-list-2017-second-update

International Labour Organization. (2018). *World Employment Social Outlook*. Retrieved from https://ec.europa.eu/knowledge4policy/organisation/ilo-international-labour-organisation_en

International Water Management Institute. (2000). *Towards Integrated Water and Land Resources Management*. International Water Management Institute.

Inyinbor Adejumoke, A., Adebesin Babatunde, O., Oluyori Abimbola, P., Adelani Akande Tabitha, A., Dada Adewumi, O., & Oreofe Toyin, A. (2018). Water pollution: effects, prevention, and climatic impact. *Water Challenges of an Urbanizing World, 33*.

ISFR. (2017). *Forest Survey of India (Published report)*. Author.

Islam, M. S., & Wong, A. T. (2017). Climate change and food in/security: A critical nexus. *Environments*, *4*(2), 38. doi:10.3390/environments4020038

Ite, A. E., Harry, T. A., Obadimu, C. O., & Ekwere, I. O. (2019). Comparison of Indoor Air Quality in Schools: Urban vs. Industrial'Oil & Gas' Zones in Akwa Ibom State–Nigeria. *Journal of Environment Pollution and Human Health*, *7*(1), 15–26. doi:10.12691/jephh-7-1-3

Ite, A. E., Ogunkunle, C. O., Obadimu, C. O., Asuaiko, E. R., & Ibok, U. J. (2017). Particulate matter and staff exposure in an air-conditioned office in Akwa Ibom State University–Nigeria. *Journal of Atmospheric Pollution*, *5*(1), 24–32. doi:10.12691/jap-5-1-4

V. Jaccarini, & E. Martens (Eds.). (1990). The Ecology of Mangrove and Related Ecosystems*: Proceedings of the International Symposium held at Mombasa*. Dordrecht: Springer.

Javed, A., & Khan, I. (2012). Land use/land cover change due to mining activities in Singrauli industrial belt, Madhya Pradesh using remote sensing and GIS. *Journal of Environmental Research and Development*, *6*(3A).

Jayasekara, M. J. P. T. M., Kadupitiya, H. K., & Vitharana, U. W. A. (2018). Mapping of soil erosion hazard zones of Sri Lanka. *Tropical Agricultural Research*, *29*(2), 135–146. doi:10.4038/tar.v29i2.8284

Jayasena, W. G. (1991). *Anuradhapura Dry Zone Agricultural Project (ADZAP)-A socio economic study of project beneficiaries*. Agrarian Research & Training Institute.

Jaypal, P. (2016). *Implementation of the 74th Constitution Amendment Act and Spatial Implications, Indian Urbanisation and Sustainable Development: Spatial Perspectives*. Available at https://www.tandfonline.com/doi/full/10.1080/19463131003704213

Jensen, J. R. (2000). *Remote sensing of the environment: An earth resource perspective*. Prentice Hall.

Jigău, G., Cernolev, E., & Acciu, A. (2016). Plant Health Risks Arising by the Soil Exhaustion. *Present Environment and Sustainable Development*, *10*(2), 185–194. doi:10.1515/pesd-2016-0036

Jitrbhiromsri, S. (2014). An inconvenient peace in the Deep South's violence: The paradox between knowing enemy hypothesis and intrinsic balancing forces. *Peace Studies Journal*, *1*(1), 155–198.

Johannes, A., Matter, A., Schulin, R., Weisskopf, P., Baveye, P. C., & Boivin, P. (2017). Optimal organic carbon values for soil structure quality of arable soils. Does clay content matter? *Geoderma*, *302*, 14–21. doi:10.1016/j.geoderma.2017.04.021

Johansson, E. L., & Isgren, E. (2017). Local perceptions of land-use change: Using participatory art to reveal direct and indirect socio environmental effects of land acquisitions in the Kilombero Valley, Tanzania. *Ecology and Society*, *22*(1), 3. doi:10.5751/ES-08986-220103

Jones-Jackson, P. (1987). *When roots die: Endangered traditions on the Sea Islands*. University of Georgia Press. muse.jhu.edu/book/11406

Jones-Jackson, P. (1987). *When roots die: Endangered traditions on the Sea Islands*. University of Georgia Press.

Jones, P. (2016a). Informal urbanism as a product of socio-cultural expression: Insights from the Island Pacific. In S. Attia, S. Shabka, Z. Shafik, & A. Ibrahim (Eds.), *Dynamics and Resilience of Informal Areas: International Perspectives* (pp. 165–181). Springer. doi:10.1007/978-3-319-29948-8_10

Jones, P. (2016b). *The Emergence of Pacific Urban Villages: Urbanization Trends in the Pacific Islands*. Asian Development Bank.

Jordan, P. K. (2016). "Ain't gonna let nobody turn me around": Spirituals as embodied acts of resistance. *The Black Scholar*, *46*(1), 37–45. doi:10.1080/00064246.2015.1119623

Justino, P. (2011). Poverty and Violent Conflict: A Micro-Level Perspective on the Causes and Duration of Warfare. *IDS Working Papers, 2011*(385), 1-25.

Kalantari, F., Mohd Tahir, O., Mahmoudi Lahijani, A., & Kalantari, S. (2017). A review of vertical farming technology: A guide for implementation of building integrated agriculture in cities. In *Advanced Engineering Forum* (Vol. 24, pp. 76-91). Trans Tech Publications Ltd. 10.4028/www.scientific.net/AEF.24.76

Kaloustian, N., & Diab, Y. (2015). Effects of urbanization on the urban heat island in Beirut. *Urban Climate*, *14*, 154–165. doi:10.1016/j.uclim.2015.06.004

Kang, T. J., Park, H. J., Chae, B. G., Jeong, N. S., & You, K. H. (2010). Analysis of landslide susceptibility in Pyeong-Chang area using fuzzy relation method. *The Journal of Engineering Geology*, *20*, 217–222.

Kanniah, K. D. (2017). Quantifying green cover change for sustainable urban planning: A case of Kuala Lumpur, Malaysia. *MIT-UTM Malaysia Sustainable Cities Program* (Working Paper Series 1). Universiti Teknologi Malaysia.

Kara, M. H., Lacroix, D., Rey-Valette, H., Mathé, S., & Blancheton, J. P. (2018). Dynamics of research in aquaculture in North Africa and support for sustainable development and innovation. *Reviews in Fisheries Science & Aquaculture*, *26*(3), 309–318. doi:10.1080/23308249.2017.1410521

Kashyap. (n.d.). *Deserts Characteristics: 21 General Characteristics of Deserts (With Maps),Yours Articles Library.* http://www.yourarticlelibrary.com/deserts- environment/deserts-characteristics-21- general-characteristics-of-deserts-with-maps/64226

Kathiresan, K., & Rajendran, N. (2005). Coastal mangrove forests mitigated tsunami. *Estuarine, Coastal and Shelf Science*, *65*(3), 601–606. doi:10.1016/j.ecss.2005.06.022

Kaul, H.A. & Sopan, I. (2012). Land use land cover classification and change detection using high-resolution temporal satellite data. *Journal of Environment*, *1*(4), 146-152.

Keesstra, S. D., Geissen, V., Mosse, K., Piiranen, S., Scudiero, E., Leistra, M., & van Schaik, L. (2012). Soil as a filter for groundwater quality. *Current Opinion in Environmental Sustainability*, *4*(5), 507–516. doi:10.1016/j.cosust.2012.10.007

Kelly, M., Yutthaphonphinit, P., Seubsman, S., & Sleigh, A. (2012). Development policy in Thailand: From top-down to grass roots. *Asian Social Science*, *8*(13), 29–39. doi:10.5539/ass.v8n13p29 PMID:23814630

Kenney, W. A., van Wassenaer, P. J., & Satel, A. L. (2011). Criteria and indicators for strategic urban forest planning and management. *Arboriculture & Urban Forestry*, *37*(3), 108–117.

Khan, M. N., & Suhail, M. (2019). Capacity Building: Satellites, Remote Sensing and GIS in the WANA Region. In M. Suhail & A. Rehman (Eds.), *West Asia and North Africa: Changing Paradigms* (Vol. 1). RawatPrakashan.

Khan, N. R., Awang, M., & Zulkifli, C. M. (2013). Small and medium enterprises and human resource practices in Pakistan. *International Journal of Asian Social Science*, *3*(2), 460–471.

Khokhar, T., & Tabary, M. E. (2016). *Five forest figures for the international day of forests.* The World Bank the Data Blog.

Klingberg, J., Broberg, M., Strandberg, B., Thorsson, P., & Pleijel, H. (2017). Influence of urban vegetation on air pollution and noise exposure–a case study in Gothenburg, Sweden. *The Science of the Total Environment*, *599*, 1728–1739. doi:10.1016/j.scitotenv.2017.05.051 PMID:28545203

Kong, F., Yin, H., James, P., Hutyra, L. R., & He, H. S. (2014). Effects of spatial pattern of greenspace on urban cooling in a large metropolitan area of eastern China. *Landscape and Urban Planning*, *128*, 35–47. doi:10.1016/j.landurbplan.2014.04.018

Konijnendijk, C. C., Annerstedt, M., Nielsen, A. B., & Maruthaveeran, S. (2013). *Benefits of Urban Parks – A systematic review.* World Urban Parks.

Koonnathamdee, P. (2013). *A Turning Point for the Service Sector in Thailand.* Asian Development Bank Economics Working Paper Series No. 353.

Kopittke, P. M., Menzies, N. W., Wang, P., McKenna, B. A., & Lombi, E. (2019). Soil and the intensification of agriculture for global food security. *Environment International, 132*, 105078. doi:10.1016/j.envint.2019.105078 PMID:31400601

Korf, B. (2002). Ethnicised entitlements in land tenure of protracted conflicts: The case of Sri Lanka. *9th Biennial IASCP Conference*, 17-21.

Koto, C. W. (2008). *Coping strategies of Fiji's urban poor: A case study of Namadai settlement, Suva, Fiji Islands* (Master's thesis). The University of the South Pacific, Suva.

Koubi, V., & Spilker, G. (2017). Natural Resources, Climate Change, and Conflict. In Oxford Research Encyclopedia of Politics. Academic Press.

Kozai, T., & Niu, G. (2020). Role of the plant factory with artificial lighting (PFAL) in urban areas. In Plant Factory (pp. 7-34). Academic Press.

Kozai, T., & Niu, G. H. (2016). Overview and concept of closed plant production system (CPPS). In *Plant Factory: An Indoor Vertical Farming System for Efficient Quality Food Production.* Academic Press.

Krzyżanowski, M., Kuna-Dibbert, B., & Schneider, J. (Eds.). (2005). *Health effects of transport-related air pollution.* WHO Regional Office Europe.

Kshetri, N. (2011). Cloud computing in the global south: Drivers, effects and policy measures. *Third World Quarterly, 32*(6), 997–1014. doi:10.1080/01436597.2011.586225

Kubiak, K., Wrzosek, M., Przemieniecki, S., Damszel, M., & Sierota, Z. (2018). Bacteria Inhabiting Wood of Roots and Stumps in Forest and Arable Soils. In Endophytes of Forest Trees (pp. 319-342): Springer. doi:10.1007/978-3-319-89833-9_14

Kumara, K. K. (2016). Agrarian change in the peasant economy of a paddy producing village in the Southern dry zone of Sri Lanka: The Gambaraya system in transition. *Sri Lanka Journal of Social Sciences, 0*(0), 77. doi:10.4038ljss.v0i0.7431

Kumar, D., & Kumar, D. (2018). *Sustainable Management of Coal Preparation.* Woodhead Publishing.

Kuroda, T. (1990). Urbanization and population distribution policies in Japan. *Regional Development Dialogue, 11*(1), 112. PMID:12316641

Lai, H. K., Kendall, M., Ferrier, H., Lindup, I., Alm, S., Hänninen, O., Jantunen, M., Mathys, P., Colvile, R., Ashmore, M. R., Cullinan, P., & Nieuwenhuijsen, M. J. (2004). Personal exposures and microenvironment concentrations of PM2. 5, VOC, NO2 and CO in Oxford, UK. *Atmospheric Environment, 38*(37), 6399–6410. doi:10.1016/j.atmosenv.2004.07.013

Lai, P., Zhang, M., Ge, Z., Hao, B., Song, Z., Huang, J., Ma, M., Yang, H., & Han, X. (2020). Responses of Seasonal Indicators to Extreme Droughts in Southwest China. *Remote Sensing, 12*(5), 818. doi:10.3390/rs12050818

Lakhiar, I. A., Gao, J., Syed, T. N., Chandio, F. A., & Buttar, N. A. (2018). Modern plant cultivation technologies in agriculture under controlled environment: A review on aeroponics. *Journal of Plant Interactions, 13*(1), 338–352. doi:10.1080/17429145.2018.1472308

Lakhiar, I. A., Gao, J., Xu, X., Syed, T. N., Chandio, F. A., Jing, Z., & Buttar, N. A. (2019). Effects of Various Aeroponic Atomizers (Droplet sizes) on the Growth, Total Polyphenol Content and Antioxidant Activity of Leafy Lettuce (Lactuca sativa L.). *Transactions of the ASABE.*

Lal, R. (2015). Restoring soil quality to mitigate soil degradation. *Sustainability, 7*(5), 5875–5895. doi:10.3390u7055875

Lal, R. (2016). Feeding 11 billion on 0.5 billion hectare of area under cereal crops. *Food and Energy Security*, *5*(4), 239–251. doi:10.1002/fes3.99

Lal, R. (2016). Global food security and nexus thinking. *Journal of Soil and Water Conservation*, *71*(4), 85A–90A. doi:10.2489/jswc.71.4.85A

Lal, R. (2018). Managing agricultural soils of Pakistan for food and climate. *Soil & Environment*, *37*(1), 1–10. doi:10.25252/SE/18/61527

Lambin, E. F., Gibbs, H. K., Ferreira, L., Grau, R., Mayaux, P., Meyfroidt, P., Morton, D. C., Rudel, T. K., Gasparri, I., & Munger, J. (2013). Estimating the world's potentially available cropland using a bottom-up approach. *Global Environmental Change*, *23*(5), 892–901. doi:10.1016/j.gloenvcha.2013.05.005

Land Watch Asia. (2012). *Land ownership and the journey to self-determination*. Sri Lanka Country Paper.

Landers, J. N., de Freitas, P. L., & Boddey, R. M. (2017). Potential for mitigation of deforestation and negative off-farm impacts with conservation agriculture: employing Zero Tillage farming in the Brazilian Cerrado. In *Savannas and Dry Forests* (pp. 253–276). Routledge. doi:10.4324/9781315243788-10

Lane, D., Chatrchyan, A., Tobin, D., Thorn, K., Allred, S., & Radhakrishna, R. (2018). Climate change and agriculture in New York and Pennsylvania: Risk perceptions, vulnerability and adaptation among farmers. *Renewable Agriculture and Food Systems*, *33*(3), 197–205. doi:10.1017/S1742170517000710

Lange, A., Siebert, R., & Barkmann, T. (2015). Sustainability in land management: An analysis of stakeholder perceptions in rural northern Germany. *Sustainability*, *7*(1), 683–704. doi:10.3390u7010683

Langeweg, F., Hilderink, H., & Maas, R. (2000). *Urbanisation, Industrialisation and Sustainable Development*. National Institute of Public Health and the Environment, Bilthoven (RIVM report 402001015). Available at https://www.pbl.nl/sites/default/files/cms/publicaties/402001015.pdf

Lans, T., Verstegen, J., & Mulder, M. (2011). Analysing, pursuing and networking: Towards a validated three-factor framework for entrepreneurial competence from a small firm perspective. *International Small Business Journal*, *29*(6), 695–713. doi:10.1177/0266242610369737

Latham, J., Cumani, R., Rosati, I., & Bloise, M. (2014). *Global land cover share (GLC-SHARE) database beta-release version 1.0-2014*. FAO.

Leach, E. R. (1959). Hydraulic society in Ceylon. *Past & Present*, *15*(1), 2–26. doi:10.1093/past/15.1.2

Leach, E. R. (1961). *PulEliya: a village in Ceylon*. Cambridge University Press.

Lee, J., Cardille, J. A., & Coe, M. T. (2018). BULC-U: Sharpening resolution and improving accuracy of land-use/land-cover classifications in Google Earth Engine. *Remote Sensing*, *10*(9), 1455. doi:10.3390/rs10091455

Lee, Y. F., Ligunjang, J., & Yong, S. C. (2004). *Urban forestry and its relevance to tourism development in Sabah* [Paper presentation]. The Asia Europe Meeting (ASEM) *Symposium on Urban Forestry*, Suzhou & Beijing, China.

Lei, Y., Yong, Z., Yun, W., & Xia, X. (2009). Equal conversion of farmland share and compensation balance based on farmland classification results. *Journal of Agricultural Engineering*, *25*(1), 244–248.

Lembrechts, J. J., Nijs, I., & Lenoir, J. (2019). Incorporating microclimate into species distribution models. *Ecography*, *42*(7), 1267–1279. doi:10.1111/ecog.03947

León, P., Espejo, R., Gómez-Paccard, C., Hontoria, C., Mariscal, I., Renella, G., & Benito, M. (2017). No tillage and sugar beet foam amendment enhanced microbial activity of degraded acidic soils in South West Spain. *Applied Soil Ecology*, *109*, 69–74. doi:10.1016/j.apsoil.2016.09.012

Lester, S. E., Gentry, R. R., Kappel, C. V., White, C., & Gaines, S. D. (2018). Opinion: Offshore aquaculture in the United States: Untapped potential in need of smart policy. *Proceedings of the National Academy of Sciences of the United States of America*, *115*(28), 7162–7165. doi:10.1073/pnas.1808737115 PMID:29991573

Lewis, I. D. (2017). Solutions to desertification. *Geodate*, *30*(2), 3.

Li & Xu. (2006). The application of agricultural land classification results in the balance of cultivated land requisition and compensation: a case study of Zhejiang Province. *China Land Science, 20*(2), 15-18.

Li, Z., Liu, J., Wang, Q., & Silva, S. S. D. (2018). Inland aquaculture: Trends and prospects. Aquaculture in China: Success stories and modern trends, 25-37.

Liang, Y. Q., Li, J. W., Lee, J., & Valimaki, S. K. (2008). Impact of urbanization on plant diversity: A case study in built-up areas of Beijing. *Forestry Studies in China*, *10*(3), 179–188. doi:10.100711632-008-0036-4

Lillesand, T.M., & Kiefer, R.W. (2002). *Remote Sensing and Image Interpretation.* John Wiley & Sons, Inc.

Lillesland, T. M., Keifer, R. W., & Chipman, J. W. (2004). *Remote Sensing and Image Interpretation* (5th ed.). John Willey and Sons.

Lim, S. S., Yang, H. I., Park, H. J., Park, S. I., Seo, B. S., Lee, K. S., ... Kwak, J. H. (2020). Land-use management for sustainable rice production and carbon sequestration in reclaimed coastal tideland soils of South Korea: A review. *Soil Science and Plant Nutrition*, *66*(1), 60–75. doi:10.1080/00380768.2019.1674121

Lim, W. S., Nisa, S., & Mojiol, A. R. (2019). Rapid observational assessment on urban forest trails established at UMS Peak of Universiti Malaysia Sabah. *Tropical Forest Journal*, *14*(1), 18–31.

Lim, W. S., & Mojiol, A. R. (2019). A Preliminary Assessment on Avian Community in the Urban Forest of Universiti Malaysia Sabah. *Transactions on Science and Technology*, *6*(3), 292–297.

Lindgren, D. (1985). *Land Use Planning and Remote Sensing*. doi:10.1007/978-94-017-2035-9

Lin, Z., Zhang, F., Xue, Y., & Yan, L. (2007). Prediction of the balance trend of cultivated land in China. *Ziyuan Kexue*, *29*(6), 114–119.

Lioy, P. J. (2017). *Toxic Air Pollution: A Comprehensive Study Non-Criteria Air Pollutants*. CRC Press.

Li, Q., Li, X., Tang, B., & Gu, M. (2018). Growth responses and root characteristics of lettuce grown in aeroponics, hydroponics, and substrate culture. *Horticulturae*, *4*(4), 35. doi:10.3390/horticulturae4040035

Liu, & Bo. (2002). The application of farmland grading and evaluation results in the balance of cultivated land requisition and compensation. *Regional Research and Development*, (3), 82-84.

Liu, C. C., Shieh, M. C., Ke, M. S., & Wang, K. H. (2018). Flood prevention and emergency response system powered by google earth engine. *Remote Sensing*, *10*(8), 1283. doi:10.3390/rs10081283

Liu, H., Ma, W., Qian, J., Cai, J., Ye, X., Li, J., & Wang, X. (2015). Effect of urbanization on the urban meteorology and air pollution in Hangzhou. *Journal of Meteorological Research*, *29*(6), 950–965. doi:10.100713351-015-5013-y

Liu, L., Li, W., Song, W., & Guo, M. (2018). Remediation techniques for heavy metal-contaminated soils: Principles and applicability. *The Science of the Total Environment*, *633*, 206–219. doi:10.1016/j.scitotenv.2018.03.161 PMID:29573687

Liu, S. H., Zeng, G. M., Niu, Q. Y., Liu, Y., Zhou, L., Jiang, L. H., Tan, X., Xu, P., Zhang, C., & Cheng, M. (2017). Bioremediation mechanisms of combined pollution of PAHs and heavy metals by bacteria and fungi: A mini review. *Bioresource Technology*, *224*, 25–33. doi:10.1016/j.biortech.2016.11.095 PMID:27916498

Liu, X., & Bae, J. (2018). Urbanization and industrialization impact of CO2 emissions in China. *Journal of Cleaner Production*, *172*, 178–186. doi:10.1016/j.jclepro.2017.10.156

Liu, Y., Langemeier, M. R., Small, I. M., Joseph, L., & Fry, W. E. (2017). Risk management strategies using precision agriculture technology to manage potato late blight. *Agronomy Journal*, *109*(2), 562–575. doi:10.2134/agronj2016.07.0418

Liu, Z., He, C., & Wu, J. (2016). The relationship between habitat loss and fragmentation during urbanization: An empirical evaluation from 16 world cities. *PLoS One*, *11*(4), e0154613. doi:10.1371/journal.pone.0154613 PMID:27124180

Livesley, S. J., McPherson, E. G., & Calfapietra, C. (2016). The urban forest and ecosystem services: Impacts on urban water, heat, and pollution cycles at the tree, street, and city scale. *Journal of Environmental Quality*, *45*(1), 119–124. doi:10.2134/jeq2015.11.0567 PMID:26828167

Li, X., Li, Z., Lin, C. J., Bi, X., Liu, J., Feng, X., Zhang, H., Chen, J., & Wu, T. (2018). Health risks of heavy metal exposure through vegetable consumption near a large-scale Pb/Zn smelter in central China. *Ecotoxicology and Environmental Safety*, *161*, 99–110. doi:10.1016/j.ecoenv.2018.05.080 PMID:29879579

Li, X., Zhou, W., & Ouyang, Z. (2013). Forty years of urban expansion in Beijing: What is the relative importance of physical, socioeconomic, and neighborhood factors? *Applied Geography (Sevenoaks, England)*, *38*, 1–10. doi:10.1016/j.apgeog.2012.11.004

Li, Y., Yang, L., Xu, Z., & Sun, Q. (2017). January. Separation and recovery of heavy metals from wastewater using synergistic solvent extraction. *IOP Conference Series. Materials Science and Engineering*, *167*(1), 012005.

Lobo, F. D. L., Souza-Filho, P. W. M., Novo, E. M. L. D. M., Carlos, F. M., & Barbosa, C. C. F. (2018). Mapping mining areas in the brazilian amazon using msi/sentinel-2 imagery (2017). *Remote Sensing*, *10*(8), 1178. doi:10.3390/rs10081178

Lomlim, C. (2015). The driving of three southern provinces' economy under the conflict situation. *Rusamila Journal, 35*(2), 25-40.

Lozano, I., Díaz, N.F., Muñoz, S. & Riquelme, C. (2018). Antibiotics in Chilean aquaculture: a review. *Antibiotic use in animals, 3*, 25-44.

Lozano-Fuentes, S., Elizondo-Quiroga, D., Farfan-Ale, J. A., Loroño-Pino, M. A., Garcia-Rejon, J., Gomez-Carro, S., ... Dominguez-Galera, M. (2008). Use of Google EarthTM to strengthen public health capacity and facilitate management of vector-borne diseases in resource-poor environments. *Bulletin of the World Health Organization*, *86*(9), 718–725. doi:10.2471/BLT.07.045880 PMID:18797648

Lucas, J. S., Southgate, P. C., & Tucker, C. S. (Eds.). (2019). *Aquaculture: farming aquatic animals and plants*. John Wiley & Sons.

Luo, K., Hu, X., He, Q., Wu, Z., Cheng, H., Hu, Z., & Mazumder, A. (2018). Impacts of rapid urbanization on the water quality and macroinvertebrate communities of streams: A case study in Liangjiang New Area, China. *The Science of the Total Environment*, *621*, 1601–1614. doi:10.1016/j.scitotenv.2017.10.068 PMID:29054671

Lu, X., Hong, J., Zhang, L., Cooper, O. R., Schultz, M. G., Xu, X., Wang, T., Gao, M., Zhao, Y., & Zhang, Y. (2018). Severe surface ozone pollution in China: A global perspective. *Environmental Science & Technology Letters*, *5*(8), 487–494. doi:10.1021/acs.estlett.8b00366

Mac Ginty, R., & Williams, A. (2009). *Conflict and development*. Routledge. doi:10.4324/9780203880005

Macher, R. (1999). *Making your small farm profitable.* Storey Publishing.

Madduma Bandara, C. M. (1985). Catchment Eco-systems and Village Tank Cascades in the Dry Zone of Sri Lanka. The Geo-Journal.

Madduma Bandara, C. M. (2009). Village Tank Cascade Systems of Sri Lanka: A Traditional Technology of Water and Drought Management. *Proceedings of the third annual workshop on disaster reduction hyperbase -Asian application.*

MaddumaBandara, C. M. (1990). Land use policy. *Economic Review, People's Bank, 15*(10).

Maharjan, U. (2019). Land Use Act 2019: An Overview. *The Rising Nepal.* Retrieved from http://therisingnepal.org.np/news/34254

Mahavansaya. (1986). *Wimalojothi Thero.* Buddhist Cultural Centre.

Mahboob, M. A., Atif, I., & Iqbal, J. (2015). Remote sensing and GIS applications for assessment of urban sprawl in Karachi, Pakistan. Science. *Technology and Development, 34*(3), 179–188. doi:10.3923td.2015.179.188

Mahdianpari, M., Salehi, B., Mohammadimanesh, F., Homayouni, S., & Gill, E. (2019). The first wetland inventory map of newfoundland at a spatial resolution of 10 m using sentinel-1 and sentinel-2 data on the google earth engine cloud computing platform. *Remote Sensing, 11*(1), 43. doi:10.3390/rs11010043

Mahmoud, S. H., & Gan, T. Y. (2018). Urbanization and climate change implications in flood risk management: Developing an efficient decision support system for flood susceptibility mapping. *The Science of the Total Environment, 636,* 152–167. doi:10.1016/j.scitotenv.2018.04.282 PMID:29705434

Majuakim, L., Lee, A. M. L., & Gisil, J. (2018). An Inventory of Flora in Urban Forests of Universiti Malaysia Sabah Campus, Sabah, Malaysia. *Journal of Tropical Biology & Conservation, 15,* 173–188.

Makowski, C., & Finkl, C. W. (Eds.). (2018). *Threats to Mangrove Forests: Hazards, Vulnerability, and Management.* Springer. doi:10.1007/978-3-319-73016-5

Malaysia, P. (2010). Food security: Concepts and definitions. *Journal of Community Health, 16*(2), 2.

Mandal, M., Kamp, P., & Singh, M. (2020). Effect of Long Term Manuring on Carbon Sequestration Potential and Dynamics of Soil Organic Carbon Labile Pool Under Tropical Rice-Rice Agro-ecosystem. *Communications in Soil Science and Plant Analysis,* 1–13.

Mangrove Management Committee. (2013). Mangrove Management Plan 2013. Author.

Manigault-Bryant, L. S. (2016). Where Black bodies lie: Historiography, race, and the place of Eros. *Theology and Sexuality, 22*(3), 165–174. doi:10.1080/13558358.2017.1329884

Mansoor, M., Jamil, M., Anwar, F., Awan, A. A., & Muhammad, S. (2018). Review A Review on Rangeland Management in Pakistan, Bottlenecks and Recommendations. *Biological Sciences- PJSIR, 61*(2), 115-120.

Mapa, R. B., Kumaragamage, D., Gunarathne, W. D. L., & Dassanayake, A. R. (2002). Land use in Sri Lanka: past, present and the future. *Proceedings of the 17th World Congress of Social Science (WCSS),* 14-21.

Marambe, B., Pushpakumara, G., & Silva, P. (2012).Biodiversity and Agro biodiversity in Sri Lanka: Village Tank Systems. In Biodiversity Observation Network in the Asia-Pacific Region. Springer.

Marambe, B., Silva, P., & Athauda, S. (2017). Agriculture and rural development under central government and provincial council setup in Sri Lanka. In *Decentralization and Development of Sri Lanka Within a Unitary State* (pp. 111–145). Springer. doi:10.1007/978-981-10-4259-1_6

Marawila, D. (2007). Revitalizing small-scale agriculture: Rental policies of alienated state lands of Sri Lanka. *Sri Lankan Journal of Agricultural Economics*, *9*(0), 23–42. doi:10.4038jae.v9i0.1831

Marichal, R., Praxedes, C., Decaëns, T., Grimaldi, M., Oszwald, J., Brown, G. G., & Oliveira, M. N. (2017). Earthworm functional traits, landscape degradation and ecosystem services in the Brazilian Amazon deforestation arc. *European Journal of Soil Biology*, *83*, 43–51. doi:10.1016/j.ejsobi.2017.09.003

Maricq, M. M. (2007). Chemical characterization of particulate emissions from diesel engines: A review. *Journal of Aerosol Science*, *38*(11), 1079–1118. doi:10.1016/j.jaerosci.2007.08.001

Markert, K. N., Schmidt, C. M., Griffin, R. E., Flores, A. I., Poortinga, A., Saah, D. S., ... Someth, P. (2018). Historical and operational monitoring of surface sediments in the lower mekong basin using landsat and google earth engine cloud computing. *Remote Sensing*, *10*(6), 909. doi:10.3390/rs10060909

Mark, M., & Kudakwashe, M. (2010). The rate of land-use/land-cover changes in Shurugwi district, Zimbabwe: Drivers for change. *Journal of Sustainable Development in Africa*, *12*(3), 107–121.

Masson, V., Lion, Y., Peter, A., Pigeon, G., Buyck, J., & Brun, E. (2013). "Grand Paris": Regional landscape change to adapt city to climate warming. *Climatic Change*, *117*(4), 769–782. doi:10.100710584-012-0579-1

Mateo-García, G., Gómez-Chova, L., Amorós-López, J., Muñoz-Marí, J., & Camps-Valls, G. (2018). Multitemporal cloud masking in the Google Earth Engine. *Remote Sensing*, *10*(7), 1079. doi:10.3390/rs10071079

Mateo-Sagasta, J., & Burke, J. (2011). Agriculture and water quality interactions: A global overview. *SOLAW Background Thematic Report-T*, *R08*, 46.

Mather, A. S. (1986). Land Use. Longman Group.

McConnell, W. J., & Viña, A. (2018). *Interactions between food security and land use in the context of global change*. Multidisciplinary Digital Publishing Institute. doi:10.3390/land7020053

McDonald, R. I., Forman, R. T., & Kareiva, P. (2010). Open space loss and land inequality in United States' cities, 1990–2000. *PLoS One*, *5*(3), e9509. doi:10.1371/journal.pone.0009509 PMID:20209082

McIntyre, K.M., Setzkorn, C., Hepworth, P.J., Morand, S., Morse, A.P., & Baylis, M. (2017). *Systematic assessment of the climate sensitivity of important human and domestic animals pathogens in European Scientific Reports*. Academic Press.

McIver, L. (2003). Blacks driven and cheated out of their land. *The Black Collegian*, *33*, 100–101.

McPherson, E. G., Nowak, D., Heisler, G., Grimmond, S., Souch, C., Grant, R., & Rowntree, R. (1997). Quantifying urban forest structure, function, and value: The Chicago Urban Forest Climate Project. *Urban Ecosystems*, *1*(1), 49–61. doi:10.1023/A:1014350822458

Meadows, D. H., Meadows, D. L., Randers, J., & Behrens, W. W. III. (1972). *The Limits to Growth*. Universe Books. Available at http://www.donellameadows.org/wp-content/userfiles/Limits-to-Growth-digital-scan-version.pdf

Meehan, J. (2013). Reinventing real estate: The community land trust as a social invention in affordable housing. *Journal of Applied Social Science*, *8*(2), 113–133. doi:10.1177/1936724413497480

Meiyappan, P., Roy, P. S., Soliman, A., Li, T., Mondal, P., Wang, S., & Jain, A. K. (2018). India Village-Level Geospatial Socio-Economic Data Set: 1991, 2001. Palisades, NY: NASA Socioeconomic Data and Applications Center (SEDAC). doi:10.7927/H4CN71ZJ

Méndez-Vázquez, L. J., Lira-Noriega, A., Lasa-Covarrubias, R., & Cerdeira-Estrada, S. (2019). Delineation of site-specific management zones for pest control purposes: Exploring precision agriculture and species distribution modeling approaches. *Computers and Electronics in Agriculture*, *167*, 105101. doi:10.1016/j.compag.2019.105101

Mersal, A. (2016). Sustainable urban futures: Environmental planning for sustainable urban development. *Procedia Environmental Sciences*, *34*, 49–61. doi:10.1016/j.proenv.2016.04.005

Metternicht, G. (2018). *Land use and spatial planning: Enabling sustainable management of land resources*. Springer. doi:10.1007/978-3-319-71861-3

Metz, B., Davidson, O.R., Bosch, P.R., Dave, R., & Meyer, L.A. (2007). *Contribution of working group III to the fourth assessment report of the intergovernmental panel on climate change, 2007*. IPCC Fourth Assessment Report (AR4).

Millar, G. (2015). "We have no voice for that": Land rights, power, and gender in rural Sierra Leone. *Journal of Human Rights*, *14*(4), 445–462. doi:10.1080/14754835.2015.1032219

Miller, N., Griffin, T., Bergtold, J., Ciampitti, I., & Sharda, A. (2017). Farmers' adoption path of precision agriculture technology. *Advances in Animal Biosciences*, *8*(2), 708–712. doi:10.1017/S2040470017000528

Ministry of Agriculture. (2015). *Circular of the Ministry of Agriculture on printing and distributing the Action Plan for Zero Growth in the Application of Fertilizer by 2020 and the Action Plan for Zero Growth in the Application of Pesticide by 2020*. http://jiuban.moa.gov.cn/zwllm/ tzgg/tz/201503/t20150318_4444765.htm

Ministry of Finance (MOF). (2018). *Economic Survey 2017/18*. Ministry of Finance.

Miranowski, J. A. (1984). Impacts of productivity loss on crop production and management in a dynamic economic model. *American Journal of Agricultural Economics*, *66*(1), 61–71. doi:10.2307/1240616

Mitchell, T. W. (2019). Historic Partition Law Reform: A game changer for heirs' property owners. In C. J. Gaither, A. Carpenter, T L. McCurty, & S. Toering (Eds.), *Heirs' property and land fractionation: Fostering stable ownership to prevent land loss and abandonment*. US Department of Agriculture, e-General Technical Report. https://www.srs.fs.usda.gov/pubs/gtr/gtr_srs244.pdf

Mitchell, T. W. (2005). Destabilizing the normalization of rural Black land loss: A critical role for legal empiricism. *Wisconsin Law Review*, 557–615.

MOF. (2020). *Budget for fiscal year 2020/2021*. Ministry of Finance.

MoFA. (2017). *Local Governing Act 2017*. Ministry of Federal Affairs and General Administration.

MoFE. (2018). *Forest Policy 2018*. Ministry of Forests and Environment.

MoFE. (2019a). *Climate Change policy 2019*. Ministry of Forests and Environment.

MoFE. (2019b). *National Forest Policy 2019*. Ministry of Forests and Environment.

MoHA. (2018). *National Policy for Disaster Risk Reduction 2018*. Ministry of Home Affairs.

Mohamed, E., Belal, A.-A., Ali, R. R., Saleh, A., & Hendawy, E. A. (2019). Land Degradation. In H. El-Ramady, T. Alshaal, N. Bakr, T. Elbana, E. Mohamed, & A.-A. Belal (Eds.), *The Soils of Egypt* (pp. 159–174). Springer International Publishing. doi:10.1007/978-3-319-95516-2_9

Moinet, G. Y., Hunt, J. E., Kirschbaum, M. U., Morcom, C. P., Midwood, A. J., & Millard, P. (2018). The temperature sensitivity of soil organic matter decomposition is constrained by microbial access to substrates. *Soil Biology & Biochemistry*, *116*, 333–339. doi:10.1016/j.soilbio.2017.10.031

Mojiol, A. R., & Bürger-Arndt, R. (2012). Urban Green Areas Management in Kota Kinabalu, Sabah-Malaysia: Concept and Sustainability. Lambert Academic Publishing.

Mojiol, A. R. (2001). *Pokok-Pokok Hiasan Bandar*. Penerbit Universiti Malaysia Sabah.

Mojiol, A. R. (2018a). Public awareness on the importance of urban forest parks in Kota Kinabalu City, Sabah. *Borneo Science*, *39*(1), 39–47.

Mojiol, A. R. (2018b). Tree Health Assessment for Roadside Tree in Kota Kinabalu City Centre, Sabah. *Borneo Science*, *39*(2), 104–113.

Mojiol, A. R., Hassan, A., Maluda, J., & Immit, S. (2008). Rapid assessment on the abundance of bird species utilizing the Kota Kinabalu Wetland Centre mangroves. *Journal of Tropical Biology & Conservation*, *4*(1), 99–107.

Mojiol, A. R., Lo, M. W., Lintangah, W., & Amat, R. (2016). *A Guide to the Plants of Kota Kinabalu Wetlands*. Sabah Wetland Conservation Society.

Mojiol, A. R., Zamri, Z., Hilmi, M. A., & Gitom, M. (2017). Visitors' Willingness To Pay (WTP) at Kionsom Recreation Centre, Inanam, Kota Kinabalu, Sabah. *Transactions on Science and Technology*, *4*(42), 174–182.

Molle, F., Jayakody, P., & de Silva, S. (2003). *Anicut systems in Sri Lanka, The case of upper Walawe basin*. IWMI.

MoLMCPA. (1964). *Land Act 1964*. Ministry of Land Management Cooperatives and Poverty Alleviation.

MoLMCPA. (2015). *Land use policy 2015*. Ministry of Land Management Cooperatives and Poverty Alleviation.

MoLMCPA. (2019). *Land Use Act 2019*. Ministry of Land Management Cooperatives and Poverty Alleviation.

MoLRM. (2013). *National Land Use Policy 2013*. Kathmandu Ministry of Land Reform and Management.

Monz, C. A., Goonan, K. A., Carr, C., Wimpey, J., Marion, J. L., & Manning, R. E. (2010). Assessment and Monitoring of Recreation Impacts and Resource Conditions on Mountain Summits: Examples from the Northern Forest, USA. *Mountain Research and Development*, *30*(4), 332–343. doi:10.1659/MRD-JOURNAL-D-09-00078.1

Monzon, J. P., Calviño, P. A., Sadras, V. O., Zubiaurre, J. B., & Andrade, F. H. (2018). Precision agriculture based on crop physiological principles improves whole-farm yield and profit: A case study. *European Journal of Agronomy*, *99*, 62–71. doi:10.1016/j.eja.2018.06.011

Moore, L. (2017). Gullah Geechee families: Land and culture. *Contemporary Rural Social Work*, *9*(1), 1–14.

Moore, R., & Parsons, E. (2011). *Beyond SDI, bridging the power of cloud based computing resources to manage global environment issues*. In *INSPIRE Conference*, Edinburgh, UK.

Moreira Barradas, J. M., Abdelfattah, A., Matula, S., & Dolezal, F. (2015). Effect of fertigation on soil salinization and aggregate stability. *Journal of Irrigation and Drainage Engineering*, *141*(4), 05014010. doi:10.1061/(ASCE)IR.1943-4774.0000806

Morgan, D. L. (1998). Practical strategies for combining qualitative and quantitative methods: Applications to health research. *Qualitative Health Research*, *8*(3), 362–376. doi:10.1177/104973239800800307 PMID:10558337

Morris Johnson, N. M. (2019). Janie's Gullah/Geechee seekin journey in "Their eyes were watching God,". *South Atlantic Review*, *84*(1), 72–90.

Moses, S. K. (2018). Enslaved African conjure and ritual deposits on the Hume Plantation, South Carolina. *North American Archaeologist*, *39*(2), 131–164. doi:10.1177/0197693118773252

MoUD. (2007). *National Urban Policy 2007*. Ministry of Urban Development.

Mounier, S. J. L., Marins, R. V., & de Lacerda, L. D. (2018). Determining the Influence of Urbanization on Mangrove Zones of Northeastern Brazil: Characterization of Ceará State Coastal Zone Organic Matter Inputs. In C. Makowski & C. W. Finkl (Eds.), *Threats to Mangrove Forests: Hazards, Vulnerability, and Management* (pp. 199–222). Springer. doi:10.1007/978-3-319-73016-5_10

Moussiopoulos, N., Kalognomou, E. A., Douros, I., Samaras, Z., Gionnouli, M., & Mellios, G. (2005). Air pollution level at hotspot areas of selected European cities. In *Proceeding of 10th Conference on Harmonization within Atmospheric Dispersion Modelling for Regulatory Purposes* (pp. 283-287). Academic Press.

Mueller Loose, S., & Remaud, H. (2013). Impact of corporate social responsibility claims on consumer food choice: A cross-cultural comparison. *British Food Journal*, *115*(1), 142–166. doi:10.1108/00070701311289920

Muerdter, C. P., Wong, C. K., & LeFevre, G. H. (2018). Emerging investigator series: The role of vegetation in bioretention for stormwater treatment in the built environment: Pollutant removal, hydrologic function, and ancillary benefits. *Environmental Science. Water Research & Technology*, *4*(5), 592–612. doi:10.1039/C7EW00511C

Mundial, B. (2008). *Land reforms in Sri Lanka: a poverty and social impact analysis*. PSIA.

Mungai, D. N., Ong, C. K., Kiteme, B., Elkaduwa, W., & Sakthivadivel, R. (2004). Lessons from two long-term hydrological studies in Kenya and Sri Lanka. *Agriculture, Ecosystems & Environment*, *104*(1), 135–143. doi:10.1016/j.agee.2004.01.011

Muñoz Rojas, M., Jordán López, A., Martínez Zavala, L. M., Rosa, D. D. L., Elmabod, A., Mohamed, S. K., & Anaya Romero, M. (2012). Organic carbon stocks in Mediterranean soil types under different land uses (Southern Spain). *Solid Earth*, *3*(3), 375–386. doi:10.5194e-3-375-2012

Muñoz-Rojas, M., Román, J. R., Roncero-Ramos, B., Erickson, T. E., Merritt, D. J., Aguila-Carricondo, P., & Cantón, Y. (2018). Cyanobacteria inoculation enhances carbon sequestration in soil substrates used in dryland restoration. *The Science of the Total Environment*, *636*, 1149–1154. doi:10.1016/j.scitotenv.2018.04.265 PMID:29913577

Murty, D., Kirschbaum, M. U. F., McMurtrie, R. E., & McGilvray, H. (2002). Does conversion of forest to agricultural land change soil carbon and nitrogen? A review of the literature. *Global Change Biology*, *8*(2), 105–123. doi:10.1046/j.1354-1013.2001.00459.x

Mytton-Mills, H. (2018). Reimagining Resources to Build Smart Futures: An Agritech Case Study of Aeroponics. In *Smart Futures, Challenges of Urbanization, and Social Sustainability* (pp. 169–191). Springer. doi:10.1007/978-3-319-74549-7_10

Naiman, R. J., Décamps, H., McClain, M. E., & Likens, G. E. (2005). Biotic Functions of Riparia. In N. Maragioglio (Ed.), Riparia: Ecology, Conservation and Management of Streamside Communities. Elsevier. doi:10.1016/B978-012663315-3/50006-X

Naiman, R. J., Decamps, H., & McClain, M. E. (2010). *Riparia: ecology, conservation, and management of streamside communities*. Elsevier.

Nair, G. V. G., Mojiol, A. R., Kamlun, K. U., & Lintangah, W. (2018). The Contribution of forest ecosystem services toward the local community living vicinity to the forest protected area : The case of Kawang Forest Reserve, Sabah, Malaysia. *Transactions on Science and Technology*, *5*(1), 25–30.

Nanayakkara, V. K. (2006). Agrarian reform and rural development: issues, concerns and future challenges: *Twenty-second meeting of CIRDAP technical committee (TC-22).*

Nasstrom, R., & Mattsson, E. (2011). *Land-use change and forestry at the national and sub-national level; country report Sri Lanka*. Focali.

Nastran, M., Kobal, M., & Eler, K. (2019). Urban heat islands in relation to green land use in European cities. *Urban Forestry & Urban Greening*, *37*, 33–41. doi:10.1016/j.ufug.2018.01.008

National Atlas. (1988). *Survey Department of Sri Lanka*.

National Geographic Society. (2019). *Noise Pollution*. Accessed 25 February 2020, https://www.nationalgeographic.org/encyclopedia/noise-pollution/

National Institute of Environmental Health Sciences. (2019). *USA.gov*. Accessed 23 February 2020, https://www.niehs.nih.gov/health/topics/agents/air-pollution/

National Land Use Policy of Sri Lanka. (2007). *Land use Policy Planning Department*. Retrieved from http://www.luppd.gov.lk/web/images/content_image/downloads/pdf/national_land_use_policy.pdf

National Landscape Department. (2008). *National Landscape Guideline* (2nd ed.). National Landscape Department.

National Research Council. (1997). *Precision Agriculture in the 21st Century: Geospatial and Information Technologies in Crop Management*. Washington, DC: The National Academies Press; doi:10.17226/5491

Nepal, P., Khanal, N. R., Zhang, Y., Paudel, B., & Liu, L. (2020). Land use policies in Nepal: An overview. *Land Degradation & Development*, 1–10.

NESDB. (2002). *The Ninth National Economic and Social Development Plan*. Bangkok: National Economic and Social Development Board. Available at: http://www.nesdb.go.th/ewt_dl_link.php?nid=3784

NESDB. (2003). *Sustainable development in the Thai context*. Bangkok: National Economic and Social Development Board. Available at: www.nesdb.go.th/ewt_w3c/ewt_news.php?nid=3157

NESDB. (2007). *The Ten National Economic and Social Development Plan*. Bangkok: National Economic and Social Development Board. Available at: http://www.nesdb.go.th/ewt_news.php?nid=5747&filename=develop_issue

NESDB. (2009). *Five Special Provinces Development Plan B.E.2552-2555*. Bangkok: National Economic and Social Development Board. Available at: http://eris.nesdb.go.th/pdf/351000-001.pdf

NESDB. (2011). *The Eleventh National Economic and Social Development Plan*. Bangkok: National Economic and Social Development Board. Available at: http://www.nesdb.go.th/ewt_news.php?nid=5748&filename=develop_issue

NESDB. (2017). *The Twelfth National Economic and Social Development Plan*. Bangkok: National Economic and Social Development Board. Available at: http://www.nesdb.go.th/ewt_news.php?nid=6420&filename=develop_issue

Neuman, W. L. (2003). *The meanings of methodology: Social research methods*. Allyn.

Nice, K. A., Coutts, A. M., & Tapper, N. J. (2018). Development of the VTUF-3D v1. 0 urban micro-climate model to support assessment of urban vegetation influences on human thermal comfort. *Urban Climate*, *24*, 1052-1076.

Nightingale, A. J. (2003). A feminist in the forest: Situated knowledges and mixing methods in natural resource management. *ACME: An International E-Journal for Critical Geographies*, *2*(1), 77–90.

Ningrum, W. (2018). February. Urban heat island towards urban climate. In *IOP Conference Series: Earth and Environmental Science* (*Vol. 118*, No. 1, 012048). IOP Publishing.

Niroula, G. S., & Thapa, G. B. (2005). Impacts and causes of land fragmentation, and lessons learned from land consolidation in South Asia. *Land Use Policy*, *22*(4), 358–372. doi:10.1016/j.landusepol.2004.10.001

Nkonya, E., Gerber, N., Baumgartner, P., von Braun, J., De Pinto, A., Graw, V., & Walter, T. (2011). *The economics of desertification, land degradation, and drought. Toward an Integrated Global Assessment*. IFPRI Discussion Paper, 1086.

Novara, A., Gristina, L., Sala, G., Galati, A., Crescimanno, M., Cerdà, A., Badalamenti, E., & La Mantia, T. (2017). Agricultural land abandonment in Mediterranean environment provides ecosystem services via soil carbon sequestration. *The Science of the Total Environment*, *576*, 420–429. doi:10.1016/j.scitotenv.2016.10.123 PMID:27792957

Novara, A., Pisciotta, A., Minacapilli, M., Maltese, A., Capodici, F., Cerdà, A., & Gristina, L. (2018). The impact of soil erosion on soil fertility and vine vigor. A multidisciplinary approach based on field, laboratory and remote sensing approaches. *The Science of the Total Environment*, *622-623*, 474–480. doi:10.1016/j.scitotenv.2017.11.272 PMID:29223076

Nowak, D. J., Hirabayashi, S., Bodine, A., & Greenfield, E. (2014). Tree and forest effects on air quality and human health in the United States. *Environmental Pollution*, *193*, 119–129. doi:10.1016/j.envpol.2014.05.028 PMID:25016465

Nowak-Sliwinska, P., Alitalo, K., Allen, E., Anisimov, A., Aplin, A. C., Auerbach, R., Augustin, H. G., Bates, D. O., van Beijnum, J. R., Bender, R. H. F., Bergers, G., Bikfalvi, A., Bischoff, J., Böck, B. C., Brooks, P. C., Bussolino, F., Cakir, B., Carmeliet, P., Castranova, D., ... Griffioen, A. W. (2018). Consensus guidelines for the use and interpretation of angiogenesis assays. *Angiogenesis*, *21*(3), 425–532. doi:10.100710456-018-9613-x PMID:29766399

NRSA. (1991). *Manual of Nationwide Land use Land Cover Mapping using digital techniques*. NRSA.

Nukala, & Mutz, D. (2015). *Strategic approach for sustainable land use in an emerging country – case of India* [Paper presention]. Linking land tenure and use for shared prosperity, Washington, DC.

Nukala, R. B., & Mutz, D. (2015). Strategic approach for sustainable land use in an emerging country – case of india [Paper presention]. Linking land tenure and use for shared prosperity, Washington, DC.

Numbere, A. O. (2018). The impact of oil and gas exploration: invasive nypa palm species and urbanization on mangroves in the Niger River Delta, Nigeria. In C. Makowski & C. W. Finkl (Eds.), *Threats to Mangrove Forests: Hazards, Vulnerability, and Management* (pp. 247–266). Springer. doi:10.1007/978-3-319-73016-5_12

Obeyesekere, G. (2008). *Land tenure in village Ceylon: a sociological and historical study*. Cambridge University Press.

Obeysekara, G. (1967). *Land Tenure in Village Ceylon*. Cambridge University Press.

Ochiai, A. (2001). The Port Royal Experiment revisited: Northern visions of reconstruction and the land question. *The New England Quarterly*, *74*(1), 94–117. doi:10.2307/3185461

Oduwaye, A. O. (2001). R*esidential Land Use and Land Values in Metropolitan Lagos* (Unpublished PhD Thesis). Urban and Regional Planning Department, Obafemi Awolowo University, Ile-Ife, Nigeria.

OECD. (2013). Southeast Asian [*With Perspectives on China and India*. Available at: http://www.oecd.org/dev/asia-pacific/Thailand.pdf]. *Economic Outlook*, *2013*, •••.

Ólafsdóttir, R., & Runnström, M. C. (2013). Assessing hiking trails condition in two popular tourist destinations in the Icelandic highlands. *Journal of Outdoor Recreation and Tourism*, *3–4*, 57–67. doi:10.1016/j.jort.2013.09.004

Oldeman, L. R., Hakkeling, R., & Sombroek, W. G. (2017). *World map of the status of human-induced soil degradation: an explanatory note*. International Soil Reference and Information Centre.

Olejniczak, M. J., Spiering, D. J., Potts, D. L., & Warren, R. J. (2018). Urban forests form isolated archipelagos. *Journal of Urban Economics*, *4*(1), 1–8.

Ooi, G. L. (2009, December). Challenges of sustainability for Asian urbanization. *Current Opinion in Environmental Sustainability*, *1*(2), 187–191. Advance online publication. doi:10.1016/j.cosust.2009.09.001

Oraby, H., Lachance, A., & Desjardins, Y. (2015). A low nutrient solution temperature and the application of stress treatments increase potato mini-tubers production in an aeroponic system. *American Journal of Potato Research*, *92*(3), 387–397. doi:10.100712230-015-9444-x

ORDPB. (1996). *Philosophy of Sufficiency Economy*. Office of the Royal Development Projects Board. Available at: http://www.rdpb.go.th/en/Sufficiency

ORDPB. (2016). *Philosophy of Sufficiency Economy*. Office of the Royal Development Projects Board. Available at: http://www.rdpb.go.th/en/Sufficiency

Orgill, S. E., Condon, J. R., Conyers, M. K., Morris, S. G., Alcock, D. J., Murphy, B. W., & Greene, R. S. B. (2018). Removing grazing pressure from a native pasture decreases soil organic carbon in southern New South Wales, Australia. *Land Degradation & Development*, *29*(2), 274–283. doi:10.1002/ldr.2560

Ortiz-Partida, J. P., Sandoval-Solis, S., Arellano-Gonzalez, J., Medellín-Azuara, J., & Taylor, J. E. (2020). Managing water differently: Integrated Water Resources Management as a framework for adaptation to climate change in Mexico. In *Integrated Water Resource Management* (pp. 59–72). Springer. doi:10.1007/978-3-030-16565-9_6

Ortiz, R. (2019). *Role of Plant Breeding to Sustain Food Security under Climate Change*. Food Security and Climate Change.

Osmond & Line. (2017). *Best Management Practices for Agricultural Nutrients*. Academic Press.

Ostrom, E., & Schlager, E. (1996). The Formation of Property Rights. In Rights to Nature: Ecological, Economic, Cultural, and Political Principles of Institutions for the Environment. Washington, DC: Island Press.

Ostrom, E. (1990). *Governing the Commons: The Evolution of Institutions for Collective Action*. Cambridge University Press. doi:10.1017/CBO9780511807763

Ow, L. F., & Ghosh, S. (2017). Urban cities and road traffic noise: Reduction through vegetation. *Applied Acoustics*, *120*, 15–20. doi:10.1016/j.apacoust.2017.01.007

Pan, Jing, Ting, Ma, Yi, & Li. (2015). Study on the sequence of agricultural land consolidation under planning guidance and cultivated land quality constraints. *China Land Science*, (8), 81-88.

Panabokke, C.R. (2009). *Small village tank system of Sri Lanka: their evolution, setting, distribution and essential functions*. Hector Kobbekaduwa Agrarian Research and Training Institute.

Panabokke, C. R. (2002). *The Nature and Prosperities of Small Tank Systems of the Dry Zone and Their Sustainable Production Thresholds*. International Water Management Institute.

Panabokke, C. R., Sakthivadivel, R., & Weerasinghe, A. D. (2002). *Small Tanks in Sri Lanka-Evolution, Present Status and Issues*. International Water Management Institute.

Panagos, P., Borrelli, P., Meusburger, K., Alewell, C., Lugato, E., & Montanarella, L. (2015). Estimating the soil erosion cover-management factor at the European scale. *Land Use Policy*, *48*, 38–50. doi:10.1016/j.landusepol.2015.05.021

Panda, S., Chakraborty, M., & Misra, S. K. (2016). Assessment of socially sustainable development in urban India by a composite index. *International Journal of Sustainable Built Environment*, *5*(2), 435–450. doi:10.1016/j.ijsbe.2016.08.001

Pande, P. C., Awasthi, P., Bargali, K., & Bargali, S. S. (2016). Agro-biodiversity of kumaun himalaya, India: A review. *Current Agriculture Research Journal*, *40*(1), 16–34. doi:10.12944/CARJ.4.1.02

Pandve, H. T. (2008). The Asian brown cloud. *Indian Journal of Occupational and Environmental Medicine*, *12*(2), 93. doi:10.4103/0019-5278.43269 PMID:20040987

Pant, N., & Verma, R. K. (2010). *Tanks in Eastern India: A Study in Exploration*. IWMI,Hydrabad, Tata Water Policy Research Program. doi:10.5337/2010.228

Parakrama, A. (2006). Rural Land Sector In Sri Lanka: Major Characteristics, Determinants and Implications for Land Policy. Institute of Policy Studies.

Paranage, K. (2018). The consequences of restricting rights to land: understanding the impact of state-land tenure policies in Sri Lanka. *Sustainability: Science, Practice and Policy*, *14*(1), 46–54.

Parente, L., & Ferreira, L. (2018). Assessing the spatial and occupation dynamics of the Brazilian pasturelands based on the automated classification of MODIS images from 2000 to 2016. *Remote Sensing*, *10*(4), 606. doi:10.3390/rs10040606

Park, M., Shin, S. K., Do, Y. H., Yarish, C., & Kim, J. K. (2018). Application of open water integrated multi-trophic aquaculture to intensive monoculture: A review of the current status and challenges in Korea. *Aquaculture (Amsterdam, Netherlands)*, *497*, 174–183. doi:10.1016/j.aquaculture.2018.07.051

Parks, S. A., Holsinger, L. M., Voss, M. A., Loehman, R. A., & Robinson, N. P. (2018). Mean composite fire severity metrics computed with Google Earth Engine offer improved accuracy and expanded mapping potential. *Remote Sensing*, *10*(6), 879. doi:10.3390/rs10060879

Parsa, V. A., Salehi, E., Yavari, A. R., & van Bodegom, P. M. (2019). Analyzing temporal changes in urban forest structure and the effect on air quality improvement. *Sustainable Cities and Society*, *48*, 101548. doi:10.1016/j.scs.2019.101548

Pascual, C., Agulto, I., Espino, A., Jr., & Malamug, V. (2019). *Effect of ground heat exchanger for root-zone cooling on the growth and yield of aeroponically-grown strawberry plant under tropical greenhouse condition*. Paper presented at the IOP Conference Series: Earth and Environmental Science. 10.1088/1755-1315/301/1/012006

Passet, R. (1979). *L'Économique et le vivant*. Payot. (in French)

Pataki, D. E., Carreiro, M. M., Cherrier, J., Grulke, N. E., Jennings, V., Pincetl, S., Pouyat, R. V., Whitlow, T. H., & Zipperer, W. C. (2011). Coupling biogeochemical cycles in urban environments: Ecosystem services, green solutions, and misconceptions. *Frontiers in Ecology and the Environment*, *9*(1), 27–36. doi:10.1890/090220

Patle, P. N., Kadu, P. R., Gabhane, A. R., Pharande, A. L., Bhagat, A. P., Bhoyar, S. M., Konde, N. M., & Rahangdale, M. K. (2020). Consequences provoked due to excess application of agrochemical on soil health deterioration–A review for Sustainable Agriculture. *Journal of Pharmacognosy and Phytochemistry*, *9*(1), 63–66.

Paudel, B., Zhang, Y., Li, S., & Liu, L. (2018). Spatiotemporal changes in agricultural land cover in Nepal over the last 100 years. *Journal of Geographical Sciences*, *28*(10), 1519–1537. doi:10.100711442-018-1559-9

Paudel, B., Zhang, Y., Li, S., & Wu, X. (2017). Spatiotemporal reconstruction of agricultural land cover in Nepal from 1970 to 2010. *Regional Environmental Change*, *17*(8), 2349–2357. doi:10.100710113-017-1164-y

Paudel, B., Zhang, Y., Yan, J., Rai, R., & Li, L. (2019). Farmers' perceptions of agricultural land use changes in Nepal and their major drivers. *Journal of Environmental Management*, *235*, 432–441. doi:10.1016/j.jenvman.2019.01.091 PMID:30710853

Paudel, K. P., Tamang, S., & Shrestha, K. K. (2014). Transforming land and livelihood: Analysis of agricultural land abandonment in the Mid Hills of Nepal. *Journal of Forest and Livelihood*, *12*(1), 11–19.

Paudel, M. N. (2016). Prospects and limitations of agriculture industrialization in Nepal. *Agronomy Journal of Nepal*, *4*, 38–63. doi:10.3126/ajn.v4i0.15515

Paul, Wolf, Dewitt, & Wilkinson. (2014). Elementary of Photogrammetry with Applications of GIS (4th ed.). Mc Graw Hill Education.

Pawson, R. (2006). *Evidence-based policy: a realist perspective*. Sage.

Peckham, S. C., Duinker, P. N., & Ordóñez, C. (2013). Urban forest values in Canada: Views of citizens in Calgary and Halifax. *Urban Forestry & Urban Greening*, *12*(2), 154–162. doi:10.1016/j.ufug.2013.01.001

Pedersen, S. M., & Lind, K. M. (2017). *Precision agriculture: Technology and economic perspectives*. Springer. doi:10.1007/978-3-319-68715-5

Peiris, G. H. (2006). Sri Lanka, Challenges of the New Millennium. Kandy Books.

Peiris, G.H. (1996). *Development and change in Sri Lanka – Geographical Perspectives*. International Centre for Ethnic Studies.

Peiris, G. H. (1978). Land reform and agrarian change in Sri Lanka. *Modern Asian Studies*, *12*(4), 611–628. doi:10.1017/S0026749X0000634X

Pellow, D. N. (2016). Environmental justice and rural studies: A critical conversation and invitation to collaboration. *Journal of Rural Studies, 47*(A), 381-386. doi:10.1016/j.jrurstud.2016.06.018

Perera, K., & Tsuchiya, K. (2009). Experiment for mapping Land Cover and its change in southeastern SL utilizing 250 m resolution MODIS imageries. *Advances in Space Research*, *43*(9), 1349–1355. doi:10.1016/j.asr.2008.12.016

Perera, M. P. (2009). Integrating Agroforestry Characteristics into Agro-well based Agricultural Lands. In *Proceedings of National Conference on Water, Food security and Climate Change in Sri Lanka*, International Water Management Institute.

Perera, M. P. (2010). *Irrigation Heritage of Sri Lanka (Sinhala Version)*. Center for Environmental Justice.

Perera, M. P. (2016). Development of Agro-well Lands and Its impact on Soil Salinity in the North Central Dry Zone of Sri Lanka. *International Journal of Scientific Research (Ahmedabad, India)*, *5*(7), 497–501. doi:10.21275/v5i7.ART2016217

Perera, M. P. (2017a). Groundwater Extraction through Agro-wells and its Impact on Groundwater Availability of Tank Cascades in the Dry Season: A Case Study in the Dry Zone of Sri Lanka. *International Journal of Scientific Research and Innovative Technology*, *4*(6), 50–62.

Perera, M. P. (2017b). Stream Reservations are at Risk?:A Case Study on the Agro-well Development in the Dry Zone of Sri Lanka. *International Journal of Scientific Research (Ahmedabad, India)*, *6*(6), 2149–2153. doi:10.21275/ART20174619

Perera, M. P., & Rekha Nianthi, K. W. G. (2016). The Impact of Agro-well Development on Floral Diversity in Tank Cascades in the Dry Zone of Sri Lanka. *International Journal of Scientific Research (Ahmedabad, India)*, *5*(6), 2061–2065. doi:10.21275/v5i6.NOV164764

Perry, K.-K. Y. (2013). *Black women against the land grab: The fight for racial justice in Brazil*. University of Minnesota Press.

Peschardt, K. K., Schipperijn, J., & Stigsdotter, U. K. (2012). Use of small public urban green spaces (SPUGS*). Urban Forestry & Urban Greening*, *11*(3), 235–244. doi:10.1016/j.ufug.2012.04.002

Petralli, M., Morabito, M., Cecchi, L., Crisci, A., & Orlandini, S. (2012). Urban morbidity in summer: Ambulance dispatch data, periodicity and weather. *Central European Journal of Medicine*, *7*(6), 775–782.

Petrova, S. T. (2020). Efficiency of Pinus nigra JF Arnold in removing pollutants from urban environment (Plovdiv, Bulgaria). *Environmental Science and Pollution Research International*, 1–17. PMID:32648225

Photongkhanong, D. (2009). *The Development Policy of Thai Government toward the Three Southernmost Provinces, A.D.1938-1986 Master*. Kasetsart University.

Phuttharak & Dhiravisit. (2014), Rapid Urbanization-Its Impact on Sustainable Development: A Case Study of Udon Thani, Thailand. *Asian Social Science, 10*(22). Available at, http://citeseerx.ist.psu.edu/viewdoc/download?doi=10.1.1.828.637&rep=rep1&type=pdf

Phuyal, R. K., Devkota, N., & Shrestha, D. L. (2017). Climate change adaptation related hindrances among rice farmers in Nepal: Farm level analysis. *Journal of Development and Administrative Studies, 25*(1-2), 1–10. doi:10.3126/jodas.v25i1-2.23434

Pieris, R. (1956). *Sinhalese Social Organization; the Kandyan Period*. The Ceylon University, Press Board.

Pimentel, D., & Burgess, M. (2013). Soil erosion threatens food production. *Agriculture, 3*(3), 443–463. doi:10.3390/agriculture3030443

Pitsuwan, S. (1985). *Islam and Malay Nationalism: A Case Study of the Malay-Muslims of Southern Thailand*. Academic Press.

Platt, P. (2007). Vertical farming: An interview with Dickson Despommier. *Gastronomica, 7*(3), 80–87. doi:10.1525/gfc.2007.7.3.80

Poncet, J., Kuper, M., & Chiche, J. (2010). Wandering off the paths of planned innovation: The role of formal and informal intermediaries in a large-scale irrigation scheme in Morocco. *Agricultural Systems, 103*(4), 171–179. doi:10.1016/j.agsy.2009.12.004

Poortinga, A., Clinton, N., Saah, D., Cutter, P., Chishtie, F., Markert, K. N., ... Bean, B. (2018). An operational before-after-control-impact (BACI) designed platform for vegetation monitoring at planetary scale. *Remote Sensing, 10*(5), 760. doi:10.3390/rs10050760

Pope Iii, C. A., Burnett, R. T., Thun, M. J., Calle, E. E., Krewski, D., Ito, K., & Thurston, G. D. (2002). Lung cancer, cardiopulmonary mortality, and long-term exposure to fine particulate air pollution. *Journal of the American Medical Association, 287*(9), 1132–1141. doi:10.1001/jama.287.9.1132 PMID:11879110

Potgieter, T. (2018). Oceans economy, blue economy, and security: Notes on the South African potential and developments. *Journal of the Indian Ocean Region, 14*(1), 49–70. doi:10.1080/19480881.2018.1410962

Poudel, U. (2020). Government preparing to set up land bank. *The Himalayan Times*. https://thehimalayantimes.com/business/government-preparing-to-set-up-land-bank/

PrabathWitharana, D. D. (2014). *The impact of land consolidation programme on land productivity in traditional agricultural land tenure system in the wet zone of srilanka* (Doctoral dissertation). Sri Lanka Institute of Development Administration.

Prakasam, C. (2010). Land use and land cover change detection through remote sensing approach: A case study of Kodaikanal Taluk, Tamil Nadu. *International Journal of Geomatics and Geosciences, 1*(2), 150.

Prashar, P., & Shah, S. (2016). Impact of fertilizers and pesticides on soil microflora in agriculture. In *Sustainable agriculture reviews* (pp. 331–361). Springer. doi:10.1007/978-3-319-26777-7_8

Premakantha, K. T., Pushpakumara, D. K. N. G., & Dayawansa, N. D. K. (2008). Identification of tree resources outside forests in the upcountry of Sri Lanka using medium resolution satellite imagery. *Tropical Agricultural Research, 20*, 354–365.

Pretty, J. (2003). Social capital and the collective management of resources. *Science, 302*(5652), 1912–1914. doi:10.1126cience.1090847 PMID:14671287

Pulido, L. (2015). Geographies of race and ethnicity I: White supremacy vs white privilege in environmental racism research. *Progress in Human Geography*, 1–9. doi:10.1177/0309132514563008

Puri, P., Nandar, S. K., Kathuria, S., & Ramesh, V. (2017). Effects of air pollution on the skin: A review. *Indian Journal of Dermatology, Venereology and Leprology, 83*(4), 415. doi:10.4103/0378-6323.199579 PMID:28195077

Qasim, S., Shrestha, R. P., & Qasim, M. (2017). A National Review of Land Degradation in Pakistan. *Current Politics and Economics of South, Southeastern, and Central Asia, 26*(1), 91–108.

Qian, Wang, Dong, Dong, Bian, & Jia. (2008). The application of Farmland Grade conversion results in the balance of farmland requisition and compensation. *Journal of Agricultural Engineering*, (8), 110–113.

Qing, W. A. N. G. (2018). Urbanization and Global Health: The Role of Air Pollution. *Iranian Journal of Public Health, 47*(11), 1644. PMID:30581779

Raats, P. A. (2015). Salinity management in the coastal region of the Netherlands: A historical perspective. *Agricultural Water Management, 157*, 12–30. doi:10.1016/j.agwat.2014.08.022

Rachel, E. (2015), *The Concept of Sustainable Development: Definition and Defining Principles*, pp. 1-3.

Rafferty, P. J. (2020). *Microclimate.* Britannica. Accessed 23 august 2020, https://www.britannica.com/science/microclimate

Ragg, A. A. (1934). The port of Suva, Fiji; its history and development. *Selected Engineering Papers, 1*(171), 3–24. doi:10.1680/isenp.1934.13635

Rahman, A. U., & Shaw, R. (2017). Fragile Mangroves and Increasing Susceptibility to Coastal Hazards in Pakistan. In R. DasGupta & R. Shaw (Eds.), *Participatory Mangrove Management in a Changing Climate* (pp. 17–30). Springer. doi:10.1007/978-4-431-56481-2_2

Rainima, T. (2016, July 24). Vatuwaqa squatters accept relocation to Makoi. *Fiji Broadcasting Corporation.* Retrieved from https://www.fbcnews.com.fj/news/ vatuwaqa-squatters-accept-relocation-to-makoi/

Rais, M., Gameda, S., Craswell, E., Sajjapongse, A., & Bechstedt, H. (1999). Decision support system for sustainable land management: A South-east Asia case. In E. K. Kersten, Z. Mikolajuk, & A. Gar-On Yeh (Eds.), *Decision support systems for sustainable development: a resource book of methods and applications.* Kluwer Academic Publishers.

Ramane, D. V., Patil, S. S., & Shaligram, A. D. (2015, February). Detection of NPK nutrients of soil using Fiber Optic Sensor. In *International Journal of Research in Advent Technology Special Issue National Conference ACGT 2015* (pp. 13-14). Academic Press.

Ramos, S., & Hesp, P. A. (2018). Mangrove Establishment in an Artificially Constructed Estuarine Channel, Sungei Api-Api, Singapore. In C. Makowski & C. W. Finkl (Eds.), *Threats to Mangrove Forests: Hazards, Vulnerability, and Management* (pp. 419–427). Springer. doi:10.1007/978-3-319-73016-5_19

Ranaweera, D. K. D. A., & Ratnayake, R. M. K. (2017). Urban land-use changes in Sri Lanka with special reference to Kaduwela town from 1975 to 2016. *International Journal of Innovative Research and Development, 6*(6), 52–64p. doi:10.24940/ijird/2017/v6/i6/JUN17014

Rathnayake, C. W.M., & Jones, S., & Benelov, M. S. (2020). Mapping LC changes over 25 years (1993-2018) in Sri Lanka using Landsat time series. *Land (Basel), 9*(27), 2–19p.

Ratnayake, J., Abeykoon, M., & Chemin, Y. (2002). *District-wise forest area variation in Sri Lanka from 1992 to 2001 for supporting the National Physical Planning Policy.* Available at: https://www.gisdevelopment.net/aars/acrs/2002/for/015.pdf

Ravanelli, R., Nascetti, A., Cirigliano, R. V., Di Rico, C., Leuzzi, G., Monti, P., & Crespi, M. (2018). Monitoring the impact of land cover change on surface urban heat island through Google Earth Engine: Proposal of a global methodology, first applications and problems. *Remote Sensing, 10*(9), 1488. doi:10.3390/rs10091488

Ray, D., & Esteban, J. (2017). Conflict and Development. *Annual Review of Economics, 9*(1), 263–293. doi:10.1146/annurev-economics-061109-080205 PMID:28202148

Redden, R. J., Upadyaya, H., Dwivedi, S. L., Vadez, V., Abberton, M., & Amri, A. (2019). *Role of Plant Genetic Resources in Food Security.* Food Security and Climate Change.

Reid, A. (1988). *Southeast Asia in the Age of Commerce, 1450-1680: Expansion and crisis* (Vol. 2). Yale University Press.

Rekha Nianthi, K. W. G., & Dharmasena, P. B. (2009). Indigenous Knowledge of Farming Practices and Water Management in the Dry Zone of Sri Lanka. In R. Shaw (Ed.), *Indigenous Knowledge and Disaster Risk Reduction* (pp. 329–348). Nova Science Publishing.

Rekha Nianthi, K. W. G., & Jayakumara, M. A. S. (2010). Progress of Research on Cascade Irrigation Systems in the Dry Zone of Sri Lanka. In R. Shaw & D. Thaitakoo (Eds.), *Water Communities* (pp. 109–137). Emerald Publishing. doi:10.1108/S2040-7262(2010)0000002010

Ren, Y., Deng, L. Y., Zuo, S. D., Song, X. D., Liao, Y. L., Xu, C. D., Chen, Q., Hua, L. Z., & Li, Z. W. (2016). Quantifying the influences of various ecological factors on land surface temperature of urban forests. *Environmental Pollution, 216*, 519–529. doi:10.1016/j.envpol.2016.06.004 PMID:27321883

Report, U. M. (2001). *Special Session of the General Assembly for an Overall Review and Appraisal of the Implementation of the Habitat Agenda.* Available at, https://www.un.org/ga/Istanbul+5/booklet4.pdf

Reyes, M. (2005). *Risk-Sensitive Land Use Planning: Towards Reduced Seismic Disaster Vulnerability.* Kassel University Press.

Rice, C., Harrison, E., & Friedman, M. (2019). Doing justice to intersectionality in research. *Cultural Studies Critical Methodologies*, 1-12. doi:10.1177/1532708619829779

Rimal, B., Baral, H., Stork, N. E., Paudyal, K., & Rijal, S. (2015). Growing city and rapid land use transition: Assessing multiple hazards and risks in the Pokhara Valley, Nepal. *Land (Basel), 4*(4), 957–978. doi:10.3390/land4040957

RitchieH.RoserM. (2020). *Urbanization.* https://ourworldindata.org/urbanization

RitchieH.RoserM. (2020). *Urbanization.* Retrieved from https://ourworldindata.org/urbanization

Rivera-Monroy, V. H., Lee, S. Y., Kristensen, E., & Twilley, R. R. (2017). *Mangrove ecosystems: a global biogeographic perspective.* Springer. doi:10.1007/978-3-319-62206-4

Rivers, F. R. (2006). Restoring the bundle of rights: Preserving heirs' property in coastal South Carolina. *Proceedings of the 17th annual estate planning symposium.* https://www.americanbar.org/content/dam/aba/events/real_property_trust_estate/symposia/2006/12_property_preservation.authcheckdam.pdf

Robinson, N. P., Allred, B. W., Jones, M. O., Moreno, A., Kimball, J. S., Naugle, D. E., Erickson, T., & Richardson, A. D. (2017). A dynamic Landsat derived normalized difference vegetation index (NDVI) product for the conterminous United States. *Remote Sensing, 9*(8), 863. doi:10.3390/rs9080863

Rodrigues, S. M., & Römkens, P. F. (2018). Human health risks and soil pollution. In *Soil Pollution* (pp. 217–250). Elsevier. doi:10.1016/B978-0-12-849873-6.00009-1

Rodríguez, F. V. L. (2018). Mangrove Concessions: An Innovative Strategy for Community Mangrove Conservation in Ecuador. In C. Makowski & C.W. (Eds.), Threats to Mangrove Forests: Hazards, Vulnerability, and Management (p. 557-578). Cham: Springer.

Rodríguez, M.C., Dupont-Courtade, L. and Oueslati, W. (2015). Air Pollution and Urban Structure Linkages.

Romero-Baena, A. J., González, I., & Galán, E. (2018). Soil pollution by mining activities in Andalusia (South Spain)-the role of Mineralogy and Geochemistry in three case studies. *Journal of Soils and Sediments*, *18*(6), 2231–2247. doi:10.100711368-017-1898-7

Rosengarten, D., & Wigfall, N. (2019, March 9). *Babylon is falling: The state of the art of Sweetgrass basketry*. Inaugural International Gullah Geechee and African Diaspora Conference, Coastal Carolina University, Conway, SC.

Rosengarten, D. (2018). Babylon Is falling: The state of the art of Sweetgrass basketry. *Southern Cultures*, *24*(2), 98–124. doi:10.1353cu.2018.0022

Rose, W. L. (1964). *Rehearsal for reconstruction: The Port Royal Experiment*. Bobbs-Merrill.

Roth, M., & Lim, V. H. (2017). Evaluation of canopy-layer air and mean radiant temperature simulations by a microclimate model over a tropical residential neighbourhood. *Building and Environment*, *112*, 177–189. doi:10.1016/j.buildenv.2016.11.026

Roy, D. P., Wulder, M. A., & Loveland, T. R. (2014). Landsat-8: Science and product vision for terrestrial global change research. *Remote Sensing of Environment*, *145*, 154–172. doi:10.1016/j.rse.2014.02.001

Roy, F., & Ferland, Y. (2015). Land-use planning for disaster risk management. *Land Tenure Journal*, 1.

Roy, P., & Roy, A. (2010). Land use and land cover change in India: A remote sensing & GIS prespective. *Journal of the Indian Institute of Science*, *90*, 489–502.

Rubio-Asensio, J. S., Parra, M., & Intrigliolo, D. S. (2020). Open field hydroponics in fruit crops: Developments and challenges. In *Fruit Crops* (pp. 419–430). Elsevier. doi:10.1016/B978-0-12-818732-6.00030-7

Ruedas, L. (2016). *Maxomys rajah. The IUCN Red List of Threatened Species 2016: e.T12904A22455724*. doi:10.2305/IUCN.UK.2016-2.RLTS.T12904A22455724.en

Rykaczewska, K. (2016). The potato minituber production from micro-tubers in aeroponic culture. *Plant, Soil and Environment*, *62*(5), 210–214. doi:10.17221/686/2015-PSE

Sabir, W. A. B. (2018). Sweeping conversations: Julie Dash's *Daughters. The Journal of Pan African Studies*, *11*(6), 231–247. https://www.jpanafrican.org/docs/vol11no6/final-Kim-26-Sabir.pdf

Saifullah, D., Dahlawi, S., Naeem, A., Rengel, Z., & Naidu, R. (2018). Biochar application for the remediation of salt-affected soils: Challenges and opportunities. *The Science of the Total Environment*, *625*, 320–335. doi:10.1016/j.scitotenv.2017.12.257 PMID:29289780

Saint-Paul, U., & Schneider, H. (Eds.). (2010). *Mangrove dynamics and management in North Brazil*. Springer. doi:10.1007/978-3-642-13457-9

Salam, A., Bashir, S., Khan, I., Shahid Rizwan, M., Afzal Chhajro, M., Feng, X., Zhu, J., & Hu, H. (2018). Biochars immobilize lead and copper in naturally contaminated soil. *Environmental Engineering Science*, *35*(12), 1349–1360. doi:10.1089/ees.2018.0086

Salfinas, N. (2008). *The Study of Bird Species Composition in Forest Plantation and Domestic Forest Areas at Kinarut, Papar, Sabah* [Unpublished Bachelor Dissertation]. Universiti Malaysia Sabah, Sabah, Malaysia.

Salin, K. R., & Ataguba, G. A. (2018). Aquaculture and the environment: Towards sustainability. In *Sustainable Aquaculture* (pp. 1–62). Springer. doi:10.1007/978-3-319-73257-2_1

Samanalawewa Hydro Electricity Project Environmental Post Evaluation Study. (1992). Ceylon Electricity Board.

Samaratunga, P. A., & Marawila, D. (2006). *Rural Land Sector in Sri Lanka: Major Characteristics, Determinants, and Implications for Land Policy (No. 7)*. Institute of Policy Studies.

Samaraweera, V. (1982). Land Reform in Sri Lanka. *Third World Legal Stud.*, 104.

Saparamadu, S., Yi, Z., & Zongping, Z. (2018). Temporal Changes of Land use Land Cover and Environmental Impacts: A Case Study in Colombo, Sri Lanka. *Int J Earth Environ Sci, 3*(1), 150. doi:10.15344/2456-351X/2018/150

Saqib, A. I., Ahmed, K., Qadir, G., Nawaz, M. Q., Rizwan, M., Zaka, M. A., & Warraich, I. A. (2017). Comparison the Efficient Reclamation of Different Inorganic Materials with Organic Amendments to Rice-Wheat Crop Sustainable Production in Salt-Affected Soils. *Cercetari Agronomice În Moldova, 50*(1), 19–29. doi:10.1515/cerce-2017-0002

Sardar, D., & Kole, R. K. (2005). Metabolism of chlorpyrifos in relation to its effect on the availability of some plant nutrients in soil. *Chemosphere, 61*(9), 1273–1280. doi:10.1016/j.chemosphere.2005.03.078 PMID:15894348

Saturday, A. (2018). Restoration of degraded agricultural land: A review. *Journal of Environmental Health Science, 4*, 44–51.

Savci, S. (2012). Investigation of Effect of Chemical Fertilizers on Environment. *APCBEE Procedia, 1*, 287–292. doi:10.1016/j.apcbee.2012.03.047

Sazib, N., Mladenova, I., & Bolten, J. (2018). Leveraging the google earth engine for drought assessment using global soil moisture data. *Remote Sensing, 10*(8), 1265. doi:10.3390/rs10081265 PMID:32021700

SBPA. (2010). *Five Special Provinces Development Plan B.E.2552-2555*. Bangkok: Southern Border Provinces Administration Act B.E.2553. Available at: www.codi.or.th/downloads/laws/law/Other-5.pdf

SBPAC. (2015). *National Security Policy B.E. 2558-2564 (2015-2020)*. Bangkok: National Security Council.

Scherr, S. J. (1999). *Soil degradation: a threat to developing-country food security by 2020?* (Vol. 27). Intl Food Policy Res Inst.

Schneider, F., & Rist, S. (2013). Envisioning sustainable water futures in a transdisciplinary learning process: Combining normative, explorative, and participatory scenario approaches. *Sustainability Science, 9*(4), 463–481. doi:10.100711625-013-0232-6

Schweninger, L. (1990). *Black property owners in the South, 1790-1915*. University of Illinois Press.

Secretariat of the Pacific Regional Environment Programme. (2013). Fiji State of Environment Report 2013. Author.

Seidl, R., Thom, D., Kautz, M., Martin-Benito, D., Peltoniemi, M., Vacchiano, G., & Lexer, M. J. (2017). Forest disturbances under climate change. *Nature Climate Change, 7*(6), 395–402. doi:10.1038/nclimate3303 PMID:28861124

Sekliziotis, S. (1980). *A Survey of Urban Open Space Using Colour-infrared Aerial Photographs. Aston*. University of Aston.

Selmi, W., Weber, C., Rivière, E., Blond, N., Mehdi, L., & Nowak, D. (2016). Air pollution removal by trees in public green spaces in Strasbourg city, France. *Urban Forestry & Urban Greening, 17*, 192–201. doi:10.1016/j.ufug.2016.04.010

Semeniuk, V., & Cresswell, I. D. (2018). Australian mangroves: Anthropogenic impacts by industry, agriculture, ports, and urbanisation. In C. Makowski & C. W. Finkl (Eds.), *Threats to Mangrove Forests: Hazards, Vulnerability, and Management* (pp. 173–197). Springer. doi:10.1007/978-3-319-73016-5_9

Shaharuddin, A., Noorazuan, M.H., Takeuchi, W., & Noraziah, A. (2014). The effects of urban heat islands on human comfort: A case of Klang Valley Malaysia. *Global Journal on Advances Pure and Applied Sciences, 2.*

Shahbaz, M., Loganathan, N., Sbia, R., & Afza, T. (2015). The effect of urbanization, affluence and trade openness on energy consumption: A time series analysis in Malaysia. *Renewable & Sustainable Energy Reviews*, *47*, 683–693. doi:10.1016/j.rser.2015.03.044

Shah, T., Samad, M., Ariyaratne, R., & Jinapala, K. (2013). Ancient small-tank irrigation in Sri Lanka: Continuity and change. *Economic and Political Weekly*, 58–65.

Shakrullah, K., Shirazi, S. A., & Sajjad, S. H. (2015). Spatio-temporal analysis of land cover changes of Dhaka City in Bangladesh. *Pakistan Journal of Science*, *67*(4), 413.

ShareSansar. (2020). Government to establish Land Banks in 300 local level units. *ShareSansar*. https://www.sharesansar.com/newsdetail/government-to-establish-land-banks-in-300-local-level-units

Sharifi, E. & Lehmann, S. (2014). *Comparative analysis of surface urban heat island effect in central Sydney*. Academic Press.

Sharma & Sen. (2015). Gurgaon-Manesar Urban Complex. *Transactions of the Institute of Indian Geographers, 37*(1), 133-146.

Sharma, N., & Shehrawat, P. S. (2019). Judging causes of soil degradation and remedial measures for reclamation in Kaithal district of Haryana state. *Journal of Applied and Natural Science*, *11*(4), 802–805. doi:10.31018/jans.v11i4.2183

Sharma, R. K. (2012). Evolution of Land Use Policy in Nepal. *Nepalese Journal of Geoinformatics*, *11*, 16–21.

Sharp, T. (2017). *Earth's Atmosphere: Composition, Climate & Weather.* https://www. space. com/17683-earth-atmosphere. html

Silberstein, J., & Maser, C. (Eds.). (2014). Land Use Planning for Sustainable Development (2nd ed.). CRC Press, Taylor and Francis Group.

Silva, M. U. (2007). History of Sri Lanka. Representative Government, 4.

Silva, R. A., West, J. J., Lamarque, J. F., Shindell, D. T., Collins, W. J., Faluvegi, G., Folberth, G. A., Horowitz, L. W., Nagashima, T., Naik, V., Rumbold, S. T., Sudo, K., Takemura, T., Bergmann, D., Cameron-Smith, P., Doherty, R. M., Josse, B., MacKenzie, I. A., Stevenson, D. S., & Zeng, G. (2017). Future global mortality from changes in air pollution attributable to climate change. *Nature Climate Change*, *7*(9), 647–651. doi:10.1038/nclimate3354 PMID:30245745

Simon, H., Lindén, J., Hoffmann, D., Braun, P., Bruse, M., & Esper, J. (2018). Modeling transpiration and leaf temperature of urban trees–a case study evaluating the microclimate model ENVI-met against measurement data. *Landscape and Urban Planning*, *174*, 33–40. doi:10.1016/j.landurbplan.2018.03.003

Singh, A. (2015). Soil salinization and waterlogging: A threat to environment and agricultural sustainability. *Ecological Indicators*, *57*, 128–130. doi:10.1016/j.ecolind.2015.04.027

Singh, A. K., Gupta, H. K., Gupta, K., Singh, P., Gupta, V. B., & Sharma, R. C. (2007). A comparative study of air pollution in Indian cities. *Bulletin of Environmental Contamination and Toxicology*, *78*(5), 411–416. doi:10.100700128-007-9220-9 PMID:17599225

Singh, A. S., & Masuku, M. B. (2014). Sampling techniques & determination of sample size in applied statistics research: An overview. *International Journal of Economics, Commerce and Management, 2*(1), 1–22.

Singh, A. U., & Prasad, D. (2016). Integrated Pest Management with Reference to INM. *Advances in Crop Science and Technology, 4*(220), 2. doi:10.4172/2329-8863.1000220

Sjöman, H., Hirons, A. D., & Bassuk, N. L. (2015). Urban forest resilience through tree selection—Variation in drought tolerance in Acer. *Urban Forestry & Urban Greening, 14*(4), 858–865. doi:10.1016/j.ufug.2015.08.004

Sklenicka, P. (2016). Classification of farmland ownership fragmentation as a cause of land degradation: A review on typology, consequences, and remedies. *Land Use Policy, 57*, 694–701. doi:10.1016/j.landusepol.2016.06.032

Skole, D. (1994). Data on global land-cover change: Acquisition, assessment, and analysis. In Changes in land use and land cover: A global perspective. (pp. 437-471) Cambridge University Press.

Smith, S. J., Schepers, J. S., & Porter, L. K. (1990). Assessing and managing agricultural nitrogen losses to the environment. In Advances in soil science (1-43). Springer. doi:10.1007/978-1-4612-3356-5_1

Smith, P., House, J. I., Bustamante, M., Sobocká, J., Harper, R., Pan, G., West, P. C., Clark, J. M., Adhya, T., Rumpel, C., Paustian, K., Kuikman, P., Cotrufo, M. F., Elliott, J. A., McDowell, R., Griffiths, R. I., Asakawa, S., Bondeau, A., Jain, A. K., ... Pugh, T. A. M. (2016). Global change pressures on soils from land use and management. *Global Change Biology, 22*(3), 1008–1028. doi:10.1111/gcb.13068 PMID:26301476

Smyth, A., Dumanski, J., Spendjian, G., & Swift, M. (1993). *FESLM: An international framework for evaluating sustainable land management.* FAO Rome.

Snow, K. C., Hays, D. G., Caliwagan, G., Ford, D. J. Jr, Mariotti, D., Mwendwa, J. M., & Scott, W. E. (2016). Guiding principles for indigenous research practices. *Action Research, 14*(4), 357–375. doi:10.1177/1476750315622542

Son, J. E., Kim, H. J., & Ahn, T. I. (2020). Hydroponic systems. In *Plant factory* (pp. 273–283). Academic Press. doi:10.1016/B978-0-12-816691-8.00020-0

Spalding, M., Kainuma, M., & Collins, L. (2010). *World atlas of mangroves.* Earthscan. doi:10.4324/9781849776608

Spielman, D., Davies, K., Negash, M., & Gezahegn, A. (2010). Rural innovation systems and networks: Findings from a study of Ethiopian smallholders. *Agriculture and Human Values, 28*(2), 195–212. doi:10.100710460-010-9273-y

Spinoff, N. A. S. A. (2006). *Progressive plant growing has business blooming.* Environmental and Agricultural Resources.

Sproles, E. A., Crumley, R. L., Nolin, A. W., Mar, E., & Lopez Moreno, J. I. (2018). Snow Cloud Hydro—A New Framework for Forecasting Streamflow in Snowy, Data-Scarce Regions. *Remote Sensing, 10*(8), 1276. doi:10.3390/rs10081276

Sri Lanka Agriculture. (2020). Retrieved from https://www.nationsencyclopedia.com/ economies/Asia-and-the-Pacific/Sri-Lanka-AGRICULTURE.html#ixzz6GxxE3Olh

Sri Lanka History Volume III . (2007). Education Publication Department.

Sri Lanka History Volume IV. (2007). Education Publication Department.

Srivastava, P., Wu, Q.-S., & Giri, B. (2019). Salinity: An Overview. In Microorganisms in Saline Environments: Strategies and Functions (pp. 3-18). Springer.

Stack, C. B. (1974). *All our kin.* Harper and Row.

Stack, C. B. (1996). *Call to home: African-Americans reclaim the rural South.* Basic Books.

Stephens, J. L. (2015). *Don't sign anything!* Center for Heirs' Property and Preservation., https://heirsproperty.org/wp-content/uploads/2018/04/2014_Fall_Newsletter.pdf

Stewart, T., Throne, R., & Evans, L. (2020). A critical review of gender parity and voice dispossession among executive women in higher education leadership. In G. Berg & L. Venis (Eds.), *Accessibility and diversity in the 21st century university*. IGI Global. doi:10.4018/978-1-7998-2783-2.ch005

Sub-Regional Plan for Haryana Sub-Region of NCR-2021, Demographic Profile and Settlement Pattern, Chapter 4. (n.d.). Available at https://tcpharyana.gov.in/ncrpb/FINAL%20SRP%20FOR%20WEB-HOSTING/04_Demographic%20Profile_Settlement%20Pattern.pdf

Sudmeier-Rieux, K., Paleo, U. F., Garschagen, M., Estrella, M., Renaud, F. G., & Jaboyedoff, M. (2015). Opportunities, incentives and challenges to risk sensitive land use planning: Lessons from Nepal, Spain and Vietnam. *International Journal of Disaster Risk Reduction, 14*, 205–224. doi:10.1016/j.ijdrr.2014.09.009

Sugau, J. B., Pereira, J. T., & Damit, A. (2017). A Guide to the Trees in Heritage Amenity Forest Reserve (HQ), Sandakan: A Revised and Expanded Edition. Sabah Forestry Department.

Sugawara, Sudin, Said, Suleiman,Gisil, & Sundaling. (2009). *Buku Panduan Hutan Bukit UMS: Tumbuh-tumbuhan.* Pernebit Universiti Malaysia Sabah.

Sullivan, P. (2004). *Sustainable soil management: soil systems guide. Appropriate Technology Transfer for Rural Areas.* ATTRA.

Sunder, S. (2018). *India economic survey 2018: Farmers gain as agriculture mechanisation speeds up, but more R&D needed.* The Financial Express.

Sun, H., Lu, H., Chu, L., Shao, H., & Shi, W. (2017). Biochar applied with appropriate rates can reduce N leaching, keep N retention and not increase NH3 volatilization in a coastal saline soil. *The Science of the Total Environment, 575*, 820–825. doi:10.1016/j.scitotenv.2016.09.137 PMID:27693153

Suthisak, D. (2014). Role of legal aid organizations in the southernmost provinces of Thailand during 2012-2013. *Peace Studies Journal, 1*(1), 221–242.

Tamang, S., Dhital, M., & Acharya, U. (2011). *Status and scope of organic agriculture in Nepal. In Food and Sustainable Agriculture Initiative, Forestaction.* Lalitpur.

Tan. (2014). Coexistence of strict control and incentive: policy context and local implementation of land increase and decrease. *China Social Sciences*, (7), 125-142.

Tandukar, H., Niroula, A., Shrestha, K., & Paudel, U. R. (2019). Assessment of national policy to promote corporate governance in Nepal. *Quest Journal of Management and Social Sciences, 1*(1), 73–95. doi:10.3126/qjmss.v1i1.25975

Tan-Mullins, M. (2009). Armed conflict and resolutions in Southern Thailand. *Annals of the Association of American Geographers, 99*(5), 922–931. doi:10.1080/00045600903260689

Ten, W. L. (2018). *Distribution of bird species and their role as ecotourism attraction in Tawau Hill Park, Sabah* [Unpublished Bachelor Dissertation]. Universiti Malaysia Sabah, Sabah, Malaysia.

Tennakoon, M. U. A. (2005). *Ellangawa (Sinhala Version).* Godage and Sons publishing.

Tennakoon, U. V. M. (1986). *Drought Hazard and Rural Development.* Central Bank of Sri Lanka.

Tessema, L., Chindi, A., Gebremedhin, W. G., Solomon, A., Shunka, E., & Seid, E. (2017). Determination of nutrient solutions for potato (Solanum tuberosum L.) seed production under aeroponics production system. *Open Agriculture, 2*(1), 155–159. doi:10.1515/opag-2017-0015

Thaman, R. R., Clarke, W., Manner, H. I., Decker, B. G., & Ali, I. (2017). *Agroforestry in the Pacific Islands: Systems for sustainability*. United Nations University Press.

Thapa, P. B. (2018). Geo-disaster and risk sensitive land use planning in Nepal. *Bulletin of Nepal Geological Society, 35*.

The Asia Foundation. (2017). *The State of Conflict and Violence in Asia* Bang Rak, Bangkok, Thailand. Available at: https://asiafoundation.org/wp-content/uploads/2017/10/Thailand-StateofConflictandViolence.pdf

The Rising Nepal. (2020). Concept of land bank for utilisation of arable land: minister Aryal. *The Rising Nepal*. http://www.therisingnepal.org.np/news/33646

The World Bank. (2016). *Arable Land (% of land area)*. Data accessed at: https://data.worldbank.org/indicator/AG.LND.ARBL.ZS

The World Cities. (2018). *The World Cities in 2018, Data Booklet*. United Nations. Available at, https://www.un.org/en/events/citiesday/assets/pdf/the_worlds_cities_in_2018_data_booklet.pdf

Thomas, M., Pennick, J. & Gray, H. (2004). *What is African-American land ownership?* Federation of Southern Cooperatives Land Assistance Fund.

Throne, R. (2018). The letter: Fidelity in researcher positionality to exhume dispossessed voices for Leavy's concept of coherence in feminist narrative research. *Gender and Women's Studies, 2*(1). http://riverapublications.com/journal/gender-womens-studies

Throne, R. (2016). Past as prologue: Sea Island Cotton as heuristic metaphor for the Port Royal Experiment. *SAGE Open, 6*(3), 1–8. doi:10.1177/2158244016662105

Throne, R. (2020). Dispossession of land cultures: Women and property tenure among Lowcountry heirs in the Gullah Geechee Corridor. In U. Onyebadi (Ed.), *Multidisciplinary issues surrounding African Diasporas* (pp. 152–174). IGI Global. doi:10.4018/978-1-5225-5079-2.ch007

Tian. (2005). It is necessary to establish the quality evaluation system of supplementary cultivated land -- further discussion on the balance of cultivated land requisition and compensation. *China Land*, (3), 36-38.

Timmins, R., Kawanishi, K., Giman, B, Lynam, A., Chan, B., Steinmetz, R., Sagar Baral, H. & Samba Kumar, N. (2015). *Rusa unicolor. The IUCN Red List of Threatened Species 2015: e.T41790A85628124*. doi:10.2305/IUCN.UK.2015-2.RLTS.T41790A22156247.en

Ting, Cui, Fan, & Xu. (2011). Land use efficiency, inter provincial differences and the balance between different regions. *Economics: Quarterly*, (3), 358-375.

Tinubu, G. B., & Hite, J. C. (1978). *Intestate holding of rural land in South Carolina: Empirical evaluation of the dimensions of the heirs' property problem. South Carolina Agricultural Experiment Station*. Clemson University.

Tiwary, A., & Williams, I. (2018). *Air pollution: measurement, modelling and mitigation*. CRC Press. doi:10.1201/9780429469985

Tobin, D., Janowiak, M., Hollinger, D., Skinner, R. H., Swanston, C., Steele, R., Radhakrishna, R., Chatrchyan, A., Hickman, D., Bochicchio, J., & Hall, W. (2015). *Northeast and northern forests regional climate hub assessment of climate change vulnerability and adaptation and mitigation strategies*. USDA Climate Hubs.

Tobin, J. (1958). Estimation of relationships for limited dependent variables. *Econometrica*, *26*(1), 24–36. doi:10.2307/1907382

Traganos, D., Aggarwal, B., Poursanidis, D., Topouzelis, K., Chrysoulakis, N., & Reinartz, P. (2018). Towards global-scale seagrass mapping and monitoring using Sentinel-2 on Google Earth Engine: The case study of the aegean and ionian seas. *Remote Sensing*, *10*(8), 1227. doi:10.3390/rs10081227

Traganos, D., Poursanidis, D., Aggarwal, B., Chrysoulakis, N., & Reinartz, P. (2018). Estimating satellite-derived bathymetry (SDB) with the google earth engine and sentinel-2. *Remote Sensing*, *10*(6), 859. doi:10.3390/rs10060859

Transforming Our World. (2018). The 2030 Agenda for Sustainable Development. In *A New Era in Global Health*. Springer Publishing Company. doi:10.1891/9780826190123.ap02

Transparency International. (2017). *Corruption Perceptions Index*. Berlin, Germany: TI. Available at: https://www.transparency.org/news/feature/corruption_perceptions_index_2017

Trnka, M., Kersebaum, K. C., Eitzinger, J., Hayes, M., Hlavinka, P., Svoboda, M., ... Možný, M. (2013). Consequences of climate change for the soil climate in Central Europe and the central plains of the United States. *Climatic Change*, *120*(1-2), 405–418. doi:10.100710584-013-0786-4

Troutman, S., & Johnson, B. (2018). Dark water: Rememory, biopower, and Black feminist art. *Taboo: The Journal of Culture & Education*, *17*(3), 73. doi:10.31390/taboo.17.3.08

Tsai, Y. H., Stow, D., Chen, H. L., Lewison, R., An, L., & Shi, L. (2018). Mapping vegetation and land use types in fanjingshan national nature reserve using google earth engine. *Remote Sensing*, *10*(6), 927. doi:10.3390/rs10060927

Tsikata, D. (2009). Gender, land and labour relations and livelihoods in Sub-Saharan Africa in the era of economic liberalization: Towards a research agenda. *Feminist Africa*, *12*, 11–30.

Tsoka, S., Tsikaloudaki, A., & Theodosiou, T. (2018). Analyzing the ENVI-met microclimate model's performance and assessing cool materials and urban vegetation applications–A review. *Sustainable Cities and Society*, *43*, 55-76.

Tuffa, S., Hoag, D., & Treydte, A. C. (2017). Clipping and irrigation enhance grass biomass and nutrients: Implications for rangeland management. *Acta Oecologica*, *81*, 32–39. doi:10.1016/j.actao.2017.05.001

Tully, K., Sullivan, C., Weil, R., & Sanchez, P. (2015). The state of soil degradation in Sub-Saharan Africa: Baselines, trajectories, and solutions. *Sustainability*, *7*(6), 6523–6552. doi:10.3390u7066523

Tunio, M. H., Gao, J., Shaikh, S. A., Lakhiar, I. A., Qureshi, W. A., Solangi, K. A., & Chandio, F. A. (2020). Potato production in aeroponics: An emerging food growing system in sustainable agriculture for food security. *Chilean Journal of Agricultural Research*, *80*(1), 1. doi:10.4067/S0718-58392020000100118

Turnbull, B. W. (1976). The empirical distribution function with arbitrarily grouped, censored and truncated data. *Journal of the Royal Statistical Society. Series B. Methodological*, *38*(3), 290–295. doi:10.1111/j.2517-6161.1976.tb01597.x

Turner, B. L., II, & Meyer, B. L. (1994). Changes in land use and land cover: A global perspective. In Global land use and land cover change: An overview (pp. 3-10). Cambridge University Press.

Turner, B. L., II, Lambin., E.F., & Reenberg, A. (2007). The emergence of land change science for global environmental change and sustainability. *Proceeding of the National Academy Sciences of the United State of America (PNAS)*.

U.S. Geological Survey. (2010). *U.S. Geological SurveyThousands of Landsat Scenes in Google's Earth Engine*. https://landsat.usgs.gov/google-earth-engine

Ugrenović, V., Filipović, V., Jevremović, S., Marjanović-Jeromela, A., Popović, V., Buntić, A., & Delić, D. (2019). Effect of Brassicaceae as cover crops. *Selekcija i semenarstvo, 25*(2), 1-8.

UN (United Nations). (2015). *World Population Prospects—The 2015 Revision: Key Findings and Advance Tables; Working Paper No. ESA/P/WP.241.* Department of Economic and Social Affairs—Population Division, United Nations. Available online: https://esa.un.org/unpd/wpp/publications/files/key_findings_wpp_2015.pdf

UN. (2015). *Resolution adopted by the General Assembly on 25 September 2015.* Washington, DC: United Nations. Available at: http://www.un.org/ga/search/view_doc.asp?symbol=A/RES/70/1&Lang=E

UNDP. (2016). *Conducting a Conflict and Development Analysis.* Available at: https://undg.org/wp-content/uploads/2016/10/UNDP_CDA-Report_v1.3-final-opt-low.pdf

UNEP. (2001). *State of the Environment Sri Lanka – 2001. United Nations Environment Programme.* Regional Resources Centre for Asia and the Pacific.

United Nations (2018). *World urbanization prospects: The 2018 revision–key facts.* Author.

United Nations General Assembly. (1987). Report of the world commission on environment and development: Our common future. Oslo, Norway: United Nations General Assembly, Development and International Co-operation. *Environment.*

United Nations, Department of Economic and Social Affairs, Population Division (2018). *The World's Cities in 2018—Data Booklet (ST/ESA/ SER.A/417).* Author.

United Nations, Department of Economic and Social Affairs, Population Division. (2019). *World Urbanization Prospects: The 2018 Revision (ST/ESA/SER.A/420).* United Nations.

United Nations. (1992). *AGENDA 21* [Paper presented]. United Nations Conference on Environment & Development, Rio de Janerio, Brazil.

United Nations. (2005). *World Summit Outcome; Resolution Adopted by the General Assembly, A/RES/60/1.* https://www.un.org/en/development/desa/population/migration/generalassembly/docs/globalcompact/A_RES_60_1.pdf

United Nations. (2020). *Cities-United Nations Sustainable Development.* Available at, www.un.org/sustainabledevelopment/cities/

Unkašević, M., Jovanović, O., & Popović, T. (2001). Urban-suburban/rural vapour pressure and relative humidity differences at fixed hours over the area of Belgrade city. *Theoretical and Applied Climatology, 68*(1-2), 67–73. doi:10.1007007040170054

USAID. (2013). *Violent Extremism and Insurgency in Southern Thailand: A Risk Assessment.* United States Agency for International Development.

Usher, A. P. (1923). Soil fertility, soil exhaustion, and their historical significance. *The Quarterly Journal of Economics, 37*(3), 385–411. doi:10.2307/1883847

Vakasukawaqa, A. (2016, July 13). You're Not Forgotten: A-G Assures Squatters. *Fiji Sun.* Retrieved from https://fijisun.com.fj/2016/07/13/youre-not-forgotten-a-g-assures-squatters/

Van Beek, C. L., & Tóth, G. (2012). *Risk assessment methodologies of soil threats in Europe.* JRC Scientific and Policy Reports EUR, 24097.

Vanos, J. K. (2015). Children's health and vulnerability in outdoor microclimates: A comprehensive review. *Environment International, 76*, 1–15. doi:10.1016/j.envint.2014.11.016 PMID:25497108

Vanslembrouck, I., Van Huylenbroeck, G., & Verbeke, W. (2002). Determinants of the willingness of Belgian farmers to participate in agri environmental measures. *Journal of Agricultural Economics*, *53*(3), 489–511. doi:10.1111/j.1477-9552.2002.tb00034.x

Veitayaki, J., Waqalevu, V., Varea, R., & Rollings, N. (2017). Mangroves in small island development states in the Pacific: An overview of a highly important and seriously threatened resource. In R. DasGupta & R. Shaw (Eds.), *Participatory Mangrove Management in a Changing Climate* (pp. 303–327). Springer. doi:10.1007/978-4-431-56481-2_19

Vengosh, A. (2003). Salinization and saline environments. *Treatise on Geochemistry*, *9*, 612.

Verhees, F. J. H. M., Kuipers, A., & Klopcic, M. (2011). Entrepreneurial proclivity and farm performance: The cases of Dutch and Slovenian farmers. *International Journal of Entrepreneurship and Innovation*, *12*(3), 169–177. doi:10.5367/ijei.2011.0039

Vernekar, K. G., Sinha, S., Sadani, L. K., Sivaramakrishnan, S., Parasnis, S. S., Mohan, B., ... Debaje, S. B. (2003). An overview of the land surface processes experiment (LASPEX) over a semi-arid region of India. *Boundary-Layer Meteorology*, *106*(3), 561–572. doi:10.1023/A:1021283503661

Versey, H. S. (2017). Caregiving and women's health: Toward an intersectional approach. *Women's Health Issues*, *27*(2), 117–120. doi:10.1016/j.whi.2017.01.009 PMID:28258803

Versey, H. S., Cogburn, C. C., Wilkins, C. L., & Joseph, N. (2019). Appropriated racial oppression and its role for health in Whites and Blacks. *Social Science & Medicine*, *230*, 295–302. doi:10.1016/j.socscimed.2019.03.014 PMID:31054520

von Bismarck-Osten, C., Birmili, W., Ketzel, M., Massling, A., Petäjä, T., & Weber, S. (2013). Characterization of parameters influencing the spatio-temporal variability of urban particle number size distributions in four European cities. *Atmospheric Environment*, *77*, 415–429. doi:10.1016/j.atmosenv.2013.05.029

Voříšek, K., Růžek, L., Svobodová, M., Šantrůček, J., Strnadová, S., & Popelářová, E. (2002). The influence of grassing and harvest management on microbial parameters after arable land setting-aside. Rostl. *Výr*, *48*(9), 382–388.

Vuran, M. C., Salam, A., Wong, R., & Irmak, S. (2018). *Internet of underground things: Sensing and communications on the field for precision agriculture.* Paper presented at the 2018 IEEE 4th World Forum on Internet of Things (WF-IoT). 10.1109/WF-IoT.2018.8355096

Vuran, M. C., Salam, A., Wong, R., & Irmak, S. (2018). Internet of underground things in precision agriculture: Architecture and technology aspects. *Ad Hoc Networks*, *81*, 160–173. doi:10.1016/j.adhoc.2018.07.017

Wallor, E., Kersebaum, K. C., Lorenz, K., & Gebbers, R. (2018). A comprehensive data set demonstrating the spatial variability of soil properties and crop growth conditions at field scale. *Open Data Journal for Agricultural Research*, *5*, 1–10. doi:10.18174/odjar.v5i0.15888

Walsh, C. (2019). *The Lagilagi controversy. Government and the People's Community Network, Part I, II and other information.* Coz Walsh's blog. Retrieved from https://crosbiew.blogspot.com/search?q=lagilagi

Wang, F., Pan, Y., Cai, P., Guo, T., & Xiao, H. (2017). Single and binary adsorption of heavy metal ions from aqueous solutions using sugarcane cellulose-based adsorbent. *Bioresource Technology*, *241*, 482–490. doi:10.1016/j.biortech.2017.05.162 PMID:28600942

Wang, J., Huang, B., Fu, D., Atkinson, P. M., & Zhang, X. (2016). Response of urban heat island to future urban expansion over the Beijing–Tianjin–Hebei metropolitan area. *Applied Geography (Sevenoaks, England)*, *70*, 26–36. doi:10.1016/j.apgeog.2016.02.010

Wang, L., Jia, M., Yin, D., & Tian, J. (2019). A review of remote sensing for mangrove forests: 1956–2018. *Remote Sensing of Environment*, *231*, 111223. doi:10.1016/j.rse.2019.111223

Wang, Y., & Zhao, T. (2018). Impacts of urbanization-related factors on CO2 emissions: Evidence from China's three regions with varied urbanization levels. *Atmospheric Pollution Research*, *9*(1), 15–26. doi:10.1016/j.apr.2017.06.002

Wanigaratne, R. D., Gooneratne, W., &Shanmugaratnam, N. (1979). *Policies and implementation of land reform in selected villages of Sri Lanka*. ARTI Research Study (Sri Lanka). no. 32.

Wanigaratne, R.D. (1995). *Informal tenure conditions in irrigated settlements in Sri Lanka: A review of empirical research evidence*. Land Tenure Center, University of Wisconsin.

Wankhade, R., Patode, R., Nagdeve, M., Gabhane, V., & Pande, C. (2017). Effect of Continuous Contour Trenches on Nutrient Status of the Micro-Catchment. *Current Agriculture Research Journal*, *5*(3), 305–311. doi:10.12944/CARJ.5.3.07

Warnasuriya, T. W. S. (2015). Mapping land-use pattern using image processing techniques for Medium resolution satellite data: A case study in Matara District, Sri Lanka. *Proceedings of the 15th International Conference on Advances in ICT for Emerging Regions*, 106–111.

Watch, D. S. (2016). *Summing up the situation of unrest in the southern border provinces in 2014*. Deep South Incident Database. Available at https://www.deepsouthwatch.org/en/node/6596

WCED. (1987). *Our Common Future*. https://netzwerk-n.org/wp-content/uploads/2017/04/0_Brundtland_Report-1987-Our_Common_Future.pdf

Webb, R., Bai, X., Smith, M. S., Costanza, R., Griggs, D., Moglia, M., Neuman, M., Newman, P., Newton, P., Norman, B., Ryan, C., Schandl, H., Steffen, W., Tapper, N., & Thomson, G. (2018). Sustainable urban systems: Co-design and framing for transformation. *Ambio*, *47*(1), 57–77. doi:10.100713280-017-0934-6 PMID:28766172

Weber, E. (2014b). Environmental change and (im)mobility in the South. In R. Anich, J. Crush, S. Melde, & J.O. Oucho (Eds.), A new perspective on human mobility in the South (pp.119-148). Dordrecht: Springer.

Weber, E. (2020). Zur Trinkwasserproblematik im Südpazifik. In M. Dickel & M. Kowasch (Eds.), Geographien Ozeaniens - Annäherungen an das Fremde. Praxis Neue Kulturgeographie. LIT Verlag: Berlin, Münster, Wien, waterZürich (pp. 77–96). Academic Press.

Weber, C., & Puissant, A. (2003). Urbanization pressure and modeling of urban growth: Example of the Tunis Metropolitan Area. *Remote Sensing of Environment*, *86*(3), 341–352. doi:10.1016/S0034-4257(03)00077-4

Weber, E. (2005). Sugar in Fiji – a dying sector? *The Indian Geographical Journal*, *80*(2), 71–86.

Weber, E. (2007). Gewalt und Staatsversagen in Fidschi. *Zeitschrift für Wirtschaftsgeographie / The German. Journal of Economic Geography*, *3-4*, 206–220.

Weber, E. (2011). Climate change and food security – some conceptual considerations. *Journal of South Pacific Agriculture*, *15*(1 & 2), 85–97.

Weber, E. (2012). Climate and environmental change and food security. *Journal of Pacific Studies*, *32*, 99–110.

Weber, E. (2014). Climate change, agriculture and food security in the Pacific Islands. *Journal of South Pacific Agriculture*, *17*(1&2), 20–35.

Weber, E. (2015). Envisioning South-South relations in the fields of environmental change and migration in the Pacific Islands-past, present and futures. *Bandung. Journal of the Global South*, *2*(1), 1–21. doi:10.118640728-014-0009-z

Weber, E. (2016). Only a pawn in their games? environmental (?) migration in Kiribati – past, present and future. *Die Erde, 147*(2), 153–164.

Weber, E. (2017). Trade agreements, labour mobility and climate change in the Pacific Islands. *Regional Environmental Change, 17*(4), 1089–1101. doi:10.100710113-016-1047-7 PMID:31258413

Weber, E. H. (2011). Climate change and food security–some conceptual considerations. *Journal of South Pacific Agriculture, 15*(1&2), 85–97.

Weber, E., Kissoon, P., & Koto, C. (2019). Moving to dangerous places. In C. Klöck & M. Fink (Eds.), *Dealing with climate change on small islands: towards effective and sustainable adaptation?* (pp. 267–293). Göttingen University Press. doi:10.17875/gup2019-1220

Weisse, M., & Goldman, E. D. (2017). *Was the Second-Worst Year on Record for Tropical Tree Cover Loss.* Global Forest Watch Blog.

Wells, K., Lakim, M. B., & O'Hara, R. B. (2014). Shifts from native to invasive small mammals across gradients from tropical forest to urban habitat in Borneo. *Biodiversity and Conservation, 23*(9), 2289–2303. doi:10.100710531-014-0723-5

WHO. (2014). https://www.who.int/mediacentre/news/releases/2014/air-pollution/en/

Wickramaarachchi, N.C., & Weerahewa, J. (2018). Relationship between Land Size and Productivity: Empirical Evidence from Paddy Farms in Irrigation Settlements of Sri Lanka. *Sri Lanka Journal of Economic Research., 5*(2), 125–142.

Wickramarachchi, N.C., & Weerahewa, J. (2016). Land Fragmentation and Land Productivity: Empirical Evidence from Land Distribution Schemes of Sri Lanka. *International Academic Research Journal of Business and Management., 5*(1), 11–21.

Wijeyewardene, E. A. L. (1956). *Report of the Commission on Tenure of Lands of Viharagam, Dewalagam and Nindagam.* Ceylon Sessional Paper, 1-1956.

Willaarts, B. A., Oyonarte, C., Muñoz-Rojas, M., Ibáñez, J. J., & Aguilera, P. A. (2016). Environmental factors controlling soil organic carbon stocks in two contrasting Mediterranean climatic areas of southern Spain. *Land Degradation & Development, 27*(3), 603–611. doi:10.1002/ldr.2417

Wilson, C., & Weng, Q. (2010). Assessing surface water quality and its relations with urban land cover changes in the Lake Calumet Area, Greater Chicago. *Environmental Management, 45*(5), 1096–1111. doi:10.100700267-010-9482-6 PMID:20364379

Wimpey, J., & Marion, J. L. (2011*). Formal and Informal Trail Monitoring Protocols and Baseline Conditions: Great Falls Park and Potomac Gorge* (Final Report). Virginia Tech, College of Natural Resources & Environmental.

Wong, Y. S., & Tam, N. F. (Eds.). (1995). *Asia-Pacific Symposium on Mangrove Ecosystems: Proceedings of the International Conference held at The Hong Kong University of Science & Technology, September 1–3, 1993.* Dordrecht: Springer.

Woodford, M. (2019). Monetary policy analysis when planning horizons are finite. *NBER Macroeconomics Annual, 33*(1), 1–50. doi:10.1086/700892

Woofter, T. J. (1930). *Black yeomanry: Life on St. Helena Island.* Holt.

World Bank Agricultural. (2014). *GDP growth indicator for countries, Nigerian GDP growth rate.* Retrieved from: https://data.worldbank.org/indicator/NY.GDP.MKTP.KD.ZG

World Bank. (2010). *Conflict and Development: Where is Conflict Concentrated in South Asia.* WB. Available at: http://blogs.worldbank.org/endpovertyinsouthasia/conflict-and-development-where-conflict-concentrated-south-asia

World Bank. (2016). *Unheard Voices: Men and Youth in Thailand's Conflict-Affected Deep South*. World Bank. Available at: http://www.worldbank.org/en/news/feature/2016/09/21/men-and-youth-in-thailands-conflict-affected-deep-south

World Health Organization. (2014). *7 million premature deaths annually linked to air pollution*. Accessed 23 February 2020, https://www.who.int/mediacentre/news/releases/2014/airpollution/en/

Wright, N. E. (2008). Property rights and possession in "Daughters of the Dust." *Melus*, *33*(3), 11–25. doi:10.1093/melus/33.3.11

WSSD. (2002). *World Summit on Sustainable Development. (September, 2002)*. Report of the World Summit on Sustainable Development. Available at: www.un-documents.net/aconf199-20.pdf

Wu, L., Zhu, Q., Yang, L., Li, B., Hu, C., & Lan, S. (2018). Nutrient transferring from wastewater to desert through artificial cultivation of desert cyanobacteria. *Bioresource Technology*, *247*, 947–953. doi:10.1016/j.biortech.2017.09.127 PMID:30060434

Wunder, S. (2001). Poverty alleviation and tropical forests-what scope for synergies? *World Devopment*, *29*(11), 1817-1833.

Wu, Y., Luo, H., Wang, H., Zhang, L., Liu, P., & Feng, L. (2014). Fast adsorption of nickel ions by porous graphene oxide/sawdust composite and reuse for phenol degradation from aqueous solutions. *Journal of Colloid and Interface Science*, *436*, 90–98. doi:10.1016/j.jcis.2014.08.068 PMID:25265590

Wynn, G., Crabtree, B., & Potts, J. (2001). Modelling farmer entry into the environmentally sensitive area schemes in Scotland. *Journal of Agricultural Economics*, *52*(1), 65–82. doi:10.1111/j.1477-9552.2001.tb00910.x

Wypych, A. (2010). Twentieth century variability of surface humidity as the climate change indicator in Kraków (Southern Poland). *Theoretical and Applied Climatology*, *101*(3-4), 475–482. doi:10.100700704-009-0221-y

Xie, C., Li, J., Li, D., Shen, Y., Gao, Y., & Zhang, Z. (2018). Grass carp: the fish that feeds half of China. *Aquaculture in China: Success Stories and Modern Trends*, 93-115.

Xie, J., Yu, J., Chen, B., Feng, Z., Lyu, J., Hu, L., Gan, Y., & Siddique, K. H. (2018). Gobi agriculture: An innovative farming system that increases energy and water use efficiencies. A review. *Agronomy for Sustainable Development*, *38*(6), 62. doi:10.100713593-018-0540-4

Xing, Y., & Brimblecombe, P. (2019). Role of vegetation in deposition and dispersion of air pollution in urban parks. *Atmospheric Environment*, *201*, 73–83. doi:10.1016/j.atmosenv.2018.12.027

Xiong. (2015). Research on fiscal and tax policies to protect the quality of cultivated land in China. *Tax and Economy*, (2).

Xu, L., Li, B., Yuan, Y., Gao, X., Liu, H., & Dong, G. (2015). Analysis on the effect of China's policy of cultivated land change and cultivated land requisition compensation balance in 2000-2010. *Ziyuan Kexue*, *37*(8), 1543–1551.

Yadav, G. S., Lal, R., Meena, R. S., Babu, S., Das, A., Bhowmik, S. N., Datta, M., Layak, J., & Saha, P. (2019). Conservation tillage and nutrient management effects on productivity and soil carbon sequestration under double cropping of rice in north eastern region of India. *Ecological Indicators*, *105*, 303–315. doi:10.1016/j.ecolind.2017.08.071

Yadav, S. K., Benbi, D. K., & Prasad, R. (2019). Effect of Continuous Application of Organic and Inorganic Sources of Nutrients on Chemical Properties of Soil. *International Journal of Current Microbiology and Applied Sciences*, *8*(4), 2455–2463. doi:10.20546/ijcmas.2019.804.286

Yang. (2013). *Study on the influencing factors and guarantee mechanism of the later stage management and protection of rural land remediation project: a case study of Yunyang County in the Three Gorges Reservoir area*. Academic Press.

Yan, G., Mas, J.-F., Maathuis, B. H. P., Xiangmin, Z., & Van Dijk, P. M.YAN. (2006). Comparison of pixel-based and object-oriented image classification approaches-a case study in a coal fire area, Wuda, Inner Mongolia. *China International Journal of Remote Sensing*, *27*(18), 4039–4055. doi:10.1080/01431160600702632

Yang, Y., Gatto, E., Gao, Z., Buccolieri, R., Morakinyo, T. E., & Lan, H. (2019). The "plant evaluation model" for the assessment of the impact of vegetation on outdoor microclimate in the urban environment. *Building and Environment*, *159*, 106151. doi:10.1016/j.buildenv.2019.05.029

Yao, W., Wang, J., Wang, P., Wang, X., Yu, S., Zou, Y., Hou, J., Hayat, T., Alsaedi, A., & Wang, X. (2017). Synergistic coagulation of GO and secondary adsorption of heavy metal ions on Ca/Al layered double hydroxides. *Environmental Pollution*, *229*, 827–836. doi:10.1016/j.envpol.2017.06.084 PMID:28760526

Ye. (2019). New law is coming into effect, and reform has a long way to go -- written at the time of the adoption of the amendment to the land management law. *China Land*, (9).

Yohannes, H. (2016). *A review on relationship between climate change and agriculture*. Academic Press.

Young, J., Udeigwe, T. K., Weindorf, D. C., Kandakji, T., Gautam, P., & Mahmoud, M. A. (2015). Evaluating management-induced soil salinization in golf courses in semi-arid landscapes. *Solid Earth*, *6*(2), 393–402. doi:10.5194e-6-393-2015

Yu, X., Gao, Z., & Zeng, Y. (2014). Willingness to pay for the "Green Food" in China. *Food Policy*, *45*, 80–87. doi:10.1016/j.foodpol.2014.01.003

Zabawa, R., Siaway, A., & Baharanyi, N. (1990). The decline of Black farmers and strategies for survival. *Southern Rural Sociology*. https://egrove.olemiss.edu/jrss/vol07/iss1/9/

Zabawa, R. (1991). The Black farmer and land in South-Central Alabama: Strategies to preserve a scarce resource. *Human Ecology*, *19*(1), 61–81. https://link.springer.com/content/pdf/10.1007/BF00888977.pdf. doi:10.1007/BF00888977

Zhang & Pingli. (2002). Quality control of newly cultivated land. *China Land*, *0*(3), 22-24.

Zhang & Zhang. (2010). The pattern of rural residential area consolidation in urban suburbs based on the current situation survey. *Geographical Research*, (5), 127–134.

Zhang, D., Liao, Y., & Jia, Z. (2005). Research advances and prospects of film mulching in arid and semi-arid areas. *Agricultural Research in the Arid Areas*, *1*, 41.

Zhang, Z., Li, N., Wang, X., Liu, F., & Yang, L. (2016). A comparative study of urban expansion in Beijing, Tianjin and Tangshan from the 1970s to 2013. *Remote Sensing*, *8*(6), 496. doi:10.3390/rs8060496

Zhao, Huang, Zhong, & Zhang, Du, & Zhang. (2012). Evaluation of the balance effect of the implementation of land supervision system on the quantity of cultivated land expropriated and supplemented. *Journal of Agricultural Engineering*, *28*(25), 1–7.

Zhao, S., Zhou, D., & Liu, S. (2016). Data concurrency is required for estimating urban heat island intensity. *Environmental Pollution*, *208*, 118–124. doi:10.1016/j.envpol.2015.07.037 PMID:26243476

Zhong, L., Cantrell, K. J., Bacon, D. H., & Shewell, J. (2014). Transport of organic contaminants mobilized from coal through sandstone overlying a geological carbon sequestration reservoir. *International Journal of Greenhouse Gas Control*, *21*, 158–164. doi:10.1016/j.ijggc.2013.12.014

Zhou, L., & Gui, J. F. (2018). Applications of genetic breeding biotechnologies in Chinese aquaculture. Aquaculture in China: Success stories and modern trends, 463-496. doi:10.1002/9781119120759.ch6_1

Zhou, Z., Liu, X., Sun, K., Lin, C., Ma, J., He, M., & Ouyang, W. (2019). Persulfate-based advanced oxidation processes (AOPs) for organic-contaminated soil remediation: A review. *Chemical Engineering Journal*, *372*, 836–851. doi:10.1016/j.cej.2019.04.213

Zubair, L. (2005). Modernisation of Sri Lanka's Traditional Irrigation Systems and Sustainability. *Science, Technology & Society*, *10*(2), 161–195. doi:10.1177/097172180501000201

About the Contributors

G. N. Tanjina Hasnat is a lecturer of the Institute of Forestry and Environmental Sciences, University of Chittagong, Bangladesh. Before joining here, she served as a lecturer at the Department of Land Administration, Faculty of Land Management and Administration, Patuakhali Science and Technology University, Bangladesh. In her career, she also worked in two national organizations named Shushilan and Community Development Centre (CODEC). She has worked in six different research projects as project director, NRM Facilitator, assistant research officer, and research assistant. Presently, she is supervising 10 BSc (Hons) students in the institute. She has twelve published research articles from ten different peer-reviewed international and national journals, and she is the lead author of ten of those. She has three book chapters as the lead author and one is published by Springer Nature. She is a reviewer of seven internationally reputed journals and also serving as an Academic Editor of 'Asian Research Journal of Arts & Social Sciences'. She is an Honorary Rosalind Member of London Journals Press.

Mohammed Kamal Hossain is the Professor of Institute of Forestry and Environmental Sciences, Chittagong University, Chittagong, Bangladesh. Dr. Hossain has a BSc (Hons) and MSc degree from the Department of Botany, Chittagong University. He has a PhD degree under the Commonwealth Scholarship Program from Aberdeen University, UK in the field of Silviculture. He has a Post-doctoral fellowship under Commonwealth Scholarship and Fellowship program in U.K. He starts his career as a *Research Officer* in the Silvicultural Research Division, Bangladesh Forest Research Institute in 1984 and continued till 1993. In July 1993, he joined the Institute of Forestry and Environmental Sciences, Chittagong University (IFESCU) as Assistant Professor and in 2001 he became the Professor of the same Institute in 2001. He has contributed more than 181 scientific articles to national and international referred journals and more than 42 publications in proceedings and in book chapters in the field of Silviculture, biodiversity and plantation forestry. He is the lead/ co-author of 12 books in the field of Silviculture and Environment. In the Institute he supervised more than 102 BSc (Hons), 66 MSc/MS and 4 PhD students. Dr. Hossain holds the life membership of Bangladesh Botanical Society; Bangladesh Association for the Advancement of Science (BAAS); Asiatic Society of Bangladesh; General Secretary, Biodiversity Research Group of Bangladesh (BRGB); Vice-President, Institution of Environmental Professionals, Bangladesh; Member, Editorial Board, Journal of Forestry and Environment, Chittagong University; Editorial Board Member, Journal of Forestry Research, China (2009 – 2018). He has visited the UK, USA, Australia, Canada, China, Sri Lanka, Japan, India, Korea, Nepal, Malaysia, Indonesia, Thailand, Vietnam, Sweden, Switzerland for academic and research purposes.

* * *

Mokbul Morshed Ahmad is an Associate Professor in Regional and Rural Development Planning in the Department of Development and Sustainability in the School of Environment, Resources and Development, Asian Institute of Technology, Klong Luang, Pathumrhani 12120, Bangkok, Thailand. Prior to that, he was an Assistant Professor in the Department of Geography and Environment, Dhaka University, Dhaka, Bangladesh. He holds a PhD in Development Geography from Durham University, Durham, UK (2000). He did his first MSc in Geography and Environment from Dhaka University, Dhaka, Bangladesh (1991) and second MSc in Rural and Regional Development Planning from Asian Institute of Technology, Bangkok, Thailand (1993). He also worked with the government of Bangladesh as a civil servant in the ministries of Public administration and Commerce. Dr. Mokbul teaches and researches on international development, NGOs, community development, human conflicts and adaptation to climate change. He has published many articles on his research areas in many journals and books. He has written/co-authored six books.

Rizwan Ahmad is a doctorate in Earth Science and has vast research & teaching experience in India and abroad. He has worked with prestigious institutes like IIRS, ISRO (Respond) project, Forest Survey of India, and Eritrea Institute of Technology (EIT), Asmara, Eritrea (North East Africa) as Assistant Professor of Geospatial technology. Dr. Ahmad is specialized in Remote sensing & GIS applications and Applied geology. His major publications are in applied geosciences using RS & GIS techniques; Dr. Ahmad worked as Knowledge Partner on UN-SDGs Goals 2030 using geospatial and statistical data in LK Singhania Education Center (participating UNESCO asp.net), Rajasthan by organizing UN-SDGs International Children's Conference 2018. Presently, Dr. Ahmad is working in the capacity of Guest Faculty in the Interdisciplinary Department of Remote Sensing & GIS Applications, Aligarh Muslim University, Aligarh, India. Recently, Dr. Rizwan has been designated as Second point of Contact for United Nations – Global Geospatial Information Management Academic Network from his University. He served as a reviewer of many reputed journals, IEEE Journal of Selected Topics in Applied Earth Observations and Remote Sensing, and Disaster Advances is one of them. He is also associated with Springer publication to review preliminary book information of book proposals.

Zahoor Ahmad is a Post-Doc Scholar at the Department of Field Crops, Faculty of Agriculture, University of Cukurova, Adana, Turkey. He has a strong background in stress mitigation in plants using innovative fertilizers and treatments.

Tasawar Ali is pursuing his PhD (Soil Science) at the Insititute of Soil and Environmental Sciences, University of Agriculture Faisalabad, Pakistan. He has specialization in Plant Nutrition and stress physiology.

Muhammad Naveed Arshad is a Post-Doctoral Modeler in Aberystwyth University, United Kingdom. He is Gold Medalist and has received his PhD from the Department of Agronomy at the University of Agriculture, Faisalabad, Pakistan and his doctoral research was based in University of California, Davis-United States. He is associated with Food and Agriculture Organization (FAO) as Consultant - Agro-Ecological Zoning, His current position focuses on the agricultural productivity potential of United Kingdom. He has vast experience in Climate Change Studies using Crop Modeling and Remote Sensing/GIS and land assessment/crop suitability mapping. He is very passionate about research on environmental issues, sustainability, and socio-ecological resilience.

Muhammad Imran Ashraf is working as PhD Scholar at the Insititute of Soil and Environmental Sciences, University of Agriculture Faisalabad, Pakistan. He has excellent expertise in soil fertility evaluation, precision agriculture, management of degraded soils and environmental pollution. His current interests are balanced use of macro and micronutrients for sustainable agriculture.

Muhammad Ashar Ayub is a PhD (Soil Science) Scholar at the Institute of Soil and Environmental Sciences, University of Agriculture Faisalabad, and working on remediation of contaminated soils using nanotechnology. The major interest of the researcher includes the Remediation of Contaminated Soils, Environmental Sustainability, Nanotechnology, and Management of Environmental Contaminants.

Tanka Prasad Dahal is Director in Land Management Training Centre, Ministry of land Management, Cooperatives and Poverty Alleviation, Government of Nepal. He has experience of more than twenty years in Land Survey, measurement and Administration, Under Government of Nepal. He has completed his Master Degree in Land Administration form Kathmandu University. He is also involved in various research work related to land administration conducted by the government of Nepal. He has worked as a project chief for using digital cadastre in Nepal. He also has experience in designing and management of training related to Surveying/Mapping, GIS/Remote Sensing and Land administration for government employees of Nepal. He is currently doing his PhD in land Administration from Kathmandu University. He is also working as a visiting faculty at Kathmandu University since 2007.

Niranjan Devkota is an economist with the special focus on agriculture, climate change and contemporary issues over a decade. He has received his PhD degree from Tribhuvan University Nepal in August, 2018. He is now working as coordinator of Research Management Cell at Quest International College affiliated to Pokhara University, Nepal. Dr. Devkota has attended UNESCAP, NDRC (China), SANDEE (ICIMOD), Hi-Aware (ICIMOD), SANEM (Bangladesh) and many other training and capacity building workshop on international co-operation, natural resource management and trade related activities in home and abroad. Dr. Devkota has been teaching economics, econometrics and research methodology in MBA and BBA since 2012. He also has worked in preparing strategic and implementation plans of several economic issues of Government of Nepal including National Planning Commission as an economist. Dr. Devkota has published dozen of articles related to agricultural economics. He has command over SPSS, STATA, GIS and R programming. He is an author of Research Methodology for Graduate Level Management Students.

Kumud Dhanwantri is an Assistant Professor at Amity School of Architecture and Planning, Amity University, Gurugram, Haryana, India, since 2013. She is pursuing her PhD in 'the domain of environmental policies and governance'. She completed a Master's in Regional Planning, School of Planning and Architecture, New Delhi (2013), and a Master's in Geography, Panjab University, Chandigarh (2008). She also poses a PG Diploma in Disaster Management, IGNOU (2012). Her major fields of study have been Geography, Regional Planning, and related GIS applications. Prior to joining Amity University Gurugram, she worked as a GIS Expert at Irrigation Department of Uttar Pradesh, Lucknow (2010-2011), and as a Project Fellow at Haryana Space Application Centre (HARSAC), Hisar (2008-2010). Therein, she worked in a World bank-aided Project as well as various National and State government projects, respectively. She has published and presented her work in various national and international journals of repute. Her research interests are in the areas of Sustainable Urban and Regional Development, Inclusive Planning, Environmental Laws, Policies, and Governance.

Hongbin Ding is a PhD Candidate of Frontier region Sociology (community&law), Sichuan University, China. He has completed his Bachelor of Environmental and Resources Law from Southwest Petroleum University (Sichuan, China) in 2014 and Master of Law from Sichuan University, China in 2017. He has three published research articles, in two of which he has contributed as the first author. His major research areas are – crowds and communities in the border areas, diversified dispute resolution mechanisms, legal governance in the border, legal problems, and countermeasure of cross-border. He has awarded the outstanding field investigator award, excellent graduate students award, and different scholarships from Sichuan University.

Samreen Fatima is working as a guest faculty in the interdisciplinary Department of Remote Sensing and GIS applications, Aligarh Muslim University, Aligarh since 2019. She has qualified for the National Eligibility Test (NET), conducted by University Grant Commission (UGC), Government of India. Ms. Fatima is actively involved in research work and academic activities.

Zia Ur Rahman Farooqi is the Doctoral Student at the Institute of Soil and Environmental Sciences, University of Agriculture Faisalabad.

Hina Fatima is a PhD Research scholar at Kyungpook National University, South Korea and pursuing PhD in soil chemistry on a fully-funded scholarship.

Danli Gao is working in Chong Zhou court for nearly seven years. In 2017, she received her master's degree from Sichuan University. During her work and study period, she wrote a paper on the status of the government in environmental public interest litigation, which won the excellent thesis award of Chinese court system. Her other paper, researching on several issues of cultivated land disputes in China won the third prize of Sichuan provincial court system.

M. D. K. L. Gunathilaka is an academician and young researcher attached to the Department of Geography. She has published several research articles in international and national level journals and conferences.

K. L. W. I. Gunathilake currently working as an Assistant Lecturer in the Department of Geography, University of Colombo. She completed her BA (Hons.) with a First Class in Geography and currently is a student of MSc in Forestry and Environmental Management in the University of Sri Jayawardenepura, Sri Lanka. Having been involved in both national and international level research publications, her major research fields include - a green environment for sustainable development and environmental management.

Dilini Hemachandra is a lecturer attached to the Department of Agricultural Economics and Business Management, Faculty of Agriculture, University of Peradeniya, Sri Lanka. She obtained her BSc and MSc degrees in Agriculture and Agricultural Economics respectively from the University of Peradeniya and PhD degree in Economics from the University of Hawaii at Manoa, US in 2015.

H.M.P. Herath is a Senior Lecturer attached to the Department of Geography and Environmental Management, Faculty of Social Sciences and Languages, Sabaragamuwa University of Sri Lanka. Currently, she is conducting her PhD at the School of Geography and Information Engineering in China University of Geosciences Wuhan. She received her M.Phil. Degree in Geography from University of Peradeniya Sri Lanka in 2017. She is a member of Geography society of Sri Lanka and major in Water Resource Management, Climate change and Watershed Management, GIS, and Disaster Management.

Irfan Iftikhar is a Ph.D. (Soil Science) Scholar at the Insitute of Soil and Environmental Sciences, University of Agriculture Faisalabad with extensive research expertise in the growth of leguminous oilseed crops under salt-affected soil conditions. His further research interests include the management and reclamation of degraded soils especially salt-affected soils and improvement in saline agriculture.

Ashok Joshi is an MBA graduate from Quest International College, Pokhara University. He received University Scholarship to pursue his MBA at Pokhara University. His research interest is in agriculture management. He has completed his MBA with the thesis entitled Youth Willingness to Accept Agriculture Entrepreneurship in Western Nepal. He is interested to work with entrepreneur and agricultural entrepreneurship management.

Mohd Nazish Khan has completed his PhD in Remote Sensing and GIS from Geology Department of Aligarh Muslim University. He is working as Guest Faculty in the interdisciplinary Department of Remote Sensing and GIS Applications, Aligarh Muslim University since 2018. He is an active researcher and academician, published many research articles and chapters in journals and books of international repute. He is also running a project entitled "GIS/GPS Mapping of Waqf Properties under Qaumi Waqf Boards Taraqqiati scheme. The project is sanctioned by Central Waqf Council, Ministry of Minority Affairs, Government of India.

Lasantha Manawadu is a senior professor renowned for land use and land cover related research studies as well as geoinformatics and published a lot of research papers, book chapters, etc.

Andy Russel Mojiol is an active faculty member at the Faculty of Tropical Forestry research fellow at the Nature Park and Recreation programme and the Small Islands Research Centre, Universiti Malaysia Sabah. His current research focuses on urban forestry, nature tourism and wildlife studies.

Muhammad Nadeem has research experiences in saline agriculture and the reclamation of problematic soils. Currently, he is pursuing his PhD in ISES, UAF.

Purna Bhadur Nepali is Associate Professor, and Program Director, Master of Public Policy and Management (MPPM), Kathmandu University School of Management (KU SOM), Balkumari, Lalitpur. Dr. Nepali is a Research Fellow (non-resident), Harvard Kennedy School and Hutchins Center, Harvard University, US where he is undertaking his research on Political Economy of Inclusive Agrarian Transformation: Comparative Analysis of Race-Caste of US and Nepal/South-Asia. He has recently completed his Fulbright Visiting Research Fellowship (2017-18) in Global Development and Sustainability at Heller School for Social Policy and Management, Brandeis University, USA. His research was on Reorienting Political Economy of Agrarian Transformations, focusing on marginalized communities in

Nepal. Previously he was the Regional Project Coordinator, Regional Food Security Governance Project in South Asia and East Asia (Nepal, India, Bangladesh, Myanmar) funded by the European Union. For the past decade, he has researched land rights and food rights, and advocates for evidence-based policy and reform in South Asia from a civil society perspective. In addition, he teaches graduate courses for masters and PhD students as an adjunct professor at the Kathmandu University and the Agriculture and Forestry University in Nepal. As a lead editor of the Journal- New Angle, he recently edited a special issue of the peer reviewed article called Agrarian and Land Issues that can be found here: http://www.nepalpolicynet.com/new/new-angle/new-angle-december-2016/

K. W. G. Rekha Nianthi is a Professor in Geography at the University of Peradeniya, Sri Lanka. She obtained her PhD in Geography (Applied Climatology) from NEHU, India. Postdoctoral qualification was obtained from the University of Minho, Portugal. She was a visiting scholar at Kyoto University, Japan and a research fellow of Mainz University, Germany. Her main research interests include Climate Change and Disaster Management. She serves as the consultant for various projects, authored many research papers and participated in many conferences. She was the Project Coordinator of the Building Resilience to Tsunami in the Indian Ocean, ADRRN-UNISDR-EU, and University Network for Disaster Risk Reduction and Management in the Indian Ocean Rim (UN4DRR). She was awarded by the UGIT Excellency Awards-2018.

Chanon Nunbhakdi has completed his masters in the field of Regional and Rural Development Planning from School of Environment Resource and Development, Asian Institute of Technology, Thailand. He was awarded AIT fellowship and Thai Government Scholarship for this Master program. His areas of research include Rural Development, Political Economy and Human Conflicts.

Muditha Prasannajith Perera is a Senior Lecturer (Grade - 1) in the Department of Geography, University of Peradeniya, Sri Lanka. He joined the Department of Geography, with the previous experience as an Assistant Lecturer of University of Ruhuna, Permanent Lecturer/Executive Officer SL-1 of the Sri Lanka Forestry Institute, Forest Department, and three-year research background inclusive of Huruluwewa Watershed Management Project (SCOR) under the International Irrigation Management Institute. Muditha Perera completed his M.Phil Degree in 2010 and the PhD in 2016. Currently he is contributing the service as a Senior Student Counselor, Warden, and as a resource person to the PGIS, PGIHS, CES, CSHR, and CDCE in the University of Peradeniya. Occasionally he is contributing his service to the Forest Department, Irrigation Department, Education Department, and to the Ministry of Mahaweli Development and Environment. He is an Editorial Board Member and Reviewer for few National /International Journals.

Udaya Raj Poudel is a PhD scholar in Tribhuvan University, Kathmandu, Nepal- working in the field of communication. His research works reflect communication, ethics, business and culture with latest practices worldwide. He has dozens of papers in the field of entrepreneurs, management and communication. He has more than two decades of educational institution management experience, and teaching English and Communication has propelled him as a communication consultant in various organizations. Mr. Paudel projects commitments in research and ethical communication and consumption. He is an author of Research Methodology for Graduate Level Management Students.

Gamini Pushpakumara is a Senior Professor and former Head of the Department of Crop Science is the current Dean of the Faculty of Agriculture, University of Peradeniya. He holds BSc degree in Agriculture from the University of Peradeniya, and a MSc and PhD degrees in Forestry and its Relation to Land Use and Forest genetics and Germplasm Conservation, respectively from the University of Oxford, UK. He is a specialist in forest tree improvement who has significantly contributed to the development of domestication of tree crops, specially underutilized tree species and agrobiodiversity. He has also made contributions to the agroforestry and perennial crop sector, particularly in the development of coconut based farming systems and smallholder farming community of Sri Lanka. He has also served as the Country Liaison Scientist to the World Agroforestry Centre, Nairobi, Kenya during the period of 2004-2015. Prof. Pushpakumara is an internationally recognized researcher with over 200 publications in peer reviewed journals. He has also made landmark contributions with the publication of books which are currently being used in the universities and centers of higher learning both in Sri Lanka and abroad. He is also a versatile academic administrator with interests in various aspects of agricultural development, education, and training.

Sudarshana Ramaraju is a policy and strategy advisor of international repute. He served the Government of India, Department of Space for two decades in various capacities. He also served the United Nations for more than 15 years and coordinated various UN programs in the Asia-Pacific region. He co-ordinated the Persian Gulf protection action plan in the Middle East of the UNEP. Moving on, he joined the United Nations Security Council and served in various important capacities including direct reporting to the Secretary General. He is an expert on serving protocol and conventions, Environmental Diplomacy, Information System and Institutional Management, Capacity building and inter-governmental project development and management. He was UNESCO consultant in East Africa and in Arab States for capacity building. He served as visiting Professor, International Institute of Geo-Information and Earth observations, Netherland and worked as an advisor to UN agencies GEF, US Aid, Islamic Development Bank, World Bank on Environmental management and also served as an advisor to Barry allebaut, Belgium. He has advised different Governments and Corporate entities on Capacity Building, Strategic planning and environmental policy and strategies. His association with the Commission will help plan new strategies that will help take Commission's policies to the newer heights.

Shahab E. Saqib has completed his Master & PhD from the Asian Institute of Technology, Thailand in the field of Regional and Rural Development Planning with excellent thesis grades. His areas of specialization are Environmental Economics, Climate Change, Food Security, and Health Economics. Nowadays, he is working as Assistant Professor in Commerce Education and Management Sciences, Department of Higher Education, Khyber Pakhtunkhwa, Pakistan.

Muhammad Shabaan is a PhD scholar at the University of Agriculture,Faisalabad. With specialization in Soil Microbiology. He is working in Soil Microbiology and Biochemistry Lab.

Lim Wing Shen is a Postgraduate Researcher at the Forestry Complex of the Faculty of Science and Natural Resource, Universiti Malaysia Sabah. His research focuses on wildlife-based nature tourism studies in Sabah, Malaysia.

Abbas Shoukat is working as Research Associate in a project at ISES, UAF as well as pursuing his PhD in Soil science.

Reshma Shrestha is an Assistant Professor in the Department of Geomatics Engineering, School of Engineering at Kathmandu University. Dr. Shrestha has more than six years of experience in the academic field. Besides academics, she has professional experience in many projects related to the application of geo-information technology in land management. She was Co-chair for the working group in FIG commission 2 from 2015 to 2018. Her research interest is in Urban Land Governance, Land Administration, Land Use Planning, Urban Planning and Management, Land Readjustment, Geo-information Technologies and Capacity Building in Geoinformatics. She has more than 15 publications including ISI publication, peer-reviewed journal articles, and conference proceedings. Her paper was awarded as an "Article of the month" by FIG. https://www.fig.net/resources/monthly_articles/2016/shrestha_etal_january_2016.asp. She obtained a review recognition from Impactful Journals like Land Use Policy (Elsevier) and Sustainability (MDPI). She holds PhD in the Title "Understanding Urban Land Governance through" Action Space": Implications for Access to Land for Low-Income Housing in Managing Informal Settlements" from the Faculty of Geo-information Science and Earth Observation, University of Twente.

Robin Throne's research agenda continues to consider voice and land dispossession from social justice research approaches. She is the author of Autoethnography and Heuristic Inquiry for Doctoral-Level Researchers: Emerging Research and Opportunities (IGI Global Research Insight Series, 2019) and editor for Indigenous Research of Land, Self, and Spirit (IGI Global, 2021).

Wajid Umar is a Ph.D. scholar at Doctoral School of Environmental Sciences, Szent Istvan University, Gödöllő, Hungary. His doctoral research investigates the use of the latest techniques to reduce nitrous oxide (N_2O) emission, to increase nitrogen use efficiency (NUE) and along with this to increase Zinc (Zn) contents in cereal grains by agronomic biofortification. He takes a multidisciplinary approach that encompasses the fields of Environmental Science, Soil Science, Chemistry, Nanotechnology, and Agronomy. He holds a master's degree in Soil Science (Plant Nutrition) from the University of Agriculture, Faisalabad.

H. Shellae Versey, PhD is a psychologist, and her research areas are health, life course, work, place, social change and intersections between gender and race. As a social psychologist, Shellae Versey's research focuses on recognizing the socioeconomic, ethnic-racial, and cultural factors that are important in African American health outcomes, particularly during later life.

Eberhard Weber is an Associate Professor at The University of the South Pacific. He has worked for the past 35 years on issues around fisheries development, food and livelihood security, rural and urban development, migration, resources management and development in South and South East Asia as well as the Pacific Islands region. Dr. Weber has a PhD in Development Geography from the University of Freiburg, Germany. He has taught Development Geography in Germany (University of Freiburg, the South Asia Institute of the University of Heidelberg) as well as in India (Madras University) and Thailand (Chulalongkorn University). Since 2000 Dr. Weber teaches Development Geography at The University of the South Pacific in Fiji.

Jeevika Weerahewa is the Professor of Agricultural Economics attached to the Department of Agricultural Economics and Business Management, Faculty of Agriculture, University of Peradeniya, Sri Lanka. She obtained her BSc and M.Phil degrees from the University of Peradeniya and PhD from the University of Guleph, Canada. She served as the Head of the Department during 2013-2016 and Chairperson of the Board of Study in Agricultural Economics at the Postgraduate Institute of Agriculture during 2011-2015. Dr. Weerahewa has been serving as an Honorary Fellow of the Faculty of Veterinary and Agricultural Sciences, University of Melbourne, Australia since 2018.

V.P.I.S. Wijeratne, is a lecturer in the Department of Geography, University of Colombo, Sri Lanka, and presently, she is a Doctoral candidate in Physical Geography at the College of Urban and Environmental Sciences, Northwest University, China. She received her MSc in GIS and Remote Sensing from the Postgraduate Institute of Science, University of Peradeniya, Sri Lanka in 2014 and BA (Hons.) First Class in Geography, University of Colombo, Sri Lanka in 2011. She is broadly interested in Eco-Hydrology, Social hydrology, GIS and Remote Sensing, Climate Change, Disaster Management and Environmental Management.

Krishan Kumar Yadav is a former Chief Town Planner, Haryana, India. His Major fields of studies are Urban and Regional Planning and Protection and Conservation of Natural Environment. He has extensively published his work in different national and international journals apart from presenting in reputed workshops and conferences in Poland, Japan and Dubai. Presently, his research interests are mainly focused on the Urbanisation and Development challenges faced by Indian Cities, Governance issues, and the Conservation of natural environment, safety and safe movement of wildlife in Aravalis, India. He has been teaching for quite some time in the capacity of Professor Emeritus and as visiting faculty in a number of Universities in Delhi and Haryana. Presently, Prof. Yadav is a visiting faculty in Ansal University, Gurugram, Haryana. He remained in the capacity of Chairman for the Haryana Regional Chapter, Institute of Town Planners, India. Recipient of 'Bharat Jyoti Award', Prof. Yadav is a Fellow member of the Institute of Town Planners of India, New Delhi. Realising the alarming negative impacts of deforestation and degradation of forest in Haryana, especially in the Aravallis mountain ecosystem, he is engaged in undertaking plantations and awareness walks through his trust, the Krishna Aravali Foundation.

Muhammad Zohaib Anjum is a PhD student (Forest Genetics), Department of Forestry and Range Management, University of Agriculture Faisalabad.

Index

G

H

I

L

M

N

O

P

R

S

T

U

V

W

Y

Z

www.ingramcontent.com/pod-product-compliance
Lightning Source LLC
LaVergne TN
LVHW062109300926
849161LV00010B/2412
* 9 7 8 1 7 9 9 8 4 3 7 2 6 *